Grand Ventures

Grand Ventures

The Banning Family and the Shaping of Southern California

by Tom Sitton

Huntington Library, San Marino, California

Sponsored by the Huntington-USC Institute on California & the West
Editing by Sara K. Austin
Production editing by Susan Green and Jean Patterson
Indexing by Jean Patterson
Book design and composition by Doug Davis
Prepress and print management by Charles Allen Imaging Experts
Printed in South Korea
15 14 13 12 11 10   1 2 3 4 5

Portions of chapters 9 and 10 originally appeared in "The Bannings on the Magic Isle: Santa Catalina Island, 1892–1919," *California History* 87 (2009): 6–23, and are reprinted with the permission of the California Historical Society.

Library of Congress Cataloging-in-Publication Data
Sitton, Tom, 1949–
  Grand ventures : the Banning family and the shaping of Southern California / by Tom Sitton.
       p. cm.
  Includes bibliographical references and index.
  ISBN 978-0-87328-243-7 (alk. paper)
  1. Banning family. 2. Banning, Phineas, 1830–1885. 3. California, Southern—History 4. California, Southern—Biography. I. Title.
  F867.S57 2010
  929'.20973—dc22
                        2010005762

CONTENTS

Foreword

S pend but a little time rummaging around the history of nineteenth-century Southern California, and you'll encounter Phineas Banning. Long characterized as a larger-than-life figure, this prime mover (literally) in the transportation history of the region, railroad builder, and "Father of the Los Angeles Harbor" cut a swath through the rough-and-tumble world of mid-nineteenth-century Los Angeles. As if straight from central casting, he was ideal for the role of "booster." Along with his peers, friends, and competitors who were similarly ambitious (if not ruthless) and forward-thinking, Phineas Banning helped organize the region's political economy in ways designed to suit the region and himself. Banning, his spouses, and their progeny became a regional First Family, important players in the community building and development of this part of the West as it was recast as an American space following the 1846–48 war with Mexico.

While Banning may be easy to encounter in the landscape of the regional past, harder to find are scholarly works that take him and his many legacies seriously. That search comes to a fruitful end with this wonderful book by the historian Tom Sitton. Almost half of it is a balanced evaluation of Banning's career as an entrepreneur and community booster, based on Sitton's meticulous reading of historical sources from myriad repositories and family collections. Unlike the breathless hyperbole of earlier characterizations, the Phineas Banning in these pages is objectively presented, evaluated, and measured. And yet, as expected, he still emerges as a dynamic and crucial figure in the early years of the rise of Southern California.

Sitton's work does not end, nor even exactly begin, with Phineas Banning. Through an innovative, multigenerational exploration, this book also looks to the accomplishments of Banning family members, from the several generations of easterners who preceded him to the dozens of those who, after his passing, made their own greater or lesser marks in Southern California.

Phineas Banning's children and their spouses carried on the legacy of the patriarch in business, politics, philanthropy, and the social life of Los Angeles and the surrounding region. His three sons continued to build a shipping business at the harbor he first developed, and they became active, important figures in the economic growth of the region as the nineteenth century became the twentieth. Sitton's narration of their development of Santa Catalina Island as a resort adds a behind-the-scenes perspective on the management of the "Magic Isle" in these years. The Banning sons also played banner roles in the social goings-on of the era, along with their spouses; one of them, Anne Ophelia Smith Banning, emerged as an early leader in social welfare and philanthropy in Los Angeles.

The next generation of Bannings, the grandsons and granddaughters, continued to play roles in diverse aspects of state and local affairs, as did their sons and daughters. We meet many of them within these pages, all cognizant of the long shadow cast by Phineas Banning, but seeking to establish legacies that they could confidently call their own. Throughout the volume, Sitton aligns biographical details and dramas with the larger context of the growth and shaping of Southern California in the late nineteenth century and much of the twentieth. This book is a superb reminder that a fine-grained biographical exploration can contribute much to our understanding of individuals and families as agents of change in the development of places, institutions, and cultures.

The Huntington-USC Institute on California and the West is particularly proud to sponsor this history of the Banning family. Special thanks to Mr. Bob Banning, whose firm hand guided the project from inception to reality; to scholarly advisers Greg Hise, David Igler, and Alan Jutzi; to Sara K. Austin, Susan Green, and Jean Patterson of the Huntington Library Press; to the John Randolph Haynes and Dora Haynes Foundation of Los Angeles; and to dozens of Banning family members and friends who saw, in the history of their forebears, an opportunity to tell an important family and California story all at once.

William Deverell, Director
Huntington-USC Institute on California and the West

L ong ago I heard the story of one of my great-aunts, who commissioned a history of our family only to destroy it upon receipt. Her reaction was probably based not on the quality of the work but on what she discovered—that some of her ancestors were not what she expected them to be. I assume (I did not read the work) that a few of my forebears were not the angels my relatives had thought them to be, as is true of any family (we are human, after all). And so that history was lost.

Family history is a complex undertaking for a historian, who must navigate events in the lives of several generations of one family, on whose interpretation the family's members might not all agree. When I started this project I knew it was fraught with the challenges of reconciling what happened with what family members wanted to hear. But it was too interesting to pass up. As it turned out, I need not have feared: the Bannings just wanted the truth, whatever it was, and to have it explained within the context of the time and place in which their ancestors lived.

With the exception of a dated hagiographical biography of Phineas Banning for young people published in 1957 and a few publications of the Banning Residence Museum, there is little in print on the history of the Bannings, and nothing treating this Southern California family over an extended span of time. Hence, there is certainly a need for a book on the life and legacy of Phineas Banning that tells the history of the entire family and their role in the evolution of Southern California.

This study was spearheaded by descendants of Phineas Banning who wanted to know more about the part the family played in the development of Southern California. I wish to thank all of the members of the family who supported the project, who spent time answering my countless questions, and who gave me access to primary source materials with which to interpret and compose this family history. Without their enthusiastic cooperation, this book could not have been written.

Among those Bannings who helped with the project, Marianne Alyce Banning Adey, Elizabeth Banning Ames, Douglas Banning, Hancock Banning III, Marian Lowry Banning, Robert J. Banning, and Nancy Morse Banning Call spent hours with me in one or more personal interviews and shared their family history materials. Marian Lowry Banning also read a draft of a portion of the manuscript to help me correct errors. William F. Banning, Francis P. Graves Jr., Marion Fitzhugh Banning Mack, Elizabeth Macfarland Brown Nordlinger, and Katharine Alice Banning Sisk answered my questions from their distant locations in one or more phone calls.

Former Banning family associates and researchers were also integral to the project. John Haskell made arrangements to be interviewed and also read and commented on the Beeco, Ltd. section in chapter 14. Two former researchers at the Banning Residence Museum were most helpful: Joyce Loranger provided me with a file of her research during her interview, and Eleanor Henry shared her research on John Banning in a telephone interview from her home in Delaware.

For assistance in my research in the East and Midwest, my thanks go to the helpful staff members of the Free Library of Philadelphia; the Delaware Historical Society, Wilmington Public Library, and New Castle County Recorder of Deeds Office in Wilmington, Delaware; the Delaware Public Archives in Dover, Delaware; the U.S. National Archives and Library of Congress in Washington, D.C; Monique Gordy, curator of the Maryland Room in the Talbot County Free Library, and the staff of the Talbot County Courthouse, both in Easton, Maryland; and the staff of the Minnesota History Center in St. Paul, Minnesota.

For their help in central and Northern California, I wish to thank Ken Kenyon of Special Collections, California Polytechnic State University in San Luis Obispo; the staff of the Bancroft Library at the University of California, Berkeley; the Special Collections Department at Stanford University Library; and California State Archives and California State Library in Sacramento.

Closer to my home in Southern California I have many individuals to thank. In the harbor area, the frequent assistance of Michael Sanborn and Tara Fansler at the Banning Residence Museum was critical to the completion of this project. Added support from volunteers Joyce Selzer and Carol Sapp was very helpful. Susan F. Ogle at nearby Drum Barracks and the staff of the Wilmington Branch of the Los Angeles Public Library provided important research materials. Historians Judson A. Grenier and Gordon M. Bakken gave helpful advice and pointed out sources for this study,

For their support of my research on the "Magic Isle" of Santa Catalina I wish to thank Jeannine Pedersen and the rest of the staff of the Catalina Island Museum; Gail Hodge, Ron Dout, Gina Long, and Cheryl Allison at the Santa Catalina Island Company; and former Avalon Mayor Ralph Morrow and First Lady Pat Morrow for their very gracious hospitality during several trips there. In addition, Santa Catalina history experts James Zordich and Patricia Moore read and provided important comments on the two Santa Catalina chapters. I also wish to thank editor Janet Fireman and three anonymous reviewers of an early draft of the Santa Catalina research for this book that was eventually published in *California History*.

For their assistance tracking down Banning-related materials elsewhere in Southern California, I am indebted to Todd Gaydowski, Mike Holland, and Jay Jones of the Los Angeles City Archives; Carolyn Kozo Cole of the Los Angeles Public Library; Dace Taube at the University of Southern California Special Collections; Simon Elliot, Jeff Rankin, and Victoria Steele at the University of California, Los Angeles Special Collections; and the staffs of the Los Angeles Harbor College Archives and Special Collections Department, the Los Angeles County Library branch in Rosemead, the San Diego Historical Society Archives, and the U.S. National Archives in Laguna Niguel, California. My very special thanks to Anne Salenger, historian and archivist for the Assistance League of Southern California Archives, who spent time pulling out collections and making arrangements for the photograph of the portrait of Anne Banning.

I want to thank my colleagues at my former professional home, the Natural History Museum of Los Angeles County and its Seaver Center for Western History Research, who have helped me in various ways with this book—John Cahoon, William Estrada, Scanmaster Brent Riggs, Betty Uyeda, and Beth Werling. I also offer my very special thanks for advice and encouragement to three retired but still invaluable curators and special friends—Don Chaput, Janet Fireman, and Errol Stevens.

Much of my research was done at the Henry E. Huntington Library in San Marino, California, where a number of people were integral to the completion of this project. My thanks to Research director Roy Ritchie and Library director David Zeidberg; curators Peter Blodgett, Bill Frank, Alan Jutzi, Dan Lewis, and Jennifer Watts; photograph specialist Erin Chase; Reader Services head Laura Stalker and staff members Christopher Adde, Bryan Dickson, Juan Gomez, and Leslie Jobsky; manuscript room supervisor Kadin Henningsen and assistants Sara Ash, Meredith Berbée, and Catherine Wehrey; and the many pages who brought out box after box of Banning Company Collection documents as well as material from other collections.

For their help in turning a rough manuscript into a finished product, I have many people to thank. Members of the Project Advisory Board who read and commented on the entire first draft included William Deverell, Greg Hise, David Igler, and Alan Jutzi. Sara K. Austin did a magnificent job in copyediting the final draft—questioning some of my assumptions and assertions, demanding clarity, and converting some of my occasionally crude prose into acceptable writing. Doug Davis designed the book and David L. Fuller created the two original maps. Huntington Library Press director Susan Green managed the progress of this publication, and Jean Patterson was responsible for seeing the book through the production stage.

Since its inception, this book has been a project of the Huntington-USC Institute on California and the West, and its director, William Deverell, has supervised and guided it at every stage. I seem to conclude my acknowledgments in every publication by thanking Bill, and he was invaluable to the success of this project.

Lastly, I again thank my spouse, Karen, who puts up with me during these long book projects. Her love and sacrifices make it all possible.

INTRODUCTION

F amily history not only records events in the lives of individual relatives. It also reflects changes in a society, and sometimes explains
how family members spurred on those changes. Placed in the context of major events and interpretive themes, history told through the
generations of a family can help us better understand the personal impact
of the larger forces that have shaped our past and present.

In the United States, this method of historical interpretation is most
familiar in narratives documenting the lives of members of America's
best-known families on the national level—families that have fundamentally affected the political, social, and cultural evolution of the nation
through successive generations. Countless textbooks and monographs
trace how these families transformed and were themselves transformed
by history. In many cases more than one member of the family was of
major significance, for example in the families of American presidents
and other national leaders.[1]

In Southern California a number of families have made vital contributions to the development of the region through several generations.
The Lugo, Coronel, Del Valle, Sepulveda, and Dominguez families are
among those who produced political and social leaders during the Spanish, Mexican, and early American periods. The Wilson, Childs, Temple,
Bixby, Workman, Keller, Watson, Ducommun, Eaton, and Newmark
clans were significant in the early American period, and their later generations also played key roles in regional history. And the Otis/Chandler,
Hellman, Hancock, O'Melveny, Garland, and Dockweiler families included several generations of important individuals, from the late nineteenth and the twentieth centuries.[2]

Prominent among the area's dynasties are the Bannings, one of
Southern California's well-established First Families. Beginning in the
mid-nineteenth century and through several generations, the Bannings

1

helped to shape the region's economic, social, and political evolution, especially in the areas of transportation, commercial expansion, harbor improvement, tourism, regional philanthropy, and preservation of history resources. More recent descendants have continued to take part in regional development, although not on as grand a scale as some of their predecessors.

The patriarch of the Southern California branch of the family, Phineas Banning (1830–1885), staked his future on a region with few apparent resources, and he became integral to the transformation of Southern California through the eras of Manifest Destiny, the Civil War, Reconstruction, and part of the Gilded Age. He was the primary agent in the early improvement of the Port of Los Angeles, now one of the largest in the world. When Phineas arrived in the region in 1851, there was no real port at San Pedro Bay and transportation methods were primitive. The region was isolated from rest of the western United States by geography and landscape, and communication and commerce were rudimentary. This was the beginning of a period of entrepreneurial expansion based on private initiatives that set the pattern for future development. Phineas arrived in Southern California poor in economic terms but rich in vision, imagination, ingenuity, and drive. Instead of traveling to the Northern California gold fields, he saw the vast potential in building a port and a transportation and shipping network that linked a sparsely settled Los Angeles to the rest of the American Southwest—before the transcontinental railroad. He then built a railroad from the city to the harbor and became a local leader in connecting Southern California to other regions in the nation by rail. Phineas was active in many other business pursuits, and he was a major community leader in Los Angeles as well as a key figure in local and state politics and philanthropy.

Banning was a fierce business competitor, always on the lookout for opportunities to expand his personal fortune. His twentieth-century business successors include leaders like Henry Kaiser, a "government entrepreneur" who used federal funding and other public resources to build his own business empire and monumental infrastructure, such as the Boulder Dam. Phineas Banning did the same thing almost a century earlier with U.S. Army contracts and Congressional funding for major harbor improvements that subsidized his own business ventures. His method has been called "enlightened self-interest," an apt description of the private and public partnerships he created to advance regional economic development while building his commercial empire. Like other major entrepreneurs in the region, he was a passionate promoter of Southern California expansion in an era when such boosters were the primary force in business and community building. These boosters envisioned the potential of the region and took advantage of whatever public and private resources they could acquire in pursuing prosperity for themselves, their families, and their community. Phineas Banning was one of the leading figures in this movement, and his descendants made their own contributions in different ways.[3]

Coming of age during the Gilded Age and the Progressive Era, Phineas's children continued their father's partnership with the Southern Pacific Railroad Company and developed and operated Santa Catalina Island—the "Magic Isle"—as a resort for almost three decades. They used their resources to defend their assets—for example, fighting the city of Los Angeles to retain their tidelands property. But they also invested substantially in their community, playing an important role in the region's economic growth. This generation also engaged in local and state politics, with family members active on various sides of political issues and partisan campaigns. The next generation continued to manage the ancestral property and family fortune created by Phineas, while also participating in politics, harbor development, social welfare organizations, and society, and contributing to regional literature. Many members of the succeeding generation, who shared in the transformation of Southern California after World War II, were especially active in promoting the Phineas Banning legacy by preserving important family documents and the family homestead in Wilmington. To varying degrees those descendants who stayed in the region carried forward the patriarch's values and his legacy by participating in the development of Southern California; the nature of the area's growth, in turn, shaped their careers.

The history of Southern California, like that of the nation itself, is composed of many patterns and events and, associated with them, individuals and groups who have contributed to change. Sometimes the driving forces of history are individuals, those who make something happen, for better or for worse. At other times, formal and informal organizations of people strive together to improve an institution, right a wrong, advance an art form or an idea, or simply make money for themselves and their clients, perhaps improving the social order at the same time.

This book is about one of those groups of people, the Banning family, over several generations, explaining how these individuals contributed to the development of Southern California as well as how they interacted with one another. It is both a story about a family as an agent of change and an interpretation of the rise of Southern California in the larger American Southwest as told through the exploits of one family.

PART 1
THE BANNINGS

Bronze statue of Phineas Banning, completed by Eugene Daub in 2004, at Banning's Landing Community Center. Photograph by Tom Sitton.

CHAPTER ONE

FROM THE OLD WORLD TO AMERICA

At the bustling Port of Los Angeles today, on a point called Banning's Landing, stands a bronze statue of a young man of the early 1850s, apparently contemplating this modern, world-class container facility. Mammoth container cranes, never-ending warehouses, huge oil-storage tanks, and countless oceangoing ships along the wharves crowd the view.

If our bronze figure turned to his left, his gaze would fall on the Pacific Ocean, where the outline of Santa Catalina Island appears off in the distance. One of the region's major resorts for more than a century, the "Magic Isle" is celebrated for its natural beauty and for the quaint architecture of its port city, Avalon. A million tourists visit each year to boat along Catalina's rocky coast, hike its canyons, dive in its coves, and play along its beaches.

If he were to turn to his right, he would face the massive expanse of housing tracts, commercial and industrial structures, and open landscapes of Southern California. The region's monumental public infrastructure snakes out from the port, with concrete and steel transportation arteries carrying people and goods around the coastal basin, out to the rest of the nation, and back again.

When the young man himself stood there in 1851, he looked out on an empty expanse of tidal flats that was anything but a natural harbor. That man's name was Phineas Banning. He and his descendants played important roles in transforming the landscape he saw then—mudflats, a rocky and virtually uninhabited isle, a dusty little town known as Los Angeles, and the rutted tracks that crisscrossed the basin—into the scene his statue presides over today. Over the past 150 years, the Banning family has been a force in shaping the economy, politics, and social life of Southern California, and their story reflects those of the many Americans of ambition and energy who remade the Southwest in their image.

Long before Phineas Banning first spied the harbor that would become his home, Bannings proudly strode the streets of a port city half a world away, where they too had become civic leaders. These Banning faces are known to millions, although few know their names. One is memorialized in *Night Watch* (1642), one of Rembrandt's most celebrated paintings. The painting depicts the members of a unit of the Dutch civic militia as they gallantly depart from their headquarters to defend law and order in urban areas. In the foreground of this colossal painting, Dr. Frans Banningh-Cocq, captain of the militia, stands out from the others, his figure a bit larger and more dignified, his costume more distinctive. The son of an apothecary and a woman of noble birth by the name of Banning (or Banningh, as it was sometimes spelled), Banningh-Cocq (d. 1655) studied law and became a magistrate, an alderman, and a burgomaster in Amsterdam. He built the Amsterdam City Hall, which later became the King's Palace, and was knighted by the king of France. Though Banningh-Cocq's appearance in Rembrandt's masterwork has assured him lasting fame, he was not the most prestigious member of the Banning family in Holland in the seventeenth century. He was just one of a number of Bannings who at that time held important positions in European society.[1]

Another Banning was immortalized in a Dutch Golden Age painting just six years later, in 1648. Jacob Banning, a wealthy Amsterdam merchant, appears as the central figure in *Banquet of the Amsterdam Civic Guard in Celebration of the Peace of Munster*. This work commemorating the Treaty of Westphalia portrays the members of the unit seated around a table celebrating the end of decades of war in Europe. The painting, by Bartholomeus van der Helst, also hangs in the Rijksmuseum in Amsterdam, giving the Bannings a prominent place in the history of Dutch art.[2] The civic pride, boosterism, energy, and ambition that are memorialized in these paintings make them apt touchstones for a story that played out among the descendants of a different branch of the Banning family, those who would help to form a land quite unimaginable to these upstanding burghers of Amsterdam.

Although the Dutch Bannings were among the oldest branches of the Banning family, by the seventeenth century the name had spread throughout Europe, and it is the English line that leads us to Southern California. The Banning name and its many variations are believed to be of Danish origin, emerging in the century after the collapse of the Roman Empire. From Denmark, the Bannings spread to Holland by about 500 AD and, later, into several parts of what is now Germany. The

Night Watch by Rembrandt. Courtesy of the Rijksmuseum Collection, Amsterdam.

English Bannings were probably descendants of these German tribes; they must have immigrated to England by the later sixth century, since Banningham in Norfolk was settled at about that time. Over the next century, the name is recorded in many regions of England, as well as in Scotland and Ireland, as Bannings acquired large landholdings and became involved in the wool trade and other business ventures. Some descendants of these early immigrants, such as London merchant, alderman, and sheriff Sir Paul Bayning, or Banning (1559–1616), and his son, the First Viscount of Bayning (1588–1629), can be traced through their political offices and religious appointments.[3] Although various branches of the Banning family, especially the more prominent ones, are frequently recorded in the British Isles during the centuries after their arrival, it is not until the sixteenth century that we can confidently trace the origins of the Southern California Bannings to a particular line.

By the sixteenth century, clusters of residents with the Banning surname were recorded in counties in northern England and in the region southwest of London. Among the southern counties where Bannings settled is Wiltshire, home of Salisbury cathedral and city, Stonehenge, the towns of Marlborough and Swindon, and a number of smaller villages, and near the ancient Roman settlement of Bath. The village and parish of Burbage, about six miles south of Marlborough, included among its citizens quite a number of Bannings, as evidenced by marriage and burial records.[4] The Bannings apparently shared in the growth of the wool industry in the area. The land surrounding Burbage had been given over to agriculture and to pasturage for sheep and cattle in the Middle Ages. By the time the Bannings settled there in the early sixteenth century, wool production had become a major industry in Wiltshire, aided by its direct connection to London by means of the Thames River.[5]

Born about 1500 in Burbage, Robert Banning is the earliest known ancestor of Phineas Banning, eventual patriarch of the Southern California branch of the family. Robert's lineal descendants remained in Wiltshire County for several generations, until Edward Banning migrated to the colony of Maryland in North America by the 1670s, where he farmed a plot called "Goose Neck." Several generations later, one of Edward's grandsons left Maryland with his family to settle in Dover, located in Kent County, one of the three Delaware counties that, along with Sussex and New Castle, comprised a colony that shared a governor with Pennsylvania. One of the children in this Dover family, John Banning, would become a prominent citizen, a major figure in Delaware's contribution to the American Revolution and the early republic, and the grandfather of Phineas Banning. (For the genealogy of this group, see appendix A.)

John Banning: Merchant and Patriot

John Banning's accomplishments foreshadowed his grandson's career. A son of the first Bannings to resettle in colonial Delaware, John was born in Dover about 1739[6] to Richard and Esther Banning. John's father died within a few years, and his mother soon married Matthew Jarrett and raised her three sons by Richard near Dover. Little is known of John's early years, but it is certain that he was well prepared for his future. Clearly he had served an apprenticeship to ready him for his working life, for he became a saddler, a respected trade for skilled craftsmen in colonial Delaware. The work was especially valued in the British colonies, for many colonists rode horses on a daily basis. John also became a merchant, selling foodstuffs and other commodities to his Dover neighbors. By the mid-1770s he had acquired quite a few parcels of land in and around Dover, which he probably rented out. He was an avid subscriber to a newspaper in the colony of Pennsylvania by 1767, a commitment that testifies to his community spirit and appreciation for the medium. Like many other

Banning family hometowns on the East Coast, from Maryland to Philadelphia.
Map by David L. Fuller.

affluent citizens throughout the colonies at this time, including many of
the Founding Fathers, Banning owned a number of African slaves, who
were his servants and workforce, and whom he occasionally leased to
others when he did not need their labor.[7]

In June 1766, John purchased from the Dover town commissioners
thirteen town lots south of Dover's central Green. One of these was on
King Street, almost adjacent to the Christ Church cemetery. There he
built a two-story brick structure that housed his home, his saddle shop,
and his mercantile business. Many years later—well after John's death—
the structure still retained evidence of its use as a store. As one writer
described it in 1824, "it had the old hooks and the other store fixtures in
the cellar where were kept hung up, hams, shoulders, middlings, and the
old time loaves of sugar and numerous other articles of trade."[8]

By the 1760s, when the relationship between England and its American colonies grew strained, John Banning had become a very successful

John Banning's 1766 house and business in Dover, Delaware, in 2007.
Photograph by Tom Sitton.

entrepreneur. His experiences as merchant and citizen until that point would have reflected the political and economic freedom permitted American colonists by the British Crown—as long as they produced resources for the mother country and continued to purchase finished goods brought over on English ships. During this period of "salutary neglect," the colonists had assumed a large measure of self-government. The region where Banning plied his trade, for example—later Delaware, but originally the southern part of the colony of Pennsylvania—had been allowed to create its own legislature in 1704. After the end of the French and Indian War in 1763, however, British authorities began to tighten their hold on the colonies and imposed new taxes to raise revenue for administration and defense and to pay for the just-ended war. Colonists, John Banning among them, objected to these measures, and protests against the Stamp Act and Quartering Act of 1765 and the Townshend Acts of 1767 resulted in boycotts of British goods, civil disobedience, and finally, bloodshed in the Boston Massacre of 1770.[9]

As the series of events that led to revolution unfolded, colonists had to decide whether to retain their allegiance to the king or to join those among their neighbors who were asserting their rights to self-governance. Although he was not apparently active early in the conflict, once he joined the cause, John Banning consistently supported those resisting British policies. In 1774 he became a leader of a Delaware political faction known for its sympathy with anti-British activists. The next year he was elected to a Kent County committee formed to raise funds for the relief of the Boston residents who had defied Parliament and its tax on tea. This committee, formed by a directive of the First Continental Congress, symbolized the connections among the several colonies, ties that would strengthen as the conflict with England escalated. This and other actions of the First Continental Congress in defiance of Britain were answered with military force in the battles of Lexington, Concord, and Bunker Hill.[10]

From 1775 onward, John Banning's service to the colonists' cause would occupy more and more of his time. In the same month that he joined the relief committee, Banning was reelected as a member of the Delaware General Assembly, having already served in 1771 and 1772. He was also appointed to the Committee of Correspondence for Kent County; these committees were charged with gathering and sharing information among the colonies. In this capacity he investigated loyalists accused of supporting the king. Given that about two-thirds of the residents of Delaware counties were loyalists, this was no small task. But, as the next few years would demonstrate, John Banning and the other committed revolutionaries proved to be a much more formidable force than the Tories. It appears that he carried out his commission well, for in early 1776 he was elected to the Council of Safety, an executive committee with the power to direct all military affairs for Delaware and to raise troops for the Continental Army.[11]

This would soon become a post of great responsibility, as the colonies began formally declaring independence from Britain. On June 15, 1776, John Banning and the other members of the Delaware General Assembly answered the call of the Second Continental Congress, unanimously passing a resolution to suspend all English authority over their government. This action, which is still celebrated as "Separation Day" in the state of Delaware, was that colony's official declaration of independence. The General Assembly also called for a state constitutional convention to meet in August that year, at which the delegates voted to remove the three Delaware counties from the authority of the Pennsylvania governor, creating a separate state. In July 1776, representatives from Delaware joined the other American revolutionaries in declaring complete independence from England. A public reading of the national Declaration of Independence took place on July 29 at the Dover Green, just two blocks north of John Banning's house, and the Delaware militiamen then prepared for war.[12]

Three months before the signing of the Declaration of Independence, John Banning, who "own[ed] a gun in good order," had joined Thomas Rodney's Dover Light Infantry Company, part of the Kent County militia, as a private. But apparently the militia needed him as an administrator more than as a soldier. In 1777 he was elected military treasurer for Kent County, in charge of supplying and paying the troops. Funding the conflict was problematic and currency was scarce in wartime, however, and he sometimes had to provide necessities from his store inventory. In 1777 he donated 650 flints from his own supply, and by the end of the war he probably added some of his own foodstuffs to the limited rations of the Delaware Regiment. He was also said to have endeared himself to the soldiers by paying them in currency and gold coin instead of the constantly devalued scrip received by most soldiers in other counties. The Delaware General Assembly seems to have found him an accurate and trustworthy manager of money, since he was appointed in 1777 and 1783 to a committee to settle public accounts resulting from the war, and to another that audited the Delaware militia in 1783. For several years he was also a justice of the peace overseeing trials for treason and other offenses.[13]

Besides this wartime service, John Banning played an increasingly active role in Delaware politics. He was elected to the Delaware State Senate three times: in 1777, 1781, and 1786, the last time while also serving as Kent County's treasurer from 1784 to 1788. During his final term as senator, he participated in the proceedings that established Delaware as the first state in the new United States of America. In 1788 he was unanimously chosen to be one of Delaware's three electors in the nation's first presidential election. Banning and his two cohorts proudly cast their votes for George Washington as president and for John Jay of New York as vice president (the latter was of course defeated by John Adams). Despite his many civic obligations, during the war and postwar years he continued to conduct his business in Dover. One of Dover's most prominent citizens, he was clearly trusted by the citizens of his town, holding bonds for many of his neighbors and serving as administrator or executor in nine Dover probate actions from the 1770s to 1791.[14]

John had apparently remained a bachelor for his first four decades, but despite his busy roster of civic duties in the 1780s he found time to take on the duties of husband. He married Elizabeth Alford, a "well-known beauty," about 1784. Elizabeth was the daughter of Charity Alston and Philip Alford of Philadelphia. Her parents had emigrated from the

British West Indies, and Philip operated a business between Philadelphia and Barbados until he was lost at sea; upon his death, Charity moved with their children to Dover.[15] Elizabeth is believed to have first married a Mr. Hudson, but he must have died a short time later, for she soon married John Casson, a hatter who had a small shop in Dover. It is perhaps as Mrs. Casson that Elizabeth came to know John Banning. Born in Dover in 1750, John Casson probably knew Banning both as a neighbor and from the military, for Casson had fought in the Revolutionary War as the captain of a cavalry unit. Casson died about 1782, and his widow and her soon-to-be spouse, John Banning, were appointed as co-administrators of the estate.[16]

John and Elizabeth Banning began their marriage in postwar Dover, a city that in 1785 had about one hundred houses and about six hundred residents, many of them involved in wheat farming. The Bannings had two children: Sarah Banning, born in 1787, and John Alford Banning, born in 1790. This marriage, like Elizabeth's first two, was not a long one. In February 1791 John died at the age of fifty-two, less than a decade after their wedding. By that time he had accumulated a large fortune in land, furnishings for the home on King Street, stock for his store, and a dozen slaves. He had promised to free some of those slaves when they reached a particular age, which several were approaching, but he died before he himself could make good on that promise. The estate was large and complex, and would take fourteen years to settle. John Banning was buried just steps from his home in the cemetery of Christ Church, where he had been a vestryman. The inscription on his gravestone reads, in part, "he was the patron and protector of the poor, an indulgent husband and an affectionate parent and a kind master." An obituary in a local newspaper noted the "confidence reposed in him by his fellow citizens" and recalled his service in the legislature since the Revolution, along with his "private virtues," including his "inflexible justice, and charity to the poor." A New York paper also mentioned his passing, praising him as a man of "exalted virtues."[17]

The Banning house and store on King Street was left to John's young son, who sold it years later, in 1816, to his brother-in-law, Henry Moore Ridgely, and the other trustees of the Dover Academy to be used as a private school. By 1829 part of it also served as a public school and as a meeting place for fraternal organizations. After a new school was constructed, the building was no longer needed, and it was converted into a carriage shop by the 1880s. In 1899 it was divided into two homes and later into apartments. Today it still stands as a private residence, with a small plaque at the entrance commemorating its builder and first resident.[18]

Within a year of John's death, Elizabeth Alford Banning remarried. Her third—or possibly fourth—husband was Dr. William McKee, a surgeon from Glasgow, Scotland, who had settled in Delaware by 1787. He owned property in New Castle County and in Camden, just south of Dover. The McKees soon moved with the Banning children, Sarah and John, to Camden. There they had two children of their own and then moved north to Wilmington in 1803, where William became a trustee of Wilmington College. In 1812 Elizabeth would pass away there, followed by William in 1816.[19]

The McKees lived very well on the proceeds of John Banning's estate, along with the income from Dr. McKee's medical practice and landholdings. Their wealth enabled Sarah Banning to attend boarding schools in Wilmington and Philadelphia in the late 1790s and early 1800s, where she was a smart and popular student. In 1802, at the age of fifteen, she was courted by Henry Moore Ridgely, a childhood friend and a member of one of the most prominent families in Dover, with whom the Bannings and McKees were well acquainted. Late the following year, Sarah and Henry were married; they would raise a family of fourteen children. Upon their marriage, Henry had just begun his career as a lawyer and a staunch Federalist. He would eventually serve the public in a series of positions—as a Delaware representative in Congress from 1811 to 1815, as Delaware secretary of state for two terms, in the state legislature for six terms, and as U.S. senator for a short term, from 1827 to 1829—before retiring from government. In addition to his political duties, he was president of the Farmers Bank of Dover for forty years and managed his large family farm, which Sarah ran during his long absences in the service of Delaware. The marriage created a much stronger bond between the Ridgelys and the Bannings, a connection that would benefit both over the next century.[20]

John Alford Banning: Gentleman Farmer

John and Elizabeth Banning's son, John Alford Banning, had a more troubled upbringing than his sister—one marred by conflicts with his mother and stepfather. Only one year old when his father died, the youngster never had a chance to know him. He did not get along very well with his stepfather, as evidenced by his protests at McKee's decisions in settling the estates of his father and his uncle, Richard Banning, and his behavior at the time of McKee's death in 1816. Like Sarah, John received a good education. He enrolled at Princeton University (then called the College of New Jersey) in 1806, graduating in 1810. He then studied law and began to manage the large landholdings left to him by his father in several counties in Delaware. In the summer of 1811, he announced his engagement to a young woman, a marriage his mother opposed because of his age—he was then just twenty—and her belief that he was not yet prepared to become "master of a family." The rest of his family also disapproved and were relieved when the engagement was broken off later that year.[21]

Early the following year Elizabeth McKee died, and her loss affected John deeply, apparently intensifying the tensions with his stepfather and spurring him to strike out on his own. For months he argued with Dr. McKee about the details of his uncle's estate. He began purchasing land in New Castle County, near Wilmington, and investing in the wheat business. By December 1812 he decided to leave Dover, where he had been living with the Ridgely family for some time, to live on a large farm about twelve miles northwest of Wilmington, which he named Oak Hill. He also became engaged again, this time to Elizabeth Lowber of Philadelphia. The two were married there in March of the following year.[22]

Elizabeth Lowber's family, like John Alford's, had long-standing ties to Kent County, where they were prosperous landholders. The patriarch of the American Lowbers, Peter Lowber (also spelled Pieter Loper), emigrated from Amsterdam and was living in New York City by 1677. He moved about 1684 to Kent County, where he purchased a large amount of farmland. His family prospered in this region, as successive generations acquired more land and a large number of slaves, many of whom continued to live in the region after they were freed. The Lowbers' wartime involvements also paralleled those of John Alford's father. At least three Lowbers from Delaware fought in units of the Continental Army or in the militia during the Revolutionary War, and Elizabeth's grandfather also served in the Delaware State Assembly in the 1790s. Her father, William, was born near Dover about 1770 and moved his family by 1805 to Philadelphia, where he was joined in 1812 by his brother Daniel; there, the two operated a leather-tanning business. The Lowbers were well known in local society, and by the Banning family in particular. In fact, like many other landowning families in Philadelphia and Delaware of this generation, who were often closely tied to one another by marriage and other social bonds, the Lowbers and Bannings were already connected by marriage: Elizabeth's uncle, Daniel Lowber, had wed Elizabeth (Betsy) Banning, a first cousin of John Alford Banning.[23]

At the time John Alford Banning and Elizabeth arrived in Wilmington, this northern Delaware city in New Castle County offered many opportunities. Although it would always be overshadowed by nearby Philadelphia as the center of economic and social activity in the vast Delaware Valley, Wilmington was Delaware's only industrial city at the turn of the nineteenth century. As a small deepwater port city located at the confluence of the Christiana (now spelled Christina) and Delaware rivers, it developed a modest but significant ocean trade. The evolution of inland transportation infrastructure, in the form of improved roads and turnpikes in the 1810s, canals in the late 1820s, and railroads in the 1830s, connected Wilmington to Philadelphia to the north and Baltimore, Maryland, to the southeast, as well as to Delaware cities to the south. These transportation improvements accelerated the creation of industrial plants in the city, provided export routes for industrial output and agricultural products, and spurred population growth. It is not surprising that John Alford's son Phineas would one day think of Wilmington when planning his own empire of transport and trade in Southern California.[24]

The society of this bustling city was considerably livelier than Dover's. At a higher elevation than the marshy lowland of Dover, Wilmington had a more pleasant climate, and many affluent families from Dover and other communities moved there in the early 1800s. And although it was not as socially important as Philadelphia, Wilmington was certainly a step above Dover. Sarah Banning Ridgely complained several times in the 1810s that isolated Dover was "dull and uninteresting as usual," lamenting that "this gloomy town affords no society" (she had similar objections to Wilmington in comparison to Philadelphia).[25] The abolitionist influence in the city also aligned it more closely with the north than was the case with other Delaware communities. Quakers with strong ties to a more cosmopolitan Philadelphia formed a significant portion of the Wilmington population. As a group Quakers were more likely to be opposed to slavery than were residents of the southern counties, who lived closer to states where the institution was more prevalent and increasingly plantation-centered. The activism of Thomas Garrett and other Quakers made Wilmington a strong center of abolitionist sympathy and an important depot on the Underground Railroad. The abolitionist and northward-looking flavor of Wilmington politics may have been influential in Phineas Banning's later decision to align himself with Union forces during the Civil War.[26]

Wilmington also became the home of the du Pont family, which established a gunpowder works along the Brandywine River in 1802 and expanded the business with cotton and woolen mills by 1810. The family soon emerged as the dominant economic and social force in the region. One of its members, Charles I. du Pont, became an important textile manufacturer and a state senator. At his first wedding in 1824, his bride was ceremoniously given away by the Marquis de Lafayette, then on a tour of America. Charles's spouse died in 1838, and while serving in the state senate in Dover in 1841, he met Ann Ridgely, the daughter of Henry and Sarah Banning Ridgely. As the traditional story goes, the abolitionist Lucretia Mott had been invited to give a speech in Dover that year, and after a tense encounter at the courthouse between opponents and supporters of slavery, Henry Ridgely (a slaveholder himself) and his friends escorted her to his home for dinner, and for her protection. The group included Charles I. du Pont and another gentleman, both of whom had asked for Ann Ridgely's hand in marriage. While in the Ridgely house, Ms. Mott accidentally fell down. Charles immediately helped her up while the other suitor began laughing. These responses helped Ann to make up her mind, and the next day Charles and Ann announced their engagement. Their marriage, which lasted until Charles's death in 1869, produced two children and a strong and long-lasting family link to the Bannings in Wilmington, Delaware.[27]

But the life of a farmer outside Wilmington would not have offered much in the way of cosmopolitan society, or even of creature comforts, at this time. The agricultural hinterland of Wilmington was primarily devoted to growing wheat that was milled locally and shipped to other markets in the early 1800s. This industry declined after 1815, shortly after John Alford and Elizabeth Banning moved there. With the end of the War of 1812 and the Napoleonic Wars, the European demand for American agricultural products receded, and Philadelphia gradually came to dominate the regional milling and grain trade. It was not a propitious time to become a farmer in Wilmington, and Banning might well not have succeeded even in good times.[28]

As it was, John Alford Banning's economic standing would not rise as he had thought it would when he moved to Wilmington to make a fresh start with his new bride. Although he had inherited quite a fortune, he proved to be a poor, or at least unlucky, entrepreneur. In 1816 he owned land in several sections of Delaware, but would eventually sell much of it except for Oak Hill, presumably for the income needed to support his family. With the wheat industry in Delaware falling into a depression, it would be a while before his remaining properties would appreciate. Unable to raise the money for taxes, he lost some of his land in Kent County in a sheriff's auction in 1815.[29]

Other evidence suggests that John was suffering from hard times. When he left Dover in 1812, John owned at least one slave named Jesse, whom he had purchased after unsuccessfully trying to buy a slave belonging to his sister and brother-in-law. Like many bondsmen of his time, Jesse ran away, in the spring of 1816, causing John to publish a reward for his return; Jesse did not reappear until five years later. During this time, Banning was presumably without the free labor that Jesse would have supplied. By at least 1828, John no longer had a slave living in his household; there is no record of his having changed his views on slavery, so we may conclude that he could no longer afford one. Indeed, slavery in New Castle County, as in all of Delaware, was declining over these years for a variety of reasons, as the slave population dropped to less than four hundred by 1850, with only two in John's district of Christiana Hundred. John also had to sell some of his inherited stock in a bank. He loaned money to his father-in-law, William Lowber, and to his former lawyer and worried about repayment. All this suggests that he did not have enough capital to weather the ups and downs of a farming life in uncertain times. Clearly, his economic prospects were gloomy.[30]

John also had troubles with his military commitment around the time he moved to Oak Hill. A year after the start of the War of 1812, Pvt. John Banning of New Castle County, a member of the Sixth Company, First Regiment, of the Delaware Militia, faced a court martial for three days' absence and was fined three dollars. Although he was clearly far from alone, judging by the long list of militiamen who were also fined, the citation did not look good on a soldier's record. The time he spent serving his country, or possibly making money to pay such fines for avoiding service, occurred just as he was starting a new life with his young family in Wilmington.[31]

For at least one period in the mid-1810s, Banning apparently often drank to excess, perhaps in response to the stresses of his recent marriage, the conflict with his stepfather, and economic ups and downs. In late 1816, a Wilmington neighbor wrote to her son in Philadelphia reporting that the "wealthy" John Banning was at present in the Pennsylvania Hospital. "The continual state of intoxication he was in has I suppose produced a species of derangement," she concluded. John recovered from his bout with liquor and resumed his career as a not-too-successful gentleman farmer and an attorney who practiced little, if any, law. In future years he would be more interested in books than in business, law, or crops. One of his daughters would remember him as a farmer, very quiet, and fond of books. His son Phineas later recalled that "In consequence of his literary tastes, and a defect in one of his eyes he was not a practical and successful farmer."[32]

John and Elizabeth raised eleven children at Oak Hill. The first was John Alford Banning Jr., born between 1813 and 1815. After him came William Lowber Banning, who always gave 1814 as his birth year, but might have been born as late as 1816, according to later census returns. Elizabeth Alice was born about 1819, Mary Lowber in 1820, and Sallie about 1821. Then Richard was born in 1822, Henry about 1825, and Alice Ponder in the following year. Phineas was certainly born in 1830, followed by Francenia Alice in 1833 and finally Cole Lowber in 1834. They were raised very strictly by their mother as Episcopalians and received modest educations. Father John managed the farm and might have practiced the law occasionally, although the census returns of 1830, 1840, and 1850 identify him as a farmer, and he never appeared in the Wilmington city directories or newspapers as a practicing attorney. He was aided on the farm by paid laborers and the children, who as they grew older pitched in with farming chores or helped to take care of their younger siblings.[33]

Life Down on the Farm

Rural life in the United States at this time was simple but laborious: farming families produced their own food and perhaps a surplus for market, made most of their own clothes, and built their own dwellings and outbuildings, among many other chores. Such a life appealed to few of the Banning children. John Alford Banning Jr. tried to leave the farm twice, but his mother always persuaded him to stay. He would remain close by and continue to help his father and the rest of the family, to the relief of his parents and some of his siblings. Living in the vicinity of his family also helped him to relieve his depression, which was exacerbated by what one of his sisters called an "unfortunate marriage."[34] Most of the other siblings also wanted to escape the farm, and some of them departed at a very early age. Perhaps they found living with a severe mother and a reserved and uninvolved father wearisome, or they saw agricultural chores as dreary and unappealing, or they thought the bustling city was more exciting or offered greater opportunities. Certainly the younger siblings would have been aware that only the eldest offspring would get what was left of the family fortune. Whatever their reasons, by 1850 only one of John and Elizabeth's children still lived with them. William Lowber Banning, the second son, decided to move out of the household by the early 1830s. He traveled on foot to Philadelphia to live with his grandfather,

William Lowber, and relied on him for advice in seeking a trade. Lowber first recommended that he learn carpentry, so William apprenticed to "an old and testy Quaker." But this occupation did not hold his interest for long, especially after the old Quaker told him to polish his shoes and William responded that he was a carpenter, not a bootblack. Lowber then recommended that William become a lawyer. After studying law, William became a Philadelphia attorney in a partnership with William Hollinshead; the firm occupied offices across the street from Franklin Square and, later, near Independence Hall.[35]

Mary Lowber Banning had moved to Philadelphia to become a teacher by 1842, and Phineas Banning, then just thirteen, followed her and his brother William to the city in the following year. Even Francenia and Cole, still teenagers in 1850, were no longer living at Oak Hill, according to that year's census. Although John Alford Banning Jr. and his wife and two children lived on a farm close by, Alice was the only one to remain on the farm with her parents. Like so many children of their generation, the Banning siblings left the farm to pursue opportunities in the big city and westward in an expanding nation during a tumultuous period in its history.[36]

PART 2

THE SOUTHERN CALIFORNIA PATRIARCH

CHAPTER TWO

A Young Delawarean in Frontier Southern California

I n 1843, young Phineas Banning decided to follow some of his older siblings, leaving the family farm at Oak Hill to seek his future and his fortune. The ninth of John Alford and Elizabeth Lowber Banning's eleven children, he was only thirteen at the time. Reminiscing much later about this time in his life, he said that his motive was merely to escape the uneventful life and "monotonous round of daily toil" and isolation he envisioned if he stayed on the farm. But he must also have known that as the fifth son, he would not be able lay claim to much of the family farm. So he begged his parents to allow him to move to the city of Philadelphia, his mecca at this young age.[1]

With a modest education and fifty cents in his pocket (as he later confided to an interviewer), Phineas left Wilmington, Delaware, and walked the thirty miles north to Philadelphia to live with his brother, William Lowber, whom he probably admired more than his own father at the time. William would be Phineas's mentor for the rest of his life, setting a high standard for the younger brother who followed his lead in business and politics. Phineas worked industriously in these pursuits to match William's success, and like his brother was known for his ambition, vision, and work ethic. Their sister Mary also lived in the city at the time, along with many members of their mother's family, the Lowbers, and other former residents of Wilmington.[2]

Phineas Banning arrived in Philadelphia at a very unsettled time. As one historian summarized it, the period from 1841 to 1854 was

> marked by unprecedented civic violence, arising from many causes: an explosive increase in population; a complex and unreconciled ethnic, racial, and religious mixture; inadequate housing; a growing and evermore obvious maldistribution of wealth; a volatile social class

structure—all exacerbated by political ineptitude or
chicanery or a combination of both.

Industrial production had taken its toll in this port city, as it became a
magnet for newcomers like Phineas and grew increasingly crowded and
congested. The economic depression following the closing of the Bank
of the United States in 1841 spurred unemployment, gang activity, and
crime. Tensions between the native population and the immigrants,
many of them divided along ethnic lines, erupted into violent con-
frontations, including a major riot in 1844 that ended with twenty dead
and over one hundred injured. Yet even in the midst of this civic
disorder, the City of Brotherly Love offered opportunity—a chance to
establish oneself.[3]

During his first few years in Philadelphia, Phineas lived and worked
with William, whose law office on North Sixth Street facing Franklin
Square had living quarters upstairs. The brick row building sat about five
blocks from the waterfront docks—close to the residence where novel-
ist Edgar Allan Poe lived from 1842 to 1844. Phineas told an interviewer
in the 1880s that he had studied law with William, but at most he might
have searched for particular cases; still just a teenager, Phineas spent the
bulk of his time on clerical duties. After about two years working at these
menial tasks, Phineas decided to change direction, and obtained a position as a clerk at Siter, Price & Company on High Street (later changed
to Market Street), about two blocks from the Delaware River and not too
far from William's future office.[4]

In the 1840s William's law partnership with William Hollinshead was
becoming more lucrative and his position in the city more prominent. He
and Hollinshead eventually moved their law office to a more prestigious
location in a red brick building on South Fifth Street, just around the
corner from Independence Hall. Both William and Hollinshead were
elected to the Pennsylvania legislature in 1845 as Democrats and served
one term. Four years later, William decided that he had finally amassed
enough of a fortune to marry and start his own family with a woman he
had courted for the previous seven years. In January 1850 he wed Mary
Alicia Sweeny, whose mother was a Pennsylvania Quaker and whose Irish
father was a direct descendant of Donal and Niall Glundubh, the mon-
archs of Ireland in the tenth century. William and Mary moved into a
rooming house in that year with a merchant and his family, besides several servants and laborers. There was no room for a younger Banning
brother in this household.[5]

By at least 1850 Phineas was living on his own, probably in a room-ing house in crowded downtown Philadelphia. He continued to work diligently at Siter, Price, a "fancy goods jobbing house" that imported and sold household goods and other commodities from Europe and else-where. He still lived close to relatives in the city, so there was no social isolation. He might have even joined in political debate at the time, as he was later reported to have spoken on the evils of slavery to a crowd at a meeting of the American Literary Union held in 1849, when he would have been only nineteen. If he did speak on the matter, he was taking a stand on what was an incendiary issue in Philadelphia, as in the rest of the nation at that time.[6]

While working at the wholesale import shop in 1851, Phineas was assigned the job of packing a large shipment of merchandise, including delicate crockery, for Dr. George East, a merchant who planned to ship the goods to California. A trader, East had lived in Chihuahua, Mexico, from the early 1830s until 1849, when he moved to California. He sold goods throughout the American Southwest and northern Mexico and hoped to sell the shipment in California, where the gold rush had brought people eager to buy luxury products such as these, which were not manu-factured locally at the time.[7]

East, then, was among those entrepreneurs who sought to capitalize on the mass migration to the American West that followed the end of the war with Mexico in 1848. Immigrants came by the thousands from around the world, and especially from the eastern United States, lured by gold prospecting and other opportunities to make a fortune. After the first an-nouncement of the discovery of gold near Sacramento in 1848, reports of newly discovered deposits and other stories about life in California con-tinually filled the front pages of newspapers throughout the East, includ-ing journals such as *Bicknell's Reporter* of Philadelphia, which printed such news in almost every issue in the early 1850s. Phineas Banning surely knew of such developments, and, still a lowly clerk after years of work in Philadel-phia, he decided to join the wave of immigration westward. His opportu-nity arrived when he met Dr. East while packing the latter's shipment of goods. The two agreed that East would pay for the cost of passage if Ban-ning would accompany him and protect the shipment en route to its des-tination. William and Mary Banning were a bit surprised by the news of Phineas's impending departure, and Mary bet him "a new velvet waistcoat" that he wouldn't leave for California. It was a bet she would soon lose.[8]

The trip from the East Coast to California could be made in one of three ways in 1851: across the country by land in a very slow wagon train;

by ship around South America, which could take up to six months; and by ship to Panama, across the isthmus on land and by river, and then by ship to the Golden State, which took at least six weeks and sometimes much longer. East chose the Panama route, which took considerably less time than rounding Cape Horn, and arranged to move his cargo, along with young Phineas, to New York. They set sail in late August 1851 on the maiden voyage of the *Illinois*, a wooden side-wheel steamer operated by the Howland and Aspinwall international importing firm.[9]

The Panama route began with a ten-day voyage from New York harbor to Chagres, on the eastern coast of Panama. From there, travelers hired guides, at whatever price the traffic would bear, for the treacherous journey across the isthmus. They were transported part of the way across the isthmus in dugout canoes on the Chagres River to Gorgona. From there they continued on foot or rode mules through mountains and jungles to the Pacific port at Panama City. The overland portion of the trip was slow and difficult and the heat unrelenting; some of the travelers enthused about the lush vegetation and varied fauna, while others complained of the "screeching of parrots" and the "howling of tigers," among other trials. Once in crowded Panama City, travelers faced the further hardships of limited provisions and uncertain accommodation while waiting for a departing steamer, often for days and sometimes longer. Tropical diseases such as malaria, cholera, yellow fever, and "Panama fever" were widespread along this route, and many travelers did not survive the ordeal. Transporting a large shipment of goods made the trek even more difficult for East and Banning.[10]

The Pacific Ocean portion of the trip, over three thousand miles, consisted of a twenty-day passage to San Francisco with stops at Acapulco, San Diego, and other ports. East and Banning stopped in San Diego and unloaded their goods. Banning stayed while East continued on the coastal vessel *Ohio* to the small port at San Pedro, arriving on November 8, 1851, to visit Los Angeles in search of a buyer for his shipment. While there, he apparently told the *Los Angeles Star* of his intention "to make Los Angeles his future residence." But, his goods unsold, he sailed on to San Francisco on the *Ohio* at the end of the month. By early 1852 he had returned to Los Angeles, and in February he agreed to sell his goods to Douglass & Sanford, a "forwarding and commission merchants" firm located in San Pedro and Los Angeles, which would sell and transport the shipment.[11] Only a month later, East became seriously ill and died.

William G. Dryden, a lawyer and future judge in Los Angeles County, had helped East to write a will, which he signed the week before his death.

In it he divided his property among his relatives and appointed Los Angeles County Clerk Benjamin D. Wilson and David Douglass, one of the partners to whom he sold the Philadelphia goods, as executors. Wilson was to handle the overall management of the estate and the disposition of East's personal property, while Douglass was responsible for taking care of the inventory of goods he and partner William Sanford had just acquired but had not yet paid for in full.[12]

East, in turn, had not fully paid Siter, Price & Company in Philadelphia for the goods and travel expenses that had been advanced, and this account too would have to be settled before the estate was closed. In order to accomplish this, all parties relied on Phineas Banning. Throughout the rest of 1852 Banning corresponded with his former employer in Philadelphia, who asked Wilson the executor to allow "our friend Phineas Banning" to act for the partners. As it turned out there was quite a bit of damage to the shipment, found too late to file an insurance claim, so the estate had to make good on the loss. The matter was finally cleared up by the end of the year, although for a number of reasons the East estate as a whole took much longer to close.[13]

Phineas Banning's work in attending to this account turned out to be his official business for a full year, since, even while he was representing Siter, Price in the probate proceedings, he had been hired as a clerk by the Douglass & Sanford company. The two young partners of this firm, New Yorker David Douglass and William Sanford of Missouri, had lived in Los Angeles since before 1850. They established a wholesale and retail business, selling and shipping general merchandise at the nascent port of San Pedro, with an office in nearby Los Angeles. They also supplied passenger service between San Pedro and Los Angeles with six horses and two mules. Their firm competed in the very early 1850s with several other concerns, whose owners included John Temple, David W. Alexander, Francis Mellus, Benjamin D. Wilson, Albert Packard, and Augustus W. Timms. Banning was, once again, only a clerk, stationed at the San Pedro store in 1852. That was his occupation as listed in the special state census of that year and as recalled by E. A. Johnson, who came to Los Angeles at the same time to drive a freight wagon. Johnson related this memory some fifty-four years later, "with his favorite pipe gripped between his toothless gums."[14]

The San Pedro harbor where Banning worked was a primitive landing site at the time. New England traders in the first half of the nineteenth century had found that the high cliffs surrounding much of the shoreline made access to the beach difficult. A crewmember aboard one of these

Carl Oscar Borg's *The Era of the Boston Ships* (ca. 1931) depicts New England
shippers trading merchandise for California cattle hides and tallow at
San Pedro Bay in the 1830s and 1840s. Courtesy of the Huntington Library.

ships, Richard Henry Dana, went so far as to call San Pedro "a miserable
hole" and the "hell of California" in 1836, as it "was designed in every way
for the wear and tear of sailors." The coastline there was crescent-shaped
for about fifteen miles. Rattlesnake Island, a five-mile strip of land slightly
higher than a sand bar, extended from the eastern side and left an opening for small ships to enter the estuary northeast of Timms Landing, near
the western point of the harbor. Deadman's Island, in the center of the
harbor, impeded navigation close in but did little to block the strong
southeasterly winds that swept the roadstead in winter. The very shallow

mudflats extending a distance from the shore forced large vessels to anchor in the much deeper and more turbulent water almost a mile away and to ferry their passengers and cargo ashore on smaller craft. The shallow lighters used for this purpose occasionally capsized, throwing their occupants and freight into the cold and sometimes rough water. Despite these shortcomings, San Pedro was the major port for Los Angeles, the center of its maritime commercial trade as well as its smuggling activity at midcentury. It was a regular stop for coastal steamers on the route between San Francisco and San Diego in the 1850s.[15]

City of Angels in the 1850s

When Phineas Banning first came to the region in late 1851, Los Angeles County was a vast expanse of about 34,520 square miles. It stretched from the Pacific Ocean at a point near the Santa Barbara County line (at that time) north of Malibu along the Santa Susana Mountains to El Tejon, and then traced a direct line northeasterly to the state line at about Daylight Springs. From there it followed the Utah and New Mexico territorial borders south to the San Diego County line near present-day Parker, Arizona, and turned westward to San Mateo Creek and then to the ocean.[16]

The landscape of this county centered on the coastal basin, a flood plain that extends northward from the Pacific Ocean at the San Pedro harbor area and eastward from Santa Monica Bay. The plain is surrounded by the Santa Monica Mountains and a series of hills that separate it from the San Fernando Valley to the north and the San Gabriel and San Bernardino valleys to the east. These valleys are surrounded on the north and east by the Santa Susana, San Gabriel, and San Bernardino mountains, the last two of which are very high ranges that form a natural barrier penetrable in only a few locations. The lower Santa Ana range completes the barrier on the southeast border from the coastline to the San Bernardino Valley. Beyond these mountains to the north and east was almost-uninhabited desert and semidesert, stretching past Death Valley and the Mojave Desert to the eastern border of the state.[17]

The county was sparsely settled in the 1850s. The population was centered in the city of Los Angeles, in towns adjacent to the Spanish-era missions of San Fernando, San Gabriel, and San Juan Capistrano, and in settlements established by Anglos at Lexington (later to become El Monte) and by the Mormons in San Bernardino. The 1850 county population of 3,530 non-Indians included twelve African Americans, all of whom lived in Los Angeles city. Approximately 4,000 Indians resided in the county by 1852, some on ranchos and on the outskirts of towns where they worked as laborers, and the others in villages in the outlying areas.[18]

The region's economy was based on cattle ranching and farming. The large ranchos surrounding the city of Los Angeles raised herds of cattle for the hide-and-tallow trade with New England merchants during the Mexican period. With the discovery of gold and the population boom in Northern California, ranchers in the southern "cow counties" found a new market for meat and made fortunes by herding their mature animals to the gold country and selling them for beef. Although the area of Los Angeles County had been considerably smaller in 1850, before Banning's arrival, it was nonetheless the home of almost a quarter of the state's beef cattle and most of its sheep at the time, and contained about one-fifth of the state's cultivated land—more than any but Monterey and Santa Barbara counties. Most of this farming acreage was located just outside of the central city of Los Angeles, where wheat, corn, barley, potatoes, fruit, and wine grapes were the principal crops. Agricultural production, like the beef cattle trade, markedly increased after the discovery of gold and the resulting opportunity to feed the rising population in Northern California. Manufacturing was nonexistent at this time; some necessities were produced by local artisans, but most of the commodities for inhabitants were imported, arriving in Los Angeles through the small port at San Pedro or overland on the Santa Fe Trail and later the Salt Lake Trail.[19]

The social structure and the economy of the region were sustained by an elite that included the ranchers who owned vast landholdings outside the city and, usually, a townhouse in the central core of the city surrounding the Plaza. The predominantly wealthy *Californios* among them fared much better than their counterparts in the north, most of whom lost their fortunes and social standing soon after the arrival of tens of thousands of Anglo immigrants in the early 1850s. In sparsely settled Los Angeles, the ranchers prospered for another decade until the cattle industry declined and they lost their empires, through foreclosure in many cases. This landed gentry was gradually joined by American and European immigrants who married into Hispanic families before statehood in 1850 or arrived soon after and created an economic foothold that granted them acceptance into the social leadership (as with Phineas Banning). These newcomers demanded more government services, improved sanitary conditions, and additional infrastructure in a region without many of these amenities. The mostly Anglo immigrants gradually joined the established gentry as the

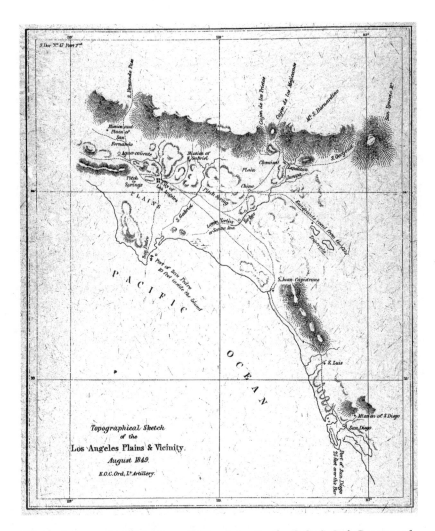

The southern portion of Southern California in 1849, by E. O. C. Ord. Courtesy of the Huntington Library.

region's urban elite, and many of them would serve in official local government positions, directing the social and economic development of the region after 1850.[20]

The city to which these future leaders came gave few hints of the megalopolis it would become. Los Angeles in 1852 was a small incorporated community of about two thousand non-Indian residents, primarily Mexicans, with a growing cosmopolitan population of Americans and Europeans. Hundreds of local Indians consigned to menial labor also lived within the twenty-eight square miles encompassed by the city limits. All of the buildings were adobe brick, with only a few rising to two stories. Commercial buildings were sparse, if growing in number, but it would be almost two decades before the first bank was established. There were no sidewalks and the streets were unpaved, turning to mud when it rained. There was only one church—the Roman Catholic Our Lady Queen of the Angels Church, facing the Plaza—but many saloons and gambling halls. A second hotel had opened the year before, but there were no hospitals or buildings devoted to social institutions. The steamer from San Francisco arrived once or twice a month, bringing passengers and newspapers to an isolated population. In many ways Los Angeles resembled the typical rugged frontier town in the American West, with all of its accompanying lawlessness, against which its citizens struggled to establish social institutions and maintain order.[21]

The single harbor for Los Angeles County at the time could boast only the tiny, quiet community of San Pedro. After witnessing a major celebration there on July 4, 1853, Horace Bell observed wryly that it was a "great place":

> it had no streets, for none were necessary. No prison admonished the evil-doer to give San Pedro a wide berth. No church invited the piously-inclined to seek religious consolation at the lively port. No! there was nothing of that sort, but the author solemnly asseverates that there was a liberty pole at San Pedro, from which proudly floated the flag of freedom. That there were two mud scows, a ship's anchor and a fishing boat, a multiplicity of old broken-down Mexican carts, a house, a large haystack and mule corral, and our old friend the gallant *Laura Bevan*, floating swan-like at her anchorage, on that beautiful Fourth of July.[22]

It was here that Phineas Banning lived in his first years in California. Working for Douglass & Sanford as a clerk in 1852, he learned the business of selling and shipping goods. The census of that year revealed that he lived very close to (possibly in the same complex as) the wealthy Sepulveda family, who owned a large ranch adjacent to San Pedro. He worked in the old "hide house," the only structure in San Pedro that dated as far back as the 1830s, which sat on a bluff above the harbor. He might even have lived there for a time between 1852 and 1853.[23]

Why did Phineas Banning stay in San Pedro instead of continuing on to the northern goldfields to strike it rich, as many '49ers and later gold seekers thought they would? Banning did not address the question in interviews later in his life, and subsequent writers have virtually ignored the point. He did sail by coastal steamer to San Francisco, the major gateway to the gold country, in May of 1852, possibly on business for his employers or perhaps to take a look at the situation for himself. Whatever his reasons for making the trip, he did not stay long. Perhaps he heard from veteran miners of the hard work and trying living conditions in the mining camps, or saw that most of them failed to get rich. In any case, he returned and chose to remain in Southern California, first helping to settle the account that had paid for his passage westward and learning his business, and then building his own empire—one whose profits would rival the earnings of some of those who did find gold. In this his chosen career resembled those of the (much more prosperous) Central Pacific Railroad's "Big Four," who made their first fortunes supplying miners rather than digging for gold themselves—or perhaps that of David Jacks, who arrived in California in 1849 and, much like Phineas Banning, decided to work as a store clerk rather than prospect for gold. Jacks, a future customer of Banning, soon became a prominent merchant and landowner, one of the wealthiest men in Monterey County.[24]

New Friends and Business Associates

During 1852 and the following two years, Banning established relationships with several important citizens in Los Angeles who would play crucial roles in his social and economic rise. These future business partners, project investors, and clients helped to bankroll or otherwise support his entrepreneurial ventures. Two of them would become his relatives by marriage, one shortly after his arrival and the other long after his death. Their stories also serve as exemplars of the extraordinarily varied and overlapping careers of the new leaders of Southern California, in whose company Banning was now taking his place.

This group included three of the more important Anglo immigrants who became members of the landed elite of Southern California in the Mexican period. All of them would provide working capital for Banning in his early entrepreneurial ventures. Among these, the earliest to arrive in Los Angeles was Abel Stearns, who migrated to California from his native New England in 1829, settling in San Pedro in 1832. Stearns became a Mexican citizen and a Roman Catholic, opened a trading business at the harbor, and eventually emerged as one of the wealthiest land and cattle barons in all of Southern California. He also served in the California legislature for two terms, and in city and county positions, and became an important customer for Banning. Another New Englander who settled in Los Angeles in this period was John Temple, who established an importing business and kept large herds of cattle and sheep on his Rancho Los Cerritos. Temple was one of the richest entrepreneurs in the region and would finance Banning's business on a number of occasions.[25]

More important to Banning was Benjamin Davis Wilson, one of the executors of the estate of George East. Born in Tennessee in 1811, Wilson became a fur trapper and trader and moved west, eventually settling in Southern California in 1841. Two years later he purchased the Jurupa ranch in the Riverside area and raised cattle. He served the Mexican government in California on several occasions until the outbreak of the war with Mexico in 1846, when he became the commander of a small unit of local volunteers in the service of the United States. After the war he moved to Los Angeles and later the San Gabriel Valley, where he became a merchant and tended a large vineyard and citrus orchard. From the beginning of the American period until his death in 1878, he was involved with many major enterprises in Southern California and held a number of official positions, including federal Indian commissioner for the region, state senator for several terms, Los Angeles County supervisor and county clerk, and Los Angeles city mayor and member of the Common Council. Long after his death his descendants would become relatives of the Bannings when one of his daughters married into the family.[26]

Several other future Banning partners arrived on the scene in Southern California at the beginning of California's American period, when the gold rush was building in the northern part of the state. "Captain" William T. B. Sanford, Banning's first boss and future brother-in-law, was born in Kentucky and raised in Missouri, where he had been a newspaper publisher. He arrived in Los Angeles in 1849 and in short order became a trader and an "expert wagon-master." In September 1850 he discovered an improved route through the Cajon Pass that would greatly ease freight hauling in the direction of Salt Lake City. He was partner to David Douglass in 1852, when their firm employed Banning; they later sold the firm's interests to Banning and a partner, but Sanford remained both a financial and working partner in the new company. He also owned a hardware store with George Carson on Commercial Street by 1854, and was involved in many other business concerns.[27]

In addition to his business interests Captain Sanford joined in the political and civic life of Los Angeles. He served on the Los Angeles Com-

Benjamin Davis Wilson. Courtesy of
the Huntington Library.

Joseph Lancaster Brent. Courtesy of
the Seaver Center for Western History
Research, Natural History Museum of
Los Angeles County.

mon Council in 1853 and 1854, and was elected as one of the first three
school trustees for the city in 1854. Appointed as the second federal postmaster of Los Angeles in late 1851, he served in that position for two
years. In the 1857 county election he was chosen one of the two justices
of the peace for San Pedro Township. Throughout the 1850s Sanford
would be another mentor and role model for Phineas Banning, who
learned both stage-driving techniques and local politics from Sanford
and soon married the Captain's sister.[28]

The lawyer in this group, Joseph Lancaster Brent, came to California from Louisiana in 1850 and established a practice representing many
of the older *Californio* families as well as newcomers. A staunch Democrat in the State Assembly for two terms, he led the party locally until he
left in 1861 to join the Confederate army. Active in many business enterprises, Brent became a political mentor and close friend to Banning, who
named one of his sons in Brent's honor.[29]

Among those brought to California in 1850 by the gold rush was John
Gately Downey, an Irish immigrant to the United States who earned
his living as a druggist. Once in the gold region, he decided instead to
settle in Los Angeles, where he established a drugstore in partnership
with James McFarland. Over the next four decades he became a major

John Gately Downey. Courtesy of the
Seaver Center for Western History
Research, Natural History Museum
of Los Angeles County.

David W. Alexander. Courtesy of the
Huntington Library.

landowner, businessman, banker, rancher, and philanthropist. He also
served in the State Assembly, on the county Board of Supervisors, and on
the city Common Council. Elected lieutenant governor of California in
1859, he became governor in 1860 when Governor Latham resigned. A
devoted Democrat who criticized the national administration during the
Civil War, Downey lost the next election.[30]

Still other Anglo elites who had arrived in the region by the 1850s
round out the group of those who were to be helpful in Banning's ventures and civic pursuits. One of them, David W. Alexander, was another
Irishman who had lived in Philadelphia with his brother George in the
1830s, at the same time as William Lowber Banning. David came to California with the Workman-Rowland party of early Anglo immigrants in
1841 and eventually settled in San Pedro, where he became a trading partner with John Temple in the 1840s. He served as county supervisor and
sheriff, as a member of the city Common Council, and was the U.S. cus-
toms collector for San Pedro in the 1850s. He would join Banning as a
business partner from 1854 to 1856 and again from 1865 to 1872. Matthew
Keller, another Irishman who settled in Los Angeles in 1850, became a
prominent vintner and civic leader, served in several city and county of-

fices, and became a close friend to Banning as well as having many business dealings with him over the years.[31]

Four of the above named pioneers (Wilson, Sanford, Brent, and Downey) combined to buy Rancho San Pedro land in 1854 for Phineas Banning's dream, a new city at the harbor that could be the terminus for a railroad in Southern California. Banning would be the driving force behind the purchase, but since he did not have the capital to buy the land himself, he relied on his friends for financial help. He would eventually return the favor in many ways.

Important contributors to Banning's pursuits who arrived in Southern California shortly after he did included a European immigrant and two Americans. Harris Newmark, a merchant from Prussia who joined his family business in Los Angeles in 1853, became one of Banning's best clients as well as a good friend. He would also develop into an important chronicler of Los Angeles history during his long life in the city. Dr. Henry Rice Myles was a dentist and a druggist who, with partner Dr. J. C. Welsh, operated a drugstore on Main Street. He supplemented his medical work by acting as the Los Angeles agent for the Alexander & Banning firm, and in 1854 he also became the local agent for Wells Fargo & Company in Los Angeles. He partnered with Wilson, Sanford, and Banning to raise and sell cattle and sheep in the mid-1850s.[32]

Another friend for whom Banning would name one of his children was Dr. John Strother Griffin, a Virginian who worked as an army physician during the war with Mexico and settled in Los Angeles in 1854. Like J. Lancaster Brent, Griffin was a staunch Southern Democrat and close friend of Phineas Banning. Besides his medical practice, Griffin busied himself with land development and other ventures with Banning, as well as many civic activities.[33]

These individuals and others, such as attorney James Lander and surveyor Henry Hancock, were just a few of Banning's close associates in the early 1850s and after. These were the men who would shape Los Angeles. Nearly all of them were involved in entrepreneurial ventures with him and distributed goods through his transportation and trading concerns. Almost all of them were involved in local and state politics and served in several government offices at these levels. All were prominent in civic organizations, and, with Phineas Banning, all were rabid boosters of Los Angeles's urban growth and prosperity, which would profit the region and themselves. And all of them played important roles in the melodrama of Banning's life in Southern California.

Harris Newmark. Courtesy of the Huntington Library.

John Strother Griffin. Courtesy of the Seaver Center for Western History Research, Natural History Museum of Los Angeles County.

Banning's year in 1852 with Douglass & Sanford proved to be a very profitable one for him, both financially and socially. He saved as much of his earnings as he could and befriended potential investors in his future enterprises. By January 1853 he established a partnership with George C. Alexander, an Irishman who had become an American citizen in New York City in 1840. George eventually moved west to follow his brother David into the import trade at San Pedro. The two new partners purchased the interests of Douglass and Sanford in the merchandise and transportation firm for which Banning had been clerking, and in February the first advertisement for "Alexander & Banning" appeared in the *Los Angeles Star.* The partners promised to store and forward goods to and from Los Angeles on the "most reasonable terms." Their stage line would carry passengers from the harbor to the city after the arrival of each steamer. Barley for livestock feed would be purchased, stored, and sold to their customers as needed.[34]

In little more than a year after his arrival in California, Phineas Banning had emerged from poverty to become a partner in a promising business concern. This firm was only the first of many ventures he would start with the aid of investors and friends, and sometimes with public funding. Not all of them would prove successful, but most would be lucrative on any terms. Alexander & Banning was the first, the beginning of the Banning family fortune in Southern California.

CHAPTER THREE

PHINEAS BANNING & THE ALEXANDERS & OTHER PARTNERSHIPS

Phineas Banning launched his own business empire at the start of 1853, and as time passed he would manage it with a succession of partners. Through his many ventures, he accumulated assets, satisfied his customers with the "accustomed promptness" he advertised, and won government supply contracts. But if his successes were great, so were his losses, including a major business failure in 1856. The erratic path of his young career echoed the uncertain if busy days of early Los Angeles, a sparsely settled and socially turbulent region where local citizens labored to establish order and economic stability.

By then a large, sturdy, and smart young man, Phineas Banning turned twenty-three in August 1853. His striking physical presence was much remarked on by acquaintances and friends. In October of that year, he met Harris Newmark, a young Prussian merchant who had just arrived by steamer to settle in Los Angeles and join his brother's mercantile business. Newmark later recalled his shock on first seeing Banning. "In European cities where I had heretofore lived," Newmark explained, "commission and forwarding merchants were a dignified and, to my way of thinking, an aristocratic class." Newmark continued:

> At any rate, upon arriving in San Pedro I had expected to find a man dressed either in a uniform or a Prince Albert, with a high hat and other appropriate appurtenances, and it is impossible to describe my astonishment when Banning was pointed out to me; for I knew absolutely nothing of the rough methods in vogue on the Pacific Coast. There stood before me a very large, powerful man, coatless and vestless, without necktie or collar, and wearing pantaloons at least six inches too

short, a pair of brogans and socks with large holes; while bright-colored suspenders added to the picturesque effect of his costume.[1]

Other observers of the early 1850s commented with similar awe on Banning's physical stamina, tremendous drive, and commanding manner. Horace Bell, never one to bestow praise or criticism lightly, remembered that Banning "could ride farther with less fatigue that any man I ever knew, notwithstanding he was never a lightweight." When "the whole country declared the impossibility" of driving a six-horse stagecoach over "an old Mexican pack trail" in 1854, "Banning willed the thing to be done." He seemed to inspire deference, even when he was not formally in charge. By the end of the 1850s Banning controlled the transportation contract to supply Fort Tejon, about seventy miles north of Los Angeles, but Bell opined that "the gallant General Phineas Banning ran the post" rather than just supplying it. He concluded (with at least a bit of exaggeration): "Whatever Banning suggested at the fort was done, and nothing was done unless he was consulted."[2]

Maj. Edward D. Townsend, an officer in the service of the army's Adjutant General's Office, met Banning in October 1855 while on an inspection tour in Southern California. He was more objective than Bell, but nevertheless effusive in describing Banning's energetic manner: "Mr B. is a rapid man, forever in a hurry and doing the business of a half dozen of men." Banning's stage-driving technique particularly impressed Townsend: "if he isn't a Yankee improvement over Jehu I don't know anything about stage driving." Anna Ogier, spouse of U.S. District Court Judge Isaac Ogier, echoed Townsend's view of Banning's energy when she reminded a friend in early 1856 that "you know what a flurry he is always in—can't wait a second if he were to make millions by it."[3]

These observations were borne out by Banning's early career and life in Southern California, which would take all his ambition, energy, and smarts. Banning seemed a perfect match for the region where he chose to live in the early 1850s, which needed people with both vision and drive to shape it into a center of transportation and commerce.

The Forwarding and Commission Business in 1850s Los Angeles

In February 1853 Phineas Banning's first partnership, Alexander & Banning, began both its forwarding and commission business and a stagecoach service for travelers between Los Angeles and the harbor at San Pedro, where freight and passenger steamships regularly docked. Since

Phineas Banning about 1855. Courtesy of the Banning Residence Museum.

Banning had been living on a clerk's wages for much of his working life, and his partner, George Alexander, was not wealthy, the two had to borrow a considerable amount of money from their associates to purchase the Douglass & Sanford firm, whose assets included wagons and lighters, draft animals, and a modest inventory of goods. George's brother David, who, with his partner Francis Mellus, was in the same business and had just returned from a trip to Europe a few months before, was probably one of those lenders. After selling out his half of Douglass & Sanford, William Sanford worked with and invested in Alexander & Banning, while also starting partnerships with several other local businessmen.[4]

The Los Angeles Plaza area in 1853, a frontier town of whitewashed adobes (from the U.S. Pacific Railroad Survey of 1853–54). Courtesy of the Seaver Center for Western History Research, Natural History Museum of Los Angeles County.

In its first year of existence Alexander & Banning ambitiously built its business and added to its transportation services. In May the company commenced construction of a "Half Way House" for travelers along the road from the harbor to Los Angeles, a structure that a local newspaper hoped might be the start of a new farming community. According to Harris Newmark, Alexander & Banning purchased fifteen additional wagons and some seventy-five mules for nearly $30,000 that summer so the company could handle more freight. Also that year, Phineas Banning began driving stagecoaches as part of the company's passenger service between San Pedro and Los Angeles on the days the coastal steamers arrived and departed. As noted above, he soon became known as an expert driver; he must have learned quickly, since he had spent his working life as a clerk and was not noted for his driving skills before arriving in Southern California. He almost certainly learned from his mentor and former boss William Sanford, who was a master driver. In future years Banning would acquire an outstanding reputation for driving stagecoaches, although he took an occasional fall, as he did on a day in February 1856, when driving from San Pedro to Los Angeles. In that incident, his team "became unmanageable" and "he was thrown forward and fell behind the horses, and becoming entangled in the geering [sic] and was dragged some hundred yards before he succeeded in extricating himself from his perilous situation." A year earlier, commercial agent Alfred Robinson accompanied Banning as he was driving a wagon. When it went out of control and tipped over, Robinson recalled, "a powerful hand prevented

San Pedro in 1855 with the facilities of Alexander & Banning, by James Madison Alden. Courtesy of the Bancroft Library.

my being pitched over the side." Then "Banning was thrown forward between the horses and how he stopped God only knows." The business of stage driving, especially along unimproved roads, was not one for the timid or physically fragile; Banning's confidence and strength no doubt contributed to his skill and growing reputation as a driver. They were certainly necessary in the fiercely competitive business into which he had entered.[5]

The year 1853 was a bustling one at the harbor for Alexander & Banning, as trading increased—and with it, competition. The previous year, Augustus W. Timms, a German seaman who had come to California in the 1840s, had purchased the only wharf in San Pedro from Diego Sepulveda, and he began competing with Douglass & Sanford and Alexander & Mellus. B. A. Townsend, who eventually sold his business to Alexander & Banning, and several others also vied for the same customers. But Alexander & Banning and Timms were the major contenders in these early days at the port, and their stagecoach drivers raced one another at breakneck speed to and from the harbor on steamer days. By 1855 there would be six major competitors for this business, including Lanfranco & Sepulveda and J. J. Tomlinson, who would eventually take over from Timms as Banning's chief nemesis.[6]

Amid this competition Alexander & Banning expanded its operations significantly in 1854 and 1855. According to a sketch of the company's complex at San Pedro and Major Townsend's notes, the site encompassed a large adobe structure, outbuildings, and associated equipment. They

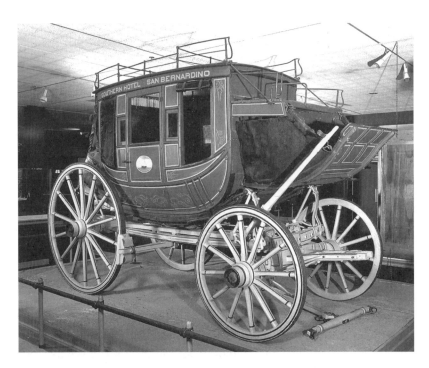

Concord stagecoach once owned by the Bannings. Courtesy of the History Collections, Natural History Museum of Los Angeles County.

acquired additional lighters to load and unload ships anchored far from the shallow depths near the wharves. With this added capacity, they accumulated new customers, for example persuading John Keys of Santa Barbara that it was faster to ship his goods to the Kern River area (northeast of Santa Barbara) by sending them south via San Pedro and Los Angeles rather than directly overland. The company also added semi-weekly stage service from the harbor to San Bernardino. Although winter rains occasionally made the crude roads impassable, the nearly year-round sunshine in the region kept shippers almost constantly busy. By September 1854 the *Southern Californian* claimed that the owners of Alexander & Banning "have upwards of 500 mules and 30 or 40 horses, 40 wagons and 15 stages running between San Pedro and this city, which are constantly employed for the accommodation of the public."[7]

Some of Alexander & Banning's stagecoaches were Concords, a model manufactured in the New Hampshire town of that name by the Abbot, Downing Company. Concords were built to swing on leather straps, which made the coach rock and roll as it passed over bumps rather than jerking like more rigid coaches. They began to appear in California in the very early 1850s. Purchasing these improved models gave the partnership a competitive advantage over companies that used more primitive vehicles. The Concord would become a favorite of Banning and his oldest son, William, who followed in his father's footsteps as an expert driver.[8]

With the expansion of its business, Alexander & Banning added another Alexander to its cast of directors. David W. Alexander, George's brother, officially joined the company as a full partner as of September 1, 1854, when the change was advertised in local papers. Another brother, Henry N. Alexander, replaced Dr. Henry R. Myles as the Los Angeles agent for the firm. W. J. Willis was listed as their agent in Lexington, a growing community east of Los Angeles that would soon be renamed El Monte. Lyman, Rich, Hopkins & Company was their agent in the Mormon colony of San Bernardino. Rankin & Company in San Francisco served as the firm's agent in that city. From then on the company name was officially Alexanders & Banning, although the old spelling would still be used in reference to the firm over the next two years, even in some court documents.[9]

The expansion of Alexanders & Banning in the late summer of 1854 was likely driven by the prospect of a new and extremely lucrative client: the U.S. Army. At about this time, the army announced plans to build a fort at the steep Tejon Pass close to the Sebastian Indian Reservation, about 70 miles north of Los Angeles. The news spurred a number of business and civic leaders in Los Angeles to demand the improvement of the primitive San Fernando Road, which led to the new fort and continued further north. Phineas Banning and his partners, who would profit from better roads when transporting supplies and passengers to the fort and surrounding community, helped to convince the county Board of Supervisors (which happened then to include David Alexander) to commit $1,000 to the endeavor if private citizens would match that amount through a subscription. Banning and friends then joined the campaign to persuade wealthy residents to contribute to the project, and $2,900 was subscribed. Banning's partner William Sanford and Sanford's hardware business partner, George Carson, were awarded the contract to grade this road over the mountains. They hired Gabriel Allen, a colorful character and jack-of-all-trades, to supervise the work, which necessitated cutting through solid rock in many places. By January 1855 the road was ready for use, and Sanford and Abel Stearns collected the subscriptions to pay for it.[10]

Phineas Banning's American Southwest, ca. 1860. Map by David L. Fuller.

The San Fernando Road project was the first of Phineas Banning's profitable ventures to be financed through a partnership of government funding and private enterprise. There would be many such in the years to come as he mastered the art of obtaining public financing to underwrite his business enterprises. In something of a celebration of this maiden voyage into the public/private entrepreneurial realm, he was allowed to test the new road in December 1854 before its official opening. As Horace Bell described the scene, before beginning the climb Banning sat ready in his stage "to which were harnessed a half dozen well-fed, panting and foaming mustangs." When he reached the summit of the San Fernando Pass, the nine observers present wondered "how that stage could ever descend, all declaring it an act of madness to attempt it. Banning laughingly assured them that it 'was all right; that a man who couldn't drive a stage safely down that hill was no driver at all, and should confine himself to ox-teaming in the valley.'" Down the hill they flew, with assorted clatters—and then a crash. Following the noise, the observers discovered "the conglomeration of chains, harness, coach, mustangs and Banning... in an inextricable mass of confusion— contusions, scratches, bruises, batter, cracks and breaks, forming a general smash and pile up in a thicket of chaparral at the foot of the mountain." "'Didn't I tell you so,' said Banning, 'a beautiful descent, far less difficult than I imagined.'" With that he immediately sent word to David Alexander to bring a work team to repair the parts of the road he had just destroyed.[11]

With the San Fernando Road improved and open, Alexanders & Banning began transporting military supplies and goods for civilians at Fort Tejon. George Alexander opened a retail store there to sell the goods. The company then extended their transportation route past Fort Tejon to the newly discovered gold mines on the Kern River. While they continued to deliver freight there, their stage line to the mines proved either too successful or not successful enough, because in February they sold this portion of their business to the California Stage Company. Headquartered in Sacramento, this firm bought up many other stage lines at that time in an attempt to coordinate and monopolize the industry. The acquisition of Alexanders & Banning's route to the Kern River allowed California Stage to consolidate the transportation network of the Central Valley.[12]

During this period of expansion, the company did not limit its sights to California. By early 1855 Alexanders & Banning was looking much further afield. The year before, Mormon leaders in San Bernardino headed by Assemblyman Jefferson Hunt had begun seeking federal and state funds to improve the "Southern Route" through the Cajon Pass and on to Salt Lake City in Utah Territory. With a coordinated effort by many interests, they secured funding from the California legislature for improving the road from San Bernardino to the state line. At the same time Los Angeles County supervisors underwrote work on the road from San Pedro harbor to San Bernardino, and the federal government appropriated funds for the Utah portion "for military and mail purposes." William Sanford and Phineas Banning then joined the campaign and began to undertake their own improvements in early 1855. Sanford had already pioneered a new, less steep section for the route back in 1850, and now he worked with Banning to grade a portion of the road, significantly reducing its angle of descent. With these modifications the lucrative Salt Lake City market and its increasing population of Mormons could be reached from San Pedro harbor with far less effort.[13]

In April 1855, Alexanders & Banning purchased about $20,000 in goods for their first freight trip to Salt Lake City. The firm assumed one-third of the debt, while William Sanford, Benjamin D. Wilson, and John Temple covered the rest. Banning and David Alexander, who had once lived in Utah, conferred with Mormon leaders in San Bernardino and were assured that their associates would be well received by the Saints in Salt Lake City. Sanford departed at the end of April with fifteen wagons, each pulled by ten mules. Together they carried a total of "60,000 pounds of assorted merchandise"; it was the largest load that any trader had yet taken to Salt Lake City. The wagon train encountered many obstacles along the way, including mountainous terrain, hostile Indians, and one broken axle. But Sanford reached his destination, sold all of the goods he had, and returned to Los Angeles in September. The trip was hailed as a financial success.[14]

Sanford's triumphant venture inaugurated a succession of similar trips to Salt Lake City by other merchants. Alexanders & Banning themselves attempted another journey in 1856, but this one would prove to be a financial disaster. On his previous trip Sanford had encountered some, apparently ineffective, opposition to his arrival by Mormon leader Brigham Young, who hoped to start his own freight hauling company and keep the merchandising profits within the Mormon community. (There were even reports that Mormon religious leaders would "preach from the pulpit cautioning the people against trading with the company," obviously to no avail.) The rejection of Sanford's venture was much more pronounced in 1856, because along with his usual merchandise, he carried a large supply of liquor to the city. This was ill advised, and not only because strict abstinence from liquor was among the religious tenets of the Mormons, who dominated the city's population and its government. As Byron Grant Pugh has concluded, Sanford's arrival also coincided with Young's increasing opposition to interlopers. When Sanford petitioned for a license to sell liquor, which was prohibited within the city limits, the city council refused to repeal the prohibition ordinance and asked Sanford to withdraw his petition, which he did.[15]

Turned away from the city, Sanford returned to Los Angeles, probably with most of the goods he had brought on the long journey to Salt Lake City. Far from yielding a profit like the previous venture, this trip cost the firm of Alexanders & Banning a small fortune. According to Phineas Banning, it permanently ended his bid to tap the lucrative market in Salt Lake City. He blamed Brigham Young, who "used his despotic power to crush out any attempt to create a business," and his "Avenging Angels" for forcing Banning and his associates "at a considerable loss to abandon the Mormon trade."[16]

Sanford's disastrous 1856 trip might not have been the determining factor in the demise of Alexanders & Banning, but it certainly contributed to the partnership's troubles. After several years of apparent success, the firm had stretched its credit to such an extent that in July 1856 six creditors launched lawsuits demanding that the company's assets be seized to repay their loans. John Temple and the executor for the estate of Charles Burrows claimed they were owed almost $6,000 each, while Banning's good friend Benjamin D. Wilson sued for almost $10,000. Several mercantile firms also sued, for smaller amounts. Wilson wrote to his wife just before the lawsuits were filed, telling her that the firm had failed and that David Alexander would "lose his intire [sic] fortune" and more; "everyone here seems to be fated to be broke," he complained. A week later he informed her that Alexanders & Banning had conducted "a careless business" and owed over $45,000. David Alexander, who two years earlier "had $60,000 and owed no one," was destitute and working on John Temple's ranch "because of his brother and Banning."[17]

The failure of Alexanders & Banning inspired a panic among creditors and a frenzy of lawsuits against various firms. An agent for the erstwhile firm's primary competitor, Augustus W. Timms, placed a large notice in the *Star* informing the public that Timms remained solvent, despite the "panic in this community, arising from the failure of a prominent business firm." He acknowledged that some lawsuits demanding the attachment of assets had been filed against his client, but "A. W. Timms is still in the field," the agent emphatically stated, "and ready to take charge of all goods with which he may be entrusted for forwarding."[18]

The assets of Alexanders & Banning spent August and September of 1856 in limbo as the lawsuits against the firm moved through the court system. A settlement was reached in October "with losses for everyone," according to one participant. Some of the creditors were awarded a combination of cash and hauling credit at Banning's new firm. Banning was able to retain some of the equipment of the failed company. Benjamin D. Wilson received personal property and equipment that had been used on the San Pedro–Los Angeles route. Dr. John S. Griffin, an investor in the business, ended up with the house William Sanford had recently bought from David Alexander, and decided to live there with his new bride. As mentioned above, David Alexander was financially ruined and resigned as Los Angeles County sheriff in order to herd cattle for his former partner, John Temple, in Tulare. Like many entrepreneurial Angelenos, Alexander would rise again, in his case in about ten years as the business partner of Phineas Banning.[19]

Banning escaped this fiasco relatively unscathed, although his reputation as a businessman was surely tarnished, to judge by Benjamin D.

Wilson's comment to his spouse about the company's carelessness. By late July 1856, before the lawsuits even reached court, Alexanders & Banning had split up and Phineas had formed a new partnership with Spencer H. Wilson, a Canadian trader in Los Angeles in the 1850s. Banning & Wilson performed the same functions in the same places as Alexanders & Banning, probably with some of the same backers and equipment and certainly with William Sanford's active participation. In late 1856 Banning & Wilson submitted bids and won a contract to deliver U.S. mail along the Los Angeles to San Pedro route. The company also arranged huge shipments by coastal steamer of local grapes, an increasingly important crop in Southern California, and other products.[20]

Banning's new company at the harbor occupied the same buildings as its predecessor. The complex included

> an extensive blacksmith shop, also a carriage manufactory, a saddlery and harness-making establishment, where the wagons, etc., required in their extensive transportation business are manufactured and repaired. There are also extensive warehouses, stables, corrals, etc. Also a grocery, provision and liquor store and hotel.

The San Pedro customhouse was at Banning & Wilson's landing, a short distance from Timms Landing and the pier there. At that time the buildings of these two firms comprised all the major structures at the harbor, still in its infancy as a Pacific port.[21]

Banning & Wilson continued in business until May 1857, when they amicably dissolved their firm. By 1863, Wilson had moved to Santa Catalina Island, where he managed trade at Wilson's Harbor with the use of his sloop, the *Ned Beal*. Meanwhile Banning's old investor and colleague William Sanford, who had been raising and selling sheep in Northern California for a firm called Sanford & Wilson (with Benjamin D. Wilson and Dr. Henry R. Myles) before and after the Alexanders & Banning failure, returned to San Pedro and Los Angeles to work again with Phineas Banning.[22]

By late 1857, Banning was finally advertising his commission and forwarding business without any partners. He had financial backers and the help of William Sanford, but he was now officially on his own. He had weathered several business highs and lows over the previous five years, but he always seemed to land on his feet. His resilience testifies to his tenacity and drive to succeed. While he did not yet own much property, his impending success would change that.[23]

City of Demons: Phineas Banning's Early Public Service

Southern California of the 1850s was a frontier, a large expanse of land with few police and an increasing influx of lawbreakers. The region attracted a number of disappointed gold seekers from Northern California and other opportunists who preyed on miners in the outlying areas of the county and also targeted wealthy ranchers, urban merchants, and Indians. A few young *Californios*—descendants of the early Spanish and Mexican settlers—rebelled against the American newcomers by forming bands that terrorized communities throughout the state, while independent groups of Indians defied "domestication" (as forced labor was called), raiding the ranches for horses and other goods. At times murders occurred daily, and local government could not curb the violence. The sum of such lawlessness made the Los Angeles area notorious as a center of civil disorder. The *Los Angeles Star* went so far as to declare that the county was "in a state of insurrection" in 1853, while Amasa Lyman of San Bernardino complained that same year of the "almost daily assassinations of our citizens." A year later Reverend James Woods wrote in his diary that conditions in the county seat of Los Angeles were so bad that although its name "is Spanish for the city of angels," it would be more accurate if "it be called at present the city of Demons." Three years later, John Forster informed a neighbor that, because of outlaw activity in the area surrounding San Juan Capistrano, "we are under a compleat state of siege and dare not go out."[24]

The lawlessness of this era was fed by the easy opportunities for theft in a sparsely settled region, by the poverty that induced some to commit crimes, by racial bigotry and violence in a time of population shifts and social change, and by the sheer size of the frontier, which was difficult to patrol and protect, given the small population. Gangs of outlaws scoffed at and frequently assaulted lawmen, who grew reluctant to extend their authority when outnumbered. In an incident made notable by the status of its victims, Sheriff James Barton and two deputies were ambushed and killed while pursuing outlaws in 1857. A posse led by Andrés Pico captured and immediately hanged most of the outlaws. The leaders of the gang, Juan Flores and Pancho Daniel, were arrested and eventually executed by vigilantes.[25]

Some citizens saw the county court system, which also struggled to find enough competent jurists, as part of the problem. Judges were few, and district attorneys and lawyers had to meet scant professional requirements to serve in the courts. Court sessions were often quite boisterous: judges and lawyers were known to carry concealed firearms during trials. A few judges, such as Augustín Olvera, were well respected and helped maintain order in the proceedings.[26]

Justice was not always as swift or sure, however, as many citizens—including Phineas Banning—demanded in an era of a seeming breakdown in law and order. Particularly in the 1850s, vigilante activity was rife when courts failed to act quickly. Over two-thirds of "popular justice" lynchings in Los Angeles County and California in the nineteenth century occurred in this decade; this surge in vigilantism was part of a nationwide trend. When it appeared that murderers might go free on technicalities, mobs often formed to raid jails and execute the accused, sometimes after impromptu trials. The most infamous vigilante hanging was that of gambler Dave Brown, who had been convicted of killing his own partner. During a tense moment after the trial, Los Angeles Mayor Stephen C. Foster tried to head off mob action by promising that he would resign from his office and personally help punish Brown if justice was not served through legal channels. When news came that Brown had received a stay of execution in 1855, Foster made good on his pledge and helped to seize Brown from Sheriff Barton and hang him. Lynchings placed a severe burden on county sheriffs who, with few deputies to assist them, had to stop the mobs.[27]

Phineas Banning was one of the first members of the Los Angeles volunteer citizen police force, founded in the 1850s. When lawlessness seemed to peak in the summer of 1853, a group of city leaders called for a public meeting in which a mounted police force of almost one hundred citizens was formed to supplement city and county officers. The Los Angeles Common Council authorized the formation of the group, called the Los Angeles Rangers, and the county supervisors appropriated $1,000 for its uniforms and equipment. Under the command of Alexander W. Hope, the Rangers began public drills to announce their presence.[28]

Banning was one of the organizers of the Rangers and, according to Horace Bell, was its most generous financial supporter. His participation in the organization's activities over the next several years has not been documented, and the actual effectiveness of the Rangers as a force for maintaining order from 1853 to about 1855 is undetermined. Its publicized arrests probably deterred some violence during this era. We do know that the group executed, mostly by hanging, about twenty-two accused felons, and launched a decade-long vigilante movement in Los Angeles.[29]

The Rangers apparently declined by 1855, because in that year Banning helped William W. Twist organize the City Guard, another mounted volunteer military unit, to aid local police. The City Guard was recognized and supplied by the state adjutant general's office, which denied a request by its captain for a field piece. The activities of this unit were reported in local newspapers during its short life, but Banning's involvement appears to have been minimal.[30]

Two years later, Banning would play a more prominent role in forming yet another volunteer military unit, this one created in response to a perceived threat from local Mormons. In 1857 relations between Mormons in Utah Territory and the U.S. government had become strained when Brigham Young refused to abide by those U.S. laws he deemed detrimental to the Mormon religion and community. President James Buchanan declared them to be in open rebellion for defying federal authority. In retaliation a group of Mormons and Indians attacked a wagon train of immigrants as it passed through Mountain Meadows in southern Utah that September on its way to California, slaughtering 140 civilians. With the U.S. Army on its way to invade Utah, further warfare seemed imminent, and the large Mormon settlement at nearby San Bernardino loomed as a major threat to citizens in Los Angeles, who were isolated and whose fears were consistently stoked by city newspapers, which often warned of the Mormon threat.[31]

When news of the massacre reached Los Angeles in October, Angelenos began agitating for a defense. Seventeen civic leaders called for a public meeting in December, which produced a pledge by forty leading citizens to prevent any sale of firearms and ammunition to Mormons. The same forty called for another public meeting on December 17 to form a new military company to meet the threat, and Phineas Banning was unanimously elected as captain of the Los Angeles Union Guards. His active leadership in this unit would be short-lived, however, because Brigham Young called for the return of the California Saints to Utah. With their departure the local crisis subsided and additional volunteer units were not needed. "Captain" Banning—as he was now known to the entire community—continued to act in the name of the unit over the next year as the "Mormon War" continued in Utah, but without a serious local threat he was unable to obtain weapons and keep the unit together. Banning's participation in military and extralegal organizations then ceased until after the Civil War.[32]

In addition to his service in these varied volunteer forces, Banning was elected one of two justices of the peace for San Pedro Township in November 1856. He served for one year, and was not too busy in this capacity since the population at the harbor was still very small and there were two justices for this township.[33]

The Banning Families

While Phineas was building his business in the 1850s, members of his family on the East Coast were also reinventing their lives. William Lowber Banning, the brother with whom Phineas had lived in Philadelphia, decided to move with his wife Mary (née Sweeny) to Minnesota Territory. They followed Mary's brother, Robert Ormsby Sweeny (1830–1902), who had relocated to the young city of St. Paul in 1852 and established himself as a druggist. Also an artist, his drawings of early St. Paul documented its rise. His depictions of local Indians and his later drawings of Civil War scenes illustrated books on these subjects. He also became a conservationist, helped found the St. Paul Academy of Natural Sciences, and served on the executive council of the Minnesota Historical Society for over three decades.[34] The civic boosterism evident in these commitments was long-standing, and among the earliest targets of his promotions was his family.

At the very beginning of his stay Robert convinced his two sisters and their husbands that St. Paul was a center of unlimited economic and social opportunity far different from the increasingly urbanized and crowded Philadelphia where they lived. In the summer of 1854 William and Mary visited Robert and were persuaded to move. The fact that William's former law partner, William Hollinshead, had already relocated to St. Paul would make the transition even easier.[35]

Before their first visit to St. Paul, William and Mary hosted the wedding of his sister Mary Lowber Banning to William Armstrong at their Philadelphia home in March. In the following month word came that John Alford Banning, father of William Lowber, Phineas, Mary (Banning) Armstrong, and their eight siblings, had passed away at the Delaware farm of Oak Hill on April 12. Then in his sixties, he signed his will only a few days before his death. In it he left half of his modest estate to his wife, Elizabeth, and the other half to "my eldest son John Banning (who has always remained with me)." He instructed Elizabeth to provide for the rest of their children in her will. When she died seven years later, the meager estate left a few hundred dollars to only some of the children. Like her husband, John, Elizabeth would be buried in Old Swede's Cemetery in Wilmington, Delaware.[36]

William wrote to inform Phineas of their father's death and to ask if he could come back home to help out the family for a while. But Phineas declined, saying that he was much too busy with his expanding business enterprise at the moment and that he therefore "must stay here a few years longer." This was a sensible explanation: given his newly established company and complex assortment of activities, his business would have been materially damaged by a long trip to the East. But the statement might also suggest that he was still not planning to make California his permanent home. In any case he did not visit his mother or his siblings living in Delaware or nearby Philadelphia upon hearing of his father's death.[37]

In the following year, 1855, William Lowber and Mary Sweeny Banning made their move to St. Paul. Like his brother Phineas, William would play a leading role in his chosen city's development. The mid-1850s was a prosperous time in this newly incorporated city of almost 5,000, although rapid population increases also brought a rise in crime and other urban problems. William had practiced law for well over a decade in Philadelphia, but decided to change professions in his new hometown. He established a bank in St. Paul in 1856 and later joined the city's Chamber of Commerce. He also served as Ramsey County auditor in 1860. Late that year he was elected to the Minnesota House of Representatives, where he took a strong interest in state finance and railroads. At the end of his term in 1861 he temporarily retired from state politics and permanently quit banking in order to join the Union army at the start of the Civil War.[38]

In 1855 William and Mary built a grand two-story brick residence with a high and "spacious portico in front, supported by Ionic columns." The house stood on the corner of Wilkin and McBoal Streets, not far from that of Governor Alexander Ramsey. In that fashionable neighborhood the Bannings were well known and respected as one of the more affluent families of the city. Their household included William Lowber Jr. (who would drown in the Mississippi River at the age of ten in 1862) and Ellen, both born in Philadelphia in the early 1850s; Evans, who was born in the later 1850s but died at the age of two; and then May (sometimes spelled Mary) Alice, Frederick, Katharine Stewart, and another William Lowber Jr., all of whom were born in St. Paul in the late 1850s and the 1860s.[39]

Most of Phineas Banning's other siblings also moved around in the 1850s as they pursued opportunities in other regions or moved back to the Delaware county of their birth. Elizabeth Alice married Isaac Elliot in 1843 and the two moved to Minnesota shortly after William did. Sallie, coincidentally, married another Isaac Elliot in Delaware in 1852, and the two stayed on a farm in the Wilmington area. Francenia Alice moved to Philadelphia and then to St. Paul, where she married Henry J. Horn, a city official and prominent lawyer, in 1859. Mary Lowber and her husband, William Armstrong, eventually moved back to New Castle County from Philadelphia. Richard, Henry, and Cole Lowber moved to Missouri, where they would remain. John Alford Jr., the eldest son, stayed in Wilmington until his death in 1885; Alice Ponder probably stayed in the general vicinity, too.[40]

Meanwhile, Phineas Banning started his own family. His biographer Maymie Krythe claims that he met Rebecca Sanford, the younger sister of his business associate William Sanford, during the spring of 1854 while she was visiting her brother on his property at the Rancho San Jose de Buenos Aires. But it seems more likely that they met when she and her mother were living with William in Los Angeles, where he brought them sometime in 1853 (they did not appear in the 1852 special state census). As the story goes, Phineas fell in love with Rebecca immediately and courted her every weekend for months until he finally asked for her hand and she consented. According to the newspapers, they were married in Los Angeles at the home of her brother William on November 16, 1854.[41]

Rebecca, born in 1834 or 1835 in Randolph County, Missouri, was about nineteen years old at the time. Her parents, John Dozier Sanford and Hannah Barnes, were both from Madison County, Kentucky, where they had owned a farm and several slaves. John died in 1835 and Hannah became head of the household with eight children. The siblings' travels as adults attest to the powerful lure of California during the 1840s and 1850s. The oldest was Phineas Banning's first employer in Los Angeles and later business partner, William Sanford, who was born in 1814, when the family lived in Kentucky. William came to Los Angeles in 1849, and two other brothers, John and Cyrus, also moved to Southern California, followed by Rebecca and her mother in 1853. One of Rebecca's sisters, Marilda, married William F. Prather and moved to Linden, California, about 1853. Only Rebecca's sisters Amanda and Frances married in Missouri and stayed there.[42]

After their wedding, Phineas and Rebecca moved into an adobe home near the Alexanders & Banning wharf in San Pedro. In time Rebecca's mother, Hannah, moved in with them and stayed until after Rebecca's death in 1868. Hannah was certainly living there by August 1857, when Judge Benjamin Hayes recorded in his diary a visit to the Banning home, where he and his wife were greeted by "Mrs. Banning and her mother, Mrs. Sanford, who had just arrived from San Francisco, and their kindness enabled Mrs. H. to pass the afternoon agreeably." Phineas and Rebecca Banning's hospitality would become legend. For Rebecca this reputation was particularly important, since the small port of San Pedro in frontier Southern California was still a sparsely inhabited, isolated community, and Rebecca's social circle was limited to Los Angeles friends and passengers arriving on steamer days.[43]

Rebecca would give birth to eight or nine infants during her marriage to Phineas, but only three would survive through their fifth year. Rebecca's fragile health and the limited medical care on the frontier were deadly hazards for her and her children, as they were for many women at the time. In August 1855 she gave birth to her first child, Fanny, who was named after Phineas's sister Francenia. In the following year John Griffin Banning was born and named for Dr. John S. Griffin, a friend and investment partner of Phineas who had settled in Los Angeles in 1854. Another son, whose name is unknown, may have been stillborn in April of 1857; there is no further mention of him. Tragedy would strike the family again that year, when Fanny died on September 22, the first of Rebecca's children to die at a very young age.[44]

Living on the Frontier

Family life at San Pedro harbor was quiet in the mid-1850s because of the minuscule population and the distance from Los Angeles. But Phineas and Rebecca Banning did their best to establish a reputation as social leaders and philanthropists in this community. They began to entertain friends and guests, some of whom would become business contacts for Phineas. These included reporters and others visiting San Pedro on "steamer day" in 1857, whom Banning treated to a dinner "which was served in excellent style and consisted of the luxuries of the season." In July 1857 Phineas and Rebecca held an impromptu "grand dance" for a group that had missed its steamer to San Francisco and was stranded in San Pedro, and he also made arrangements for their overnight accommodations. Another reporter in the same year observed that San Pedro was "dreary" and the "only agreeable thing about the place is the cordial hospitality of Messers Banning and Sanford." Phineas was also thanked the same year for offering his coaches to transport Los Angeles schoolchildren to and from a picnic arranged for them.[45] In 1854 Banning hosted a barbeque celebration for the Fourth of July; he would become notorious for his annual Independence Day orations. The enthusiastic speech of this "go-ahead 'forwarding merchant' of San Pedro, fast stage driver and earnest man of the times" on July 4, 1857, "tickled and edified the crowd hugely."[46]

These modest early contributions to local society would become the foundation for the Bannings' civic engagements in the next three decades. Over these years, the family would emerge as one of the major social, civic, and economic forces in the growing community that Phineas Banning played a crucial role in developing.

CHAPTER FOUR

DELAWARE ON THE PACIFIC

The year 1858 was transformative and busy, even for the legendarily ambitious and energetic Phineas Banning. Not only did he win his first important political office and continue to build his company, he also founded his own town at the harbor as a competitor to San Pedro. Not all his ventures were immediately successful; some languished over the next few years. But during the period from 1858 to 1861, he would set the future course of his business and ensure the prosperity of his family.

New San Pedro and Wilmington

It is ironic that Banning would name his new community in Southern California after the Delaware hometown he had fled at age thirteen. Wilmington, Delaware, was the center of agricultural production for its surrounding area, but it was merely a small port city with a modest amount of manufacturing. It had little to excite Phineas in his youth, or to offer him in the way of opportunity. He readily abandoned it in 1843 to seek his fortune in what was then one of the nation's largest cities, Philadelphia.

The first notice of his dream of building a city at present-day Wilmington, California, appeared in a letter published in the *Los Angeles Star* in February 1854. The writer recalled the federal railroad survey investigating routes for the transcontinental railroad the previous December, which had stirred local excitement, and revealed that a small group of local businessmen were interested in establishing a new town at a harbor site about six miles closer to Los Angeles than San Pedro. This venture became more of a reality later in the year, as described in the *Southern Californian* in November 1854. Under the caption "New City," that paper reported that "several capitalists" hoped to prepare for the coming of the transcontinental railroad to Southern California by

Manuel Dominguez, owner of
the Rancho San Pedro.
Courtesy of History
Collections, Natural History
Museum of Los Angeles
County.

purchasing 2,400 acres of land from Manuel Dominguez and his family
on his Rancho San Pedro "with the intention of laying out a new city."
The location would accommodate a fine harbor, and "in case the Pacific
Railroad makes its terminus in this valley," it would "build up a city of
considerable importance, and enrich the gentlemen who have embarked
on this new enterprise."[1]

The first purchase of land for the new city was financed in 1854 by
J. Lancaster Brent, John G. Downey, Dr. Henry R. Myles, William Sanford, and Benjamin D. Wilson, all good friends and business partners of
Phineas Banning. Banning himself was not among the original investors
because he did not then have enough capital to participate, but he is
universally credited with being the chief promoter of the purchase.
Lt. Edward O. C. Ord drew up a survey and subdivision map of "New
Town" and gave it to Sanford several months later, but for a time nothing was done to develop the property. Rather, Banning and the five investors waited for Congress to approve funding for the railroad that
would jumpstart the founding of the new settlement.[2]

Progress in planning for the railroad in Washington, D.C., was ex-
cruciatingly slow, however, and the always-impatient Banning finally decided to forge ahead. By 1858 he had recouped his losses from the demise

of Alexanders & Banning, and he began purchasing some of the land investment from Downey and others. In July he acquired half of Henry R. Myles's interest in this parcel, and he bought more of Myles's portion the following year. He also purchased several hundred additional acres near the original parcel for himself and partner Henry N. Alexander from other members of the Dominguez family in 1858, and another thirty-five acres of waterfront property from the original five investors the following year. In June 1860, he filed the map of "New Town" with the county recorder and continued to acquire property there from the original five partners and their successors.[3]

As soon as he acquired land, Banning set about developing it in preparation for moving his harbor business there. His planned relocation was not solely spurred by the possibility of a railroad terminus. It would also allow him to beat out his transportation competitors by offering a shorter and faster route from the harbor to Los Angeles. He further hoped, with the help of government grants, to create a more sheltered harbor than San Pedro by partially enclosing the inner harbor and then dredging it to accommodate larger ships. The expanding maritime trade lured by these improvements would, he predicted, enhance the value of land and facilities along the waterline, and further development would increase the price of lots in the surrounding subdivisions of commercial and residential real estate. Thus, the venture could hold the promise of vast profits from trade, transport, and real estate alike.

As Richard Barsness and others have noted, the wisdom of Banning's relocation to "New San Pedro" was less than universally hailed at the time. Much of the land bordered on shallow mudflats intermittently inundated by "floods from the Los Angeles River and high tides from the bay," so competitors and other critics referred to it as "Banning's Hog Waller" or "Goose Town." But Banning persisted and had his men busily building his new city in the summer of 1858.[4]

By September 25, the town had enough infrastructure for Banning to begin loading and unloading freight and transporting passengers. To celebrate the event he invited a large number of guests to "assist" him with the first landing. As the *Star* glowingly described it:

> The ceremony of inauguration consisted in towing a line
> of barges, containing passengers and freight, to the land-
> ing place. In ascending the channel, all hands, the ladies
> included, assisted in hauling the hawser; and when the
> passengers were landed, and the first bale of goods, the

company united in wishing prosperity to Capt. Banning and the New Town, pledging the same in bumpers of "sparkling California." Afterwards, a sumptuous entertainment was provided for the guests; next day was devoted to the pleasing amusements of yachting and fishing. This was one of the most agreeable parties of the season; and was conducted with that liberality and hospitality for which Captain Banning is so famous.[5]

Banning had initially planned to continue operating his original business at San Pedro while conducting his main operation in his new town, and he secured approval from the county Board of Supervisors to begin building a new 350-foot wharf at the old port in August 1858. This wharf would not last long, however. Only two weeks after the celebration in New San Pedro, the heavy winds of "a regular south-easter" accompanying a violent storm at the harbor sent much of the flooring of this wharf to the sea. "Mr. Banning's famous yacht, 'Medora,'" was broken up, along with one of his large barges and other property. With this further reminder of the dangers inherent to the old port, Banning decided to move his entire operation to the safer New San Pedro over the next several years.[6]

New San Pedro required two major improvements to accommodate Banning's business plans. The first was a better road to and from Los Angeles. Banning had already arranged to have Los Angeles improve the city portion of the road to the harbor, which passed the new port on its route from Los Angeles to old San Pedro, while he served on its Common Council that summer. In October he began building a road from his new landing to the county road that picked up at the city limits to continue the road from Los Angeles out to the harbor. He successfully petitioned the county Board of Supervisors for an appropriation for his road, in return for which he agreed to deed the land for the road to the county and pay to build a bridge over a waterway along its route. In late December a story in the *Star* reported that a number of improvements had been made, "and the place generally had a thriving, bustling, go ahead appearance, so indicative of the enterprise of Capt. Banning." By January 1859 Banning began advertising that he would receive goods at New San Pedro and transport them to Los Angeles on a regular basis.[7]

The other needed improvement was a deeper harbor. To initiate that project Banning and Benjamin D. Wilson lobbied for federal funding of a survey of the inner harbor, known as "Wilmington Estuary" to Banning, the "creek" to Wilson, and the "lagoon" to critics of the scheme. Banning

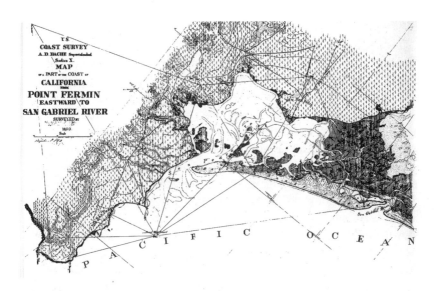

San Pedro/Wilmington harbor, 1859 (from the U.S. Coast Survey).

and Wilson's pleas to congressmen and letters to newspapers concerning the hydrology of "Banningsville," convinced authorities to order a survey of the entire harbor area by the U.S. Coast Survey in 1859. Although the survey did not lead immediately to government-funded improvements, it established the potential of the inner harbor and would help Banning secure federal appropriations after the Civil War.[8]

New San Pedro did not immediately boom in population; most house lots and commercial property outside of Banning's operation remained unsold. The partners in the investment in the town sometimes changed, but they continued to share the idea that it would eventually be profitable, and they agreed to a division of real estate parcels among themselves that was finalized in 1862. By the following year New San Pedro would grow larger, as maritime trade increased and a U.S. military force was stationed there for the duration of the Civil War. Banning then convinced his partners that the town should be renamed so that it would not be confused with the much older San Pedro a few miles away. He suggested the name Wilmington, the Delaware hometown that he had abandoned in 1843. The partners agreed and the state legislature approved the change in 1863. Thereafter, the name of the city would serve as a reminder of Phineas Banning's central role in remaking the region's primary harbor.[9]

Banning's Business

After the amicable dissolution of his second partnership in May 1857, Banning began advertising his business simply as "Phineas Banning." His mentor and brother-in-law, William Sanford, again was his partner, and Benjamin D. Wilson and others continued to finance him. But as he expanded his empire over the next three years, Banning himself would be the name and face of his firm.[10]

Banning's business grew at this time in part thanks to changes in how the U.S. Army supplied its western outposts. During the 1850s the army Quartermaster General's Office found that it was cheaper to supply its installations in the vast American West by contracting out the work to private entrepreneurs. This privatization would have its own downsides, for the process of assigning contracts was from the start riddled with favoritism and corruption. Secretary of War John B. Floyd himself was implicated in a scandal involving the firm of Russell, Majors & Waddell, the largest contract shipper in the West, and many other instances have been documented since the 1850s.[11]

But, corruption or not, the new system was a boon for those involved in trade and transport in the region. With his transportation system already in place and his good relationships with U.S. Army officers stationed in Southern California, Banning was well situated to tap into some of this business. Alexanders & Banning, after all, had been purchasing, shipping, and selling supplies at Fort Tejon since it was completed in 1855. When the army requested bids for a contract to ship freight to Fort Tejon from San Pedro in 1858, Banning submitted his proposal to his good friend and the fort commander, Gen. Benjamin L. Beall, and was present when the bids were opened. His rate of $4.74 per one hundred pounds of supplies underbid his major competitor Augustus W. Timms by just one cent per pound, a suspiciously small margin that suggests he may well have had insider information when drafting his bid. Having won that contract, Banning joined a group of Los Angeles citizens to raise another subscription to repair the road to Fort Tejon and successfully petitioned the county supervisors to contribute to it. With the improved road, Banning was able to run seventeen wagons every few months on the one-hundred-mile route from the harbor; he was said to have netted about $10,000 from the contract that first year. While he charged the government for these shipments, he happily transported free of charge the natural history specimens collected by officer John Xántus, thus simultaneously nurturing his connections at the fort.[12]

No doubt pleased with this regular and lucrative trade, Banning looked eastward for further government military contracts. Fort Yuma, about 250 miles east of Wilmington on the Colorado River, had been established in the early 1850s to protect immigrants traveling to Southern California in wagon trains. The small garrison tried to pacify the nearby Yuma Indians. When violence between the tribes and incoming settlers escalated in 1858 and 1859, the army increased its military presence in the area and so needed more supplies. In 1859, the army would build Fort Mojave, near present-day Needles, Arizona, to prevent incursions by the Mojave Indians, and this fort would need supplying, too.[13]

In March 1858, with these conflicts on the rise, Banning was awarded the contract to escort an army detachment from San Pedro to the Colorado River and to transport supplies to Fort Yuma. In December he accompanied an army exploring party in search of an appropriate site for the new fort. Thanks to the contacts made on these trips, he secured the contract to supply Fort Mojave in May 1859. Banning used pack mules, which could handle rough terrain, for the first trip over the untested overland route to the fort. Having determined that wagons could traverse it, he then dispatched seven ten-mule teams carrying a total of 28,000 pounds of supplies in heavy wagons. Banning charged the army $210 per day, with no limit on the number of days the trip could take; the wagon train therefore had little incentive to hurry. As a result, although the leisurely journey allowed Banning's men to make some improvements in the road and discover water resources along the way, the cost of the trip proved to be exorbitant compared to current freighting rates. The huge profit Banning made at the army's expense was notorious: the "Banning's Wells" his men dug were quickly renamed "Government Holes." The army soon determined that it would be more advantageous to ship supplies by steamboat from Fort Yuma on the Colorado River. The contract Banning then lost would probably not have made a great difference to his fortune, however, for Fort Mojave would close just two years later.[14]

But toward the end of the 1850s, the era of little competition and easy government money was fading fast. Both the government and private business benefited from increasingly intense competition in the stage and freighting business in Southern California. New companies opened stage lines from Los Angeles to San Luis Obispo, San Bernardino, and San Diego. The Utah Territory trade—closed to Banning by Brigham Young in 1857, as noted in the previous chapter—grew as the Mormon War with the U.S. government subsided, and Banning's competitors dominated that market.[15]

In 1858 Augustus W. Timms was still Banning's major rival in transportation matters and primary adversary in the numerous lawsuits stemming from their fierce competition. The year before, Timms had hired away, at a higher salary, one of Banning's most competent employees, Frank Lecouvreur, to manage the Timms office in San Pedro. This was, however, one of Timms's last victories against Banning. After a few financial reverses in 1858, Timms began selling out his interests to his primary creditor, wagonmaker John Goller, who joined with another competitor, J. J. Tomlinson, to form Goller & Tomlinson. This firm soon surpassed Banning's company in volume of freighting and passenger business. Goller sold out his portion of the company in 1861 to Tomlinson, who then formed a new partnership with his brother-in-law, John M. Griffith, and continued to battle Banning until Tomlinson's death in 1868.[16]

The early history of the firms' rivalry reflects the risky and improvisational nature of frontier business. Shortly after partnering with Goller, Tomlinson had to accompany a large freight shipment on an extended trip to Salt Lake City. Because Goller was still learning the business and could not have run it in Tomlinson's absence, Goller & Tomlinson rather naively rented to Banning all of its equipment, storage facilities, and animals in San Pedro for six months, entrusting them to their competitor rather than leaving them idle. Banning made the most of these assets to increase his business by employing Edward McDonald, who had worked for Banning since his arrival in San Pedro from New York in 1853, to set up another business advertising the exact same rates. The new company thus gave the appearance of competition but did not actually benefit customers, who paid the same rates at both. Near the end of this period many of Goller & Tomlinson's assets were seized from Banning by the county sheriff in court actions, and they sued Banning for unpaid rent and failure to take care of the property, but to no avail. The two firms finally settled their differences to the satisfaction of no one.[17]

Even facing this competition, Banning's company was thriving in 1858, to judge by the size and assets of his operation. Newspaper reports stated that he employed sixty men in his complex of shops in old San Pedro before his move to the new location. Besides blacksmithing, stevedoring, and driving stages and freight wagons, they were manufacturing stagecoaches fitted out with harnesses made by Elijah Workman in Los Angeles. By midyear Banning owned twenty-one freight wagons, six stagecoaches, six large lighters and smaller boats, warehouses in Los Angeles and at the harbor, and a wharf, along with two hundred mules and one hundred workhorses. He would soon add two steamers, the *Comet* and the *Clara*.[18]

By 1860 Banning would also be importing and selling lumber from Northern California. That year he won a contract with a private firm to transport redwood poles for the southern section of the telegraph line between San Francisco and Los Angeles. His teams began hauling the 250-pound poles to the central California town of Visalia that summer for the portion of the line running south from there. The completion of this line in October was a communications breakthrough: while before it could take days for national and international news and other information to reach Los Angeles, now it took just minutes. With improved communication with San Francisco and the rest of the nation, the status of Los Angeles began to change, from a distant frontier outpost to a more important economic and political center in a region of growing potential.[19]

Banning's fortunes seemed to thrive, but by late 1860 there was a general business downturn in the region that, coupled with the increased competition from Tomlinson, encouraged him to take on a partner. August F. Hinchman was the brother-in-law of John Temple, and probably had access to Temple's wealth, which would certainly help Banning weather economic ups-and-downs. He had also been the superintendent of schools in Santa Barbara County and a businessman in Los Angeles in the 1850s. The Banning & Hinchman partnership lasted from October 1860 to February 1862, after which Hinchman stayed on as Banning's agent in Los Angeles while serving for a year as superintendent of the city schools.[20]

Banning & Hinchman carried on the same business that Banning had pioneered as "Forwarding & Commission Agents," with Banning headquartered at the port and Hinchman in the city. They advertised themselves in San Francisco newspapers as dealers in lumber, coal, iron, flour, and grain, and proprietors of the U.S. mail stage line between New San Pedro and Los Angeles.[21]

The firm also subcontracted with various companies and individuals to transport large and heavy objects, as well as merchandise, throughout Southern California and Arizona Territory. In fact, the company established a reputation for such difficult moves. In 1861 Banning & Hinchman agreed to haul a four-ton iron boiler from the harbor to a mining area in the San Bernardino Mountains for Francis Mellus, a Los Angeles merchant who also financed a mining company. The trip involved carrying the cumbersome boiler over Cajon Pass and up a steep mountain, and many observers thought it impossible. Banning & Hinchman was not dissuaded, however, and employed William Sanford to accomplish the task. As promised, the boiler reached its destination in

August 1861 and was put to use powering several stamp mills crushing gold-bearing quartz.[22]

Not content simply with transporting goods, the firm ventured into processing as well; in 1861 Banning & Hinchman added a "cattle-killing and trying works" to its list of assets. The hide-and-tallow trade had been a staple of the California economy since the Mexican period, when *Californio* ranchers raised large herds of cattle and sold them to New England merchants for their hides, used to manufacture shoes and other leather goods, and tallow, which was made into soap, candles, and other products. This business had waned since statehood, when most cattle began to be raised for their meat and sent north to feed hungry miners in the gold fields. Banning decided to start a business that used all the parts of the cow, processing meat as well as hide and tallow. Ranchers herded their cattle to New San Pedro to be slaughtered and skinned by inexpensive local Indian laborers. The meat was dried, salted, and preserved as jerky, while hides were dried and prepared for market, and the cattle fat was boiled in try-pots, cooled, and then packed for shipment to the east. Finally, meat byproducts of the boiling process were sold as hog feed. Banning envisioned a huge profit in this very efficient enterprise, aiding the ranchers, local businessmen and, of course, his own firm. Unfortunately, the cattle industry was soon hit by several consecutive years of drought, a turn of events that killed off the initiative in just two seasons.[23]

Fortunately for the partners, the trying works was but one portion of Banning & Hinchman's operation in 1861, which had expanded its inventory of equipment and animals since it was last described by reporters in 1858. At New San Pedro—"a little village or town, perhaps an incipient commercial metropolis," thought one reporter—were the company's substantial wharf, warehouses, workshops, engine house, stores, and other buildings, along with about twenty dwellings, which included a hotel, two rooming houses, and family residences. Most, possibly all, of the residential structures housed Banning's employees, for the community was still little more than a company town. A stack of redwood poles rested nearby, awaiting the realization of Banning's plan to extend the telegraph line to his office in Los Angeles. In the city, Hinchman supervised warehouses, a large lumberyard containing building materials and coal, and stables for their equine "locomotive power." Clearly the business was booming by the start of the Civil War. A reporter described Banning at this moment with something like awe (and perhaps a hint of sarcasm): "His capacity to manage and carry on a large business, one with innumerable, but slightly connected branches, filled with intricate ramifica-

Los Angeles Plaza area in the 1860s. Courtesy of the Seaver Center for Western History Research, Natural History Museum of Los Angeles County.

tions, is only equaled by his unlimited ambition to do all the business that comes within his line, or has any legitimate connection, however feeble, with it."[24]

The Banning Family Moves to New San Pedro

Although Phineas and Rebecca suffered the death of a son in the period between 1858 and mid-1861, their fortunes in general seemed to reflect the prosperity of Banning's business. Another son, William Sanford Banning, was born in October 1858. He was named after Rebecca's oldest brother, and probably Phineas's, too, and was destined to be the family patriarch after his father's death. For just two years later, John Griffin, the Banning's first son, died at the age of four while Phineas was on a business trip to San Francisco. This was just three years after the death of Francenia, their first daughter and the first of many Banning children to die at an early age; the chain of losses must have felt like a curse to Rebecca and Phineas.[25]

Before John Griffin's death, Phineas had a new home built in New San Pedro to house what seemed a rapidly growing family. The structure was located on Canal Street, not far from his wharf. He wrote to his sister-in-law, Mary, in October 1859 that the house was "almost completed" and he would move his "tribe" into it very soon. The house would serve as the family residence for five years, when a new and much larger home was completed on an elevation further north of the waterline. The 1859 residence would later become part of the Wilmington Exchange, the premier hotel in town.[26]

The new Banning home in New San Pedro was finished and fully occupied in time for the census taker to record its occupants for the 1860 federal census. Besides Phineas and Rebecca and their young sons John and William, the household included Rebecca's mother, Hannah, and Rebecca's brother, William Sanford. Rebecca's niece Hannah Young and Emma Griffin, both from Missouri and both sixteen years old, and Harriet, a fourteen-year-old African American who was probably the daughter of a family slave in Missouri, lived with them, along with Banning's bookkeeper, Tom Workman, and his wife, Alice. With the exception of Alice, Phineas, and the two Banning boys, all had been born in the slaveholding South. As historian Joyce Loranger has noted, the residents overwhelmingly had Southern accents and sympathies in the years before the beginning of the Civil War.[27]

The residence next door to the Bannings housed eight of his male employees at the time. They received room and board along with their wages, meaning that Rebecca probably had to make arrangements for their meals and living quarters. One of these workers was Herman W. Hellman, a sixteen-year-old clerk who had come to the U.S. from Prussia in 1859 and was employed by Banning from June of that year to the end of 1860. He left Banning's company that year and eventually entered the wholesale business in Los Angeles, where he became a competitor of Harris Newmark and one of the city's leading businessmen.[28]

With his new home, his enlarged family, and a prospering business in New San Pedro by 1861, Phineas invited his older brother William Lowber to leave chilly Minnesota and bring his family to Southern California and enjoy the fruits of its abundance. As historian Kevin Starr has observed, Phineas embodied the California Dream at this time, "acting out the myth of Southern California as land of plenty and promise for poor boys from the East." Phineas pointed out "how things have declined in Minnesota" and urged his brother to take advantage of opportunities for raising cattle on one of the "great many Ranchos for sale." "Stock raising has always been a good business in California," he wrote, "and there never was so good a time to commence it as the present." Since he had just expanded into that field, he would be able to help William get started and get rich if he would retire from banking and politics in St. Paul.[29]

Fortunately for William, he did not heed his younger brother's advice, for Mother Nature would not cooperate with Phineas's optimistic vision of the future. That very winter, heavy rain inundated the region, causing flooding that damaged property, drowned cattle, washed out roads, and harmed business in general throughout the state. A severe drought of two years followed the flood. Without rain the grasses dried up and cattle starved. This drought, historian Robert Cleland later concluded, marked the end of the domination of the region by the beef cattle industry and set the stage for the "new economic order" that would replace it. Bad timing, it would seem, for brother William's new investment.[30]

Adventures in Politics

In the same year that Phineas Banning founded his new town, he entered a major political contest for the first time. Politics in Southern California in the 1850s often dealt with issues of great moment, and passions could run high. National questions such as whether slavery should be extended enflamed political rhetoric in the region, especially as the nation grew closer to the beginning of civil war. Major state issues such as the repeated proposals to divide California into two entities, forming a "Territory of Colorado" of the southern counties, could also be highly controversial, especially when the outcome affected the pocketbooks of the more affluent. The area was overwhelmingly Democratic before 1861, both because most recent immigrants were Southerners and because the *Californio* landed elite aligned themselves with the party of the Southern landed elite. Even so, elections were hotly contested by the Whig and then the Republican parties.[31]

Municipal elections in the small city of Los Angeles were not always quite so bitter. Although some candidates evoked national issues to drum up partisan support, citizens generally ignored city contests. During this period in Los Angeles municipal politics, historian Robert Fogelson has commented, "power was so extraneous to the interests of the townspeople that politics attracted little attention. Candidates occasionally contested for office, but citizens seldom voted in elections, and legislators rarely met to conduct public affairs."[32]

Holding a city office, however, could be helpful to a young man with ambition and a desire to succeed like an older brother in Philadelphia politics. In early 1858 Banning decided to run for a seat on the Los Angeles Common Council, although he and his family resided many miles outside the city limits. The election drew scant attention from the *Star*, other than an editorial asking voters to support the most competent and honest candidates. On May 3, Banning came in seventh, the last to qualify for the seven available seats. John Goller, one of Banning's major competitors, along with John S. Griffin, Antonio F. Coronel, Stephen C. Foster, Cristobal Aguilar, and David Porter joined him on the council for that year. Two of Banning's associates were also elected to city offices: James Lander as city attorney, and Henry N. Alexander as city treasurer.[33]

Banning served in this office for one term, from May 10, 1858, to May 9, 1859. While he began conscientiously, he soon resembled Fogelson's typical officeholder. After two months he began missing meetings, and after October 1, when New San Pedro was in full operation, he attended very few. When present, he served on the finance, street grading, and police committees of the council. He also joined the entire council on the Board of Equalization, which heard appeals to the city's tax assessment roll. His most notable political act was to get the council to empower Mayor John Nichols to order that the city portion of a road between San Pedro and Los Angeles be surveyed, mapped, and declared a public street. This street, not surprisingly, was the one that Banning used for his express business to and from the harbor. Given the city's small population, Banning and his cohorts had little business to conduct and not much tax revenue to work with. The experience in local government, however, enhanced his political reputation, which would aid him in the future.[34]

The burden of traveling to meetings in Los Angeles, which took time he needed to devote to building up his new community, certainly played a role in Banning's absences. In the following year he would cite this as his reason for deciding to forgo another local race. By this time he had established a reputation as a business and community leader and had impressed a number of staunchly Democratic friends and business partners. In 1859 these friends nominated him as a candidate for supervisor at the county Democratic convention. He now knew that he would have little time for the office and immediately declined the nomination in an advertisement in the *Star*, saying that "his business would preclude his attending to *both* with his accustomed promptness."[35]

Phineas might also have been unsure of his party affiliation in 1859. Although he would become well known as a Republican by the end of the Civil War years, in the 1850s Banning was a Democrat, like his brother William Lower Banning. In fact, a Democratic Party leader who was also Banning's lawyer claimed years later that Banning was a very active Democrat in the 1850s, working for local party leader J. Lancaster Brent and with his politically oriented partner William Sanford. The Democrats who nominated him as a county supervisor in 1859 certainly thought he was. But he, like his brother William Lower in St. Paul, also opposed the impending secession of the South, and that conviction was more important to him than party loyalty. As a staunch Unionist in 1860, when the nation seemed headed toward certain division, Phineas is reported to have supported the Constitutional Union Party ticket of John Bell and Edward Everett in the national election. This party provided an alternative for conservative voters who wanted to uphold the Union but feared that a focus on the question of slavery, central to Democratic and Republican platforms alike, would force secession. However he voted that year, 1860 apparently marked a political watershed for Phineas, as for his brother, and he would soon profess himself a Republican, an affiliation he retained for the rest of his life.[36]

In Social Spheres

In the years from 1858 to 1861 Phineas and Rebecca stepped up their social and philanthropic activity as they became more affluent and prominent. Phineas was mentioned in city newspapers as the generous host of parties and excursions such as the opening of New San Pedro in September 1858. His hospitality was celebrated by his guests, including almost a dozen passengers who, caught in a storm as they arrived in New San Pedro, stayed at his home through Christmas Day in 1860. He frequently entertained military officers serving in the area. One officer warmly recalled "a most sumptuous" dinner at old San Pedro for a large party of gentlemen, including officers of the Sixth Infantry and Banning's former partner George C. Alexander, at which "the finest quality of champagne flowed freely." Other invited officers included Winfield Scott Hancock, the U.S. Army quartermaster in Los Angeles, who arrived in the city in late 1858 and became a regular guest and a good friend. These social occasions cemented Banning's relationship with army officers, and no doubt he reminded them of his friendship when he sought government contracts for transportation and supply of military installations.[37]

Banning soirées sometimes included dancing, even though Phineas would generally beg off. He once told his sister-in-law that he could not dance because his feet were too big. In later years the dinner parties would reach epic proportions, becoming true banquets; Rebecca's duties as a menu planner and hostess expanded with the number of guests at these events. When Lady Franklin, widow of Arctic explorer Sir John Franklin, visited Los Angeles in 1861, the Bannings hosted a large reception for her at their home in New San Pedro.[38]

Phineas also continued to donate his services and equipment for social occasions, several of them reported by the *Star*. On two occasions in

Winfield Scott Hancock.
Courtesy of the
Huntington Library

1859 he supplied stagecoaches for the leg between Los Angeles and San Pedro for excursions to Santa Catalina Island. Through this generosity, according to a reporter, "he almost excelled himself, and added another claim to the respect and confidence of the community, which he so largely enjoys and has so nobly earned." On another occasion he offered his coach to take the city sewing circle out to Benjamin D. Wilson's Lake Vineyard residence and back for their regular meeting. And in the same year he acceded to the request of several churchwomen by contributing toward the purchase of a melodeon for Protestant worship and then transported it from the harbor to Los Angeles free of charge.[39]

In many cases, we know of his activities because local newspapers saw them as newsworthy, demonstrating how dramatically Phineas Banning's stature in Southern California had risen since his arrival a decade earlier in 1851. He had transformed himself over those ten years into a prominent business, civic, and social leader, promoting the region and leading the quest to develop San Pedro harbor. But he was far from finished: while he would continue to advance his standing along with that of his family and close associates in the Civil War years, he would face new challenges when the nation exploded in bloody conflict in 1861.

CIVIL WAR SOUTHERN CALIFORNIA

O n April 12, 1861, the forces of the Confederate States of America fired on Fort Sumter in South Carolina, plunging the nation into four years of bloody civil warfare. Known variously as the "War Between the States" or "War of the Rebellion," depending on the speaker's sympathies, the conflict ripped the nation apart. Often family members fought one another as the industrializing North battled the agrarian South, whose economy depended on slave labor. The war left well over 600,000 combatants dead and about the same number wounded, and it caused countless civilian casualties and major property and environmental destruction, especially in the South. The legacy of the war continued to be felt in national politics, sectional development, and race relations for almost a century and a half.

Southern California was far from the battlefields of this conflict, but the war still affected regional politics and society. While historians have disagreed on the nature and extent of pro-Union sentiment in the southern counties, there was certainly persistent and vocal opposition to the federal government and frequent demonstrations of support for secession, particularly by newcomers from the South. Approximately 250 citizens of Los Angeles County, including Gen. Albert Sidney Johnston and Phineas Banning's good friend J. Lancaster Brent, traveled east to join the Confederate forces. Union military leaders were concerned enough about local sympathy for the Southern cause and the remote possibility of a Confederate invasion to establish several military camps in Southern California to maintain federal authority. Tension between pro- and anti-Union groups exacerbated partisan and interparty political differences and invited restrictions of civil liberties. National issues, previously only a backdrop to local and regional concerns, came to the fore of the political scene.[1]

For the Banning family, the war years likewise highlighted the divided sectional loyalties of its members. Phineas was a passionate Unionist who loudly denounced secession and helped supply the U.S. Army. Rebecca retained her Southern sympathies and reportedly retreated upstairs when Phineas entertained Union officers in their home, as he often did. The tensions that kept them apart were probably as stressful as those facing any American family with divided loyalties in the early 1860s.[2]

William Lowber Banning in the War

When the war began, Phineas and his brother William Lowber Banning immediately decided to defend the Union. In 1861 William joined the Third Regiment of Minnesota Volunteers and headed to Washington, D.C., to seek a commission worthy of his talents. He was allowed an interview with President Abraham Lincoln in August and afterward wrote to his wife that Lincoln had agreed to approve the appointment if Secretary of War Simon Cameron concurred. Cameron finally did, and William received a commission as "Commissary of Subsistence," an officer charged with provisioning the army, with the rank of captain, and was assigned to the Missouri Department of the U.S. Army.[3]

Rebecca's home state of Missouri, where Phineas's brothers Richard and Henry had lived since at least 1850, was then experiencing an intrastate conflict within the larger U.S. Civil War. The internal struggle in this slave state pitted slaveholders against a recent influx of antislavery residents. The state witnessed continual and bloody fighting between these two groups, as well as between federal and rebel troops hoping either to keep the state in the Union or to force it to join the Confederacy. Contingents of irregular troops on both sides raided the communities of their opponents. Under the command of William Quantrill, "Bloody Bill" Anderson, and others, they inflicted the worst atrocities against civilians of the entire war.[4]

William served in Missouri under Gen. John C. Frémont and his successor, Gen. Samuel R. Curtis. Stationed at various times in St. Louis, Jefferson City, Warsaw, Pilot Knob, and other venues in Missouri, he was responsible for procuring supplies for the U.S. Army of the Southwest. He saw very limited battlefield action, but did become involved in preventing local residents from supporting the Confederates during the army occupation. In 1863 he was stricken with malaria and compelled to resign his commission that July. His military career over, he returned home to St. Paul.[5]

William Lowber Banning
during the Civil War.
Courtesy of the
Huntington Library.

Defending the Union in Southern California

Phineas, too, was ardently pro-Union. A former employee later recalled a conversation Banning had before the war began with Albert Sidney Johnston, a California-based U.S. Army officer who would soon become a Confederate general, about the possibility of secession. Phineas, he reported, emphatically declared his allegiance to the undivided Union. When Johnston asked if Banning would support the decision of his native state of Delaware on whether to secede, Banning answered: "Yes, if my state goes right, but if she attempts to leave the Union, I hope that the Government will send troops enough to forever wipe her out. But, I know that Delaware will never secede."[6]

When the war did begin, Phineas, like his older brother, decided to join the Union army. He arranged to leave his business under the management of his brother-in-law William Sanford and headed to San Francisco to take a steamer to Washington, D.C., and there seek a military commission. While in San Francisco, Banning heard that a Confederate army from Texas had invaded New Mexico Territory in July and was planning to continue westward into California. In order to stop it, a Union force would be raised in Northern California, transported to

Southern California, and then sent eastward into New Mexico Territory. With his new home state threatened, Banning thought he could better serve the federal government from New San Pedro, so he headed back home. As a result, his life during the war was like that of most in the far West. While few saw the battlefield, the war would nonetheless profoundly affect Californians by transforming the economy and politics of the state over the next several years.[7]

Phineas would eventually receive the military commission he coveted, but too late to serve in the military during the war. He requested a commission in the state militia from Governor Frederick Low, whose campaign he supported in 1863. He would not receive it until April 1866, however, when he was at last appointed a brigadier general of the First Brigade of the new California National Guard. The unit was never called to service, but he retained his new title, a promotion from "Captain," his title after his 1857 election to the Union Guards, and "Major," as he had begun referring to himself by the summer of 1859. From April 1866 to his dying day, he called himself "General" Banning and insisted on using this title to enhance his position in Southern California.[8]

While not a soldier, Banning did support the Union cause in other important ways. As the most outspoken defender of the Union in a region dominated by Southerners and Confederate sympathizers, he made numerous speeches excoriating secessionists in the face of hostile crowds. He came to the defense of military officers by protecting their supplies from local opponents, and he helped the U.S. Army station troops in the area to keep the peace and prevent the "Monte Boys" and other secession advocates from intimidating local Unionists.[9]

Banning also led the local subscription crusade for the Sanitary Fund, a national organization that raised money to care for wounded U.S. soldiers and their families. Before his participation, the fund had done well in Northern California, but poorly in the south, where Confederate sympathy was much stronger. Banning had raised some money in New San Pedro in 1863, but little was done elsewhere. He helped to revitalize the campaign in early 1865, and, boosted by recent Union victories, the county effort raised a substantial amount of money.[10]

Working with the U.S. Army

Banning's primary contribution to the Union cause, however, came through his business, fulfilling the many transportation, supply, and construction contracts the U.S. government awarded him during the war. In 1861 he persuaded Gen. James Carleton, commander of the Southern

California district, to locate the army's supply depot in New San Pedro. Having ensured that the army's supplies would all go through his harbor, Banning then obtained contracts to supply Carleton's California Column as it moved eastward to New Mexico Territory; his steamers also transported provisions through the Gulf of California to Fort Yuma. He supplied the Owens River expedition to suppress the Paiute Indians, and his employees provided miscellaneous services to the troops, such as shoeing horses. Sometimes the military officers praised Banning's work, but they also complained about the tardiness of his teams and his high freight rates.[11]

Banning also received a short-lived contract to construct buildings for a U.S. outpost on Santa Catalina Island. The army took possession of the island in 1863, intending to use it for an Indian reservation, primarily for "hostiles" in Northern California. A small army post was planned for the central isthmus, and in 1864 Banning was apparently chosen to erect the buildings. Only a few had been completed by the summer, however, when government policy changed and the reservation idea was scrapped.[12]

In securing government contracts, Banning relied on his friendly relationships with army commanders, including Gen. Benjamin L. Beall at Fort Tejon and Gen. Winfield Scott Hancock in the Quartermaster's Office in Los Angeles. His efforts were further cemented by his work to enhance the position of New San Pedro as the primary seaport in Southern California and at the same time to promote the Union cause by establishing a federal base there. In early 1862, shortly after securing the army's agreement to locate its depot at their harbor, Banning and partner Benjamin D. Wilson sold thirty acres of their property to the U.S. government for one dollar in order to ensure that a military installation would be built there. The camp, named in honor of Richard C. Drum, for several years adjutant general of the Army of the Pacific, was built in 1862–63 in New San Pedro by—who else—Phineas Banning, who had of course won the construction contracts as well. Army authorities claimed that the complex cost nearly one million dollars, a stunning amount at the time. This was probably an exaggeration, but the post was extensive, and erecting it was undoubtedly lucrative. The camp boasted separate quarters for officers and junior officers, five barracks for the troops, an office for the quartermaster, a hospital, commissary, guardhouse, bakery, blacksmith shop, and ammunition magazine, along with stables and other outbuildings, all surrounded by a tall picket fence. In addition, Banning built a government depot and warehouse further south at his wharf.[13]

Drum Barracks Junior Officers' Quarters as it looked in 1928. Courtesy of the Huntington Library.

Camp Drum, or Drum Barracks, as it was more commonly called, replaced several smaller, temporary camps and became the major depot for army supplies and a way station for troops in the Southwest, as well as a deterrent to local secessionist activity. The government presence there served to build up Banning's town of Wilmington and contributed to the Los Angeles regional economy. When the post eventually closed in 1866, the loss of revenues was sorely felt in Wilmington and at the county seat. Phineas Banning may have pocketed just one dollar for the camp land, but many more dollars followed in its train, in the form of government contracts. As an investigator for the Quartermaster's Office concluded in 1867, Banning, referred to as the "general Government Contractor for Southern California and Arizona," probably received every single U.S. Army contract for supplies in the region, as well as many for construction and other purposes during the war.[14]

The remarkable extent of Banning's influence with local quartermasters was formally documented when Bvt. Brig. Gen. James F. Rusling investigated the controversy over the Drum Barracks' water system just after the war. The system had been created when the army discovered, after the camp was occupied, that there was not enough clean drinking water to supply it. Banning convinced the army authorities that the government should build a facility to bring water from the San Gabriel River to the camp, and he of course offered to help with the construction—in return for a franchise to sell any surplus water in Wilmington. He then arranged for Assemblyman E. J. C. Kewen to introduce a bill in the state legislature authorizing Banning and his partners to build a dam on the San Gabriel River and "to construct a water course, consisting of ditches and flumes" from the river to Camp Drum and Wilmington after securing the proper right-of-way agreements. The bill, approved April 1, 1864, also allowed Banning to set the rates for selling the surplus water.[15]

Construction of the twelve-mile watercourse began almost immediately. Los Angeles County Surveyor George Hanson was the engineer for the project, which involved digging and reinforcing a four-foot-wide canal that carried water most of the way from the dam and then building an elevated wooden flume for the last three miles into the harbor. Banning agreed to provide 100,000 feet of lumber for the flume, a small portion of what was needed, while the government supplied the rest plus all other materials, as well as the labor of some four hundred soldiers over the course of eight months. It was not until October, when the project was nearly complete, that an official contract was finally approved giving Banning all of the surplus water from the system. By the beginning of 1865 he was already using this water to irrigate his Wilmington barley fields, which supplied feed for the many animals employed in his transportation business.[16]

Criticism of the cost of this joint venture, and the benefits that flowed to Banning from it, began almost immediately. The *Los Angeles News*, then edited by one of Banning's political opponents, reported in late January 1865 that army inspectors might recommend a reconstruction of "The Great Government Ditch" using iron pipes, which would "leave the present structure in the hands of Mr. Banning" and result in vast new government expenditures for another water system. In the following month a San Francisco newspaper published a story describing a number of lavish expenditures for supplies and structures by quartermasters at Drum Barracks, the centerpiece of which was the new water system, built at taxpayers' expense but profiting private citizens. The U.S. quartermaster general ordered an investigation, but Maj. Gen. Irvin McDowell, another good friend of Banning, stopped it. Several ranking officers suspected nonetheless that at least some of the accusations were well founded.[17]

Some of these suspicions were substantiated by the February 1867 inspection by General Rusling. Rusling submitted a long report to the U.S. quartermaster general of his findings. His assignment was to assess the entire installation, which had then been closed for several months, with an eye to its future disposition. But he had many things to say beyond the present condition and the value of this camp to the army.

On the camp's "irrigating ditch," Rusling concluded that it was no longer needed, and that after the camp closed and local farmers began to tap the river for their own irrigation purposes, the flume had run dry. The consensus of local opinion, he claimed, was that the ditch was really built to supply water to the town of Wilmington, and the matter "is the staple subject for laughter by all officers I met." He reported that when General McDowell, newly appointed as commanding officer for the department, had visited Drum Barracks in 1864, he was astounded to learn that the U.S. Army had built the system but Banning actually controlled it. McDowell had then forced Banning to transfer ownership to the United States in return for receiving the surplus water. By the time of Rusling's visit in 1867, however, it was virtually worthless to the U.S. government and, he concluded, "there it stands to-day, a gigantic monument of the folly + extravagance of <u>somebody</u>."[18]

On a larger scale, Rusling charged that Drum Barracks itself never should have been built in New San Pedro in the first place. San Diego was a much more appropriate location, he thought, despite the assertions of Banning and others that it was too close to the border with Mexico and could therefore easily be invaded. San Diego had a much better natural harbor than Wilmington (where "there is really no harbor at all") and was half the distance to Fort Yuma and Arizona Territory. Banning even admitted that he had persuaded the authorities to choose his harbor over San Diego because his own interests lay there. Rusling cast aspersions on several quartermasters who had reputedly made fortunes during their service at Drum Barracks. They were responsible for approving the extravagance, he said, including the high rates Banning charged for supplies such as barley. Rusling's overall conclusion was that the entire complex—buildings, flume, and all—should be dismantled and the materials sold, and that the camp should be removed to San Diego.[19]

In a note to his report, Rusling regretted having to "speak so unfavorably" about Phineas Banning, because he was grateful for the many courtesies that Banning had extended to him. During Rusling's visit Banning had taken him on a tour of Los Angeles, entertained him, and loaned him a wagon for the trip to Arizona. Obviously, Phineas did not know what Rusling would report to the U.S. quartermaster general. "I must say I admire his genius & audacity in getting Drum Barracks to become what it is," Rusling admitted, but he was emphatic that he had to report what he actually found. Rusling's characterization of Banning in his later book *Across America* (1874), which documented his travels in 1866–67, was far more complimentary. In that work he referred to Banning thus: "A man of large and liberal ideas, with a great native force of character and power of endurance, he was invaluable to Southern California and Arizona, and both of these sections owe him a debt of gratitude, which they never can repay." Banning "was a good second edition of Mr. Ben Holliday [*sic*], yet without his bad politics," he wrote.[20]

Banning's Other Business

While Banning devoted most of his company's resources to government contracts during the war, he also continued his usual work as a "Forwarding and Commission Agent, and Dealer in Lumber, Flour, Grain, &c," as his advertisements stated. His company operated lighters and small steamers between his wharf and ships anchored outside the harbor to shuttle passengers and freight, and his coaches transported them to and from Los Angeles. He also sent teams to transport equipment and commodities to sites such as the Cerro Gordo mining region in Inyo County for private enterprises. Although competitor J. J. Tomlinson did more stage and freight business during the depressed California business climate of the early 1860s, and many Southern sympathizers avoided doing business with Banning because of his pro-Union stance, Banning's company did well. In early 1865 he was listed as by far the largest taxpayer in Los Angeles County (although others may have underreported their incomes to reduce their taxes). Despite his prosperity, Banning decided by the end of the war to take on a former partner, David Alexander. While this time the firm name remained Banning & Company, the additional capital Alexander brought would allow the company to expand its private staging and freight business after the war, when government contracts declined.[21]

According to Harris Newmark, Banning also expanded his business by taking a stand against a few anti-Semites in Los Angeles who had hoped to drive Newmark and other Jewish businessmen out of the city. In the summer of 1865 Newmark heard of the plan and offered Banning a deal in order to thwart it. If Banning & Company offered him lower transportation rates, Newmark proposed, he would import goods from San Francisco and sell them much more cheaply than the gentile conspirators could sell theirs and thus damage their business. Banning agreed to help his good friend and good customer, and at the same time spite some of the merchants who had given their business to his competitors. After about six months the opposition gave in, Newmark's business expanded, and Banning & Company split the profits with him.[22]

As his business grew larger, so did Banning's city, known as New San Pedro in 1861. Its name was officially changed by the California legislature to Wilmington in 1863. A typical small seaport, it was described by Rusling in the 1860s as "a village of shanties, with an unsettled and changing population." Others observed that the approximately sixty-five dwellings were served by "a number of saloons." Flooding at high tide was always a problem; one reporter wryly noted that "what the city lacks in the elevation of its site it makes up in the elevation of its water-lines, many of them being higher than the surrounding objects." Its fate remained tied to Banning and his business, and it rose in prosperity, as did he, during the war years. As J. Ross Browne commented on Wilmington in 1864: "The city fathers are all centered in Banning, who is mayor, councilman, constable, and watchman, all in one . . . Big of heart, big of body, big of enterprise, is Phineas—the life and soul of Los Angeles county." With the departure of troops beginning in 1865, Wilmington would become much less active and prosperous, but Phineas would still be proud of his creation.[23]

The First Banning Oil Venture

Phineas Banning embarked on still another commercial venture at this time—a pioneering effort in an industry that would pay huge dividends to many of his descendants, if not to him. For during the Civil War he became interested in extracting petroleum in Southern California and marketing it at a profit.

The presence of petroleum in the region was by then well established. Tar found on the Rancho La Brea had been used for some time to waterproof the canoes of Native Americans and the roofs of Spanish- and Mexican-era adobe houses, as well as to caulk ships calling at nearby ports. (From the Ice Age on, the pools of tar had also trapped numerous animals, some of whose fossil remains are now housed at the Natural History Museum of Los Angeles County and the George C. Page Museum, at the La Brea tar pits.) In other locations in Los Angeles County and present-day Ventura County, oil leaked to the surface in small quantities.

By 1861, George S. Gilbert, a whale oil merchant near Ventura, was

Wilmington Exchange Hotel in the 1860s. Courtesy of the Huntington Library.

refining a small amount of kerosene from oil seepage there. Railroad magnate Thomas Scott, who had purchased and developed oil fields in Pennsylvania in the late 1850s, sent a chemist to investigate mineral deposits in the West in 1864; the chemist discovered Gilbert's operation and raved about its financial potential. Banning evidently heard of this discovery and hatched a plan to look for oil in Los Angeles.[24]

In December 1864, Banning wrote to the Los Angeles Common Council to ask for permission to drill on city lands. He had, he said, "dispatched his first Engineer to the East to observe and procure the most approved apparatus for making perforations into the bowels of Mother Earth." Drilling would be "an undertaking of great expense, with a view of developing more effectually the resources of our favored county." In return for his investment, he wanted a two-year quitclaim deed to a city lot for "experimental purposes." The city agreed to this arrangement and gave Banning five years to strike oil in paying quantities or the contract would be void.[25]

Banning immediately organized several of his associates as the first investors in the Los Angeles Pioneer Oil Company, incorporated on February 24, 1865. Banning was elected president, merchant Charles Ducommun was chosen treasurer, and Banning's clerk Patrick H. Downing was the secretary. Other directors included Gen. Winfield Scott Hancock, Matthew Keller, Benjamin D. Wilson, Dr. John S. Griffin, former Governor John G. Downey, and Drum Barracks officers J. S. Curtis and W. F. Swasey. The company soon began issuing stock certificates to raise capital to pay for equipment and drilling rights.[26]

Pioneer Oil began its drilling operations by May 1865, and during its first year newspaper reports were very favorable and expectations were high. The company secured drilling rights for sites in Los Angeles, in Wilmington, near the coastline on the Palos Verdes Rancho, on the San Pasqual Rancho (present-day Pasadena), and other locations. The company's superintendent, A. A. Polhamus, the engineer Banning had sent to Pennsylvania to learn drilling procedures, began operations in the San Fernando Valley that year. By the summer of 1866 newspapers reported that the company was "prepared to furnish merchants and others with illuminating and lubricating oils."[27]

The expenses of production for this venture, however, were not matched by the proceeds. The equipment was primitive and the geological strata difficult to penetrate. In some cases the drills could not reach the black gold; in other cases they struck saltwater or nothing at all. Furthermore, in the days before internal combustion engines, the market for the final product was limited. In the following decade others developed successful wells in the San Fernando Valley, and by the 1890s oil would be found in much larger quantities—just before its use by the railroads made it more valuable. But the demand in the late 1860s could not support several companies drilling in Southern California. The Los Angeles Pioneer Oil Company eventually folded and the Los Angeles Common Council reclaimed its 1865 deed.[28]

Although this venture did not profit Phineas Banning, his project laid the groundwork for the more lucrative efforts of later oil drillers in the region. He and his partners drilled in the wrong places, but others would find the right spots just outside downtown Los Angeles in the 1890s, and in Santa Fe Springs, Signal Hill, Wilmington, Huntington Beach, and other locations in the early twentieth century. Petroleum extraction and refining would become one of Southern California's major industries, and would fuel in turn the railroad, automobile, and aircraft industries, as well as regional manufacturing generally. And although he did not find it himself, Phineas passed on a fortune in oil, for he owned parcels in Wilmington and later in Orange County that would eventually produce a bonanza for his heirs in the twentieth century.

Family Triumphs and Tragedies

During the Civil War years, Rebecca Banning gave birth to two more sons who, along with their brother William, would carry the family business into the next century. Both were named after good friends—friends whom the Civil War would drive far from Phineas and Southern California. In August 1861, Joseph Brent Banning was born. Phineas named him after J. Lancaster Brent, a lawyer and good friend who was one of the five original investors in the Wilmington property in 1854. A fierce proponent of the Southern cause, Brent departed soon after the child's christening to join the Confederacy as a general, never to return to California. Before he left, however, he presented young Joseph with a deed for a lot in Los Angeles that skyrocketed in value when the city grew larger, and on which Joseph would build a substantial home three decades later for his own family.[29]

Then, at the close of the war in May 1865, Rebecca and Phineas welcomed Hancock Banning to their family. As Joseph was named after a staunch Confederate, Hancock was named for one of Phineas's friends who had steadfastly defended the Union. Winfield Scott Hancock had been a lieutenant in the U.S. Army during the war with Mexico before his promotion to captain and assignment as quartermaster in Los Angeles in late 1858. There he became close to Phineas Banning and rewarded the latter for his business abilities and friendship with a number of army supply contracts for transport, firewood, and other commodities. Hancock was promoted to brigadier general after the outbreak of the Civil War and led Union troops in a number of battles, most notably at Gettysburg in 1863. After the war he served as a commanding officer in the West and in 1880 was nominated for president as a conservative Democrat, but lost to Republican James A. Garfield.[30]

Before Hancock, Rebecca had had another son who, like most of her other children, died not long after birth. This time, however, the child was a victim of a catastrophe that claimed the lives of over thirty, many of them Banning family and friends. Rebecca was pregnant in April 1863 when disaster struck what was meant to be a joyful journey. Late on the afternoon of the 27th, a crowd of fifty-eight people, including many Banning family members and friends, gathered at Banning's wharf and boarded his tugboat, the steamer *Ada Hancock* (named after Winfield Scott Hancock's daughter). This small craft was bound for the *Senator*, a coastal steamer lying about a mile out, which was going to take some of the party to Northern California. The Banning family group accompanied Dr. Henry R. Myles and his fiancée, Miss Medora Hereford (sister of Benjamin D. Wilson's spouse, Margaret), who were to be married in San Francisco.[31] The *Ada Hancock* was about a half mile along its route and rounding a sharp bend "when a squall of wind arose suddenly and struck her, causing her to careen so much that her port guard was under water." As the ship was righted, cold water washed over the hot steam engine and blew up the boiler. The explosion tore the boat apart and left the harbor area littered with the body parts of many of its passengers. Twenty-nine people were killed instantly in the explosion, one more died in a few hours, and Medora Hereford died nine weeks later, "suffering terribly the whole time." The news reached Los Angeles at 8 p.m. and Dr. Griffin and many others rushed to the scene to do what they could to help the victims of what was seen as one of the region's worst disasters. A number of officers and troops stationed at nearby Drum Barracks also aided the injured and would be commended for their actions.[32]

Among Banning family members, company employees, and close friends killed in the *Ada Hancock* tragedy were Rebecca's brother William Sanford, Dr. Henry R. Myles, Banning & Company bookkeeper Tom Workman, *Ada Hancock* Captain Joseph Bryant, and later Medora Hereford. Also among the dead were Captain T. W. Seeley of the *Senator*, the son of Confederate General Albert Sidney Johnston, several wealthy businessmen, and two Mormon missionaries on their way to Hawaii. The injured included Rebecca, her mother, Hannah Sanford ("dangerously" hurt and almost drowned), Ruth Wilson (a daughter of Benjamin D. Wilson), and Banning sons William and Joseph. Rebecca's servant, Harriet, who was also injured, was reported to have "behaved nobly, in the estimation of all," grabbing the two boys and supporting them until they could be pulled from the water, and then assisting others. Phineas, the only survivor of those in the forward portion of the boat, which took the brunt of the blast, was blown out of the vessel and finally rescued some five hundred feet away from the wreck.[33]

Phineas, whose boat had brought about this catastrophe, was as devastated with guilt as he was injured. He tried to make amends with the victims as best he could by paying for most of their medical expenses. But the most painful of his losses was yet to come, for the disaster probably also caused the death of his unborn son. In the accident, Rebecca Banning had suffered a "contusion of the head and probably some internal injuries." About three months pregnant at the time, she gave birth in October to a child who did not live long enough to receive a name.[34]

A violent death met another of Rebecca's brothers before the year was out. John Sanford lived near Fort Tejon, where he raised sheep. On December 6 he was driving a buggy near Elizabeth Lake and gave a ride to a stranger walking along the road. The stranger, Charles Wilkins, took Sanford's gun, fatally shot him, and stole one of the horses. Wilkins eluded troops from the fort but was captured in Santa Barbara five days later and escorted to Los Angeles for trial. It was soon discovered that Wilkins had a long record of crime and violence, including eight murders, grand larceny, an escape from San Quentin Prison, and participation in the 1857 Mountain Meadows massacre as one of "Brigham Young's Destroying Angels."[35]

Wilkins would confess to Sanford's murder, but was himself killed before he could be sentenced. The vigilantism that took his life fed off the outlawry and violence still common in the region. J. Ross Browne commented about "the lively condition of society in and around Los Angeles" during his travels in 1864: "It is not considered safe for a man to travel about, even within a few miles of camp [Camp Drum], without a double-barreled shotgun, a revolver, a bowie-knife, and two Derringer pistols." Vigilante action in Los Angeles, so prevalent in the 1850s, was still in fashion during the war, when crime seemed on the rise. Browne noted: "Running down, catching, shooting, and hanging suspicious characters was esteemed the very best kind of sport, being dangerous as well as exciting...Whether the country will be permanently benefited by these acts remains to be seen. I hope it will, for it certainly needs reformation of some sort." Late in the same year as Sanford's murder, former Los Angeles County lawman Boston Daimwood and three others suspected of theft and threatening the lives of local residents were arrested and imprisoned by Sheriff Tomás Sanchez. On November 21, a group of about two hundred citizens stormed the jail before their trial, removed the four and another prisoner, and hanged them all. A couple of weeks later, Manuel Cerradel, thought to have taken part in the killing of rancher John Rains, was hung on one of Phineas Banning's own boats. Sentenced to ten years' hard labor for a different crime, Cerradel and several other prisoners were being taken by Sheriff Sanchez to San Quentin. They had boarded Banning's *Cricket* for the short ride to the awaiting coastal steamer when a group of passengers suddenly seized the convict and lynched him "from a yardarm, and the body was dropped overboard."[36]

Whether or not Banning was involved in that incident, he was well practiced in the "sport" of lynching; Wilkins was, then, most unfortunate in his choice of victims. He freely admitted his guilt and was quickly indicted by a grand jury in the Court of Sessions on December 16. When he faced Judge Hayes the following day, he again admitted killing Sanford, and Hayes ordered him back the following morning for what would probably have been a death sentence. Suddenly, a "mob from Wilmington headed by Banning" stormed into the courtroom, dragged Wilkins

The Banning family residence in 1870. Courtesy of the Banning Residence Museum.

off to "Banning's corral" and hanged him. Three reliable eyewitnesses later confirmed that Phineas Banning had commanded the mob of vigilantes. On the following day Banning even wrote to another community leader offering to hang another accused murderer "if we are very sure he deserves it." No one, least of all Banning, was arrested for Wilkins's lynching, which the newspapers reported in a matter-of-fact manner. Still more revealing of the general attitude of the time toward vigilantism was the county Board of Supervisors' decision, many months later, to reward Banning with $200 for arresting Wilkins. Clearly, the public sentiment that had encouraged the extralegal bursts of violence of Banning's Los Angeles Rangers in the 1850s had not changed much by the mid-1860s, and neither had Banning's willingness to lead the charge.[37]

Amid these many traumatic deaths among family and friends, Phineas Banning seems to have been spurred on to rebuild his household and social circle on a yet grander scale. The year after these tragedies, Phineas and Rebecca built a new home that would become the premier residence in Wilmington. The design of the house was Greek Revival, a style much favored by wealthy easterners of the previous century, whose homes Phineas remembered from his native Delaware. He envisioned an imposing structure, one that would accommodate more children, a larger extended family, and many guests. The house consisted of three floors of living and working spaces with a large basement and a cupola, added to the roof soon after construction. The façade featured a raised portico with columns supporting a second-story porch. The architect of this mansion, which dominated the landscape north of the Wilmington harbor, is unknown. Since there were few experienced architects in Los Angeles at the time, the building may have been based on available design plans and built by local craftsmen, who did most of the construction with redwood shipped from Northern California.[38]

Construction of the house probably began in the spring or summer of 1864, since a visitor to Wilmington in late August reported that "its exterior is in an unfinished state." The family moved in by early 1865 and filled the home with furniture, wall coverings, fine-dining implements, and other furnishings that spoke to the Bannings' self-image as social elites. These included a library of books, particularly poetry, which Phineas loved to read in his spare time. When the residence was finished, Banning began building a wooden fence around his 333-acre property and the larger Benjamin D. Wilson lot that adjoined it, and constructing a barn and other outbuildings. He also supervised the digging of an artesian well on the property, and here again he did not stint; it was the first in the county and "the largest in America," according to later newspaper reports, "with a winding stairway leading down to great pumps."[39]

By the end of the Civil War Banning had completed the new family homestead, much of which survives to this day. The house would not only serve as the family home, but also as Wilmington's community center, where business deals were negotiated, political moves discussed, and social affairs celebrated throughout the rest of Banning's life.

Civil War–Era Politics

During the Civil War years, state and local contests for office in Southern California became more highly spirited events, physically as well as intellectually. Tensions between the large cohort of Southern sympathizers and the Union soldiers stationed there to contain them were constantly inflamed by news of the bloody warfare in the East, and the national issues of slavery and secession were injected into every election. One of Phineas Banning's former employees, Frank Lecouvreur, recounted his experience as an election inspector in San Pedro in 1862, when about twenty "Arch Yankees" intimidated him into arming himself with two pistols as protection from attack. In the same year a Republican State Assembly candidate accused the county Board of Supervisors, predominantly Democrats, of illegally disqualifying ballots cast by U.S. soldiers. In the following year Republican Francisco P. Ramírez, publisher of the Spanish-language Los Angeles newspaper *El Clamor Público* in the 1850s, filed a petition to contest the election of Henry Hamilton to the

State Senate, charging Hamilton with disloyalty and ineligibility. Ramírez also claimed that the Board of Supervisors had deliberately failed to appoint election inspectors in four precincts, and appointed aliens in two others, in order to nullify votes in those strongly pro-Union precincts. His complaints were likely justified. In 1864 the county Board of Supervisors—Democrats all—would throw out enough votes in four pro-Union precincts to give presidential candidate and Democrat George McClellan a majority in the county.[40]

In the midst of this political maelstrom, Phineas Banning stood fast, a dedicated Unionist, "staunch Republican and Abolitionist," as Harris Newmark recalled. A moderately liberal Republican in the 1860s, Banning advocated federal authority over the states, the abolition of slavery, and public funding of major infrastructure improvements such as railroads and harbors. Local Democrats were, of course, much more conservative on all these issues. Banning's many pro-Union speeches and friendships with the officers stationed at Drum Barracks fed the animosity of his political opponents. In 1863 he supported the state Republican ticket in opposition to his business associate and friend John G. Downey, and in 1864 he was elected to represent Los Angeles as a state delegate to the Union Party national convention, with instructions to again nominate President Abraham Lincoln. (Because of the supervisors' vote-disqualification scheme, however, Los Angeles County went to McClellan instead.) Later that year, when *Los Angeles Star* editor Henry Hamilton lost his adamantly Democratic newspaper, Banning bought its assets and moved it to Wilmington to become the pro-Union, pro-Banning *Wilmington Journal*.[41]

As the war came to an end in the spring of 1865, Banning decided to run for state office to advance his plans to get government funding to improve the harbor and build a railroad from it to Los Angeles. A leader of the Republican wing of the Union Party, he contested Andrés Pico and John Mallard for the party nomination to the office of state senator from Los Angeles County. Banning was opposed by those who did not share his aims, such as J. J. Tomlinson, whose stage line would be driven under by a rail line, and many Democrats temporarily in the Union Party because of their opposition to splitting the nation in half. Although Banning missed the party convention, his supporters secured the nomination for him. The opposition claimed that Banning had purchased votes; one of Banning's employees, A. A. Polhamus, later recalled that an opposition delegate had suddenly received some money and a job offer that precluded his attendance at the convention in favor of a Banning delegate.

Phineas Banning, about
1865. Courtesy of the
Huntington Library.

Such shenanigans were, however, common in those years, and the
charges were never investigated.[42]

In the general election campaign Banning faced off against Democrat Murray Morrison, supported by Democratic leader Volney Howard,
who was also Banning's attorney. Phineas was now much more actively
involved. Herman Hellman, a former employee who accompanied him in
the campaign, remembered that "there was hardly a ranch house in the
whole County we did not visit. His special delight was to kiss every baby
he found." Morrison's supporters charged again that Banning was buying
votes, but if he was, it seems they were equally guilty. Just before the general election, A. A. Polhamus learned that two companies of cavalry
troops at Drum Barracks that had supported Banning were being paid to
vote for the other ticket. Banning's forces did not let on that they knew
of the scheme and told the soldiers that Banning's stages would carry

them to Los Angeles for the election. On the day of the election, however, no stages appeared, and the soldiers' horses were hidden near the San Gabriel River so that they would have to walk the long distance if they wished to vote. Few showed up, and those who did were too late to cast a ballot.[43]

Banning's opposition also charged that he had conspired with Democrats to win the election and was ruining the Union Party collaboration. But his Democratic friends also complained of his electioneering tactics. One of these remarked to another that Phineas had taken advantage of them by pouring Benjamin D. Wilson's and Matthew Keller's fine wine at one of his campaign barbeques. "I hope it will make them so drunk that they cannot get to the poles [sic] on election day," he wrote.[44]

Banning's campaign nonetheless was supported by many Democrats; after all, he had been a Democrat and always had many friends and business associates in the party. They had nominated him for county supervisor in 1859 when he was a member of the party. With the war ending, Banning focused his State Senate campaign on building up the harbor and attracting the railroads, goals shared by many local Democrats. He was the only Republican from the county to win in the general election. In December he traveled to the state capitol in Sacramento to begin serving his four-year term.

On April 10, 1865, news flashed over the telegraph wires to Los Angeles that Confederate General Robert E. Lee had surrendered his troops to Union General Ulysses S. Grant. The "rebellion is crushed," cried the *Los Angeles News*, as cannons boomed out the news from Drum Barracks. Celebrations of the victory by Phineas Banning and other Unionists lasted for several days.[45]

The festivities ended abruptly on April 15, when news of the shooting of Abraham Lincoln by John Wilkes Booth reached Los Angeles by telegraph. Quite a few Southerners, embittered by the Union victory, expressed joy over this tragedy, and within days at least six were arrested by Union soldiers for "allegedly glorifying the murder of Lincoln." Harris Newmark recalled that staunch Southerner John S. Griffin, his own physician and Banning's frequent business partner, was in Newmark's office when they heard the news. Griffin "was on his feet instantly, cheering for Jeff Davis" and preparing to run out into the street in an "unbalanced condition" to proclaim his loyalty to the South. Newmark stopped him from this folly, and later was thanked by Griffin, who "frankly admitted that I had undoubtedly saved him from certain death."[46]

Phineas Banning's assistant, business associate, political ally, and good friend Albert Alexander Polhamus (1837–1913). Courtesy of the Huntington Library.

News of the death of the president the next day brought the temporary "ill-advised exultation" to an end, "promptly suppressed, either by the military or by the firm stand of the more level-headed members of the community." As things settled down, the city made plans to honor the martyred president, and on April 19, the day of Lincoln's funeral, Los Angeles closed down while dignitaries, fraternal and religious organizations, and community groups marched solemnly through the streets. The procession was followed by memorial services in the Temple Block and several other locations.[47]

In Wilmington, "all business places in town were draped in black and no trade was carried on. There were salutes from Drum Barracks" as Phineas Banning led memorial services for President Lincoln in front of the Wilmington Exchange Hotel.[48]

Phineas Banning had one more special tribute to make to the fallen president. When the new California legislature took up its business in December 1865, one of the first items on its agenda was ratification of the Thirteenth Amendment, which abolished slavery. The measure had been approved by Congress the preceding January, and by the time the Golden State representatives considered it at their regular session, enough states had already ratified it to make it law. California finally approved it on December 19, and Senator Banning proudly signed his name to the document celebrating its passage.[49]

Phineas Banning emerged from the Civil War as a hero to many Unionists and a scoundrel to the political opponents who could not stop him. His Union ties had benefited his business as well, adding massive government contracts to his work for private customers. Although the departure of Union troops would soon take its toll, his company town of Wilmington was thriving. His family, battered by the tragedies of the early 1860s, had nonetheless grown and now lived in the largest residence south of Los Angeles. And by the end of 1865 he was a California legislator, ready to promote in the statehouse his dreams for the future of Wilmington and Los Angeles. This future would unfold in an era during which the nation would try to heal its wounds after a long conflict. Citizens like Phineas Banning would learn to work with former enemies to establish a new social compact at the outset of an era of rapid modernization in industrial production, transportation, communication, and race relations.

CHAPTER SIX

WILLIAM AND PHINEAS: RAILROAD ENTREPRENEURS

Railroads were a key force in modernizing nineteenth-century America. Beginning with the building of the first "iron horses" and routes in the 1820s, railroads connected communities and opened undeveloped regions to economic growth and opportunity. Networks of rails spread throughout New England and the mid-Atlantic and Great Lakes states by the 1850s. And fulfilling the nation's "Manifest Destiny" to expand westward demanded a transcontinental railroad that would run to the Pacific Ocean, an objective achieved by the end of the 1860s. The last quarter of the century would be a golden age for railroad building: competing companies and routes proliferated, until at last economic and political necessities brought mergers and regulation.[1]

Railroads tied America together socially, economically, and sometimes politically. They spanned vast distances and quickened the pace of travel, seeming to draw the country's far-flung regions closer together. They offered new access to previously unreachable markets for agricultural and factory goods, spurring industrialization. They drove the growth of cities by offering faster and more convenient passenger transportation to population centers along the tracks. Not only did they move people and goods, but the rails also spread standards and expectations throughout the country, unifying its economy and culture. They fostered standardization in the manufacture of their equipment, for example, and they made accurate timekeeping crucial for scheduling, for companies and individuals alike.

As their industry exploded, railroad executives emerged as economic titans of the nation. James J. Hill of the Great Northern, J. Edgar Thomson and Thomas A. Scott of the Pennsylvania, Franklin B. Gowan of the Philadelphia and Reading, Jay Gould of the Union Pacific, Jim Fisk of the Erie, and the Central Pacific "Big Four"—Collis P. Huntington, Leland Stanford, Charles Crocker, and Mark Hopkins—became some of the most powerful men in the American economy and wielded great influence in federal, state, and local government. With fortunes gained from lavish federal land grants, local government subsidies, construction contracts, and operational income, they set about acquiring social prominence as well, establishing and enhancing their status in all sectors of Gilded Age America.[2]

The railroads not only made a new American elite but also helped to build, and sometimes destroy, the fortunes of the many entrepreneurs who caught railway fever in cities and regions throughout the country. In the American West, railroads created an abundance of opportunities as they transformed the trans-Mississippi region from frontier to settlement. From the 1860s onward, railroads would shape the West, and individuals with vision and ambition seized the chance to build and operate them. Two of those were the Banning brothers—William and Phineas.

William Lowber Banning and His Railroad

William Lowber Banning worked tirelessly during and after the Civil War as a director and later as the president of the Lake Superior and Mississippi Railroad (LS&M). Along with other local businessmen and, later, prominent eastern investors, he established this railroad as the first shipping link between the twin cities of St. Paul and Minneapolis—the hub of agricultural, timber, and mineral production in southeastern Minnesota—and Duluth on Lake Superior, which would be developed as a port. Once Great Lakes shipping was improved, commodities such as grain could be transported to the East Coast, which in turn gave Minnesota access to international trade. When the LS&M was at length taken over by the Northern Pacific Railroad, it became part of the transcontinental line, linking the Great Lakes to the Pacific Coast as well.

Attempts to build a rail line serving Minnesota trade date to 1854, the year before William moved to the state. In 1857 the Minnesota territorial legislature chartered a line known as the Nebraska and Lake Superior Railroad, which was organized by local businessmen, and granted it almost 700,000 acres of land. Like other state and federal grants to railroads during this era, the grant was intended to help railroad companies raise capital to build their lines by reselling the land. The acreage was all swampland, however, and the company executives could not accumulate enough capital to get started. As wheat production continued to increase in central Minnesota, however, the need for a shipping outlet to the East became urgent, and a group of St. Paul businessmen led by Lyman Dayton lobbied in 1861 to revive the company as the LS&M.[3]

William Lowber Banning was involved in this venture while he served in the state legislature in 1860–61, and no doubt helped to get approval to transfer the land grants to the new company. The first years of the Civil War stalled the project, but upon his return from military service in 1863, Banning took an active role in securing land and money for the line. In that year he spearheaded a drive that resulted in a St. Paul municipal bond issue of $250,000, an infusion of capital and public confidence that he hoped would attract wealthy private investors. In 1864 he helped to form a lobbying group to obtain a grant of federal lands along the LS&M's proposed route. Minnesota Representative Ignatius Donnelly was the front man for this and later LS&M lobbying efforts, for which Banning paid him generously with company stock certificates. Banning spent much of the 1864 congressional session in Washington, D.C., working for passage of the grant. When Congress awarded the grant not directly to the company, but instead to the state of Minnesota, he moved back home to lobby in the state capitol. There the LS&M was opposed by St. Paul's rival city, Minneapolis, and by Wisconsin economic interests trying to keep competitors out of Lake Superior shipping. Banning's group nonetheless won the grant for the LS&M, which increased its total landholdings to over 1.6 million acres, small by the standards of transcontinental lines, but, according to historian John L. Harnsberger, "liberal considering the length of the road and the fact that it was to be built in one state."[4]

Banning might have intended to push for further legislation in favor of his railroad in 1865, when he again ran for a Minnesota State Senate seat as a candidate of the Union Party. He was defeated by Democrat George L. Otis. But if the voters did not want him, the railroad certainly did: when LS&M President Lyman Dayton died that October, William Lowber Banning was elected to that office. With government land grants in place, he now had to raise capital on a large scale to begin the work of building. He commissioned surveys by the William Branch Company in St. Paul, a firm that had done work for his bank in the 1850s and would later participate in the construction phase. And, having been unsuccessful at convincing American investors, he decided to try those in England.[5]

In January 1866, William obtained a letter of introduction from Minnesota Governor William R. Marshall and embarked on his voyage to London, hoping to sell millions of dollars of bonds to build his railroad. In an odd coincidence, while there he ran into his friend, the mayor of St. Paul, but his almost two-year trip was otherwise uneventful and

William Lowber Banning
in the 1870s. Courtesy of
the Huntington Library.

unprofitable. As he later wrote to an associate, he encountered "a profound ignorance on the part of the most intelligent English capitalists
in regard to American enterprise." Past bad investments in American
ventures had clouded their judgment about such undertakings, he concluded, and the advantages of his proposed route were lost on people
who knew nothing of the geography of the nation or of Minnesota.
Disappointed, Banning would have to find another source of capital for
the LS&M.[6]

That new source of funding would be his wealthy neighbors from
his years in Philadelphia. Jay Cooke, whose banking house had helped to
finance the Union cause in the Civil War, already had an interest in the
Duluth area. Although Cooke had declined to finance the LS&M in 1865,
when Banning first asked him, Banning had helped him buy land in the
port city. In 1868 Banning induced him to visit the region, inspect his
holdings, and judge for himself the potential of the venture. This time
Cooke was convinced, and along with another banking firm, E. W. Clarke
and Company, and railroad magnates J. Edgar Thomson of the Pennsyl-

vania Railroad and Thomas A. Scott, then with the Union Pacific, Cooke began to inject funds into the railroad project, while at the same time speculating heavily in land near Duluth. With this infusion of cash, construction began seriously and quickly. The timing must have seemed propitious: quite a number of other railroads throughout Minnesota and the rest of the nation were just being launched.[7]

Cooke's stake in the railroad company brought him into its leadership. He and his Philadelphia associates assumed financial control of the LS&M, and Banning directed its operation on a more limited basis in Minnesota. While Cooke's bank sold bonds in the eastern investment market, Banning supervised the actual construction of the 155-mile route from St. Paul through the city of Carlton and along the banks of the St. Louis River to Duluth. In 1869 he began advertising the 1.6 million acres of railroad lands for sale to settlers and speculators. The proceeds from these transactions helped to add operating funds to the company's coffers, as well as to increase the population served by the rail line.[8]

In the spring of 1870 Banning represented the Philadelphia directors as manager of a lobbying campaign in Congress. They sought to finance a major harbor improvement at Duluth, the terminus of the railroad, with a grant of a half million acres of land to the railroad. Atypically for a federal land grant, the proposal did not stipulate that the land had to be in alternating sections. If the land granted was a contiguous allotment, it would have given the railroad directors "control of nearly all the land within a hundred miles of Duluth, including every possible approach to the harbor." It would also have given them control of valuable mineral rights in the area, a fact that Banning hoped to keep quiet for the moment. Banning hired his good friend, former U.S. Representative Ignatius Donnelly, to lobby Congress for this harbor grant. He personally wrote a considerable number of letters to senators and representatives asking for their vote, while also organizing local support. He reminded Minnesota Senator Alexander Ramsey on several occasions of "the urgent appeals of the people of Minnesota and the Railroads we represent" to improve the harbor for transport of the state's products "to eastern and European markets." Donnelly worked diligently to get the bill passed, but opposition in the Senate stemming from the enormous size of the grant and the (no longer covert) mineral rights giveaway delayed a final vote until the end of the session, when the bill was at last voted down. This failure was a personal defeat for Banning, who had led the campaign, as well as for Cooke, who had thought he could develop Duluth as a competitor to Chicago, the reigning shipping hub for the region.[9]

During the lobbying and the political debates over the harbor bill, construction of the LS&M continued. By March 26, 1870, over one hundred miles of track had been laid and 3,000 men were at work on the remainder. By the middle of September the line was completed and ready for regular service. In the months before its official opening, several special trains toured the line. Historian Don Hofsommer described one of these trips "as that of August 1, headed by the locomotive *W. L. Banning* and bearing among other notables Banning and his family, Chief Justice Salmon P. Chase, and his daughter, Kate Chase Sprague." William's eldest daughter, Ellen, christened the *W. L. Banning* for the trip that day with "two glasses of water—one from Lake Superior and one from San Pedro Harbor, California sent by her uncle, Phineas Banning."[10]

With the railroad built, William Lowber Banning submitted his resignation to the board of directors on December 2, 1870. In a newspaper story at the time he claimed that, now that construction was finished, he was no longer "essential" and wanted to retire from active management. Historian John L. Harnsberger claims that Banning was actually forced to resign as part of a plan by the Philadelphia directors to wrest Banning's remaining authority away from him. If this was the case, the Philadelphians did not do any better than Banning at making the line pay. A rival railroad launched a shipping-rate war in the region at this early juncture, when Cooke's development costs at Duluth were high and money was tight. Although the LS&M shipped a considerable amount of wheat in its first year, profits were nowhere near what Cooke had expected.[11]

In order to reduce his costs, Cooke leased the LS&M in 1872 to the Northern Pacific Railroad, which he also controlled. But this solution would not last. As one historian observed, "Mr. Cooke's schemes were based on the delusive idea that the pendulum of trade and finance always swings upward," and he had not set enough capital aside to weather the "inevitable downward movement." During the national Panic of 1873, Cooke had to declare bankruptcy. The Northern Pacific continued to operate, but was forced into foreclosure in 1877. Its LS&M line was then reorganized as the St. Paul and Duluth Railroad Company. The new company continued shipping Minnesota goods to the growing port at Lake Superior, from which they could reach eastern and foreign markets, much as William Banning had planned. In 1900 the railroad was absorbed by a revitalized Northern Pacific to become part of the two systems, one serving the East and the other the West, that Jay Cooke had envisioned over a quarter of a century earlier.[12]

The first Lake Superior and Mississippi Railroad depot at its terminus in Duluth, 1872. Courtesy of the Minnesota Historical Society.

Phineas and His Railroads

Like William, Phineas Banning was an early railroad booster in his region, and he followed his older brother's path, involving himself with legislation, lobbying, and construction. The year after the Pacific Railroad Survey was completed, in late 1853, he had convinced five investors to purchase land in present-day Wilmington as a future site for a West Coast terminus for the transcontinental railroad. The prospect of the railroad, then, was the initial impetus behind Banning's "New City": the idea was to "build up a city of considerable importance," home to both a railroad terminus and a key seaport. Los Angeles newspapers hailed this venture and followed the progress of the railroad project, but the bill stalled in Congress for years. As we have seen, the ever-impatient Phineas decided to build his city anyway beginning in 1858, before the transcontinental route was chosen.[13]

Other like-minded local leaders proposed a local railroad from Los Angeles to the harbor in the early 1860s, in anticipation of the transcontinental line, but could not put their plan into action. In 1861

State Senator Abel Stearns passed a bill in the legislature to construct such a line. According to the bill, the project was to be managed by unnamed investors on the East Coast and financed by subscriptions of capital stock by the county and city of Los Angeles. The Civil War, however, slowed the undertaking. At length the owner of the Rancho San Pedro, over which much of the track would be built, Manuel Dominguez, and several of his business partners were granted a franchise in 1863 for building a railroad on this route with the same local government funding arrangement. Public opposition to subsidizing the project with government bonds, however, killed this latest version of the plan. Late in 1864 a committee made up of local businessmen, including Benjamin D. Wilson, David Alexander, Matthew Keller, and Francis P. F. Temple, was created to plan the road. At the December public meeting to discuss the proposal, Phineas Banning and others spoke in its favor, but again nothing was done to bring it to fruition.[14]

Banning had as much to gain as anyone from such a railroad, since if he could control it, he would dominate the transportation business from the harbor to Los Angeles, his landholdings at Wilmington would grow in value, and, of course, he would make money from the railroad itself. To make it happen, however, he needed political pull and government financing, and he set out to get it. Like his brother William, he ran for the State Senate in 1865; unlike his brother, he was elected. His twin campaign promises had been to pass a law approving the construction of the harbor railroad and to lobby for federal funding to improve the harbor. In early 1866 he introduced his railroad bill and several others that would underwrite construction by allowing the county Board of Supervisors and the mayor and Common Council of Los Angeles to subscribe a combined $300,000 in capital stock. All of these measures were defeated that year due to strong local opposition from his stage and freight competitors, from farmers who raised barley for animals pulling the freight wagons, and from those who objected to higher taxes or Banning's participation in the project. Some civic leaders in Ventura, furthermore, feared the proposal because they thought Banning would try to annex a portion of that Santa Barbara County property to help pay for the subsidy. Although Banning was a pragmatist who worked well with members of both parties, he had failed to line up enough support for his proposals or any of the related bills he offered in that legislative session.[15]

Banning busied himself with other railroad schemes while pursuing funding for the harbor line. In that same year Banning became a director of the Atlantic and Pacific Railroad, a project created by former California Senator John C. Frémont and chartered by Congress to build a line from Springfield, Missouri, to California. Banning appeared on the initial list of almost one hundred directors along with railroad moguls Frederick Billings, J. Edgar Thomson, and Thomas A. Scott, and distant Banning relatives Charles I. du Pont and Henry Moore Ridgely of Delaware. This venture was not successful, however, and ultimately lost its lucrative land grants. Publicity about Frémont's involvement in a major railroad scandal finally drove the Atlantic and Pacific into bankruptcy, and it was taken over by the Atchison, Topeka and Santa Fe. Banning gained nothing financially from this speculation, but it did give him all the more impetus to create a local railroad: whoever built it, a transcontinental would arrive someday soon in Southern California, and he should be in a position to profit from it.[16]

In the 1867–68 session of the legislature Banning again introduced the bills to construct and finance the local railroad. This time he first lobbied the county Board of Supervisors and a number of prominent businessmen to support them. The measures called for the county to subscribe $150,000 worth of railroad stock and the city $75,000, if approved by popular vote. Banning also included a stipulation that the railroad could assign its stock to the Atlantic and Pacific or another major railroad if they connected to Los Angeles, a possibility that might enhance his recent investment in the Atlantic and Pacific and, as historian Charles Westbrook has noted, entice the Southern Pacific Railroad in Northern California to enter the region. This time Banning's measures passed. The governor signed the legislation and the election was set by the Board of Supervisors for March 24. In the meantime Banning and the other leaders of the railroad project formed a company in February to build and operate the line. It was headed by John G. Downey, their fellow Wilmington landowner and former governor.[17]

The first duty of the directors of this company was to win the voters' approval of the referendum. In the short campaign they spoke out for the railroad as necessary to the region's economic development, and Banning "flooded Los Angeles with circulars and posters urging the railroad subsidy." The county Board of Supervisors and the members of the Common Council endorsed it, as did many civic leaders whose businesses would profit from the project. The editor of the only major newspaper in Los Angeles at the time, the *News*, was a rabid political opponent of Banning, but still a promoter of the city and county—and, therefore, of the railroad. The smaller *Los Angeles Republican* also supported the referendum. Banning's chief rival for the stage and wagon trade between

Wilmington Harbor with a Los Angeles and San Pedro Railroad engine on Banning's Landing, 1870. Courtesy of the Huntington Library.

the city and the harbor, J. J. Tomlinson, led the opposition, charging that the railroad would only benefit Banning, creating a monopoly for him at the harbor. Tomlinson was joined by farmers and cattle ranchers who thought they would bear most of the cost of the railroad through their property taxes and at the same time lose a market for their feed crops. This opposition waned in the last days of the election campaign after Tomlinson's untimely death. Banning's referendum ultimately passed by a slim margin.[18]

The construction of the railroad began soon after the election. It was no surprise that of the several bidders, mostly in Northern California, Phineas Banning won the contract. The contract's terms were lucrative: he would be paid for each mile of track as it was laid and would also make considerable profits by selling some of his Wilmington land for a depot and other uses, and some of his vessels for water transportation related to the railroad. The entire project was to be completed by January 1, 1870. As Banning later recalled, he had at the time just suffered huge losses from his investments in La Abundancia Mining Company in Sonora, Mexico, which left him short of the cash he needed to start construction. He therefore assigned his contract to Henry Baldwin Tichenor in San Francisco. Tichenor was well known to Banning as a lumber merchant who had built sawmills, toll bridges, and a small railroad in Northern California. Banning paid Tichenor in stock, and the merchant soon held a substantial stake in the Los Angeles and San Pedro Railroad (LA&SP).[19]

Despite a number of delays due to late shipments of building materials, Phineas Banning promised that the railroad would be completed on schedule with his "accustomed promptness." The twenty-one miles of track were in fact actually laid early—by October 1869. Banning built a large depot in "downtown" Los Angeles on the southwest corner of Alameda and Commercial streets, and altered a building in Wilmington to serve as the terminus depot there. He purchased two engines, along with passenger and freight cars and other railroad vehicles, and supplied lighters, steamboats, and other floating vessels that would shuttle between oceangoing ships and the depot. A grand ball and other festivities celebrated the opening of the railroad on October 26, and trains began rolling on a regular schedule on November 1.[20]

Although Banning's promptness could not be questioned, his methods often were. Over the next three years the LA&SP operated amid accusations of mismanagement and extravagance. The directors repeatedly requested more county financing for the company, even as their other businesses reaped sizeable rewards from the operation. Banning & Company (with partner David Alexander) and Tichenor were reimbursed handsomely for the construction from the government subsidies, and Banning forged a monopoly on the lightering business at Wilmington. Feeling that they had been taken, the county Board of Supervisors, the city's Common Council and the *News* questioned many of the payments to and purchases by the contractors as well as the high freight rates charged by the LA&SP. The *News* consistently criticized the "Railroad Ring" of LA&SP directors as "Subsidy Hunters" and called for investigations, resulting in one lawsuit by the city. Banning, labeled the "Duke of Wilmington," orchestrated the company directors' decisions, the *News* said, charging him with mismanagement. The *Los Angeles Republican* compared Banning to the notorious Jim Fisk, each of them being a "gobbler-up of railroads." Meanwhile, the company's negotiations with representatives of towns that wanted connections to the line ended in arguments over the payments the railroad demanded in return. The directors even argued among themselves: the first president, John G. Downey, complained loudly that the line should have been built through his own property and that his son-in-law should have received the construction contract instead of Banning and Tichenor. Beyond the accusations and the drama, the railroad was a success for merchants in Los Angeles, for the development of Wilmington, for the shippers and passengers who used it, and—of course—for the directors, such as succeeding President Benjamin D. Wilson and Vice President Phineas Banning, who operated the line.[21]

With the LA&SP in operation by 1870, Banning turned his attention to a new railroad venture. In December he incorporated the California and Arizona Railway, a narrow-gauge steam railroad, to run between Wilmington and the gold-mining town of Wickenburg in Arizona Territory, by way of San Bernardino and the San Gorgonio Pass. The line would also have a branch to the silver mines in Inyo County, so that it could replace Banning's wagon trains to both destinations, just as the LA&SP had replaced his stage business from the harbor to the county seat. This railroad, however, would not be built. Unable to secure private funding or government subsidies, Banning ceded the route to others with more resources.[22]

Another reason Banning gave up on his railroad to Arizona was that a transcontinental railroad might soon build a route close to his own proposed line, making it redundant. In fact, Banning later claimed that he and Benjamin D. Wilson came up with the idea to have the Southern Pacific Railroad Company extend its planned route, to run south from San Francisco through central California and then east to Arizona and beyond, in order to give Los Angeles direct access to eastern markets. The Southern Pacific had been originally chartered in 1866 to build such a road, and in the following year that company was taken over by the Central Pacific Railroad "Big Four"—Collis P. Huntington, Leland Stanford, Mark Hopkins, and Charles Crocker—who were planning to build another transcontinental line along a southern route. There were several courses that it could follow, and Stanford sent a special agent, William Hyde, to Southern California in 1869 to investigate the possibilities. While in Los Angeles, Hyde consulted with Banning, former Governor Downey, Benjamin D. Wilson, and other community leaders about the feasibility of having the railroad continue southward through Los Angeles County. Hyde then departed and was not seen again for some time.[23]

Hyde's appearance seems to have sparked Banning's campaign to bring the Southern Pacific to Los Angeles. At the time of the visit, Benjamin D. Wilson had just been elected state senator succeeding Banning, and the two began political efforts to lure the railroad southward. In early

1870 Wilson introduced and passed a bill in the state legislature that would allow several central California counties to grant subsidies of up to 5 percent of their assessed property values to aid prospective railroads. A second bill allowed all counties to grant such subsidies through special elections. But later in the year a Southern Pacific official jeopardized the plan, saying that the mountainous terrain surrounding Los Angeles would probably preclude building the route through the city. So in 1871 Wilson and Banning traveled to Washington, D.C., where Congress was considering a bill to authorize the Southern Pacific to build on public land. With some concerted lobbying, they were able to insert the phrase "by way of Los Angeles" in that bill's description of the route, thus ensuring that Los Angeles would have at least a chance of being located on the main line.[24]

Like other cities along the route, however, Los Angeles would have to grant the Southern Pacific a large subsidy or it would be bypassed. In early 1872, the Southern Pacific was building southward and soon would have to decide how close it would come to Los Angeles. Wilson, Banning, and other civic leaders organized a "Committee of Thirty" to negotiate with the Southern Pacific. In the best deal the negotiators could get, the county would have to pay a subsidy equal to 5 percent of the assessed value of Los Angeles County property in 1872, give Southern Pacific the stock held by the county and city in the LA&SP and land for a depot, and pay for a spur line to Anaheim—a total of $602,000. These harsh terms ignited vocal opposition among county taxpayers with large landholdings, including even members of the Committee of Thirty. Banning had earlier written to Wilson that he expected the same opposition to the proposal as had fought the LA&SP subsidy—some farmers in the San Gabriel Valley and most of those in what would eventually become Orange County—while "nearly every merchant and lawyer" in the county seat would vote for it.[25]

Wilson, Banning, and others defended the deal as the only way to bring the railroad to Los Angeles and guarantee the city's future development and prosperity. In August, in the middle of the debate, Thomas A. Scott, president of the Texas and Pacific Railroad, suddenly arrived and announced that his company was ready, for a smaller subsidy, to continue his southern line by joining a local railroad to be built from San Diego to Los Angeles. He had already received congressional approval to build from Texas to San Diego, and the spur to Los Angeles would be relatively inexpensive. The members of the Committee of Thirty were unsure that he would actually build the extension, however, and if he did, San Diego would be his railroad's primary terminus in Southern California, relegating Los Angeles to secondary status. Suddenly there were two possibilities, besides outright opposition to any railroads, and public opinion was further aroused.[26]

"The town is in an uproar," wrote one member of the Committee of Thirty in July to Wilson, noting that Southern Pacific agent William Hyde was back and concerned about the controversy. The county Board of Supervisors had been wavering over the Southern Pacific proposal, inundated with petitions from proponents and opponents of various subsidies. Before the Texas and Pacific proposal surfaced, the Southern Pacific had requested a county election to decide the matter, and the district attorney concluded that the supervisors could be held liable if they did not submit the proposition to a vote. Once the Texas and Pacific made its offer, that proposal's adherents petitioned the supervisors to put it before the voters at the same time; the Southern Pacific forces of course objected to the competition. On September 17, a divided Board of Supervisors argued over whether to put one or both of the proposals on the ballot. After considerable debate, they voted three to two to let the voters choose the better of the two measures or to vote down both of them.[27]

In the short election campaign, the commercial interests in the city, led by Special Agent Hyde, united behind the Southern Pacific proposal. Hyde made ruthless demands and threatened retaliation by the railroad if they were not met. As the campaign progressed in October he reported to his boss, Leland Stanford, "The furnace is getting hotter and hotter daily" and complained to Collis P. Huntington that he had never been in "such a venal community in all my life as Los Angeles." But he was certain that, if the vote was successful, "we can make this county one of our most valuable tributaries and most delightful places of resort for tourists and any other man." Speaking of one of his closest allies in the campaign, he wrote to Huntington that "Gen'l Banning was one of our staunchest friends" in this contest. Banning was "a thorough soldier, erect rotund and solid in appearance . . . with all of a natural soldier's brusqueness," Hyde wrote, and "he has enlisted the sympathy and dislike of his fellow citizens of this County in about equal proportion."[28]

Shortly before the election Banning informed Wilson that victory was assured: his brother William had talked to Thomas A. Scott in Philadelphia and reported that Scott had given up on his extension from San Diego to Los Angeles for the time being. Phineas nonetheless continued his many activities in the campaign and played a key role in the Southern Pacific effort, along with Wilson, the *Star*, and Judge Robert

Widney, who wrote a widely distributed pamphlet aimed at the business community and advocating the subsidy for the Southern Pacific. Governor Downey, Volney Howard, Frank Ganahl, and the *News* campaigned for the Texas and Pacific. Opposition to the railroads' proposals was disorganized; a few rallies were held in distant farming areas that might not profit from a railroad. Vote buying by both railroads was blatant and, for the Southern Pacific at least, more extensive than necessary. On November 5 the county voters approved the Southern Pacific proposal by a wide margin. As Banning had predicted a year before, it fell short of votes only in the communities that would be included in Orange County almost two decades later.[29]

With this victory the Southern Pacific continued construction of its line to Los Angeles, which was completed in 1876. Banning was a featured speaker at the celebration for the driving of the last spike at Lang Station, some forty miles north of Los Angeles. As expected, the railroad expanded the transportation network, making it possible to move goods much further and faster and contributing to the commercial and agricultural growth of the county. By this measure boosters could argue that the huge subsidy paid by county taxpayers was well worth the investment. On the other side of the ledger, however, the Southern Pacific would refuse to pay its fair share of taxes in the coming years and would offend, among others, many of its 1872 supporters. The Southern Pacific's interference in local and state politics for decades to come would reveal all of its economic and political power, and its arrogance in using it.[30]

The passing of the ballot measure also meant that the Southern Pacific would acquire the LA&SP and its harbor business from Banning and his associates in May 1873. Banning still continued some of his lumber and other operations at the new wharf he had built at Wilmington in 1873. But now that his railroad and his harbor lightering concession were in the Southern Pacific's hands, Banning primarily worked for and with the railroad to establish its operations at the harbor. He brokered the sale of additional warehouse, depot, and wharf facilities needed by the railroad in 1874 and both sold some of his own land to the company and negotiated others' land sales.[31]

Banning was also of modest assistance to the Southern Pacific when another railroad threatened to expand into Los Angeles County in the 1870s. The Los Angeles and Independence Railroad was chartered in 1874 to connect the silver-mining region in Inyo County to Los Angeles and then continue to the Pacific Ocean at Santa Monica. Southern Pacific officials kept a close eye on the company since it not only represented transportation competition but also the threat of a competing harbor at the Santa Monica terminus. This was of course also a threat to Wilmington and to Phineas Banning's remaining interests there. Financed by Nevada Senator John P. Jones and a few other investors without a government subsidy, the company completed the portion of its road from Santa Monica to Los Angeles. But the failure in 1875 of one of its principal investors, the Temple and Workman Bank, and competition from the Southern Pacific aided by Banning doomed the new venture, and the railroad was eventually sold to the Southern Pacific in 1877.[32]

Banning was much more active in his role as an agent and lobbyist for the Southern Pacific in Yuma, California, and in towns in Arizona Territory. As one historian of that region has opined, with the LA&SP "came General Phineas Banning, and the SP soon found the charm, tact and persuasive powers of that man to be invaluable" in managing the extension of the line into Arizona. With his experience in arranging freighting of supplies to Fort Yuma and other sites near the Colorado River, Banning was chosen by Southern Pacific official David D. Colton to negotiate the property purchases for the railroad as the Southern Pacific continued to build eastward. In November 1876 he concluded a pact in which the Common Council of "Yuma Village" in California agreed to sell to the Southern Pacific a one-hundred-acre plot of land, then a part of Fort Yuma but soon to be granted to the village, for a railroad depot and bridge. This agreement was a necessary step in the Southern Pacific plan to cross the Colorado River itself and to prevent the Texas and Pacific Railroad from advancing westward along the same path and collecting its federal land grants.[33]

Banning's next assignment was to lobby the territorial legislature to grant a franchise for the Southern Pacific to lay track from the town of Yuma to the eastern border of Arizona Territory. He spent most of January in Tucson persuading many of the legislators and the city's civic leaders to support the franchise, for which the Southern Pacific paid him handsomely. After much bickering among lawmakers from rival areas of the territory, a few legislators hammered out a compromise bill "at a meeting held in Charley Brown's Congress Hall saloon." The full legislature then approved the franchise in early February. As a bonus, Banning also convinced Tucson municipal officials to donate land for the depot plus $10,000 for additional railroad expenses.[34]

Banning's lobbying skills were apparently given a considerable boost by Southern Pacific money. Anticipating the need to pay legislators for their votes, Collis P. Huntington concluded as early as September 1875

Collis P. Huntington. Courtesy of the
Huntington Library.

Charles Crocker. Courtesy of the
California History Room, California
State Library.

that Arizona Territorial Governor A. P. K. Safford should call the legislature together to pass the franchise "at a cost of say $25,000." Safford
replied to Huntington soon after the franchise was approved, in a letter
that would cost him a re-appointment to the governorship just over a
decade later. In it he noted that he was returning $20,000 of the sum to
"fix" the legislature, "noting dryly that Huntington had overestimated the
legislature's price." Whether Safford kept the balance of the money himself (the Southern Pacific reportedly paid him a monthly retainer while
he was in office) or actually used it to pay off the legislators is uncertain,
but obviously Southern Pacific leaders thought that bribery was needed
as a supplement to Phineas Banning's powers of persuasion.[35]

With the franchise approved, the Southern Pacific continued building eastward in California toward Yuma, on the Colorado River. Banning
briefly moved to the town in April 1877 to take possession of steamboats
and docks just purchased by the Southern Pacific. He was reported to
have been in a railroad crash in which a conductor was killed, but Banning suffered only a few bruises. He returned to Yuma in August, when
the Southern Pacific was approaching Fort Yuma on the California
side of the river. At that point a dispute between the railroad and the
U.S. government over the right-of-way on fort property prevented the
Southern Pacific from crossing the river into Arizona. Huntington and

the other Southern Pacific leaders would not wait for the dispute to be legally settled, however. In the early morning of September 30, Southern Pacific crews quietly laid rails across the bridge after the commander of the fort had forbidden it. A loud noise at 2 a.m. alarmed the few soldiers at the fort; they failed to stop the crew, however, and the railroad triumphantly entered Arizona on its march eastward. The U.S. government refused to take action against the Southern Pacific, which continued to trump the Texas and Pacific in their competition to complete a southern transcontinental route.[36]

Despite the rewards of his work as agent for the Southern Pacific, Banning soon found that Wilmington was calling him home. After several years of experience at the harbor, Southern Pacific officials found that the lightering and tugboat business in Wilmington was more trouble than it was worth to them. In 1878 the Southern Pacific offered to sell it back to Phineas Banning in a lucrative proposal—one he would not refuse. Late that year he began accumulating capital for part of the purchase, while the railroad gave him uncharacteristically generous terms on a loan to complete the deal. By late October, Charles Crocker reported to Collis P. Huntington in New York that "General Banning is now in full charge at Wilmington." Crocker was both relieved to be rid of the business and pleased that Banning would now operate it. As one of Crocker's correspondents later recalled, the railroad executive told him, "I was so taken with General Banning that I would have scorned to have imposed on him any exacting conditions in our arrangements. He is a man of nerve as well as a man of honor."[37]

In closing this deal, Phineas proved to be just as shrewd as the Big Four and other Southern Pacific officials in business negotiations, in this case managing to secure his harbor monopoly in perpetuity. When railroad representatives signed the 1878 agreement to sell Banning's lightering and other facilities back to him, they pledged to give him all of the harbor business of the railroad and construction companies for specific rates. Four years later, Charles Crocker wrote to Collis P. Huntington that, in examining a plan for a wharf extension, he had discovered that "we had bound ourselves to give him this business for all time regardless of any extension or wharves or improvements. There was no limit to the duration of the contract. He had us in the door and could squeeze it very tight."[38]

Whether or not the company resented his monopoly, Banning was not finished with his work for and with the Southern Pacific. In the early 1880s he would help to build the extension of the railroad from

Wilmington to San Pedro, thus transferring harbor leadership from his own Wilmington back to the older port. He would also continue to operate his lightering business serving the Southern Pacific, a relationship that would eventually harm his image in Southern California. The railroad was already widely despised for its monopoly of transportation, its high freight rates and high-handed tactics, and its political corruption. The publication in 1883 of the correspondence among its leadership further blackened its reputation. The specter of the "Octopus," as the Southern Pacific was derisively labeled, would unfortunately reflect to some degree on Phineas Banning in the last years of his life, counterbalancing much of the good he had done for Southern California.[39]

There is a striking parallel between two Banning brothers, in their roles in railroad building and the political activity necessary to make it successful. Although neither would stay in the industry long, both transformed their respective regions by helping to establish and improve rail transportation. The railroads in turn brought economic development and modernization to Minnesota and to Southern California. While the Bannings' influence was restricted by their limited capital and clout, the brothers can be credited with playing crucial roles in bringing the railroad to their communities, a development that also benefited them and their families personally.

CHAPTER SEVEN

The Postwar Years and the Death of
Phineas Banning

By the end of the Civil War, Phineas Banning had entered middle age, but his legendary energy barely flagged, and the accomplishments of his final two decades reflected his boundless ambition even when his health began to decline. The end of the war forced him to re-invent his work once again, as lucrative army supply and construction contracts disappeared. He responded by becoming a lobbyist and power broker focused on the improvement of "his" harbor and, as we have seen, on the railroads. His success at these ventures helped drive the region's transformation from a local economy dominated by the landowning elite to the national trade and export powerhouse it would become. During these years he also lost his wife and remarried, helped to raise an even larger immediate family, participated in politics and social events, and even had a town named for him. To say that his last years were busy ones is simply to say he was Phineas Banning.

Banning's entrepreneurial activities just after the close of the Civil War were dominated by his railroad interests, but he continued operating his stage and lightering business for several years. By May 1865, his former partner David Alexander had joined him again, although the firm name remained Banning & Company. His company clerk was Eldridge E. Hewitt, who would become an officer of the Los Angeles and San Pedro Railroad and later the Southern Pacific. The company had offices in the Temple Block in downtown Los Angeles and in Wilmington, where Banning also sold lumber and other commodities on a retail basis. In the postwar years, he added to his Wilmington complex with the Union Wagon Factory, which manufactured Concord-style coaches and a variety of other horse-drawn vehicles. The concern must have prospered, for he vastly expanded it in 1867.[1]

The conclusion of the war, however, also brought the end of most of Banning's highly lucrative military supply contracts, a loss that must have hit the company hard. Fort Tejon had already closed, and the contract for Fort Yuma was awarded to a supplier whose practices and cozy relationship with quartermasters were just as controversial as Banning's had been. Its freight wagons freed for other work, Banning's company continued to ply the road to Arizona through Yuma in the late 1860s, this time in a profitable venture supplying mining towns in the territory. He also freighted goods to Utah as well as Nevada, as he had in the company's early days. A new competitor, Remi Nadeau, challenged his ongoing business moving goods to and from the Inyo County mining country and other areas in California, and their rivalry became very personal. Nadeau's grandson later wrote that once, when his grandmother and family arrived in San Pedro on the coastal steamer, his father hired a boat to bring them ashore to avoid patronizing one of Banning's lighters.[2]

Banning also established new regular stage lines just after the war. His passenger and mail service to Yuma began in 1866, although a lack of profits and water along the route caused him to abandon the line in March 1867. He kept a triweekly run to San Bernardino carrying passengers, the mail, and Wells, Fargo & Company express materials a bit longer. His existing stage line from the harbor to Los Angeles operated continuously until the Los Angeles and San Pedro Railroad made it obsolete in 1869. Before the railroad was completed, Banning's stages continued to compete with those of J. J. Tomlinson, racing at breakneck speed from the harbor to Los Angeles on steamer days. Such contests between stage drivers were as much business as sport, because the winner could claim the mail contract between the two points.[3]

The thrill and competitiveness of stagecoach driving often attracted remarkable characters, and Banning's stable was no exception. One of Banning's drivers in the 1860s, John J. Reynolds, was among the most notable. He held the speed record for the trip between the harbor and the city and was known to have a special relationship with his animals. Reynolds was described as a "courtly, good-looking man who swore infrequently and never drank whiskey" (Banning required his drivers to be polite and sober). As Reynolds confided to a writer at the time, "I delighted in fast driving and making myself solid with the ladies." When the run was finally replaced by the railroad, he became the proprietor of the Pioneer Hack Line in Los Angeles, supplying coaches and drivers for excursions and parties.[4]

The colorful reputation of Banning's coachmen apparently fed into the story that a very young Wyatt Earp once drove Banning stages from San Bernardino to Los Angeles for a very brief period in the summer of

1865. This myth seems to have first appeared in Stuart N. Lake's biography of Earp in 1931, and was repeated in subsequent publications. Although it is appealing to think that these two larger-than-life characters crossed paths, there is no evidence in Banning's financial records or in Stuart Lake's research materials, or anywhere else, that it actually happened. Since Earp was the source for much of Lake's narrative, the story probably stems from the old frontier lawman and entrepreneur's well-known tendency to play fast and loose with the facts.[5]

In the course of the early 1870s, by the terms of the agreement that brought the Southern Pacific to Los Angeles, Banning would have to sell most of his harbor lightering and storage operation to the railroad. Anticipating this loss, he solicited new business from other small ports, such as Anaheim Landing farther south, and increased the number of his vessels, including "Banning's uncomfortable tugs," as one passenger described them at the time. He also built another wharf in 1873 and established a new lumberyard nearby. After the Southern Pacific took over the harbor, he began spending more of his time working for the Southern Pacific as a lobbyist and a facilities agent, and sold off many of his shops and other buildings to the railroad and to businessmen like Benjamin D. Wilson. But Banning was far from ready to abandon his ambitions for his empire in Wilmington, although he apparently sought to share the risk. At this time Banning joined Wilson, Leonard J. Rose, Francis P. F. Temple, and other Los Angeles entrepreneurs in establishing the Co-operative Warehousing and Shipping Association at Wilmington to perform the same warehousing, wharf construction, and transportation functions that Banning had been carrying out for the last twenty years. The group's innovation was a plan to extend a wharf to deep water while promoting dredging operations to improve the port over a number of years.[6]

Banning also retained some of his property in Los Angeles related to the harbor business. Not far from one of these parcels, and the LA&SP depot he had helped to create, was Banning Street, named in his honor in 1869, when it was included as part of the Aliso Tract. This subdivision was developed by the Aliso Homestead Association, which included many of his business partners hoping to cash in on its proximity to the new railroad depot. The original two-block road was extended from Alameda Street to the Los Angeles River in 1876. It was mostly residential, except for the lot that would later house the Los Angeles Soap Company complex.[7]

Banning was ingenious in seeking novel ways to increase his fortune as well, and he subscribed to *Scientific American* in search of creative inspiration. In 1876 he obtained a patent for his own invention, a "car-trucks and wheels" vehicle in the form of a flat railroad carriage that moved on rollers along a wooden plank surface. According to Banning, the "track" for this vehicle could be laid very cheaply and easily in sparsely settled regions, making the system economical to build and operate. Apparently he could not find a financial backer for this invention, or perhaps he was dissuaded from developing it by his new employer, the Southern Pacific. In any case, the invention was never manufactured.[8]

Like many prominent citizens of Los Angeles County, Phineas Banning was active in real estate transactions during this time as well. He promoted some of the property he owned in Wilmington and sold a few lots to new residents and speculators. He also partnered with Benjamin D. Wilson and John S. Griffin in several development ventures in which they borrowed money from each other, using land in the Pasadena area as collateral. Banning even helped to settle a dispute between the two others in 1873 over selling part of the Rancho San Pasqual to members of the Indiana Colony, the group that would found Pasadena the following year.[9]

Among the many effects that the war's end had on the region, the closing of the Drum Barracks military installation, deemed unnecessary by the U.S. Army, probably hurt the economy of Wilmington most. But here, too, Banning demonstrated his inventiveness in his campaign to wring still more revenue from a project that had already benefited him handsomely. Banning hoped to bolster his business empire by reacquiring the property he and partner Benjamin D. Wilson had donated to the government in order to bring the camp to Wilmington. At first he tried to convince the federal authorities simply to give back the now-more-valuable land along with the buildings to him and Wilson, although he could not legally compel them to do so. He then offered to supply Drum Barracks with water for fifteen years in return for the rights to the flume he had built in 1864 to supply the camp. This offer was also turned down. The army did allow him to control the quartermaster's depot while its disposition was debated. Meanwhile, army officials consulted a private attorney to determine who owned what at the camp and composed reports on its condition, most of which recommended that the empty buildings be dismantled and the materials used elsewhere or put up for public auction.[10]

Unable to make headway against the army, Banning traveled to Washington, D.C., in early 1873 to lobby Congress to appropriate more to improvements at Wilmington harbor and to pass a bill giving the entire Drum Barracks property and its buildings to him and Wilson. The

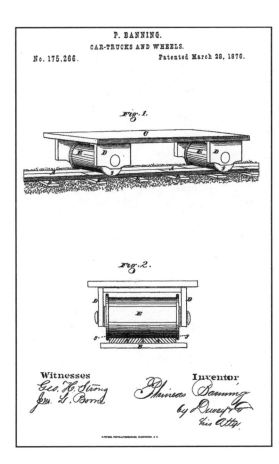

Phineas Banning's
"Car-Trucks and
Wheels" patent, 1876.
United States Patent and
Trademark Office.

reports of army inspectors such as Bvt. Brig. Gen. James F. Rusling, which concluded that the entire project had primarily benefited Banning and his businesses, aroused opposition, however, and the amended bill only granted the return of the original plot of land. The secretary of war left it to the quartermaster general to determine the fate of the buildings. A congressman later told Banning that, "as so much of irregularity has heretofore been charged at Drum Barracks," the buildings would be sold in a public auction in July. If the quartermaster's intention was to upbraid Banning for enriching himself at the government's expense, the punishment was light: on that day Banning and Edward McDonald purchased the buildings for themselves and Benjamin D. Wilson at very advantageous prices.[11]

The land and buildings Banning acquired from the U.S. government were immediately incorporated into his business. Most were used as warehouses; the blacksmith shop and wheelwright shop continued as such. The old warehouse depot on Banning's wharf stored goods lightered by his stevedores. The 300-foot-long barracks building some distance away would serve as a barley warehouse by 1878, when he regained his harbor business from the Southern Pacific.[12]

Benjamin D. Wilson had more philanthropic plans for his part of the purchase. He donated the hospital, another building, and ten acres of property to the Methodist Episcopal Church South for a "literary college." Established in 1874, Wilson College served students from throughout the area, providing them with a "thorough classical and practical education." The college ultimately fell victim to a change in emphasis by the trustees and its lack of endowment, but it survived for over a decade. Wilson College certainly raised the educational and cultural status of Wilmington and reflected Wilson's philanthropy in the region.[13]

Building a Harbor

One of Banning's major postwar accomplishments was to lead a campaign to improve the harbor at Wilmington and San Pedro, a quest that would eventually turn it into the busiest container port in the nation. This was no mean feat, considering both the natural features of the coastline and the political opposition he faced in later years. While "General" or "Admiral" Banning, as he was labeled in city newspapers, was not alone in this project, he certainly was the driving force, for both the betterment of the region and his own personal interest.

Before 1865 Banning had made only modest improvements to his Wilmington shoreline. The prospect of the railroad line to the harbor, for which he lobbied as a state senator in 1865 and 1867, spurred him on to make the changes needed to accommodate the Pacific trade that he envisioned. In 1866 he invited U.S. Senator Cornelius Cole, whose campaign he had supported, to inspect the harbor and then to help secure federal appropriations for its improvement. These would be used to construct a breakwater to protect ships and to dredge the shallow inner harbor. With further cajoling Banning also arranged for Rear Admiral N. K. Thatcher of the North Pacific Squadron to inspect the harbor in 1867. After wining and dining Thatcher, Banning was elated to learn that the admiral had written a glowing description of the Bay of San Pedro, recommending to the secretary of the navy that he obtain federal improvements in order to make the harbor a naval station. Banning sent copies of the letter to California senators and representatives as ammunition for the coming debates in Congress concerning appropriations.[14]

In late 1870 Banning began his major lobbying campaign for government funding. He convinced Senator Cole to offer a harbor bill. To ensure its passage, Banning traveled to Washington, D.C., in January 1871 to buttonhole anyone who could help pass the legislation. His efforts yielded $200,000 to begin the improvements. Energized by this victory, he pressed Cole repeatedly for more help with harbor matters and enlisted other business associates and civic leaders to use their influence to get further federal aid.[15]

The first federal improvements began in September 1871 and were supposed to be completed by the following March. The plans called for a one-mile breakwater running from the tip of Rattlesnake Island to Deadman's Island, which would control the flow of sand into Wilmington Slough. Once the sand was blocked, dredgers could deepen the main channel to ten feet. But the project was slowed because of design problems, inadequate funding, and inappropriate building supplies. The original contractor quit and the project was delayed. Banning decided to ask for more money and again traveled to the nation's capitol to lobby Congress. He obtained another $150,000, enough to get the project going again. The project supervisor brought in a large workforce to speed the work, and the breakwater was completed in 1881 at a cost of about $480,000. In the meantime, dredging in the inner harbor commenced, and State Senator Benjamin D. Wilson continued to write to congressmen asking for more federal money.[16]

Even after the initial dredging, however, larger ships still had to anchor outside the harbor and have their cargo transferred to the wharf by expensive lighters. So in that same year Banning gathered a group of prominent Los Angeles citizens to petition Congress for an additional $200,000 to deepen the harbor further. This time Congress provided only meager funding, but it would appropriate more over the next few years. By 1893, almost one million dollars had been expended on the overall project, and the inner harbor channel was eventually dredged to a depth of sixteen feet. Phineas Banning would not survive to see the full result, but the expanded capacity of Los Angeles harbor would lead to its becoming a world-class port in the next century.[17]

The improvement to the harbor was a boon to the town of Wilmington. Banning had been promoting the town since he established it in 1858 and had raised its status when he convinced the U.S. Army to relocate its main post there in 1862. During the war he directed his farflung supply operation for the government from Wilmington as the town grew. Its larger population required an expanded infrastructure, however, and

Bird's-eye view of Wilmington, 1877. Courtesy of the Huntington Library.

so Banning also directed his postwar efforts to building up the town's resources.

When the army canceled his "government flume" project toward the end of the war, Banning began searching for additional water sources for the town. He had artesian wells drilled in the vicinity, but they could not supply enough water for the town's needs, and in 1871 he began negotiations with Manuel Dominguez to obtain water from Rancho San Pedro. In the following year he incorporated the Wilmington Canal and Reservoir Company to build a canal from the San Gabriel River; the canal would transport passengers and freight to Wilmington while also providing irrigation and waterpower. His nephew William L. Banning and business partner David Alexander were also trustees of this company. As historian Robert Gillingham has noted, Phineas's talks with Dominguez about purchasing a parcel of land for a reservoir failed when Dominguez refused to sell, fearing that winter flooding might wreck the reservoir and damage his land. Never one to back down from a plan, Banning then sued to condemn the land and won, and immediately established his new business. The decision in his favor, however, was reversed by the California Supreme Court in 1875, forcing Banning to dissolve the company. As shipping traffic increased at the harbor by 1881, he began pumping water to supply the ships from a well he had dug in Wilmington. And by late 1883 he was reported to be building a reservoir to hold 1,500,000 gallons of water on his own homestead to serve the thirsty residents of Wilmington and San Pedro, and the ships in the harbor.[18]

With the harbor improvements beginning by 1872, dredging began to fill in the submerged lands just offshore in the inner harbor, increasing their value and attractiveness to investors. In order to protect these tidelands for the public, State Senator Benjamin D. Wilson took the advice of engineers and sponsored a bill in the legislature, supported by Phineas Banning, to incorporate Wilmington as a city, since state law at that time forbade granting to individuals tidelands located within two miles of an incorporated city. Having celebrated the incorporation, the new city's residents elected city trustees. But the trustees were never to govern. As several observers had noted in the 1860s, Phineas Banning was himself the government of Wilmington, the "mayor, councilman, constable, and watchman, all rolled into one." The new trustees did not meet once during their two-year terms, and there would never be another election. In 1887, two years after Banning's death, the state legislature would disincorporate Wilmington because of its failure to organize a city government. The town would be incorporated again in 1905, this time by the vote of its residents, and then consolidated with the city of Los Angeles in 1909.[19]

The incorporation of Wilmington might have blocked others from purchasing harbor tidelands, but not Phineas Banning. In the 1860s he had relied on an 1863 California law allowing private citizens to purchase "swamp and overflowed lands" to buy over 600 acres of tidelands adjacent to Wilmington, and he continued to buy such land in the years to come. State Senator Wilson, while publicly reiterating that the tidelands could not be privately owned, composed a bill in 1872 to allow Banning to purchase tidelands at the harbor. In 1878 the tidelands became an issue when, during discussions of a harbor bill in the legislature, Banning, the Southern Pacific Railroad, and advocates for Wilmington fought over the ownership of submerged acreage. Banning said in 1880 that, for his part, he was just trying to prevent "some San Francisco shark" from seizing the lands and would gladly deed them to anyone who promised to improve harbor facilities. Apparently Banning saw it as his duty to manage these lands, since there was no city government in Wilmington to perform that function. Banning would pass on his substantial tidelands holdings to his heirs, who would face a lengthy legal challenge from Los Angeles in the next century over their ownership.[20]

The incorporation of Wilmington did not spur a population boom, but the number of residents of the new city climbed to about 550 by early 1874. More important for Banning, the name of the harbor was changed by a congressional act in 1874 from San Pedro Harbor to Wilmington

Harbor. His face "was all beaming with joy" the day he visited a newspaper office to spread the news. He was likely the major lobbyist behind the act, though his cause was helped by the political clout of his friends in the executive offices of the Southern Pacific Railroad.[21]

Banning's focus on the Wilmington harbor deepened further once the Southern Pacific sold him back his business lightering freight and passengers and selling ballast material and water to ships. As in the past, Banning was accused of taking advantage of his position by demanding high rates for supplies, lightering, and stevedoring. It was also alleged that he descended to crime in defending his monopoly: a small competitor, Captain John F. Janes, charged Banning with ordering the sinking of his boat. Janes had started a modest but profitable sand ballast and lightering business at the harbor that undercut Banning's prices by a wide margin. But one night in January 1879 a "gang of Wilmington thugs" scuttled his lighter, which was anchored near those of Banning. Janes blamed Banning, although Banning's representative (who must have been an underling, since he was a "Commodore" rather than an "Admiral") told a reporter that a bunch of drunken toughs were probably the guilty party. Several years later Janes would edit an occasional local newspaper, the *San Pedro Shipping Gazette*, in which he consistently attacked Phineas Banning as "a natural born leech and blood sucker" and the "tool and hireling of a rotten, corrupt and thieving railroad monopoly." Janes ranted against the Southern Pacific and the Chinese in California in equally derisive terms.[22]

Many of Banning's customers between 1878 and 1882 accused the company of charging excessive rates, padding its bills, and being slow to unload ships. Although such accusations were probably common across the business, a San Francisco agent for Balfour, Guthrie & Company threatened in 1880 that British ships would avoid the port if Banning did not lower his rates. Most vessels had to take on ballast in the harbor after discharging their cargo, since San Pedro still exported little in comparison to its imports; the ship captains Banning dealt with objected to the high prices he charged for ballast. Representatives from Goodall, Perkins & Company, a frequent customer, issued many protests about overcharges and late deliveries. San Francisco agents for the Central Pacific Railroad wrote the company about their customers' many grievances over Banning's service. The agent of the Pacific Coast Steamship Company, one of Banning's best clients, frequently complained; in their occasional blowups, he and Banning exchanged angry letters accusing one another of insult. Additional complaints came from local merchants about overcharges or damage to their goods. Business was good during these years, but pleasing customers was certainly not easy.[23]

Although some of Banning's methods also raised the ire of representatives of the Southern Pacific Railroad, he was granted the contract in 1880 to extend its tracks from Wilmington to San Pedro. Over the next year he had piles driven on Mormon Island and in the bay and built track to new Southern Pacific depots. Although the construction revenues were welcome, this project ultimately worked to Banning's detriment, because it moved a substantial amount of harbor business back to San Pedro, reducing the need for his lighters. In 1888 the tracks were continued another two miles to Timms Point at the southern tip of the bay, where the railroad began construction of a long wharf. With these projects completed, San Pedro replaced Wilmington as the chief port district. Fortunately for him, Banning would not live to see his own city surpassed.[24]

While building the Southern Pacific line, Banning also tried to expand his Wilmington business by building new wharves and adding new excursions. In his 1881 application to the county Board of Supervisors, he offered to put up $30,000 in bonds and donate 200 feet of land fronting San Pedro in return for a wharf franchise at Wilmington. The supervisors, who had often approved Banning's previous applications, demurred this time, explaining to Banning's lawyer that they believed that he had a monopoly and that his rates were excessive. They also suspected that he might have forced an earlier applicant for the franchise to withdraw. In February 1885 Banning tried to block the granting of another wharf franchise, this one sought by the Kerchoff Lumber Company at San Pedro. Both Banning and the Southern Pacific Railroad opposed this franchise, and both were chastised by the *Times* for trying to thwart any competition at the harbor. On March 5, the supervisors voted four to one in favor of the franchise, the lone dissenter being Banning's good friend, Supervisor George Hinds.[25]

On a more positive note for the "General," his company began regular summer excursions to Santa Catalina Island in 1883. Banning's old competitor, Augustus W. Timms, had been bringing vacationers to the resort area for years for camping, fishing, and swimming, and by the early 1880s the number of visitors was increasing. Over the previous two decades, some of Banning's former employees, among others, had started various businesses on the island. In 1883 Banning was considering purchasing and developing Santa Catalina and decided to establish a regular weekly run on his steamboat *Amelia* during the summer season. Banning went all out for the first excursion, arranging special trains from Los Angeles to San Pedro, providing bait and tackle for fishing, erecting bathhouses on the island for swimmers, and hiring a brass band for dancing during the cruise. Captain A. A. Polhamus commanded the ship, and General Banning "entertained the representatives of the press and several friends in royal style, preparing a most sumptuous repast for their benefit." Many of the passengers became seasick on the trip, but other than that it was a success. Visitors to Santa Catalina increased that summer and the schedule was renewed in following years. The 1883 season was the precursor of the major investments the Bannings would later make in Santa Catalina, when Phineas's three sons assumed control of the company.[26]

By 1884 Banning's health was deteriorating, and he began to make plans for his sons to take over his businesses. In that year he incorporated two companies to carry out different aspects of his harbor operation, naming as trustees himself, his oldest son, William, his employees Patrick H. Downing and Frank B. Fanning, and lawyer George S. Patton. The Wilmington Transportation Company would be responsible for the "general transportation, towing, lightering, storing, wharfage and warehouse" operation. The Wilmington Development Company would take care of ship agency, stevedoring, furnishing supplies and ballast, and maintaining shops, equipment, and shipyards for the harbor. These companies would function without much of Banning's assistance or supervision, as he became increasingly absent due to health problems. They would operate profitably for many years after his death, in fact, simply by continuing the businesses Phineas had so thoroughly mastered over his busy career.[27]

An English shipmaster visited the port of Los Angeles around this time and offered a mixed assessment of what Banning had achieved there. Writing to the British Consul in Los Angeles, he described Wilmington as "a wretched place" and San Pedro as made up of "about thirty wooden shanties, seventeen of those are drinking and gambling dens." Merchants of the towns were "scoundrels," and lowlifes tried to sneak on board ships with whiskey to induce crews to desert. Although Banning had a monopoly on almost everything, he was a "good man," and his nephew, William L. Banning, was the "only reliable storekeeper" in the harbor. Phineas would have been incensed to have heard his harbor described in this way, but the positive characterization of him and his nephew in the midst of a rough port environment speaks volumes about his personal stature near the end of his business career.[28]

Phineas Banning's efforts over several decades to develop Los Angeles harbor and the surrounding area were critical to the expansion of the port over the next century and a half as it became one of the largest in the world. His alterations also severely affected the regional environment. The massive dredging to deepen the port and the diversion of rivers and streams to bring in more fresh water destroyed much of the original wetlands and flora, and wildlife deserted the area. This was evident during Gen. James Rusling's visit in 1867, when he noticed the changing landscape and Banning told him that the "vast flocks of wildgeese" there "were even more numerous in former years." The plowing of Banning's farmland and, later, the development of parts of Banning's property changed the natural watershed, leading to serious problems with flooding in the late nineteenth and twentieth centuries. And the expansion of harbor shipping and industries in the twentieth century has caused severe problems with air and water pollution that have yet to be solved. In short, while the harbor improvements helped to build the region's economy, the overall changes to the port and its surroundings damaged the environment in lasting ways, as has often been true of "progress" in Southern California.[29]

Banning Families, 1865–1885

With the Civil War over, the tension in the Banning family resulting from sectional rivalries probably eased a bit. Phineas and Rebecca had three young sons to care for when Phineas decided to run for the State Senate in May 1865, adding another duty to his busy life. Rebecca continued to take care of her sons and run the Banning household with the help of her mother and their teenaged servant, Harriet. She and Phineas regularly entertained business associates, neighbors, and others in their mansion, and their "sumptuous" and elaborate dinners followed by "wine and wit" became famous. Rebecca also became an important property owner, at least on paper: she was listed in Los Angeles County assessment records as the owner of and taxpayer for the Banning residential lot and house.[30]

Rebecca assumed another responsibility for the couple when she gave birth to a daughter in the fall of 1866. Elizabeth, also called Bessie, was named for Phineas's mother and sister. Unfortunately, she was another of Rebecca's offspring who did not survive childhood: Bessie died in January 1867 and was buried on the family property. Around this time, Phineas took Rebecca and the boys to visit her sister Marilda in the San Joaquin Valley, a trip that might have been intended to help both of them deal with their grief.[31]

It would not be long before Rebecca was pregnant again, and this childbirth would be her last. In January 1868 another boy, Vincent Edgar Griffin Banning, was born. Complications from the birth soon endangered her life, and she died within days. Her funeral arrangements were rushed because Phineas decided to leave Wilmington almost immediately, to arrive in Sacramento in time to serve in the legislative session. While he was gone, his occasional business partner former Governor John G. Downey and his devoutly Catholic spouse decided to have the baby baptized at the Plaza Church in Los Angeles in May. How the non-religious Phineas reacted to this event is not known, but the Downeys probably felt justified when Vincent died the next month. He was buried near his mother and siblings.[32]

With three young sons to raise, a yearning for a new mate, and a desire to enlarge his family, Phineas did not wait very long to end his mourning for Rebecca. In the same month that she died, he was paying considerable attention to a young lady in San Francisco. The wife of one of Banning's business partners wrote Benjamin D. Wilson's wife that the General "had a new 'true love' while here—a 'Miss Marianna' this time, and he was terribly devoted to her." But soon "his ardor cooled down considerably, and he even began to mention another young lady's name. He's a fickle General isn't he?"[33]

Shortly after that romance, Phineas began pursuing a young lady from the San Luis Obispo area. Mary Elizabeth Hollister was the daughter of Joseph Hubbard Hollister, whose ancestors had emigrated from England in the mid-1600s and fought in the French and Indian and Revolutionary Wars. Just after 1800 Joseph's father moved to Ohio, where Joseph was born in 1820. He married Ellen Mossman in 1842, and they had five children, the eldest of whom was Mary, born in 1846. In 1853 Joseph and his brother drove a herd of sheep across the plains to California. There they joined Thomas and Benjamin Flint and Llewellyn Bixby (who later purchased the Rancho Los Cerritos and Rancho Los Alamitos in present-day Long Beach), who helped them bring the sheep to Los Angeles. The venture proved so profitable that the Hollister brothers did it twice more. After the third trip Joseph decided to stay, settling with his family on property he bought in Santa Barbara County. In the 1860s the Hollisters purchased the Chorro and San Luisito ranches and other property further north, and by 1867, the year Ellen Hollister died, Joseph was one of the largest landowners and possibly the largest sheep farmer in the state.[34]

Although we do not know how Phineas and Mary Hollister met, Banning likely knew her father from his business dealings in the 1850s, when Phineas partnered with Benjamin D. Wilson and William Sanford to herd sheep from Los Angeles County to better pasturage in Northern California. Hollister might also have been a customer of Banning's freight business at Wilmington harbor. They most certainly met as members of the Masonic Lodge in Los Angeles in the 1850s and early 1860s. They might have also met while Banning was a state senator, since Hollister would no doubt have had an interest in state legislation.[35]

In any event, Phineas surely met Mary through her father. By early 1868, not long after Rebecca's death, he decided that he wanted to wed Mary. In the spring of that year she embarked on a trip to New York, sailing from San Francisco. So Phineas sent a letter to his old friend Harris Newmark, who was living in New York for a time, asking him to deliver a sealed envelope to Mary when she arrived. Newmark complied, discovering later that the envelope contained a letter proposing marriage. She turned Banning down at first, but—as we might predict from his business dealings—he did not easily accept rejection, writing love letters and visiting her at the family home in San Luis Obispo. Although her father disapproved of the marriage, Mary finally gave in over a year later, on August 1, 1869. Before the end of that year, friends of Phineas knew that "he is certainly going to be married to Miss Hollister." The wedding took place on Valentine's Day, 1870, at the ranch and elaborate home of Mary's uncle William W. Hollister, in Goleta, a few miles from Santa Barbara.[36]

When the Bannings returned to Wilmington after the wedding, the occupants of his mansion were fewer in number. Rebecca's mother, Hannah, had moved to Linden, California, to live with Rebecca's sister, Marilda Prather. Phineas had arranged this so that Mary would not have to live with his first wife's relations. Hannah was not happy about her removal; she believed Phineas had promised her that she would be able to live with him in Wilmington for the rest of her life. She reportedly consulted a lawyer about suing Phineas but probably found that she had no case. In 1883 she passed away in Linden. Harriet, the African American servant who had performed so valiantly in saving lives during the 1863 *Ada Hancock* explosion, accompanied Hannah to Linden. The fate of the rest of Rebecca's family is quickly told. Rebecca's only surviving brother, Cyrus, had returned to Southern California in 1860, and this time purchased farmland in the La Ballona area near a relative, John Young. He fell victim to intemperance and in 1877 he and his wife, Lucy Ann Sanford, separated and then divorced. She continued to raise their nine children and manage the farm, which became very profitable. Cyrus, meanwhile, died in Stockton about 1890.[37]

Mary Elizabeth Hollister about 1864. Courtesy of the Banning Residence Museum.

Phineas and Mary wasted little time in enlarging the Banning family of three sons. In January 1871, Mary gave birth to a girl, whom they named Mary Hollister Banning. Unwilling as usual to interrupt his work for family reasons, Phineas left four days later on a trip to Washington, D.C., to lobby Congress, so his spouse was left to recuperate from childbirth and manage the household with the help of their servants. In July 1874, another daughter was born, named Ellen Mossman Banning after Mary's mother. Like many of Rebecca's children, Ellen did not live very long. She died eight months later and was buried on the Banning property. Almost one year later, Lucy Tichenor Banning was born in February 1876. Lucy was named after Mary's aunt and sister, and Phineas's business partner in San Francisco. "Ginger," as her father called her, would be Mary and Phineas's last child, and the fifth of his children to reach adulthood.[38]

Over the fifteen years of their marriage, Phineas was frequently absent on business trips, and Mary ran the household. The three boys did not care much for their young stepmother, but upon their father's insistence they accepted her and soon became very protective of their two half sisters. Mary also traveled when she could, especially to Northern California to visit her relatives there. She took her two girls on a trip to visit friends and relatives in Ohio in 1881, and accompanied Phineas on a journey to the East Coast in 1884.[39]

The Banning boys, meanwhile, attended the Burton School in Los Angeles and Wilson College. William soon became his father's right-hand man in the business and would eventually lead the company. Joseph decided to study law, and in 1881 he was accepted into the office of his parent's lawyers, the Los Angeles law firm of Andrew Glassell & George H. Smith. He apparently flourished there, even accompanying Glassell on a business trip to the East Coast in 1883. He never did become a practicing attorney in California, however, preferring to use his legal knowledge for business while also becoming an accomplished photographer. The youngest son, Hancock, remained in school throughout the postwar years.[40]

Phineas had a wonderful relationship with his sons as they grew to manhood. Unlike his own father, he spent time with his sons, rarely disciplined the three, and loved to kid around with them. He gave each a nickname: William was "Captain," the same title as William Sanford, for whom he was named, and a harbinger of his future sailing abilities; Joseph was "Judge," in reference to his desire to become a lawyer; and Hancock was called "Uncle" for reasons unknown.[41]

At home Mary played hostess at Phineas's many parties and elaborate "regales." Their cuisine was customarily described as "the best this side of the continent," and their guest lists were long and varied. Mary had help with these parties and household chores from their several servants. In 1870 the crew included three "domestics," and in 1880 there were two Chinese cooks, an Irish maid, and a coachman. In these years Mary directed several changes to the 1864 house, adding the present kitchen and changing the functions of upstairs rooms. Not long before their wedding Phineas had imported seeds from Australia for eucalyptus trees and planted them on both sides of the entrance to the mansion, making for a distinctive approach to the home, witnessed by an engraving of the homestead in an 1880 county history.[42]

Mary had a more forceful personality than Rebecca, and her assertiveness showed early on. A lonely Phineas wrote to her often while on his numerous trips, but she rarely answered him (according to *his* correspondence, of course). In a note she sent inviting a friend to lunch, she playfully noted that her "youthful husband" was delivering the message, but added sternly, "please see that he starts for home at an early hour."[43]

While monitoring his social life, Mary also influenced her husband's religious practices. Phineas had little interest in religion after his upbringing by an extremely religious mother, and he enjoyed poking fun at clergymen. Mary, by contrast, was a devout Episcopalian, and since there was no Episcopal church in Wilmington she arranged to have services in her basement in the 1870s. In 1882 she invited Reverend Carlos P. Linsley to come to Wilmington and build a church. Mary became the chief donor to the building fund; her contributions paid for the windows in the chancel and part of the structure. Appropriately enough for a church in a port, the bell came from one of Phineas's steamboats, the *Amelia*, accompanied by more money. By 1883 the church was nearing completion and the entire Banning family was attending Sunday services. The *Los Angeles Times* reported, perhaps sarcastically, the noticeable change in Phineas later that year, remarking that "Admiral Banning has been converted and allows no work to be done on the wharf on Sunday."[44]

During this post–Civil War era, another Banning family member arrived in the harbor area. William L. Banning, the son of Phineas's oldest brother, John Alford Banning Jr., moved to Southern California about 1867 after serving in the Union army and went to work for his uncle. He married Adelaida Mellus, the daughter of merchant Francis Mellus, who had come to Los Angeles from Boston in the 1840s and was a business partner of David Alexander when Phineas Banning first arrived in California. When Alexander was elected county sheriff in 1875, he appointed William L. Banning his undersheriff. After a failed bid in 1879 for the job of sheriff, however, William apparently abandoned his political ambitions. He remained a shopkeeper and businessman in San Pedro, tied to his uncle's firm, and brought his brother-in-law, Frank Mellus, into the Banning business circle.[45]

The "other" William Lowber Banning (actually there were four in two generations), Phineas's older brother, made a similarly ill-fated political bid during these years, when Phineas had apparently decided that his interests were served better by lobbying politicians than by becoming one. In 1877 William entered the race for the highest office he would seek: governor of Minnesota. This time he was nominated as a Democrat, running against the incumbent Republican, John S. Pillsbury, and representatives of the Greenback Party and Prohibition Party. This

The Banning residence in 1879. Courtesy of the Huntington Library.

election focused on whether the fiscal policies of the Republican administration had effectively addressed the devastation of the 1873 depression. William's friend, Ignatius Donnelly, was a major figure in the national and state Greenback Party, which argued that the government should issue paper money rather than specie, permitting mild inflation in order to help farmers. Banning ran as a Democrat with considerable Greenback support, although his position on currency was mixed. The newspaper headline announcing the results, "Bouncing of Banning," succinctly describes the drubbing he suffered from the incumbent.[46]

The defeated gubernatorial candidate withdrew to the business side of civic life, continuing his active involvement in the St. Paul Chamber of Commerce, serving for several years as its president. In that capacity he became known for leading the opposition to a state bill to give a railroad a $5,000,000 loan, which he considered a giveaway. By 1884 he was also the president of the St. Louis River and Dalles Improvement Co.[47]

During these years William Lowber and Phineas and their families met on only a few occasions. Phineas managed to visit William's home in St. Paul on the way back from his lobbying trip to Washington, D.C., in 1871, and in 1884 both Phineas and Mary would visit him on a long trip to the East Coast and other destinations. William returned the favor in 1882, when he brought his eldest daughters Ellen and May Alice to Wilmington for a short stay. It was the first time these two girls met their Southern California cousins, and Phineas's sons were immediately smitten. In later years all three would become infatuated with the girls' younger sister, the beautiful Katharine.[48]

Sheep and the Town of Banning

Given Phineas Banning's close identity with the port, it may seem peculiar that one of his legacies in Southern California—the town that bears his name—sits many miles from the coast. His connection to the town, however, derived not from his harbor business but through his wife's family and the Southern Pacific Railroad. While Banning was once again in Washington, D.C., to lobby Congress for more harbor improvements in January 1873, Mary's father, Joseph Hubbard Hollister, died, leaving a fortune in land and sheep to his children. Over the next three years the Bannings made a number of trips to San Luis Obispo to help settle the estate. Mary's brother-in-law, Robert Edgar Jack, was the administrator and worked diligently to keep all of the siblings satisfied. Most of the land was sold and the proceeds paid to the heirs in lump sums. Some was leased to a land company, which became insolvent in 1879; that land would be split among the siblings. Mary and Phineas hired real estate agents to manage their share of the property in San Luis Obispo, which they rented out for farmland and pasture, and Los Angeles lawyer John D. Bicknell handled the legal aspects of this investment. Mary also inherited a lot in Ohio that her father had retained through the years.[49]

During the negotiations concerning the sale of the Hollister sheep, Mary arranged with her brother to keep her portion of the herd. She and Phineas planned to move the sheep south to Wilmington and to follow her father's example in raising them for wool, which had become a booming industry in Southern California. During the early 1860s farmers had reacted to the drought in Southern California by replacing their dying herds of cattle with sheep, and the cessation of the Confederate cotton trade during the war had driven wool prices up dramatically. By 1874 there were an estimated 500,000 head of sheep in Los Angeles County alone, most of them in what is now Long Beach and Orange County.[50]

In order to pasture her herd of about 2,600 head of sheep, Mary used $17,500 from her inheritance to buy more than 4,000 acres of land near the Santa Ana River in present-day Newport Beach. This property had been part of the Rancho Santiago de Santa Ana, partitioned between Los

Angeles lawyers Andrew Glassell and Albert Chapman in 1868. Mary bought a parcel belonging to Glassell, who would eventually be related to her by the marriage of one of her stepsons.[51]

Phineas knew something about sheep from his work with William Sanford herding Benjamin D. Wilson's flock in the 1850s, and he had owned a few since at least the 1860s. He arranged to have the Hollister sheep moved south to the new property, which he called the "Banning Ranch," and hired a sheep man to care for them. He then had an artesian well sunk there to supply water. Ever attentive to the potential value of waterfront property, by the end of the year Banning was reported to be subdividing some of the acreage fronting on Newport Harbor that was unneeded for the sheep.[52]

But the timing of this new venture was unfortunate. The early 1870s had seen limited rainfall in the region, and the drought of 1876–77 destroyed the Southern California sheep ranges just as the early 1860s drought had wiped out the range cattle pasturage in the region. Looking for alternate grazing land, Banning turned his attention toward western Arizona Territory, where water and green pastures had lured California sheep herds for several years. Since he was then working for the Southern Pacific to gain approval to build through the territory, Banning knew the area well. By early 1877, the railroad was approaching the Arizona border along the same route his freight wagons had followed to Fort Yuma. This made it convenient for Banning to have his sheep herded to a point along the tracks in the San Gorgonio Pass about twenty-eight miles east of Riverside, where the railroad had a station and he had built sheep corrals. He would then ship them on Southern Pacific railroad cars bound for Yuma and have them driven from there to pastures in the Santa Cruz Valley.[53]

The railroad named its depot in the San Gorgonio Pass Banning Station by early 1877, obviously in honor of its political and business agent who owned sheep corrals there. The station marked the proposed city of Moore, a town as yet without inhabitants, owned by Ransom B. Moore, a former Texan who had lived in El Monte and had once served as a Los Angeles County supervisor. The depot was at the terminus of a long water flume built by a private company to bring water along with lumber for railroad ties and firewood to Moore City. The San Gorgonio Fluming Company—one of whose investors was Banning's own attorney, John D. Bicknell—did not deliver the lumber when the railroad required it, however, and soon failed. The "Great Flume" survived to provide water for the settlement until it was finally dismantled in 1884.[54]

Two stories have emerged to explain how "Moore City" became the town of Banning. The first is that San Gorgonio Fluming Company manager Dr. Welwood Murray, who had met Banning earlier in Los Angeles, perhaps through Bicknell, offered to have the settlement named in his honor if "the General would do something nice for the town in return," such as making a contribution to the construction of the local Baptist church. Banning city historian Tom Hughes believes that the General came through with this donation and the name was changed. The other story, told by one of Moore's daughters, is that Moore and Banning had been close for some time, and that Moore simply changed the name of his planned settlement as a tribute to his friend. The first explanation is certainly the most plausible and the one that historians have accepted.[55]

In any case, the Banning name appeared on the printed letterhead of businesses there by early 1877. A post office was established in that year, and by the end of 1878 Banning "could boast four small houses, several tents, three saloons, a boarding house, and a store." The rough beginning of the small town, "glamorized by brawls, street killings and at least one lynching," quickly changed as the rougher element moved out and real estate dealers moved in. By 1884 residential lots in "Banning Colony" were advertised in Los Angeles, and the population grew and then declined as the Southern California real estate boom of the 1880s dwindled. The town was finally incorporated as a city in 1913. In a later connection to Phineas Banning, during World War II General George S. Patton Jr., a close relative of the Bannings, built a hospital in the area for his tank-training operation. Today, Banning celebrates Phineas Banning's most famous business with its nickname for Old Town Banning— "Stagecoach Town U.S.A."[56]

The town of Banning survived, but Phineas's sheep business was not long-lived. Many other stockowners had also moved their sheep and cattle to the region, overgrazing the western Arizona pastures. As the area reached capacity, even Arizona stockmen such as Walter Vail, owner of the vast Empire Ranch near Fort Crittenden, had to look elsewhere; he eventually leased land during another drought in the 1890s on Santa Catalina Island, then owned by Phineas Banning's three sons. When Phineas moved back into the harbor business on a large scale in 1878, he and Mary decided to abandon the sheep business and lease the Newport Beach property for farming. The land would profit their descendants handsomely, especially when oil was discovered there a few decades later.[57]

Two Decades in Politics

The post–Civil War era saw Phineas Banning take an active role in local and state politics, largely in order to build up his interests through the passage of railroad issues, harbor improvement grants, and tidelands legislation at the federal, state, and local levels from the 1860s until his death in 1885. Although he began this period as an elected official, he soon moved to influencing legislation through lobbying, a decision that probably helped his cause, since he could inspire fierce opposition as a public figure.

In 1865 he had emerged as the leader of one wing of the Union Party when he won his seat in the state senate. As one of the few Republicans in this coalition dedicated to preserving the Union, Banning became the target for Democrats, who then outnumbered Republicans by a wide margin. His most consistent political enemies in the decade to come included *Los Angeles News* editor A. J. King, a fierce and racist Southern Democrat who attacked Banning in print whenever possible, King's successor Charles E. Beane, and some of the later editors of the *Herald*, *Express*, and the early *Times*.[58]

In addition to working for bills that benefited his business, Banning was willing to cross the aisle to pass legislation for long-standing business and political allies among the old elite. The Republican Banning joined the opposition Democrats in voting in December 1867 to continue printing the governor's message and reports of state officers in Spanish as well as English. He stated that he had to do so to help his many Spanish-speaking constituents keep abreast of civic affairs. This vote was an affirmation of his relationships with the *Californio* elite, which dated from his first years in Southern California when he lived on or near the Sepulveda Ranch at San Pedro harbor. He had worked with many *Californio* customers since the early 1850s both in his transportation business and in his short-term venture in the cattle industry in 1861, and had cooperated with *Californio* political leaders in the Democratic Party before the Civil War.[59]

Banning had risen to prominence when some of the *Californios* still retained wealth and power in Southern California. But 1867 witnessed the continuation of the old landed elite's downfall, as the post–Civil War wave of immigrants from other states began to transform the region into an Anglo community where adobe structures were replaced by red brick, religious celebrations gave way to secular events, and Spanish disappeared from official publications. Ironically, considering his vote in 1867, many of the objectives Phineas Banning worked for—such as building the railroad and developing the harbor—brought more newcomers who gradually replaced the former civic and economic leadership, Americanizing the region.[60]

When Banning left the state senate in 1869, his good friend and business partner Benjamin D. Wilson won his seat, and from that point Banning worked with and through Wilson when he needed a government connection. This alliance was especially important for securing federal harbor funding and passing state bills to incorporate Wilmington, acquire tidelands, and other Banning objectives. Banning also asked Wilson to aid his political allies when possible.[61]

Wilson was not Banning's only "inside man." The General claimed that he had been instrumental in electing Cornelius C. Cole as U.S. Senator from California in 1865, and he certainly lobbied Senator Cole to get federal funding for Wilmington harbor improvements. In 1871 Banning promised to work for Cole's re-election; in return, the senator would lobby the secretary of war to order a harbor survey for dredging purposes, and help Banning purchase the old Drum Barracks buildings. In the same year he asked Cole to replace the deputy collector of the Port of San Diego with a candidate he and his friends in San Diego favored. Senator Cole agreed.[62]

Other friends and political confidants among California officeholders exchanged political favors for his support. Banning used his influence to gain votes for the election of Governor George C. Perkins in 1880, and Perkins subsequently made at least two appointments at Banning's request. Congressman Romualdo Pacheco usually won approval for Banning's many applications for federal aid and contracts. And Banning was a friend and supporter of General George Stoneman, elected governor in 1883.[63]

Banning was often himself the target of lobbying. As state senator, of course, he received many requests for help from citizens and political leaders. But even after he left office, his political pull drew supplicants. In 1872 a representative of Anaheim citizens opposed to their new city charter asked him to convince State Senator Wilson to repeal it. In the early 1870s, former State Senator William Gwin asked Wilson to use his influence in getting Banning to "put his herculean shoulder to the wheel" to promote Gwin's Pacific Transfer Company of San Francisco. Banning's clout was further enhanced when he went to work for the Southern Pacific Railroad as a special agent and lobbyist in the mid-1870s.[64]

After his term as state senator was up in 1869, Phineas Banning did not run for elected office again, although he continued to participate in local and state Republican Party activities. In 1868 he was elected a delegate to a state convention that in turn chose delegates to the Republican national convention. In the 1880s he was active in local Republican conventions and at party meetings, which he sometimes chaired.[65]

Banning also participated in national elections, and was particularly conspicuous in 1880. The Democratic nominee for president that year was General Winfield Scott Hancock, an old friend who had helped Banning with U.S. Army contracts, and the namesake of his youngest son. The two had kept in contact, writing and meeting occasionally after Hancock left Los Angeles in 1861 for an assignment with the Army of the Potomac during the Civil War. Banning had even listed him among the initial directors of the Los Angeles Pioneer Oil Company when it was formed in early 1865. Although Phineas was a staunch Republican in 1880, he could not desert his old friend, and his vocal support for a Democrat irked his fellow Republicans.[66]

As the campaign developed, Banning found that their connection was being used as evidence of Hancock's corruption. A Republican newspaper in Stockton printed an editorial criticizing Hancock, claiming that the Democrat had helped Banning to get a government contract twenty years earlier for building a federal water structure that would never work. The accusation referred to the "government flume" for Drum Barracks, which was actually approved while Hancock was serving in the East. Although the accusation probably had little impact on the national campaign, all of Banning's support locally could not help his friend defeat the Republican James A. Garfield. Three years later Hancock would visit Wilmington, where he was hailed in speeches and entertained by his old friend for four days.[67]

Banning's pull in Southern California politics meant he was often invited to speak at local civic celebrations such as the Fourth of July, the 1876 U.S. Centennial festivities, and an 1872 grand ball and celebration, for which he was the grand marshal. Always burnishing his political and civic persona, he loved to be addressed by the official and unofficial titles he acquired over his career. He promoted himself from captain of the local Union Guards in 1857 to major in 1859, and became a general in 1866 when he was appointed to a California National Guard unit that was never activated, although he would hold this commission from 1866 to 1870, again from 1872 to 1876, and for a short time in 1882. He would proudly insist that others use these grandiose titles, even though he was a man who did not fear physical or dirty work, a hands-on entrepreneur who rolled up his sleeves every day at work, drove his own stagecoaches, and was seriously injured in 1863 while moving large piles of lumber with his men. Newspapers, business associates and even his second spouse, Mary, frequently called him "General." Others dubbed him "Admiral," evoking his domination of the harbor and his fleet of steamers and tugboats. Some of Banning's critics ribbed him for this display of vanity; one newspaper story in 1880 referred to Charles Dickens's mockery of the proliferation of American titles, calling "our militia 'Generals,' and corner grocery 'Judges' and Town Council 'Honorables' as ridiculous as our spittoons and our dollar aristocracy," an obvious slap at Banning. Another newspaper announcing his retirement from the National Guard in 1882 sharply criticized him for using the title "General," which implied he was on a par with a military leader like George Washington. Possibly as a good-natured response to such teasing, his own lawyer once addressed a letter in 1881 to "Hon. General Admiral Phineas Banning."[68]

The Patriarch Passes On

In the decades following the Civil War Phineas Banning continued to work at his usual rapid pace. Even while planning future investments and lobbying investors and politicians, he frequently pitched in with the tough manual labor that his stevedores and other employees did each day. These labors, along with his penchant for overconsuming fine food and spirits, began to affect his health by the 1870s, while he was still just in his mid-forties.

Despite his continual hard work, Banning's rising economic fortunes were reflected in his increasing waistline. Photographs of him in his early twenties depicted a man of solid frame and muscular build. But by the 1860s, he had expanded noticeably, and early in the following decade an acquaintance would comment on the "Falstaffian rotundity" of Banning's "bulky physique." His frequent entertaining at home was doubtless to blame, particularly the "regales" that had become so noteworthy. Banning was remembered by an associate as "an ideal host," and his frequent dinner parties were nothing short of feasts, with elaborate cuisine, an assortment of wines, champagne, and other liquor, and lively discussion and entertainment. One participant at Banning's birthday party in 1881 called the meal "as sumptuous a repast as it has been our fortune to be a partaker of in many a day. Course after course followed in charming time, each washed down with the finest vintages of this as well as foreign climes."[69]

He also dined extravagantly while on his many business trips. In 1873 the San Francisco *Alta California* reported that during his many visits to

Phineas Banning with good friend Matthew Keller and father-in-law Joseph
Hubbard Hollister, about 1873. Courtesy of the Huntington Library.

San Francisco he occasionally missed regular meals and had to request
late dinners. At one of these repasts at the Occidental Hotel, he and three
friends devoured a boiled turkey and "twelve hundred oysters," according to a reporter. As he left the dining room, an acquaintance greeted
him and invited him to dinner, but Banning declined. "Oh no, I don't feel
hungry; I just had a glass of water and a soda cracker, and that is all I care

for tonight," he replied. "I am going to bed soon and I never like to risk anything hearty just before retiring." After Banning left, the acquaintance entered the dining room to find that Banning and friends had cleaned out the kitchen. The next day he ordered a basket of eggs and a box of oyster shells sent to Banning's room as a reminder of the "light supper" he had the night before.[70]

Banning was also known as a hearty drinker, which was certainly not uncommon among Los Angeles area residents in the frontier years. Saloons were ubiquitous, and whiskey was heavily consumed at all levels of society. Quite a number of local civic leaders, including prominent judges and lawyers, drank throughout the day, and "court often recessed because of judicial incapacity." Judson Grenier has described how one of the participants in the legal affairs of the last decade informed J. Lancaster Brent in 1865 that the "the old guard . . . had done itself in through intemperance," many of them physically incapacitated or dead from the consequences of drink in the 1850s and 1860s.[71]

Banning had a particular fondness for champagne, which flowed freely at his dinners and parties and, according to a friend of his, "was always on tap." His consumption of alcohol was noted by contemporaries such as General Winfield Scott Hancock, who warned Matthew Keller that if he and Banning brought a large stock of Keller's wine to the 1876 Centennial celebration there would be so much "jollification" that they might not return home. One of Banning's grandsons recalled meeting a woman in Oakland who had encountered Phineas when he exited a stagecoach in a state of inebriation and stepped on her daughter's foot. The woman said she angrily hit him with her umbrella, and on the next day he rode a long distance to apologize for the incident. Another grandson said that Banning's second wife, Mary, claimed that Phineas required a half-pint of champagne with peaches and cream by his bed every evening.[72]

The combination of rich food and drink and a hardworking, fast-paced life took its toll on him by 1876. In that year Edward L. Watkins, a nephew of J. Lancaster Brent who had moved to Southern California from New Orleans the previous year, was working for Banning and Benjamin D. Wilson observing the harbor dredging and managing other operations. In early May, Banning became seriously ill and Watkins stood vigil at his bedside for a good month. On May 8 Watkins wrote to Wilson, "We found the Genl much worse on our return last night + he is now about as bad off as when at his worst. I sat up with him last night + I am now on watch for tonight. I have but little hope for the Genl now, he is passing large quantities of blood + also expectorates the same." On

May 13 Watkins informed Wilson that this was the tenth day that Banning had passed blood, and on the 25th that the General was "much worse yesterday + Dr. Orme was down + remained last night with him." On June 5 Watkins reported that Banning was so bad that "last night I thought every moment would be his last."[73]

Watkins did not reveal Banning's affliction, assuming Dr. Orme indeed diagnosed one. This episode may have been the beginning of the liver and kidney problems that would become more serious later in his life. Despite his apparently dire condition, Banning recovered to some extent from this particular illness by the beginning of July, when he gave a very short speech at the Fourth of July ceremonies in Los Angeles. In a few more months he was well enough to travel to Arizona to continue his work for the Southern Pacific Railroad.

In the next several years Banning lost two of his closest friends, which was certainly a cause for some distress, although he was not one to show it. Benjamin D. Wilson, the Tennessean who had come to Southern California in the early 1840s and forged a varied career as, among other things, a merchant, vintner, citrus grower, and politician, died in March 1878. He was one of the first local residents Banning had met when he arrived in Southern California, had been his business partner and financier since the mid-1850s, and had joined him in ventures such as the Los Angeles and San Pedro Railroad and the transfer of land to the U.S. government for Drum Barracks. Their families had been very close, especially when the Wilsons stayed in Wilmington. The two families would continue their intimacy through the following generations and would eventually be bound through marriage.[74]

Three years later, Matthew Keller passed away at the age of seventy. Keller had known Banning since the mid-1850s, and was one of his best long-term customers. He and Banning had loaned money to each other on several occasions. The two were members of the local Masonic Lodge and occasionally traveled together; they shared a love of humor and an occasional practical joke. Like the Wilsons, the surviving members of the Keller family remained close to the Bannings, and were further connected to them by land transactions.[75]

His close friends' deaths did not appear to check Banning's consistently fast pace. In June 1882, however, he resigned his final appointment as brigadier-general in the California National Guard. His reason for leaving the First Brigade was "on account of continued severe attacks of neuralgia in the head," a condition not very well understood at the time. Perhaps the bedside champagne kept the pain at bay.[76]

Benjamin D. Wilson (on porch) and family with son-in-law James de Barth Shorb, about 1877. Both Shorb and Wilson were business partners with Phineas Banning. Courtesy of the Seaver Center for Western History Research, Natural History Museum of Los Angeles County.

In July 1883, Phineas set off north to the mineral resort of Bartlett Springs for some "rest and health renewal." He stopped in San Francisco to meet his friend James de Barth Shorb to discuss his plan to purchase and develop Santa Catalina Island, and at the same time perhaps to speak with trustees of the Lick Trust, which owned the island. While in San Francisco, however, Banning stepped off of a cable car and was "knocked down and run over by a passing express wagon." He had to stay in the city to recover from the accident because, as he wrote to Shorb, it was impossible for him "to stand or ride in my bruised condition." He canceled his stay at the resort, and several days later he was back in Wilmington and resuming his normally busy schedule, including a trip to Santa Catalina Island in early August. The pace must have been exhausting, as his liver and kidney ailments were no doubt exacerbated by the accident. During these years, as Harris Newmark recalled, Banning remained at home much of the time and sent a locomotive to Los Angeles to fetch his physician, Dr. Joseph Kurtz, whenever he needed him.[77]

In 1884 Banning decided to seek help for his condition further afield. After transferring his business to his two new companies, the Wilmington Transportation Company and the Wilmington Development Company, and giving power of attorney to his son William, he departed for a long trip east for medical treatment and to visit his hometown in Wilmington, Delaware, as well as Philadelphia, New York, and his brother's home in St. Paul, Minnesota. He spent time in Hot Springs, Arkansas, and then White Sulphur Springs, West Virginia, where the mineral waters were said to cure a wide assortment of maladies that nineteenth-century medicine could not. After various treatments he wrote to his son Hancock that he was "getting better every day." Visiting the sites of his boyhood and William's family probably had a curative effect on his mind as well. After his return he planned to visit the Bartlett Springs resort closer to home in Northern California.[78]

Phineas arrived home still sick after this trip of several months. In late November he journeyed to San Francisco to visit a homeopathic physician recommended to him by a friend. As his son Joseph related to his uncle William Lowber Banning, Phineas improved while in San Francisco, then caught a cold and a severe chill. He recovered enough to come home for Christmas, and was even able to spend time in his San Pedro office conducting business for a while, but decided on more treatment. Accompanied by his wife Mary and children Joseph and Lucy, he returned to San Francisco to see his medical specialist in mid-January of 1885. He caught another cold on the very night of his arrival, however, and never recovered, although he kept his spirits high and joked with his doctors. On March 8 he died in his room in the Occidental Hotel.[79]

On the following day a Southern Pacific train carried Banning's body to Los Angeles. He then took his last ride to Wilmington on the tracks of the old Los Angeles and San Pedro Railroad that he had helped create. On March 12 Wilmington closed its businesses as its residents and hundreds of others came from miles away to participate in his funeral. A procession of mourners "half made up of foot-passengers walking four abreast, was a mile in length." The twenty-four pall bearers included David Alexander, Eldridge E. Hewitt, A. A. Polhamus, E. F. Spence, George Hinds, John M. Griffith, and other prominent citizens of Wilmington and Los Angeles, many of them former business associates and employees of Banning & Company. The service was conducted at the Banning residence, and Phineas was buried in the Banning section of nearby Wilmington Cemetery.[80]

Phineas Banning has been frequently described as the stereotypical ambitious, energetic, self-made American man of the nineteenth century. He has been credited with dominating the stage and freight system in Southern California, with almost single-handedly building a railroad and the Los Angeles harbor, with helping to save the region for the Union during the Civil War, and a host of other altruistic accomplishments. This version of his legacy was shaped by the reminiscences of those who loved or at least admired him, and has been carried on and embellished by those who accepted that perspective.

The voices of Banning's critics are rarely heard today, although they were certainly loud while he was alive. Opposition newspapers complained of his politics, his monopoly at the harbor and close relationship to the Southern Pacific Railroad, and his seemingly unending new ventures, all calculated to make money at others' expense. But even these critics mingled praise with their accusations. Gen. James F. Rusling, who castigated Banning in his 1867 report on Drum Barracks, nonetheless referred to him in a later book as "A man of large and liberal ideas, with great native force of character and power of endurance." A newspaper that occasionally opposed him (depending on its editor) admitted in 1879, "It is difficult to say just how much this section [region] has been indebted to him. Few men who have made California their homes have shown the dauntless and all conquering energy of the wheel-horse of Wilmington." After Banning's death the same paper eulogized him as a hero of the region:

> He saw in the distance the coming greatness of Southern California, and worked wisely to hasten the day of its coronation... He was the embodiment of good humor, a felicitous public speaker and tireless in his labors for promoting public welfare... Like the rest of us he had his faults. He was apt at times to be preemptory and domineering, but his heart was always in the right place.

Even though they attacked him on occasions, these and other critics found qualities in him that they admired.[81]

Phineas Banning in his
later years, about 1881.
Courtesy of the Banning
Residence Museum.

The true character of Phineas Banning may not have reached the heights implied by the adulation of his gushing admirers, but still rose well above the harsh condemnation of his most ardent detractors. He was certainly the "active, energetic, irrepressible Phineas Banning," jumping from one venture to another while holding all together. He was a prime example of the nineteenth-century entrepreneurs in Southern California who, as Steven Erie has observed, built the original growth machine before the boom of the 1880s. These elite commercial leaders shaped the economy of the region through private enterprise, rabid boosterism, a prickly partnership with the region's largest corporation, the Southern Pacific Railroad, and public resources in the form of city, county, state, and federal subsidies for major infrastructure. Banning was a key member of this group, which dominated regional development into the early twentieth century and whose vision of the region affects us still.[82]

Phineas Banning started with nothing in Southern California and built an empire with hard work and with the help of many individuals and the government at key moments. He was a man of huge appetites who loved his family and friends, while always keeping a shrewd eye on the next opportunity. His contributions to Southern California development, to the crude transportation system he helped to mold into a road and rail network, to a harbor that would eventually become one of the world's busiest, and to community institutions in the region cannot be doubted. He was out to seize opportunities and make money for himself, but his quest for wealth also resulted in major contributions to the development of Southern California at critical junctures. With his death in 1885 it would be time for others to assume his mantle in the rise of Southern California. And it would be an opportunity for his children to take over his business and show what they had learned from him.

PART 3

THE BANNING BROTHERS AND SISTERS

THE SONS TAKE OVER

P hineas Banning died a wealthy man. After more than three decades of working hard to amass property (and losing some of it in
unsuccessful ventures), he left a large estate to his family. With his
departure, however, there was no one to stop his second wife and her
three stepsons from acting on their mutual animosity. The conflict
between Mary Elizabeth Hollister Banning and the boys delayed the
settlement of the estate and set the stage for future infighting.

William, Joseph, and Hancock disliked Mary from the start. After
their mother, Rebecca, died in 1868, the boys found it hard to accept this
young substitute. Phineas forced them to obey and be civil to Mary. She
showered attention on her two daughters, letting Phineas manage the
boys. His death removed the peacemaker in the family and set mother
and stepsons against each other. One month after Phineas's death, both
Mary and Hancock participated in the same Easter celebration at the
Episcopal Church in Wilmington, but that would be the last such public
show of unity. Soon the boys avoided her at all costs, referred to her as "a
very cruel person," and impressed this view on their children. Hancock
Banning's oldest son, Hancock Jr., recalled that he was never allowed "to
have anything to do with her" and never encountered his grandmother
until he was about twenty years old. They met accidentally when Mary
came to visit her daughter, who was staying at his parents' home while they
were out of town. Hancock Jr. had climbed out of a bathtub and was
wandering the house in a pair of wet "BVD drawers" when he and Mary
were introduced. He later quipped: "I haven't seen the old bag since."[1]

Six months after Phineas died, Mary arranged to memorialize him
with a stained-glass window in the chancel of St. John's Episcopal
Church in Wilmington. By that time the Southern Pacific Railroad
officials who had worked so closely with Phineas for over twenty years
had told her that it was not in their interest "to have a lady" heading the

Banning business at the harbor. Although she was not happy with how William and Joseph were running the companies Phineas left behind, she knew she could not buck the railroad; she soon sold her interest to the two. By early 1886, Joseph wrote his uncle that she "expressed a desire to have nothing more to do with us boys—we are consequently not on speaking terms." Mary and her two girls, Mary Hollister and Lucy Tichenor Banning, moved to Los Angeles and then to Oakland, where the girls were privately schooled. The boys moved to the Long Beach Hotel, and the Wilmington mansion stood virtually empty. The heirs arranged through a lawyer to remove family heirlooms from their one-time home when the other parties were not present, so as not to start an argument.[2]

In the meantime Mary E. H. Banning initiated probate proceedings to settle Phineas's will. The document specified that she would receive one-half of the property and that the five living children would be entitled to one-tenth each. Because of the vast amount of real estate involved, no fewer than three referees were appointed to assess the value of all the parcels. Progress on such a complicated case was slow, and the boys worried that Mary would try to take the best property for herself. In July 1887, they filed suit to partition the real estate, specifically over 4,000 acres in Newport Beach that Mary had received as part of her inheritance from her father. Mary responded with a suit arguing that she alone owned that property. When it came time for the trial a year later, Mary refuted the boys' claim that she had given them 1,000 acres of that land in 1883, but she nonetheless lost the suit. She appealed the decision to the California State Supreme Court in 1889, and lost again. In 1890 the Newport Beach property was finally divided among Mary and the three boys, but not the two girls, both minors who would eventually share their mother's estate after she died. The boys complained for years that their stepmother had secured the best farmland, while they ended up with "saltflats and deadpan." Time, and luck, would heal that wound when oil was later found on the portion allotted to the boys. The division of the rest of the property after the final decree was approved in 1891 was less contentious, although Mary had disagreements with her lawyers. Halfway through the proceedings she had to fire her first lawyer, John D. Bicknell, because he was also representing her stepsons and their primary business partner, the Southern Pacific Railroad. Months later she would instruct her new lawyer to bring in Alfred B. Chapman, with whom she and Phineas had done business in the past, because she did not "wish him to be on the other side."[3]

The Passing of William Lowber Banning

Before we usher Phineas's children and their ventures onstage, a member of the former generation must take his bow. William Lowber Banning, whose career in Minnesota closely paralleled his brother's in Southern California, was bringing his story to a close, though he survived Phineas by a few years. Like Phineas in many ways, William also had strong personal ties to his brother's family, and at first it seemed that he might come to take Phineas's place as a father figure to his boys.

The Banning brothers had hoped that William and his family would move to Wilmington, and had even offered their uncle the Banning mansion as a lure. But he had declined their offer during a visit in 1887, preferring to live out his life in St. Paul, also the home of his sister and her husband, who had followed him there in the 1850s. There he was nearer his oldest daughter, Ellen Barrows Banning, who had married in 1884 and now lived in Lowell, Massachusetts. Her husband, Frederick Ayer, was a prominent textile manufacturer and the wealthiest man in Lowell when he proposed to Ellen in St. Paul. A descendant of a family from the same Wiltshire County in England as that of the Bannings, Ayer was sixty-two when he wed his second wife, who was then thirty-one, and the two had three children of their own.[4]

So William returned to Minnesota after his 1887 visit to Wilmington. Within a few years, he had become enfeebled by age, however, and in the winter of 1892 he again visited Southern California, this time in hopes of improving his health. There he stayed at the Banning mansion with the family of Joseph Brent Banning. In November of the following year, back in St. Paul, he suffered a stroke. He died soon after and was buried in Oakland Cemetery. His obituary in the *St. Paul Pioneer Press* recounted his accomplishments, as did a tribute in the *Los Angeles Times*, composed by a writer who had interviewed him the year before.[5]

William's contributions to the development of St. Paul and Minnesota are still remembered in the state. Northeast of St. Paul at White Bear Lake, a Banning Avenue extends for several blocks. But William Banning's primary monument in Minnesota is Banning State Park. Established in 1963 by the Minnesota state legislature, the park of over 5,000 acres along the Kettle River had been the site of a town named Banning and its nearby sandstone quarries. Almost 500 stonecutters worked at the site in the 1880s, carving stone for buildings such as the Minneapolis Courthouse. The town's postmaster, Martin Ring, named it for Banning, the former president of the railroad that connected the city to St. Paul and Duluth. The trend away from stone as a building material after 1900 led to the demise of the quarry and that, combined with frequent fires, led to the rapid decline of Banning, Minnesota, leaving it a virtual ghost town by 1912. The absence of urban development, however, helped to revitalize and conserve the natural landscape, and today, along with the ruins of the town and the quarry, the park boasts an abundance of flora and fauna, as well as campgrounds and hiking trails. The park is a fitting memorial to William Lowber Banning and his many gifts to his adopted home.[6]

Phineas Banning's Sons

In the spring of 1887, William Lowber Banning had brought his family out to Wilmington to visit the children of his late brother, Phineas. While there, he met John D. Bicknell, his nephews' lawyer, and the two had long discussions on the front porch of the Banning mansion. In letters they exchanged the following year, they assessed the characters of the three Banning boys, who were then taking over their father's business. Bicknell believed that the eldest, William, or "Captain," was "a remarkable businessman for his age." Joseph, the middle son, "attended to business and is doing well in every respect," although his health was a concern: an injury had left him partially lame, and it was well known that Banning boys played "rough sports." The youngest, Hancock, had also been diligent in business and had a new yacht that he would race in San Diego on July 4. All three of them had been looking to him for fatherly advice since Phineas died, Bicknell said, and all three were doing well.[7]

In his response to Bicknell's letter, William Lowber agreed with Bicknell's characterizations and offered some of his own. Hancock displayed a "winning smile and jolly laugh that cannot be resisted." Joseph had a "warm heart and level head" and "wise conservatism trying to hold the Capt. back, who needs that check perhaps, not more however, than Joe requires the fervid and forward impulses of the Capt. to urge him onward." All three of them "represent what is good in human nature."[8]

"Captain" William Sanford Banning, the "remarkable businessman for his age," would take the reins to serve as patriarch of the next generation. Named president of the Wilmington Transportation Company after Phineas's death, he led the various Banning companies established over the next three decades. He also followed his father in becoming an expert stagecoach driver and was nationally known for preserving this skill in the automobile age. William led the fight with stepmother Mary to protect the boys' inheritance and would become the guardian of the entire family in the years to come. He remained a bachelor; family

William Sanford
Banning, about 1880.
Courtesy of the
Huntington Library.

tradition holds that there was only one love in his entire life—his cousin
Katharine—who married one of his brothers. He often lived with his
brothers' families, however, so he was not isolated from family life. He
shared a home for ten years after March 1897 with Hancock's family, and
then joined Joseph's; he also lived on his own at times, in a large mansion
in Los Angeles and on a ranch in eastern Los Angeles County. He spent
most of his career directing the Banning companies, but found time to
devote to his interests in stagecoach driving, boating, and camping. He
belonged to several elite men's clubs, horse racing associations, and
gun clubs. On civic occasions, he was often charged with providing a coach
for dignitaries, including, in 1891, the president of the United States.

Joseph, or "Judge," was three years younger than William. Joseph had
studied law in the office of his parents' attorneys, Glassell, Smith &
Patton, in 1881 but decided to pursue a business career instead. After his
father's death, Joseph served as vice president and treasurer of two
Banning companies—those responsible for shipping, stevedoring,
ballasting, lightering, and other services at the harbor. He also directed

William S. Banning with friends and relatives in their elaborate costumes at
the 1895 La Fiesta de Los Angeles Parade. Courtesy of the Huntington Library.

the Banning businesses concerned with agriculture, sheep, grain, and
lumber. Joseph became an accomplished amateur photographer and took
a number of photographs of the family and of the harbor region from
about 1880 to the early 1900s, documenting the expansion of the port. He
also attempted to breed dogs for a time in the 1890s. By 1888 he joined
the prestigious California Club in Los Angeles, an elite men's organization of which all three brothers became members.[9]

In March 1887, when William Lowber Banning brought his family
from St. Paul to visit their California cousins, both Joseph and William
immediately fell in love with Katharine Stewart Banning, their uncle's
youngest daughter. Joseph emerged as the victor in the quest for their
first cousin's hand, and in April 1888 he and Katharine were married in
her parents' home in St. Paul. Joseph's brothers gave the couple the
Banning mansion in Wilmington, which the boys had inherited, as
their wedding present. Joseph refused to accept it as a gift, but he and
Katharine agreed to move in, and it was in this home that their first two
children were born—Joseph Brent Banning Jr. in 1889 and Katharine Mary,
or "Kash," in 1890. After several years in Wilmington, however, Katharine
yearned for surroundings more akin to the affluent St. Paul neighborhood
where she had grown up. So in 1894 she and Joseph decided to move to

Joseph Brent Banning, about 1887.
Courtesy of the Huntington Library.

Katharine Stewart Banning in 1884.
Courtesy of the Huntington Library.

Los Angeles, where they built a substantial home on a lot given to Joseph
in his childhood by Joseph Lancaster Brent, friend of his father and
Joseph's namesake. The family moved into their new two-story residence
on the corner of Tenth and Westlake Avenue in April 1895, and their
second son, William Phineas Banning, was born four years later.[10]

Although William Lowber Banning could not bring himself to leave
Minnesota, after his death his widow, Mary Alicia, and daughter May
Alice moved to Southern California to live with Mary's daughter Katharine and Joseph Brent in the Westlake home. They would join the family
for summers on Santa Catalina Island and in frequent social gatherings in
Los Angeles, many of them hosted by Katharine. They also assisted
Katharine in her work for Childrens Hospital in Los Angeles, which would
be established at the start of the new century. Katharine was a founding
member and an original director and was active in raising funds, re-
cruiting volunteers to donate and sew clothing for the children and to
sell. Apparently inheriting her father's business sense, she "demonstrated
considerable talent at devising engaging ways to raise money" and enticed
other civic-minded women in the city to join her cause. It was Katharine
who, in 1901, created the forerunner of the doll fairs that served as the
hospital's major fundraising events for over seventy years.[11]

Joseph and Katharine's house on Westlake Avenue about 1895. Courtesy of the Huntington Library.

The youngest son of Phineas Banning, Hancock was nineteen when his father died in 1885. Soon after that he moved to Pasadena, where he lived with his friend William Staats. While living at "The Shanty," as it was known, Hancock often practiced the cornet accompanied by Staats on the violin and his sister May Staats on the piano. In later years Hancock would play at benefits in Los Angeles and with the Santa Catalina Island Marine Band during the summer seasons and on a tour of California in 1895.[12]

After taking a course in a local business college, Hancock decided to make his fortune in Pasadena. He founded the Pasadena Transfer and Fuel Company, establishing a coal yard on Los Robles Avenue and building a three-story brick building on Fair Oaks Avenue at Colorado Boulevard. There he sold the coal and kept animals for transport. His horses were notoriously lively. "Anyone traveling by No. 6 South Fair Oaks Avenue was living dangerously for that was the address of the Pasadena Transfer Company and Banning's team of 'fiery blacks' were always ready to run away at the slightest provocation," wrote early Pasadena resident Henry Markham. The young Hancock was the chief organizer of the local Salvation Army unit and was still listed as living and working in Pasadena in the 1890 city directory. That would not last much longer, however, as he was about to be married and join his brothers in the family business.[13]

On November 12, 1890, Hancock married Anne Ophelia Smith, daughter of George Hugh Smith and Susan Glassell Patton. Given the closely interwoven familial network that bound the Los Angeles elite at the time, their meeting seems to have been foreordained. Anne's father was an attorney for the Banning brothers in their suit against their mother. And Susan Glassell Patton also had several connections to the Bannings. Her brother, attorney Andrew Glassell, had sold the Banning Ranch to Phineas and Mary E. H. Banning in the 1870s and was the first president of the Los Angeles Bar Association, serving from 1878 to 1880. Her first husband, George Smith Patton, had served as a Confederate officer and was killed in the Battle of Winchester in 1864. Their eldest son, also called George Smith Patton, married Ruth Wilson, the daughter of Benjamin D. Wilson, Phineas Banning's business partner and friend. The Wilsons and the Bannings had been inseparable since the 1850s, and Ruth Wilson's 1884 marriage brought the younger George S. Patton into the circle. He became a lawyer in the firm of Glassell, Smith & Patton (which included his stepfather and his uncle), was elected county district attorney in 1884, and would father George S. Patton Jr., the famous World War II general. Hancock's brother Joseph had also apprenticed in the office of Glassell, Smith & Patton in the early 1880s, and might have met his brother's future bride then. Any of these connections could have been responsible for bringing Hancock and Anne together (see Banning Family Connections chart, appendix D).[14]

After the Civil War and the death of her first husband, Anne's mother, Susan Glassell Patton, had brought her four children to Los Angeles in 1867. They lived at first with Susan's brother, Andrew Glassell, who until then resided in San Francisco. Susan ran a private school for girls for a few years. In 1870 she married her late husband's first cousin, Col. George Hugh Smith, another Confederate Army officer who had wooed her once before, in Virginia in the 1850s. They had two children, Anne and Eltinge, before Susan died of breast cancer in 1883. Born in Los Angeles in 1871, Anne Ophelia Smith was named after her grandmother on her father's side. Anne was educated in private schools in Virginia, and returned home to marry Hancock at St. Paul's Episcopal Church, a few months before her twentieth birthday.[15]

As Hancock would later note, Anne, just like his mother, Rebecca

Hancock Banning, about 1890.
Courtesy of the Huntington Library.

Anne Ophelia Smith about the time
of her marriage in 1890. Courtesy of
the Banning Residence Museum.

Sanford, was proud of her Southern family and their attachment to the
Confederacy during the War Between the States (as her family pointedly
called it). Her father and her mother's first husband had both been
officers in the Confederate Army, and her uncle, William Thornton
Glassell, was the Confederate commander of a torpedo boat, the first to
seriously damage a major warship. The incident occurred on October 5,
1863, in Charleston harbor, when Glassell's almost completely submerged
vessel rammed a torpedo into the USS *New Constitution*, seriously
damaging it and sending Union sailors into the water. Unfortunately for
Glassell, the explosion also disabled his engine, and he was captured and
held in a military prison. After his release and the end of the war he
moved to Los Angeles to join his brother Andrew working in real estate
development and then ranching in Santa Cruz until his death from
tuberculosis in 1879.[16]

The Glassells, Pattons, and Smiths, in short, were fiercely committed
to the Southern cause, and the South's defeat greatly affected them. The
Smith home became a gathering place in Los Angeles for the postwar

influx of Southerners traumatized by the horrors of warfare and needing a sympathetic ear. As a child Anne was noticeably moved by their reminiscences, and she formed the "Southern Secret Society" for local children whose parents had suffered during the war. The members would meet in the Smith barn loft to talk about what the war meant to their families and share their pride in their parents' defense of the "Lost Cause."[17]

Like her sister-in-law, Katharine Stewart Banning, Anne was proud of her lineage, and she not only celebrated her roots in the South but also took pains to uncover further illustrious ancestors. With the help of a genealogist, she traced her ancestors back from prominent American families in the East through English nobility to King Edward III and Alfred the Great. According to the rather inventive compiler of the list, Anne could claim as relations William the Conqueror, Charlemagne, El Cid, Constantine, Alexander the Great, King Solomon, King David and last, but certainly not least, Lady Godiva. Anne would have no trouble joining the Colonial Dames of America.[18]

After their wedding Hancock and Anne lived in her father's house on Fort Hill, only one block away from Hancock's stepmother, Mary, and his two sisters. Over the next few years their three children were born there: Hancock Jr. in 1892, Eleanor Anne in 1893, and George Hugh in 1895. Childbirth and Hancock's devotion to his businesses took their toll on Anne in the 1890s; plagued by headaches and backaches, she often sought relief in travel and at sanitariums in Northern California and Baltimore, Maryland. She also suffered from anemia and, probably, stress, exacerbated no doubt by Hancock's frequent insistence that she control her lavish spending habits while they tried to build their fortune. Despite the tensions of their early married life and her frail health, Anne and Hancock survived the 1893 depression and other calamities to live happily, and luxuriously, thereafter.[19]

Whether living with Anne's father and family made their burdens lighter or heavier is uncertain. George H. Smith, a prominent lawyer in Los Angeles, had helped to reestablish the county bar association in 1888, and in 1898 he was a founding trustee of the University of Southern California Law School, where he would sometimes teach. He served as California Supreme Court Commissioner from 1899 to 1904 and as a justice on the State Court of Appeal for the Second District from 1905 to 1907. He was also a state senator from Los Angeles from 1877 to 1888. At the same time his "writings on jurisprudence gained him considerable reputation in the legal profession in the United States and England." These included his treatises *Right and Law* (1877), *Theory of the State* (1895), and

Hancock and Anne's house on Fort Hill. Courtesy of the Seaver Center for Western History Research, Natural History Museum of Los Angeles County.

Logic, or the Analysis of Explicit Reasoning (1901). As one historian has noted, Smith was an intellectual who "wrote in a flowing if somewhat archaic style, using an impressive vocabulary, but never with pretension and always with clarity." Living with Hancock and Anne, in short, was one of the most important attorneys and legal minds in the city and the state. The esteemed jurist was not always at his books, however. He enjoyed making extended late-night rounds of some of the city's finest saloons, forcing a worried Hancock to search for him during Anne's absences in the 1890s.[20]

Also living with Hancock, Anne, and her father on Fort Hill during the 1890s was Hancock's older bachelor brother, William, and Anne's half sister, Susie Patton. Susie had come to Los Angeles with her mother and the rest of the family in 1867, and she and Anne remained close throughout their lives. Susie later married Dr. W. Lemoyne Wills and had left the Banning household by 1904. Besides Susie Patton, George H. Smith, and William, the Bannings lived with four servants by 1900, evidence that they were doing well at the turn of the new century.[21]

In the 1890s Anne entertained Angelenos and others at the Banning home on Fort Hill and in a summer home on Santa Catalina Island. Hancock joined a number of business and civic associations, such as the

George H. Smith with two of his grandchildren, 1902. Courtesy of the Huntington Library.

Chamber of Commerce, apparently as a family representative. As a member of the chamber's executive committee for many years, he played a key role in the single most important commercial and civic organization in the region, one that contributed greatly to the growth and prosperity of Southern California. Hancock was especially active in planning several La Fiesta parades in the 1890s, major celebrations of Los Angeles's romanticized past, and festivities like those surrounding the visit of President William McKinley in 1901. He also joined elite men's clubs, such as the California Club (by 1888) and the Jonathan Club, formerly a young men's Republican club but transformed in 1895 into a men's social club that counted Hancock among its founding members. He spent much of his free time on the water. Like his older brother William, Hancock loved ships and sailing. He earned a mariner's license in 1886 and frequently took friends on pleasure cruises and raced his yacht *La Paloma* in contests off the California coast. Drawing only three feet of water, the *La Paloma* was very fast, but also very "touchy," and his brothers referred to it as "Hancock's Coffin."[22]

In the years after their father's death and before the turn of the century, the Banning brothers were a tightly knit trio. The three banded together against their stepmother in order to ensure what they saw as their rightful inheritance. Together they also sued others who contested their claims to land they believed their father had owned. After his few years in Pasadena, Hancock would join his two brothers in the family business at the harbor. During the late 1880s, before their inheritances came through, they pooled their resources to purchase land throughout the Los Angeles area.[23]

Their largest joint purchase of the decade, in 1888, was an 8,000-acre ranch straddling the border of Los Angeles and Ventura counties, just southwest of present-day Thousand Oaks. The ranch was first a business investment managed by Joseph, providing a source of income from the sale of beef cattle, pigs, and agricultural crops—hay, alfalfa, and corn. But it also became a recreational destination where the family and their friends often camped. William Banning frequently drove groups of family members and friends in a stagecoach from Wilmington to Los Angeles to the Conejo Ranch for weekend stays in the early 1890s. A Banning cousin from Minnesota printed a bound memorial of a two-week vacation trip to the ranch from Wilmington in 1889, complete with drawings of the vehicles and guests and poetry written by the participants. The Bannings held the Conejo Ranch until 1896, when they sold it to F. W. Matthiesson of Pasadena, using the proceeds for other ventures.[24]

In 1892, the brothers together bought Santa Catalina Island, a purchase that would shape the family and its business for years to come. They decided during the ensuing 1893 depression that in order to keep and develop the resort, they would have to devote all of their resources to the island and the harbor. The three brothers decided to pool all of the company assets and some personal property in order to provide the capital they needed. This included their homes, and businesses they owned individually, such as Hancock's coal business. The decision certainly demonstrated their fraternal trust, but would also contribute to dissension: Hancock and Anne immediately clashed over the constraints this decision put on her spending, and the brothers later argued over how to manage the arrangement and whether each was contributing his fair share.[25]

Their need for capital also led to fierce fights with others as they sought to protect their assets. In 1891 the Banning brothers and the Southern Pacific Railroad were sued by the daughters of Manuel Dominguez, who had sold parts of his Rancho San Pedro land to Phineas Banning, who had in turn sold some of it to the Southern Pacific. Both Dominguez and Banning died in 1885, and in the following year the executors for the Dominguez estate claimed that Mormon Island in the

Banning excursion group at the Conejo Ranch, about 1889. Courtesy of the Huntington Library.

Wilmington estuary still belonged to the Dominguez estate, as shown by the original land grant confirmation. The Dominguez daughters then set about selling the property, which the Southern Pacific had begun developing in 1890, to the Los Angeles Terminal Railway to serve as part of its entrance to the harbor. Meanwhile, the Superior Court ruled against their claim; they appealed the case to the California State Supreme Court, which initially ruled for the Dominguez estate, but reversed itself after another hearing. Finally the Los Angeles Terminal Railway, which had by then bought the island, appealed to the U.S. Supreme Court. John D. Bicknell and U.S. Senator Stephen M. White argued for the Bannings, and in May 1897 the federal court affirmed the state court ruling. William Banning expressed the Bannings' gratitude to Senator White, saying that even "should it have gone against us, we would have felt that everything possible had been done." The Bannings would retain possession of Mormon Island for another five decades.[26]

If the three Banning brothers were inseparable in these years, their wives, Katharine Stewart Banning and Anne Banning, seemed to share in their fellow feeling. Only a few years apart in age, their relationship was initially amiable. Anne and her children stayed at the St. Paul home of William Lowber Banning, Katharine's father, for several months in late 1893, just before he died, and all seemed to enjoy the visit. Katharine and

Anne also hosted social gatherings together in their first decade as sisters-in-law. The friendliness of these early years contrasts sharply with their interactions in the years after 1900. The two wives were increasingly at odds as their husbands intensified a rivalry that would split the family in several directions. Both women would develop into very strong-willed matriarchs, ironically not unlike the brothers' step-mother, whom they so detested.[27]

Banning Daughters

Katharine's and Anne's strength of purpose and firmness of character formed a striking contrast with the Banning girls, whose privileged upbringing seemed at times to have been more of a curse than a blessing. The oldest of the two daughters, Mary Hollister Banning, was fourteen years old when her father died. She spent her school years in Oakland, where she attended a private boarding school and Ellis Villa College in the late 1880s. She lived with her mother and sister in Los Angeles after her schooling was completed. Wealthy from her share of the Banning estate, Mary was an intelligent young woman who participated in social events with her mother in 1890s Los Angeles and was said to have in-spired an intense rivalry between two suitors. In November 1897 she made her choice, marrying Wilt Wakeman Norris, a mining engineer from a wealthy family in New York. The two lived in Los Angeles for a while, and then moved to Mexico City at the turn of the century. But Norris would die just seven years after they wed, while visiting New York in 1905. After burying her husband in Los Angeles, Mary continued her cosmopolitan life there, and later in New York City, Paris, France, and finally in Los Angeles again. She occasionally stayed at Hancock's West Adams home, relying on him for help with her investments, and she was a favorite aunt of many nieces and nephews.[28]

Whereas Mary seemed relatively well adjusted, her younger sister, Lucy Tichenor Banning, definitely was not. Lucy had just turned nine when Phineas died, and she spent the rest of her life apparently searching for a father figure. Chronically insecure, despite being considered one of the most beautiful women in the Golden State, she abandoned four husbands for paramours. "Her beauty was her ruin," recalled Katharine S. Banning after Lucy died, and although her brothers tried to help her, they could not save her from herself and her hunger for love. Katharine concluded, "She injured only those who loved her most!"[29]

Lucy left Wilmington with her mother and older sister and divided her time between her mother's home in Los Angeles and the Field

Mary Hollister (left) and
Lucy Tichenor Banning,
about 1890. Courtesy of
the Huntington Library.

Seminary in Oakland. Her oldest brother, William, predicted she would soon abandon boarding school, but she stayed long enough to gain a basic understanding of French and music, and other attributes necessary to a girl of her social standing. She was much more interested in men than in her studies. In December 1893, at the age of seventeen, she traveled to San Francisco, where she rendezvoused with John Bradbury, the son of a Los Angeles mining millionaire, who was ostensibly on a business trip. Joined by several of her friends, she and Bradbury crossed the bay to Oakland for a quiet wedding, and returned to the Palace Hotel in San Francisco, where they telegraphed the news to their parents. The Bannings were not united in their approval. Writing to Anne, Hancock mused, "I wonder how long they will stay together," and blamed his stepmother's lack of common sense and decency for Lucy's plight. William Banning's salutation in an 1894 letter to Lucy's husband, "Dear Johnny," might have reflected the family's estimation of John Bradbury's immaturity.[30]

Lucy and her husband made their home in Los Angeles in the Bradbury mansion atop Bunker Hill, an ornate Victorian residence designed by the noted San Francisco architect Joseph Cather Newsom. There the couple joined Bradbury's mother, Simona, who presided over numerous social events in the city. Lucy doubtless attended many of these, and was soon celebrated in that circle for her beauty; readers of a social magazine, the *Capital*, voted her the most beautiful woman in the city in 1895.[31]

Marital bliss was fleeting for Lucy and John Bradbury. In 1897 she met H. Russell Ward, "who is English, bald-headed, middle-aged and married," according to a reporter, and with his "wiles and fascinations," he swept her off her feet. The two left Los Angeles in early July for San Francisco, where they were greeted by the press as "elopers," although both were already married to others. San Francisco newspapers reported their arrival as a special event and described the two going about their business, both looking over their shoulders. Their apprehension was sensible, for on the next day Lucy and Ward were arrested for adultery and soon "rubbed shoulders with the outcasts and drunkards who the regular Saturday roundup takes in droves to the City Prison." The two denied the charges and soon were out on bail and quarrelling. At first Lucy agreed to testify against Ward if the charges against her were dropped, but she then decided to face the charges. The case was finally dropped when her mother arrived and convinced her to repent. Amid rumors that they had been paid off, the Society for the Prevention of Vice agreed that the charges against Lucy should be dismissed and that Ward alone should be tried. She promised that "she will have nothing more to do with 'that scoundrel, Ward,' the polo-player who made her the victim of his hypnotic wiles." With that public vow, she and her mother headed to Chicago to meet her husband, who had agreed to forgive her infidelity.[32]

Lucy's mother, Mary, made sure that her daughter and the millionaire reconciled, whether or not it was heartfelt. According to a reporter, she "told them they had acted like naughty little children long enough. The husband was generous enough not to demand a weeping repentance, and the wife refrained from vowing eternal faithfulness. Then all three had a nice little lunch together." After the repast Mary arranged to head home to Los Angeles and the Bradburys went shopping for a contemplated trip to Europe. All were satisfied, at least for a while. That is, all except for the unfortunate Mr. Ward, who later died after a fall from a train; whether this was a suicide or an accident is unknown.[33]

In the midst of this episode Lucy had written to her brothers in Southern California, begging their forgiveness for her actions. She asked for their sympathy and showered praise on her two sisters-in-law, Anne and Katharine, who should, she said, be the true role models for their daughters. Hancock wrote to a family friend, the operator of the Occidental Hotel, where Lucy was staying (and in which Phineas Banning had died in 1885), asking him to present a proposal to her and her mother. Hoping to help Lucy "remedy the mistakes of the past" and "live a different life," Hancock offered to move his family and his brother William to the capacious Wilmington mansion, at a great cost to himself. Lucy could then join them for a year, learning from their example "to mend her ways." Suggesting that Lucy's upbringing was responsible for her failings, he noted, "Her sister Mary is erratic and excitable" as well, and that her sister's and "her mother's idea of propriety are not in harmony with those of my family." Whether Lucy ever heard the proposal is unknown. If so, she did not accept the offer.[34]

Lucy's reconciliation with her husband would not endure. The two moved to Mexico for a few years after the 1897 split, returning to Los Angeles and the Bradbury mansion in 1901. Rumors of their marital problems were rife that year, and in December John Bradbury admitted to the press that Lucy had fled to San Francisco again, followed by her mother. Over the next year the relationship worsened, and in December 1902 Lucy was quietly divorced from her husband on the grounds of nonsupport. The *Times* story about the split recalled Lucy in her youth as "airy, headstrong, little Lucy Banning," who "was determined to have her own way" and usually did. Society had responded to her antics since then by abusing her, "its most delicious recreation." Her husband, the paper concluded, certainly had not been "a great success as a moral ballast."[35]

Lucy Banning would continue to build her reputation as a thoroughly spoiled, "man crazy" young woman. Less than two months after her divorce was final, she was rumored to be engaged to Charles Hastings, a wealthy young man from Pasadena. Seven months later she was said to be making plans to wed another wealthy member of California society. A year and a half later she was reported to be engaged to Hastings again. None of these predictions bore fruit, although Lucy would marry again, in 1906. This time it was to Mace Greenleaf, the leading man at the Burbank Theater. A *Times* story observed, "The Burbank's patrons have noted for some time that since Greenleaf's appearance Mrs. Bradbury and her mother never missed a performance," and that the actor and Lucy had eyes for no one else. The fact that Greenleaf was playing Romeo might have had something to do with Lucy's infatuation. Less than a year later the two were said to be planning a vaudeville act in which they would star. Like her first marriage and reported engagements, however, this theatrical union would not last long. Lucy's ill-considered decisions and promiscuity would be a recurring trial for the Banning family in the decades to come.[36]

Stepmother Mary

The stepmother of the Banning brothers, Mary Elizabeth Hollister Banning, was almost forty when Phineas Banning left her a widow in 1885. Immediately at loggerheads with her stepsons, she had fought them throughout the long probate process, changing her legal representation and resorting to lawsuits to enforce her inheritance. Even the arrangements for Phineas's monument at the Wilmington Cemetery had devolved into arguments over who would pay for the fountain's water supply. When probate finally closed in 1891, she was a very wealthy woman. She had already abandoned her home in Wilmington, and even though William Banning had eventually agreed to provide the water for his father's memorial, she decided to move the remains of her husband and their infant daughter Ellen to Rosedale Cemetery in Los Angeles in 1887. From that time she divided her residence between a house on South Main Street and a home on Telegraph Avenue in Oakland, where she could keep an eye on her two daughters and their schooling.[37]

In May 1886 Mary purchased several lots on Fort Hill, between Broadway (then Fort Street) and Hill Street, which included the old Jake Phillipi beer garden. She spent a considerable amount of money to remodel the structure and landscape the grounds, transforming it into a residence fit for entertaining society. Her home was only one block from Hancock's, but the two would never visit each other. Although she was wealthy, she took in boarders at times, and sued at least one for unpaid rent (he responded that he was her guest rather than her tenant). A habitual litigant, Mary lodged other suits against individuals who owed her money and against the city when officials tried to cut a street through her property in 1896. When not managing her real estate and investments, or involved in society functions in Los Angeles women's clubs such as the Friday Morning Club and the local chapter of the Daughters of the American Revolution, Mary spent much of her time traveling in Europe with her pampered daughters.[38]

The Banning Business Continues

The Banning brothers took over their father's business at a time of great opportunity for Los Angeles entrepreneurs involved in trade. With the initial federal improvements to the San Pedro Bay harbor completed, shipping was on the rise, and with it demand for all of the harbor services provided by the Bannings. A second railroad, the Atchison, Topeka and Santa Fe, entered the city in 1885, offering access to more places and promising competition in freight rates, which could lower expenses and therefore the prices of goods shipped. The population boom that followed the new railroad into town expanded the local consumer base, even though the boom abated by 1888. A chamber of commerce was reestablished in 1890 to further promote economic expansion. Manufacturing was still limited to local needs, but would begin to take off in the 1890s, and the local service sector was substantial in comparison with that in other cities of the same size. Although a national depression in 1893 would dampen growth for a time, the business atmosphere would soon turn around and the new century would usher in an economic boom in Los Angeles.[39]

William and Joseph led both of the Banning harbor companies in 1885. William was president and manager and Joseph the vice-president and treasurer of both the Wilmington Transportation Company (WTC) and the Wilmington Development Company (WDC); the WTC managed company vessels and the WDC services to shippers. By early 1889, Hancock joined his two brothers and brought along his coal business, with locations in Pasadena, Los Angeles, and now Wilmington. He also acted as the company's general passenger and freight agent for WTC vessels, and helped Joseph manage the family's Conejo Ranch. In the meantime, William directed overall business affairs for both companies, including securing franchises to build and operate wharves in the harbor.[40]

Other family relatives were also associated with the business. One was the "other" William Lowber Banning, the son of Phineas's eldest brother, John Alford Banning Jr. This William had lived in the harbor area since about 1867, first working for Phineas and later conducting his own business. He had married Adelaida Mellus, the daughter of Francis Mellus, who had become a prominent Los Angeles merchant before California statehood and a partner of David Alexander, who also partnered with Phineas. In 1890 William died in Wilmington at the age of forty-eight and was buried by several fraternal societies.[41]

After 1890, William and Hancock helped Adelaida manage her real estate properties and other business. The three Banning sons also looked after her son, John, while he was going to school in the 1890s. The family ties earned their ongoing concern for John's welfare, but they drew the line when it came to business. When William was consulted about John's application for employment in 1909, he kept his distance by asking a subordinate to reply to the letter but noted that as far as he knew John "is a man of limited ability and not much energy."[42]

The Banning brothers also worked with Adelaida's brother, Frank Mellus, in these years. Mellus was in the general commission business, dealing primarily in agricultural products and wool; he also sold insurance locally and represented a Pittsburgh lock manufacturer. William Banning asked him to act on the brothers' behalf to create a wharf space and a county road in Santa Monica because he feared the company's close connection to the Southern Pacific Railroad would lead to local opposition. In other situations the Bannings employed Mellus in procuring supplies and making arrangements for inspections. Mellus also insured some of the Banning buildings until 1898, when they switched to the company they represented as agents. Despite the end of this business, they remained friendly.[43]

The other officers in the brothers' companies, which sometimes went by the name "Banning Brothers," included several employees who had worked for their father. William G. Halstead, superintendent of the Wilmington Transportation Company until 1894, had worked for Phineas Banning's rival Remi Nadeau in the Cerro Gordo mining region before accepting the job with Phineas in 1883. Andrew Young, the superintending engineer at Wilmington, was an expert marine engineer and had worked for the company since the early 1880s. Although he was nearly let go several times, he stayed with the business for decades and named one of his sons Banning Young. After Joseph moved out of the Banning mansion, Young lived there for about a decade. Edward Mahar, assistant superintendent (and soon to be WTC superintendent), would be elected mayor of San Pedro in 1905 and later created his own company to buy out the Banning harbor business. The other officers included Frank H. Lowe of Pasadena, who was assistant general passenger and freight agent for Hancock's company, and Edwin Stanton, superintendent at Santa Catalina Island, who joined the Bannings after moving to the area from Philadelphia in 1891.[44]

In their relationship with their workers, primarily longshoremen, the Bannings followed what would come to be called the "open shop" approach of the local business establishment, which had united to thwart union organizing and worker militancy. Their father was known for his excellent rapport with his employees, but labor relations on the docks became strained in the 1880s, when the Shipowners' Association fought wage increases for members of the Coast Seamen's Union, which had organized with the help of the San Francisco chapter. The Shipowners' Association virtually locked out union members, and in 1886 the union called a strike in protest. The fallout from the strike hit the Banning operation: in October William and Joseph had to convince their nonunion dockworkers that it was safe to continue to work. William wrote to his sister that the two of them with several employees and three deputy sheriffs "have been standing guard with shot guns" to keep the union men away, in order to protect their workers from retaliation "at their homes this evening." While this incident did not escalate, labor unrest would continue at the waterfront in the 1890s, and the Bannings' business would be affected, like other companies that served shipping interests. William Banning played down the conflicts, informing a Southern Pacific official in 1894 that "we have never had any trouble with any of the Unions" because his men did not belong to unions. In all such situations the Bannings would abide by the demands of local employers, who were increasingly adamant about stopping all labor union advances in Los Angeles.[45]

The Bannings found that the close relationship their father had forged with the Southern Pacific Railroad benefited them enormously. Joseph admitted to his uncle in 1893 that when the brothers were starting out on their own in 1885 they "were inexperienced in business matters and without the R.R. Co. assistance we certainly would not now occupy the position we do in transportation matters." From that time on the Banning brothers' business was inseparable from the railroad. "Our business has been almost exclusively with them," Joseph wrote in another letter, "and it would not be to our advantage to do anything opposed to their interests." This sentiment was echoed by William, who told his uncle in 1893 that "about all we have was acquired through their influence and assistance," and he warned others to refrain from antagonizing railroad officials. As William wrote to a customer in 1897, "It is thought by many people here we are standing in with Southern Pacific Company," and local newspapers like the *Times* were quick to make the cozy relationship public. The Southern Pacific helped the brothers create a monopoly in stevedoring and towing at San Pedro harbor and promised a similar monopoly at the Santa Monica Bay port being built in the early 1890s. After 1900 the railroad and the Bannings would become tied even more closely through their mutual ownership of harbor tidelands and through social connections between the family and railroad executives.[46]

Sometimes, however, the close relationship with the railroad harmed the Bannings' other business. A contract Phineas had made with the Southern Pacific, for example, required that they lease a wharf that belonged to the railroad; this agreement necessitated high freight rates, for which the Bannings took the brunt of abuse from customers. During political fights over the best location for a harbor in the 1890s, the Bannings felt compelled to back the railroad's choice of Santa Monica, even though most of their land was elsewhere. When more harbor improvements began at the turn of the century, the Bannings hoped to again receive the contract for supplying rocks to build the breakwater, but the Southern Pacific made sure that the railroad would be awarded that honor and the federal funding that came with it. (The Bannings concluded that the Southern Pacific had bribed federal officials.) The Bannings decided to protect their investment by absorbing these losses without a stir, knowing that any protest they had made about the railroad, often portrayed in the press as a villain, would quickly have been broadcast by local newspapers.[47]

The Bannings' purchase of Santa Catalina Island in 1892 (see chapter 9) fundamentally transformed their harbor business. In order to develop the island as a resort and pay the mortgage as the 1893 national depression enfolded, they not only had to raise capital but also had to cut costs in other areas and reorganize their assets and operation. In 1894 they incorporated the Banning Company to encompass all of their holdings except for those related to Santa Catalina Island. The Wilmington Development Company was virtually dissolved, while the Wilmington Transportation Company continued to manage shipping. Although the company still made a profit in the 1890s, they had to fire many employees in 1894 and, until the Conejo Ranch was sold, sometimes came close to being unable to make payroll.[48]

And yet, as the purchase of Santa Catalina and other ventures would prove, the Banning brothers, like their father, were relentlessly ambitious, always looking for new sources of profit. In 1899 they joined in a franchise with the Southern Pacific to establish a new ferry service in the harbor. In the same year they created the Banning Drilling Company to search for oil, which was fast replacing coal as the major energy source for the railroads and other industries. New oil wells were being opened daily by 1895 and, William Banning concluded, would soon overtake the Banning coal business. The brothers finally decided to join the search, but they were not real oilmen, at least not at that time, and this venture died without a trace. They knew where to find water, though, and in 1900 the brothers incorporated the San Pedro and Wilmington Water Company to supply homes, farms, and vessels in the harbor area with water pumped from local wells and other sources. Their father had started this company's predecessor when he launched his effort to bring water to the area in the 1870s. The brothers continued the company under its new name for a short time amid many complaints by residents, businesses, and ship captains about their high rates. Customers also complained that the water had a strong sulphur taste until it stood for a while. On the bright side, as one local newspaper stated, the mineral-rich water was reportedly "of great aid to invalids." In 1901 the Bannings sold the company to a Long Beach development firm, which consolidated it with three other concerns to create the Seaside Water Company.[49]

By the turn of the century the Banning brothers ran their company from three locations. Edward Mahar oversaw day-to-day harbor operations from his office in San Pedro. Edwin Stanton was stationed in Avalon on Santa Catalina, where Joseph and Hancock also managed the resort when they lived there during the summers. William, who was frequently absent on business trips, directed the company from his downtown Los Angeles office on Spring Street, in a two-story brick building sandwiched between the taller Stowell Block and the Workman Block. Hancock too was usually stationed downtown when not at Catalina.

The Banning brothers' devotion to shipping was always on display in the streetside window of their downtown office on Spring Street, in the form of a model of the steamship *Vanderbilt*, which they proudly exhibited there for many years. The *Vanderbilt* was considered the largest wooden steamship in the world when it was launched in 1856. It first plied the Atlantic Ocean on cruises between New York and Le Havre, then served the U.S. government during the Civil War. In the 1870s, it was converted into a sailing vessel and renamed the *Three Brothers*. The vessel had called at least once at San Pedro Bay during Phineas's lifetime, in 1881. The exquisite scale model was built in the 1880s by G. C. Fowler and purchased about 1889 by Hancock Banning, who first displayed it in his Los Angeles office on North Main Street. When the Bannings finally sold their business in 1920, William brought the model home, and the family later donated it to the Natural History Museum of Los Angeles County, where it has been exhibited in a California history gallery for decades.[50]

Gilded Age Politics

Like their father, the Banning brothers wielded a fair amount of political influence, although none of them ever ran for a major office. They did, however, play a role in local politics as members of the conservative Republican business establishment that dominated Southern California politics in the Gilded Age and helped to advance their company interests into the new century.

The Southern California political milieu between 1886 to 1900 was in many ways similar to that of the preceding era. Competition between

Republicans and Democrats in elections and policymaking was still to some extent based on national partisan politics, at least in rhetoric, although local issues usually determined the outcome. The Democratic Party had the advantage of seasoned leaders from the era of its dominance, but the newcomers who flooded the region during the 1880s allied themselves with the Republicans, and the GOP increasingly captured elections and offices. By 1895, just one of the twenty-three top Los Angeles County officials was a Democrat.[51]

National politics of the era also saw the rise of the Populist Party, formed in response to continuing discontent among the nation's farmers. Populism was very strong in California, where a number of the party's candidates were elected to the state legislature in the 1890s. Populists embraced a number of political and social reform objectives, such as direct legislation, unemployment relief, and restraints on corporations, which aligned the party on occasion with urban reformers on the Left. As was true at the national and state level, local Populist chapters frequently joined with Democrats (and occasionally with Republicans) to support candidates when their political interests overlapped. While some of these candidates won, disagreement within the Populist Party over the practice contributed to the party's limitations.[52]

Of the many political issues that would arise between 1886 and 1900, anger over the economic practices and political power of the Southern Pacific Railroad Company stands out as a constant and significant variable, organizing and energizing groups of all political stripes. After 1876, the railroad had helped to bring prosperity to the region by transporting agricultural goods and—when faced with competition—lowering its rates, sparking the population boom in 1886–88. But many residents had mixed feelings about the corporation because of its often-highhanded business methods and political tactics. The Southern Pacific also fought with the county Board of Supervisors over delinquent property taxes, was ordered to repair roads it had altered without authorization, and was blamed for flooding caused by the design of its bridges. The *Times* and other papers railed against the Southern Pacific for these local sins as well as its political influence at the state level, which enabled it to thwart competition, charge exorbitant freight rates, and avoid paying taxes. The railroad's partners, including the Banning brothers, would bear some of this criticism.[53]

Southern Pacific leaders understood their political quandary early on. As Charles Crocker wrote to Collis P. Huntington in 1883, railroad officials had a bad reputation because they took part in the affairs of both political parties in California. The candidates they did not nominate "become our enemy immediately." And the candidates the Southern Pacific did support "are so anxious to prove that we did not help them, that they are the worst men we have to deal with. The result is that the men whom we have spent our money in the electing, are the ones on whom we can rely least."[54]

The Southern Pacific's major involvement in 1890s politics—national as well as local—was its role in the "Free Harbor Fight." Since the early 1870s, when Phineas Banning personally lobbied Congress for appropriations to build a world-class port, most area civic leaders had backed San Pedro–Wilmington as the best site for a Los Angeles–area harbor, supporting the project with official resolutions to Congress in the 1870s and 1880s. The Southern Pacific, which owned considerable property in San Pedro, agreed: company executive Charles Crocker stated in 1888 that the federal government should create a deepwater port there. But when the Los Angeles Terminal Railway brought competition to San Pedro harbor, Southern Pacific President Collis P. Huntington began buying property further north along the coast with the idea of developing a harbor at Santa Monica instead. When an 1891 U.S. Army engineering report recommended San Pedro for harbor appropriations, Huntington threw all of the political might of the Southern Pacific into diverting those funds to Santa Monica, where the railroad owned the surrounding property and could exclude all competition.[55]

Opponents of the Southern Pacific fought back for a variety of self-interested motives: shippers hoped to prevent the monopoly, while others wanted to protect their own financial investments in San Pedro or in the competing railroad. They formed a coalition made up of hundreds of commercial interests and individuals, the Los Angeles Chamber of Commerce, the Los Angeles Terminal Railway (which had its terminus in San Pedro), and the *Times*. Senator Stephen M. White, one-time lawyer for the railroad and the Bannings, championed the San Pedro cause in Washington, D.C. This group was opposed by the Southern Pacific and a number of business leaders who demanded that the federal appropriation go either to Santa Monica alone or to both, but with a much larger share earmarked for Santa Monica. In 1895 the San Pedro forces founded the Free Harbor League to press for their favorite location and conducted an extensive political campaign, seeking to demonize the Southern Pacific and portray its president, Collis P. Huntington, as unethical. League leaders included *Times* publisher Harrison G. Otis, lawyer George S. Patton Sr., and many members of the Los Angeles Chamber of Commerce.[56]

The Banning brothers would be caught in the middle of this battle. Their property was in Wilmington and San Pedro, so an improved harbor there would enhance their land values while increasing their company's business. If, on the other hand, the harbor appropriations went to Santa Monica, the Southern Pacific would relocate almost all of its business there; shipping at San Pedro would decrease and the port's value would decline. But by 1893 they had hedged their bets, signing an exclusive contract with Collis P. Huntington for all stevedoring work at the new Santa Monica harbor. Close partners of the railroad, they feared that if they supported the Free Harbor League, they would antagonize the railroad leadership and jeopardize this opportunity. The Bannings chose to stand with the railroad and therefore, as Joseph told his uncle in St. Paul, felt "called upon to do all in our power in favor of Santa Monica." Hancock was a director in 1895 of the Chamber of Commerce and may have used his position to sway members to support Santa Monica or both harbors. But whatever the brothers did for the railroad, they did it quietly. Word of their advocacy never reached the newspapers, which were always hungry for stories about the machinations behind the potential monopoly at Santa Monica.[57]

The Banning contributions to the Southern Pacific's fight were not enough to tip the scales in its favor. In 1897, after a long and bitterly fought struggle—"a remarkable fight between a community and a powerful corporation," according to the *Times*—San Pedro harbor was chosen for appropriations by the Senate Commerce Committee. The decision was commemorated with a grand jubilee, attended by those who supported San Pedro. Among the organizers was Hancock Banning, proud member of the water carnival committee, who attended the celebrations with those who had actually fought the defeated Southern Pacific.[58]

From about 1890 the Banning brothers used their growing economic clout and the political connections their father had made to work within the state and local Republican Party, supporting their allies and electing their friends, and calling on them to promote the region and their business. They frequently took advantage of their partnership with the Southern Pacific Railroad in political circles, asking its officers and operatives, such as U.S. Senator Leland Stanford and lobbyist George Hatton, to help appoint their favorites to offices. They also worked with others to enlist officials like William F. Herrin, chief counsel and political strategist for the Southern Pacific, to their cause. They backed perennial Southern Pacific candidates such as Hervey Lindley and Col. Daniel Burns to retain their credentials as Southern Pacific allies.[59]

Republican Party stalwarts, the Banning brothers loyally supported GOP candidates for almost all offices. They lobbied and helped finance legislation at the state and local levels to advance their interests, and ensured the loyalty of at least one local politician, Judge William Savage, during a crucial period by keeping him on a retainer. But they also campaigned tenaciously for friends and family, whatever their politics. The brothers backed James de Barth Shorb—family friend, business partner of their father, and Democrat—in his winning run for county treasurer in 1892. And for almost an entire decade they supported the candidacies of John Cline, a former county sheriff and good friend, for various political offices. Although they failed to get their cousin's brother-in-law appointed to a federal office in 1897, they were generally successful in their political pursuits in the 1890s.[60]

The Bannings also sought political favors from their attorney, Stephen M. White, both when he was a member of the state legislature in the late 1880s and after he was elected U.S. senator from California in 1892. In partnership with John D. Bicknell, White had also represented the Southern Pacific, but broke with the railroad during the Free Harbor fight. He continued to represent the Bannings, however, and argued their side in the Dominguez de Guyer case before the U.S. Supreme Court. Apparently unconcerned that he opposed the railroad and was a Democrat, the Bannings called on him to appoint friends to federal offices and to expedite important business matters for them.[61]

By the turn of the century the Banning brothers had established themselves as influential players in local politics and conservative Republican affairs. As the state assemblyman from the harbor area admitted to another political figure, the Banning brothers "are quite a power in my district." They would continue to wield that power in the new century.[62]

The 1885–1900 period was one of expansion and prosperity for the immediate descendants of Phineas Banning. Successful in further developing his business enterprise, increasing family wealth, sustaining the Baning political influence, marrying well (for the most part), and enlarging the immediate family and its network of relatives, friends and business allies, the next generation had flourished. One more Banning venture begun in the early 1890s would capture the family's attention for three decades—the ownership of the Magic Isle. The fascinating story of the Banning years of Santa Catalina Island unfolds in the next two chapters.

SANTA CATALINA ISLAND ADVENTURE:
THE EARLY YEARS

About five years after the Banning brothers began to expand their harbor and associated businesses during the Gilded Age, they embarked on their boldest venture—one that would become their signature enterprise—the purchase of Santa Catalina Island. For almost thirty years, from 1892 to 1919, Catalina would shape their business and become the focus of the entire family's social life. The first decade of this adventure would prove to be the most rewarding for them, as business and family connections melded in Wilmington, Los Angeles, and Santa Catalina. The venture's success seemed to confirm that the Banning sons had inherited their father's almost unerring sense for Southern California's next big thing, as well as his energy and ambition in bringing that vision to life.

The Gilded Age was a fortuitous era to invest in a resort. If that resort was in California, all the better. In the late nineteenth century, commodious seaside and inland hotels offering long summer vacations for the wealthy and shorter stays for the middle class became popular destinations on both coasts. Eastern resorts such as Saratoga Springs and Coney Island in New York, Newport in Rhode Island, and White Sulphur Springs in West Virginia offered a variety of living accommodations and amusements for those seeking recreation and rejuvenation. After the Civil War, and especially once the transcontinental railroad was completed, the American "Wild West" became a tourist favorite. Eastern visitors were enamored of Yellowstone and the Grand Canyon, wild buffalo herds on the open plains, and Rocky Mountain hunting grounds. Eventually the ski slopes of Colorado and the Sin City casinos and shows in Las Vegas, Nevada, became favored destinations.[1]

California became the "ultimate goal of western travel" at this time because it combined cosmopolitan centers with scenic beauty. Grand hotels such as the Del Coronado in San Diego and the Del Monte further north, and in beach cities in between, offered luxury and phenomenal views. These venues would later compete with the California missions and other sites for tourists, but before 1900 they were the places to see and to be. Southern California was particularly rich in tourist venues after the railroads began bringing in easterners and midwesterners. In addition to the Del Coronado, tourist hotels sprang up in the 1880s on the beaches of Santa Barbara, Santa Monica, and Redondo, and in suburban towns such as Pasadena, Pomona, and Riverside. Regional boosters helped to promote these destinations by popularizing the image of California as a paradise like the Mediterranean in landscape and climate, a perception that had captivated the health seekers and homebuilders who flocked to Southern California in the 1880s. The Bannings would capitalize on this marketing of the region and on the increasing popularity of recreational activities for less-sedentary visitors at the turn of the century to create a retreat for the wealthy on Santa Catalina. There the economically fortunate could relax, socialize, and play on an island that offered an abundance of opportunities for pleasure.[2]

"The Magic Isle"

Santa Catalina is one of eight islands, a group known as the Channel Islands, that dot the coastal waters of California between Santa Barbara and San Diego. Santa Catalina lies about twenty-two miles from the closest point on the mainland, and is certainly "26 Miles Across the Sea"—the distance given in a popular song of the 1950s—from several places along the California coast. About twenty-two miles long, the island ranges from a half mile wide at the isthmus to eight miles at its widest point. It comprises almost seventy-five square miles of mountains and canyons. Its coast might at first make it appear unpromising for a resort: as one historian wrote, "There are no beaches excepting in the crescent-shaped cañons, for bold rocks stand out in the water, in some places like immense granite walls, against which the ocean dashes its fury."[3]

The island was inhabited by Tongva Indians when Spanish explorer Juan Rodríguez Cabrillo arrived there in 1542 with three ships. Cabrillo named the island San Salvador, after his flagship. During his stay that winter, he was injured in an altercation between the Tongva and his men, possibly near present-day Wells Beach on the north side of Catalina Harbor, which lies to the west of the isthmus. He died from his wounds, and some scholars believe he was buried somewhere on the island. Sixty years later, Spanish adventurer Sebastian Vizcaíno explored the California coastline and renamed many of the locations that had earlier been christened by Cabrillo and others. Vizcaíno landed on San Salvador on the feast day of Saint Catherine and called the island Santa Catalina in her honor.[4]

After the Spanish colonization of California beginning in the 1760s, the Native population of the island slowly dwindled. Many Indians moved back to the mainland, where they were removed to the missions or to the large cattle ranchos. Santa Catalina became instead a base for Russian otter hunters living in Northern California, for New England smugglers hoping to avoid Mexican trade laws and taxes, and for various fishing enterprises. Several California residents petitioned the government in the 1820s and 1830s to grant them the island to raise sheep or cattle, but were denied. Finally, during the war between the United States and Mexico, Governor Pío Pico issued a grant for the island as one of his last official acts before he fled the capital at Monterey. The grant gave the entire island to his friend Thomas Robbins, a Massachusetts trader who had moved to Santa Barbara in the 1830s. Over the years to come, the land would rarely stay in the same hands for more than a few years. After five years Robbins sold it to another Santa Barbara resident, José María Covarrubias, for $10,000. Covarrubias tried to raise goats there but was not successful and sold half of his interest in the island within three years to San Francisco merchant Albert Packard, a business partner of Benjamin D. Wilson at San Pedro harbor. Various parts of the island changed hands until 1867, when James Lick of San Francisco, who had gradually been acquiring island land, finally became its sole owner.[5]

During the 1850s and 1860s, when mostly absent landlords owned portions of the island, a number of squatters ran businesses there. Phineas Banning's chief nemesis in the harbor trade, Augustus W. Timms, raised sheep and goats on the island and brought visitors from the mainland to his landing there to swim and fish all day for a fee of $4. Banning's former business partner Spencer Wilson and former employee Ed McDonald raised sheep there from 1859 until 1862. Another former Banning employee, Frank Lecouvreur, visited Santa Catalina in 1856 and found it a "very romantic island," although the lack of a dependable freshwater source meant that the only available drinking water was "decidedly disagreeable to the newcomer on account of its salty taste." A mining boom in the early 1860s brought mining claims for the property, and Union troops arrived during the Civil War to establish a camp and explore the possibility of using the island as a reservation for hostile Indians in Northern California. Banning himself organized several excursions to the island for friends on his ships over the years, and by the early 1880s his steamboat *Amelia* shuttled vacationers to Santa Catalina weekly.[6]

In fact, shortly before his death, Phineas Banning was planning to acquire the island for himself. In 1883 he tried to interest Benjamin D. Wilson's wealthy son-in-law, James de Barth Shorb, in purchasing the island with him, with the idea of establishing a resort and mines. Banning contacted the trustees of the trust that held the island at that time and offered to consult with them about its disposition. "This is a good time to strike for the island," he wrote to Shorb in one of several letters asking him to join in this venture. Before Shorb could agree, however, Banning was struck down by an express wagon in San Francisco while on the way to Bartlett Springs for a vacation, and his ill health became his more immediate concern.[7]

James Lick had purchased Santa Catalina Island to exploit its mineral wealth. He moved to chase off squatters and those taking timber from the island, but was unconcerned with the few visitors who visited for camping and health reasons. He eventually gave up on his mining idea and tried to sell the island in 1872, but the deal fell through when one of the investors died. In 1876 Lick himself died and his ownership of Santa Catalina reverted to the Lick Trust, which was controlled by the University of California. The trust held the island until 1887, when it sold Santa Catalina for $200,000 to Los Angeles real estate developer George Shatto, who hoped to create a pleasure resort at Timms Landing on the island. He first renamed the site Shatto but, perhaps recognizing that this was not an especially attractive moniker for a resort, later changed it to Avalon, a name said to have been proposed by his sister-in-law after she read Tennyson's *Idylls of the King*.[8]

Shatto set out town lots to sell in Avalon and built the Hotel Metropole as a center for the populace and his real estate promotions. In order to finance the venture he enticed the International Mining Syndicate of Birmingham, England, to purchase a large portion of the island from him over three years. The syndicate leaders believed they could make a profit mining silver if they could send the ore back to England as ballast in returning ships, but within a short time they defaulted on their payments. With that failure Shatto was short of cash, as his expenses for surveying and promotion mounted. Meanwhile potential buyers were reluctant to purchase home sites so soon after the real estate bust that ended the "Boom of the Eighties" in Southern California.[9]

With Shatto vulnerable, the Banning brothers decided to make their move. Like their father, they had had a special interest in Santa Catalina for years. All three had spent time on the island in the 1880s, when Banning boats regularly transported visitors back and forth from the mainland. They also vacationed there: Hancock visited the island on his yacht and was even listed as the musical editor of its first newspaper, the *Catalina Jewfish*, in the summer of 1889. The Bannings increased the number of Wilmington Transportation Company ships serving the island that year and expressed an interest in building a hotel there. In 1890 William Banning wrote to George Shatto, saying that the brothers had heard a rumor of the impending failure of the English mining syndicate to make good on the payments and informing him that they were prepared to purchase the island. This advance notice apparently prompted Shatto to try to strengthen his negotiating position by telling the Lick Trust that the English syndicate would be able to pay its debt very soon and that they need not foreclose.[10]

At the same time William reported to the secretary of the Lick Trust on the state of the talks, saying that Shatto wanted $300,000 for his investment and the Bannings had only half that amount. William then asked influential Southern Pacific officials W. W. Stow and Charles Crocker and other Lick trustees to demand prompt mortgage payments from Shatto, traveling to San Francisco to lobby for their support. Phineas Banning's Southern Pacific Railroad friends came through for his sons. With further lobbying assistance from James de Barth Shorb and the legal help of John D. Bicknell, lawyer for both the Bannings and the Southern Pacific Railroad, the road was paved for the Lick Trust to foreclose on Shatto's mortgage.[11]

In January 1892, the *Express* announced that the Bannings, the Lick Trust, and Shatto had reached an agreement to transfer ownership of Santa Catalina to the Bannings. The sale was in escrow, and Hancock Banning promised the reporter that the brothers would make the resort a success through frugal management. The Bannings assumed the mortgage of over $127,000 owed to the Lick Trust and paid Shatto $25,000 for his interest. The final deed document was dated September 20, 1892. With the deal concluded, the Bannings took control of the entire island except for the lots Shatto had already sold to individuals and one mining claim, with each brother owning one-third of the land. Shatto had made out relatively well considering his vulnerable position, one that had prompted even his own lawyer to admit that his client could not operate the island by himself.[12]

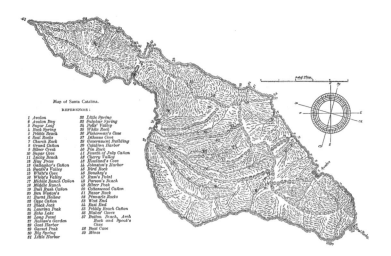

Santa Catalina Island in 1892. Courtesy of the Huntington Library.

Banning Santa Catalina

When the mining syndicate failed and its assets were sold in January 1892, the Banning brothers assumed de facto ownership of Santa Catalina and immediately began major improvements to accommodate the large crowds of vacationers expected during the coming summer. The *Falcon*, a Wilmington Transportation Company steam tugboat, was remodeled as a double-deck passenger ship; together with the steamboat *Warrior*, it would shuttle visitors to Santa Catalina. Carpenters were brought in to repair and enlarge the Hotel Metropole, while outside parties constructed additional hotels in Avalon. A pavilion ninety feet in diameter was built near the beach "for dancing and other amusements." An army of engineers repaired and expanded the waterworks, streets, and the sanitation system; fences were erected around the town to keep out stray animals, bathhouses were built for swimmers, trees were planted, and the county franchise for a new wharf for Banning steamers was secured.[13]

Unlike George Shatto and most Southern California real estate developers of the time, the Bannings preferred to lease rather than sell lots outright, a policy that allowed them to control the property but irritated lessees who wanted to buy their home or business sites. The Bannings, however, were not primarily real estate speculators, at least not yet. Their objective in developing Santa Catalina as a resort and Avalon as a quaint and picturesque village was instead to make money by transporting pas-

Avalon harbor, early 1890s. Courtesy of the Huntington Library.

sengers there. They sponsored free amenities and events, such as band concerts, to lure customers who could enjoy them for the price of a round-trip ticket on a Banning vessel. In return for spending large sums on improvements, the Bannings believed that they should have a monopoly on transportation of visitors to and from the island. Those who arrived by some other means should not have access to the Bannings' improvements. This idea would soon evolve into a policy of physically preventing "tramp boats" (as the Bannings called them) from sneaking passengers onto the island.[14]

Customers who purchased Wilmington Transportation Company tickets to Santa Catalina certainly had plenty of options for recreation. The island quickly became legendary for sportfishing after photographs of anglers and their catches began appearing on postcards and promotional material for the island. A fleet of yachts, power launches, and rowboats were available for fishing or pleasure boating. Many visitors swam in the Pacific along the crescent-shaped Avalon beach. Hunting wild goats and quail was allowed in some portions of the interior of the island. Some visitors enjoyed shooting flying fish as they rose from the water, although this practice was not encouraged. Hiking around the

Stagecoaching around the Farnsworth Loop. Courtesy of the Huntington Library.

island to see its natural beauty and to explore the remains of Indian villages was also popular. A well-designed nine-hole golf course and a tennis court were available for those who enjoyed less rugged sport. Stagecoach rides from Avalon and the isthmus to Eagle's Nest and other locations could be thrilling in the hands of drivers such as Jack Goodwin and occasionally William Banning himself, who took passengers down steep grades and around tight curves in Concords and other coaches pulled by six spirited horses. William Banning claimed the privilege of driving on the inaugural trip along several of the roads that the brothers built on the island.[15]

For those seeking less strenuous activities the pavilion was open for dancing every night during the season. Concerts by Porter's Santa Catalina Island Marine Band, sometimes with Hancock Banning on cornet, were held every day. A concessionaire operated a "monster skating tent." In July 1899, an aquarium displaying sea creatures of the region opened, and tours in glass-bottom boats, which allowed passengers to view fish while cruising in comfort, were very popular, as they are to this day.[16]

The island was even proposed as a venue for a heavyweight prizefight between "Gentleman Jim" Corbett and Peter "Black Prince" Jackson in 1894. Newspapers reported that a "so-called Santa Catalina Athletic Club" had subscribed $35,000, along with another $5,000 from individuals, to hold the event at Avalon that June. But because prizefighting had been banned in California by the legislature the year before, a backlash

Porter's Santa Catalina Island Marine Band, 1898. Courtesy of the Catalina Island Museum.

against the contest emerged immediately. The Banning brothers considered supporting the fight on their island but soon backed down. "I suppose we should not allow two 'mugs' to fight there," Joseph wrote to an uncle in South Carolina, "particularly as public sentiment might overwhelm us; not to speak of the disapproval of my wife and my brother's wife." Unable to find an alternate site, promoters of the contest were forced to cancel the event.[17]

Island visitors could choose among accommodations ranging from the elegant Hotel Metropole and other hotels in Avalon, to the few houses and cottages owned by the Bannings and other residents, to tent cottages available for rental from concessionaires or the Bannings. "Canvas cities" featuring row upon row of such tents sprang up at several locations. Many visitors later remembered the communal life of the tent cities with fondness. As Marshall Stimson, a frequent camper in his youth and later an attorney and civic leader, recalled, "Camp life at Avalon had many amusing episodes. Amateur cooks produced various odors, appetizing and otherwise. Silhouette night tent scenes and loud conversations contributed to community entertainment." A typical day for him and other young people at the camp included fishing and swimming in the morning, rowing with girls after lunch, making fun of the new arrivals (many of whom were seasick) when the steamer arrived about 6 p.m., then attending a band concert after dinner and dancing until 11 p.m. at the pavilion. "No place on earth could have provided a more lovely

Hotel Metropole and beach, ca. 1890. Courtesy of the Huntington Library.

opportunity for good, healthy enjoyment and informal social intercourse than Catalina Island," he wrote.[18]

Santa Catalina's visitors had few options for communicating with the mainland in the days before the coming of the telephone, but the Bannings came up with a playful solution to help long-term visitors stay in touch. Besides carrying messages and mail on their steamers, they established a novelty carrier pigeon service in 1894. The Zahn brothers, their good friends, trained the birds that shuttled between Avalon and the Zahns' home near the State Normal School in Los Angeles. Messages were attached to the birds' legs with string, and many of them made the cross-channel trip much faster than ships. This ancient method of sending messages attracted interest for several years, although it was not very dependable because of hazards such as hungry hawks and sharp-shooting bird hunters. The novelty eventually wore off and the service was discontinued. By 1903 a radio-transmission service had taken its place.[19]

Besides providing amenities, the Bannings worked to protect the natural beauty and animals of the isle and its surroundings. While they encouraged visitors to hunt the abundant quail and overabundant goats and participate in sportfishing, the Bannings and other residents tried to protect other species. The Bannings led campaigns to lobby the county

Postcards of sportfishing at Santa Catalina. Courtesy of the Seaver Center for Western History Research, Natural History Museum of Los Angeles County.

Board of Supervisors for various ordinances to preserve the wild environment. They helped to pass laws protecting seals, sea lions, and some birds in 1892, restricting the use of fishing nets in 1902, prohibiting the killing of seals and sea lions near Avalon in 1914, and restricting the cutting of kelp along the coastline in 1916. In 1897, William Banning persuaded a state senator to offer a bill prohibiting the use of nets along the Catalina coastline. Sportfishing enthusiasts, including the Bannings, formed the Santa Catalina Tuna Club to preserve game fish as well as smaller prey fish like sardines. Their work was particularly important after 1900, when the increasing popularity of sportfishing at the resort threatened to deplete the adjacent waters if steps were not taken to protect the marine population.[20]

In the meantime, Joseph Brent Banning busied himself with the island's flora. He had planted trees in Avalon just after the brothers bought the island, and later he obtained seeds and saplings for Catalina from family friend and reforestation expert Theodore Lukens. Joseph planted over a hundred blue gum eucalyptus trees across the isthmus, in part to act as a windbreak. Along with protecting wildlife on the island and in its waters, these efforts helped to make the island a mecca for naturalists from California universities, whom the Bannings encouraged in their investigations.[21]

Improving transportation on the island meant building roads, and the Bannings were masters of that business. They built a system linking the major sites, many previously accessible only by boat along the coast or by muletrain over steep mountainous terrain. They commissioned roads from the isthmus to Little Harbor and from Avalon to Middle Ranch and on to the isthmus, connecting the main attractions on the southern portion of the island by 1898. Other roads linking spots such as Eagle's Nest and Middle Ranch were completed by 1904. The Bannings offered stagecoach rides for visitors on some of the new roads. They also hoped to develop new recreational facilities in the interior along the route: a newspaper reported in 1893 that the Bannings intended to build "commodious buildings" on a stage road, "both to be used as old-time hostelries, where the wants of the inner man will be cared for after the style of old." The roads also provided access to land that the Bannings leased to private businesses or used for their own satellite enterprises.[22]

Having sunk substantial capital into developing the resort, the Bannings had to entice visitors in order to make back their investment and turn a profit, and to that end they carried out an increasingly ambitious promotional campaign. In the early years, railroads that stopped at the harbor at San Pedro Bay advertised the island for free to increase ridership and to assist the Bannings, their business partners at the harbor. Soon the Bannings began advertising in newspapers and magazines in California and Arizona just before and during the tourist season. Instead of spending money on advertising in the Midwest and on the East Coast, they lured reporters from newspapers in those regions, and these visits often resulted in flattering stories about the island "Where Every Prospect Pleases." The campaign helped to build the growing tourist industry in California in the 1890s and early 1900s and worked hand in glove with various promotions, by railroads, print media, real estate concerns, and other vested interests, that touted Southern California as a place to visit and to live, and in which to invest.[23]

The Banning promotional machine for Santa Catalina was especially indebted to Charles Frederick Holder, a professor of zoology at the Throop Institute in Pasadena (which later became the California Institute of Technology) and a writer and sportsman who tried to preserve and popularize the natural setting of the island. Holder authored many books and countless essays on the natural history, archaeology, and history of Santa Catalina for local and national magazines and science journals. Many of the articles were devoted to sportfishing, his chief interest. In 1892, the Bannings hired Holder to stimulate popular interest in and visits to the island. He became their in-house promoter extraordinaire, penning volumes such as *An Isle of Summer, Santa Catalina* (1901), *The Adventures of Torqua* (1902), and *The Channel Islands of California* (1910), and articles in *Scientific American* and *National Geographic*. Holder had written so many articles by 1907 that he began submitting them under different names so that they did not appear to be duplications. The Bannings reviewed drafts of some of his work and asked him in 1894 to interview elderly Indians about where Juan Rodríguez Cabrillo's bones might be buried. A decade later they suggested that Holder compose a biography of the explorer Cabrillo. Holder never did write that book, but he did continue to promote Santa Catalina and sportfishing, to the point of personally revitalizing the Santa Catalina Tuna Club in 1907.[24]

In order to manage and properly finance their island business, the Bannings incorporated the Santa Catalina Island Company in October 1894. The purpose of the new company, they said, was to carry on a general hotel and restaurant business and related operations, "To lay out parks, race courses, places of amusement and entertainment, and conduct the same," to establish a telegraph and telephone business between the island and the mainland, to build a bathhouse, and to create a waterworks to supply water for irrigation and domestic use. The directors were the three brothers, who each held 1,665⅓ shares, and Katharine and Anne, who each held two shares. Edwin Stanton would manage the company on the island, with Joseph joining him on site during the summer season to oversee all operations.[25]

Business flourished in the first decades of this venture. The *Times* reported that about 36,000 passengers visited the island in the eighteen months between May 1892 and December 1893. Hancock wrote to Anne that business had suffered in 1894, the worst year of the depression locally, but that the 1895 season had been a real moneymaker. By 1898 the Bannings put a third Wilmington Transportation Company steamer, the *Hermosa*, back into service carrying passengers to the island. They had just refitted the boat in San Francisco to transport stampeders from Seattle to the Klondike gold country in Alaska, but it had unfortunately arrived in Washington just as that boom began to peter out.[26]

Besides operating their principal business transporting and entertaining visitors, the Bannings exploited other resources on the island. The

Professor of zoology, sportsman, and Santa Catalina Island publicist Charles Frederick Holder. Courtesy of the Huntington Library.

brothers supplied the first contractor charged with construction of the breakwater at San Pedro in 1893 with rock from the island. Unfortunately, their friends at the office of the Southern Pacific Railroad saw the profit in this venture and arranged through Collis P. Huntington to have Congress change the stipulations for the outer breakwater, put out for bid in 1900. This time rock from Chatsworth and Riverside County (some of it said to be much inferior to that from Catalina) was shipped to the harbor by the Southern Pacific. As Hancock Banning Jr. later observed, "The S.P. had the political club and used it. Too bad for us."[27]

Avalon street scene. Courtesy of the Huntington Library.

The Bannings also quarried soapstone on the island and marketed it as Serpentine Marble, also known as Catalina Marble or Catalina Soapstone. In this operation, overseen by Hancock and managed by Frank Carey, the soapstone was split into large pieces on the island and then transported to a yard in Los Angeles where it was cut and finished. Serpentine, which had a mottled green appearance, became fashionable in decorative furnishings at the turn of the century. Larger pieces were also used on the exterior of a number of buildings in downtown Los Angeles in the 1890s and early 1900s. Hancock tried (evidently unsuccessfully) to sell some Santa Catalina soapstone in 1893 to the architect of the acclaimed Bradbury Building, so called after the father of John Bradbury, who married Lucy Banning later that same year. The quarrying continued until the Bannings sold the island and the new owner deemed it unprofitable.[28]

Much of the mountainous interior of the island was not suited for recreational use, and it had been used for many years to pasture livestock. The Bannings continued the tradition, and soon after taking over the island William Banning enticed his father's old friend, Walter Vail, to graze his sheep and cattle there. Vail, owner of the Empire Ranch in Arizona, had known Phineas since the 1870s, when the latter had moved his sheep to Arizona Territory during the drought in Southern California. Vail in turn looked to Santa Catalina for pasturage when Arizona endured overgrazing and a long drought in the early 1890s. He decided to lease a majority of the island for $2,000 per year. The Bannings rented vessels to move Vail's cattle and sheep from San Pedro, and named the island entry point Empire Landing in honor of Vail's homestead.[29]

This particular lease was not among the successful Catalina ventures. There was not enough water on the island for the human population (the Bannings had to bring it in by ship), much less for a large herd of cattle, and not enough fencing to contain Vail's livestock, which roamed even into the streets of Avalon. At a huge loss, Vail had to move his animals to Santa Rosa, another of the Channel Islands, by 1896. Still, he remained a close family friend, and spent quite a bit of time with the Bannings after moving to Los Angeles in 1895.[30]

Raising sheep for wool, however, would continue on the island. In 1898 the Bannings incorporated the Banning Wool Company to manage the sheep already there. The three brothers controlled most of the company and Joseph was president. Frank O. Whittley, a sheep man with many years' experience on the island, served as the resident superintendent and owned one-quarter of the stock. Hancock reported in 1904 that the operation at Middle Ranch, Whittley homestead, was prospering and wool was selling as expected. But the other brothers lost interest after expenses increased and the sheep developed health problems. In 1907 the directors voted to sell the company to the Bannings' Santa Catalina Island Company. The officers of the latter company then leased the flock to John Maurer, who in 1912 cleared out most of the existing sheep, by then wild and unsheared, and brought in Merinos. Maurer tended this flock until 1919, when the island and sheep were sold to the new island owner.[31]

Social Life at Santa Catalina

While the ownership and management of Santa Catalina was a business venture for the Bannings, the island was also the center of their social and family lives every summer, and sometimes during the off-season. Joseph, and to a lesser degree Hancock, spent considerable time there during the tourist season, managing the operation and supervising the construction of additional amenities. In 1897 Joseph built a cottage at Avalon where he and his family lived much of the year during the Bannings' first decade running the island. After living at the Metropole with his family early on, Hancock moved in 1897 into the large two-story residence formerly occupied by Joseph's family in Descanso Canyon, a short distance from Avalon by boat, and Anne spent most of her summers

Hancock and Anne's Descanso Canyon house. Courtesy of the Huntington Library.

there entertaining relatives and friends. During these summers the Bannings were the center of the Santa Catalina social world, and were consistently mentioned in the frequent descriptions of news and social
events on the island in Los Angeles newspapers. This social circle was
primarily peopled by the more affluent members of society who could
afford to stay on the island for prolonged periods. Over the course of
each season the list of visitors to the island included countless members
of the social elite in Southern California, as well as many of their counterparts from throughout the nation.[32]

   Life on the island during the tourist season was one of relaxation,
recreation, and social intercourse for the Bannings and their friends. The
wives and children of the affluent families who summered on the island
generally stayed there almost the entire time, whereas the husbands frequently returned to their occupations in Los Angeles, Pasadena, and
other cities during the week. Owners of many of the island's accommodations, the Bannings often invited family and friends to stay with them
in company cottages. Over the years the George S. Patton family stayed
there regularly, and distant relatives such as the Frederick Ayer family from
Massachusetts and Katharine Stewart Banning's siblings from Minnesota

visited on occasion. Robert Hord Ingram, a Southern Pacific Railroad executive who had arrived in Los Angeles in 1902 and who worked with the Banning brothers on many business projects, regularly stayed with his family on the island the whole summer as a guest of the Bannings.[33]

Ingram's spouse, Selena Gray Galt Ingram, became an intimate friend of Katharine and kept a diary recording her life in Southern California. Her entries every summer detailed the many activities she enjoyed on the island. The older women spent much of their time in genteel pursuits such as playing bridge and planning parties and luncheons. Both men and women played golf and tennis, went boating, attended concerts and dances, and occasionally visited the many tourist sites. Young adults spent their time swimming, fishing, sailing, horse riding, hiking, dancing, and visiting other island attractions. The long and full summer days together cemented personal and business relationships that would continue throughout the year and into the future.[34]

Good part-time citizens of their town, the Bannings participated in the civic life of Avalon. Joseph was elected as one of the two justices of the peace for the island and served in that capacity from 1892 to 1896, thus justifying his nickname, "Judge," which his father had given him many years before. In order to hold offenders found guilty of various crimes, the brothers obtained permission to build a small county jail in Avalon in 1896. In the following year Joseph was elected to the school board for the island, which would oversee the two-room school built in 1901 to accommodate fifty-nine students.[35]

In order to protect Santa Catalina's image as a family resort, the Bannings carefully restricted drinking and other adult pleasures and tried to keep them inconspicuous. The upscale Metropole got its liquor license right away, but other watering spots posed problems. William told Joseph in 1897 that he had heard unfavorable comments about their plans to turn Joseph's former home at Descanso into a restaurant and beer garden, and warned that if the wrong characters "and particularly women" are seen there, it might reflect badly on the family. He recommended that they rent the home out as a residence (Hancock's family moved into it later that year) and quietly establish the beer garden some place less noticeable. Drinking was also an occasional problem on Wilmington Transportation Company vessels transporting island visitors. In 1900, for example, William had to ask a company superintendent to investigate a report that a "partly intoxicated" man on the *Hermosa* had vomited on a child whose mother then issued a formal complaint. Two years later William instructed Joseph to screen potential lessees of the Seal Rock Sa-

The young summer beach crowd at Avalon in the early 1900s always included a number of Bannings and their friends. Seaver Center for Western History Research, Natural History Museum of Los Angeles County.

loon as carefully as his older brother monitored the operation of the bar on the *Hermosa* to avoid bad publicity from incidents involving liquor.[36]

Saloons on the island were a particular challenge because their owners often allowed illegal gambling on the premises. At first the Bannings turned a blind eye. Writing Joseph in 1896, William advised that until the "gambling proposition becomes noticeable and objectionable it would be well to leave it alone." They would gain patronage by tolerating gaming as long as it was discreetly managed, and if it did become a problem they could ask the new justice of peace to close the saloons down. Gambling became more open and prevalent, however, and William heard reports of gamblers hustling residents of the Metropole. On several occasions after 1900 he recommended prohibiting saloons on Banning property to protect the company from bad publicity. But gambling would continue in saloons operated by Ben Rosin and Dan Jerrue, punctuated by occasional raids by law enforcement authorities.[37]

The island's most notorious gambling haven was the Pilgrim Club, built in 1902. Financed by several New Yorkers, the Pilgrim was an opulent recreational center that "operated as a miniature Monte Carlo." It was "exquisitely furnished with Turkish rugs, heavily stuffed leather furniture, and works of art," and the center of the gaming room was dominated by an ornate chandelier. The Pilgrim Club was sometimes a thorn in the side of the Bannings; in 1906 William had to inform its director that he could not solicit customers while at the Metropole. The club also brought unwanted publicity when the county district attorney investigated gambling there, ordering the establishment raided on several occasions.[38]

Protecting the image of the island in those years also meant adhering to formal and informal codes of racial segregation. Resorts throughout the nation enforced strict rules on interracial relationships, barring nonwhites from staying at the more affluent establishments. Jews were also turned away from many resorts. On Santa Catalina Island, Mexican ranch hands, Asian food preparers, and African American servants of Caucasian visitors were welcome as employees, but not as social equals. This was especially important to the many island residents and visitors, such as George S. Patton and Selena Ingram, who had been raised in the South, where strict rules governed relations between the races.[39]

Although few Mexican or Asian families could have afforded to stay on the island in those years, on at least two occasions middle-class African Americans faced discrimination when visiting the island. In 1904 William Banning informed the manager of the Metropole that a number of "colored delegates" to a Methodist convention had asked if they would be accommodated if they came to Santa Catalina. Lawyers for the company advised them to say that the Metropole was full, so William suggested they look for rooms elsewhere. He instructed an aide to tell the party that they could eat at restaurants around town, but that the Metropole's employees "would refuse to wait on them if they went in [the] dining room and a number of [the hotel's] guests would leave." If they still insisted on eating at the hotel, William said, "put them in the small dining room and we'll send over a colored waiter if we can find one." The following year, T. Harry Jones purchased a ticket to Santa Catalina, but was denied a room at the Metropole by the hotel clerk, who told him that "colored people" were not allowed. He was then addressed by one of the Banning brothers, who allegedly told him, "You can't stop here; you ought to know that." Jones was later denied a tent at another location. He accused hotel employees of intimidating him and filed suit against the company.[40]

Preserving an image of affluence, social appropriateness, and family values in the 1890s and early 1900s required the company to abide by strict rules or find ways around them. By barring poor and nonwhite people from their facilities, the Bannings hoped to keep their island true to the image they projected to their wealthy clientele. As William wrote to one of the company managers in 1900, their advertisements concerning dancing at the pavilion that season did not exclude anyone for reasons of "nationality" or occupation, but when they built a new pavilion for the public "we may generally exclude all objectionable persons as heretofore." In enforcing the unwritten rules of race during this era, the Bannings were as vigilant as the owners of such resorts anywhere.[41]

Protecting an Investment

The Bannings invested a small fortune in the infrastructure and amenities at Santa Catalina Island in the early 1890s, and they did not charge visitors an admission fee, only requiring tickets for passage on a Wilmington Transportation Company vessel. It took no time at all for other ship captains to offer cut-rate transport to the island, where their customers could take advantage of the free amenities. The Bannings decided to protect their investment and their monopoly by enforcing a prohibition on all non-Banning ships on the island, a tactic that would result in a long war with intruders and protests from some Avalon residents, who demanded an end to the monopoly.

The Bannings established the policy soon after assuming control of the island. Although William opposed it at the start, anticipating adverse publicity from their "stopping the little guy," he soon changed his mind. By early 1893 he was using various methods to thwart the competing "tramp steamers," restricting their use of wharfs, manipulating hotel availability, and turning non-Banning visitors away from amenities such as the new pavilion and tents. He consulted lawyers to be sure that his tactics were legal. Soon the Bannings began building fences and hired a security force, including former and future county sheriff John Cline, to stop the increasing traffic. The stealthy approach of some of the vessels became a major safety concern. In 1895 a U.S. Revenue cutter reportedly almost ran down a boat without lights that was attempting to land twenty-two passengers at 3 a.m.[42]

In the following year the non-Banning ship *Point Loma*, sailing from Long Beach, made several landings at Avalon. William informed Joseph that they would have to stop it by charging its passengers the price of passage on a Banning vessel to disembark and by restricting access to the amenities. On June 23, however, Joseph, Banning Company Secretary Frank H. Lowe, and John Cline confronted the passengers upon landing, refusing to let them disembark at all; one of them, attorney Charles Wellborn, cannily demanded access to the U.S. Post Office, which was legally government property and so not under the Bannings' control. Wellborn was accommodated, and the ladies on the boat were allowed to go into the Metropole while the Banning forces and the ship captain discussed the situation. The *Point Loma* then returned with its passengers to Long Beach. This incident and others like it resulted in public discussions in Avalon about the Banning policy, and most of those residents who owned lots sided with the Bannings, noting that the company had made huge expenditures and that their wishes should be respected.[43]

When incursions by competing boat captains continued into 1897, William again consulted lawyers and was told to post "Private Property" signs on the wharf. Additional "special officers" were hired, such as Tom Savage, a political figure in the Los Angeles Tenderloin district, whom Cline recommended because "he does not drink, is cool and level headed and is afraid of no body." In 1899 a former George Shatto associate, C. A. Sumner, protested the Banning policy before the county Board of Supervisors. Around that time, another launch from Long Beach approached the island and was turned back, but not before one of its passengers, lawyer John Kemp, tried to get ashore, only to be chased down by the Banning security force and allegedly dumped into the water. Kemp later filed suit against the Bannings for $50,000, but the jury could not agree on a verdict and the case was eventually dropped.[44]

Under pressure from court actions and with bad publicity from the landing incidents mounting, William Banning suddenly announced in September 1899 that his company would throw open the port of Avalon to all ships, but that the Bannings would move all of their amenities to another location, where they would again prevent landings by other ships. Newspaper stories reported that the Bannings were moving their resort business to the isthmus. Avalon residents dependent on the tourist trade were alarmed and some offered to assist the Bannings in preventing the landings if they promised to keep the amenities in town. Although they would continue to plan for improvements at the isthmus, the Bannings ultimately decided to leave matters in Avalon as they were, including their policy on intruders.[45]

Keeping the bulk of Avalon residents on their side in the war against trespassers was crucial to the Bannings, and this was not the first time that the company reminded the town of what it stood to lose. When the stories concerning the *Point Loma* incident were circulating, William instructed Joseph to muster support from the hotel owners and businessmen to back the Banning policy on tramp steamers; otherwise, he threatened, the Bannings might not spend any more money in Avalon than was necessary. Regarding residents who helped intruders land, William was firm: "If anybody at Avalon takes a decided stand against us please let me know, and we may be able to find some way to bring them in line." In 1900 William informed an Avalon civic leader that all property owners at Avalon would have to sign an agreement allowing the Bannings to prevent landings on their property, and he told Joseph that if they objected the company would not build the new sewer. While the Bannings hoped to retain good relations with their neighbors, they were not shy about demanding adherence to their policy.[46]

In 1903 an assault on the Bannings came from another direction. State Senator Orrin Z. Hubbell introduced a bill stating that private vessels and individuals could not be hindered from landing on islands off the coast of California. The Bannings and the *Times* agreed that the bill was aimed specifically at Santa Catalina, and the Bannings used their political influence to convince other senators to defeat it. They were joined by most Avalon property owners, who sent a petition to Sacramento. The opposition campaign proved effective and the bill failed.[47]

The Banning policy would finally be overruled by the courts as a result of a dispute with one of the company's concessionaires, the Meteor Boat Company, which ran power glass-bottom boats in Avalon harbor. When a new combination tour package was announced that excluded this company, its owners determined to challenge the Banning monopoly. Meteor officials petitioned the county Board of Supervisors for a franchise to build a wharf at Avalon that would be available to all vessels at the usual fee. Three months later one of the proponents of the Meteor petition ferried over a large group of passengers, who broke through the ranks of the Banning security force to enter the island. In response to this assault, residents called a meeting three days later at which they voted to back the Bannings. On the following day Captain Oliver Hollar led three power launches from Long Beach with about two hundred "volunteers" to invade the Magic Isle. They were met this time by "Two hundred deputy constables, many of them Mexicans employed on the Banning ranch," a barbed wire barricade, and blasts from fire hoses. The intruders still managed to reach the shore, where the captain and two others were arrested for trespassing and then released. Apparently no one was injured, and Hancock Banning was cited for his chivalry in politely ushering a dozen young women from the invasion force onto the island. After that concession, more of the men "soon began to trickle through the barricade, and in half an hour the bands were playing and the beer was flowing."[48]

The *Times* continued to support the Bannings, who kept residents and visitors satisfied and safe by operating Avalon "more like a private country club than a public resort." But when residents protested vehemently at further Banning plans for the beach, the Bannings announced that they would let the residents of Avalon decide whether the port should be open or closed. When another independent steamer arrived in late October, no resistance was offered. As Hancock told a *Times* reporter, the Bannings were tired of fighting and would stop. From now on they would operate on a more profitable basis and charge for everything they supplied, while public facilities would have to be paid for by a newly formed municipality. The new Banning policy became law in 1907, when the Meteor lawsuit was finally decided and Judge Nathan Conrey ruled in favor of an open port. Although one last boat was prevented from landing, the island was now free to all comers. Some older residents worried that the resort would now change, and not for the better.[49]

Expansion and More Investment

The Banning brothers' occasional announcements of plans to develop the isthmus were not merely threats to keep Avalon residents on their side. Even as they were protecting their investment in Avalon, the Bannings had decided to develop another location on Santa Catalina in order to expand their operation and boost profits. The western end of the island stood virtually empty, ripe for further development. At the same time that they launched this project, they also added new facilities in Avalon as relations with town residents improved.

The drive to make the isthmus into another attraction began in 1899. The Bannings owned all of the land there and could lease the lots. They hoped to build a resort that would rival Avalon and could accommodate the overflow of visitors every season. They built water and sanitation facilities, erected a new pier in 1903, and planted a large number of eucalyptus trees for shade and as a windbreak, at Joseph's direction. Hotels, a tent city, and attractions like those in Avalon were planned, along with a resort hotel more opulent than even the Metropole. The *Times* reported in 1903 that a million dollars would be spent on the improvements, and that the Bannings had hired Olmsted Brothers, the most renowned landscape architecture firm in the nation, to design the grounds and link the isthmus to Emerald Bay to the northwest and to Middle Ranch and Avalon to the southeast with a tree-lined boulevard.[50]

The possibility of commissioning the prestigious Olmsted Brothers had first been raised by Frederick Ayer, who visited the island in 1902. Hearing about the directors' vague plans for the isthmus, he recommended that the Santa Catalina Island Company hire the firm from Brookline, Massachusetts, to design and oversee the landscaping. Soon after that, one of the directors contacted the Olmsteds to assess their interest in the project, now planned to be "much more elaborate" than Avalon. The landscape firm agreed to send out a representative and began assembling reference books on Southern California flora and other materials in order to make appropriate recommendations. Two members of Olmsted Brothers then spent several days at the isthmus in April 1903 with William Banning, inspecting the site for themselves.[51]

In June, John C. Olmsted sent a forty-five-page report outlining his proposals. He recommended a long, undulating road for horses and carriages, lined with a guardrail and decorative plantings, to connect the several attractions. He also suggested locations for a first-class hotel like the Metropole, a possible second-class hotel, and other buildings. A cottage village, Olmsted proposed, could be laid out around an ornamental "pleasure ground" near a large pool of seawater at a distance from the ocean. Lastly, he addressed practical matters, such as plans for utilities and sites for service buildings. In all, the report conjured a vision of a resort paradise still more elaborate and picturesque than the existing town of Avalon.[52]

The Olmsted project, which would have been an expensive proposition if brought to life, would eventually be abandoned. Since the Bannings had just planted a large number of trees at the isthmus to act as a windbreak, they decided to delay the project at least until the following year to give the saplings time to mature. The Olmsted firm agreed, and held off preparing more specific plans until the Bannings were ready. The following year was not a good one for such an expensive outlay, and in early 1905 a severe storm devastated the entire area. Many trees were blown down by the strong winds and the soil turned to mud. This setback caused the brothers to rethink the project, and plans for the major buildings, attractions, and infrastructure were put on hold. The Bannings would eventually build at the isthmus, but not based on the elaborate Olmsted plan. Much later, after the Bannings sold the island, engineer J. B. Lippincott tried to interest the island's new owner in hiring the Olmsted firm in 1919, as he believed the millionaire wanted to rebuild the island "and make something 'as big as Atlantic City' out of it." But nothing came of the suggestion, and so the Olmsteds' vision for the island died.[53]

Meanwhile, the Bannings had continued making improvements and adding attractions at Avalon. Joseph supervised the installation of a power plant for electric lighting in 1901. A "Greek Amphitheater" was built along a hillside under the direction of Hancock Banning. The Santa Catalina Island Marine Band played regular concerts there for over twenty years, with Hancock occasionally joining the group on the cornet. A scenic incline railway was built to transport tourists from Avalon to Lover's Cove for a breathtaking view of the bay and a chance to view the marine gardens there from a glass-bottom boat. Beginning in 1905, the Bannings put on a fireworks show every Saturday night during the season to illuminate Avalon Bay.[54]

Expecting large crowds to flock to these new amenities, the Bannings added two new steamers to their regular schedule in the early 1900s. *Hermosa II* replaced its namesake in 1902, and the *Cabrillo* (originally called the *San Salvador* after Juan Rodríguez Cabrillo's flagship) was launched in 1904. Both were built by expert shipwright William Muller at the Banning shipyard on Mormon Island. The *Cabrillo* was touted as perhaps the fastest vessel in her class on the California coast. These two steamers increased the number of passengers the company could bring to the island and added a degree of luxury to the trip.[55]

In order to finance this latest expansion the Bannings needed an infusion of capital. Starting the year after they purchased the island, they had searched for ways to improve their investment position. William requested changes in the mortgage payment schedule several times in the early 1890s, asking the Lick Trust for payment extensions and to release parcels in Avalon so that the Bannings could borrow money against them. He made the same request in 1897 and 1901 of the California Academy of Sciences, which took over the mortgage after the Lick Trust dissolved. In 1895 William asked his cousin's stepson, Charles F. Ayer, if he was interested in purchasing one-quarter interest in the island and three ships, because the Bannings needed cash for major improvements and would not be able to weather any further financial downturns if they used up all their own capital. Soon, he promised Ayer, Santa Catalina would be the "best paying private enterprise on the Pacific Coast."[56]

Ayer declined the offer, but another relative would sign on in 1901. George S. Patton Sr., Hancock's half brother-in-law, was brought in as a partner, keeping ownership within the extended Banning family. Patton was in the process of retiring from practicing law and would soon become the vice president and general manager of the land company of electric railway magnate Henry E. Huntington. By the terms of the deal,

Patton would own one-seventh of the Banning property on Santa Catalina and one-seventh of the Wilmington Transportation Company (with
each brother owning two-sevenths of both these companies), and one-
seventh of three-quarters interest in the Banning Wool Company, all for
$80,000. The deal also made Patton a company director with full
voting rights.[57]

With this infusion of cash, the island owners could pay for the permanent improvements planned for Avalon and the isthmus, sometimes
called Catalina City (now Two Harbors), and borrow more funds as
needed. The future looked bright for the company, and other investors
were drawn to the light, some from great distances. Two months after
the announcement of Patton's purchase, the newspapers reported that a
New York millionaire with a summer residence at Avalon had offered
$3 million for the island but had been turned down. Before the end of
the year another New Yorker seeking to purchase the island contacted
William Banning. William responded that they were not interested in
selling the entire island, but perhaps they might be willing to sell their
Avalon property for $2 million; he would consult the other directors. The
directors agreed to allow William to negotiate on those terms, but the
investor backed out when he could not have the entire island. Despite
the failure of this sale, these investors' interest increased the brothers'
confidence in their future. In the very early 1900s Santa Catalina seemed
the perfect place for the Banning family.[58]

CHAPTER TEN

A Family Rift and the Remaining Years at
Santa Catalina

Family Feud

D uring the period from the early 1900s to 1919, the brothers' amiable
relations soured, a development that affected their intertwined
family and business lives on Santa Catalina and elsewhere. A feud
pitted one brother against another and soon enveloped other members of
the family. The brothers' troubled management of the family holdings on
the "Magic Isle" was typical of the ways their business suffered from this
tension. They had banded together to buy and run Santa Catalina, but
their disagreements about how to manage the island would drive them
apart, ultimately forcing the brothers to relinquish control of it.

Family Feud

The strain in family relations began as early as 1903. A split between two
of the brothers, Hancock and Joseph, set off a rivalry that became increasingly bitter over the next decade, eventually drawing their brother
William and their spouses into familial competition and animosity. The
personal differences among the Banning brothers stemmed from disagreements concerning their conduct of the business, exacerbated after
1910 by heavy drinking. William, who according to tradition drank too
much alcohol at a party in Chicago sometime before 1900 and who thereafter never drank, arbitrated arguments between the other two. Hancock
was not known to drink to excess, but he did drink regularly, particularly
later in life: his daughter-in-law confessed that she had never kissed her
father-in-law without smelling liquor on his breath. Another Santa Catalina Island Company director, George S. Patton Sr., was known to drink
quite a bit in the early 1900s and much more in the years before his death
in 1927. Whether his and Hancock's drinking affected company management is difficult to determine.[1]

But the fourth of five company directors and its first vice president,
Joseph Brent Banning, definitely had a problem with alcohol by the early

years of the century. Hancock was well aware of it by late 1903, when he criticized his brother for injuring their business. Joseph, he said, "drinks too much and has some worthless, dishonest employees which he leaves in charge when he is away." Although William tried to find a way to ameliorate their differences, the friction between his brothers grew. Joseph resigned as a company director in 1903 but then returned in 1904, only to complain that he had no more voice in company management. By 1905 the problem had become more serious, and William tried to find a loan for Joseph to start his own business, something that could draw his attention from the feud. Joseph was so disturbed by the situation that he offered to sell most of his interest in the company to streetcar magnate Henry E. Huntington or to Patton. Around the same time, William told Hancock to refrain from asking Joseph to call a meeting about a company policy because "nine chances to one the meeting would end in a row."[2]

The emotional conflict also spilled over into the relationship between Hancock and Katharine S. Banning. In 1905 Katharine wrote to Hancock about a conversation during which, she claimed, he had criticized her husband Joseph in front of her. She regretted not having said something to him about it at the time. She then upbraided Hancock, saying that although she still considered him a friend, he should not have doubted "my undying love for my husband." In his reply, Hancock denied having said anything bad about Joseph to her, or indeed to Joseph himself. In fact, he was no longer in communication with his brother: "he does not speak to me and has not for some time." Furthermore, he was indeed expecting an apology from Hancock, and without that, "I can never feel the same towards him that I used to."[3]

Over the next few years Joseph's status with the company fluctuated with his health. He frequently missed company directors meetings, and in September 1907 he was demoted to company "traffic manager," charged with distributing promotional material and advertising, a task with reduced responsibilities. Although he remained involved with plans to expand the operations at the isthmus, reports of Banning employees drinking at the isthmus that year reflected on his supervision. (Intemperance seemed to be common on the island; the company superintendent at Avalon was having his own problems with liquor and soon would be "on the water wagon.") In 1908 Joseph proposed to do some landscaping work at the isthmus; William thought it a good idea, since Joseph's doctor had repeatedly asked William to find an occupation for him. Joseph also spent several months with Katharine at "the Springs"—

White Sulphur Springs in West Virginia. This spa and vacation resort was famous for its mineral waters, recommended by doctors for treating liver and kidney diseases as well as many other afflictions. (His father, Phineas, had visited the same resort in the year before his death to seek a cure for his maladies.) At the same time Joseph apparently turned to religion for help. By early 1909 William reported to Hancock, "I am satisfied from personal observation and from what I hear that the influence of the Christian Science Church has made a great change in J.B. It has not only enabled him to control his appetite for drink but has changed his disposition to a marked degree." Soon after that Joseph accompanied his family on a trip to New York and seemed fine.[4]

In the summertime, however, things deteriorated. In June 1909 William telegraphed Katharine, who was in the East visiting her sister Ellen Banning Ayer, that her husband was under the care of a physician for the "same complaint" but was doing well. Joseph's condition suddenly worsened, however, and William again contacted Katharine, saying that the doctor now thought she should return home. She set off to California, and William sent telegrams almost daily to her as she traveled, noting changes for the better and for the worse. In a letter to Hancock, William reported that Joseph was seriously ill and would be for some weeks or months to come: "His liver is in very bad condition, and it was very serious for a couple days last week." That the episode was serious was confirmed by Katharine's sister May, who confessed to a family friend that Joseph had been "desperately ill" for six weeks. By October Joseph seem to be well over the emergency and ready for work. Katharine's note of 1916 that Joseph had been restored to health again might have referred to further such problems, but could also have been a response to a different malady.[5]

As Joseph's drinking continued during these years, Hancock became increasingly frustrated with the company's management of Santa Catalina and other Banning businesses. In January 1907 he was given more authority over affairs in Avalon, and thought by the end of that year that he had done an excellent job in increasing profits, especially by adding some amenities and by building up departments such as the sheep business. The rest of the directors did not agree, however, and in late 1907 they decided to dissolve departments they thought to be extravagant and return to the original plan of concentrating on transportation. Hancock protested, but William pressed for the change in policy, and Joseph, George S. Patton Sr., and attorney James A. Gibson, the company's fifth director, agreed.[6]

Defeated on this vote, Hancock considered himself removed from management and began agitating for a division of the overall family investment so he could manage his share by himself. The board accepted the proposal as the only way to settle the feud. At first Joseph and Hancock exchanged letters over how to divide the property. Then they consulted their lawyers. The process would be drawn out for years, with William in the middle defending Joseph and replying to Hancock's many complaints. He recommended to Hancock that he work out with Joseph how to split the property; they could then run the business themselves and William could retire. But he felt that, as things stood, they could not manage in his absence. After many exchanges, William ultimately warned Hancock that he and Joseph had to either agree on a plan or hire a manager to run the business because "in case of my death, with the feeling that exists between you, the chances are that notwithstanding your enormous resources, you might lose everything you have." Until they did, William resolved to manage the business himself with advice chiefly from George S. Patton Sr.[7]

Hancock always wanted William to continue as president in order to keep Joseph from taking over, but he constantly criticized William's leadership. William's health deteriorated by 1911, and, weary of the fight between his brothers, he told them he had to take time off from the business to rest. An executive committee composed of Joseph, Hancock, and General Manager A. M. Jamison was appointed to run the island while William took an indefinite leave of absence. (At the same time family friend John Schumacher replaced lawyer James A. Gibson as a director.) When Joseph was away on various trips, furthermore, Hancock was left in charge of the operation. All three brothers, then, led the company at various times; they were forced to compromise to keep some semblance of continuity in the management of the island. Both Hancock and Joseph continued to claim that they had no say in the management of the island, but they certainly did, at different times and in various capacities.[8]

The Banning family feud was not a private affair. News of it spread throughout the business community and was whispered in the halls of the elite California Club and Jonathan Club by 1909. It also profoundly affected the two brothers' wives. As Joseph's drinking impacted the family business, Katharine S. Banning's relationship to Hancock and Anne was strained. While they seemed to be accommodating in family situations, Katharine and Anne were less frequently seen at social functions together. Selena Ingram, who met the two in 1902 and thought that Katharine was "the dearest sweetest woman in the world," spent many summers with both of them in Avalon, and frequently socialized with them in Los Angeles. She heard Katharine's side of the story several times, and finally had a long talk with Anne at her Descanso home in 1909, where she heard Anne's version of the conflict and could see "how much right is on this side too."[9]

Katharine and Anne both sided with their husbands, seeing the other couple as the offending party. Their differences may have had something to do with their lineage as, respectively, daughters of Union and Confederate officers, for Hancock described the family situation as "the War Between the States." But while the wives also belonged to opposition political parties, the conflict seems to have centered more on their competition for social status and their personality differences. As Ben Truman wrote in the *Times* in 1911, Katharine was "quiet and reserved in all her social ways," while Anne "was a leader in Los Angeles society and a great favorite with all who know her." All of these factors could have contributed to Truman's description of the relationship between these two "skirmishing girls," but the feud between their husbands surely deepened the rift between their wives. And this divide would eventually have an effect on more than just the family business at Santa Catalina Island.[10]

The Island Business in Flux

In the meantime, however, the Bannings had to manage their several companies, including Santa Catalina Island, in the midst of family turmoil. In 1903 they obtained a loan to pay off debts and to finance expansion at Avalon and at "Catalina City" on the isthmus. In 1905 the *Times* reported that the brothers planned to double the size of Avalon, laying out a tract of lots along a terraced hillside for lease, or, in a change of policy, for sale in fee simple. Nine hundred lots were surveyed, and a few of them sold. The incline railway, which ran from a point near the amphitheater, provided access to these lots. This was the same year, however, that strong winds devastated the isthmus, delaying development for a time.[11]

At the same time that they were expanding the business, the brothers were often rumored to be selling the island. Newspapers reported in 1904 that Santa Catalina was going to be sold to Henry E. Huntington, and Hancock had to deny it publicly. The same story appeared again in 1905, when Joseph did offer to sell his share to Huntington. In 1906 Selena Ingram wrote in her diary that her husband, Southern Pacific Railroad manager Robert Ingram, had been given an option to sell all but Hancock's portion of the island within sixty days. Robert Ingram tried to convince Southern Pacific President E. H. Harriman to buy, without success. Two years later, another railroad magnate, Great Northern Railroad President James J. Hill, visited the island and asked if it was for sale. Joseph told him it could be purchased for the right price, but whatever the amount was, apparently it was too steep for Hill. Then, in 1910, William tried to interest New York investment banker Otto M. Kahn in becoming a part owner of Santa Catalina Island, and Kahn also eventually declined. Clearly the persistent rumors of the sale of at least a large part of the island were not unfounded.[12]

As mentioned above, in 1907 the company directors decided over Hancock's protests to focus the business more narrowly on transport, selling off or shutting down the company's peripheral businesses on the island. This was, as it happened, also the year that the Meteor Boat Company decision officially opened the port of Avalon to independent boat owners. These changes not only contributed to the conflict between William and Hancock over the direction the company was taking but also loosened the family's control over some aspects of the island. This would come as welcome news for those Avalon residents who resented Banning policies and their monopoly on transportation to and from the island.[13]

After the 1908 season the Bannings again looked to the isthmus as a place to develop a profitable resort on their own terms, without some of the limitations they faced in Avalon. By this time Joseph was working on landscaping the grounds as part of his rehabilitation. William had just purchased a large amount of lumber very cheaply and sent it to the isthmus, where contractors began building necessary structures. The start of construction startled some Avalon residents, who were afraid the Bannings would desert their town, so William halted it temporarily in an attempt to appease them. But as negotiations over division of the island among the family continued, Joseph decided he wanted the isthmus for himself, as the focus of the property he hoped would be allotted to him. Joseph developed his own plans for the isthmus and had a rendering made, and he commissioned Los Angeles architect Carroll H. Brown to design a home for his family there on an elevation overlooking the bays on both sides of the island. The building of this structure in 1910 spurred increased interest in that area, and predictions that it would one day rival Avalon. Joseph continued to press the directors for more development of the isthmus, but the company was unable to find financing. Rumors that the Bannings intended to move their entire operation to the area, however, would continue to surface whenever they faced community opposition in Avalon. And they would.[14]

Joseph Brent Banning's vision for Catalina City at the isthmus, 1911. Courtesy of the Huntington Library.

The Anti-Banning Backlash

Relations between the Bannings and the residents of Avalon had been generally good since 1892, although there had always been specific complaints from a few business proprietors and homeowners over company policies. After the turn of the century, however, the dissenters gradually increased in number and became vocal critics of the Banning monopoly, even to the point of helping "intruders" land on the island without Wilmington Transportation Company tickets. Eventually led by *Catalina Wireless* newspaper editor Willis M. LeFavor and Avalon building contractor Arthur G. Woodson, they also complained about the state of Avalon's streets and water system, the Bannings' refusal to offer reduced fares for Avalon residents, and the company policy of prohibiting lessees from buying their residences. This opposition became the nucleus of a movement to take control of the town by incorporating it as a city and electing representatives to direct its management.[15]

The protesters were countered by a group of property owners who, fearing the loss of company-provided amenities, tried to ameliorate the situation by working with the Bannings to make improvements to Avalon. William Banning reported to the other Santa Catalina Island directors in 1908 that a permanent committee of "conservative property owners at Avalon" had formed to work with them on needed upgrades and to again close the port to tramp steamers. William met with leaders of this group in November 1908 and came to an agreement with them, promising to improve streets and provide electric lighting, a fire hose, and a military band, among other provisions.[16]

Joseph and Katharine's residence at the Santa Catalina isthmus (now the Banning House Lodge). Courtesy of the Banning Residence Museum.

The success of these negotiations led to the formal incorporation of the Freeholders Improvement Association of Avalon in May 1909. The association arbitrated disputes between the Bannings and their opposition, even though the Freeholders were known to be Banning sympathizers. In fact, one of their directors was Frank H. Lowe, a company official, and the Santa Catalina Island Company was one of the first one hundred members. Over the next few years the association worked to resolve and diffuse complaints against the Bannings and to operate some of the facilities and infrastructure at Avalon. These included the "Pleasure Pier," built by the Bannings in 1909 and given to the association, which provided services to sightseers. As historian James Zordich has noted, the agreement between the association and the Bannings also restored the old monopoly on transportation to the island at the expense of the independent vessels arriving from Long Beach and other coastal points.[17]

The partnership between the Bannings and the Freeholders Improvement Association of Avalon resolved some of the conflicts between the town and the company, but not all. During the negotiations between the two, William Banning ordered a study of the voting population of Avalon in case the company could not reach agreement with the association and had to settle the dispute through a public referendum. In 1911 the *Times* reported that independents besides the Meteor Boat Company would continue to bring passengers to Avalon, preventing the association from keeping its end of the bargain by blocking landings. And in the following year Hancock Banning cautioned company officials about signing a five-year agreement with the association in which the company would be bound by certain restrictions but would still have to compete with independent shippers.[18]

Proof that the partnership would not dissuade Banning critics from action came in February 1913, when two Avalon merchants filed a complaint against the Wilmington Transportation Company, still the only common carrier between the mainland and the island, for charging excessive freight and passenger rates. The complaint was heard by the California Railroad Commission, which regulated companies transporting passengers and freight. The defense argued that the commission had no authority in this case because the Banning ships traveled for the most part outside of California waters. Even with the Freeholders Improvement Association of Avalon intervening on their behalf, the Bannings lost on the issue of jurisdiction and their petition for a rehearing was denied. The Bannings appealed the ruling on jurisdiction to the California Supreme Court and then to the U.S. Supreme Court in 1915, but lost again in both cases. When the original issue of excessive fares was finally considered in 1915, however, the Railroad Commission decided that the rates were fair, considering the risks the company undertook.[19]

Outright opposition to Banning control of the island came to a head in 1913 as well. In the previous general election, a county home rule charter had been approved for Los Angeles, giving the county Board of Supervisors the power to establish local option restrictions on liquor sales and delivery in unincorporated areas, but not in cities. Residents of Avalon had been trying to limit saloons in town since at least 1895, when a petition protesting the granting of a liquor license for a saloon had been presented to the Board of Supervisors. By 1912 such sentiment throughout Southern California was much stronger, and saloon interests fought to protect their businesses from county restrictions. On Santa Catalina they joined with those who opposed the Banning monopoly to press for the incorporation of Avalon as a city and began collecting signatures for the petition. As the *Times* pointed out, before 1913 the saloon owners had adamantly opposed incorporation and more taxes, "But today, incorporation to the 'wets' means liberty, better conditions and representative government and, it is alleged, several saloons."[20]

The incorporation of Avalon was also expected to end the Banning transportation monopoly and lower fares, once the city approved new franchises. The *Times* further predicted that the Pilgrim Club (closed since a raid in 1909) would reopen for gambling, among many other changes. The Bannings claimed to be neutral on the issue, but they certainly had a lot to lose. A spokesman for the company was quoted as saying that "If the residents and property owners desire to incorporate and will continue to maintain the standard of peace and quietness for the port which has existed during the past four years, we shall not oppose them." The Bannings were not prepared to allow cityhood to jeopardize their investment, however, and it was understood that, after years of threats, they might finally close their amenities, end financial support for Avalon utilities, and move their operation to Catalina City at the isthmus. Although William had been preparing for a vote of this kind for several years, and consulted his lawyers about how to register company employees in 1908, the company officially tried to remain aloof from the fray and played no public role. The prevailing sentiment in Avalon was not with the Bannings or the Freeholders Improvement Association, and in the June 1913 election incorporation was favored by a vote of 132 to 88.[21]

Defeated by the city backers, the Bannings adjusted to cityhood. Initially, the company continued to operate the water, sewer, and electric light utilities in the new municipality. The company did hedge its investment though: the *Times* reported in August that the directors were again making plans to develop the isthmus as a resort. In the meantime, the Freeholders supported the Bannings by continuing to prevent independent vessels from landing. This vigilance included spraying men and women trying to disembark at Freeholders' Pleasure Pier with fire hoses; they justified this by noting that the intruders had not paid a wharfage fee and were bringing in liquor, which contributed to rowdy behavior and the littering of city streets.[22]

The availability of liquor on the island was itself a major issue for residents, as the incorporation campaign had demonstrated. The Bannings hoped to limit the number of saloons on the island in order to preserve the resort's family appeal and company profits. An ordinance passed by the new Avalon city trustees allowed for just one liquor license, which the Bannings promptly secured for the Metropole (although they failed to pay for it). Since the Metropole closed for the season on September 15, no place in Avalon could legally sell liquor from that date until the beginning of the next tourist season. The two saloon owners on the island immediately began circulating a referendum petition to bring the city ordinance to a popular vote. Three proposals were approved for the referendum: one, put forward by the "drys," prohibited all saloons; the second, supported by the two saloon owners, the city trustees, and the Bannings, mandated only two saloon licenses; and the third allowed for three sa-

Avalon Harbor in 1911. Courtesy of the Huntington Library.

loons and permitted some other liquor sales. Both the liquor interests and the Bannings worked to register voters for the September 11 election, in which the two-saloon measure was passed (additional hotel and club licenses were also made available).[23]

By 1914, just one year after becoming a city, Avalon's finances were already strained and the trustees turned to the Bannings for help in financing civic improvements. But the Bannings were increasingly hostile to the trustees' goals and unwilling to support city improvements as they had in the past. In order to gain city control of utilities, the trustees called for an election to approve $130,000 in bonds to purchase the Banning sewer system, electricity plant, water system, and gas plant. Opposed by the Bannings, the proposal was overwhelmingly defeated in March by residents unwilling to take on such debt. In May the Wilmington Transportation Company expressed further displeasure with city management, which had by then nearly depleted the municipal treasury. William Banning told the trustees that his company would no longer collect the head tax imposed by ordinance on passengers landing on its own wharf and would no longer donate several hundred dollars per month to the city. Amid discussions of belt-tightening and even disincorporation, the

trustees raised revenue by approving licenses for more saloons and allowing them to open on Sundays, a move that infuriated those opposed
to more liquor establishments and potentially created more work for the
city marshal, who had to police the barrooms.[24]

The city's financial problems and a dismal summer season spurred
further negotiations with the Bannings, resulting in an agreement at the
end of 1914 that allowed the Freeholders Improvement Association to
again manage municipal affairs in partnership with city officials and the
Santa Catalina Island Company. The Bannings promised to provide a free
band for concerts and dancing, to take care of city sewers, garbage collection, street maintenance, and lighting, to donate land for a city cemetery, and to allow the Freeholders to conduct a competing transportation
service at their own wharf. The three entities began implementing the
agreement soon after, and in June the Freeholders took back the Pleasure
Pier, which they had sold to the city for $5, and began operating it again.
The new officers of the Freeholders Improvement Association included
Banning friends and even the general manager of the Santa Catalina Island
Company. "Freeholders Rejoice Over Avalon's Prospect" declared a *Times*
story describing these developments in mid-1915, and all three partners
looked forward to a better relationship and a more prosperous season.[25]

A Great Fire and Its Aftermath

The tranquility brought to Avalon by this pact was shattered just hours
before dawn on November 29, 1915, when a devastating fire destroyed a
large section of the city. Beginning about 3:30 in the morning at or near
the Hotel Rose, the inferno was fanned by strong winds and traveled rapidly though the eastern and downtown districts, burning over half of the
city's structures to the ground. The poorly equipped Avalon volunteer
fire department was no match for the conflagration, even with an entire
ocean of water at its disposal. The Metropole, five other major hotels,
and several smaller hotels and rooming houses were consumed, along
with the Pilgrim Club, the Tuna Club, the main bathhouse, several substantial residences, a number of waterfront shops, and countless wooden
and tent cottages. An estimated two hundred persons were left homeless,
but at least there were no fatalities and no major injuries. The damage,
only half of which was covered by insurance, was estimated the next day
at a half million dollars.[26]

The fire was believed to have been set deliberately, although no one
was ever convicted of the crime. Some Avalon residents believed it was
started by the owner of a small hotel in Avalon who owed a considerable

Ruins of Avalon after the 1915 fire. Courtesy of the Huntington Library.

amount of money and hoped to collect on the insurance. Others thought that a group of residents opposed to the Bannings' ownership of much of Avalon had started the fire, since it appeared to have been ignited in several locations simultaneously. Joseph Brent Banning, who was present and took photographs of the conflagration and its aftermath, reported that he had heard a number of rumors concerning the explosion that started the fire, and all pointed to the same perpetrator. The Los Angeles County District Attorney's office investigated the blaze for quite some time, and even arrested "a former Avalon resident who was unpopular there" as the arson suspect, but no one was ever prosecuted. Hancock Banning Jr. later noted that when he returned to Avalon the day after the catastrophe, he spoke to a priest about the cause of the fire, which had stopped just short of the Catholic church at one point and of Ben Rosin's saloon at another. The padre concluded that the Lord must have intervened to save the church. Banning wryly responded that if that were true, then the devil must have saved the saloon.[27]

Immediately after the fire, the Bannings were asked if they planned to rebuild the destroyed structures at Avalon or move their main operation to a new town at the isthmus. The Metropole and other Banning buildings were insured, but rebuilding Avalon's infrastructure would require a major outlay. The directors differed among themselves. Hancock advocated rebuilding Avalon and erecting a replacement for the Metropole as soon as possible. He cautioned against borrowing money and making any further investments at the isthmus at a time when Avalon needed so much attention; unlike Joseph, he had no personal interest in the west end of the island. Hancock even suggested that he and William could buy out Joseph and George S. Patton Sr.'s shares, and Hancock could manage the operation himself. Four of the five directors also considered selling most of the island at this point. In December they awarded an option to Patton to buy all but Hancock's share of the company along with several Wilmington Transportation Company ships and equipment, at a price that would have brought them a handsome profit. A week later the directors were entertaining enquiries about such a sale from an agent who thought he might have a solid buyer, but an offer was never made.[28]

By early 1916 the directors announced that they would spend a quarter of a million dollars to rebuild their "high class pleasure resort" at Avalon for the coming summer season by clearing away the wreckage, rebuilding the bathhouse and the streets, and erecting a new tent city and a "first class café" for visitors. Patton agreed to hold onto his share of the island so as not to burden the Banning brothers with any further debt. Still, it would be impossible to build a hotel such as the Metropole in the few months before the start of the season, so that project would wait until after the resort opened. The brothers were again in conflict over the site of the new luxury hotel: Hancock wanted it in Avalon, but Joseph and William already had plans to build one at Catalina City on the isthmus. Tent cottages would have to suffice for visitors for the summer of 1916 while the family feud continued.[29]

As expected, the 1916 tourist season was dismal for Banning profits. Brochures for Santa Catalina Island reminded guests that Wilmington Transportation Company tickets were required to take advantage of Banning amenities, but few amenities existed that year. Tent cottages were the only available Banning accommodations, which certainly kept away those seeking more luxurious housing. After the season the Bannings negotiated a trust deed for $850,000 to pay off debts and build a new major tourist hotel in or near Avalon, and began planning the improvements.[30]

The resort hotel became one focus of another family dispute by late 1916. In December Hancock complained to a family lawyer that William was willing to give away an immense lot of valuable property to a San Francisco hotel builder. Furthermore, he said, the other three directors were reluctant to borrow enough money to expand the operation and to reestablish the units that had been closed in order to keep the entire venture afloat—businesses that he had developed when he managed the

island on his own in 1907. He thought he should again be put in charge
of the entire island operation, to recreate these "revenue-bearing departments" to complement the transportation enterprise. With a satis-
factory loan from one of the Bannings' banks, he could buy out the other
owners and make the island profitable again. In January 1917 he confronted William in a letter in which he criticized the latter's plan to sell
lots in Avalon and give away hotel sites and other privileges as "dangerous and outrageous." Hancock warned that he would inform one of their
bankers, Jackson A. Graves (father of a future Banning relative), of William's proposed actions so Graves could prevent William from "throwing
the company into bankruptcy."[31]

The directors finally approved a motion to build and finance the hotel
themselves in January 1917, but Hancock voted against the proposal because it did not specify a location. He likely feared it would be built at
Catalina City instead of Avalon. Several months later a site near Avalon
was chosen and work was begun, but had to be abandoned because of tidelands issues with the federal government. After an even more unprofitable
tourist season than 1916 and more management infighting, the directors finally agreed in December 1917 to erect a hotel on the tidelands site later on
(it was never built) and in the interim to construct an annex for it at Descanso Canyon, after moving Hancock Banning's summer home to the rear
of the property. This annex became the St. Catherine Hotel. Ground was
broken in the spring of 1918 under Hancock's direction, and the hotel was
completed in June, just in time for the start of the season.[32]

The opening of the St. Catherine could not arrest the downward tra-
jectory of the Banning investment in the island. As several historians
have noted, the nature of American tourism across the nation was beginning to change in the 1910s with the increasing popularity and af-
fordability of the automobile. While older and wealthier Americans
continued to spend long summers at major resort hotels, middle-class
and affluent families—even the Bannings—spent some of their vacation
and idle hours motoring to tourist destinations for sightseeing and recreation. The "Good Roads" movement in California, which stimulated highway construction and repair after 1909, made more localities conveniently
accessible and leisure pursuits more varied. As historian Jane Wilson has
observed, in Southern California the older set might continue to spend
their vacations at Avalon with its social order and limited amenities, but
"their motoring children preferred more sophisticated entertainments"
at a multitude of other venues easily reached by automobile. Combined
with the disruptions of the Banning shipping and harbor business brought

about by World War I, the loss of tourists to the automobile dealt a fatal blow to the Bannings' venture on Santa Catalina Island.[33]

Near the close of the 1918 season Hancock was again criticizing the other directors, especially William, for allowing their island investment to deteriorate. In a memorandum he cited a long list of policies that needed to be changed to create additional income and to avoid selling the island at a sacrifice. In December he again expressed to the company officers his hope of obtaining a loan to buy out the other Santa Catalina Island Company owners and manage the island himself based on his previously successful policies. But Hancock did not have the loan in hand, and by this time he had probably alienated the other directors with his constant complaints. In the following month, an opportunity would surface that other directors could not pass up.[34]

The Sale of Santa Catalina

The conclusion of the Banning story on Santa Catalina was written in early 1919, when a new buyer emerged. William Wrigley Jr. was a Chicago chewing-gum magnate and owner of the Chicago Cubs baseball club of the National League. According to Hancock Banning Jr., Wrigley had told William Banning that he had been "a good boy all through the war, and paid his taxes, and now he was going to play with the island." Since 1914 Wrigley had owned a winter home—actually a large mansion—in Pasadena and was well aware of the charms of Santa Catalina Island. With two partners, he offered to purchase the Banning interest in the island and the Wilmington Transportation Company for about three million dollars. They would place the management of the company in the hands of one of the partners, David Blankenhorn, a Pasadena investment banker and developer who had just returned from wartime service in the U.S. Army. Blankenhorn, along with his business associate and the third partner, Robert Hunter, represented Wrigley's business interests in Southern California and had convinced the gum magnate that the island and its transport operation would be a wise investment. The sale and transfer of stock was negotiated by lawyers representing the Bannings and Wrigley, and was announced in February 1919.[35]

The owners' decision to sell was not unanimous, but the majority was in perfect agreement. William Banning arranged the protocol and headed the negotiations. He was probably relieved to bring an end to declining profits and the family feud that still hampered management of the island. He may also have been pressured to sell by lenders who had helped to finance the St. Catherine Hotel and found it could not be in-

The St. Catherine Hotel, completed in 1918. Courtesy of the Huntington Library.

sured at a reasonable price because, even after 1915, the island lacked adequate firefighting resources. Joseph Brent Banning, who usually sided with his older brother in such matters, and George S. Patton Sr., who probably feared further losses, deferred to William, who became the spokesman for a majority of the stockholders in order to approve the sale. In February the company directors and officers resigned and were replaced by Wrigley's team.[36]

Hancock, the lone dissenter, tried one last time to thwart the sale. Refusing to sell his shares, he warned William that "you have gotten into the hands of a dangerous outfit." Before the sale Blankenhorn and Hunter had apparently tried to smooth the waters, asking Hancock if he was willing to manage the company as a minority stockholder, and they consulted him about selling off a large portion of property in Avalon, which Hancock had always opposed when the Bannings owned the island. When the time came for the newspaper stories announcing the sale, however, Hancock claimed he had had nothing to do with the deal and had not been offered a price for his own shares. His protests proved fruitless, however, and eventually he transferred his stock to William in return for property in downtown Los Angeles and cash to pay off a debt, and the sale was completed.[37]

William was asked to remain on the board of the Santa Catalina Island Company to help with the transition, and he would stay for another decade. The sale also included the Wilmington Transportation Company, owner of the *Cabrillo* and the *Hermosa II*, the luxury steamers that plied the route between the island and the mainland. This company was acquired by Wrigley in the same manner and on the same day as Santa Catalina, with its directors and officers resigning one at a time in favor of Wrigley's slate. (William also stayed on with this company until 1929.) With the ownership of these companies transferred, the Bannings then sold their remaining shipping operations in the harbor area, which were held by the Banning Company, and that company was dissolved and finally disincorporated in August 1920. By that time the family was no longer involved with the resort business the three brothers had started, nor with the shipping business their father had begun almost seven decades earlier. The new owners of Santa Catalina lifted the ban on selling lots to private owners and permitted independent vessels to land there. As an old resident later summed up the Banning rule of the island for twenty-seven years, it "wasn't democratic, but they did maintain order."[38]

The closing of the Banning era at Santa Catalina Island brought new owners with new dreams for the "Magic Isle," and deep pockets to match. Wrigley added many amenities over the years, including a baseball field and other facilities for his Chicago Cubs, who would spend their spring training on the island. Santa Catalina became a playground for film and sports celebrities, a set for motion pictures, and a training center for the armed forces during World War II, while always remaining the popular summer resort that the Bannings had created. In 1975 the Wrigley family deeded most of the island to the Santa Catalina Island Conservancy, a nonprofit organization responsible for the conservation of most of the interior and coastline of the island. While Avalon, Two Harbors at the isthmus, and other points are still dedicated to sports, recreation, and tourism, most of the island is now protected from development and its natural landscape preserved, a setting for science education programs devoted to its natural history and that of the ocean surrounding it. For the Bannings, of course, protecting the natural features of the island was in their own economic interest, since this enhanced its lure for tourists and seekers of pleasure and recreation. To a large degree, they were good stewards of this island paradise and left it to future owners and residents to do the same.[39]

The first two decades of the twentieth century were years of increasing family disagreements for the Bannings and brought an end to their venture in the Southern California tourist industry as well as their inherited harbor business. Although they invested substantial energy and capital in remaking Santa Catalina, they ultimately could not overcome their own shortcomings, their differences with others on the island, and gradual changes in regional and national tourism. As we will see in the following chapter, however, the Magic Isle was not their only concern during these years: the Banning brothers were also involved in state and local politics, protecting their tidelands property, and, of course, raising the next generation of Bannings.

THE BANNINGS IN THE PROGRESSIVE ERA

T he two decades after the turn of the century saw the nation transformed in the realms of politics, the economy, and culture. Public sentiment turned against the business magnates and their
political allies who had put the gold in the Gilded Era—precisely the
circle in which the Bannings moved and that patronized Santa Catalina
in its heyday. The family split over how to respond to the intense political reformism of this new era, which brought an end to almost everything they had built together. The feuds that plagued the management
of Santa Catalina frayed the bonds that held the brothers and their businesses together. And finally, although only the younger generation of
Bannings directly participated in the War to End All Wars, its economic
aftershocks contributed to the destruction of all that remained of the
Banning Company.

Historians of American history have dubbed the decades around the turn
of the twentieth century the "Progressive Era." Beginning in the 1890s
and continuing through World War I and into the 1920s, a reformist
cultural and political movement swept the nation. Progressives sought to
modernize the political, economic, and social institutions of America,
reduce the power of large corporations, eliminate corruption, and ameliorate the social ills caused by industrialization and urbanization.[1]

The progressives also fought to alter politics at the state and local
levels. In Los Angeles urban reformers shook up the old political system,
in which elected representatives had confined their policymaking to providing basic municipal services and keeping taxes low. These incumbents
reflected the views of their backers, an entrepreneurial elite of business
and professional leaders, including the Banning brothers, who wanted

to spur growth through private development, rabid boosterism, and anti-union policies. This elite collaborated with the political arm of the Southern Pacific Railroad, the state's single most important economic power, to influence legislation, most effectively through the Republican Party, but also with Democrats. Partners in business, the Banning brothers and the leaders of the Southern Pacific were partners in politics, too.[2]

Los Angeles city and county progressives—many of whom were also active in the statewide movement—were a disparate yet highly organized group of middle-class business leaders and professionals. These men and women did not always agree on specific reforms but banded together to change the political structure and gain a voice in urban policy making. Many reformers, but not all, supported women's suffrage, direct legislation, and election reform, and fought to eliminate municipal corruption and "vice" businesses like saloons, gambling establishments, and brothels. A smaller subset worked with labor unions and reached out to the poor. In the early 1900s their leaders organized against the Republican political establishment, which was managed by agents of the Southern Pacific Railroad. Exploiting public outrage over vice scandals involving city officials, progressives took over city hall in 1909 and then the county courthouse one year later. They also contributed to the statewide movement that stormed Sacramento with Governor Hiram Johnson's victory in 1910. Once in office they would shake up the existing system and contest the influence of the Banning brothers and other defenders of the old order.[3]

Banning Politics

In the maelstrom of reformist politics and social change in the Progressive Era, the Banning brothers almost always stood pat. Staunch Republicans, the three brothers supported the party at all levels. Joseph even made it a point to travel back east to attend the inauguration of President William Howard Taft in early 1909. Locally they backed GOP candidates: in the 1890s, John Cline for county sheriff and, in 1906, mayoral candidate Dr. Walter Lindley, on whose campaign committee Hancock served. Since the Bannings' principal business partner, the Southern Pacific Railroad Company, effectively chose the Republican candidates for state and local offices, the Bannings found it to their mutual benefit to cooperate with railroad political agents such as Walter F. X. Parker and Republican officeholders. When it was in their interest, however, they also courted Democrats such as Senator Stephen M. White and associates of family member George S. Patton on specific matters.[4]

After 1900 the Banning brothers veered away from this conservative course only once, in 1911, when Joseph contributed to the campaign of Mayor George Alexander, a progressive reformer and a member of the Republican Party. In the primary election Alexander and the conservative Republican candidate ran far behind Job Harriman, a leader of the Socialist Party who received nearly enough votes to win the office outright. Certain that reformers would win, in a fit of panic the city's business and social elite turned to Alexander as the progressive candidate most acceptable to them. Family friend Selena Ingram, who came from a very conservative Democratic family, wrote in her diary, "We trust Alexander will surely beat Harriman, the Socialist—although we do not really care for Alexander!" Joseph contributed to his campaign and offered Banning automobiles to transport his supporters to the polls. Alexander and the good government forces (the "Goo-Goos" to conservatives) triumphed.[5]

The two Banning wives—now matriarchs—differed radically in their approach to politics. Katharine does not appear in any reports of party activity in this period. Her father, William Lowber Banning, had been a lifelong Democrat in Pennsylvania and Minnesota, and her husband, Joseph, was a staunch conservative Republican. But she apparently decided to stay out of politics, becoming a prime example of the American woman lauded by opponents of women's suffrage: the angel of the house who stayed on her pedestal, far above the political fray. In fact, the only mention of her interest in politics is a note that she hosted a speech by a critic of women's suffrage in her Westlake Avenue home in 1911; she was most likely a member of the group that organized the meeting.[6]

On the other hand, Hancock's spouse, Anne, was deeply involved in politics throughout most of her life. In the Progressive Era and after she was a leader in the Democratic Party at the local, state, and even national levels. Her political heritage as a Southerner and daughter of a devout Democrat was directly opposed to that of her husband, and they disagreed on most partisan political issues. In the late 1890s she supported Democrat Meredith P. Snyder for mayor of Los Angeles, and in the 1900s she backed mostly moderate Democrats. In the summer of 1912 she and many of her relatives in the Wilson and Patton families were members of the social committee of the California Democratic Women's League, which was preparing to campaign for the Democratic candidate for president as soon as he was nominated. Anne devoted so many hours to party work and on political issues throughout her life that it is difficult to imagine how she managed at the same time to run a household and participate in her many charitable and social activities.[7]

Anne's half brother, George S. Patton, was also a staunch Democrat, although of a very conservative bent, which allowed him to collaborate happily with the Banning brothers in managing Santa Catalina Island. George had served as district attorney in Los Angeles County in the 1880s and ran unsuccessfully for Congress as a Democrat in the next decade. He was a member of the Democratic County Central Committee for many years and was influential in party decisions. When the Democrats won the presidency in 1912, George thought he might be chosen for a national post, but was not offered one. By then his political ideology was described as "sort of a reactionary royalism," this at a time when the progressive movement was at its zenith. In 1916 he ran for the U.S. Senate against progressive Republican Hiram Johnson and was crushed in the balloting.[8]

Phineas Banning's daughters Mary and Lucy spent much of the Progressive Era away from Los Angeles and probably did not participate in politics. Their mother, Mary E. H. Banning, did become involved in local politics, as well as women's clubs and society events. Like Anne, she was a member of the Friday Morning Club, a women's organization formed by Caroline Severance in Los Angeles, whose members became increasingly active in political and social reform activities after 1900. Many of the women in the club were married to leaders of the progressive movement and worked together with them to achieve women's suffrage and other goals.[9]

Mary E. H. Banning joined the nonpartisan municipal reform movement by 1913, just as many of its adherents again banded together with conservatives to defeat Socialist Job Harriman in his second bid for mayor. In May she hosted a public reception at her home for candidates of the Municipal Conference of 1913, a fusion coalition that drew together some reformers and many of the city's worried conservatives. The reception was well attended, and almost one hundred people took seats on her expansive front porch. Mayoral candidate John Shenk spoke in favor of city investment in San Pedro Bay infrastructure as he stood next to an oil portrait of Phineas Banning, "the pioneer promoter of harbor improvements." In the coming primary election the Socialists would be defeated, but many conservatives then deserted the Shenk coalition, and he lost the general election. Mary continued to support the nonpartisan reformers as a member of the executive committee and was active in other campaigns.[10]

One of the most prominent issues of the era was women's suffrage, on which the Banning family was completely split. The movement to get the

Mary E. H. Banning's house on Fort Hill about 1890. Courtesy of the Security
Pacific Collection, Los Angeles Public Library.

vote for women in California had been gaining steam since the 1890s,
when several advocacy organizations were formed. In Los Angeles the
Suffrage Club, founded by women, and later on the Political Equality
League, formed by wealthy men, worked together to bring the issue to
a vote. Women's suffrage was opposed by conservatives who believed
that a woman's place in society was in the home, not engaged in the sometimes seedy world of politics, and by "vice" entrepreneurs who feared that
women would vote to suppress their businesses. When progressives took
over the state government, they placed a constitutional amendment on
the November 1911 ballot allowing women to vote in state and local offices
in California, and launched a political campaign to win its approval.[11]

Most of the Bannings opposed the women's suffrage amendment.
Hancock and Joseph remained silent in public, but privately they did not
favor it. Katharine probably belonged to the anti-suffrage group that had
met at her home. William Banning was more vocal, becoming a prominent member of the Men's League Opposed to Extension of Suffrage to
Women, a group of fifty conservative businessmen and professionals that
also included George S. Patton, Senator Frank Flint, and banker Jackson A.
Graves, a future Banning relative by marriage. The conservative *Times* saw
the organization simply as a group of concerned community leaders, while
the reform-minded *Tribune* painted the committee as the engine of the
Southern Pacific political machine. Patton's wife, Ruth Wilson Patton,

belonged to the Southern California Association Opposed to the Ballot for Women, a group of women who claimed they already had all the political power they needed.[12]

On the other side of the issue were two, perhaps three, Banning women. Mary E. H. Banning, the brothers' stepmother, clearly supported the suffrage amendment through her women's clubs. After its passage, she helped raise campaign funds for pro-suffrage groups in other western states. Anne was an outspoken advocate, an "out and out" suffragist, according to Hancock and to Selena Ingram. Her activism was certainly in keeping with her liberal reform politics. Anne's daughter Eleanor, who was still a teenager in 1911 but had "the greatest kind of interest in politics," according to her father, was believed to be against the amendment. However, Hancock wrote, "she would surely put in a vote if she were old enough to do so." Eleanor would continue to be engaged with politics in later years and was probably pleased that the women's suffrage amendment passed in 1911, if only by a close margin.[13]

Another progressive political issue that affected the Bannings—and their pocketbooks—was the fight for government control of public resources and utilities. Progressives championed this cause in order to end corruption in government and to rationalize urban development. Private owners of such resources, they argued, tended to get their way by paying off officeholders and could refuse to participate in projects that would benefit the public. Conservative business interests, too, supported municipal control of infrastructure like the water system, because this tended to improve service and keep costs low, thereby attracting new industries and residents. In Los Angeles, the campaign focused specifically on achieving city control of the harbor at San Pedro. An alliance of municipal reformers and the Los Angeles Chamber of Commerce wanted to acquire a deepwater port for landlocked Los Angeles to prepare for the boom in trade promised by the completion of the Panama Canal. They proposed to get their port simply by expanding the city boundary southward to encompass the entire harbor area, a move opposed by the Bannings, the Southern Pacific Railroad, lumber companies, and other port property owners, who wanted government funding for improvements, but not government restrictions.[14]

In 1900 the harbor included the city of San Pedro, incorporated in 1888, and Wilmington. The latter district, established by Phineas Banning in 1858, had been incorporated by the state legislature in 1872 but had never formed a municipal government. With Phineas no longer able to stop it, the legislature disincorporated this city without a government in 1887, and it again fell under the jurisdiction of the county Board of Supervisors. In 1905 the adjacent city of Long Beach attempted to increase its own harbor frontage by annexing Wilmington, but the proposition failed to win enough votes. Wilmington residents fought back against this threat by voting overwhelmingly for incorporation that same year. After a long court battle spearheaded by Los Angeles business interests that coveted the Wilmington waterfront, the vote was upheld in 1909.[15]

In the meantime the Los Angeles boosters had annexed a "shoe-string" addition in 1906 as part of their campaign to take over the harbor. This long, narrow corridor of land connected the southern city limits to Wilmington and San Pedro. During the next three years they negotiated a plan to consolidate the three cities, giving Los Angeles its harbor. Consolidation was opposed by Long Beach, which still hoped to create a joint harbor with Wilmington and San Pedro; by the Southern Pacific Railroad, which owned considerable property in San Pedro and hoped to keep this harbor subservient to its primary port in San Francisco; by the Bannings and harbor lumber companies; and by some residents of the harbor towns who expected to pay higher taxes after consolidation. The proponents were finally victorious in 1909, and both Wilmington and San Pedro gave up cityhood in return for a never-fulfilled promise to retain some measure of self-government as a borough within the municipal government.[16]

The victory for Los Angeles harbor advocates did not come easily. The Southern Pacific Railroad and the Bannings, threatened with losing some of their property along with their influence in port development, waged a fierce campaign against the proposal. While the Southern Pacific used its usual political tactics at the state level, the Bannings pressed their agenda in local elections. In the San Pedro city election of 1906 they supported an anti-consolidation "Citizens" ticket that included the superintendent of the Banning Company and other candidates for city trustees. In that same year they backed a slate of candidates, including one of their own employees, in the Wilmington city election against an anti-Banning and anti-saloon "People's Ticket." The Bannings did well in both elections, winning most of the slots in Wilmington when they promised to pay for dredging the inner harbor. As the court battle over the incorporation of Wilmington dragged on, William Banning asked his business allies to intervene with members of the Los Angeles Chamber of Commerce who, he asserted, were delaying harbor improvements with their suit. He even offered to give up Banning property in the inner harbor to resolve the issue.[17]

While the Bannings fought against consolidation in San Pedro and Wilmington, the Southern Pacific and dissident harbor residents took on the Los Angeles delegation in Sacramento. City representatives pushed through the bill and brought it to a vote, however, backed by the *Times*, the Chamber of Commerce, the city administration, and the local representative of the Army Corps of Engineers, which was responsible for harbor improvements. When the consolidation measure passed, Los Angeles had completed its march to the sea and its harbor commission at last had a harbor to rule.[18]

The Tidelands Issue

The takeover of the harbor in 1909 not only wrested control of the harbor's future from the Bannings, the Southern Pacific, and other companies, but also set the stage for the taking of some of their property. The progressives and their business allies presented their campaign to develop the port as the struggle of "the people" for the common good against selfish private interests, but to the owners of waterfront property it looked like a land grab, and they fought to protect their investments. Because many Los Angeles residents were hostile to the economic and political power of the Southern Pacific Railroad, the drive to take harbor property from the railroad and its friends soon gathered speed.

This effort centered around the status of the harbor tidelands: who could and did own the land within the harbor that was above water at normal low tide and submerged at normal high tide? California laws passed in the 1860s allowed such "swamp and overflowed lands" to be sold to private parties, and Phineas Banning had purchased quite a bit of it for next to nothing. The state legislature altered the law in 1870, when it prohibited the sale of tidelands within two miles of incorporated cities. Phineas Banning supported the incorporation of Wilmington in 1872 specifically in order to thwart future sales of tidelands to private interests— a fact that would later become key in the argument over ownership.[19]

Once construction of the breakwater began in the early 1900s, the tidelands suddenly looked to be very valuable. This acreage represented much of the waterfront in the harbor, and dredging within the port would supply material to raise the land above the high water mark so that wharves, warehouses, and shipping facilities could be built on it. Because they owned the tidelands that would have to be dredged to accommodate oceangoing ships, the Bannings, the Southern Pacific, and other corporations could also block any attempt by municipal authorities to plan and expand public harbor operations. Once they had dredged the harbor, the

Bannings hoped to use and lease their tidelands property to companies doing business there. In 1905, William Banning asked the chief of the U.S. Army Corps of Engineers, the federal agency responsible for harbor improvements, to expedite the drawing of improved harbor lines so that the Bannings could determine the best place to dredge the inner harbor. E. E. Calvin, general manager of the Southern Pacific, wrote in support of the request, which would also speed the railroad's plans for the harbor. These requests spurred activity in the Los Angeles office of the Army Corps of Engineers: Captain Amos Fries and civilian engineer David E. Hughes studied the technical and legal aspects of the tidelands issue and recommended that the state act to reclaim the privately held tidelands. Both Fries and Hughes would aid Los Angeles in the consolidation campaign and the effort to obtain the tidelands.[20]

In response, the Bannings, the Southern Pacific, and other private harbor interests lobbied federal officials for permission to begin their harbor operations before the city could act. The Bannings paid Thomas E. Gibbon, a lawyer for the Los Angeles and Salt Lake Railroad who would later oppose the Bannings as a member of the harbor commission, to travel to Washington, D.C., and other points east to obtain political support from Secretary of War William H. Taft, who oversaw the U.S. Army Corps of Engineers. Senator Frank Flint was recruited to introduce a bill in Congress instructing Taft to establish harbor lines at Wilmington that would benefit private owners. Hancock Banning tried to persuade his friend, Southern Pacific official Robert Ingram, to have the railroad's powerful president, E. H. Harriman, forward the request to the secretary of war, but was rebuffed. On the local front the Bannings tried to build bridges with the trustees of Wilmington in case they needed the support of their hometown on the tidelands issue.[21]

The Bannings nearly extricated themselves from this fight when William concluded an arrangement to sell most of their tideland property to the Southern Pacific for $250,000 in 1908. By the terms of the deal, the Bannings would have retained their ownership of Mormon Island, which they could continue to develop by dredging. Everyone thought it was a good deal except Hancock, who protested that it would actually put the Banning Company in financial trouble. The sale was contingent, however, on the tidelands issue being settled in their favor, so the Bannings still had to work with the Southern Pacific to win that battle before any of the property could change hands.[22]

In the meantime, although the consolidation vote was still pending and the harbor was still outside city boundaries, the city of Los Angeles and its boosterish business partners entered the fray. In early 1907 the harbor committee of the Los Angeles Chamber of Commerce protested to the Army Corps of Engineers over the private owners' plan to reclaim tidelands by dredging the deeper navigable areas, noting, "We believe in a harbor built by government, because in that way only is it possible to secure development and adoption of a comprehensive plan." "Private interests," the committee argued, could not "carry out so broad a scheme." In June 1908 the newspapers reported that Judge Joseph Call might be sent to Washington, D.C., to lobby the president and attorney general on the city's behalf. In a hearing that month, the city, its primary business organization, and the Army Corps of Engineers joined publicly to advocate for government development of the harbor and government ownership of its tidelands. In the following month the city's harbor commission voted to ask the state attorney general to file a suit to settle the validity of the tidelands grants.[23]

The state began legal action at the end of 1908, and the first of a dozen cases involving the Bannings and other private owners would be heard the following year. The very long judicial process centered on whether the tidelands were granted while Wilmington and San Pedro were incorporated cities and what early California laws said about submerged and navigable lands. City attorney Leslie R. Hewitt and the private firm of Anderson & Anderson argued for the state, while George H. Smith and lawyers for the Southern Pacific represented the defendants. In January 1911, Judge Walter Bordwell ruled in the first of the cases that tidelands awarded to the Bannings and later sold to the Southern Pacific should not have been awarded in the first place, that Wilmington was legally incorporated from 1872 to 1887, when some of the grants were made, and that the private parties should not be compensated for their losses.[24]

With the initial court proceedings favoring public ownership, the progressives and their allies asked the state legislature to transfer these lands from the state—to which the tidelands would revert if the ruling held—to the city. A delegation of Chamber of Commerce members and reform activists headed by former Banning lobbyist Thomas E. Gibbon traveled to Sacramento to urge passage of the Los Angeles Tidelands Act. With the defeat of the Southern Pacific political machine in the 1910 election, the legislature was in the hands of the progressives, and advocates doubtless expected the bill to pass easily. San Francisco commercial interests tried to block the bill, however, fearing the effects of a competing harbor in Los Angeles. The Los Angeles delegation finally persuaded their counterparts in the north to cooperate by helping them to push

The Banning's Mormon Island tidelands location about 1910. Courtesy of the Huntington Library.

through similar measures for tidelands in the San Francisco Bay, and the bill for the southern port finally passed.[25]

The public acquisition of the harbor, however, was far from complete. The Southern Pacific and the Bannings appealed Judge Bordwell's decision to the State Supreme Court. In several decisions over the next two years, the Supreme Court ruled in favor of the state, and thereby Los Angeles, in nine cases—those concerning tidelands within two miles of the Wilmington and San Pedro city limits. The court also agreed to re-hear arguments that the statute of limitations for challenging the private owners' claims had run out. The Bannings and the Southern Pacific then appealed to the U.S. Supreme Court for relief on rulings concerning the use of the property adjacent to the tidelands, but the state was victorious again. Hancock Banning hit on the only bright side to the loss of the family tidelands when he remarked to Banning Company officer David P. Fleming: "Just got some good news, Dave; we won't have to pay taxes on that tide land anymore."[26]

Throughout this long court battle the Bannings had tried to compromise with the city, offering to donate some of their own land in order to reach an agreement outside the courts. City officials did allow the Bannings to continue their business during the appeals, but could not accept any land without acknowledging that the Bannings owned it in the first place. When the U.S. Supreme Court decision was announced in 1916, the Bannings and the city finally negotiated an end to their differences. The Bannings would transfer their title to their tidelands to the city in return for a thirty-year lease on the property. When the Southern Pacific finally agreed in 1917 to give up its right-of-ways on harbor land, all parties signed the lease, and the city was free to develop the harbor.[27]

With the ten-year battle over the tidelands finally at an end, the city began to expand the harbor into a port that would eventually become one of the largest in the world. Over three million dollars in municipal bonds approved in 1910 were available for building harbor infrastructure and, with the court battles settled, federal and private improvements could also resume. Foreign trade grew rapidly in the coming years. The tidelands cases paved the way for that expansion and would later provide precedents when the court was asked to determine the legal status of oil drilling along the coastline in the next several decades.[28]

Banning Businesses

While they fought for their property at the harbor, the Banning brothers continued to operate their businesses there until 1920. In that year the three brothers would divest themselves of all their companies, although they would continue to hold commercial and residential investment properties in Wilmington, San Pedro, and elsewhere as investments.

From 1900 to 1919, Santa Catalina Island and the company that owned it remained a major focus for the Bannings, but harbor operations were integral to their business. The Wilmington Transportation Company owned and managed the ships that brought visitors to and from the Magic Isle, the vessels that serviced ships in the harbor, and those that shuttled passengers and freight—less necessary as the harbor was deepened. The Banning Company performed the same functions as the old Wilmington Development Company, owning and operating shipyards and providing ballast, water, repairs, and stevedoring for incoming ships. It also encompassed the Banning real estate interests, purchasing, developing, and managing land in Southern California. All three companies worked in overlapping harmony, so much so that at times it was difficult to determine which one was responsible for a particular function.[29]

The Banning Company continued to be one of the key contributors to the growth and economic success of the port. The Banning Company's stevedoring business grew dramatically in the early 1900s as San Pedro became the busiest port on the coast for lumber, needed in vast quantities for building in Southern California. As the region became a center for the oil industry, the Bannings' harbor companies got into that profitable business, transporting machinery and petroleum products. With continued federal breakwater and dredging activities and the ever-increasing private trade passing through the harbor, the company's towing, shipping, storage, and service functions flourished.[30]

For the first decade of the twentieth century, the Bannings continued to work diligently to enhance the value of their property at the harbor, improving it by themselves and soliciting the help of the federal government. While the Army Corps of Engineers planned and supervised construction of the outer breakwater and other infrastructure, the Bannings paid private companies to dredge some of the inner harbor adjoining their own property to allow larger vessels to dock closer to Banning warehouses. When the tidelands issue moved to the courts, however, they decided to stop dredging, and once they lost their tidelands property they had little reason to resume. In the meantime they continued their transport and storage services and made plans to lease their property on Mormon Island to other businesses during their thirty-year agreement with the city harbor commission.[31]

In their harbor concerns the Bannings continued to work closely with officials of the Southern Pacific Railroad, their major client thanks to an exclusive contract to transport the railroad's freight in San Pedro and Wilmington. The Bannings were also tied to the Southern Pacific through their interconnected tidelands claims. The Bannings moved their downtown company offices to the Pacific Electric Building that housed the railroad headquarters in 1902, making communication between them convenient. The Southern Pacific was expanding its operations in Southern California in the early 1900s. The region's burgeoning production of agricultural and other commodities drove demand for swift transportation to markets, and the Bannings benefited from this growth. In other cases, however, the Bannings suffered from their association with the Southern Pacific because of the railroad's reputation for cutthroat business practices and hardball politics. But as long as the two were economic partners, the Bannings felt they had to do whatever they could to keep good relations with the California "Octopus"—so called because its many-tentacled business seemed to touch all aspects of the state's economy and politics. As William Banning reminded Hancock in 1913, "These people have always treated us with great consideration in every way," and they could not afford to antagonize them.[32]

Partnering with the Southern Pacific in these years meant working closely with its leaders, especially Robert Ingram, the general manager in Los Angeles. Ingram's wife, Selena, often noted in her diary that William and Hancock had met with or traveled with her husband on harbor business involving their companies. The Ingrams must have become like family, because the brothers invited them to stay at Santa Catalina every summer at no charge for cottage rental and transportation. Ingram returned the favors by singing the Bannings' praises to his superiors at key junctures. The Bannings also worked with other Southern Pacific officials and entertained them at various social and business events.[33]

As major employers in Southern California, the Bannings continued to discourage unionization by maintaining an "open shop," like most of the regional mercantile establishment. The three brothers were members of the pro-business Los Angeles Chamber of Commerce and became even more militant when they joined the local chapter of the Citizens Alliance at its founding in 1904. This unit of a national association devoted to curbing the advances of labor unions was a subsidiary of the Los Angeles Merchants' and Manufacturers' Association, the most strident opponent of organized labor in the region. In answering the call of streetcar and real estate magnate Henry E. Huntington to join the Citizens Alliance, the Bannings signaled their commitment to fighting unions at the harbor, usually with the support of the Southern Pacific Railroad and other powerful companies.[34]

As president of the Banning Company, William was the individual most closely associated with the Banning stance in labor relations. He was as fiercely anti-union as any "open shop" leader. As he had in the 1880s, he again demonstrated his determination in 1906, when he chaired a committee of wharf owners, lumber dealers, and railroads working to break a strike by sailors against ship owners; they succeeded by using nonunion labor to unload ships very quickly at San Pedro. He told a reporter, "As far as the Banning Company is concerned, it never has, and never will, recognize a labor union, even though its boats should rot at the docks." Eighteen of his men had walked out in protest, but most of his crew did not. "Los Angeles must be kept an open shop city," he declared, "and all property owners, merchants and citizens must bear whatever burdens are necessary to defeat the demands of labor unions for the closed shop."[35]

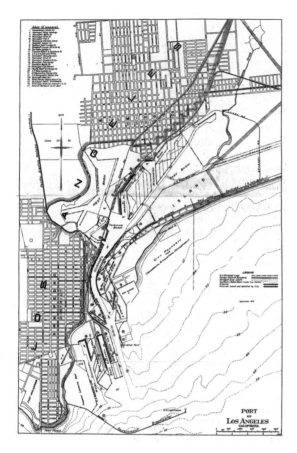

The Los Angeles harbor in the early twentieth century. Courtesy of the Seaver Center for Western History Research, Natural History Museum of Los Angeles County.

In other instances William hired attorneys to file injunctions against longshoremen and tried to arrange for a boarding house for wharf laborers on railroad property in order to keep a crew of nonunion men close at hand in San Pedro in the event of a strike. In 1912 the Banning Company became the primary target of the Industrial Workers of the World during a strike in San Pedro because of its exclusive contracts with the Southern Pacific and the Pacific Steamship Company. During the longshoremen's strike at the harbor in 1916–17, the Bannings were among the major companies that obtained an injunction against workers who had resorted to violence when the conflict dragged on. The Bannings were finally defeated, in a sense, by a major union in 1919, when the Pacific Steamship Company decided to award its stevedoring contract, which the Bannings had held for years, to a labor union, the International Longshoremen's Association (ILA). The change spurred the independent longshoremen who worked for the Bannings to protest to local business organizations that they were being forced out of work: because they had stayed neutral during the dock strike three years earlier, they were barred from joining the ILA.[36]

The Bannings lost the contract with the Pacific Steamship Company just one month after selling Santa Catalina Island. Once William Wrigley Jr. purchased their island and their ships, their harbor business shrank and the Banning brothers decided that it was time to dispose of the rest of their holdings. In 1920 they sold the Banning Company assets to Edward Mahar, their superintendent for thirty-five years, and officially dissolved the company on August 25. From that point on their connections to the harbor were limited to the lease on Mormon Island, the residential and business lots they owned as investments, and the old Banning homestead their father had built.[37]

The only family business that the Bannings retained after 1920 was the Townsend Land Company, a firm they had created in 1908 to manage the approximately 575 acres of land in Orange County near Newport Beach known as the Banning Ranch. This property was part of the much larger parcel that Mary E. H. Banning had purchased in 1874 with her inheritance from her father. The three brothers formed the company with Long Beach real estate agent Stephen Townsend, who managed the property leased for agricultural purposes. The directors also planned to explore the property for water and mineral resources, although many years would pass before they found enough to justify the search. The wait, however, would be well worth it for their descendants.[38]

Family Relations and Relatives

In the first two decades of the twentieth century, the members of the Banning family in Southern California were closely knit by business and social ties, yet frequently in conflict. The rivalry between Hancock and Joseph could make social events tense affairs and their business life a trial, but each tried to accommodate the other to hold the family together in sometimes trying circumstances.

Joseph Banning's drinking problem, which had seriously affected the management of Santa Catalina Island, was less harmful to his personal relationship with his brothers. Joseph's behavior had irked the businessman Hancock so much by 1908 that he had insisted on managing their island business and sought to divide up their property, but in the end, little of the property was actually split up. And although Joseph and Hancock often argued about their business affairs, the two were far more cordial in family situations. The same could be said of William, who tried to arbitrate his brothers' business arguments in order to keep peace in the family and the Banning companies alike.[39]

After 1900 Joseph spent less time during the year at Santa Catalina, staying instead with his family at their home in Los Angeles. In fact, he appeared infrequently in family business records and hardly at all in local newspapers after 1909. During these years, Joseph and Katharine's children were being educated in private schools, young Katharine Mary at Miss Spence's School for Girls in New York City and Joseph Brent Jr. at Yale University. Katharine Banning's mother, Mary Sweeny Banning, lived with the family from shortly after the death of her husband in 1893 until her death in 1910. Katharine's sister May Alice also stayed with them for many years after moving from Minnesota. William Banning, who had been living with Hancock and Anne, moved in with Joseph's family in 1907; he had grown impatient with Hancock over his feud with Joseph.[40]

Katharine Banning spent much of her time attending and hosting social events, especially with her mother and sister May, Selena Ingram, and relatives in the Patton and Wilson families. Katharine also continued her volunteer work with the Childrens Hospital. In 1914 she chaired a sewing committee for the hospital. Putting out a public call through the city's newspapers for donations of materials and volunteers to sew practical gifts for the children, she hosted much of the sewing work at her home. The response was overwhelming and the effort a great success.[41]

Katharine and Joseph also entertained her oldest sister, Ellen, and her husband, Frederick Ayer, during these years. The Ayers often came out to California to visit Ellen's mother, Mary, and the Bannings, and occasionally spent time at Avalon (also, as it happened, the name of the Ayer summer home in Massachusetts). In 1902 the entire Ayer family and almost all of the Bannings, a few Pattons and Wilsons, and George H. Smith posed for a photograph at the Hancock Banning residence in Descanso Canyon on Santa Catalina. The Ayers' visits would become less frequent after the death of Ellen and Katharine's mother and finally stopped in 1918. In March of that year, Frederick Ayer died at the age of ninety-five. Less than three weeks later Ellen died, just short of her sixty-fifth birthday.[42]

Hancock Banning held various positions of authority in the several Banning companies in rapid succession during this period, while he increasingly disagreed and argued with his brothers over business. By 1908 he had forced them to take the first step toward dividing up the property they owned together and was making plans to start a separate shipping and warehouse business in Wilmington, where he could live in the old

Banning house built by his father. He began searching for a loan to start the business, since much of his fortune was tied up in the Santa Catalina venture at that time.[43]

In 1907 Hancock and Anne had sold their house on North Broadway and moved to a Mission-style residence on the corner of West Adams Boulevard and Grand Avenue, then an extremely fashionable section of Los Angeles. The house had been designed by local architect Carroll H. Brown and built in 1897 for John J. Fay, a wealthy businessman who arrived in the city in that decade. Anne loved the home from the time they purchased and remodeled it, and though she would live in others over the years, this was the one that in her "heart, she could never quite give up."[44]

Although Anne and Hancock moved into the West Adams home by 1907, they would live there only sporadically after that. As part of the family property split in 1908, Hancock received the Wilmington mansion, which Joseph and Katharine had left in 1895 in order to live in Avalon and Los Angeles. It had been occupied since by the family of Andrew Young, chief engineer of the Banning companies. When Hancock took it over he divided the machinery housed there among his brothers and began remodeling the house for Anne. They converted the fireplaces from coal-burning back to wood, replaced doors and windows, transformed the basement into a grand ballroom, and added many amenities to the grounds, including a Japanese garden, about 1911, and a small amphitheater for outdoor theatrical productions. William Banning helped them acquire carved wood furniture and antiques. These improvements to their "country home" made it grand enough for the couple's friends from the city, and Anne loved to host "large entertainments" there. Although Anne yearned for her home and social life in Los Angeles, Hancock was proud of his renovation of the old homestead, which was close to his nascent business in Wilmington. And, of course, when they tired of either, they could visit their large summer house at Descanso on Santa Catalina Island.[45]

Anne and Hancock's children attended private schools throughout the country. Hancock Jr. went to the Virginia Military Academy, as had his uncle George S. Patton and his cousin George Jr., and then to Cornell University. Eleanor attended Miss Spence's School for Girls in New York City, Marlborough School in Los Angeles, and then the University of California, Berkeley. George Hugh was educated at the Harvard School in Los Angeles, the Lawrenceville School in New Jersey, and then the University of California, Berkeley.[46]

Despite the time demanded by her political activities and busy home

The Ayer–Patton–Banning family party at Avalon in 1902 (most likely photographed by Joseph Brent Banning, missing from the group). Courtesy of the Huntington Library.

life, Anne continued her volunteer work in this period, redoubling her efforts after the 1906 San Francisco earthquake and fire. Since the mid-1890s she had been a member of an "Assistance League" of affluent women in Los Angeles who raised funds for charity through social events, a group that became less active in the early 1900s. When Anne heard about the 1906 catastrophe, she immediately organized a local "Ladies of Assistance" group, which gathered food, clothing, and other necessities to send the victims. Her evident commitment to charity eventually led to her work for the Red Cross during World War I and then to her founding of the Assistance League of Southern California in 1919. This organization devoted to helping those in need remains active today. Anne served as president of the local chapter for almost three decades and later built the Assistance League into a national organization. She also participated in many other philanthropic activities during the Progressive Era, including benefits for the Childrens Hospital, Katharine's favorite charity. In 1917 she donated her collection of bisque dolls, given to her by William S. Hart and other theater personalities, to an auction for the hospital.[47]

At the same time, Anne emerged as the acknowledged leader of Los Angeles society. Her name was frequently mentioned in the newspaper society pages, and rumors of her possible competition with other socialites grabbed the attention of columnists. She further enhanced her position by staging theatrical presentations by the Amateur Club of Shakespeare in the amphitheater of her Wilmington home. As director of this benefit for two years, she took full charge of the arrangements, setting, and promotion for the plays. And besides all of her activity as mother, philanthropist, society leader, and political activist, she found time to travel frequently to other cities in California, to the East Coast, and to Europe, often without her busy husband.[48]

As in the 1890s, Anne and Hancock's lavish lifestyle periodically forced him to economize and to beg Anne to do so as well. They could not afford to maintain three large houses—on West Adams Boulevard, in Wilmington, and on Santa Catalina. After 1908 they lived most of the time in Wilmington, and Hancock convinced Anne at least to rent out the West Adams home, since she could not bring herself to sell it. (According to her son George Hugh, it sat vacant most of the time.) Renters such as a very sickly Senator John P. Jones and Baron Alfred de Ropp of the American Trona Corporation occupied the home sporadically from 1912 to 1919. Three servants and expensive boarding schools for the children also added to their financial burdens. Moving the children to less expensive schools and canceling expensive club memberships helped the situation somewhat, but Anne continued to spend and Hancock to complain.[49]

Hancock and Anne's household was reduced a bit in these years, with the subtraction of one renowned lawyer. Anne's father, George H. Smith, had lived with them ever since they were married, when they had moved into his house on Fort Hill. After they sold that house in 1907, he moved into the West Adams home and stayed there until his daughter started to rent it, eventually taking up residence in the University Club. He continued his law practice in the firm of Smith, Phelps, and Miller and his legal writings, and he served as the Banning family lawyer in cases involving the tidelands and other issues. In January 1915 he suffered a stroke while working at his desk, and passed away within weeks. He left most of his fortune to Anne and his granddaughter Eleanor.[50]

For a short while around 1910, Anne's half sister, Eleanor Patton Brown, and four of Eleanor's children lived in the West Adams house. Eleanor's husband, Thomas Bruen Brown, was a Los Angeles attorney who had died in 1893 when his children were very young. The family was

The George S. and Ruth Patton family with Henry E. Huntington and Hancock Banning (far right) in 1903. Courtesy of the Huntington Library.

close to the Bannings, and the Brown children spent many summers with their cousins at Santa Catalina. Their stay at Anne's home was temporary, however, and Eleanor soon moved to a home further west while her children started their own families. Several of the Brown children would consult on business matters for some of the Bannings and Pattons over the next several decades.[51]

The Patton family members were devoted to both Anne, their blood relative, and her sister-in-law Katharine, even as the two Banning matriarchs were growing distant from each other because of the rivalry between their husbands. Ruth and George S. Patton and their children, along with Ruth's sister, Anne ("Nannie"), lived close by in the Lake Vineyard home of pioneer Benjamin D. Wilson. Ruth and Nannie were almost constant companions of both Banning spouses at social events, card parties, outings, and summers on Santa Catalina. At one of these Avalon get-togethers, Ruth's son, George S. Patton Jr., met Beatrice Ayer, daughter of Katharine's sister Ellen Banning Ayer. The young George and Beatrice would meet again—many times—and in 1910 they were married. George Jr., a West Point graduate, participated in the 1912 Olympic Games in Stockholm, Sweden, and then embarked on a career in the

U.S. Army, a choice that would force his family to move frequently in the years to come. Over the decades he would see action in several wars, as well as fame and controversy during World War II.[52]

The oldest Banning brother, William, continued staunchly to fulfill his role as patriarch of the family and president of all of the Banning businesses. In the early years of the new century he was invited to be a member of the Los Angeles County Highway Commission, which supervised construction of hundreds of miles of new roads, to join the foundation committee for the Southwest Museum, and to be a trustee of the Independent Church of Christ, among other positions, but declined all of them because of his heavy workload. He seemed to be everywhere in these years, spending parts of his summers on Santa Catalina, shuttling frequently to San Francisco to confer with Southern Pacific Railroad officials, traveling to the East Coast for business and lobbying, and even making a shopping tour of London and other destinations in 1910 to furnish the mansion he was building.[53]

This mansion would be the first house William had lived in that was his alone. In the first years of the century he had lived with Hancock's family on North Broadway. When Hancock bought the West Adams home William moved with him, but soon decided to move to the Westlake Avenue home of Joseph and Katharine. He would stay there until 1912, when his new house on the corner of Hoover and Thirty-first streets was completed. The mansion was designed by Carroll H. Brown, a prolific architect in Southern California since his arrival in the 1880s who had also planned an elaborate granite monument for Phineas Banning in Wilmington (1885), the Joseph Brent Banning house at Catalina City (1910) and the Catalina Yacht Club on Terminal Island (1898), George S. Patton's house on Broadway (1886), the Fay Residence purchased by Hancock Banning (1897), the landmark Thomas D. Stimson Residence on Figueroa Street near Adams Boulevard (1891), and several downtown Los Angeles business blocks in the 1890s. William Banning's massive two-story structure featured a number of separate suites for family members surrounding an inner courtyard, an enormous ballroom for social events, and many rooms for servants and for other functions. It was furnished with expensive antiques he had purchased on the East Coast and in Europe. Adjacent to the living quarters, a huge barn accommodated up to thirteen horses and his collection of horse-drawn vehicles. In front of the property he installed a cast-iron fence with columns shaped liked cornstalks, which he had purchased in New Orleans. The fence, which formerly stood before a home at the corner of

William Banning's Compton "Halfway House" barn and his friends. Courtesy of
the Huntington Library.

Julia and St. Charles streets in the Crescent City, caught William's eye
while he was there in 1910. The finished property, which he referred to
simply as "The Barn," was the scene of a celebrated housewarming in
December 1912.[54]

The barn section of the "Barn" was emblematic of William Banning's
attachment to horses and his apathy toward automobiles and the growing Los Angeles car culture. After building his dream house, he purchased a lot of fifteen acres in Compton, about halfway to Wilmington.
There he built his "Halfway House," a modest home where he stayed
overnight while on the road to either Los Angeles or the harbor. He
leased the rest of the property, except for the structures, to cover some
of his costs. He also built a barn with stables and four windows with elaborate exterior frames, perhaps, as Hancock Banning Jr. suggested, "so the
horses could look out and not be lonely."[55]

As family patriarch, William presided over the two branches headed
by his brothers. Although they had their differences in the early years
of the century, the families jointly participated in many activities un-
connected to the business arrangements that both united and divided
them. The common thread was Santa Catalina, where the Bannings, their
relatives, and their friends spent much of their summers. The three
brothers usually had to return to the mainland for days at a time, but
Anne and Katharine often stayed all summer. The two matriarchs did
not always attend the same fetes, and sometimes relations between the

two were tense. Selena Ingram, a good friend of both, noted that during the summer of 1913 Anne's two sons were asked to invite Katharine's party of guests on a family picnic. Katharine was "in a perfect rage" because the boys' chaperone did not do the inviting. Selena tried to help smooth out the situation but Katharine argued with her until she left in tears. The boys told Selena that they had "cordially" invited Katharine's group but that their offer could have been misinterpreted. This blowup over an apparently innocent invitation shows how touchy the relationship between the families had grown.[56]

Other family occasions seem to have transpired more peacefully. These included many other Santa Catalina events, a number of camping trips to Yosemite and the Santa Monica Mountains, and vacation jaunts to other locations. In 1908 both sides celebrated a major event at the harbor when the Great White Fleet passed by San Pedro. During many of these meetings, the calming presence of William Banning and members of the Patton, Wilson, and Ingram families probably helped to diffuse tensions.[57]

No such ceasefire would interrupt the hostilities between the Banning brothers and Mary E. H. Banning, who remained persona non grata as far as her stepsons were concerned. She seemed, however, largely unaffected by the rift. Besides her political activity during the Progressive Era, Mary was active in the Daughters of the American Revolution, the Friday Morning Club, and other women's organizations. With her wealth still intact—she owned many parcels of land throughout the region—she was frequently mentioned on the society pages of the newspapers, though never in the same paragraph as Anne and Katharine. She was also known for her religious work and her quiet philanthropy, only occasionally reported in the press.[58]

While the brothers and Mary were rarely in contact, they probably were aware of one another's doings and may have competed at times. Mary commissioned noted architect Irving Gill to design her Los Angeles dream house in 1911, just as William was building his and shortly after Hancock renovated the Wilmington mansion. A very modern structure compared to the "gingerbread" mansions she had lived in, the house was so unique in style that it made the front page of the *Times* real estate section. "California's First Cubist House" was built using the tilt-slab construction that the "architectural heretic" Gill helped to pioneer, and the house became the sight to see on Commonwealth Avenue at Fifth Street.

A Banning camping trip to Yosemite in 1902. Courtesy of the Huntington Library.

Despite the very modern exterior, on the inside Mary was less adventurous, installing the traditional furniture she had acquired when she presided over the Banning homestead in Wilmington and the house on Fort Hill.[59]

Mary would not have long to enjoy her avant-garde home. She suffered a stroke in 1918 and recovered to some degree, but in August 1919 she had another stroke, and this time it was more serious. Her daughter Mary was with her at the time and Lucy was summoned from New York to help out. On August 22 she died in her home at the age of seventy-three. Her funeral took place two days later, "attended only by the members of the family and intimate friends." She was buried at Rosedale Cemetery alongside her husband, Phineas.[60]

The oldest of Mary's daughters, Mary Hollister Banning Norris, had lived with her husband in New York City and Mexico City until his death in 1905. After that she returned to New York only to move later to Paris, France, and finally back to Los Angeles in the 1930s. She occasionally visited her siblings while staying at her mother's home on Commonwealth Avenue. In the early 1900s she also stayed with her half brother, Hancock, on occasion, and as William remarked to a correspondent in 1907, she "looks to him for advice in almost every thing she does." When her mother died, Mary H. B. Norris inherited the Newport Beach property and would soon be sued by the state for the large estate tax.[61]

One of the younger Mary's visits to Los Angeles concerned a lawsuit initiated in 1918 by her nephew Thomas B. Brown Jr., a son of Anne Banning's half sister, Eleanor Patton Brown. Thomas argued that she owed him $21,000 for handling her financial interests since 1911, based on a contract the two had signed. Mary rebutted his claims in court, saying that Brown had never presented a bill to her, that he had been taking double commissions on property transfers, charging both her and the other party, and that she had intended to reward him with a considerable sum by including him in her will. The judge in the suit sided with Mary, and Brown lost the case. When Mary died decades later, however, Brown was not among the many beneficiaries of her estate.[62]

The youngest Banning sister, Lucy, also lived her life largely outside the Banning circle during these years; her troubled romantic life extended her exile. After her divorce from John Bradbury and many rumored engagements and entanglements, the "willful and ill-starred daughter of Mrs. Mary Banning" had married actor Mace Greenleaf in 1906. The two considered creating a vaudeville show that they would premiere on the East Coast and then tour throughout the country, but the relationship began to sour before the show was ready to be staged. By 1910 Lucy had reunited with Robert Ross—a childhood friend, a newspaper reporter, and the son of U.S. Circuit Judge Erskine M. Ross—who was said to have stood by her as her marriage to Greenleaf crumbled. In October of that year, Lucy and Ross "eloped" to Tijuana, Mexico, vowing never to return to the United States. Exercising her flair for drama, Lucy initially told reporters that Mace had mistreated her, but she later admitted that she was just unhappy with him. Ross thought that they might

Mary E. H. Banning's "Cubist" house by Irving Gill. Courtesy of the Seaver Center for Western History Research, Natural History Museum of Los Angeles County.

make their home in India, but instead they sailed to Yokohama, Japan, where they lived for just a year before again crossing the ocean to alight in Vancouver, Canada.[63]

Newspapers in San Francisco and even New York avidly followed the continuing saga of Lucy's romances, and they took note when, in November 1911, Greenleaf finally filed for divorce on the grounds of desertion. Before the case could be settled, he died while on tour in Philadelphia in late March of the next year, rendering the divorce unnecessary. Within days of learning the news, Lucy and Ross "found the path to the altar cleared of all obstacles—and followed it." Returning to her mother's home in Los Angeles as she always did after her elopements, Lucy once again walked down the aisle, in Riverside on April 1. The couple then moved to New York City, returning to Los Angeles only after the death of Lucy's mother, who bequeathed her Commonwealth Avenue home and ranch property in San Luis Obispo to her wayward daughter. This marriage had an unusually successful run, lasting almost fourteen years before Lucy lost interest in Ross and found another lover in the mid-1920s. Lucy's rebellious restlessness remained much the same, although the mood of the times seemed to catch up with her; Phineas Banning's youngest daughter seemed more at home in the turbulent modern age than the staid Victorian era of her childhood.[64]

The Bannings in World War I

In June 1914, Joseph Brent Banning and his family arrived in New York via the transcontinental railroad and set sail for their European vacation on the *Lusitania*, a British liner bound for Liverpool. After a luxury cruise across the Atlantic, the family spent about six weeks touring London, Paris, Genoa, and other cities, and returned to the U.S. in August on the *Baltic*. Their pleasure tour was shadowed by the gathering clouds of war. While they were in Europe, Archduke Franz Ferdinand of Austria–Hungary was assassinated in Sarajevo, igniting the War to End All Wars. Conversation on their uneventful trip back to the U.S. was dominated by news of the war and rumors of the presence of German spies. While again crossing the Atlantic the following year carrying civilians, many of them members of the international elite, the *Lusitania* was torpedoed by a German submarine off the coast of Ireland. Almost 1,200 passengers and crew lost their lives, 128 of them Americans. This catastrophe, among other events, turned public sentiment against Germany, eventually drawing the U.S. into World War I in 1917.[65]

Hancock's family learned of the official outbreak of the war just after one of Anne's many social events. As Hancock Banning Jr. recalled, his mother was hosting a high tea at their home on West Adams Boulevard in August 1914, attended by officials from the German, English, and French consular offices in Los Angeles. Fritz Demmler, a local businessman attached to the German consulate, was called to the phone during the party and came away "white in the face." He asked young Hancock to convey his apologies to Anne and quickly left. The French officer soon got his call and did the same, followed by the English representative. As the rest of the party soon discovered, England had just declared war on Germany.[66]

Joseph Brent Banning Jr. enlisted in the Navy in April 17, in the first month of U.S. involvement in the war. He was first stationed at the naval training station in San Pedro, where he taught courses in navigation and seamanship, both Banning specialties, and patrolled the coast. Later he was transferred to the twelfth naval district in San Francisco as an ensign and served as the assistant to the head of the Joint Naval Vessel Board and Naval Overseas Transportation Service until he was discharged in 1919 as lieutenant junior grade.[67]

While Joseph Jr. trained sailors, Hancock Banning's youngest son, the adventurous George Hugh, taught aviators. After graduating from the University of California, Berkeley, he attended the San Antonio Flying School. When America entered the war he enlisted in what became the U.S. Army Aviation Service and was initially stationed at Post Field, Fort Sill, Oklahoma. He studied flying and then taught it at installations in San Antonio, Texas, San Diego, and Sacramento. He was discharged from the service in 1919 as a second lieutenant.[68]

Hancock Banning Jr. was an apprentice electrical engineer at the General Electric Company plant in Schenectady, New York, when Congress declared war. He immediately enlisted in the navy and attended Navy Officers School at Columbia University for most of 1917. He then was commissioned a lieutenant junior grade and assigned to the battleship USS *New York* as a gunnery officer on one of the main gun turrets. The *New York* patrolled the North Sea in 1918 but, to Hancock's disappointment, never had the opportunity to fire on the enemy. After the war he tested new destroyers in San Francisco as an engineering officer for the U.S. Navy Trial Board until he was discharged in 1919.[69]

While aboard the *New York* in November 1918, young Hancock witnessed the surrender of the German High Seas Fleet, and his account of it in letters home was published in the *Los Angeles Herald*. He described the celebration by allied seamen when they heard of the German capitulation on the night of November 11, along with his excitement at sighting the Duke of Wales on a nearby vessel. The ceremony of surrender itself took place on November 21, when a squadron of about two hundred British and American ships formed two columns facing east while "The Hun Fleet" of about seventy ships steamed west between them. Although the allies expected the Germans to fight or at least to try to scuttle their ships, not a shot was fired. Hancock Jr. saw the surrender as dishonorable, "the lowest of the low of the whole war," because the German navy handed over its ships "without raising a finger to save them or put them out of every ones reach at the bottom of the North Sea."[70]

A more distant Banning relative, one related to the family through both his father and his wife, spent the war in Europe, eager to serve on the front lines. Lt. George S. Patton Jr., the son of Anne Banning's half brother and the husband of one of William Lowber Banning's granddaughters (Phineas Banning's great-niece), was by then a career officer in the U.S. Army. In the midst of the Mexican Revolution decade, in 1915 and 1916, he had policed the border in the Eighth Cavalry Regiment in Texas under General John J. Pershing. When the U.S. declared war on Germany, Patton was ordered to join Pershing's Allied Expeditionary Force headquarters staff. Once in Europe he transferred to the Tank Corps and finally got his wish to see action in August 1918. As the commander of 150 tanks in the attack on St. Mihiel near Verdun in September, Patton won the praise of American newspapers for his leadership and the criticism of his commander for moving so far ahead of his headquarters that they lost communications. Two weeks later, while leading an attack in the Meuse–Argonne offensive, he was wounded while trying to direct his tanks and organize scattered troops from other outfits. He recovered in an army hospital, where he was promoted to colonel and then released two weeks before the November 11 armistice that ended the war. Patton was awarded the Distinguished Service Cross for his bravery and returned to the U.S. five months later to continue the military career that would make him a legend in the next world war.[71]

While the previous generation of Banning men mostly attended to their businesses during the eighteen months that the U.S. was at war, the Banning matriarchs and their daughters supported the war troops on the home front. Although both Katharine and Anne Banning worked for the war effort, and both volunteered for the Red Cross, the nature of their activities was in keeping with their sharply different politics and personalities. Anne was drawn to work that took her, quite literally, out of her home and into shops and cities. Katharine's charity, by contrast, focused on activities more traditionally associated with women, for example gathering clothing and personal items for soldiers, and while she shared Anne's entrepreneurial bent, unlike Anne she brought her philanthropic "business" into her home.

Anne served in many organizations, one of them the Los Angeles chapter of the women's section of the Navy League, which promoted Americanization and national defense programs. A leader in society, she was asked to persuade women in the region to volunteer their skills and time for the war effort.[72]

Anne was involved most intensely with the Red Cross. She took this commitment very seriously as a means to support Allied troops and civilians in Europe and America during the conflict. Before the war, she had come up with the idea of the "Grey Sisterhood," a relief organization affiliated with the Red Cross that would serve in urban centers throughout the United States. The Red Cross approved her plan, and volunteers adopted a uniform consisting of a gray gown with a white apron; many images of Anne during and after the war show her in it. She was also credited with originating the Red Cross Shop, an institution that quickly spread from Los Angeles to the rest of the nation. As general manager of the first Red Cross Shop, she solicited donations of money and goods to sell in the store. She also organized volunteers to repair donated clothing, furniture, and other items for sale and to handle publicity, bookkeeping, and other administrative functions for the shop. Anne also aided the Red Cross by staging at least one benefit performance at William's "Barn" in 1914. Some of the players included family members. Although the presentation of *Patience* received only mixed reviews in the city's

Anne Banning in her
favorite Red Cross
uniform. Courtesy of the
Huntington Library.

newspapers, it did raise a modest sum for Anne's favorite charity.[73]

The combination of her Red Cross and other war relief work took a
toll on Anne in early 1918. By then she had moved into an apartment on
Scarff Street in order to be close to her war work in the city. While
preparing to visit her son, George Hugh, who had just suffered an attack
of appendicitis at his base in Texas, she apparently had a nervous breakdown. Anne recovered quickly and went back to her work, however, and
continued until October of that year. By then she had decided that she de-
served a vacation, and so she and several other Red Cross Shop officials
resigned and allowed others to take their places in the relief effort.[74]

Katharine S. Banning worked for the Red Cross during the war as
well, as an official in the Los Angeles chapter. In April 1917, the same
month the U.S. declared war, she was elected chair of the Gift Garments
Committee, which gathered and made clothing and other items for soldiers headed overseas. The activity sparked a controversy in the following month when the organization was criticized for collecting tobacco
products for the soldiers. Katharine was in charge of collecting, and had
relied on the advice of veterans, who told her that tobacco was important
to soldiers during wartime. When the board of managers for the local

Katharine S. Banning with one of her "Bill's Comfort Bags" (on right) and grandchildren in Vermejo, New Mexico, 1927. Courtesy of the Huntington Library.

unit decided to discontinue tobacco collections rather than risk alienating the protestors, Katharine felt slighted, and she resigned. The board refused to accept her resignation and reversed their decision, apparently in order to mollify her. Katharine did not rejoin the Gift Garments Committee, although she continued to support the Red Cross in fundraising campaigns. She also helped to sell war bonds as chair of the California state chapter of the National Women's Liberty Loan Committee.[75]

As part of her fundraising for the Red Cross, Katharine demonstrated her own entrepreneurial talents, perfecting, manufacturing, and marketing a kit bag for servicemen. "Bill's Comfort Bag" was a waterproof leather pouch with pockets for toiletries, mending implements, and other necessities. The basic idea was not new, since similar "handbags" and strapped pouches already existed. But Katharine's design, based on her motorcamping experience, caught on. She turned her home on Westlake Avenue into a factory to make the bags and sell them and related accessories; the purchasers would then give them to soldiers, and the profits were donated to the Red Cross. Newspaper stories in the *Times* and the *Examiner* ran pictures of Katharine Stewart and her daughter Katharine Mary sewing the bags and explained how her marketing and philanthropy worked. Katharine was so proud of this venture that she patented the bag in 1919 and continued to market it long after the war ended.[76]

The war in many ways marked a generational and cultural turning point for the Bannings, as it did for the nation at large. The men of the younger generation, now adults, had served their country and were now looking to make their mark in civilian life. The Banning matriarchs had discovered new purpose in their work supporting the war effort. At the same time, the transformation of politics, the economy, and public sentiment, in combination with ongoing personal conflicts, had gradually pulled the Banning brothers and the Banning Company apart. With the end of the Great War came the end of the Banning businesses, and soon after the generation that had created and managed them. It was time for the next generation to claim its birthright and lead the family through the peaks and valleys of the postwar era: through prosperity, a catastrophic depression, and finally another world war.

PART 4

THE NEXT GENERATIONS

THE SECOND GENERATION EMERGES—THE 1920S

D uring the Roaring Twenties Phineas Banning's grandchildren
launched their adult lives, and his surviving three sons and two
daughters began to cede the stage, though several remained active for decades to come. With this generational shift, the pursuits of the
once close-knit clan grew ever more separate and diverse. As the decade
opened, the Banning brothers had essentially dissolved the business ties
that had built their fortunes and bound them together. The next generation became more dispersed still, divided by personalities, politics, and
an increasingly mobile and metropolitan life. Three of Phineas's children
would die in the course of the decade, and the careers of the next generation would have been almost unrecognizable to him—they were builders
and makers and entrepreneurs, but not of towns and harbors and roads.
Instead they built portfolios, erected philanthropic organizations, broke
literary ground, and expanded trade from executive offices. They were as
much the children of the newly modern and cosmopolitan Southern
California as of their parents.

The 1920s ushered in major changes for the United States and for the
burgeoning metropolis of greater Los Angeles. The gradual shift of the
U.S. population from rural to urban areas had finally tipped the scale by
1920, when the census revealed that, for the first time, most Americans
were living in urban centers. The end of the war brought economic prosperity and unleashed pent-up consumer demand. Industry, no longer
limited to producing armaments, turned to manufacturing consumer
goods, the sales of which contributed further to the booming economy.
The popularity of the automobile and the development of public transportation, combined with the dispersal of industrial plants, meant that

Joseph Brent Banning in the 1910s. Courtesy of the Huntington Library.

individuals and families increasingly lived and worked in widely separated places. These and other factors contributed to a trend that transformed community life. These economic and social revolutions felt like liberation to some, but to others augured the loss of traditional values. An apparent loosening of social mores in the celebrity culture of the postwar years was met by a resurgence of conservative political and religious activity, each competing for the attention of Americans who had just weathered the War to End All Wars.[1]

These national trends were mirrored in the Banning family's Southern California. The vast metropolis of Los Angeles came of age in this era of urbanization and rapid suburbanization, setting the course for many modern American cities. This physical expansion, coupled with economic development in the form of increased manufacturing, harbor expansion, more financial institutions, and growing entertainment, service, and tourism industries, drove modernization and social change. The 1920s saw prosperity for many in the region, but not all. The rising tide of the economy benefited the established elite like Phineas Banning's children, whose investments afforded them lives of comfort. It also offered

The Joseph Brent Banning memorial at Avalon. Courtesy of the Huntington Library.

many opportunities for those in the younger generation blessed with resources, ambition, and motivation. Just as the nation seemed poised between familiar social structures and values on one hand and the forces of modernization on the other, the established power of the Banning elders was balanced against the energies of the next generation.[2]

A Decade of Banning Deaths

Joseph was the first of the elder Bannings to pass away. He had suffered various health problems, some of them serious, over the previous twenty years. In late 1920, at almost sixty years of age, he suffered what his physician identified as a stroke and cerebral hemorrhage. Critically ill, he lay comatose for several days, showing no signs of recovery, and he died on November 4. Hundreds of friends attended his funeral two days later at Inglewood Cemetery. Mourners filled a special boat that brought Santa Catalina Island residents to the mainland for the burial. Two weeks later a memorial service was held at Avalon, where he had spent much of his time over the previous three decades. Many of his old friends, along with the new officers of the Santa Catalina Island Company, spoke at this gathering and began planning a monument to the "Father of Catalina."[3]

Joseph Brent Banning's estate was valued at about one million dollars, half of which went to Katharine, while the other half was divided

Hancock Banning in his
later years. Courtesy of
the Huntington Library.

equally among his three children. Katharine would soon sell their Westlake Avenue residence and move into her brother-in-law William's mansion at Hoover and Thirty-first Streets, where her children and, soon,
their spouses would join her.[4]

Joseph's brother Hancock enjoyed the fruits of the Roaring Twenties for a few more years. The brothers had divided among them their
gains from the sale of the Banning companies, and Hancock now occupied himself with managing his holdings. Among other investments, he
owned business property in downtown Los Angeles and at the harbor,
residential lots in Wilmington, and ranch land in Fresno County. He also
managed the remaining jointly held property at the Port of Los Angeles,
including the lease of over 3.5 million square feet of warehouse space.
With Anne he continued to improve the old Banning mansion, their primary residence, stocking it with furniture from their former summer
home on Santa Catalina and adding a solar heating unit in the house's
cupola in the early '20s. He still kept an office in the Pacific Electric Build-

Lucy Banning
Greenleaf, about 1910.
Courtesy of the
Huntington Library.

ing in downtown Los Angeles, although he visited it less frequently. The "jolly Hancock—cordial as ever" was an active member of many of his clubs, including the Jonathan and California Clubs, the Los Angeles Athletic Club, the Bohemian Club of San Francisco, and the Southern California Yacht Club, which he joined in 1921. He continued to question Anne's spending on the household and to grumble about her many social and philanthropic pursuits—as he had from the beginning of their marriage.[5]

Hancock had been ill for some time when, in July 1925, he suffered an attack of appendicitis. He was brought to the Good Samaritan Hospital and underwent three operations there but would not recover. On the morning of August 7 he passed away. His funeral took place on August 10, and as at Joseph's burial a special ship brought "a delegation of island residents" from Avalon, where flags were lowered to half-mast. The feud between the brothers now finally over, Joseph's sons served among the pallbearers. Hancock was buried at Inglewood Cemetery while another service was held concurrently at St. John's Episcopal Church in Wilmington. On that night Porter's Santa Catalina Island Marine Band, an ensemble he had joined with his cornet on many occasions, played at a special memorial concert for him at the Greek Amphitheater in Avalon. On August 13 the *Times* published a touching "appreciation" of Hancock by his good friend, columnist and banker Jackson A. Graves. Hancock "was a man of the highest principles and of sterling worth," wrote Graves. He "had a good word for everybody" and "possessed a brave and generous spirit. His heart went out to those in distress."[6]

Like brother Joseph, Hancock divided his estate, leaving half to Anne and half to his three children in equal shares. Hancock's estate was much larger, however, because of the investments he had made in his later years. Instead of selling assets and distributing the funds, his family kept the estate intact, to be managed by Hancock's sons and son-in-law, who would live off the interest and royalty income. In order to pay the inheritance taxes on the estate, however, they soon were forced to sell the old Phineas Banning homestead. Given his pride in his renovation of the family home, this was not a decision that Hancock would have approved.[7]

Although her romantic sagas seemed tailor-made for the new liberated age, Phineas's youngest daughter, Lucy, did not long survive her brother Hancock. Lucy Banning had shocked many Southern Californians in the 1890s and early 1900s when she repeatedly married and then left her husbands for other lovers. Her life seemed to mirror that of actress Evelyn Nesbit and other women whose sexuality was the focus of newspaper scandals of the early 1900s, stories that anticipated the mores of a later age. By the postwar 1920s, gender roles had become less rigid, and Lucy was considered emancipated by some Americans. By the spring of 1926 she had taken refuge in her mother's former home on Commonwealth Avenue after separating from her third husband, Robert Ross. Lucy then sailed to Japan, where she and Ross had lived for a year after their marriage, and before the end of the year Ross began a divorce action based on her desertion; it was granted in January 1927. Within months California newspapers announced that "the vivacious Mrs. Ross" was now engaged to Charles Hastings, a wealthy wine grower originally from San Francisco who had settled in Los Angeles and owned an estate in nearby Pasadena. The two, who had known each other since before her first marriage and had, rumor said, been engaged many years before, would probably be married in Paris, she told the press.[8]

This marriage, however, would not take place. Even before her estrangement from Ross in 1926, Lucy had become infatuated with an-

Setsuzo Ota "wrestles" with an elephant in a promotional image from the 1920s. Courtesy of the Seaver Center for Western History Research, Natural History Museum of Los Angeles County.

other man, a Japanese judo expert whom she first noticed at a wrestling match in Los Angeles in early 1926. Setsuzo Ota, graduate of the University of Tokyo and a top jujitsu expert in Japan, came to the U.S. in 1922 and eventually made his way to Los Angeles to establish himself as a professional wrestler. At this time many Americans were intensely anti-Asian, and especially anti-Japanese, because Japan was thought to have imperialist designs on territory in the Pacific. Asians were barred from becoming U.S. citizens, and California law prevented them from owning property. In the face of this racism, Ota became a hero to Japanese residents in Southern California. Lucy first attended one of his wrestling matches in January 1926 and returned for many more. Enamored of this athlete nineteen years her junior, she took him with her to Japan that summer during her separation from Robert Ross. At the time Ota was thought to be her chauffeur; the *Times* identified him as such when Ota, Lucy, and another woman were involved in a car accident on the road to San Diego.[9]

In January 1928, Lucy and Ota left California, where state laws prohibited marriages between Caucasians and Asians, and were wed in

Seattle. The Banning family was mystified by the news, claiming to know nothing about Lucy's new husband. After returning to Los Angeles, Ota was reported to be unhappy in his marriage. Old acquaintances kidded him "because of his defiance of traditions in his efforts to disprove that east and west never can be happily united at the altar." The two decided to travel to Japan and Europe on a long honeymoon vacation, but Lucy discovered that by marrying a Japanese national she had lost her U.S. citizenship and had to apply for an alien permit. Talking to a reporter asking about the loss, and anti-Japanese sentiment in general, she said, "I think our people are too narrow-minded." At length she got her permit, and the two departed for France in late September to visit Lucy's sister, Mary, who had lived in Paris since 1920, and begin their belated European honeymoon.[10]

In February 1929, Lucy was hospitalized with influenza and pneumonia in Florence, Italy, and on the 20th she died, with Ota and Mary at her bedside. Ota brought her body back to the U.S. the following month and placed it in a vault until Mary arrived in May for the services. Lucy's reputation as a California beauty and a "man crazy" romantic became her legacy, her posthumous fame based largely on the number and names of her romantic partners.[11]

Lucy's fourth and last husband was the major beneficiary of her wealth, estimated to be about $450,000, but he would have a difficult time acquiring any of it. Much of the inheritance was bound up in real estate, which Ota, as a Japanese national, was prohibited from owning, and the early years of the Great Depression were an unpropitious time to sell property. Ward Chapman, the administrator of the estate and a beneficiary himself, offered to sell the old Mary E. H. Banning home on Fort Hill to the city, but municipal funds were lacking. (Los Angeles County finally purchased it in 1942.) Chapman still had not sold any of Lucy's property by 1940, when Ota was arrested by the FBI. Along with two policemen and several others, he was charged with the 1938 kidnapping of a Japanese national. The FBI alleged that the conspirators had taken their captive, who was an underworld figure in Southern California, back to Japan. Ota spent five years in prison and emerged penniless; soon after his release, he began working as a gardener in Nevada. With the help of another attorney he tried to sue for the residue of Lucy's estate in 1947, but was denied the last remaining share. Newspapers stated that he received in all a total of $122,000 from the estate, but he claimed that after deducting lawyer fees and other expenses it was only about $6,000, enough, he noted, for an expensive party. In 1951 Ota returned to Japan, where he was believed to be very wealthy, but could only afford to live in a modest Tokyo hotel. His health gradually declined, and in the summer of 1963 he took his own life.[12]

A close Banning relative in the brothers' Southern California circle, May Alice Banning, had died the year before Hancock. May, daughter of William Lowber Banning and sister to Katharine Stewart Banning, had come to Los Angeles with her mother after her father died in 1893. May had lived with Katharine and Joseph, but moved after Joseph's death. In October 1923 she embarked on an extended tour of Europe with Anne Wilson, a relative of Anne Banning and devoted friend of May and Katharine S. Banning. While in Paris May was hospitalized with heart disease, and she died there in December 1924. She would be buried in St. Paul, Minnesota, where she was born.[13]

Relatives in the Patton family, who, like the Wilsons, formed an inner circle of friends with the Bannings, also passed on in the 1920s. Anne Banning's half brother, George S. Patton Sr., died in June 1927 after being ill for several months. The former co-owner and director of the Santa Catalina Island Company and unsuccessful candidate for the U.S. Senate in 1916 had served as the first mayor of San Marino and was chairman of the board of trustees of the Huntington Library at his death. One year later his spouse, Ruth Wilson Patton, died while on her way to visit her son, Major George S. Patton Jr., in New Mexico. A daughter of Benjamin D. Wilson, one of Phineas Banning's closest friends and business partners, Ruth had been a frequent companion of the Bannings in family gatherings at Santa Catalina, Los Angeles, and in the San Gabriel Valley. The deaths of George and Ruth loosened almost three decades of close business and family ties that bound the three Banning brothers and their spouses to the Wilson and Patton clans.[14]

Survivors of the Older Generation

While several members of the generation of Phineas Banning's children passed away in the 1920s, the others continued to hold considerable sway in Los Angeles society, business, and politics—even as the next generation emerged to carry on the family name and legacy in Southern California and elsewhere.

The oldest Banning daughter, Mary Hollister Banning Norris, spent the 1920s and half of the 1930s living in Paris. She kept her family investments intact and relied on Hancock and then Hancock Jr. to help her keep track of her oil royalties and leased land income. She was a favorite of many of the young members of the family, but quite proper and elitist, a trait she conveyed in a letter to Hancock questioning the appropriateness of George Hugh Banning's writing about "common" people, and in comments to relatives belittling women who worked for a living. After Adolf Hitler came to power in Germany in the mid-1930s, she returned to Los Angeles and lived out her days in luxury at the Biltmore Hotel.[15]

"Captain" William Banning continued to work as a vice president for the Santa Catalina Island and Wilmington Transportation companies until 1929, advising the new owners in the transition from Banning management. In 1920 he was sent to New York to negotiate the purchase of the *Avalon* as an addition to the fleet carrying visitors back and forth to the island. While there he also conferred with U.S. Navy officials about purchasing decommissioned ships for Los Angeles harbor shippers and investors, including *Times* publisher Harry Chandler.[16]

During the 1920s he also managed his own considerable real estate interests, including tidelands leased from the city under the 1917 agreement. He was a director of a stock brokerage firm managed by his two nephews, although agreeing to list his well-known name on their letterhead was probably his main contribution. In 1920 he arranged to sell Banning family property in Fresno County to Henry Keller, a member of a family that had been close to Phineas and his sons for many years. This sale proved a disaster for Keller, who rented the land for agricultural use until the Great Depression impacted the farming sector. William had the luxury of forbearance and declined to foreclose on the mortgage, telling Henry to pay interest alone during those lean years. As the economy gradually improved, the Kellers were at long last able to make their final payment in 1944.[17]

With his Santa Catalina playground for stage coaching now owned by another, William found new open spaces for his hobby at Harry Chandler's Vermejo Park Ranch in New Mexico, where he spent his summers with Katharine S. Banning and some of her family from about 1927 to 1930. This venue was too far away, however, and in 1929 he decided to purchase a ranch about thirty miles east of Los Angeles in present-day Walnut, near his old friend, stage driver Tom Green. There he began erecting a complex of buildings that would become a summer resort for his nieces and nephews during the Depression. For the present it served as the new storage and exhibition facility for his vehicles and home for his horses, which were in frequent demand for special events, such as parades at the harbor. In 1920 William's restored Concord coach, finished by the expert shipwright William Muller, was featured in the Los Angeles Automobile Show—right next to a booth showcasing a brand new Cadillac limousine.[18]

Soon after the death of his brother Joseph, William invited Joseph's widow, Katharine, to move into his mansion at Thirty-first and Hoover in Los Angeles along with her three grown children. Katharine, who thought him to be perhaps the most "noble man" she had ever met (as she frequently wrote in her family scrapbooks), accepted. William, believed by later generations to have been in love with Katharine before her marriage to Joseph, was happy to have the family there, and she became the hostess of the many social functions held at the "Barn." She also found time for more charitable work raising money for the indigent children cared for at Childrens Hospital, and was honored for her involvement in founding the institution at its silver anniversary celebration.[19]

While living at the "Barn" during the 1920s, Katharine continued to manage her Bill's Comfort Bag business. She had manufactured these bags at her home during the war, donating proceeds to the Red Cross, but the operation became a for-profit venture after 1918. She contacted a company to make patterns for the bag and then found a manufacturer to make them. She obtained U.S. and Canadian patents and became the focus of an advertising campaign featuring photographs of people using the bags, testimonials from soldiers, and the story of how she designed the first one for her son Bill in the navy. Eventually the bags were re-designed for specific uses such as automobile camping, cruises, and sports. The DuPont Company, founded in Delaware by a distant relative of the Bannings, produced the fabric for the bags, which sold quickly at first. By the late 1920s, however, the bags declined in popularity, and by the onset of the Depression the business was no longer profitable.[20]

While she was happy to be taken in herself, Katharine was less welcoming when her sister-in-law moved to Los Angeles in the 1920s. Her younger brother William Lowber Jr. (actually the second William Jr., since his older brother, the first William Jr., drowned as a child) had been out West to visit his cousins at the Banning's Conejo Ranch in the late 1880s, and he produced several accounts of vacations there for the family at his printing plant in St. Paul, Minnesota. In his hometown he married Evangeline Ruth Gauthier, a member of several cultural clubs in the city, and they had three children. In the early 1920s, however, marital problems drove the two apart, and he eventually moved to Washington, D.C., while a penniless Evangeline brought her children to Los Angeles to seek help from their more prosperous relatives. The recently widowed Katharine offered little assistance, so the St. Paul contingent had to fend for themselves. The cold greeting offered the Minnesota natives by their

Southern California relations has kept these two branches of the family apart ever since.[21]

Evangeline's son, William Lowber Banning III, had served in the U.S. Army during the war and was decorated by the Italian government for his valor. He then attended Wooster Academy in Massachusetts for two years, during which time he married Florinda Steffer at home in St. Paul. When he moved with his mother and siblings to Los Angeles, he became an advertising executive with the pioneering political consultant and public relations firm of Lord & Thomas, conducting marketing surveys in the 1920s. He would eventually start his own ad company. A resident for many years of Beverly Hills, William Lowber III's ambition and drive made him an important figure in Southern California advertising and social life. His sister, Beatrice, would marry Ted Braun, an influential lobbyist and adviser to U.S. presidents and a consultant to Nelson Rockefeller and other important politicians, as well as less savory characters in the 1960s. Their mother, however, never completely adjusted to her new life in Los Angeles. She suffered from heart trouble, and in 1937 she was found dead in her car, which was parked in the garage with the motor running.[22]

Anne Banning's philanthropic, political, and social work continued unabated during the 1920s. Throughout the decade she was lauded in city newspapers for her work with the Red Cross and the Assistance League of Southern California, which she founded in 1919 to continue some of the Red Cross programs she had started. She found a promising location for the Assistance League's headquarters, across the street from the William Fox Studios in Hollywood, which was still in its infancy as the center for the region's film industry. The Tea Room at the headquarters became a favorite lunchtime venue for motion picture celebrities, who were then approached for charitable contributions. The community welfare programs of the Assistance League offered childcare for women who worked in the industry and anyone else in need of a helping hand. In 1920 Anne came up with the idea of renting the homes and other real estate of Assistance League members and their allies to motion picture studios as film locations, with the proceeds going to the charity. Her own residence in Wilmington was used several times for this purpose, along with hundreds of other locations over the next several decades.[23]

In 1920 Anne was chosen to serve on the general committee of the Southern California unit of the European Relief Committee, which raised money for starving children in Central and Eastern Europe, and she hosted fundraising gatherings for the committee at her home. In 1922 she was named an officer in the French Academy in Paris for her wartime relief work, which had been of tremendous benefit to France. Her newspaper appeals for the Red Cross appeared frequently; in one of them, Mary Pickford and Douglas Fairbanks, in costume, joined her at a filling location to make a pitch for donations. Anne was also known for her services to cultural organizations such as the Southwest Museum.[24]

At the same time Anne was active in politics and a reluctant leader in Los Angeles society. She attended the 1920 Democratic convention in San Francisco as a delegate pledged to William Gibbs McAdoo, who lost the nomination after a marathon forty-four rounds of balloting. Three years later she was appointed by Los Angeles Mayor George C. Cryer to a committee to entertain President and Mrs. Harding on their trip to the West Coast, for which Anne was planning an excursion to Santa Catalina Island. (The president died in San Francisco on his way south.) In 1925 she joined the mayoral campaign of Judge Benjamin Bledsoe, a Democrat who contested incumbent Mayor Cryer and his manager, Kent Parrot. The *Times* had branded Parrot as a city boss and Cryer as his puppet in order to stymie efforts by city progressives to acquire public hydroelectric plants. Parrot responded by depicting Bledsoe as the pawn of wealthy *Times* publisher Harry Chandler and private power interests. With municipal ownership the major issue, the progressives won the election and Anne's candidate again lost.[25]

As a society matron Anne was still a frequent hostess, although more often of charitable benefits than strictly social events. When she was mentioned in the society columns it was usually to depict her as the city's queen, albeit "an unwilling sovereign" who "refuses to take the job seriously." Uninterested in protecting the Los Angeles elite "from encroachments of social climbers," she left that responsibility to others, few of whom could replace her, even at a job she would not accept. "Mrs. Banning won't sit on the throne or wear the crown, but she still reigns—mildly, reluctantly, all too kindly."[26]

While Anne and Hancock lived in Wilmington in the first half of the 1920s, Anne leased their twenty-four-room home on West Adams Boulevard as "La Casa de Flores," an exclusive club and home for affluent bachelors and professionals and a site for weddings and other special occasions. After Hancock's death in 1925, Anne was faced with the dilemma of where to live. By that time the area surrounding the Wilmington homestead seemed increasingly unsafe; Hancock had informed a relative in 1923 that he sometimes had to fire his shotgun over the heads of "undesirables" to keep them away. The mansion was far from the rest of the family, who had no interest in living there, and the upkeep was expensive. The burden of the inheritance taxes on Hancock's estate finally forced Anne to follow her sons' advice to sell the home and move back into the West Adams residence when her tenant's lease expired.[27]

Anne and her family offered to sell the house and grounds to the city, and a number of Wilmington residents wanted the city to buy it for a park. The Los Angeles City Council was then in the process of acquiring five other sites for parks in the area, a plan backed by the Cryer-Parrot city administration. According to local real estate brokers, one of the sites, owned by Cryer-appointed Harbor Commissioner Walter Allen, had been assigned a suspiciously high value by appraisers. The Banning proposition was forwarded to the park commission, which recommended that the city buy the five sites plus the Banning parcel. The city council, however, voted to decline the Banning lot, and Wilmington residents were up in arms. Mrs. A. S. C. Forbes, a noted local historian, helped to organize civic groups to demand the purchase of the historic Banning property, which cost only one-third of the price of the other five sites combined. In the face of massive opposition at the next hearing, the council relented and agreed to purchase the Banning site, letting the other five properties go.[28]

In October 1926, the city council ordered the city attorney to plan an election to ask voters to approve $275,000 in bonds for the purchase. In the ensuing plebiscite the measure passed, and residents of Wilmington were assessed additional taxes to pay for the acquisition. The sale of the property was finally consummated in June 1927, and the park opened soon after. Plans called for the mansion to become a museum related to the history of the harbor area and a community center. Immediately, it began serving as the primary community venue for social and civic functions, just as it had in the days of Phineas Banning, and it has been a vital and vibrant community asset ever since.[29]

The New Generation

The children of Hancock and Anne resembled one another in some respects, but differed markedly in their political views and interests, just as their parents had. Anne strongly influenced her daughter Eleanor's views, and both Anne and her father, George Hugh Smith, shaped the life of George Hugh Banning, named in honor of his grandfather. Hancock Banning Jr., on the other hand, was truly his father's son. The younger Hancock overcame a rebellious adolescence to assume his father's conservative nature. At the Thatcher School for Boys in the Ojai Valley, he was reprimanded for using profane language, among other transgressions. His father thought him both selfish and self-centered and prescribed the discipline of a military school, so it was off to the Virginia Military Institute (VMI), which several members of Anne's family had attended. There he was promptly dismissed along with seventy-nine other cadets for defying authority; the group had made a collective demand that two dismissed fellow cadets be reinstated. This action, various romantic scrapes, and his continuing expressions of disrespect for his mother and his siblings deeply disturbed his parents. With the help of his family, Hancock was readmitted, although his poor grades forced him to repeat a year in order to catch up academically.[30]

Hancock Jr. graduated from VMI in 1914, completed his bachelor's degree in mechanical engineering at Cornell University, and began technical training with the General Electric Company. After his service in the navy during the war, he returned to General Electric's headquarters in Schenectady, New York, for several years and then relocated to Southern California. He found a home in San Marino, not far from the Patton family, and worked as a sales engineer for Union Iron Works. After his father died in 1925, he took his place managing the family's property from an office in Wilmington, work that would occupy him for the next few decades. He also played a pivotal role in preserving the Banning's nonmonetary legacy, saving family documents and recording his memories of events.[31]

In 1919 Hancock Jr. had married Florence Lewers Johnston, granddaughter of former Los Angeles County district attorney and judge James Robert Dupuy. Born in Kentucky, Florence became a close friend of Hancock's sister after moving to Los Angeles, spending many summers with the Bannings at Santa Catalina. After graduating from the Marlborough School in Los Angeles, she attended college in Brooklyn, New York. She and Hancock lived in Schenectady while he worked there, and then returned to Los Angeles County to raise their three children—Hancock III, Robert, and Elizabeth—born between 1921 and 1932. After several years of marriage she became active in civic and cultural organizations; a highlight of her early service was speaking to the League of Women Voters on parenthood in 1927. In her many charitable and civic commitments, Florence closely resembled her mother-in-law, Anne, who frequently leaned on her for assistance, often asking Florence to drive her to appointments in the 1920s. Florence welcomed the addition of another daughter-in-law to share the burden. She also joined organizations separate from Anne's in order to find her own niche in the family and in the larger society of Southern California by the 1930s.[32]

Eleanor Anne Banning, Anne and Hancock's middle child, attended the Marlborough School—where all of the young Banning women and many of their friends matriculated—and then moved on to the University of California, Berkeley. There she majored in political science and history, graduating in 1915. Initially she planned to teach at the college level, but such opportunities, especially for women, were few at the time. Although devoted to her family and engaged in Los Angeles society, Eleanor was quite independent and interested in politics and the local Democratic Party. In 1917 she married John C. Macfarland, and the two would have four children; one, the first, died in infancy, and another was adopted. Like Hancock, they lived in the San Gabriel Valley, purchasing a home in South Pasadena in 1921. Over the next two decades Eleanor would become an important player in state and local politics, education, and Depression-era relief efforts.[33]

John Cobb Macfarland became a pillar of the entire Banning family by serving as its legal adviser. Macfarland had emigrated west from his native Nebraska and was a graduate of Harvard School in Los Angeles, Stanford University, and Harvard Law School. One of the region's most distinguished attorneys, he had a long and illustrious legal career as a member and, by 1928, a partner in the prestigious law firm of Gibson, Dunn & Crutcher. He was also deeply involved in service to the profession, a large and ever-expanding cohort in Southern California, and would be elected president of the Los Angeles Bar Association in 1941. Macfarland would be of inestimable value to the Banning family in their legal battle with the Los Angeles Board of Harbor Commissioners over property ownership in the 1930s. A devout Republican, he was a good debating partner for his Democratic spouse during the New Deal era.[34]

The third child of Anne and Hancock, George Hugh Banning, was the most independent and artistic of the three. While attending the University of California, Berkeley, in 1916, he considered becoming an admiralty lawyer, so he joined the crew of a "tall ship" lumber schooner sailing to Australia in order to gain some practical experience. When he returned to California he briefly resumed his studies, enlisting in the armed forces in 1917 when the U.S. entered the war. After his service in the Army Air Corps, he returned to Berkeley and graduated in 1919. With his degree in hand he joined the staff of the *San Francisco Chronicle* as a reporter.[35]

In April 1920, George and Gladys Armstrong surprised their families by announcing their engagement in Berkeley. Born in Oregon in 1899,

Gladys was then a junior at the university, the only daughter of Dr. and Mrs. Maurice Armstrong, who lived in Los Angeles. The two had been "sweethearts," the *Times* reported, for at least three years. Their engagement was not a long one, for the couple would marry four days later. They made their home in Berkeley in the 1920s, where their only child, Douglas, was born in 1923.[36]

George had embarked on his career as a writer before his marriage. Besides composing his graduating class play, *Adonis Falls*, in 1919, he also wrote a book of poems entitled *Found in a Derelict: "Queen of the Night" and Other Poems*. It was based on his recent experience on the tall ship as a "sailor!—a long haired, tar-dobbed, hickory-clad, sun-blacked, sea-dog!" The book was published in conjunction with his mother's charities and all of the proceeds donated to the Red Cross. The *Los Angeles Times* gave the production a very positive review, possibly in part because of Anne's connection to it. George then began working on a novel that also centered on life at sea. *Spun Yarn* was published in London in 1923, and although it was not very widely circulated, it did help to establish his name as a writer.[37]

In that same year George embarked on a cruise with G. Allan Hancock, a good friend of his father's, that would lead to a notable book. Hancock planned a long trip on his *Velero II* from Wilmington down the coast of Baja California and then along Mexican beaches in order to explore the region with an eye to strengthening its commercial ties with Southern California. The voyage was supported by the Los Angeles Chamber of Commerce as part of its continuing effort to promote trade. Hancock's crew was composed of expert sailors, along with a marine biologist recruited to study sea life and George to write about the trip. When they returned, George composed *In Mexican Waters*, an account of the expedition that won him an international audience, as it was published in French and German as well as English. One reviewer of the tome commented, "The humor runs occasionally to facetiousness, but it is an entertaining book."[38]

After the publication of *In Mexican Waters*, George became caught up in his uncle William's obsession with horse-drawn vehicles, particularly the stagecoaches that grandfather Phineas Banning had mastered two generations earlier. George began his own extensive historical research into the history of stagecoaches in America and worked with William to write *Six Horses*, which appeared in 1930. The book paid tribute to James Birch, John Butterfield, the firm of Majors & Russell, and Ben Holladay, pioneers who built networks of stagecoach transportation in the 1850s and 1860s before the transcontinental railroad was completed. Descriptions of their careers and the coaches they operated were animated by George's lively writing and informed by William's technical knowledge and his passion for the vehicles and the steeds that powered them. Professional historians, particularly those specializing in the American West, were almost unanimous in their praise of a book they found to be authentic, authoritative, and entertaining, some noting the zeal of the authors as a positive feature. Ironically, the book paid no attention to the important staging career of family patriarch Phineas Banning.[39]

Besides this book, George published several related essays in local magazines on stage driving. An amateur sailor and watercolorist during the 1920s, he also wrote freelance essays and short stories on sailing, travel, and other subjects for national publications.[40]

The unpredictable life of a peripatetic writer like George Hugh must have been almost unimaginable to the children of Katherine Stewart and Joseph Brent Banning. Katharine and Joseph were far more conservative in every way than Anne and Hancock, and their children, drawn to careers in finance and business, and bound together in an almost clannish family life, reflected their upbringing. After Joseph died, Katharine tried to keep a firm hold on her children to further mold them as much as possible in the image of their parents.

Their first child, Joseph Brent Banning Jr., was the oldest of his generation. His mother was devoted to him, and he returned the favor by looking after her during his father's illness and after his death. His uncle Hancock held Joseph Brent Jr. up as model to his rebellious son Hancock Jr., saying that the obedient Joseph never hid anything from his mother. He was certainly much less assertive than the children on Hancock's side of the family. As a child, Joseph participated in family performances with his cousins and learned to play the violin. Like his parents, young Joseph was conservative in social values and politics. His uncle William, who liked to give everyone a nickname, as Phineas did his sons, dubbed Joseph "Doc."[41]

After graduating from Yale in 1914, Joseph Jr. worked with his father in the Banning Company for a year and then found a job in the trust department of the Security Trust and Savings Bank. He served in the U.S. Navy in California during the war, spending much of his time in San Francisco. After the war he was appointed secretary of the Pacific American Steamship Company, his first step in what would become a career as an executive in the international shipping industry. This vocation would keep him near the ocean, where he spent some of his free time sailing, like his two uncles and his cousins.[42]

In 1922 Joseph Jr. married Alice Mira Morse, born in 1895 in San Francisco. Her father, John Frederick Morse II (1857–1898), had been a physician and surgeon in that city, where he built a distinguished reputation for improving public health. Her grandfather, John F. Morse (1815–1874), had also been a physician and an early California pioneer of 1849 who had established the *Sacramento Union*, written the first history of that city, and helped to found state medical societies.[43]

After their wedding in San Francisco and their honeymoon, Joseph brought his bride home to live at the "Barn" together with his siblings and their spouses, as well as his mother and his uncle William. Their first daughter, Nancy Morse Banning, was born while they lived there, and their youngest child, Katharine Alice, was born in 1931, just after they moved away. Joseph and Alice were said to be opposites in personality: he was quiet and unassuming while she was assertive, and a very fast driver. The chemistry must have been just right, as they would have a long marriage.[44]

During the 1920s Joseph Jr. moved up the ladder in the steamship industry. In 1920 he was hired as an agent by the Matson Navigation Company and in late 1921 he opened its Los Angeles office. He was charged with building the trade between Southern California and Hawaii, continuing to develop the Los Angeles harbor, and "maritime management and labor relations." By 1926 he had acquired a license as a Master of Steam Vessels, which gave him a technical background in the steamships he managed. Before the end of the decade he was the general manager for Matson operations in Australia and New Zealand and directed its expansion. When Matson merged with the Los Angeles Steamship Company in 1930, Joseph Jr. was promoted to the freight division and made assistant to Vice President Ralph Chandler. This was a prestigious and influential post, and he would rise even higher in the decades to come. More than anyone else in the family, Joseph Jr. carried on the Banning family tradition of developing the harbor and its businesses.[45]

Joseph's sister, Katharine Mary Banning, had attended boarding school in New York. After that she returned home and is recorded only as a companion to her mother at social events for quite some time. Two years after her father's death in 1920, Katharine married Francis Porter Graves, the son of Banning family friend Jackson A. Graves. The elder Graves was a conservative banker in Los Angeles, and his son followed in his footsteps. Francis was born in nearby Alhambra in 1895, attended the University of California, Berkeley, and served in the U.S. Navy during the war. In the early 1920s he established the stock brokerage house of Francis P. Graves & Company, which purchased a seat on the New York Stock Exchange in 1927. In the following year he reorganized his company as Graves, Banning & Company, with his brother-in-law William Phineas Banning as a partner.[46]

Katharine Mary and Francis were married in the elder William Banning's palatial "Barn," and after a honeymoon in China they returned to live with her extended family for the rest of the decade. All three of their children were born at the "Barn"—Francis Jr. in 1923, Jane in 1924, and Selwyn in 1928. When the rest of Joseph and Katharine Stewart's extended family moved to Hancock Park by 1930, Katharine Mary and Francis chose to assert their independence from the clan by moving instead to a series of houses, including his boyhood home, in the Pasadena area.[47]

The third child of Katharine and Joseph, William Phineas Banning, was born in 1899 at Avalon, at a time when his parents lived on Santa Catalina for much of the year. The baby of the family, William was even closer to his mother, Katharine, than his two siblings were. He attended the University of California, Berkeley, where he served in the naval reserve during the war. After graduation in 1921 he worked in the stock-brokerage firm of Hunter, Dulin & Company until 1926. He then joined the firm of his brother-in-law, Francis Graves, and in 1928 became a partner in Graves, Banning & Company.[48]

In late 1920 William married Evangeline Victoria Grier, whom he had known since high school. Evangeline was born in 1899 in Lead, South Dakota, where her father, Canadian-born Thomas Johnston Grier, was the superintendent of the Hearst family's Homestake Mining Company. She arrived in Los Angeles in 1914 and finished her education, attending the University of California, Berkeley, in 1918–19. During the 1920s she joined the Junior League and volunteered at the Childrens Hospital promoting a lecture series.[49]

Unlike Joseph Jr. and Alice, who seemed to thrive on their differences, William and Evangeline's contrasting personalities led to conflict. She was free-spirited, while he had close bonds with his comparatively conservative mother. Upon their return from their honeymoon, they immediately moved into the "Barn" with his mother, uncle, and other siblings—which probably did not help matters. Their marriage did survive the 1920s, however, during which time they had two children, Evangeline Victoria and William Phineas Jr.[50]

⁓

This second generation of Bannings came into its own in the 1920s, when postwar economic expansion was transforming Los Angeles into a booming metropolis. The opportunities they found in stock exchanges and shipping companies were created by the mushrooming regional economy, as branch plants of major industries from the East sprung up, and ancillary businesses arose to support the expanding entertainment industry. Professionals such as attorneys and architects had plenty of wealthy clients to keep them busy. New and extensive petroleum fields enriched property owners and many oil company executives, such as C. C. Julian, and that money also poured into the local economy. The discovery of black gold added a speculative craze to the magnet drawing in residents from other parts of the nation and spurring suburban growth in the areas surrounding established urban centers.[51]

Each of the Bannings of this generation and their spouses had been afforded excellent educations, and most of them had inherited some money and other resources with which to establish their young families. The scions of the two branches, however, followed quite different paths in their family lives. The children of Anne and Hancock tended to strike out on their own, putting down roots in various places rather than building a close-knit circle around their elders. In this they reflected the more elective, mobile, and dispersed model of family and community that was taking shape in Los Angeles, as in many modern American cities. Both Hancock Jr. and Eleanor and their spouses chose to live in the San Gabriel Valley, in San Marino and South Pasadena respectively, and commuted to Wilmington or Los Angeles for work. George Hugh and Gladys would remain in Berkeley until after 1930, when they also moved to South Pasadena. Although the children of Anne and Hancock were close to their parents, they chose to live far away from the Banning homes in Los Angeles and Wilmington.

The children of Katharine S. and Joseph, however, kept close to the widowed matriarch in these years, perhaps in part because of their more socially conservative bent, and in part because of their mother's great force of will. In any event, their tightly intertwined family more closely resembled that of the three Banning brothers of the previous generation, who lived for better and for worse in great physical and psychic proximity. After Joseph's death Katharine had moved into the "Barn" with her brother-in-law William and her three grown children. The mansion was huge, with

Facade of William Banning's "Barn" at Thirty-first and Hoover Streets. Courtesy of the Huntington Library.

suites of rooms for all of them. As they married, all three within two years, they brought their spouses to the "Barn" and began raising their children born in the 1920s. One of those children recalled the decade in which the three young wives—Katharine, Alice, and Evangeline—took turns managing the entire household for three months at a time. Evangeline, the free spirit of the family, apparently found the arrangement oppressive. She confessed to her mother that her mother-in-law, Katherine, and William Banning frequently criticized her, and confided to her diary that she did not wish to have another child in this environment.[52]

The Katharine Stewart Banning family's residence at the "Barn" would last until 1929. With the coming of the Olympic Games to Los Angeles in 1932, city planners were launching a number of projects to improve transportation flow and beautify the city, as well as building infrastructure for the international competition. In 1928, the city decided to widen Hoover Street, near the Coliseum and other Olympic venues, in part by taking property on one side of William Banning's estate. When William learned that the city was ready to exercise eminent domain, he decided that it was time for everyone to relocate. The family would gradually move out over the next two years, and the "Barn" would finally be razed in 1936.[53]

Interior courtyard of the "Barn" with family apartments. Courtesy of the Huntington Library.

The family reconstituted their compound elsewhere in the city. Joseph Jr. had heard of Paul Williams, a young African American architect who had been making a name for himself designing elegant residences and office buildings in Los Angeles, and he made an appointment to see him about housing the Bannings. As Joseph's daughter, Nancy, recalls, her father and mother were very impressed when Williams began drawing an elevation of a residence at his desk as they talked. The Bannings were sitting on the opposite side of the desk, facing Williams, who actually sketched upside down so that they could see the drawing properly. The immediate result of that virtuoso performance was two commissions, and another followed soon after. Joseph Jr. asked Williams to design two homes next door to each other in fashionable Hancock Park. One was for Joseph Jr. and Alice and their family, and the other for his mother, Katharine, with a suite of rooms in the rear of the house for Uncle William. Both residences were done in the American Georgian style and finished in red brick. William Phineas then commissioned Williams to plan a home directly across the street from his mother's house. This one was in a French Provincial style with a stucco exterior.

With the completion of these residences, Katharine Stewart's family, except for Katharine Mary and Francis Graves, was again together; Joseph Jr. could look after her and she could keep a close eye on all of them.[54]

The 1920s were years of transition for the Banning family as the second generation began to assert itself, even as the living members of the previous generation still exerted considerable control. In the course of the next two decades, the transition would be complete. But even by the '20s, the family had largely walked away from the legacy that Phineas had built and that the Banning brothers had built upon. The Banning companies were dissolved, Santa Catalina sold, the harbor properties largely gone, the homestead now a park and museum. Ironically, even as the harbor chapter was closing for the Bannings, Phineas, the Southern California patriarch, was remembered by his adopted hometown, when in 1926 Wilmington High School was renamed General Phineas Banning High School. The Banning name would live on in Wilmington even though all the Bannings had left.

CHAPTER THIRTEEN

The Bannings in the Great Depression and Second World War

The prosperity of the 1920s would not last. The 1929 stock market crash ignited the worst economic downturn in U.S. history, and another world war soon followed. The Bannings' personal wealth cushioned the financial blow to the family and put them in a position to help others, an opportunity that several of the women of the family eagerly embraced, working through charities to assist those in need and supporting the campaigns of progressive politicians. Still, the family was under increasing financial pressure, until their losses were reversed by the discovery of oil on their Wilmington lands. Once again the Banning fortunes would parallel the rise of a major industry that shaped Southern California. The success of this venture helped them to weather the economic storm and the catastrophic war that followed in its wake.

A decade of postwar mass consumption, easy credit, and artificially high stock prices came to a sudden halt in 1929, when the stock market crash ushered in the financial calamity known as the Great Depression. Industrial production plummeted, many factories and banks closed, and unemployment in the nation reached 25 percent by 1932. Countless citizens lost their homes and savings, and breadlines in major cities seemed to have no end. The crisis was felt throughout the world and remade the global political landscape. Laissez-faire capitalism, it seemed, had failed, and alternative ideologies emerged, offering a desperate populace systemic solutions but also breeding demagogues on the left and the right.[1]

One major result of the onset of the Depression in the United States was the election of Franklin D. Roosevelt in late 1932. His New Deal administration was an experimental exercise that quickly established new government agencies to restructure the economy, create jobs and relief resources, spur recovery, and reform and regulate economic institutions. The economy improved by 1936, but a recession the following year lasted until the beginning of the arms buildup at the start of World War II. FDR also tried to remake the judiciary, and to protect his reforms he fought to prolong his presidency beyond the generally accepted two terms—actions that lost him some of his early supporters, including several Bannings.[2]

The Depression hit a little later on the Pacific Coast, where the economy was more regional, but it hit just as hard. By early 1931, the unemployment rate for male workers in Los Angeles was almost 20 percent. Homeownership, a major index of prosperity in the Southland, declined for the first time, and breadlines were rivaling those in the rest of the nation. The region's tourist industry plummeted and service jobs almost disappeared; poor migrants took the place of tourists, filling the roads into the state. Hampered by limited resources, county and municipal governments tried ineffectually to address the situation, while the state was slow to react. Federal help and private charities stepped in as major providers of social welfare until the economy finally turned around with the advent of World War II, when Southern California became a center for war-related manufacturing and troop training. In the 1930s even wealthy families such as the Bannings had to change their spending habits and join with other civic leaders in meeting the crisis.[3]

The Bannings in the Great Depression

In Los Angeles, municipal and county governments were ill equipped to respond to the economic devastation. Local officials moved slowly, perhaps persuaded by the pronouncements of stockbrokers such as Francis Graves and William Phineas Banning, who were quoted in the *Times* almost weekly just after the Wall Street crash, cautioning against panic and predicting "that the market is now fairly well stabilized" and that there would be a quick turnaround. Los Angeles Mayor John Porter and other conservatives felt government should not lead the way, believing, as President Herbert Hoover did, that the market would correct itself and the emergency would end soon. Private charities, such as Anne Banning's Assistance League of Southern California and religious organizations, therefore provided much needed relief efforts at the local level. Anne was a driving force in these groups and in countywide advisory committees made up of charities and business organizations, along with her daughter, Eleanor, and daughter-in-law Florence (Hancock Jr.'s wife). In 1935, when the local economy was much improved, Anne was heralded as one of Los Angeles's principal "Depression Heroes and Heroines" for her efforts both locally and nationally.[4]

On the state level, the administration of Governor "Sunny Jim" Rolph also did little to stem the tide of unemployment in the early years of the Depression. Several political movements aimed specifically at altering the state economic system emerged in the 1930s; these would electrify Golden State politics and usher in a wave of new legislators who would gradually change its political system to some degree, but too late to help those suffering from the Depression. On the statewide front, too, Anne Banning was active in California's limited efforts to address the economic calamity by encouraging the California self-help movement and as a member of the State Emergency Relief Commission in 1933.[5]

For the Banning political activists of the 1930s—Anne, Eleanor, and Florence—participating in government relief efforts went hand in hand with electing more progressive and activist representatives. For the three of them this meant working for the Democratic Party, the party of their Southern heritage. Anne continued to support the party at all levels, as she had in her earlier years, when she and Hancock regularly voted for different candidates. Although a well-known Democrat, she was congratulated for her "splendid record" in politics in 1934 by *Times* publisher and Republican stalwart Harry Chandler, who cheered her on and told her not to be deterred by her "narrow-minded and bigoted" critics. A strong supporter of William Gibbs McAdoo when he ran for president in the 1920s, Anne was a leader of his campaign committee when he was elected U.S. Senator in California in 1932. In that year she was also an early advocate of Franklin D. Roosevelt in his quest for the presidency, and while campaigning for him she was chosen as one of the California electors who voted FDR into office.[6]

As an officer in the Women's Democratic League in Los Angeles, Anne supported FDR's New Deal administration and hoped it would influence relief and recovery efforts at the state and local levels. In 1936 she again was chosen as an FDR elector and loyally campaigned for him. Her position in the national party boosted her influence on the local level during the 1937 race for mayor of Los Angeles. During that campaign, the *Times* had endorsed incumbent Frank Shaw, a moderate Republican who claimed that he had brought the New Deal to Los Angeles. A political column in the paper further claimed that the "better elements of the Democratic Party" in the city were working for Shaw. A telegram reply from the Democratic headquarters corrected the record, offering a long list of "unquestionably high-minded" Democrats, Anne among them, who were backing liberal Democrat John Anson Ford for mayor. The re-tort did not have a major effect, however, and Shaw narrowly defeated Ford in the general election.[7]

Anne's daughter-in-law Florence Johnston Banning, a leader in local society by 1931, was recognized as a key figure in the Council of Social Agencies, although she played only a minor role in Democratic politics. She too was a strong supporter of FDR and the New Deal, in contrast to her husband, Hancock Jr., who was adamantly opposed to both. But Florence's chief public statement on national politics was in conflict with Anne's. Like some other Democrats in 1940, Florence criticized FDR's quest for a third term because it broke with tradition and smacked of ambitions for presidential dynasty. The *Times*, which supported Repub-lican Wendell Willkie in this race, proudly headlined a story on her views "Mrs. Banning to Aid Willkie." The best-known Mrs. Banning, Anne, was predictably upset to hear from friends and associates who thought that *she* had switched parties and quickly spread the word that the *Times* and her daughter-in-law had created that misapprehension. Florence continued to campaign for Willkie, saying that she had never voted for a Republican for president but would do so this time. Not enough other voters would join her protest, however, and FDR won again. Anne eventually forgave her eldest son's spouse for breaking party ranks.[8]

Eleanor Banning Macfarland took after her mother in political ac-tivism, although not always in her choice of candidates. Her husband was as much a moderate Republican as she was a moderate Democrat. After spending part of her youth as a Democratic Party worker, beginning with her uncle George S. Patton Sr.'s senatorial campaign in 1916, she became a leader in the 1930s. She joined her mother in party organizations for women and supported FDR in 1932. In the following year she, along with rising Republican political strategist Asa V. Call and others from both major parties, was elected a delegate to the state convention that ratified the repeal of national Prohibition. She then worked for the National Recovery Administration in trying to curb unemployment.[9]

In 1936 Eleanor was still a proud FDR campaigner and served as a delegate to the Democratic National Convention that nominated him for a second term. But like many loyal FDR supporters she changed her mind in 1937, when Roosevelt attempted to "pack" the U.S. Supreme Court with five additional justices in order to obtain rulings more favorable to his legislative program. The following year, Eleanor Macfarland was chosen to present Eleanor Roosevelt with a resolution conferring on her the title of "honorary first citizen of Los Angeles County" during the First Lady's visit, and she did it graciously. But she no longer supported the New Deal, although she was more critical of FDR's political advisers than of the president himself.[10]

Eleanor concentrated her political energies at the state level, where she was much more involved than her mother. In 1934 California's moderate Democrats saw a chance to replace a conservative Republican governor with one of their own. Noted writer and socialist Upton Sinclair upset that plan when he won the Democratic nomination based on his End Poverty in California (EPIC) plan, which would have allowed the unemployed to re-open closed factories and till unused farmland in the state, and permitted the state to issue scrip, among other strategies for economic recovery. Most conservative and many moderate Democratic leaders broke ranks with their party that year and campaigned vigorously for incumbent Frank Merriam, and Eleanor was one of them. As chair of the women's division of American Democracy of California, she took her campaign to the radio waves, arguing that the EPIC agenda would result in economic and social chaos. Two years after Sinclair's defeat, Eleanor won a seat as a state delegate to the Democratic national convention as one of eight replacements for representatives of the EPIC forces, who had been snubbed by the national committee.[11]

In what might have been a reward for her defection from the Democratic ranks in 1934 and a bid for her support in anticipation of the 1938 election, Governor Frank Merriam appointed Eleanor a regent of the University of California in December 1937. She surely was qualified for the position, but her political credentials and willingness to cross party lines certainly benefitted the governor, who had won her support in 1934 and would retain it in 1938. In that year former EPIC candidates Culbert Olson and Sheridan Downey won the Democratic nominations for governor and senator. Eleanor, who had backed her mother's friend Senator William Gibbs McAdoo for the Democratic nomination, again jumped ship. She became one of the most prominent figures in the Nonpartisan Committee of California, a group of well-known conservative Democrats, and a few moderate Republicans, who pledged to elect Republicans to state office. She then joined the "Good Government Democrats" (the same group, without the Republicans) to defeat Olson, Downey, and lieutenant governor nominee Ellis Patterson, who were much too far to the left for them. Eleanor explained that the three Democratic nominees had supported EPIC in 1934, and still did. "I have no hesitancy in recommending to all Democrats that they vote to save the State from this threat of unsound government," she advised her audience.[12]

After four decades of Republican governors, however, most California Democrats chose not to pass up the opportunity for change, and they rallied behind their party's nominees. Olson, Downey, and Patterson were elected. Commenting to Senator McAdoo on the local support for the much more liberal Democrats in the primary, Eleanor said that she "would like to disenfranchise all Los Angeles County citizens for ten years because of [their] failure to use the brains God gave them." But Eleanor and her fellow moderates had delayed the coming of the New Deal to California, and the weak Olson administration made the party's victory a hollow one. By this time, the reform impetus of the New Deal was also on the wane. Eleanor would not have another opportunity to play a role in a major federal or state election: she became ill during the first half of 1940 and died that summer.[13]

Family Matters

Not all members of the Banning family became active in politics during the tumultuous 1930s. Like all American families, however, the Bannings were affected by the Great Depression in myriad ways—in getting and giving, economically and socially, at work and at home.

The Depression intensified Anne Banning's involvement with her many social and philanthropic interests. Besides her political work, which was at least partly motivated by a search for government help with her social agenda, she was increasingly active in philanthropic campaigns. She led the local chapter of the Assistance League of Southern California, which by 1938 was aiding over 2,000 individuals each month and providing daily childcare for seventy-five children. Chapters of the successful group spread throughout the nation, and in 1935 Anne co-founded the national organization, headquartered in Los Angeles. She also coined the League's motto: "All for Service and Service for All." Described as a "porcelain, delicate figure with a mind of a military commander," she enlisted film celebrities and society figures, and anyone else she could persuade, in her charitable campaigns. She also served on several national social welfare committees created by private citizens and the New Deal administration, and as vice president of the Fatherless Children of France. With these new responsibilities she continued to add to her reputation as one of the most active and respected leaders in Southern California philanthropy.[14]

In addition to her charity work, Anne helped build educational programs aimed at preserving peace during this decade of social and political turmoil. She served as co-chair of the Los Angeles chapter of the

Philanthropist Anne
Banning's portrait at
the headquarters of
the Assistance League
of Southern California.
Photograph by Bart
Bartholomew.
Courtesy of the
Assistance League of
Southern California
Archives.

United States Society, a national organization that supplied pedagogical
materials and created programs to increase citizen awareness of governmental activities and political issues. She took part in an Assistance League
program that helped a segment of the Russian colony in Los Angeles raise
funds for a clubhouse, an event that strengthened ties between communities within the city. Along with her daughter, Eleanor, she was also a
member of the Pan-American Fellowship, whose Los Angeles leaders
tried to forge stronger ties to countries in Central and South America to
dispel "alien propaganda" designed to divide the Americas as Europe was
preparing for armed conflict.[15]

At the same time, she used her position as a leader in regional society to advance her philanthropic endeavors by organizing social events
for the Los Angeles elite, who were then invited to contribute to her
causes. In the 1930s she continued to be seen as the reluctant leader of
Los Angeles society, wearing a crown that "has been forced upon her
through the years as her natural right by birth, authority, inherent leadership." She still disclaimed the honor, explaining, "There are so many

more interests demanding the attention of intelligent women." But she was not averse to using her royal reputation to attract socialites to her parties who might aid her charities.[16]

Despite her position and her fortune, like most Americans even Anne Banning was hurt financially by the Depression. In past decades she had lived well and spent her money lavishly, to her husband's chagrin. After Hancock's death, Anne owned much property but had little cash. With the onset of the Depression, her property declined in value and she was not always able to pay her bills on time. Her son Hancock Jr. managed her finances and took on his father's monitory role, frequently reminding her to restrain her spending. Throughout the 1930s she sometimes had to lease her opulent residence on West Adams Boulevard to pay for her expenses and live in a smaller and less costly Craftsman home in South Pasadena, next door to her daughter Eleanor.[17]

Anne's predicament caused some embarrassment in 1932, when the *Times* reported that her West Adams Boulevard home and its expensive furnishings would be auctioned. The paintings that would be put up for bid, the newspaper said, included a number of works that Anne had ordered from a London gallery in the late 1920s but had not paid for yet. As it turned out, most of the paintings and other furnishings on the block belonged to Madame Julia Rodenzo, a wealthy resident of Paris who had occupied the home over the previous year. The house was removed from the auction before it started, as it could not have fetched a good price with the economy so bad. Anne kept some of her paintings, sold a few of them and relied on her son and her lawyer to negotiate with the gallery to delay her payments until the end of the decade. As it turned out, some of the pieces in her collection were later found to be counterfeits, according to an expert at the art gallery of the Huntington in nearby San Marino.[18]

While overseeing his mother's finances, Hancock Jr. made a career of administering the Hancock Banning estate and its property. He also supervised the Townsend Land Company, which still held some parcels of land for both sides of the family, and helped his uncle, "Captain" William Banning, manage his land and other assets, acting as an insurance agent for William's collection of stagecoaches. Besides leading the fight to stop the city of Los Angeles from taking family property at the harbor, he oversaw the finances for his "Greasy Spoon" restaurant on Mormon Island during the early 1940s. His spouse, Florence, was busy raising their sons and daughter and working for her substantial portfolio of social welfare organizations, which included the Pasadena Council on

Social Agencies, the California Conference on Social Work, the Pasadena
Junior League, and the Visiting Nurse Association.[19]

Eleanor Banning Macfarland raised her three children during the
1930s while serving in various civic and philanthropic organizations. Her
political activism earned her appointments to federal National Recovery
Administration and Farm Security Administration advisory committees,
the Los Angeles County Citizens' Relief Commission, and to the Board
of Regents of her alma mater, the University of California. She also
worked with a number of private humanitarian groups such as her
mother's Assistance League of Southern California, along with the English Speaking Union and the Pan-American Fellowship. Her husband,
John, continued to build his reputation as a partner in the law firm of
Gibson, Dunn & Crutcher, while serving as the Banning's legal counsel.[20]

In early 1940 Eleanor was diagnosed with multiple sclerosis and had
to curtail her ambitious schedule as her condition worsened. In June her
oldest daughter, Anne Banning Macfarland, married Lt. Samuel Robbins
Brown Jr., of the U.S. Navy, in a ceremony attended by the immediate
family and a few friends. Just over a month later, Eleanor died at the age
of forty-seven. She was buried at the San Gabriel Cemetery after a service attended by "scores of persons prominent in civic, social and business affairs." Although she died much too young, Eleanor had followed in
her mother's tradition, making many important contributions to the social and political development of the region. The great significance of
these achievements was witnessed by an obituary in the *New York Times*,
as well as tributes in local papers.[21]

Eleanor's younger brother, George Hugh, returned to Southern California from Berkeley in the early 1930s and continued his writing. Besides short articles for books, essays for magazines, and another story on
stagecoach history, he published *Sailor Ways*, a book for children, in 1932.
By 1934 George had moved his family to South Pasadena, just a few
blocks from his mother and sister. His writing income could not support
them during the Depression, so he sought the position of postmaster of
the city. His mother Anne's influence with the national administration
and friendship with Senator William Gibbs McAdoo smoothed the way,
and McAdoo obtained an appointment for George as acting postmaster
in November 1934. EPIC Democrats in South Pasadena, annoyed at
George for opposing the EPIC campaign of Upton Sinclair, protested that
he was unqualified. The job had been nominally temporary for a very
long time, but after going through a background investigation and com-
plying with other regulations George finally removed the "acting" from

his title in 1937. Until 1946, when he resigned to resume his career as a writer, he carried out his duties well. During his tenure, he was no doubt pleased to be able to commission a mural by John Law Walker for the new South Pasadena Post Office that depicted a Concord mail coach like those he had described in *Six Horses*.[22]

While George's new South Pasadena job was successful, his marriage was not. He and Gladys, both described as free spirits by their descendants, divorced after eighteen years of marriage in 1938. Gladys married twice more before her death in 1980. Their son Douglas spent most of the 1940s at boarding school, serving in the army, and attending college. George soon remarried, in 1940, this time to Helen Shoff, a New Yorker who lived in the same apartment building as he did. The two raised one daughter, Marianne Alyce, and Helen's son Kent from her previous marriage, moving to their "One Horse Ranch" in La Jolla, California, in the early 1950s.[23]

Most of Hancock Banning's children and their families got along well together, except for the business-like Hancock Jr. and the creative George, who clashed over financial affairs. Their long-standing sibling rivalry, fed by their different temperaments, divergent political views, and their mother's apparent preference for her younger son, erupted over the handling of their father's estate. This rivalry was also fueled by too much alcohol, as Hancock Jr.'s drinking did not mix well with his management of the family assets. George admitted that he also imbibed too much, and he certainly took after his spendthrift mother. He nonetheless accused Hancock Jr. of charging too much for managing the estate and shortchanging him when portioning out the proceeds. Hancock Jr., in turn, was convinced that George had persuaded their mother, Anne, to put the estate funds in trust to keep him from managing them, and he moved the funds to a different trust to prevent George from withdrawing the principal. Writing about George's supposed machinations, Hancock Jr. said, "He was good at that . . . always a hindrance . . . mean + greedy." John C. Macfarland, their brother-in-law, legal adviser, and occasional arbitrator, counseled Anne not to worry about their differences. "If they can't act like grown men and talk their opposite views out objectively it is too bad but I don't think you should lose any sleep over it," he wrote to her in 1942. In the early 1950s the brothers quarreled over the disposition of their mother's personal property after her death. The bitter feelings never ceased, though the brothers could set them aside at times for the sake of the family—such as a Thanksgiving feast George arranged at his house in 1943 for the whole family, including Joseph Brent Banning's branch.[24]

While Anne Banning kept busy with her many political, philanthropic, and cultural pursuits in these years, Katharine S. Banning spent most of her time keeping a close eye on her children and grandchildren. From her home in one of the three neighboring Banning residences in Hancock Park, she could oversee the activities of her two sons and their immediate families, who lived next door and across the street. She rarely appeared in the newspapers at social events, and the lone public notice of her doings was a description of her annual Christmas party in 1938. She began holding these elaborate celebrations just after her marriage to Joseph, and continued into the 1940s. In 1941 she had to cancel the party because of the war, after having sent out about 300 invitations to family and friends.[25]

While Katharine watched over her branch of the family, her oldest son, Joseph Brent Jr., cared for her. Joseph Jr.'s career as a shipping executive continued to thrive in the early 1930s when he was promoted to general superintendent of the Matson steamship line. The Banning name continued to resonate in the harbor area as he led the shipping companies in their negotiations with city government, commercial organizations, and labor unions.[26]

In 1934 he played a key role in a major labor dispute at the harbor. The International Longshoremen's Association was then in the midst of an organizing campaign to unionize longshoremen, raise low wages, and improve working conditions. The first action on the Pacific Coast took place when union leaders in San Francisco called a strike in October 1933 to protest the firing of several union members who had worked for Joseph Jr.'s firm, the Matson Navigation Company; the strike was called off when their co-workers were reinstated. The increase in this union activity in California would lead to a major strike along the Pacific Coast the following year.[27]

In San Pedro the unionists created their own hiring hall for assigning jobs to workers, which competed with the shippers' Marine Service Bureau, of which Joseph Banning Jr. was a leader. One of his primary duties was labor negotiations, no doubt challenging work for a man remembered by many of his family members as rather meek. When the dockworkers voted overwhelmingly to be represented by the union in January 1934, he was among the company leaders who agreed to a number of minor concessions in the form of a small wage increase and bonuses for certain types of work. The Pacific Coast unionists then presented a number of demands to the shippers, including recognition of the union hiring hall and a coastwide wage scale, which the companies rejected. When workers along the coast voted to walk out in late March, the San Pedro longshoremen agreed to follow. In preparation for the strike, Joseph Banning Jr., as head of a special committee of the Marine Service Bureau, arranged for members of the regional Merchants' and Manufacturers' Association to contribute to a large fund for additional private guards. These guards would assist the forces of Captain William F. "Red" Hynes and his notorious Los Angeles Police Department "Red Squad" in defending harbor property at San Pedro.[28]

Although President Roosevelt intervened to delay the walkout, the strike finally began on May 9, when dockworkers left their jobs in ports all along the coast from Seattle to San Diego. Los Angeles and Long Beach were the only ports to remain open; the Merchants' and Manufacturers' Association had hired thousands of strikebreakers to load and unload ships under the protection of armed guards. The company also housed the strikebreakers in fortified compounds, one of which became the scene of the most serious conflict between local unionists and the police. In the early hours of May 15, strikers stormed a compound at the West Basin to disperse the strikebreakers, and police and special deputies opened fire with rifles and tear gas. Two unionists were killed, five were seriously wounded, and many others were clubbed and arrested. Thousands attended the funerals in San Pedro and a memorial service in San Francisco, where two striking unionists were also killed by police in a similar incident on Thursday, July 5. The twin tragedies are still remembered in San Francisco and at the Los Angeles harbor as "Bloody Thursday."[29]

With San Francisco and other ports closed, Los Angeles harbor gained some of the trade originally destined for elsewhere. When unionists and employers began negotiating to end the conflict in San Francisco and San Pedro, Joseph Banning Jr. served as the spokesman for the Southern California shipping companies, and some of the sessions were held in his office. Armed with financial aid from businesses and with a large pool of potential strikebreakers, thanks to the Depression, Joseph refused union demands for a closed shop and a coastwide labor agreement. Despite the standoff, harbor business in San Pedro was already starting to return to normal by the end of May. The strike along the coast continued into June, when President Roosevelt again intervened and the conflict was sent to arbitration. Picketing continued, however, and further clashes between the union and police resulted in more deaths in San Francisco and Seattle. On July 31, the strikers finally went back to work, and in San Pedro observers were sent to Joseph Banning Jr.'s Marine Service Bureau to prevent discrimination in the rehiring of union members.[30]

The 1934 harbor strike would be the most serious labor dispute Joseph Jr. faced, but certainly not the last. In November 1934 he was the company spokesman during a dispute on a Matson liner between union and nonunion crewmembers. Four years later he was among the leaders of the Waterfront Employers' Association (successor to the Marine Service Bureau) when dock unions held a work stoppage in support of another union seeking increased wages and other objectives in a new contract with shipowners. When the deadline set for ending the dispute passed, the employers halted all shipping at San Pedro for ten days. The conflict was finally resolved by a federal arbitrator in favor of the employers. After that victory Joseph Jr. continued his work with the Matson line, untroubled by serious conflicts with unions until his retirement in 1954. By that time he had spent almost forty years as an influential figure in the expansion of the harbor and of international trade in San Pedro, which in turn fueled the economic growth of Southern California.[31]

Katharine S. Banning's daughter Katharine Mary—known as "Kash"—and her husband, Francis Graves, and family lived in the San Gabriel Valley not far from many of Hancock Banning's descendants during the 1930s. Francis continued as managing partner of the stockbrokerage, but lost a considerable portion of his own investments after the stock market crash. He also felt compelled to try to repay clients whose funds he had invested and lost, and the combination of his losses and these debts forced the family to move out of their substantial residence in Pasadena into smaller quarters. They moved into the old Graves Homestead in Alhambra after his mother's death in 1939 (his father had died in 1933). By 1942 they were in a still smaller home in nearby Altadena, two years after Francis had retired from his business, which was then reorganized with several new partners as Bogardus, Frost, and Banning.[32]

Katharine S. Banning's youngest son, William Phineas Banning, lived across the street from his mother in the 1930s while continuing his partnership in the stockbrokerage firm with brother-in-law Francis Graves. In 1933 his marriage to Evangeline Grier—"Muddie" to family members—began to fall apart after their son underwent an operation late in that year. Several family members tried to help mend the rift, but to no avail. In February 1934 she sued him for divorce, charging that her husband "frequently refused to kiss her" and was "consistently surly and inclined to ignore her." William kept the two children and the house in Hancock Park and Muddie was awarded stocks, furniture, and cash. She eventually remarried and moved to San Francisco and then Sausalito, where she died in 1988.[33]

After the divorce, William's mother, Katharine, raised William Phineas Jr. while Evangeline Victoria, known as Paddy, attended boarding school. Four years later, William Sr. married Helen Large in Cleveland and adopted her daughter, Cynthia. Helen proved to be quite erratic in her behavior, however, and this marriage also ended in divorce, in 1944. Undeterred, in 1947 William married Janet Kirby Chappell in a small family ceremony in Arizona. She was the daughter of Rollin Kirby, the noted political cartoonist for several New York newspapers in the early 1900s. The two moved from the family residences in Hancock Park to their Bradbury Ranch in Duarte, where both remained for the rest of their lives.[34]

Meanwhile, "Captain" William Banning devoted more time to his passion of stagecoach driving and to taking care of the growing Banning family. Newspapers and other publications occasionally ran stories with illustrations of William pursuing his coaching hobby, whether driving his stages in parades such as La Fiesta de Los Angeles of 1931, which commemorated the city's 150th anniversary, or communing at his Walnut Ranch with others of like mind. In 1932 he gave actor Will Rogers and California Governor "Sunny Jim" Rolph wild rides on one of his stages at the Kellogg Ranch in Pomona when W. K. Kellogg gave his Arabian horse stables to the University of California. William commissioned a perfect one-third scale replica of one of his Concords, and the *Times* celebrated the completion of the project in 1933 by featuring a photograph of the model and the actual coach along with William and his niece Nancy Morse Banning on the front page of its second section. William proudly displayed the model at his ranch; it was eventually donated to the Natural History Museum of Los Angeles County in the 1960s. William also founded the Overland Stage Coach Club for former drivers and served as its president for several years. In 1941 he was described as the only remaining member of the club, although his nephew George Hugh was considered an associate member because of all he had done to help his uncle promote this pastime. The Captain freely admitted that he had never driven an automobile, and by this point it was obvious that the octogenarian never would.[35]

In the 1930s and after, Anne and Katharine S. Banning apparently carried on the tradition of rivalry between the Hancock and Joseph Brent branches of the family to some degree, albeit quietly. Rumor held that

William Banning gives Will Rogers a ride at the Kellogg Ranch in Pomona.
Courtesy of the Huntington Library.

early in the century the two spouses were seldom on Santa Catalina at the same time, or at least not in the same part of the island. Even after their husbands' conflicts were long over, they apparently avoided each other at social events, except on special occasions for close family members. They only once appeared in the same newspaper story, one that listed both as local hostesses for the 1932 Olympic Games in Los Angeles; whether they actually met at this function is unknown. They did serve together on a family reception committee at the dedication of the Banning mansion as a museum in 1936.[36]

Captain William Banning tried to ameliorate the old family rift for the next generation by hosting summertime vacations for all of the Banning children at his Walnut Ranch. The ranch was far from their homes in the San Gabriel Valley and in Los Angeles, so the occasion re-quired an automobile trip along Valley Boulevard through La Puente, described by one of the participants as "the town where all the road agents and horse thieves lived." Thanks to William, the ranch became a haven for Phineas Banning's great-grandchildren; they and some of their cousins and friends spent their summers riding horses and stagecoaches, playing games, and getting acquainted with ranch animals—and wild animals such as rattlesnakes, bobcats, tarantulas, hawks, coyotes, and mountain lions. The dozen or more children who were there at any given time had to follow the rules "Uncle" set for meals, and observe early bedtime and nighttime silence (or at least a reasonable facsimile), but found many opportunities to bend the rules and have more fun.[37]

More than just a vacation venue, the Walnut Ranch would serve as a community center for this generation of cousins in the 1930s and early '40s. Along with the Catalina Island School for Boys, where several of the boys went to school together, "Uncle" William Banning's Walnut Ranch served to strengthen the bonds of this generation and lay to rest the ghosts of their grandparents' feuding.[38]

Unlike Phineas Banning's 1864 home, William's Walnut Ranch could not be saved through a declaration of landmark status. In 1975, the existing main ranch house was approved as a Los Angeles County Point of Historical Interest. Suburban encroachment brought housing tracts ever closer, however, and by 1980 the last structure of the original complex had disappeared.[39]

Banning Fortunes in Dire Circumstances

The Bannings were well off when the Depression began, but because most of their assets were invested in real estate that had plummeted in value, they felt the pinch of the depressed economy. Family members managed their parents' estates and had to fight off attempts to seize some of their property. By the end of the decade, however, they would be saved by the discovery of oil on their lands. Once again, the Bannings would ride the wave of a burgeoning industry, as Southern California continued to be a major source of petroleum in the nation.

After Joseph Brent and Hancock died, in 1920 and 1925 respectively, their real estate and other property was held through estates created by their families. Their sons managed the estates in order to reap income from leases, rentals, and royalties. The estates could look rich on paper—the Hancock Banning estate was valued at well over $1.3 million in 1929. But this figure represented the appraised value of the land, which depreciated quickly in the early 1930s and would have been difficult to sell in a depressed real estate market. The situation was so bad at one point that banks declined to foreclose on some of the Hancock Banning estate property because it was worth less than the amount owed; they allowed Han-

William Banning driving a stagecoach at his Walnut Ranch, about 1940. Courtesy
of the Huntington Library.

cock Jr. to continue managing the estate in the hope that he could recoup
their earlier values.[40]

Both estates would continue into the 1940s, their value depressed in
the early '30s but then boosted by oil royalties, which began to make a
difference by later in the decade. With that infusion of income the
family of both branches would shore up their financial situation in the
decades to come.[41]

The settlement reached among the Bannings, the Southern Pacific
Railroad, and the city over the harbor tidelands in 1917 became an economic issue for the Bannings once again during the Depression. Shortly
before his death in 1925, Hancock Banning had sold to the city of Los
Angeles about five acres of his remaining property on Mormon Island, a
valuable plot of land in the inner harbor just south of Wilmington, which
the city then leased to an oil company. This lot was one of several parcels
owned by the Banning family that was not considered to be tidelands
and so not subject to the 1917 agreement. After Hancock's death the
city tried to buy another twelve acres of waterfront land along the
West Basin held by Hancock's estate in order to build a highway. City officials balked at the high price asked by the estate, which estate executor

John C. Macfarland explained included damages to other Banning property as a result of the construction. The harbor commission instead ordered condemnation proceedings on a small portion of the property, which allowed them to complete the highway while discussions over the sale continued, and the two sides eventually settled on a price.[42]

In 1929 the harbor commissioners initiated a court suit to take a valuable strip of Mormon Island acreage from the Bannings and the Pacific Coast Borax Company, which had purchased part of the site from the Bannings and built a large factory there. The city claimed this was tidelands property, covered by the 1911 state tidelands law, and should revert to the city without compensation to the private owners. At issue was where the mean high tide mark was when William Banning received the patent in 1882; if parts of the island had been below that mark, they were the city's to take. Hancock Jr. and Joseph Jr. led the fight for the Bannings. Negotiations between the major parties dragged on for two years until a compromise was reached in 1931 and a purchase price set. The city rescinded its offer, however, and the issue was ordered for trial in 1933. In the meantime John C. Macfarland directed a lobbying campaign in Washington, D.C., from his Los Angeles office at Gibson, Dunn & Crutcher on behalf of the Bannings. Hancock Jr. charged that the city responded by harassing the Bannings, withdrawing police services near their property, and requiring unnecessary improvements. The Bannings refused to back down, however, and near the end of 1933 the *Times* announced that the city and the Bannings had reached agreement on the sale of the critical plot of land in the suit. The city council hastily approved the purchase the following day to avoid a longer fight and more legal expenses.[43]

Since the Bannings no longer owned it, the parcel held by the Pacific Coast Borax Company was not part of the deal, and the city continued to pursue their suit against the company. Borax won one ruling in 1934, and the city unsuccessfully appealed it to the U.S. Supreme Court in 1935. The city persisted with another appeal in the U.S. District Court, but was defeated again. In the final court action in 1939, the U.S. Circuit Court in San Francisco upheld the previous ruling, which concluded that the city had lost any claim to the property after it induced Pacific Coast Borax to spend over $1.5 million improving the land. Hancock Banning Jr., who had few good things to say about the harbor commission after several decades of experience with some of its members, must have loudly cheered the news of this outcome.[44]

The sinking value of the Banning estates was sharply reversed in the mid-1930s when their long-held property in Wilmington and then New-port Beach began producing oil in vast quantities. Although Phineas Ban-ning and others, hampered by primitive equipment and low demand, had been unable to make a profit from oil extraction in the 1860s, discover-ies in Ventura County and in portions of the city of Los Angeles in the 1890s and in the San Joaquin Valley in 1910 marked the region as a major oil field. With the growing demand for oil to fuel railroads and automo-biles after 1900, drilling increased and major deposits were struck at Huntington Beach, Santa Fe Springs, Signal Hill, Torrance, and other lo-cations in the 1920s. Southern California became the nation's center for oil extraction and refining, and oil from the region became the harbor's major export in the 1920s and a primary driver of the expansion of trade at the port. Investments in this industry by large corporations and smaller companies alike also helped to build the region's banking sector and to spark the population boom of the 1920s. Oil fueled the 1940s U.S. war effort, and in the postwar era led to the boom in automobile ownership and contributed to suburban sprawl.[45]

One of the 1920s booms—actually a boomlet—occurred at Newport Beach near the old Banning Ranch property, where Phineas had tried to raise sheep in the 1870s. By 1925 several profitable wells had been drilled in the Newport field, and Mary Hollister Banning Norris, who had in-herited a large parcel of land there from her mother, hoped to profit by leasing her land to an oil company. This boom would not last long, how-ever, as the crude discovered then was of poor quality. Additional drilling was done there in the 1930s, but nothing more would be found until the next decade. Mary soon sold her portion of the ranch, while the descen-dants of her brothers retained their much smaller parcel.[46]

The three Banning brothers and their spouses owned a considerable amount of property in Wilmington, and had been hoping to strike oil there since 1899, when they created the Banning Drilling Company. That venture did not work out, and the Bannings then leased some of their land to an oil company until 1921. By 1932 oil was being extracted at Wilming-ton, and residents were even pumping crude on their homesteads from shallow depths and in small quantities for their own use and to sell to their neighbors and others. After a story appeared in the *Times* and *West-ways* about Cristóbal Salcido striking oil while digging a large hole for a cesspool on his lot on Banning Avenue, then covered with sand from dredging the harbor decades earlier, drilling continued at a faster pace. By May 1936, the Sovereign Oil Company, having leased land from the Bannings, was boring new holes in the Wilmington oil field.[47]

In December 1936 three additional zones of the field were discovered and the boom was on. Within several years the Wilmington field was one of the most productive in the nation in total output, ranking second in the Los Angeles basin after the Torrance field. It contained one of the largest reserves in California, and the gasoline refined from the crude had the highest octane rating in the state. The drilling and the addition of heavy industry in the area actually caused the earth to sink as oil was pumped out, a problem that forced the city of Los Angeles to undertake various measures beginning in the 1940s to prevent flooding, sinkholes, and structural damage to harbor facilities. The Wilmington field, though it had considerable environmental impact, was one of the most valuable in the state for decades; it continues to be considered for expanded production whenever oil prices rise.[48]

The Wilmington boom dramatically increased the wealth of the Bannings, whose property was suddenly much more valuable. Hancock Jr. and his uncle William handled the negotiations with several oil companies, who agreed to lease Banning land and to pay them royalties and a portion of the net proceeds. These arrangements netted both sides of the family a considerable income, which shrank somewhat in 1947, when their leasehold on Mormon Island reverted to the city along with the proceeds from oil extraction there. By that year, however, the oil income the Bannings lost when the leasehold expired was already being replaced with income from the Banning Ranch property in Newport Beach, which began producing crude early in the 1940s. This property had been managed since 1908 by the Banning family's Townsend Land Company, but since it was much more valuable for its lease and oil royalties than as a site for future development, the company was dissolved in 1945. The Bannings would negotiate a new arrangement to manage the land they owned together in the following decade.[49]

Another World War

The second "war to end all wars" had a profound effect on the generations of Americans and others throughout the world who lived through the conflict. Of those Americans in military service, hundreds of thousands fought overseas; many of them were killed and still more returned with physical injuries or psychological scars or both. Those on the home front witnessed upheaval in their neighborhoods, as almost 20 percent of Americans relocated in these years, and in the workplace, where the need for workers to manufacture munitions and other goods brought women and minorities into industries previously dominated by white men. The population shifts exacerbated racial tensions, leading to riots in some cities, and shortages in housing, food, fuel, and other commodities strained families in many ways. These changes in economic and social conditions would set the tone for the nation when it entered the Cold War era a few years later.[5]

The changes roiling the nation at large afflicted Southern California as well, and in some ways were even more disruptive there than in the rest of the country. The flight to the suburbs accelerated, especially when war workers flooded the region and African Americans and other minorities moved into the neighborhoods from which Japanese Americans had been expelled. Factory jobs increased with the demand for war-related goods, attracting more workers and creating a serious housing crisis. Shortages of everyday goods were rife. But in spite of hardships, Southern Californians adapted to the crisis, as did their counterparts throughout the nation.[51]

The Bannings were no exception. The men continued their careers, although their work was sometimes modified by military needs and material shortages. Hancock Jr. managed family lands near the harbor, including a site on Mormon Island leased to the U.S. Navy. Joseph Jr. worked in a much busier harbor, where naval vessels and war munitions carriers competed with other ships for access to berths. The women of this generation were consumed with volunteering for social welfare organizations, as well as managing their households and raising children.[52]

The two family matriarchs drew upon their charitable experience in the previous war and were heralded for their significant contributions to the war effort. Katharine S. Banning resurrected her garment-making campaign at her house on McCadden Place, which became known as the "McCadden Unit" of the local American Red Cross Service. Before the U.S. declared war, she made bandages for the British War Relief organization. Anne Banning had never suspended her involvement in the Red Cross and other humanitarian groups, and she continued to be a leader in these efforts throughout the war.[53]

When the war began, some of the Banning males were too old or too young to join up, but many of the rest volunteered for service. Donald Macfarland and William Phineas Banning Jr. were not even teenagers in 1941, although both would later serve in the U.S. armed forces. Of those who were active during World War II, Hancock III was a U.S. Navy aviator who flew off of a carrier in the Pacific Theater and left the service as a lieutenant junior grade. His brother, Cpl. Robert J. Banning, served in the Army Air Corps for three years, part of the time as a weather observer in the Pacific ("Never saw a shot fired in anger," he once boasted). Douglas Banning joined the army and was stationed in Australia; the ship that brought him to his troop transport in San Francisco was the *Catalina*, which had often carried him to and from Santa Catalina Island in more carefree times. Francis Graves Jr. and his brother Selwyn were in ROTC programs at the Culver Military Academy in Indiana and received officer commissions in the U.S. Army right after they graduated. Francis was sent to Italy as a forward observer directing fire to an artillery unit, then to France, where he was wounded in late 1944. He was finally reassigned to the Third Army, where for a short time he served as an assistant to Banning relative General George S. Patton Jr.. Selwyn suffered a severe hearing loss while assigned to the 13th Armored Division, which cut short his career in the armed forces. After his discharge he returned home and entered graduate school in 1945.[54]

Three newcomers to the Banning family were also stationed overseas during the war. Lt. James Totten, who had married Ruth Ellen Patton, the daughter of General George S. Patton Jr. and Beatrice Ayer (both Banning relatives) in 1940, served as an army artillery officer in Europe. Lt. Col. John K. Waters, husband since 1934 of the General's other daughter, Beatrice, served in North Africa, where he was captured by the Germans in 1943, imprisoned in Germany, and then rescued by his father-in-law in 1945. U.S. Navy Lt. Samuel Robbins Brown Jr., who had married Eleanor Banning Macfarland's daughter Anne in 1940, was stationed aboard the USS *New Orleans* in the Pacific. This heavy cruiser was fired on at Pearl Harbor during the December 1941 attack and later participated in the battles of the Coral Sea, Midway, the Eastern Solomons, and many others.[55]

The major family figure in the war, of course, was General George S. Patton Jr., the nephew of Anne Banning and husband of Phineas Banning's great-niece Beatrice Ayer. From his tank training program in the Southern California desert in 1941–42, through major campaigns in Europe, postwar reconstruction, and his death in late 1945, Patton was heralded as one of the most competent and fearless military leaders of any nation during the war, while also inspiring controversy with his style and temperament.

The books devoted to General "Old Blood and Guts" Patton and his World War II experience would probably fill a small library. The brief version of the story begins with his role as commander of the I Armored Corps, training his tank warfare troops in the blistering heat of the Imperial Valley desert at Chiriaco Summit, when the U.S. entered the war.

General George S. Patton Jr. and Lt. Francis P. Graves Jr. during World War II.
Courtesy of the Huntington Library.

In the following year he moved his troops to Morocco and was eventually placed in command of the American forces that helped to push the
Axis armies out of North Africa in 1943. Later that year he was given
command of the Seventh Army, part of the invasion force that took Sicily.
He participated in the several campaigns to deceive the Germans about
the Allies' planned targets, and after the Normandy invasion he was
placed in command of the Third Army. Moving it quickly to help liber-
ate Paris and then heading toward Germany, he used various tactics to
help his highly mobile force avoid large enemy concentrations and instead attack at weak points—until his army literally ran out of gas near
Metz, France. In the winter of 1944 Patton's army was instrumental in
turning back the last German offensive in the Battle of the Bulge, and
then turned its sights toward Berlin. When the war in Europe ended,
Patton was put in charge of the occupation forces in Bavaria, where he
died from injuries sustained in an accident between his staff car and an
army truck in December 1945.[56]

Christening of the SS *Phineas Banning* by his great-granddaughter Evangeline
Victoria Banning, in 1943. Courtesy of the Huntington Library.

Patton's military accomplishments made him a national hero, although some of his more controversial actions tarnished this image. A
flamboyant and arrogant leader, he was blunt and frequently too quick to
act, often arguing with his superior officers. He came close to losing his
wartime commands altogether on several occasions, and was temporarily removed once. He was strict and demanding with his troops, and on
two separate visits to army hospitals he slapped enlisted men he thought
were malingerers (one of them had malaria, the other was shell-shocked).
On two occasions after his rousing and spirited speeches, his troops killed
a total of seventy-six unarmed Italian and German prisoners of war, later
saying that they thought they were following his orders. While supervising Bavaria after the German surrender, he made racist remarks about
the victims of the Holocaust, while at the same time he worked to keep
former Nazis in government positions to avoid chaos in the civil bureaucracy. For these actions he was fiercely criticized in U.S. newspapers and
finally removed from his command in 1945. He also smuggled an original
copy of the 1935 Nuremberg Laws signed by Adolf Hitler out of Germany

without authorization and gave it to the Huntington Library (where it remained until 1999, when it was placed on a permanent loan at the Skirball Cultural Center in Los Angeles). Clearly, Patton was as controversial as he was successful during these years.[57]

Like most Americans back home who followed military events, the Banning family looked up to Patton for his exploits in battle. The adults were duly proud of him and his tough reputation and battlefield glory. The children worshiped him as larger than life. Joseph Jr.'s daughters, Nancy Morse and Katharine Alice "Kay" Banning, collected issues of *Time* magazine that featured Patton prominently, and Nancy was so impressed with her trip to the Desert Training Center to visit the General that over sixty-five years later she could recall some of the military tactics he taught her. Nancy's cousin, Marion Fitzhugh Macfarland, recalled her first meeting with Patton when she was about ten years old. "Typically dressed in his Army uniform, his chest full of medals, and his famous pearl-handled pistols in their holsters above each hip," he was a commanding sight for the entire family. When he asked young Marion what he could do for her, she asked him to swear (he was known for his profanity). After he "roared with laughter," he accommodated her.[58]

A final Banning contribution to the Allied war effort was the SS *Phineas Banning*, the 136th Liberty ship built by the California Shipbuilding Company in its Wilmington yard. Christened in early 1943 by Phineas Banning's great-granddaughter Evangeline Victoria "Paddy" Banning, this freighter was a welcome addition to the nation's wartime shipping capability. Newspapers in Delaware saluted its launching as a tribute to one of its native sons, who had migrated to the Pacific Coast almost a century earlier. One said of Phineas, "He believed in long term planning—a philosophy strange to the get-rich quick Californians of those golden pioneering days." As that newspaper reporter probably realized at the time, long-term planning was also critical in bringing the war to a close.[59]

With the end of the war in 1945, prosperity would return to the United States and to the Bannings in Southern California. Another generation would pass on and yet another would take its place. Petroleum would continue to support the family and historic preservation would become a major Banning cause.

CHAPTER FOURTEEN

ANOTHER GENERATION AND PRESERVING THE BANNING LEGACY

With the end of World War II, the great-grandchildren of Phineas Banning began to take their place on stage, and their grandparents and parents to take their bows. Many of those who have stayed in Southern California are making their own marks in its history, although the time to measure their contributions awaits a future historian. But already apparent is their commitment to preserving the legacy of Phineas Banning and the next two generations of his family as a reminder of the role of Banning family members in the shaping of the region. In this sense they have already "made history," by making it possible to tell more fully the story of Southern California.

Even as the social, political, economic, and technological changes that have swept through America since World War II speak to a seemingly restless quest for the new, they also reflect our roots in the entrepreneurial, visionary spirit of Phineas Banning's generation. Tracking these changes, we discover stories that are familiar in many ways. The era of national prosperity in the late 1940s and 1950s recalled the boom years of the Gilded Age in the wake of the Civil War. The reformist promise of the Progressive Era was renewed in the 1960s, when causes such as civil rights for people of color, women's liberation, and opposition to the war in Vietnam challenged the status quo. Like the political scandals and economic depression that inspired Progressive Era reforms, the Watergate scandal and rising energy prices in the 1970s cast suspicion on national leaders in government and business. In more recent years, the computer and communications revolution is fueled by the belief forged in the Roaring Twenties that modernity and technology are inextricably linked. And as in the years of economic depression and political radicalism leading up to World War II, we are today constantly reminded of the threats as well as the promise of the interconnected global economy.[1]

In the midst of these changes many Americans, like the Bannings of Southern California, have looked to the past for guideposts. They have sought to reflect on it and to glean from it stable values, even as the present threatened to erase the world they remembered. Part of that search for the past included preserving historical records, to better understand how past generations coped with and participated in the changes that made our world. This quest has driven the growing interest in genealogy, a search for an understanding of ourselves through our family histories. It has also expanded preservation efforts directed at historic architecture and landscape, as the built environment of the past helps us to comprehend the nature and magnitude of our society's transformation.

The Passing Banning Generations

Unfortunately for those who sought to preserve the Banning story in the postwar years, the era began with the disastrous loss of many irreplaceable family records. William Banning had built a brick blockhouse at his Walnut Ranch to store and preserve his silver saddles, weapons, and other treasures along with important family documents and business records, but had left some of them out in a barn to review for their historical content. In March 1944, the structure was consumed by fire, thought to have been set by a caretaker's cigarette. Six horses perished in the inferno, along with five of the Captain's stagecoaches and his collection of saddles, harnesses, and accoutrements. Overnight, the home of William's hobbies and the summertime haven for his brothers' grandchildren had been devastated, along with a large cache of Banning family papers.[2]

Eighty-five-year-old "Uncle" Banning was living in a sanitarium when the blaze occurred, and his doctor thought it best not to tell him the news at that time. When he eventually learned of it, "he took it like a soldier" despite being seriously ill, according to his nephew and the co-author of his stagecoach stories, George Hugh. William would recover and move back to a house he had recently purchased a block north of the one he had lived in with Katharine S. Banning in Hancock Park, but he was never the same. In January 1946 he died at his home of several maladies, including a cerebral hemorrhage. He was buried at Inglewood Cemetery with his brothers, rather than at Rosedale, where his father, stepmother, and half-sisters Ellen and Lucy were interred. A special tribute for him was planned for March at the Butterfield Stage Stop in Beaumont, California, by a group of surviving stage drivers who remembered him well. Obituaries appeared in magazines devoted to the history of the American West.[3]

William was certainly up in years when he passed away, but still "the loss of the barn and the horses and stages could not have been blameless" for his death, one of his grandnephews surmised. All of the children who spent their summers at his ranch paid tribute to him, many of them possibly unaware of all his quiet acts of generosity to the family, which included paying their school tuition when times were bad for their parents. Joseph Jr. and Hancock Jr. served as executors of his estate, which, in a final contribution to peaceful family relations, was distributed to the entire family.[4]

In the same year as the Walnut Ranch fire, another Banning relative passed away in Los Angeles. Adelaida Mellus Banning, the daughter of pioneer merchant Francis Mellus, was said to have been born in the old adobe home of Manuel Requena, first alcalde of Los Angeles, near the Plaza in 1853. She had married Phineas Banning's nephew William L. Banning (the son of his eldest brother, John Alford Banning Jr.) and lived for most of the rest of her life in San Pedro. William and Hancock Banning counseled her on financial and family matters after she became a widow.[5]

In 1951 one of the two original Banning matriarchs died at her home in San Marino. Anne Ophelia Smith Banning was eighty years old, and had resigned from her leadership position in the Assistance League of Southern California and its national organization just three years before. Only in her last years had this crusader for many charitable causes and political issues finally slowed down due to age and declining health. Her presence would be keenly missed in philanthropic circles in the region, and the Assistance League of Southern California would pay homage to her work on many occasions.[6]

Anne's matriarchal competitor in the family, Katharine S. Banning, outlived her by three years. In 1954 Katharine passed away at Good Samaritan Hospital at the age of eighty-eight after a lengthy illness. Her obituary noted her volunteer work with the Red Cross and the Childrens Hospital of Los Angeles. With her death both of the wives of the sons of Phineas Banning were now gone, leaving only one more member of the original generation of siblings and spouses.[7]

That member, Mary Hollister Banning Norris, one of Phineas's two daughters by his second wife, was still installed at the plush Biltmore Hotel across the street from Pershing Square when she died in January 1956. She was not the latest-born of that generation, but had survived all of her siblings and their mates. Mary was buried in the family plot at

Rosedale Cemetery with her father, mother, and sisters. Like her older brother, she left some of her estate to her brothers' descendants, but designated the largest individual distributions for some of her old friends in New York.[8]

∿

As was the case for the generation of Phineas Banning's children, those in the next generation either died relatively soon after their parents, in this case in the 1960s, or lived remarkably long lives to witness yet another generation's rise. On the Joseph Brent Banning side of the family, Joseph Jr. retired as a shipping executive in 1954 and served on the county grand jury two years later. He died in 1969 at the age of seventy-nine, followed only one year later by his spouse, Alice Morse Banning. Her death was also noted in newspapers in Sacramento, where her grandfather had been a pioneer physician, editor, and important community figure.[9]

Katharine Banning Graves, or "Kash" as she was called, had been the last member of her generation to be born in the old Banning mansion in Wilmington. After a long illness, she died in 1965. Her husband, Francis Porter Graves, had retired from his stock brokerage firm in 1940 and died in 1963, two years before his spouse.[10]

William Phineas Banning, the youngest child of Joseph Brent and Katharine S. Banning, married three times. He was living on his Bradbury Ranch in Duarte when his third spouse, Janet Kirby, passed away in 1977; he died there in 1981.[11]

Of the members of the Hancock Banning branch, Hancock Jr. continued his family property management with the help of members of the next generation; he died in 1982 at the age of ninety. His wife, Florence Johnston Banning, was still active in philanthropy when she passed away in January 1989.[12]

John C. Macfarland, the widower of Hancock Jr.'s sister, Eleanor, who had died in 1940, had also served as the family's legal adviser. He married Elizabeth Bodine Stephenson in 1947. They were living in Pasadena when he died in 1966, and Elizabeth passed away there in 1989.[13]

The younger brother of Hancock Jr. and Eleanor, writer George Hugh Banning, had also remarried after his divorce in 1938. His second wife, Helen Shoff, died in early 1967. Later that year George married Ruth Lockett, a family friend who had been involved in Democratic Party politics and state relief efforts with Anne Banning. This marriage lasted until George's death at his home on the One Horse Ranch in La Jolla in 1989.[14]

The Next Generation

A new generation of Bannings started their professional, civic, and social careers soon after the close of World War II. Many stayed in the area to participate in the continuing development of Southern California, while others departed to make their mark in other communities and in other countries. While it might be too early to judge some of these contributions in the broader context of the region's history, it is already evident that a few have been instrumental in the area's transformation over the past few decades. The members of this Banning generation who stayed in Southern California were involved in a wide range of economic interests, civic concerns, and social and philanthropic endeavors that have sustained the region in a variety of ways.

Hancock "Bill" Banning III, the oldest son of Hancock Jr. and Florence, graduated from the University of California, Berkeley, and married Julia McCook in San Gabriel in 1949. Bill became a real estate developer and bank executive during the residential and commercial boom in Southern California in the 1950s and 1960s. He and Julia lived at first in South Pasadena, where their five children were born, then in Santa Monica, where he opened the Beverly Hills branch of Coldwell Banker. In 1962 they left for Newport Beach, where he took over management of the Banning family property. There he became a trustee of the Newport Beach Art Museum and a civic figure in the local community. His spouse, Julia, earned a degree in history from the University of California, Irvine, in 1973 and has been active in several civic and social organizations, including Planned Parenthood of Orange County and the Diggers Garden Club, a favorite of several Bannings.[15]

Hancock's younger brother, Robert Johnston Banning, returned from World War II to earn his degree in economics from the University of California, Berkeley. His career saw him rise to senior administrative posts in several departments of Los Angeles County government in an era of tremendous population expansion, which led to increasing demands and mandates for new government services, and the modernization of the county bureaucracy. In the 1970s and '80s he was a trustee and officer of the California Historical Society, at one time serving as its president. In 1954 he married Joan Spain Bridge, a native of Vermont, who was a partner in a flower-arranging business for a time. They raised two sons in Pasadena.[16]

The youngest of Hancock Jr.'s children, Elizabeth Banning, received her BS in zoology from the University of California, Los Angeles, in 1956. Two years before that, she married Charles Burton Ames Jr., then an electrical engineering student at the University of California, Berkeley. After graduating, Charles worked for Hughes Aircraft in Alaska and in Southern California, a center for aviation research and production in the postwar era. Elizabeth was active in the Junior League and Planned Parenthood, both organizations that her mother had belonged to, as well as the Friends of Banning Park. They raised four children in San Marino and later Santa Monica. Charles retired and became a citrus orchardist before he passed away in 2004.[17]

The adopted son of Eleanor Banning and John C. Macfarland, Donald Macfarland, was born in the United Kingdom and served in the U.S. Navy before marrying Diane Elizabeth Woodford in 1956. At that time he was studying electrical engineering at Pasadena City College. He managed their investments to great effect, while she was active in a number of civic organizations before her recent death. They raised three children at their home in San Marino.[18]

Douglas Banning, the only child of George Hugh Banning and Gladys Armstrong, returned from World War II to attend Pomona College and then earned an MBA from Stanford University in 1950. He was hired as the treasurer-controller of a pharmaceutical company, where he worked for over twenty years, and is now retired. He is the author of *Techniques for Marketing New Products* (1957), which he wrote at the urging of a publisher who had read some of his work on the subject.[19]

Moving now to the Joseph Brent Banning branch of the family, the eldest of Joseph Jr. and Alice Morse Banning's children is Nancy Morse Banning Call. Educated at the Marlborough School and Stanford University (economics, 1947), she became active in a number of civic, cultural, and philanthropic organizations such as the Junior League, the Los Angeles Philharmonic and Hollywood Bowl Associations, the Huntington Library, the California Arts Commission, and the California chapter of the Mount Vernon Ladies Association. She also emerged as the leader of the campaign to improve the old Banning homestead in Wilmington in the early 1970s by initiating restoration and preservation efforts, establishing a research and education program, and creating a fundraising organization for the improvements. In 1952 she married Dr. Richard W. Call, and they had three daughters. He is also a graduate of Stanford and a physician who became the medical director of the Union Oil Company. He has been a trustee and one-time president of both the Seaver Institute and the Natural History Museum of Los Angeles County Foundation, as well as the chair of the board of trustees of the Childrens Hospital of Los Angeles and a trustee of several investment firms.[20]

With this marriage Nancy became the daughter-in-law of Asa V. Call, then president of Pacific Mutual Life Insurance Company and a director of many other firms, as well as a leader in commercial organizations. He was deeply involved in most campaigns for the expansion of civic infrastructure and with many major philanthropic and cultural organizations in the region. Call was also one of the most influential power brokers in Los Angeles from the late 1930s to the 1970s, the head of informal political groups that chose and financially supported candidates for local, regional, and statewide offices. Coincidently, his father (Richard's grandfather), prominent attorney Joseph Call, was one of the progressives who fought to take harbor tidelands property away from the Banning family and the Southern Pacific Railroad just after the turn of the century.[21]

Selwyn Jackson Graves, the youngest child of Francis and Katharine Banning Graves, returned from the army to attend Claremont Men's College (1945–49), the American Institute for Foreign Trade (1950), and Pomona College (1950–51). He moved to Costa Rica, where he and a Mr. Heaven formed a company known as "Graves and Heaven," later joined by his cousin William Phineas Banning Jr., but the business failed. While there he met and married Fay Ann Sweetland, a nurse from Atlanta, Georgia, in 1954. The two then moved to San Diego, where he managed investments and she volunteered in community welfare organizations while they raised their four children. He passed away in 2008.[22]

The son of William Phineas Banning and Evangeline "Muddie" Grier, William Phineas Banning Jr. had been raised by his grandmother, the redoubtable Katherine S. Banning, after his parents' divorce in 1934. His early career paralleled his cousin Selwyn's: he served in the U.S. Navy, attended Pomona College, and graduated from the American Institute for Foreign Trade in 1953; he then joined Selwyn Graves in the ill-fated business venture in Costa Rica. After that he worked for Cutter Laboratories and Litton Industries as a Latin America sales and marketing manager selling pharmaceuticals, and for Airshields (a medical equipment company). In 1950 he married Suzanne Boushey, a Los Angeles native and graduate of the Marlborough School, and the two raised five children in Los Angeles, Newport Beach, and Duarte. They divorced in early 1985, and later that year he married Marian Lowry Winter, the director of the Banning Residence Museum at the time. A graduate of Immaculate Heart College in Los Angeles with a degree in history, she already had three children of her own. William passed away in 1994 at the age of sixty-four.[23]

❧

Descendants of William Lowber Banning (Phineas's brother) also made their lives in Southern California. William Lowber Banning III, who had moved to Los Angeles with his mother and sister in the early 1920s, had in the prewar years been a successful advertising executive with the public relations agency of Lord & Thomas, a pioneering firm in political campaigning, and on his own. William and his family eventually moved to Beverly Hills. He died on a yacht at Newport Harbor in 1950 and his spouse, Florinda Steffer, remarried the following year. Their son, William Lowber Banning IV, married Ursula Frei in 1947, and the couple lived in Los Angeles while he took over his father's advertising business, which became an even more important industry in the Southland in the later twentieth century. They eventually moved to Montecito, where he passed away in 2008.[24]

All of these descendants of Phineas Banning contributed to the development of Southern California in various ways and to different degrees. (For those in this generation who did not remain in Southern California and made their mark elsewhere, see appendix B.)

Beeco, Ltd.

In the postwar era, the Bannings were held together both by family ties and through their joint ownership of property, specifically through a company called Beeco, Ltd. This entity became the family's property holding company, managing petroleum rights and royalties and developing real estate holdings on the family's behalf for three decades.

In 1945, the Bannings dissolved their land management entity, the Townsend Land Company, because their real estate was by then either managed through the two family trusts or leased to oil companies opposed to development close to their oil-pumping operations. With the tremendous residential and commercial growth in Southern California after the war, however, it became evident that the family could profit handsomely by developing and selling much of its vacant property, along with additional land purchased from others, as shopping centers, housing tracts, and the like.

The principal tract that launched the Beeco venture was the Banning Ranch near Newport Beach, originally 4,077.51 acres, purchased by Mary E. H. Banning in 1874 with the proceeds of her inheritance and used by Phineas Banning for raising sheep. The ranch had been split in the division of property after Phineas's death, when his sons received part of it and their stepmother the rest. Her portion was inherited by her daughter Mary Hollister Banning Norris, who sold it before the property produced oil on a large scale. The remaining five hundred acres owned by the three sons became immensely profitable in the 1940s, when the leaseholders of the ranch began extracting oil in great quantities.[25]

This remaining portion of the Banning Ranch was owned by members of both branches of the family, and it was William Phineas Banning, the stockbroker and youngest son of Joseph Brent Banning, who thoughtfully forged a consensus on how it should operate. William created the family's investment company as Beeco, Ltd. in 1958, managing it for the first few years with the help of Douglas Banning as secretary and several other relatives as the other directors. During this period, relations with the oil companies drilling on the leased property were the directors' chief concern. Because these lessors opposed any construction close to their drilling sites, even to the point of suing the Bannings to prevent it, there was very little development in the early years of the company.[26]

That would change in the next decade, after Hancock "Bill" Banning III took over as the leading officer of Beeco in 1962. Now that Southern California's population and business opportunities were exploding, Beeco began a program of development. The first projects consisted of a residential community on the eastern side of the Banning Ranch, plans for a marina where the Santa Ana River meets the Pacific Ocean, and a shopping center in Wilmington, among others. In 1966 John Haskell, then working for Coldwell Banker, was hired by Beeco, and he would be a key figure in the company's work and the family's oil interests for the next three decades.[27]

Managing the Banning Ranch property was not a simple task by the early 1980s. In 1981 the City of Newport Beach attempted to annex five acres of the ranch in order to control some of the slanted wells that were pumping oil from city-owned tidelands. The issue was actually a dispute between the city and the oil company that it contracted with, but Beeco had to join its own leaseholder oil companies in blocking the annexation in order to protect its overall holdings.[28]

In the same year, a Beeco project became entangled in a battle between city officials and residents over the scale of development being approved in Newport Beach. During the campaign of residents to stop a Newport Center project already approved by the city council, Beeco proposed a development of residential, commercial, and light-industrial units on seventy-four vacant acres of its property that had been annexed to the city in the early 1960s. The Beeco project was approved by the city planning commission, but several homeowners in the vicinity protested against the plan, demanding that the office units be replaced by residential housing to reduce pollution and traffic congestion. Beeco offered to pay for highway construction to mitigate traffic concerns and dropped some of its plans for commercial units when it discovered that the buildings would be on an earthquake fault. (The revised plan called for this site to become a residential area.) As both the Beeco project and the more controversial Newport Center project were being considered at the same council meetings, the two issues were considered by many residents to constitute a pattern of city hall caving in to wealthy developers.[29]

In February 1982, the city council rescinded its approval of the Newport Center project and tentatively approved a compromise version of the Beeco plan that pleased no one. The project's opponents launched a referendum campaign to overturn the decision. The *Times*'s editors printed many letters on the issue, alternately condemning the city council and questioning statements by Hancock Banning III, or praising the "Banning plan." With the referendum question slated for the November election, the campaign became a battle over how Newport Beach should grow and how much. Beeco's plan was backed by the local chamber of commerce and residents supporting increased development, and opposed by homeowners' associations, such as the alliance that defeated Newport Center, and slow-growth advocates. Beeco officials were afraid that if the referendum passed, the property would be less desirable to potential buyers, and contributed generously to defeat it. This support, as well as the confusing ballot wording (one had to vote "yes" to kill the Beeco project and "no" to approve it), probably played a part in the defeat of Proposition N that year.[30]

With the Beeco victory, Hancock Banning III made plans to submit his proposal to the California Coastal Commission for its consideration. But the project never got off the ground. Fatigued by the long delay caused by the referendum, and with an eye to the termination of the oil leases on the property in only a few years, the Banning family instead agreed in 1983 to sell the Banning Ranch property to the two oil companies that then held the leases, retaining only the very deep mineral rights. John Haskell completed the final details of the sale in 1984 and continued to manage some of the Banning family oil properties in Wilmington for another five years.[31]

The Banning Ranch continues to produce oil to this day. The remaining 402 acres of unincorporated property, still coveted by Newport

Beach as well as neighboring Costa Mesa, continues to attract developer interest in both good and depressed markets. Even in 2008, plans to develop the property were inspiring opposition by environmentalists and others. With its gushing oil and ideally located real estate, the ranch holdings combined two of the great economic engines of the region, generating wealth for the family in every period of Southern California history since Phineas Banning arrived in the region.³²

Preserving the Banning Legacy

In the long European and American tradition of preserving the memory of ancestors, often creating new memories in the process, the Banning family worked diligently since the early 1900s to burnish their forebears' legacy, remembering their patriarch as the "Transportation King" of Southern California and a major figure in its social, economic, and political history, and his three sons as the developers of Santa Catalina Island for almost three decades. Joseph Brent Banning began this work in 1905, when he collected information about Phineas for one of the ubiquitous local history volume sets that included histories of the region and biographies of prominent citizens. Joseph also asked three of his father's good friends for their reminiscences, and the contributions of A. A. Polhamus, Herman Hellman, and Ben C. Truman have been invaluable resources for understanding Phineas's personality and some of his activities. At the same time, Hancock and Anne Banning commissioned genealogies of both of their families when Anne applied for membership in the Colonial Dames, and that report shed light on many ancestors of the Bannings and the Smiths in America and Europe.³³

The letters and papers Joseph Brent collected were kept by his spouse, Katharine S. Banning, who also gathered information and stories about the Phineas Banning and William Lowber Banning sides of the family, which she kept in scrapbooks. Phineas's eldest son, William S. Banning, preserved many of the family papers and business records at his Walnut Ranch, where some were lost in the 1944 fire. Hancock Banning Jr. also saved a large collection of his father's personal and business papers along with family photographs, which he labeled with historical information. All of these materials, along with another large photograph collection from the Joseph Brent Banning descendants, were eventually donated to the Huntington Library, where they are preserved and made available to scholars. George Hugh Banning donated his collection of family papers and research for his works on stage coaching to the library of the Banning Residence Museum in Wilmington.

In addition, Hancock Banning Jr. completed an interview for the Center for Oral History Research at UCLA, which recorded his particular reminiscences of the Banning family in the region during his lifetime. A number of family members also contributed to broader state and local history preservation efforts over the years. Evangeline Grier "Muddie" Banning was a member and sponsor of a group in 1931 that aided the California Landmarks and Historical Records Bureau, which aimed to spark interest in state history by establishing an historical landmark designation program for important sites in the Golden State. Both Hancock Jr. and his wife Florence were members of the California Historical Society and contributed to special projects at El Molino Viejo, its Southern California headquarters. Robert J. Banning, their youngest son, was a long-time trustee of that organization, serving as its president and in other offices over the years. He has become the genealogist of the family and spearheaded the creation of the Banning Family History Project through the Huntington-USC Institute on California and the West—the major result of which is this book. And several others, including Anne Banning, Nancy Morse Banning Call, Elizabeth Banning Ames, and Marian Lowry (Winter) Banning, worked diligently to create the major venue for commemorating the family's legacy in Southern California, the Banning Residence Museum.[34]

The transformation of the old Banning homestead in Wilmington into an educational site was part of a broader historic preservation movement in the twentieth century in California. The rich and diverse built heritage of the Golden State, created through the interplay of its landscape and environment with the peoples who have settled here, has become home to various cultural resources that teach us about different eras in the development of the state and its regions. The earliest Southern California conservation drives, before 1925 or so, were the campaigns to save the California missions and the adobe and wooden structures of the 1800s by organizations such as Charles F. Lummis's Landmarks Club and the Native Sons and Daughters of the Golden West. The state became involved in preservation by the 1930s and a state commission, aided by Evangeline Grier Banning and others, was formed to identify significant sites threatened with destruction and to draw attention to their plight. After World War II, the impending centennial celebration of the discovery of gold sparked a "preservation consciousness," building support for more state

The Banning residence as a city facility in 1930. Courtesy of the Huntington Library.

and local programs in history and archaeology. By the late 1960s the federal government had increased funding for state projects, and California's state agency for historic preservation expanded its role, helping identify and preserve historic sites with matching grants, commissioning experts to advise on historical accuracy, assisting local interpretive and educational programs, and encouraging community support for preservation. By the 1970s, the statewide programs and funding were developed and available, awaiting energetic local citizens who could use them to preserve the important reminders of our past.[35]

The structure now known as the Banning Residence Museum was built in 1864 by Phineas and Rebecca Banning. The three-story Greek Revival mansion contained thirty rooms plus a cupola, and was reminiscent in style of many of the dwellings of Phineas's childhood home in Delaware. The house was significantly enlarged over the years; Joseph Brent Banning installed its first bathroom in 1893, and Hancock added the kitchen and other rooms in the rear, a ballroom, and the adjacent sunken garden about 1911, among many other changes.[36]

Anne Banning sold the Phineas Banning mansion to the city, ostensibly to raise enough cash to pay the taxes from the estate of her husband,

Hancock. Wilmington residents campaigned aggressively to force the city to purchase it in 1927, and the twenty-acre property quickly became a popular park and community center. In 1930 the city parks board decided to use the 1864 house as a museum and to replace the original furniture, removed by the family. The *Times* supported this endeavor with a feature story on Banning Park and its "Banning Hall" late that year, a glowing description of the property that stretched a few facts. The parks department did not get far with this initiative, however, until the California Landmarks and Historical Records Bureau worked out an agreement with the city to furnish the homestead with "treasured antiques and heirlooms" provided by pioneer families in the area. Anne Banning was enlisted to join the project as a member of the exhibit committee, and William S. Banning endorsed it, appearing on his stagecoach in front of the house in photographs that were reprinted in newspaper announcements.[37]

In early 1936 a pact was signed between the parks commissioners and the Banning House Memorial Association in which the city promised to permanently maintain the house as a museum. The association, whose members included Anne Banning, Dr. Owen C. Coy of the University of Southern California, and several others, would represent the families who were supplying the furnishings in their dealings with the city and sponsor much of the exhibition work. The association put out a call for donations of furniture and furnishings, specifying no particular provenance, in order to fill the house. The city began refurbishing the structure, adding a sprinkler system and putting up Civil War–style wallpaper donated by several motion picture studios. With this work still in progress, Anne assembled the executive board of the Association at her Los Angeles home in May 1936 to plan the formal dedication. The June 6 ceremony was attended by a number of state and city officials, celebrities, prominent society figures, history organization members, and many others. The reception committee included both Anne Banning and Katharine S. Banning, their children and spouses, and "Captain" William Banning and Mary Hollister Banning Norris. The mansion was also marked as State Historical Landmark Number 147.[38]

The momentum generated by the 1936 celebration was followed, unfortunately, by years of neglect. The Banning mansion did not receive much financial support from the city, and most of the museum work was done by volunteers. Acquisitions, such as furniture formerly belonging to Joseph P. Widney, Phineas Banning's associate in promoting the harbor, were sponsored by members of history organizations. During World

War II, almost half of the park was taken over by the U.S. Army and temporarily christened "Camp Banning," with the mansion serving as headquarters. After the war the park accommodated temporary housing for veterans and their families in the Keppler Grove complex until 1949. In 1952 the mansion was reopened for tours, which were conducted by the Native Daughters of the Golden West and others on Sunday afternoons between April and October over the next two decades. An annual Wisteria Festival in the spring drew attention to the large wisteria planted in 1910 behind the house and attracted thousands of visitors "both to admire the great vine and to be conducted through the mansion by a corps of pretty girls dressed in the picturesque costumes of pioneer days." The mansion received additional recognition when it was listed as the city's Historic-Cultural Monument Number 25 in 1963 and placed on the National Register of Historic Places on May 6, 1971.[39]

In the early 1970s, city Recreation and Parks Department General Manager William Frederickson met Nancy Morse Banning Call, who was then chair of the Junior Arts Center at Barnsdall Park, and asked for her help in improving the situation at Banning Park. She agreed and contacted several experts and friends to participate in various elements of this campaign. Robert B. Haas of UCLA advised on interior design, and William E. Jones at the Los Angeles County Museum of Art helped choose and place appropriate furniture. Christine Shirley, Nancy's friend from her college days at Stanford, was asked to establish a research program as the foundation for interpretation and tours. Shirley Low of Colonial Williamsburg was brought in to set up the interpretive program in cooperation with officials from the Los Angeles city school system. The Junior League of Los Angeles was enlisted to start a volunteer program and supply volunteers, and both Nancy and her sister Katharine "Kay" Banning Sisk loaned original pieces of Banning furniture for exhibit. Nancy also worked with Los Angeles City Council member John Gibson, a former business associate of Hancock Banning Jr., to secure more funding from the city.[40]

Of equal importance was the creation of the Friends of Banning Park, organized by Nancy Morse Banning Call in 1974. This organization became the support group for the site, raising money to hire experts to plan and implement restoration and enhancement of the building and grounds. These projects included restorations of various parts of the house in the late 1970s and of the barn in the late 1980s, and furnishing all of the structures with appropriate historical objects, many of them from the Banning family itself. In 1984 the 1850s cornstalk fence that

William S. Banning had purchased in New Orleans to surround part of his "Barn" residence in Los Angeles was retrieved from storage and installed around the patio. A further conservation project encompassing reroofing, painting, and replacement of non-historic features was begun in the early 1990s as part of a long-range plan for further preservation efforts, and additional work has been done since.[41]

Nancy Banning Call has certainly been the driving force in the campaign of over three decades to transform the Banning Residence Museum into the historic and interpretive center it is today. Many other Bannings have also been critical to its success. Anne Banning led the initial effort to preserve the building as a historic site. William Phineas Banning Sr. donated $25,000 in stocks to assist the 1970s effort to rejuvenate the site. Elizabeth Banning Ames, an early member and treasurer of the Friends of Banning Park, devoted many hours to the enhancement of the site. Marian Lowry (Winter) Banning served as director of the Banning Residence Museum in the 1980s and again in 1995–96. Julia Banning and others were volunteers there. Nancy Banning Call, her sister Katharine "Kay" Banning Sisk, George Hugh Banning, Hancock Banning Jr., and William Phineas Banning Jr. all donated collections to the facility. All of the other members of the family helped with financial contributions to make the improvements possible.

In varying degrees, three generations of Bannings and their descendants have made the Banning Residence Museum their family project. It has become the primary institution for preserving the legacy of Phineas Banning and his descendants in the broader context of the development of Southern California over the last century and a half.

Yesterday and Today

Following the last generation of Bannings discussed in this book, many younger descendants of Phineas have spread throughout Southern California, the rest of the nation, and other parts of the world. Like their primary family patriarch, some have played important roles in the development of their community and the country, many in Phineas's adopted home in Southern California.

None, however, could boast of the same degree of accomplishment as Phineas, passionate participant and, frequently, leader in the quest to re-create Southern California—a region that was sparsely settled upon his arrival and, by the time he died thirty-four years later, was well on its way to becoming a thriving metropolis. The "Transportation King," he established a network of roads from the harbor area and Los Angeles to destinations throughout the American Southwest and played a critical role in establishing two railroads to modernize transport and spur economic growth; he created a seemingly endless stream of businesses that served residents and newcomers, and enriched him and his family; he was a fiercely vocal patriot during the Civil War who defended the Union in the context of strong regional sympathy for the Confederacy; he served as a state senator for four years in the best interests of California and his region, while also furthering his entrepreneurial goals; he was a generous philanthropist, a leader in local society, and a community booster who knew no limits in promoting his adopted home; and he was a family man, the patriarch who built a wide-ranging business empire in order to improve his family's fortunes.

Phineas Banning's nickname—"Father of the Los Angeles Harbor"—accurately describes his major role in developing this world-class port. When he first saw it, San Pedro Bay was a shallow harbor rimmed with mudflats. It was frequently buffeted by storms. Of the several entrepreneurs who had interests there, he was indeed the driving force in improving the harbor: he had a vision of its potential and the drive to make it a reality, lobbying for federal funding to begin its eventual transformation into a deepwater port of international importance. Today the Port of Los Angeles has grown to about 7,500 acres, with 270 berths and 76 container cranes along 43 miles of waterfront. As of 2008 the port provided about 1.1 million jobs in California and brought in $89.2 billion of California's trade income. It is the busiest container port in the United States; combined with the neighboring Port of Long Beach, it comprises the fifth-busiest container port in the world. Phineas is honored there with a bronze statue at Banning's Landing Community Center.[1]

Other tangible reminders of Phineas Banning's contributions to Southern California include the Banning Residence Museum and Banning Park in Wilmington; Banning Street in downtown Los Angeles and Banning Boulevard and Banning Avenue in Wilmington; Phineas Banning High School in Wilmington; the city of Banning in western Riverside County, California; the government barracks building on Santa Catalina Island and, to some degree, the remaining Drum Barracks building in Wilmington; and the Phineas Banning Alumni House on the campus of the University of California, Irvine, funded by the Banning family in the 1980s.

The children of Phineas Banning made their own mark in Southern California with their continuation of their father's harbor business and support for harbor improvements, their development of Santa Catalina Island as the popular resort it remains to this day, and their participation, along with their spouses, in the political, civic, philanthropic, and social life of the region. The Banning sons are still remembered for their contributions to and stewardship of the "Magic Isle." Joseph Brent Banning's memorial stands at Avalon, and his home at what is now known as Two Harbors at the isthmus of Santa Catalina survives as the Banning House Lodge. William Banning's Walnut Ranch, however, no longer exists as a historic site.

The spouses of these Banning sons have also left their mark in the development of Southern California, especially in philanthropy. Anne Ophelia Smith Banning is revered as a leader in social welfare efforts in the region, most notably as the founder of the Assistance League of Southern California. Today this multimillion-dollar operation continues to salute her role in its founding and her contributions to its growth over four decades. One of its units, the Anne Banning Auxiliary, is especially active in educational and social-welfare programs in greater Los Angeles such as Operation School Bell. The national organization that she cofounded now includes 123 chapters. And Katharine Stewart Banning is remembered as a leading force in the founding and success of Childrens Hospital in Los Angeles.

The grandchildren of Phineas Banning managed the family property, while making their mark in the region as authors, business leaders, philanthropists, social welfare advocates, and political activists. Their children have made similar contributions in these areas, and have also worked to preserve the family legacy. They have been especially successful in the rehabilitation of the Banning Residence Museum, which has allowed historians and visitors to interpret the larger context of the development of Southern California through the prism of one of the major characters who shaped its direction and its contours.

One of Phineas Banning's ancestors and one of his siblings have also been remembered with physical tributes. The Dover home of his grandfather, Revolutionary Era patriot John Banning, is a well-preserved historical landmark. And Banning State Park in eastern Minnesota is a reminder of the contributions made to that state by one of Phineas's brothers, William Lowber Banning, whose daughter Katharine married one of the three Banning brothers and made her own contributions to Southern California social life and philanthropy.

The Banning family is still a First Family in Southern California in more than just a chronological sense, although its heyday was a long time ago. Phineas Banning and his descendants have been entrepreneurial, political, and social leaders in the region since the early 1850s. Fortunate recipients of the patriarch's fortune, the family has managed to increase the estate through good investments and fortuitous petroleum discoveries. They still hold important economic and social positions in their communities and are active in philanthropy and regional history preservation. It appears certain that the Banning family's role in the economic and civic life of Southern California will continue well into this new century.

THE BANNINGS FROM ENGLAND TO AMERICA

The Banning family in Southern California can trace its lineage back to the English county of Wiltshire in the sixteenth century. Wiltshire County, southwest of London, is home to the village and parish of Burbage. Burbage has been in existence as an agricultural community since at least 1000 AD. A number of Bannings had settled there by the early 1500s, including Robert Banning, who was living there in 1539 and is the earliest known direct ancestor of Phineas Banning of Southern California. The family's genealogists believe that Robert was probably born just before 1500 and was still alive in 1565. He was the father of John Banning, a resident of Burbage in 1565, who was the father of another John, who was living there in 1613. The third John in this line received an MA in 1634 from Magdalen College and appeared on the Subsidiary Roll in 1642 as a contributor to the less fortunate. His son Stephen lived out his life in Burbage, dying there in 1688. Stephen's son, also named Stephen, was resident there as a very old man in 1714. He had at least two sons: John—who married an heiress and raised a family in Milton, Wiltshire—and Edward.[1]

The younger son, Edward Banning, was the first Banning in this line to immigrate to the British colonies in North America. Edward is believed to have left England in the mid-1600s, during the tumultuous years of the English Civil War. This conflict led to the rise of Cromwell and the execution of Charles I in 1649. The monarchy was restored in 1660 with Charles II, who favored France and Roman Catholicism; at the "Glorious Revolution" in 1688, his younger brother, James II, who had succeeded him, was removed from the throne. This prolonged struggle for political power and English souls affected places as far away from London as the village and parish of Burbage, where nonconformist religious leaders were active from the late 1640s through the 1660s. Many Anglicans, Puritans, and Roman Catholics—all subject to persecution at various phases of the conflict—fled England during the seventeenth century to begin new lives in the colonies.[2]

Edward Banning settled on the Tobacco Coast in Maryland, one of the early proprietary British colonies in North America. Maryland was founded in 1632 as a haven for Roman Catholics, although it also attracted Puritans facing repression in England in the 1640s and other religious dissidents by the 1650s. Tobacco was the primary crop, harvested by indentured servants at first and by African slaves after 1639. By 1678 Edward was renting about fifty acres of land off the eastern shore of the Chesapeake Bay in Talbot County when this land was surveyed for its owner, Anthony Mayle. The farm was on the north side of the Choptank River, where it split into the Tred Avon River, and on the western side of Plaindealing Creek (see map on page 11). The plot was directly south of the land where Edward's more affluent kinsman, Robert Banning, would have his plantation, Royal Oak. Edward's parcel was known as "Goose Neck," and he finally purchased it in 1691 after Mayle died. He raised tobacco and was taxed in kind; the province assessed three hundred pounds of that crop from him in 1678 to help pay for the "public charges of this province." His planting must have proved successful, as he was able to cover that assessment and, in that same year, also pay to avoid military service in an expedition to pacify the Nanticoke Indians.[3]

Edward was followed to America by a number of other Bannings, including a possible cousin, John, who settled in Lyme, Connecticut. These immigrants established families and new generations of Bannings throughout the colonies by the mid-1700s. Quite a number of them lived in Maryland, including Jeremiah, Anthony, Robert, and other prominent Bannings. Meanwhile, Edward Banning continued to farm at Goose Neck, raising six children by his first wife (whose name is unknown) and two children by his second wife, Susannah, whom he married about 1698. He died in 1710, leaving some of his estate to Susannah as long as she remained unmarried, and the rest to his older sons. He bequeathed 1,500 pounds of tobacco to his younger son, Andrew, further evidence that his yields were substantial.[4]

Edward's second son by his first spouse was John, born sometime in the 1680s. John married Mary Parnell and lived on a farm called "Golden Lyon," given to them by Mary's father in 1715, in neighboring Queen Anne County, Maryland. Both John and Mary died by 1719, when his brother Thomas assumed custody of their three young sons, William, John, and Richard. Five years later, the three chose to live with another uncle, Andrew, instead.[5]

The youngest son of John, Richard, eventually married Esther Wilson, also from Queen Anne County, in 1737. Soon after their marriage the two moved from Maryland to the town of Dover in Kent County, Delaware. Delaware was then a semi-autonomous union of three counties that had previously comprised the southern part of the colony of Pennsylvania. There they raised their sons Richard Jr., John, and Phineas (named after Esther's brother) together for a very short time. Richard Sr. was dead by 1742, when his will was opened to probate. His widow married Matthew Jarrett within two years and remained in the Dover area, where her three sons by Richard grew up and started their own families. One of them, John Banning (ca. 1739–1791) would become a Revolutionary War hero in Dover and the grandfather of the patriarch of the Banning clan in Southern California.[6]

Phineas Banning's Great-grandchildren Who Left Southern California

When they came of age, some members of the generation of Phineas Banning's great-grandchildren departed Southern California, scattering to many destinations and adjusting to an assortment of circumstances in their new hometowns and homelands.

The oldest daughter of Eleanor Banning and John Macfarland, Anne Banning Macfarland, married just before her mother died in 1940. Her spouse, Lt. Samuel Brown Jr., was a Chicago native and a 1934 graduate of the U.S. Naval Academy who served in World War II and then in the Bikini Islands. Serving at the Pentagon in Washington, D.C., he was promoted to the rank of rear admiral. The two had four daughters and eventually moved to Florida. Both died there, Samuel in 1991, and Anne in 2008.[1]

Marion Fitzhugh Macfarland, the youngest child of Eleanor and John, attended Stanford University and married Randall Jaeger Worthington in 1953. They moved to Hawaii, where he lived and worked as an insurance agent and investor, and where their three children were born. They divorced in 1972, and he passed away in 1985. She moved to Northern California and eventually married John Eric Mack, a childhood friend originally from Pasadena.[2]

Marianne Alyce Banning, daughter of George Hugh Banning and his second wife, Helen C. Shoff, was educated at Mt. Holyoke College and Stanford University, where she received a master's in teaching. She married John Fuller Adey, a native of the United Kingdom, in 1965. After he received his MBA from Harvard in 1972, they moved to England, where they raised four children. Marianne taught there, and she still reviews children's books for various publications. John managed the U.K. National Blood Authority and held several other administrative positions.[3]

Katharine (Kay) Alice Banning, the youngest daughter of Joseph Jr. and Alice, was a graduate of Marlborough School and Stanford, where she received a degree in Spanish in 1953. The following year she married Daniel Arthur Sisk, who received his BA and law degree from Stanford. The two then moved to Sisk's native New Mexico and raised three children. Katharine became active in church and community organizations, while Daniel joined a law firm and became a partner. In 1970 he was appointed to fill a vacancy in the New Mexico State Supreme Court but lost the ensuing election.[4]

Francis Porter Graves Jr., oldest son of Francis and Katharine Banning Graves, returned from World War II to attend Pomona College, graduating with a degree in English literature in 1949, and then enrolled in the American Institute for Foreign Trade (1959). He married Donna Mary Wendel, a New Yorker, in 1957 and they moved to Central America for several years. The couple eventually settled in St. Paul, Minnesota, where they raised four children, and Francis was involved in several businesses. They later moved to Bayview, Wisconsin.[5]

Jane Banning Graves, the daughter of Francis and Katharine, graduated from Pomona College in 1948 and then earned a degree in occupational therapy from the University of Southern California. She was working at the Letterman Hospital in San Francisco when she met Henry Charles Otten, who was recuperating from the loss of a leg in the Korean conflict, and they married in 1954. They moved to New York, where Charles taught at the U.S. Military Academy at West Point, and raised three daughters. He retired as a colonel and they relocated to his native Montana, where he died in 1984; she passed away in 1999.[6]

Evangeline Victoria Banning, the daughter of William Phineas Banning and Evangeline "Muddie" Grier, attended Pomona College, where she met and married Richard S. Harding of San Antonio, Texas, in 1948. They soon moved to Mill Valley, where he worked as a geological engineer and she studied at a theological institute. The Hardings raised four children in Northern California but were later divorced; she died in 1974.[7]

A more distant and very noteworthy relative of this generation of Bannings was Robert Channing Seamans Jr., who married Eugenia Ayer Merrill, a great-granddaughter of William Lowber Banning (brother of Phineas), in 1942. Seamans became a professor of aeronautics and instrumentation at the Massachusetts Institute of Technology, an engineer at RCA, and an administrator at the National Aeronautics and Space Administration before his appointment as secretary of the Air Force by President Richard Nixon in 1969. His career included a number of other prestigious appointments to educational and governmental organizations and awards for service. He passed away in June 2008.[8]

PHINEAS BANNING GENEALOGY

Information about Phineas Banning's ancestors and siblings is partial; his great-grandchildren's spouses and children are not listed.

Phineas Banning's Ancestors and Siblings

John Banning ca. 1739–1791
  m. Elizabeth Alford ca. 1760?–1812
    Sarah 1787–1837
      m. Henry Moore Ridgely 1779–1847
      Ann Ridgely 1815–1898
        m. Charles I. du Pont 1797–1869
    John Alford 1790–1854
      m. Elizabeth Lowber 1794–1861
      John Alford Jr. ca. 1813–1885
          William Lowber ca. 1842–1890
            m. Adelaida Mellus 1853–1944
      William Lowber ca. 1814–1893
          m. Mary Alicia Sweeny 1826–1910
          Ellen Barrows 1853–1918
          May Alice 1858–1924
          Katharine Stewart 1866–1954
      Elizabeth Alice ca. 1819–?
      Mary Lowber 1820–1877
      Sallie ca. 1821–1891
      Richard 1822–ca. 1898
      Henry ca. 1825–1860
      Alice Ponder ca. 1826–?
      Phineas 1830–1885
      Francenia Alice 1833–1904
      Cole Lowber 1834–1913

Phineas Banning's Family

Phineas Banning 1830–1885
- m1. Rebecca Sanford ca. 1835–1868
    - Francenia Allibone 1855–1857
    - John Griffin 1856–1860
    - Infant son? 1857
    - William Sanford 1858–1946
    - Joseph Brent 1861–1920
        - m. Katharine Stewart Banning 1866–1954
    - Infant son? 1863
    - Hancock 1865–1925
        - m. Anne Ophelia Smith 1871–1951
    - Elizabeth 1866–1867
    - Vincent Edgar Griffin 1868
- m2. Mary Elizabeth Hollister 1846–1919
    - Mary Hollister 1871–1956
        - m. Wilt Wakeman Norris 1869–1905
    - Ellen Mossman 1874–1875
    - Lucy Tichenor 1876–1929
        - m1. John Bradbury 1872–1913
        - m2. Mace Greenleaf 1873–1912
        - m3. Robert E. Ross 1875–1960
        - m4. Setsuzo Ota ca. 1897–1963

Joseph Brent Banning Branch

Joseph Brent Banning 1861–1920
- m. Katharine Stewart Banning 1866–1954
    - Joseph Brent Banning Jr. 1889–1969
        - m. Alice Mira Morse 1895–1970
            - Nancy Morse Banning 1925–
            - Katharine Alice Banning 1931–
    - Katharine Mary Banning 1890–1965
        - m. Francis Porter Graves 1895–1963
            - Francis Porter Graves Jr. 1923–
            - Jane Banning Graves 1924–1999
            - Selwyn Jackson Graves 1928–2008
    - William Phineas Banning 1899–1981
        - m1. Evangeline Victoria Grier 1899–1988
            - Evangeline Victoria Banning 1922–1974
            - William Phineas Banning Jr. 1929–1994
        - m2. Helen Large ?–?
            - Cynthia Banning ?–?
        - m3. Janet Kirby de la Chesnaye Chappell 1907–1977

Hancock Banning Branch

Hancock Banning 1865–1925
m. Anne Ophelia Smith 1871–1951
Hancock Banning Jr. 1892–1982
m. Florence Lewers Johnston 1895–1989
Hancock Banning III 1921–
Robert Johnston Banning 1924–
Elizabeth Banning 1932–
Eleanor Anne Banning 1893–1940
m. John Cobb Macfarland 1885–1966
Anne Banning Macfarland 1918–2008
Donald Macfarland 1931–
Marion Fitzhugh Macfarland 1932–
George Hugh Banning 1895–1989
m1. Gladys Armstrong 1899–1980
Douglas Banning 1923–
m2. Helen Christianne Shoff 1908–1967
Marianne Alyce Banning 1941–
m3. Ruth Lockett 1910–

APPENDIX D

BANNING FAMILY CONNECTIONS

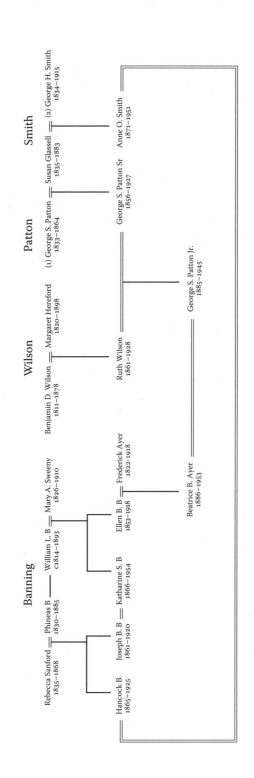

Banning

Wilson

Patton

Smith

Rebecca Sanford = Phineas B
1835–1868   1830–1885

William L. B —— Mary A. Sweeny
c1814–1893   1826–1910

Benjamin D. Wilson = Margaret Hereford
1811–1878   1820–1898

(1) George S. Patton = Susan Glassell = (2) George H. Smith
1833–1864   1835–1883   1834–1915

Hancock B
1865–1925

Joseph B. B = Katharine S. B
1861–1920   1866–1954

Ellen B. B = Frederick Ayer
1853–1918   1822–1918

Ruth Wilson = George S. Patton Sr = Anne O. Smith
1861–1928   1856–1927   1871–1951

Beatrice B. Ayer = George S. Patton Jr.
1886–1953   1885–1945

Notes

List of Abbreviations

ALSCA	Assistance League of Southern California Archives, Los Angeles, Calif.
BANC	Bancroft Library, University of California, Berkeley, Calif.
BRM	Banning Residence Museum Library, Wilmington, Calif.
CIM	Catalina Island Museum, Avalon, Calif.
CPSU	Special Collections, California Polytechnic State University, San Luis Obispo, Calif.
CSA	California State Archives, Sacramento, Calif.
CSL	California State Library, Sacramento, Calif.
DHS	Delaware Historical Society, Wilmington, Del.
DPA	Delaware Public Archives, Dover, Del.
EBA	Elizabeth Banning Ames Collection
HEH	Henry E. Huntington Library, San Marino, Calif.
LACRC	Los Angeles City Records Center, Los Angeles, Calif.
LAPL	Los Angeles (Central) Public Library, Los Angeles, Calif.
LCW	Library of Congress, Washington, D.C.
MABA	Marianne Alyce Banning Adey Collection
MHC	Minnesota History Center, St. Paul, Minn.
MLB	Marian Lowry Banning Collection
RJB	Robert J. Banning Collection
SCICA	Santa Catalina Island Company Archives, Avalon, Calif.
SCWHR	Seaver Center for Western History Research, Natural History Museum of Los Angeles County, Los Angeles, Calif.
SU	Special Collections, Green Library, Stanford University, Stanford, Calif.
UCLA	Department of Special Collections, Young Research Library, University of California, Los Angeles
USNALN	U.S. National Archives, Laguna Niguel, Calif.
USNAW	U.S. National Archives, Washington, D.C.

INTRODUCTION

1   Examples of histories of nationally significant families include: Richard
Brookhiser, *America's First Dynasty: The Adamses, 1735–1918* (New York:
Free Press, 2002); Doris Kearns Goodwin, *The Fitzgeralds and the Kennedys*
(New York: Simon and Schuster, 1987); Paul C. Nagel, *The Lees of Virginia:
Seven Generations of an American Family* (New York: Oxford University
Press, 1990); William R. Polk, *Polk's Folly: An American Family History* (New
York: Doubleday, 2000); Karl Schriftgiesser, *The Amazing Roosevelt Family,
1613–1942* (New York: Wilfred Funk, 1942); John D. Gates, *The du Pont
Family* (Garden City, N.Y.: Doubleday, 1979); Alden Hatch, *The Lodges of
Massachusetts* (New York: Hawthorn Books, 1973); Clare Brandt, *An Ameri-
can Aristocracy: The Livingstons* (Garden City, N.Y.: Doubleday, 1986); and
R. W. B. Lewis, *The Jameses: A Family Narrative* (New York: Farrar, Straus,
and Giroux, 1991).

2   The wide variety of regional family histories include: Leo Newmark, *Califor-
nia Family Newmark: An Intimate History* (Santa Monica, Calif.: Stern, 1970);
Roy E. Whitehead, *Lugo: A Chronicle of Early California* (Redlands, Calif.:
San Bernardino County Museum Association, 1978); Francis J. Weber, *Southern California's First Family: The Dohenys of Los Angeles* (Fullerton, Calif.:
Lorson's Books and Prints, 1993); and, to some extent, Robert Gottlieb and
Irene Wolt, *Thinking Big: The Story of the Los Angeles Times, Its Publishers,
and Their Influence on Southern California* (New York: G. P. Putnam's Sons,
1977); Judson A. Grenier with Robert C. Gillingham, *California Legacy:
The James Alexander Watson–María Dolores Domínguez de Watson Family,
1820–1980* (Los Angeles: Watson Land Company, 1987); Frances Dinkelspiel,
*Towers of Gold: How One Jewish Immigrant Named Isaias Hellman Created
California* (New York: St. Martin's, 2008).

3   Richard White, *"It's Your Misfortune and None of My Own": A New History
of the American West* (Norman: University of Oklahoma Press, 1991), quote
on 499. On the roles of private elites and public entities in the growth of the
region, see Steven P. Erie, "How the Urban West Was Won: The Local State
and Economic Growth of Los Angeles, 1880–1932," *Urban Affairs Quarterly* 27
(June 1992): 519–54. The "enlightened self-interest" description is a staple of
interpreters at the Banning Residence Museum in Wilmington, California.

CHAPTER ONE

1   Banning genealogies with accounts of the painting include: Pierson Worrall Banning, "The First Banning Genealogy" (typescript, Chicago, 1908), 1–2
(copy at LAPL); *Genealogical and Biographical Records of the Banning and
Allied Families, Prepared for Miss Kate Banning* (New York: American Historical Society, 1924), 11–16; Mary Marjorie Tyler, "Banning and Aliied [*sic*] Families," *Americana* 22 (January–December 1928): 89–90; *Banning-Bradley and
Allied Families* (Hartford, Conn.: States Historical Society, 1930), n.p.;
E. D. Clements, "Banning and Allied Families," *Americana Illustrated* 26, no. 4
(1932): 516–17; Leroy B. Banning, *Banning Branches* (Bowie, Md.: Heritage

Books, 1994), i; Elizabeth van Schaick-Banning, *The Book of Banning* (Westminster, Md.: Willow Bend Books, 2005), 108–23. A limited amount of Banning genealogical material without the *Night Watch* discussion can also be found in *Colonial Families of the United States of America*, 7 vols. (Baltimore: Seaforth, 1912), 1:25–31; and Zella Armstrong, comp., *Notable Southern Families*, 6 vols. (Baltimore: Genealogical Publishing, 1974), 6:25–29. On Rembrandt and his *Night Watch* see, among many others, Gary Schwartz, *Rembrandt: His Life, His Paintings* (New York: Viking, 1985), 209–13.

2   Van Schaick-Banning, *Book of Banning*, 122–24.

3   On Sir Paul Bayning, see ibid., 47–301.

4   Distribution of the Bannings in the U.S. and U.K. can be found on Ancestry.com, at http://www.ancestry.com/learn/facts/Banning (accessed 27 August 2007). On the history of Wiltshire County, see Alice Dryden, ed., *Memorials of Old Wiltshire* (London: Bemrose and Sons, 1906); D. A. Crowley, ed., *History of Wiltshire*, 17 vols. (London: Institute of Historical Research, 1999), vol. 16; R. B. Pugh and Elizabeth Crittall, eds., *History of Wiltshire*, 17 vols. (London: Institute of Historical Research, 1956), vol. 13; and Pamela Street, *Portrait of Wiltshire* (London: Hale, 1971).

5   The history of the village of Burbage is traced in Crowley, *History of Wiltshire*, 16:70–82. Evidence of Bannings there can be found in the documents published online by Colin Younger in the Family History section of the Burbage, Wiltshire, website, http://www.burbage-wiltshire.co.uk/burbageindex.html (accessed 27 August 2007). Some of these Bannings are listed in van Schaick-Banning, *Book of Banning*, 301–4.

6   John Banning's gravestone in Dover's Christ Church cemetery indicates that he died on 15 February 1791 in "his 52nd year," which puts his birth date between February 1739 and February 1740.

7   For accounts of the importance of saddlery in the period, see John W. Sherwell, *A Descriptive and Historical Account of the Guild of Saddlers of the City of London* (London: Harrison and Sons, 1889), 7; *The Leatherworker in Eighteenth Century Williamsburg* (Williamsburg, Va.: Colonial Williamsburg, 1967), 19–20; Russell H. Beatie, *Saddles* (Norman: University of Oklahoma Press, 1981), 34; Lee M. Rice and Glenn R. Vernam, *They Saddled the West* (Cambridge, Md.: Cornell Maritime, 1975), 1. For John Banning's acquisition of land, see copy of indenture for land conveyance from William Pollard to John Banning, 5 August 1774, box 6, Christine Shirley Collection, BRM. For his newspaper interest, see *Pennsylvania Chronicle*, 10 August 1767. John Banning's property at his death is listed in his probate file, Kent County Register of Wills, RG3545.00, microfilm roll 009, DPA; notations on his prominence in the community and purchase of property can be found in J. Thomas Scharf, *History of Delaware, 1609–1888*, 2 vols. (Philadelphia: L. J. Richards, 1888), 2:1047–48, 1065.

8   Scharf, *History of Delaware*, 2:1047 (on the early history of the house); Harold Donaldson Eberlein and Cortlandt V. D. Hubbard, *Historic Houses and Buildings of Delaware* (Dover, Md.: Public Archives Commission, 1962), 57–59, quote by George Purnell Fisher on 58.

9   Emil G. Sammack and Don O. Winslow, eds., *Dover: The First Two Hundred and Fifty Years, 1717–1967* (Dover, Del.: City of Dover, 1967), 19.

10 George H. Ryden, ed., *Letters to and from Caesar Rodney, 1756–1784* (Philadelphia: University of Pennsylvania Press, 1933), esp. 28, 50–53, 101–2; Delaware Public Archives Commission, *Delaware Archives*, 5 vols. (Wilmington, Del.: various pubs., 1911–19), 2:986; John Munroe, *History of Delaware*, 5th ed. (Newark: University of Delaware Press, 2006), 64–67.

11 On Banning's offices and activities during this period, see Delaware Public Archives Commission, *Delaware Archives*, 2:987; Scharf, *History of Delaware*, 1:224–25; and Jane Harrington Scott, *A Gentleman as Well as a Whig: Caesar Rodney and the American Revolution* (Newark, Del.: University of Delaware Press; Cranbury, N.J.: Associated University Presses, 2000), 75–76, 121. On Delaware Tories, see Harold B. Hancock, ed., "The Kent County Loyalists," *Delaware History* 6 (September 1954): 92–139.

12 Claudia L. Bushman, Harold B. Hancock, and Elizabeth Moyne Homsey, eds., *Proceedings of the Assembly of the Lower Counties on Delaware, 1770–1776, of the Constitutional Convention of 1776, and of the House of Assembly of the Delaware State, 1776–1781* (Newark: University of Delaware Press, 1986), 557, 570; Scharf, *History of Delaware*, 1:241–42.

13 The succession of John Banning's offices is noted in Delaware Public Archives Commission, *Delaware Archives*, 1:613; 2:1008; 3:1088, 1191, 1238, 1240 (quote), 1286, 1335; and Scharf, *History of Delaware*, 242. On the donation of flints, see Leon Valinger Jr., ed., "Rodney Letters," *Delaware History* 3 (September 1948): 107. The story of Banning providing hard money for the devalued Continental scrip is mentioned in an abstract of Mrs. Charles I. du Pont to Nicholas Johnson, 10 April 1893, in Leon Valinger Jr. and Virginia E. Shaw, comps., *A Calendar of Ridgely Family Letters, 1742–1899, in the Delaware State Archives*, 3 vols. (Dover, Del.: Public Archives Commission, 1948–61), 3:313.

14 Henry C. Conrad, in *History of the State of Delaware*, 3 vols. (Wilmington, Del.: for the author, 1908), 1:157, 266; 2:611, mentions John Banning's state senate and county treasurer elections; see H. Clay Reed, "Presidential Elections in Delaware, 1789–1829," *Delaware History* 14 (April 1970): 1–20; Leon Valinger Jr., comp., *Calendar of Kent County, Delaware, Probate Records, 1680–1800* (Dover, Del.: Public Archives Commission, State of Delaware, 1944), 251, 270, 283, 297, 335, 355, 396, 439.

15 Charity loved to tell the story of the death of her mother, whose funeral was delayed for days so that another daughter could be present. When the lid was finally being placed on her mother's casket, "signs of life were visible, and she was restored to her rejoicing family." Each year thereafter the event was commemorated as the mother and her children "would go to the graveyard and take their tea upon the headstones as a reminder of the uncertainty of life." See Joyce Loranger, research notes (quotes), BRM. Elizabeth Alford Banning's date of birth is not known. Since she first married about 1780 and gave birth to three children in the 1790s, it is probable that she was much younger than John Banning and probably born about 1760.

16   On Philip and Charity Alford, see Ruthanna Hindes, "Delaware Silversmiths, 1728–1830: New Discoveries," *Delaware History* 19 (Spring–Summer 1981): 129–31; Valinger, *Calendar of Kent County, Delaware, Probate Records*, 355; Delaware Public Archives Commission, *Delaware Archives*, 3:1183, 1261; and research files on Charity Alston's will, BRM. John Casson had previously been married in 1773 to Elizabeth Parke in Kent County; see Ancestry.com entry for Casson as extracted from Jordan Dodd, Liahona Research, comp., *Delaware Marriages, 1645–1899*, http://www.ancestry.com. Former Banning Residence Museum volunteer and researcher Eleanor Henry has found evidence that Elizabeth had married a Mr. Hudson before she married John Casson; Eleanor Henry, telephone interview by the author, 16 December 2007.

17   John Banning probate file, Kent County Register of Wills, RG3545.00, microfilm roll 009, DPA; Katharine S. Banning's notes in a book (quoting the headstone), photocopy in box 8, Los Angeles Harbor Area Collection, Archives and Special Collections Department, Los Angeles Harbor College, Wilmington, Calif.; *Pennsylvania General Advertiser*, 2 March 1791; *New York Journal & Patriotic Register*, 14 March 1791.

18   This history of the house is based on Scharf, *History of Delaware*, 1:1047; and Eberlein and Cortlandt, *Historic Houses and Buildings of Delaware*, 57–59.

19   For the McKee family's residences, see abstract of Willemina Ridgely to Ann Ridgely, 19 September 1806, in Valinger and Shaw, *Calendar of Ridgely Family Letters*, 1:274, and notes, 2:88–89. McKee's early residence in Delaware and appointment as trustee of Wilmington College are noted in Scharf, *History of Delaware*, 2:686, 884, 902.

20   Abstract of William McKee to Mrs. Ann Ridgely, 10 February 1795, in Valinger and Shaw, *Calendar of Ridgely Family Letters*, 1:135, and notes, 2:87–90 (quote on 89). On Ridgely's careers, see Scharf, *History of Delaware*, 1:572; Conrad, *History of the State of Delaware*, 1:261, 3:898–900. Letters collected in Mabel Lloyd Ridgely, ed., *What Them Befell: The Ridgelys of Delaware and Their Circle in Colonial and Federal Times; Letters 1751–1890* (Portland, Maine: Anthoensen, 1949), 259–353, shed light on Sarah's life during her marriage to Ridgely.

21   John Alford Banning's early life can be followed in Mrs. John Davis to Sarah Ridgely, 24 January 1816, Ridgely Family Collection, DPA; abstracts of Mrs. Elizabeth McKee to Sarah Ridgely, 11 August 1811, Miss Elizabeth McKee to Sarah Ridgely, 24 October 1811, and Sarah Ridgely to Henry M. Ridgely, 21 November 1811, in Valinger and Shaw, *Calendar of Ridgely Family Letters*, 2:138–40. Copy of Jean W. de Ved (Office of the Secretary, Princeton University) to Mrs. Herbert E. McQuesten, 28 February 1946, Family Files, RG 9225.001, DPA, contains biographical information on John Alford Banning.

22   These events in John's life can be followed chronologically in abstracts of Sarah Ridgely to Henry M. Ridgely, 2 February 1812, Henry M. Ridgely to Sarah Ridgely, 22 March 1812, in Valinger and Shaw, *Calendar of Ridgely Family Letters*, 2:147–48, 156; Sarah Ridgely to Henry M. Ridgely, 28 December 1812, folio 245, Ridgely Family Collection, DPA. His land purchases are listed in Index to Deeds (1640–1873), New Castle County Recorder of Deeds

Office, Wilmington, Del. The present-day location of Oak Hill Farm would be just off the north side of Barley Mill Road, about two miles west of Monroe Park on the Kennet Turnpike; see D. G. Beers, *Atlas of the State of Delaware* (Philadelphia: Pomeroy & Beers, 1868), Christiana Hundred.

23   Early generations of Lowbers are listed or discussed in Donald Odell Virdin, *Some Pioneer Delaware Families* (Arlington, Va.: Virdin, 1977), 151–53; Evelyn Jackson Tubbs Metzler, "The Lowbers of Kent County, Delaware: Moving South from New Amsterdam (New York) to Kent-on-Delaware," *Maryland and Delaware Genealogist* 19, no. 3 (July 1978): 80–81; F. Edward Wright, *Colonial Families of Delaware, Vol. 1* (Westminster, Md.: Willow Bend Books, 1999), 131–36. Elizabeth's parents and grandparents can be found in the Lowber family file in the Joseph Brown Turner Collection, and probate files for Lowber family members, Kent County Register of Wills, both in DPA; U.S. Census Office, Population Schedules, 6th Census (1840), New Castle County, Del., microfilm roll 33; and Henry C. Peden Jr., *Revolutionary Patriots of Delaware, 1775–1783* (Westminster, Md.: Family Line, 1996), 161. The Ponders of Philadelphia are listed in *McElroy's Philadelphia City Directory* (Philadelphia: A. McElroy) in 1837 and 1844.

24   Wilmington's economic development is traced in Carol E. Hoffecker, "Nineteenth Century Wilmington: Satellite or Independent City?" *Delaware History* 15 (April 1972): 1–18; Peter C. Welsh, "Merchants, Millers and Ocean Ships: The Components of an Early American Industrial Town," *Delaware History* 7 (September 1957): 319–36; Carol E. Hoffecker, *Delaware: A Bicentennial History* (New York: W. W. Norton, 1977), 48–50; and Munroe, *History of Delaware*, 103–10. The city's transportation links are discussed in Bruce E. Seely, "Wilmington and Its Railroads: A Lasting Connection," *Delaware History* 9 (September 1980): 1–9.

25   Richard L. Bushman, *The Refinement of America: Persons, Houses, Cities* (New York: Knopf, 1992), 219–21, 233, quotes on 220. The geography was pointed out to me by Eleanor Henry in a telephone interview, 16 December 2007.

26   Munroe, *History of Delaware*, 96–101; James A. McGowan, *Station Master on the Underground Railroad: The Life and Letters of Thomas Garrett* (Moylan, Pa.: Whimsie, 1977); Patience Essah, *A House Divided: Slavery and Emancipation in Delaware, 1638–1865* (Charlottesville: University Press of Virginia, 1996), 70–78.

27   Du Pont connections to the Banning family in Wilmington can be found in Valinger and Shaw, *Calendar of Ridgely Family Letters*, 3:140–47, and leading du Pont figures in Delaware and their businesses are noted in Conrad, *History of the State of Delaware*, 1:179, 265; 2:514–55; 3:884, 888–89. Overall family histories include Marc Duke, *The du Ponts: Portrait of a Dynasty* (New York: Saturday Review, 1976); and William H. A. Carr, *The du Ponts of Delaware* (New York: Dodd, Mead, 1964), which includes the stories of the 1824 marriage, 114–15, and Lucretia Mott, 155–57.

28   Scharf, *History of Delaware*, 1:321. The state of agriculture in Delaware in the early 1800s is described in C. M. Allmond, ed., "The Agricultural Memorandums of Samuel H. Black, 1815–1820," *Agricultural History* 32 (January 1958):

56–61; and Hoffecker, *Delaware*, 43–48. Orchards and other new crops would later turn the agricultural situation around, and by the early 1840s New Castle County was being described as "the paradise, the garden spot of the State"; see H. Clay Reed, ed., *Delaware: A History of the First State*, 2 vols. (New York: Lewis Historical, 1947), 1:373–77, quote on 376.

29   Advertisement in the *American Watchman*, 7 October 1815; Scharf, *History of Delaware*, 2:1118.

30   Advertisements in the *Delaware Gazette and Peninsula Advertiser*, 30 May, 4 November 1816, and in the *Delaware Gazette and State Journal*, 11 December 1821. On John Alford Banning's attempt to purchase a slave from his sister, see Henry M. Ridgely to Sarah Ridgely, 27 December 1812, folio 268, Sarah Ridgely to Henry M. Ridgely, 18 January 1813, folio 245, and John A. Banning to Henry M. Ridgely, 15 December 1814, folio 248, Ridgely Family Collection, DPA; *William H. Williams, Slavery and Freedom in Delaware, 1639–1865* (Wilmington, Del.: Scholarly Resources, 1996), 114. The persons living on the Banning farm in 1830 are enumerated in U.S. Census Office, Population Schedules, 5th Census (1830), New Castle County, Del., microfilm roll 12.

31   The court martial listing can be found in Delaware Public Archives Commission, *Delaware Archives*, 5:680–88, and it is also mentioned in Henry C. Peden Jr., *The Delaware Militia in the War of 1812* (Lewes, Del.: Colonial Roots, 2003), 13. The only other John Banning appearing in the Delaware census at the time lived much further south, in Sussex County.

32   Mrs. John Rumsey to William Rumsey, 23 November 1816 (quote), folder 3, box 35, Rumsey Family Collection, DHS; Lionel A. Sheldon, "Biographical Sketch of Phineas Banning," 1888, MSS C-D 771, BANC, quote on 3. The eye problem was probably retinitis pigmentosa, which causes retinal degeneration and deteriorating vision. Several of his descendants were also afflicted with this inherited disease.

33   Banning, *Banning Branches*, 98–102 (although this information is not always correct and many dates are uncertain or unlisted); Sheldon, "Biographical Sketch of Phineas Banning," 3; U.S. Census Office, Population Schedules, 5th Census (1830), New Castle County, Del., microfilm roll 12; U.S. Census Office, Population Schedule, 6th Census (1840), New Castle County, Del., microfilm roll 33; U.S. Census Office, Population Schedules, 7th Census (1850), New Castle County, Del., microfilm roll 1. On the Banning children teaching their siblings, see abstract of Elizabeth Banning to Nicholas Ridgely, 11 April 1841, in Valinger and Shaw, *Calendar of Ridgely Family Letters*, 2:336. The U.S. censuses of 1860, 1870, and 1880, scanned and available to subscribers of Ancestry.com, were also used to determine birth dates for the siblings, but these census schedules and the others list inconsistent ages and dates of birth. The birth years for John and William, which varied considerably in the census schedules from 1850 through 1880, are based on the most likely of the years listed in them, along with the 1820 census. Also, their father John Alford Banning had two sons between the ages of ten and fifteen in 1830; they were, then, born between 1815 and 1820. Finally, their father claimed in his will that John was his eldest son.

34   Elizabeth Banning to Nicholas Ridgely, 22 September (quote), 9 October 1839, folio 289, Ridgely Family Collection, DPA.

35   Katharine S. Banning, notes from a reminiscence of her mother in 1905 (quote), scrapbook 11, 1996 Addendum, Banning Company Collection, HEH; *McElroy's Philadelphia City Directory for 1844*, 15.

36   Abstract of Mary Lowber Banning to Rev. Nicholas Ridgely, October 1842, in Valinger and Shaw, *Calendar of Ridgely Family Letters*, 3:74; U.S. Census Office, Population Schedules, 7th Census (1850), New Castle County, Del., microfilm roll 1, p. 720.

CHAPTER TWO

1   Phineas Banning, "Settlement of Wilmington," 1883, transcribed and edited by Edward P. Newkirk, MSS C-E 139, BANC, quote on 1; Lionel A. Sheldon, "Biographical Sketch of Phineas Banning," 1888, MSS C-D 771, BANC, 4. James M. Guinn, *A History of California and An Extended History of Los Angeles and Environs*, 3 vols. (Los Angeles: Historic Record Company, 1915), 2:29–30, is based on details supplied by one of Banning's sons and contains a number of discrepancies (such as the date of Phineas Banning's birth).

2   Banning, "Settlement of Wilmington," quote on 4. The locations of family members can be found in *McElroy's Philadelphia City Directory* (Philadelphia: A. McElroy, 1844), 15, 187, 253, and 287.

3   Elizabeth M. Geffen, "Industrial Development and Social Crisis, 1841–1854," in *Philadelphia: A 300 Year History*, ed. Russell F. Weigley (New York: W. W. Norton, 1982), 307–62, quote on 307–8; Michael Feldberg, *The Philadelphia Riots of 1844: A Study of Ethnic Conflict* (Westport, Conn.: Greenwood, 1975), esp. 3–18; Sam Bass Warner, *The Private City; Philadelphia in Three Periods of Its Growth* (Philadelphia: University of Pennsylvania Press, 1968), 49–157.

4   Banning, "Settlement of Wilmington," 1–2, 5; Ernest Hexamer and William Locher, *Maps of the City of Philadelphia* (Philadelphia, Pa.: E. Hexamer & W. Locher, 1858–60), 1:13; available on the Greater Philadelphia GeoHistory Network website at http://philageohistory.org/rdic-images/HXL 1860v1/pl13.htm (accessed 14 January 2008); Federal Writers' Project, Works Progress Administration, comp., *Philadelphia: A Guide to the Nation's Birthplace* (Philadelphia: William Penn Association of Philadelphia, 1937), 384–88.

5   Katharine S. Banning, notes, box 2, 1996 Addendum, Banning Company Collection, HEH; Charles H. Browning, *Americans of Royal Descent*, 3rd ed. (Philadelphia: J. P. Lippincott, 1894), 92–93; U.S. Census Office, Population Schedules, 7th Census (1850), New Market Ward, Philadelphia, 377.

6   Banning, "Settlement of Wilmington," 2; *Los Angeles Express* clipping, March 1885, box 4, 1996 Addendum, Banning Company Collection, HEH. The Philadelphia newspapers and the abolitionist *Pennsylvania Freeman* did not mention the speech by Phineas at the time.

7   *Los Angeles Star*, 20 March 1852; passport for George East, signed by Luis Ramirez, Mexican vice-consul in St. Louis, Missouri, 27 April 1833, document RI 144, William G. Ritch Collection, HEH.

8   *Bicknell's Reporter* (Philadelphia), 11 February–8 July 1851; *Alta California*
    (San Francisco), 22 October 1861, mentions the trip with Dr. East a decade
    earlier; Katharine S. Banning, notes based on an interview with Mary Sweeny
    Banning, 1905, box 4, 1996 Addendum, Banning Company Collection, HEH.

9   *Los Angeles Star*, 8 November 1851; *New York Tribune*, 29 September 1851
    (on the departure of the *Illinois*); John Haskell Kemble, *The Panama Route,
    1848–1869* (Berkeley: University of California Press, 1943), 145–65, 219, 231.

10 *Alta California* (San Francisco), 3 December 1851. On the Panama trips to
    California, see Kemble, *The Panama Route*, 166–99; James P. Delgado,
    To California by Sea: A Maritime History of the California Gold Rush
    (Columbia: University of South Carolina Press, 1990), 47–54, quote on 51;
    and Aims McGuinness, *Path of Empire: Panama and the California Gold
    Rush* (Ithaca, N.Y.: Cornell University Press, 2008), 33–35, 46–49. On
    Phineas Banning's trip, see Carol G. Wilson, *California Yankee: William R.
    Staats, Business Pioneer* (Claremont, Calif.: Saunders, 1946), 18. For two sto-
    ries of other groups of easterners who came to California the same year via
    the same route, see Elizabeth I. Dixon, ed., "Early San Fernando: Memoirs of
    Mrs. Catherine Dace," *Southern California Quarterly* 44 (September 1962):
    223–25, 263, and Isaac Read, "The Chagres River Route to California in 1851,"
    California Historical Quarterly 8 (March 1929): 3–16. Panamanian robbers
    made the trip even more treacherous. See Read, "Chagres River Route," 13,
    and *Alta California* (San Francisco), 3 December 1851, for two examples.

11 *Los Angeles Star*, 8 November 1851; *Alta California* (San Francisco), 1 Decem-
    ber 1851; Delgado, *To California by Sea*, 54–55; agreement of sale, 2 February
    1852, Estate of George East, probate file 51½, box 8, Los Angeles County
    Court Records, SCWHR.

12 *Los Angeles Star*, 20 March 1852; documents in East probate file, box 8,
    Los Angeles County Court Records, SCWHR.

13 Benjamin D. Wilson to Siter, Price & Company, 10 December 1852, box 3,
    Baily East to Wilson, 17 December 1853, box 3, Siter, Price & Company to Wil-
    son, 16 October 1852, box 17, copy of Siter, Price & Company to Phineas Ban-
    ning, 16 October 1852, 4 November 1852, box 17, Addendum II, Benjamin D.
    Wilson Papers, HEH.

14 *Los Angeles Star*, 14 February, 7 August 1852; Phineas Banning to Nicholas
    Blair, 3 September 1852, box 21, Abel Stearns Papers, HEH; California Census
    of 1852, Los Angeles County, 12 (microfilm at HEH); *Los Angeles Times*, 26
    January 1908 (quote). Partners in the competing firms can be found in 1851–
    53 advertisements in the *Los Angeles Star*.

15 Robert F. Lucid, ed., *The Journal of Richard Henry Dana, Jr.*, 3 vols. (Cam-
    bridge, Mass.: Harvard University Press, 1968), quotes on 1:251–52; Del-
    gado, *To California By Sea*, 109 (on smuggling); John Albert Wilson, *History
    of Los Angeles County, California* (Oakland, Calif.: Thompson and West,
    1880), 141.

16 Owen C. Coy, *California County Boundaries: A Study of the Division of the
    State into Counties and the Subsequent Changes in Their Boundaries* (Berke-
    ley: California Historical Survey Commission, 1923), 140–44.

17   Howard Nelson, *Los Angeles Metropolis* (Dubuque, Iowa: Kendall-Hunt, 1983), 16–19.

18   U.S. Census Office, 7th Census (1850), *Statistical View of the United States* (Washington, D.C.: A. O. P. Nicholson, 1854), 200; *Governor's Message; and Report of the Secretary of State on the Census of 1852, of the State of California* (San Francisco: State Printer, 1853), 19–21.

19   U.S. Census Office, 7th Census (1850), *Statistical View of the United States*, 200; Robert Glass Cleland, *The Cattle on a Thousand Hills: Southern California, 1850–1870* (San Marino, Calif.: Huntington Library, 1941), 102–16.

20   On the Anglo newcomers and their desire for more services, see Leonard Pitt, *The Decline of the Californios: A Social History of the Spanish-Speaking Californians, 1846–1890* (Berkeley: University of California Press, 1971). Robert Fogelson, *The Fragmented Metropolis: Los Angeles, 1850–1930* (Cambridge, Mass.: Harvard University Press, 1967), 8–23; and Frederic Cople Jaher, *The Urban Establishment: Upper Strata in Boston, New York, Charleston, Chicago and Los Angeles* (Urbana: University of Illinois Press, 1982), 578–87.

21   Harris Newmark, *Sixty Years in Southern California, 1853–1913* (New York: Knickerbocker, 1916), 60–127; H. D. Barrows, "Reminiscences of Los Angeles in the Fifties and Early Sixties," *Annual Publications of the Historical Society of Southern California* 3 (1893): 55–62.

22   Horace Bell, *Reminiscences of a Ranger: or Early Times in Southern California* (Santa Barbara, Calif.: Wallace Hebberd, 1927), 124–25.

23   California Census of 1852, Los Angeles County, 12 (microfilm at HEH); Katharine S. Banning, notes in scrapbook 5, 1996 Addendum, Banning Company Collection, HEH. On the hide house and surrounding area, see Hallock F. Raup, "Rancho Los Palos Verdes," *Quarterly Publications of the Historical Society of Southern California* 19 (March 1937): 10.

24   *Alta California* (San Francisco), 24 May 1852, lists Banning as a ship passenger to San Francisco; Arthur Eugene Bestor Jr., *David Jacks of Monterey and Lee L. Jacks, His Daughter* (Stanford, Calif.: Stanford University Press, 1945), 3–21.

25   On Stearns, see Ronald C. Woolsey, *Migrants West: Toward the Southern California Frontier* (Sebastopol, Calif.: Grizzly Bear, 1996), 1–15; and Cleland, *Cattle on a Thousand Hills*, 243–73. On Temple, see Marco R. Newmark, "The Life of Jonathan (John) Temple," *Historical Society of Southern California Quarterly* 36 (March 1954): 46–49; and Walter H. Case, *History of Long Beach* (Long Beach, Calif.: Press-Telegram, 1935), 14–16.

26   Summary report and letters in Benjamin D. Wilson Papers, HEH; Gary F. Kurutz, "Don Benito Wilson: A Pioneer in Transitional Southern California, 1841–1854" (master's thesis, University of San Diego, 1972).

27   Richard O. Johnson to Marshall Duell, 23 July 1982, vertical file, BRM; Vernetta Ripley, "The San Fernando Pass and the Pioneer Traffic That Went Over It," *Quarterly Publications of the Historical Society of Southern California* 29 (March 1947): 39; John Robinson, *Gateways to Southern California: Indian Footpaths, Horse Trails, Wagon Roads, Railroads and*

Highways (Arcadia, Calif.: Big Santa Anita Historical Society, 2005), 193–95, quote on 194.

28   *Los Angeles Star*, 7 May 1853, 6 May 1854, 15 August, 5 September 1857; Newmark, *Sixty Years in Southern California*, 105, 327.

29   Summary report and assorted documents in boxes 1–8, Joseph Lancaster Brent Papers, HEH; Newmark, *Sixty Years in Southern California*, 47; Woolsey, *Migrants West*, 57–71.

30   "Downey, John Gately," California Biography File, LAPL; H. Brett Melendy and Benjamin F. Gilbert, *The Governors of California: Peter H. Burnett to Edmund G. Brown* (Georgetown, Calif.: Talisman, 1965), 101–14.

31   "Alexander, David Watt," California Biography File, LAPL; H. D. Barrows, "Don David W. Alexander," *Annual Publications of the Historical Society of Southern California* 3 (1897): 43–45; Jane Apostol, "Don Mateo Keller: His Vines and His Wines," *Southern California Quarterly* 84 (Summer 2002): 93–114.

32   Newmark's career is described in Newmark, *Sixty Years in Southern California*. On Myles, see William Sanford to Benjamin D. Wilson, 20 June 1856, Wilson to Margaret Wilson, 20 October 1856, box 5, Benjamin D. Wilson Papers, HEH; *Southern Californian*, 5 October 1854, 25 April 1855; Newmark, *Sixty Years in Southern California*, 109–11.

33   Newmark, *Sixty Years in Southern California*, 47, 107; Woolsey, *Migrants West*, 80, 134.

34   *Los Angeles Star*, 12 February 1853; "Great Register of Los Angeles County," 1872, SCWHR.

CHAPTER THREE

1   Harris Newmark, *Sixty Years in Southern California, 1853–1913* (New York: Knickerbocker, 1916), 23.

2   Horace Bell, *Reminiscences of a Ranger: or Early Times in Southern California* (Santa Barbara, Calif.: Wallace Hebberd, 1927), quotes on 335, 340–41.

3   E. D. Townsend, *The California Diary of General E. D. Townsend*, ed. Malcolm Edwards (Los Angeles: Ward Ritchie, 1970), quotes on 102, 104; Anna Ogier to Margaret Wilson, 4 February 1856 (quote), box 4, Benjamin D. Wilson Papers, HEH. Jehu was a king of Israel in the ninth century BC, hailed as a masterful chariot driver; "Jehu" became a nickname for a coach driver, especially a fast or reckless one.

4   *Los Angeles Star*, 21 August 1852, 12 February 1853.

5   *Los Angeles Star*, 28 May 1853, 23 February 1856 (quote); *Los Angeles Times*, 26 January 1908; Newmark, *Sixty Years in Southern California*, 24. The Robinson incident is related in Alfred Robinson to Abel Stearns, 20 April 1855, box 54, Abel Stearns Papers, HEH. My thanks to Karen Jenks for bringing this letter to my attention.

6   On Banning's competitors, see advertisements in the *Los Angeles Star*,
     2 April 1853, 22 April, 1 September 1854; Richard W. Barsness, "Los Angeles'
     Quest for Improved Transportation, 1846–1861," *California Historical Society
     Quarterly* 46 (December 1967): 293; Newmark, *Sixty Years in Southern
     California*, 23; and Oscar Osborn Winthur, *Express and Stagecoach Days
     in California* (Stanford, Calif.: Stanford University Press, 1936), 95. One
     of Timms's stages broke the record for the twenty-five-mile ride from
     San Pedro to Los Angeles in 1855 with a time of one hour and fifty-five
     minutes; *Los Angeles Star*, 6 October 1855.

7   *Southern Californian*, 14 September 1854 (quote), 1 February 1855;
     Franz Stenzel, *James Madison Alden: Yankee Artist of the Pacific Coast,
     1854–1860* (Fort Worth, Tex.: Amon Carter Museum, 1975), 51; Townsend,
     California Diary of General E. D. Townsend, 102; Alexanders & Banning to
     John Keys, 17 February 1855, box 2, 1996 Addendum, Banning Company
     Collection, HEH; Edward O. C. Ord notes Banning business activities in
     his diaries: 1: 30 December 1853, 1 February 1854, and 2: 19, 20 April 1854,
     12 December 1854, 28 February 1855, box 7, Edward Otho Cresap Ord
     Papers, BANC.

8   The appearance of the Concord in California is noted in *Sacramento Union*,
     7 December 1851; and Winthur, *Express and Stagecoach Days in California*,
     96–98. The coach is described in Captain William Banning and George
     Hugh Banning, *Six Horses* (New York: Century, 1930), 23–26, 358–60,
     photographs facing 4 and 25.

9   See advertisements in *Los Angeles Star*, 1 September 1854; and *Southern Cali-
     fornian*, 13 June 1855.

10   Los Angeles County Board of Supervisors, Minutes of Meetings, 1: 11 August
     1854, 2 January 1855, Los Angeles County Board of Supervisors Office, Los
     Angeles, Calif.; *Southern Californian*, 28 December 1854; Vernetta Ripley,
     "The San Fernando Pass and the Pioneer Traffic that Went Over It," *Quar-
     terly Publications of the Historical Society of Southern California* 29 (March
     1947): 34–48. On frontiersman Gabriel Allen's more illustrious exploits, see
     Newmark, *Sixty Years in Southern California*, 222–23; Horace Bell, *On the
     Old West Coast: Being Further Reminiscences of a Ranger*, ed. Lanier Bartlett
     (New York; Grossett & Dunlap, 1930), 165.

11   Bell, *Reminiscences of a Ranger*, quotes on 336–37.

12   *Alta California* (San Francisco), 23 January 1855; *Los Angeles Star*, 19 January
     and 23 February 1856; *Southern Californian*, 1 and 13 February 1855. The Cali-
     fornia Stage Company is discussed in Winthur, *Express and Stagecoach Days
     in California*, 91–96.

13   John W. Robinson, *Gateways to Southern California: Indian Footpaths,
     Horse Trails, Wagon Roads, Railroads and Highways* (Arcadia, Calif.: Big
     Santa Anita Historical Society, 2005), quote on 203; Edward Leo Lyman,
     *The Overland Journey from Utah to California: Wagon Travel from the City
     of Saints to the City of Angels* (Reno and Las Vegas: University of Nevada
     Press, 2004), 156–57.

14   *Los Angeles Star*, 14 April, 28 April (quote), 22 September 1855; settlement of
accounts with Sanford, Banning & Co., 28 April 1855, box 4, Benjamin D.
Wilson Papers, HEH. For details of the trip, see Robinson, *Gateways to
Southern California*, 203; Lyman, *The Overland Journey from Utah to California*, 157; Byron Grant Pugh, "History of Utah–California Wagon Freighting" (master's thesis, University of California, Berkeley, 1949), 35–36, 45–48.

15   *Los Angeles Star*, 22 September 1855 (quote); Pugh, "History of Utah–
California Wagon Freighting," 49–50; Lyman, *The Overland Journey from
Utah to California*, 157–58. The actions of the Salt Lake City Council are
covered in Edward W. Tullidge, *History of Salt Lake City and Its Founders*
(Salt Lake City, Utah: E. W. Tullidge, 1886), 866.

16   Phineas Banning, "Settlement of Wilmington," 1883, transcribed and edited
by Edward P. Newkirk, quotes on 4–5, MSS C-E 139, BANC; *Los Angeles
Star*, 19 December 1857.

17   *Executor of Estate of Charles Burrows v. Alexander and Banning*, case 353,
John Temple v. Alexander & Banning, case 354, *Benjamin D. Wilson v.
Alexander & Banning*, case 355, *Bachman & Co. v. Alexander & Banning*,
case 356, *Rich, Newmark & Co. v. Alexander & Banning*, case 357, *Elias &
Brother v. Alexander & Banning*, case 358, box 11, Los Angeles Area Court
Records, HEH; Benjamin D. Wilson to Margaret Wilson, 4 July (quotes),
13 July (quotes) 1856, box 5, Benjamin D. Wilson Papers, HEH. Obviously,
the plaintiffs in these cases did not get the news of the firm's name change
to Alexanders & Banning.

18   *Los Angeles Star*, 26 July 1856.

19   *Los Angeles Star*, 2 and 9 August 1856; James H. Lander to Wilson, undated
(October 1856?), quote, and Wilson to Margaret Wilson, 20 October 1856,
box 5, Benjamin D. Wilson Papers, HEH.

20   *Los Angeles Star*, 30 August, 27 September, 18 October 1856; receipts for
firm of Banning & Wilson, 23 July 1856 to March 1857, box 5, Benjamin D.
Wilson Papers, HEH. The mail contract is listed in U.S. House, 35th Cong.,
1st sess., 1857–58, series 951, H. Doc. 96, XI:458.

21   *Los Angeles Star*, 16 May 1857, as quoted in Henry P. Silka, *San Pedro:
A Pictorial History* (San Pedro, Calif.: San Pedro Bay Historical Society,
1984), 25.

22   *Los Angeles Star*, 30 August 1856, 19 May 1857; William Sanford to
Benjamin D. Wilson, 5 February 1856, box 4, 20 June, 7 November 1856,
box 5, Benjamin D. Wilson Papers, HEH. Spencer Wilson eventually
returned to Los Angeles and was a merchant there until his death in 1877.
His activities are covered in U.S. War Department, *The War of the Rebellion:
A Compilation of the Official Records of the Union and Confederate Armies*,
70 vols. (Washington, D.C.: Government Printing Office, 1880–1901),
series 2, 50:682; and *The First Los Angeles City and County Directory, 1872*
(Los Angeles: Ward Ritchie, 1963).

23   *Los Angeles Star*, 17 October 1857.

24   Robert G. Cleland, *The Cattle on a Thousand Hills: Southern California,
      1850–1870* (San Marino, Calif.: Huntington Library, 1941), 90–97; *Los Angeles
      Star*, 16 July 1853; Ronald Woolsey, "Crime and Punishment: Los Angeles
      County, 1850–1856," *Southern California Quarterly* 61 (Spring 1979): 79–98;
      Leonard Pitt, *Decline of the Californios: A Social History of the Spanish-
      Speaking Californians, 1846–1890* (Berkeley: University of California Press,
      1966), 148–80. The individual observations are from Amasa Lyman to Benja-
      min D. Wilson, 18 July 1853 (quote), box 2, Benjamin D. Wilson Papers, HEH;
      John Forster to Cave J. Couts, 27 January 1857 (quote), CT732, Cave J. Couts
      Papers, HEH; and James Woods, diary, 12 November 1854, 57 (quote), HEH.

25   Woolsey, "Crime and Punishment," 80–81; *Los Angeles Star*, 31 January,
      2 February 1857. For Barton's career, see Ronald C. Woolsey, *Migrants West:
      Toward the Southern California Frontier* (Sebastopol, Calif.: Grizzly Bear,
      1996), 77–84; and Los Angeles County Sheriff's Office, *150 Years: A Tradition
      of Service* (Paducah, Ky.: Turner, 2000), 9–14.

26   Los Angeles court sessions at the time are described in Newmark, *Sixty
      Years in Southern California*, 45–59; W. W. Robinson, *Lawyers of Los Angeles*
      (Los Angeles: Los Angeles Bar Association, 1959), 37–38; Paul Spitzzeri,
      "On a Case by Case Basis: Ethnicity and Los Angeles Courts, 1850–1875,"
      California History 83, no. 2 (2005): 22–39.

27   *Los Angeles Star*, 18 January 1855, 26 July 1856, 2 March 1857; Robert W. Blew,
      "Vigilantism in Los Angeles, 1835–1874," *Southern California Quarterly* 54
      (Spring 1972): 11–30; Paul Spitzzeri, "Judge Lynch in Session: Popular Justice
      in Los Angeles, 1850–1875," *Southern California Quarterly* 87 (Summer
      2005): 83–97.

28   Los Angeles County Board of Supervisors, Minutes of Meetings, 1: 11 August
      1853, Los Angeles County Board of Supervisors Office, Los Angeles, Calif.;
      Los Angeles Star, 6 August 1853; Woolsey, "Crime and Punishment," 89–90.

29   Bell, *Reminiscences of a Ranger*, 102; Robinson, *Lawyers of Los Angeles*, 42.

30   *Southern Californian*, 15 April 1855; J. M. Scammell, "Military Units in
      Southern California, 1853–1862," *California Historical Society Quarterly* 29
      (September 1950): 234.

31   Lyman, *The Overland Journey from Utah to California*, 133–40.

32   *Los Angeles Star*, 17 October, 12, 19, 26 December 1857, 23 January 1858;
      "Inventory of the Military Department, Military Companies Records,
      1848–1880," item 3412-3, CSA; Scammell, "Military Units in Southern
      California," 236–37.

33   *Los Angeles Star*, 22 November 1856.

34   Mary Dunning Nagle, "A Sweeny Sampler," *Minnesota History* 41 (Spring
      1868): 29–33. Three books illustrated with Sweeny's work are Mary Wheel-
      house Berthel, *Horns of Thunder: The Life and Times of James M. Goodhue*
      (St. Paul: Minnesota Historical Society, 1948); William L. Shea and Earl J.
      Hess, *Pea Ridge: Civil War Campaign in the West* (Chapel Hill: University of
      North Carolina Press, 1992); and R. O. Sweeny, *Sketches and Reminiscences of*

the City of St. Paul as I First Saw It in the Spring of 1852 (St. Paul: Minnesota Historical Society, 1991).

35   Robert Ormsby Sweeny to William Lowber Banning, 19 August 1852, Phineas Banning to William Lowber Banning, 24 June 1854, box 2, 1996 Addendum, Banning Company Collection, HEH.

36   *Philadelphia Public Ledger*, 31 March 1854 (notice of Mary's wedding); *Delaware Gazette*, 18 April 1854 (obituary); John Alford Banning and Elizabeth Lowber Banning probate files, Register of Wills, New Castle County, RG 2545.001 (microfilm), DPA. J. Thomas Scharf, in *History of Delaware, 1609–1888*, 2 vols. (Philadelphia: L. J. Richards, 1888), 2:842, notes the cemetery where John and Elizabeth are buried.

37   Phineas Banning to William Lowber Banning, 24 June 1854 (quote), Francenia Alice Banning to William Lowber Banning, 15 June 1854, box 2, 1996 Addendum, Banning Company Collection, HEH.

38   Advertisement in *St. Paul Daily Pioneer and Democrat*, 17 June 1856. William Lowber Banning's life is chronicled in John H. Guthman, "William L. Banning," Biography Files, MHC; *Saint Paul City Directory* (St. Paul, Minn.: Goodrich and Somers, 1856–57); J. Fletcher Williams, *A History of the City of St. Paul and of the County of Ramsey, Minnesota* (St. Paul: Minnesota Historical Society, 1876), 367–68, 396; T. M. Newsom, *Pen Pictures of St. Paul, Minnesota* (St. Paul: for the author, 1886), 505–6.

39   Photograph of W. L. Banning Residence (from a drawing, 1857), MR2.9SP3.2gp99, Photograph Collection, MHC; Evadene A. Burris, "Building the Frontier Home," *Minnesota History* 15 (March 1934): 53–54 (quote). The family is noted in Alice Monfort Dunn, "People and Places in Old St. Paul," *Minnesota History* 33 (Spring 1952): 4; and Marion Ramsey Furness, "Childhood Recollections of Old St. Paul," *Minnesota History* 29 (June 1948): 118, 121. William Jr.'s death is noted in a newspaper clipping, July 1862, box 2, 1996 Addendum, Banning Company Collection, HEH. Birth dates for the children were derived from the U.S. census of 1880 population schedules for St. Paul, Minn., as scanned on Ancestry.com, http://www.ancestry.com.

40   Phineas Banning to Francenia Alice Horn, 16 October 1859, box 2, 1996 Addendum, Banning Company Collection, HEH; abstract of Elizabeth A. Elliot to Mrs. Ann du Pont, 27 August 1890, in Leon Valinger Jr. and Virginia E. Shaw, comps., *A Calendar of Ridgely Family Letters, 1742–1899, in the Delaware State Archives*, 3 vols. (Dover, Del.: Public Archives Commission, 1948–61), 3:308. The marriages of Elizabeth and Sallie are noted in *Delaware Gazette*, 10 March 1843, 3 December 1852. The complete list of siblings, with some inaccuracies, appears in Leroy B. Banning, *Banning Branches* (Bowie, Md.: Heritage Books, 1994), 100–102.

41   Maymie Krythe, *Port Admiral: Phineas Banning, 1830–1885* (San Francisco: California Historical Society, 1957), 58–59, 65; *Alta California* (San Francisco), 28 November 1854. The residence of Rebecca and Hannah in Los Angeles is mentioned in Benjamin D. Wilson to William Sanford, 9 July 1853, Margaret Wilson to Benjamin D. Wilson, 12 September 1853, box 3,

Benjamin D. Wilson Papers, HEH. It is most likely that Rebecca did not arrive until 1853, as in the last letter cited here, Mrs. Wilson reported that "Mr. Sanford's relations have not arrived yet."

42 Richard O. Johnson to Marshall Duell, 23 July 1982, Vertical File, BRM.

43 Marjorie T. Wolcott, ed., *Pioneer Notes from the Diaries of Judge Benjamin Hayes, 1849–1875* (Los Angeles: McBride, 1929), quote on 154.

44 Phineas Banning to Mary Sweeny Banning, 16 October 1859, box 2, 1996 Addendum, Banning Company Collection, HEH; Phineas Banning to Benjamin D. Wilson, 21 February 1856, box 4, Benjamin D. Wilson Papers, HEH; *Los Angeles Star*, 11 April, 26 September 1857; Joyce Loranger (former BRM research specialist), interview by the author, 14 November 2007. Rebecca was thrown from a carriage and injured in February 1855, but it is difficult to know how this accident affected her; she gave birth to many children after the accident. *Southern Californian*, 22 February 1855. Banning himself stated that he had eight children with Rebecca. See Col. J. J. Warner, Benjamin Hayes, and J. P. Widney, *An Historical Sketch of Los Angeles County, California* (Los Angeles: Louis Lewin, 1876), 119.

45 *Los Angeles Star*, 28 March, April 1857, clippings in vol. 46, Hayes Scrapbooks, BANC; *Alta California* (San Francisco), 27 July, 12 November (quote) 1857.

46 *San Francisco Bulletin*, 13 July 1857 (quote); Newmark, *Sixty Years in Southern California*, 157.

CHAPTER FOUR

1 *Los Angeles Star*, 1 February 1854; *Southern Californian*, 30 November 1854 (quotes).

2 On the purchase of the 2,400 acres, see Index of Deeds, book 1, and Deed Book 1:208, Los Angeles County Recorder's Office, Norwalk, Calif.; notes on Rancho San Pedro, folder 15, box 23, Solano-Reeve Papers, HEH. The map is mentioned in the entry for 28 February 1855, diary 2, box 7, Edward Otho Cresap Ord Papers, BANC. U.S. Army Lt. Edward Otho Cresap Ord (1818–1883) drew the first city map of Los Angeles in 1849 and surveyed portions of the San Pedro Bay region for the coastal survey in the early 1850s. He later served in the Union army during the Civil War and eventually reached the rank of major general.

3 Banning's purchases can be traced in Deed Book 4:3, 175, Deed Book 5:9, Los Angeles County Recorder's Office, Norwalk, Calif.; notes on Rancho San Pedro, folder 15, box 23, Solano-Reeve Papers; map of "Banning's Reserve" with ownership notes by Frank Lecouvreur, 3 February 1872, box 16, Benjamin D. Wilson Papers, HEH; *Los Angeles Star*, 27 March 1858; Joyce Freeman Loranger, "Phineas Banning: The Stories vs. the Record," *Shoreline* 27 (August 1999): 6–9.

4 Richard W. Barsness, "Los Angeles' Quest for Improved Transportation, 1846–1861," *California Historical Society Quarterly* 46 (December 1967): 297–98, quote on 297.

5   *Los Angeles Star*, 2 October 1858 (quote); *Alta California* (San Francisco),
     8 October 1858.

6   *Los Angeles Star*, 6 March, 14 August, 9 October 1858 (quotes). Although
     badly damaged, the *Medora* was scheduled to be repaired and put into serv-
     ice once again; *Los Angeles Star*, 16 October 1858. J. Ross Browne observed
     that Banning still had an office and a warehouse in old San Pedro in 1860;
     A Tour Through Arizona, 1864; Or, Adventures in the Apache Country
     (repr., Tucson, Ariz.: Arizona Silhouettes, 1951), 32.

7   *Los Angeles Star*, 30 October, 6 November, 25 December 1858, 15 January 1859.
     Banning's road to the harbor appears on a map of the Abel Stearns rancho in
     1868. See W. W. Robinson, *Maps of Los Angeles, From Ord's Survey of 1849 to
     the End of the Boom of the Eighties* (Los Angeles: Dawson's Bookshop, 1966),
     plate 62.

8   *Los Angeles Star*, 12 February (quote), 11 June 1859; Wilson to Rep. William M.
     Gwin, 7 October 1858, box 7, Benjamin D. Wilson Papers, HEH.

9   Copy of *Phineas Banning, Benjamin D. Wilson, and Henry Myles v. John
     Downey, James McFarland, Edward McDonald, and Manuel Dominguez*
     (suit to partition the 1854 New San Pedro/Wilmington purchase), 1862, box 6,
     Banning Company Collection, HEH; Judson A. Grenier with Robert C. Gilling-
     ham, *California Legacy: The James Alexander Watson–María Dolores
     Domínguez de Watson Family, 1820–1980* (Los Angeles: Watson Land Com-
     pany, 1987), 190–91.

10   *Los Angeles Star*, 17 October 1857; Herman Hellman to Joseph Brent Banning,
     18 February 1905, box 4, 1996 Addendum, Banning Company Collection, HEH.

11   Erna Risch, *Quartermaster Support of the Army: A History of the Corps,
     1775–1939* (Washington, D.C.: Office of the Quartermaster General, 1962),
     312–15.

12   The El Tejon contract is covered in *Los Angeles Star*, 24 April, 12 June 1858;
     Alta California (San Francisco), 29 May 1858; Earle Crowe, *Men of El Tejon:
     Empire in the Tehachapis* (Los Angeles: Ward Ritchie, 1957), 62, 95, 98; Helen
     S. Giffin and Arthur Woodward, *The Story of El Tejon* (Los Angeles: Daw-
     son's Bookshop, 1942), 97. See also Ann Zwinger, *John Xántus: The Fort Tejon
     Letters, 1857–1859* (Tucson: University of Arizona Press, 1986), 137, 156, 185.

13   *Los Angeles Star*, 19 March, 27 August 1859.

14   *Los Angeles Star*, 14, 20 March, 15 December 1858; *Alta California* (San
     Francisco), 18 June 1858; Dennis Casebier, *The Mojave Road* (Norco, Calif.:
     Tales of the Mojave Road, 1975), 95–96. For an overall treatment, see John W.
     Robinson, *Gateways to Southern California: Indian Footpaths, Horse Trails,
     Wagon Roads, Railroads and Highways* (Arcadia, Calif.: Big Santa Anita His-
     torical Society, 2005), 208–11.

15   *Los Angeles Star*, 6 November 1858, 11, 26 February, 11 June 1859.

16   Two such lawsuits are *Phineas Banning v. Aug. W. Timms*, case 489, filed
     5 January 1858, box 14, and *Phineas Banning v. Augustus W. Timms et al.*,
     case 525, filed 12 May 1858, box 15, Los Angeles Area Court Records, HEH.
     On Lecouvreur and Goller, see Frank Lecouvreur, *From East Prussia to the*

Golden Gate (New York: Angelina Book Concern, 1906), 310–11; and John Baur, "John Goller: Pioneer Angeleno Manufacturer." *Quarterly Publications of the Historical Society of Southern California* 36 (March 1954): 21–22.

17   *Los Angeles Star*, 5 April 1859; "Dictation of E. N. McDonald of Wilmington," ca. 1888, box 3, Miscellaneous California Dictations, BANC; *J. J. Tomlinson, Rufus S. Ellis, and Alexander M. W. Ball v. Phineas Banning*, case 695, filed 10 February 1860, box 20, Los Angeles Area Court Records, HEH.

18   *Los Angeles Star*, 7 May, 16 October, 25 December 1858; *Alta California* (San Francisco), 18 June 1858.

19   Harris Newmark, *Sixty Years in Southern California, 1853–1913* (New York: Knickerbocker, 1916), 283–85; Crowe, *Men of El Tejon*, 98–99.

20   A. A. Polhamus to Joseph Brent Banning, 4 April 1905, box 4, 1996 Addendum, Banning Company Collection, HEH; Newmark, *Sixty Years in Southern California*, 67, 313.

21   *Alta California* (San Francisco), 22 October 1861.

22   *Los Angeles Star*, 17 August 1861; Robinson, *Gateways to Southern California*, 221–22.

23   Robert G. Cleland, *The Cattle on a Thousand Hills: Southern California, 1850–1870* (San Marino, Calif.: Huntington Library, 1941), 63. The entire operation was described by a reporter in the *Alta California* (San Francisco), 22 October 1861.

24   *Alta California* (San Francisco), 13 October (first quote), 22 October (remaining quotes) 1861.

25   *Los Angeles Star*, 30 October 1858; Phineas Banning to Mary Sweeny Banning, 16 October 1859, box 2, and A. A. Polhamus to Joseph Brent Banning, 4 April 1905, box 4, 1996 Addendum, Banning Company Collection, HEH. William Sanford Banning rarely used his middle name. It is clearly listed in an indenture in which his father donated a lot of land to three of his sons in 1868; indenture, 12 February 1868, box 6, Banning Company Collection, HEH.

26   Phineas Banning to Mary Sweeny Banning, 16 October 1859, box 2, 1996 Addendum, Banning Company Collection, HEH; Newmark, *Sixty Years in Southern California*, 237.

27   U.S. Census, Population Schedules, 8th Census (1860), San Pedro Township, 480 (microfilm); Loranger, "Phineas Banning: The Stories vs. the Record," 5–6; Joyce F. Loranger, "Women of This House—Who Were They?" (lecture for Banning Museum Residence volunteers, 2007), in possession of author.

28   Loranger, "Women of This House"; Herman Hellman to Joseph Brent Banning, 18 February 1905, box 4, 1996 Addendum, Banning Company Collection, HEH; Newmark, *Sixty Years in Southern California*, 248.

29   Phineas Banning to William Lowber Banning, 3 September 1861, box 2, 1996 Addendum, Banning Company Collection, HEH; Kevin Starr, *Inventing the Dream: California through the Progressive Era* (New York: Oxford University Press, 1985), quote on 52.

30   Cleland, *Cattle on a Thousand Hills*, 127–37, quote on 137. Thousands of carcasses littered the ranchos during the drought; cattle prices plummeted.

J. Ross Browne wrote of the town of San Pedro in 1864: "The principal inhabitants are wild geese, sea-gulls, and dead cattle." Over 70 percent of the cattle in Los Angeles County perished. Cattle ranchers lost their fortunes and allowed their taxes to become delinquent, and many would ultimately lose their land. Merchants also suffered because ranchers could no longer afford to buy their goods. Although agriculture was also adversely affected, the local vineyards survived and helped the region avoid economic devastation. See *Los Angeles Star*, 16 January 1864; Browne, *A Tour Through Arizona, 1864*, quote on 32.

31   *Los Angeles Star*, 12 March 1859; John Shore to Benjamin D. Wilson, 13 June 1858, box 7, Archibald H. Gillespie to Wilson, 4 August 1859, box 8, Benjamin D. Wilson Papers, HEH. On the *Californios* and the parallel between their use of Indian labor and the owners of slave plantations in the South, see Paul Bryan Grey, "Francisco P. Ramirez: A Short Biography," *California History* 84 (Winter 2006–7): 24–25.

32   *Los Angeles Star*, 8 November 1856, 30 January 1858; Robert Fogelson, *The Fragmented Metropolis: Los Angeles, 1850–1930* (Cambridge, Mass.: Harvard University Press, 1967), quote on 205.

33   *Los Angeles Star*, 1, 8, 15 May 1858. Banning might have used his office address in the city to fulfill the residential requirements for the council, loose as they were at the time.

34   Los Angeles Common Council, Minutes of Meetings, vol. 1: 10 May 1858– 7 May 1859, esp. 7 June 1858, LACRC .

35   *Los Angeles Star*, 11 (quote), 18 June 1859.

36   *Los Angeles News*, 9 September 1871; [Joseph Brent Banning?], biographical statement on Phineas Banning, n.d., box 2, and A. A. Polhamus to Joseph Brent Banning, 4 April 1905, box 4, 1996 Addendum, Banning Company Collection, HEH. On the 1860 election, see Ella A. Ludwig, *History of the Harbor District of Los Angeles* (Los Angeles: Historic Record Company, 1926), 322. In the summer of 1854 Phineas's sister Francenia informed their brother William that Phineas had sent her a "paper" with a lead article claiming a "Great Whig victory" for "Mayor Banning," who won in San Pedro by a majority of one vote, with two votes cast. San Pedro was not a city at the time, so there was no municipal election there. Phineas's letter to his sister was probably in jest, but might have revealed the possibility of his sympathy with the Whigs that year before he became active in local Democratic Party politics. See Francenia Alice Banning to William Lowber Banning, 15 June 1854 (quotes), box 2, 1996 Addendum, Banning Company Collection, HEH.

37   *Los Angeles Star*, 12 December 1858; Jane Apostol, "An Army Bride Goes West," *Southern California Quarterly* 72 (Winter 1990): 305–6 (Christmas 1860 story); David M. Jordan, *Winfield Scott Hancock: A Soldier's Life* (Bloomington: Indiana University Press, 1988), 29.

38   Phineas Banning to Mary Sweeny Banning, 16 October 1859, box 2, 1996 Addendum, Banning Company Collection, HEH. On Lady Franklin's visit, see Newmark, *Sixty Years in Southern California*, 306; and Maymie R. Krythe, "The Senator . . . Favorite Coastwise Steamer," *Quarterly Publications of the Historical Society of Southern California* 40 (March 1958): 47.

39   *Los Angeles Star*, 30 April, 15 October 1859. On the Catalina excursions, see *Los Angeles Star*, 11 June 1859 (quote); John Albert Wilson, *History of Los Angeles County, California* (Oakland, Calif.: Thompson and West, 1880), 95.

CHAPTER FIVE

1   Ronald C. Woolsey, "Disunion or Dissent? A New Look at an Old Problem in Southern California Attitudes toward the Civil War," *Southern California Quarterly* 66 (Fall 1984): 185–205; John Robinson, *Los Angeles in Civil War Days, 1860–1865* (Los Angeles: Dawson's Book Shop, 1977), 50–166.

2   Joyce Loranger, interview by the author, 14 November 2007.

3   Katharine S. Banning's transcription of William Lowber Banning to Mary Sweeny Banning, 23 August, 29 October 1861, box 2, 1996 Addendum, Banning Company Collection, HEH.

4   See "The Civil War in Missouri" website, Missouri's Civil War Heritage Foundation, http://www.mocivilwar.org/home.html (accessed 24 September 2007); William E. Parrish, *Turbulent Partnership: Missouri and the Union* (Columbia: University of Missouri Press, 1963), 15–207.

5   *St. Paul Pioneer Press*, 27 November 1893; *National Cyclopaedia of American Biography*, 63 vols. (New York: James T. White, 1898–1984), 16:244; U.S. War Department, *The War of the Rebellion: A Compilation of the Official Records of the Union and Confederate Armies*, 70 vols. (Washington, D.C.: Government Printing Office, 1880–1901), ser. 1, 8:363.

6   A. A. Polhamus to Joseph Brent Banning, 4 April 1905, box 1, 1996 Addendum, Banning Company Collection, HEH.

7   Ibid.; Robinson, *Los Angeles in Civil War Days*, 66.

8   "California Militia Staff Brigadier General, 1861–1866," 15:5, 124, and "Register of Commissions," 17:5, 18:26, California Adjutant General Office, California Military Records in the State Archives, 1858–1923 (on microfilm at the Los Angeles County Library, Rosemead, Calif.); California Adjutant General, *Report of the Adjutant General of the State of California, 1865–1867* (Sacramento: State Printer, 1867), 99; *Los Angeles Star*, 19 December 1857, 11 June 1859; Remi Nadeau, *City-Makers: The Men Who Transformed Los Angeles from Village to Metropolis during the First Great Boom, 1868–1876* (Garden City, N.Y.: Doubleday, 1948), 25–26.

9   *Los Angeles Times*, 7 March 1886; Robinson, *Los Angeles in Civil War Days*, 56–57, 148–49.

10   Robinson, *Los Angeles in Civil War Days*, 109–10, 157; John Albert Wilson, *History of Los Angeles County, California* (Oakland, Calif.: Thompson and West, 1880), 97.

11   U.S. War Department, *War of the Rebellion*, ser. 1, vol. 50, pt. 1: 146–49, 625–626, 653, 677–79, 853, 911–12; pt. 2: 1281–82. See also Aurora Hunt, *The Army of the Pacific: Its Operations in California, Texas, Arizona, New Mexico, Utah, Nevada, Oregon, Washington, Plains Region, Mexico, etc.,*

1860–1866 (Glendale, Calif.: Arthur Clark, 1951), 42–43; Robinson, *Los Angeles in Civil War Days*, 88–91.

12   Donald Chaput, "The Civil War Military Post on Catalina Island," *Southern California Quarterly* 75 (Spring 1993): 37–50; R. C. Drum to J. F. Curtis, 26 December 1863, U.S. War Department, *War of the Rebellion*, ser. 1, vol. 50, pt. 2, p. 709. See also documents relating to the military takeover of Santa Catalina Island, documents 646–50, folder F3753, Military Department—Adjutant General—Indian War Papers, CSA; and Theodore Kornweibel Jr., "The Occupation of Santa Catalina Island during the Civil War," *California Historical Society Quarterly* 46 (December 1967): 345–57; *San Pedro News-Pilot*, 23 November 1911. The barracks building still survives as the Isthmus Yacht Club.

13   *Alta California* (San Francisco), 22 August 1864; Quartermaster General M. C. Meigs to the secretary of war, 19 August 1872, box 527, Quartermaster Consolidated Correspondence File, RG 92-225, USNAW; plan of Drum Barracks buildings, folder 196 B, Solano-Reeve Papers, HEH; Hunt, *The Army of the Pacific*, 42–44; Don McDowell, *The Beat of the Drum: The History, Events and People of Drum Barracks, Wilmington, California* (Santa Ana, Calif.: Graphics, 1993), 35–37. Some of Banning's charges for work on the buildings can be found in January and February entries in his daybook for 1863, volume 85, Banning Company Collection, HEH.

14   Bvt. Brig. Gen. James F. Rusling, "Report of Inspection of the Depot and Post at Drum Barracks, Wilmington, Cal.," February 1867, box 527, Quartermaster Consolidated Correspondence File, RG 92-225, USNAW, quote on 53; Robinson, *Los Angeles in Civil War Days*, 164; Hunt, *The Army of the Pacific*, 43.

15   *The Statutes of California and Amendments to the Codes* (Sacramento, Calif.: State Office), 5th sess., 1863–64, 289–90 (quotes).

16   Rusling, "Report of Inspection of the Depot and Post at Drum Barracks," 30–36, and Agreement, Phineas Banning and United States, 15 October 1864, box 527, Quartermaster Consolidated Correspondence File, RG 92-225, USNAW; *Alta California* (San Francisco), 23 August 1864; drawings of Drum Barracks Aqueduct and proposed Wilmington Ditch and Reservoir, folders 196A and 197, Solano-Reeve Papers, HEH; Erna Risch, *Quartermaster Support of the Army: A History of the Corps, 1775–1939* (Washington, D.C.: Office of the Quartermaster General, 1962), 471.

17   *Los Angeles News*, 21 January (quote), 26 February, 25 March 1865; Rusling, "Report of Inspection of the Depot and Post at Drum Barracks," 31; Maj. Gen. W. H. Halleck to Lt. Gen. U. S. Grant, 8 December 1865, U.S. War Department, *War of the Rebellion*, ser. 1, vol. 50, pt. 2, p. 1290.

18   Rusling, "Report of Inspection of the Depot and Post at Drum Barracks," 32–39, quotes on 37.

19   Ibid., 4–5, 27, 41–42, quote on 5.

20   Ibid., 2–4, quote on 3–4, 48–49, quote on 48; James F. Rusling, *Across America: or, The Great West and the Pacific Coast* (New York: Sheldon, 1874), 331–33, 339–40, quote on 331. See chapter 7 of this volume for the later disposition of Drum Barracks.

21   *Alta California* (San Francisco), 24 October 1859; *Los Angeles News*,
      25 March 1865; *Phineas Banning v. Mitchell and Owens Mining Co.*, 1865,
      case 1112, box 33, Los Angeles Area Court Records, HEH; E. E. Hewitt to
      Benjamin D. Wilson, 17 May 1865, box 10, Benjamin D. Wilson Papers, HEH;
      Harris Newmark, *Sixty Years in Southern California, 1853–1913* (New York:
      Knickerbocker, 1916), 342–43.

22   Newmark, *Sixty Years in Southern California*, 342–45.

23   Rusling, "Report of Inspection of the Depot and Post at Drum Barracks,"
      quote on 45; *Alta California* (San Francisco), 22 August 1864 (quote); J. Ross
      Browne, *A Tour Through Arizona, 1864; Or, Adventures in the Apache Coun-
      try* (repr., Tucson, Ariz.: Arizona Silhouettes, 1951), quotes on 34, 36.

24   W. H. Hutchinson, *Oil, Land, and Politics: The California Career of Thomas
      Robert Bard*, 2 vols. (Norman: University of Oklahoma Press, 1965), 1:48–132;
      James J. Rawls and Walton Bean, *California: An Interpretive History*, 5th ed.
      (New York: McGraw-Hill, 1988), 289–90.

25   Phineas Banning to the mayor and Common Council of Los Angeles,
      12 December 1864, and Ordinance, 16 July 1865, Los Angeles Municipal
      Records, Archives, 6:544, 616, Los Angeles Pioneer Oil Company Collection,
      HEH.

26   *Los Angeles News*, 4 February 1865. Wilson's importance to the venture is
      noted in Patrick H. Downey to Benjamin D. Wilson, 3 April 1865, box 10,
      Benjamin D. Wilson Papers, HEH.

27   *Los Angeles News*, 9 May 1865, 23 February 1866; *Wilmington Journal*,
      27 September 1866 (quote); *Los Angeles Herald*, 11 February 1906; William
      Bracken to trustees of Los Angeles Pioneer Oil Company regarding lease of
      land for 99 years, 11 February 1865, box 1, Matthew Keller Papers, HEH;
      Phineas Banning v. Jose L. Sepulveda et al. (including Los Angeles Pioneer
      Oil Company), 1865, case 1110, box 32, Los Angeles Area Court Records,
      HEH; John W. Shore to J. Lancaster Brent, 9 July 1865, document BT202,
      Joseph Lancaster Brent Papers, HEH; Hiram A. Reid, *History of Pasadena*
      (Pasadena, Calif.: Pasadena History Company, 1895), 76–77.

28   Los Angeles City Council revocation of Los Angeles Pioneer Oil Company
      deed and other documents, 1886, Los Angeles Pioneer Oil Company Collec-
      tion, HEH.

29   Deed to Lot 2, Block A, Bonnie Brae Tract, box 2, 1996 Addendum, Banning
      Company Collection, HEH. On Brent, see Ronald C. Woolsey, *Migrants
      West: Toward the Southern California Frontier* (Sebastopol, Calif.: Grizzly
      Bear, 1996), 57–71.

30   A. A. Polhamus to Joseph Brent Banning, 4 April 1905, box 1, 1996 Adden-
      dum, Banning Company Collection, HEH. On Hancock, see David M. Jordan,
      Winfield Scott Hancock: A Soldier's Life (Bloomington: Indiana University
      Press, 1988).

31   *Los Angeles Star*, 2 May 1863; Newmark, *Sixty Years in Southern California*,
      319–21.

32   Ibid.; *Alta California* (San Francisco), 2 May 1863; Benjamin Hayes to
      A. S. Ensworth, 29 April 1863, Hayes Biography File, San Diego Historical

Society Archives, San Diego, Calif.; Phineas Banning to J. Lancaster Brent, 3 August 1865 (quotes), document BT10, Joseph Lancaster Brent Papers, HEH; U.S. War Department, *War of the Rebellion*, ser. 1, vol. 50, pt. 2, p. 424.

33 *Los Angeles Star*, 2 May 1863 (first quote); A. A. Polhamus to Joseph Brent Banning, 4 April 1905, box 1, 1996 Addendum, Banning Company Collection, HEH; Benjamin Hayes to A. S. Ensworth, 29 April 1863 (quote), Hayes Biography File, San Diego Historical Society Archives, San Diego, Calif.

34 John S. Griffin to Benjamin D. Wilson, 27 October 1864, Benjamin D. Wilson Papers, HEH; *Alta California* (San Francisco), 2 May 1863; Joyce Freeman Loranger, "Phineas Banning: The Stories vs. the Records," *Shoreline* 27 (August 1999): 17.

35 *Los Angeles Star*, 19 December 1863; *Alta California* (San Francisco), 18 December 1863; A. A. Polhamus to Joseph Brent Banning, 4 April 1905 (quote), box 1, 1996 Addendum, Banning Company Collection, HEH; Paul R. Spitzzeri, "Judge Lynch in Session: Popular Justice in Los Angeles, 1850–1875," *Southern California Quarterly* 87 (Summer 2005): 101.

36 Browne, *A Tour Through Arizona, 1864*, quotes on 37, 38; Spitzzeri, "Judge Lynch in Session," 97–100; Robert W. Blew, "Vigilantism in Los Angeles, 1835–1874," *Southern California Quarterly* 54 (Spring 1972): 23–24, quote on 24.

37 *Alta California* (San Francisco), 23 December 1863; John W. Shore to J. Lancaster Brent, 9 July 1865 (quote), document BT202, Joseph Lancaster Brent Papers, HEH; Phineas Banning to N. A. Potter, 18 December 1863 (quote), box 18a, Banning Company Collection, HEH; Los Angeles County Board of Supervisors, Minutes of Meetings, 3: 15 August 1864, Los Angeles County Board of Supervisors Office, Los Angeles, Calif.; Spitzzeri, "Judge Lynch in Session," 101. The eyewitnesses were Harris Newmark, H. D. Barrows, and Banning employee A. A. Polhamus, who wrote: "We hung him from a gate beam." Newmark, *Sixty Years in Southern California*, 327; W. W. Robinson, *Lawyers of Los Angeles* (Los Angeles: Los Angeles Bar Association, 1959), 42–43; A. A. Polhamus to Joseph Brent Banning, 4 April 1905 (quote), box 1, 1996 Addendum, Banning Company Collection, HEH. The envelope holding the case records for this trial concludes with: "Taken from the custody of the Sheriff and hung by a mob." *People v. Charles Wilkins*, 17 December 1863, case 667, Criminal Box 2, Los Angeles Area Court Records, HEH.

38 Mesick Cohn Waite Architects, "Historic Structure Report: General Phineas Banning Residence, Wilmington, California," 1992, 4–15, BRM; John Leonard Connoly Jr., "A Survey of Nineteenth Century Building in Los Angeles" (master's thesis, University of Southern California, 1962), 129–30. For an extended discussion of the context of Phineas Banning and the architecture of the house, see James J. Yoch, *Visionary on the Golden Shore: Phineas Banning in Southern California, 1851–1885* (Wilmington, Calif.: Banning Residence Museum, 2002), 74–89.

39 *Alta California* (San Francisco), 23 August 1864 (first quote), 29 September 1868; Marian Winter, "Phineas Banning's Dream House," *Shoreline* 9 (April 1982): 5–8; Phineas Banning to Benjamin D. Wilson, 15, 16 December 1864, box 10, Benjamin D. Wilson Papers, HEH; unidentified newspaper clipping,

ca. March 1885 (quote), box 2, and A. A. Polhamus to Joseph Brent Banning, 4 April 1905, box 1, 1996 Addendum, Banning Company Collection, HEH.

40   Frank Lecouvreur, *From East Prussia to the Golden Gate* (New York: Angelina Book Concern, 1906), 313; Woolsey, "Disunion or Dissent," 190, 203–5; Robinson, *Los Angeles in Civil War Days*, 152–53.

41   *Los Angeles News*, 20 September 1864; *Stockton Daily Independent*, 14 March 1864; Newmark, *Sixty Years in Southern California*, quote on 296; Robinson, *Los Angeles in Civil War Days*, 149–51. On the Union Party convention, see Hubert Howe Bancroft, *History of California*, 7 vols. (San Francisco: History Company, 1884–90), 7:307–8.

42   Polhamus to Joseph Brent Banning, 4 April 1905, box 1, 1996 Addendum, Banning Company Collection, HEH; *Los Angeles News*, 27, 30 June, 11, 28, 22 July 1865.

43   Hellman to Joseph Brent Banning, 18 February 1905, Polhamus to Joseph Brent Banning, 4 April 1905, box 1, 1996 Addendum, Banning Company Collection, HEH.

44   John S. Griffin to Benjamin D. Wilson, 27 October 1864 (quote), box 10, Benjamin D. Wilson Papers, HEH; *Los Angeles News*, 2, 5, 9, 19 September 1865.

45   *Los Angeles News*, 11 April 1865 (quote); Robinson, *Los Angeles in Civil War Days*, 158–59.

46   Robinson, *Los Angeles in Civil War Days*, quote on 161; Newmark, *Sixty Years in Southern California*, quotes on 337.

47   Newmark, *Sixty Years in Southern California*, 338–39, quotes on 338; Robinson, *Los Angeles in Civil War Days*, 159–62.

48   Maymie Krythe, *Port Admiral: Phineas Banning, 1830–1885* (San Francisco: California Historical Society, 1957), 137.

49   Kilbee Brittain, *The General Phineas Banning Residence Museum*, rev. ed. (Wilmington, Calif.: Friends of Banning Park, 2008), 19. Although California approved the amendment two weeks after the official ratification, it was much further ahead than Phineas's native state of Delaware, which rejected the amendment in 1865 and did not ratify it until 1901. See Steve Mount, "The U.S. Constitution Online," http://www.usconstitution.net/constamrat .html (accessed 10 June 2008).

Chapter Six

1   John F. Stover, *American Railroads*, 2nd ed. (Chicago: University of Chicago Press, 1997); Robert L. Frey, ed., *Railroads in the Nineteenth Century* (New York: Facts on File, 1988), xiii–xxxiii.

2   Frey, *Railroads in the Nineteenth Century*.

3   J. Fletcher Williams, *A History of the City of St. Paul and of the County of Ramsey, Minnesota* (St. Paul: Minnesota Historical Society, 1876), 421; John L. Harnsberger, "Land, Lobbies, Railroads and the Origins of Duluth," *Minnesota History* 37 (September 1960): 89; Theodore C. Blegen, *Minnesota: A History of the State*, rev. ed. (Minneapolis: University of Minnesota Press, 1975), 296–97.

4   Harnsberger, "Land, Lobbies, Railroads," quote on 90; Blegen, *Minnesota*,
      297; Martin Ridge, *Ignatius Donnelly: The Portrait of a Politician* (Chicago:
      University of Chicago Press, 1962), 96–97. The early chronology of Banning's
      involvement is noted in *St. Paul Pioneer Press*, 11 December 1870.

5   Ledgers, vols. 6, 8, box 1, vols. 12, 15, 16, box 2, William Branch and Company
      Records, MHC; John H. Guthman, "William L. Banning," Biography Files,
      MHC.

6   William R. Marshall, letter of introduction for William Lowber Banning,
      20 January 1866, box 6, 1996 Addendum, Banning Company Collection,
      HEH; copy of William Lowber Banning to Jay Cooke, 20 December 1868,
      box 1, Jay Cooke Papers, MHC; T. M. Newsom, *Pen Pictures of St. Paul,
      Minnesota* (St. Paul, Minn.: for the author, 1886), 505–6.

7   Harnsberger, "Land, Lobbies, Railroads," 92–93; Frey, *Railroads in the Nine-
      teenth Century*, 57–63, 289; Jocelyn Wills, *Boosters, Hustlers and Speculators:
      Entrepreneurial Culture and the Rise of Minneapolis and St. Paul, 1849–1883*
      (St. Paul: Minnesota Historical Society Press, 2005), 114–19.

8   Newspaper clipping (ca. 1869) for land sale, microfilm roll 46, Ignatius
      Donnelly Papers, MHC; Harnsberger, "Land, Lobbies, Railroads," 93; Don L.
      Hofsommer, *Minneapolis and the Age of Railways* (Minneapolis: University
      of Minnesota Press, 2005), 32–33; Harold F. Peterson, "Early Minnesota Rail-
      roads and the Quest for Settlers," *Minnesota History* 13 (March 1932): 37.

9   William Lowber Banning to Donnelly, 2, 8, 13, 16, 18, 19, 20, 25 April 1870,
      microfilm roll 43, Ignatius Donnelly Papers, MHC; William Lowber Banning
      to Alexander Ramsey, 8, 26 March 1870 (quotes), microfilm roll 19, Alexan-
      der Ramsey Papers, MHC; Harnsberger, "Land, Lobbies, Railroads," 95–100;
      Ridge, *Ignatius Donnelly*, 129–31.

10   William Lowber Banning to Alexander Ramsey, 26 March 1870, microfilm
      roll 19, Alexander Ramsey Papers, MHC; Hofsommer, *Minneapolis and the
      Age of Railways*, quote on 32; Frederick Ayer, *Reminiscences of Frederick Ayer*
      (Boston: Merrymount, 1923), quote on 69.

11   Newspaper clipping (1870), scrapbook 9, 1996 Addendum, Banning Company
      Collection, HEH; Harnsberger, "Land, Lobbies, Railroads," 93; Hofsommer,
      Minneapolis and the Age of Railways, 32–34.

12   Frey, *Railroads in the Nineteenth Century*, 62, 287–89; Eugene Smalley,
      History of the Northern Pacific Railroad (New York: Putnam, 1883), 163–89,
      quote on 164, 293–95; Louis T. Renz, *The Northern Pacific Railroad* (Fairfield,
      Wash.: Ye Galleon, 1980), 34, 38, 40–41, 200; C. C. Andrews, *History of
      St. Paul, Minnesota* (Syracuse, N.Y.: D. Mason, 1890), 414–15.

13   *Southern Californian*, 30 November 1854 (quote), 8 February, 25 April 1855;
      Los Angeles Star, 27 March 1858.

14   George Goss to Phineas Banning, 3 June 1861, box 32, Abel Stearns Papers,
      HEH; John W. Robinson, *Southern California's First Railroad: The Los
      Angeles and San Pedro Railroad, 1869–1873* (Los Angeles: Dawson's Book
      Shop, 1978), 26–27; Judson A. Grenier with Robert C. Gillingham, *California
      Legacy: The James Alexander Watson–María Dolores Domínguez de Watson
      Family, 1820–1980* (Los Angeles: Watson Land Company, 1987), 190–91;

Harris Newmark, *Sixty Years in Southern California, 1853–1913* (New York: Knickerbocker, 1916), 318; William P. Reynolds to Benjamin D. Wilson, 30 November 1864, box 10, Benjamin D. Wilson Papers, HEH.

15   *Journal of the Senate during the Sixteenth Session of the Legislature of the State of California, 1865–1866* (Sacramento: State Printer, 1866), 209, 216, 236; *Los Angeles News*, 9 February 1866; Robinson, *Southern California's First Railroad*, 28–29; Grenier, *California Legacy*, 207.

16   Southwest Pacific Railroad Company, Atlantic and Pacific Railroad Company, *Statutes, Conveyances and Documents* (New York: Stockholder Job Printing Office, 1867), 4, RB 36101, HEH; Frey, *Railroads in the Nineteenth Century*, 303, 389; H. Craig Miner, *The St. Louis–San Francisco Transcontinental Railroad: The Thirty-fifth Parallel Project, 1853–1890* (Lawrence: University Press of Kansas, 1972).

17   *Journal of the Senate during the Seventeenth Session of the Legislature of the State of California, 1867–1868* (Sacramento: State Printer, 1868), 141; Charles Ruggles Westbrook, "The Securing of a Transcontinental Railroad Tie for Los Angeles and the Development of the Adjoining Port Facilities, from the Founding of San Pedro to 1881" (master's thesis, University of Southern California, 1966), 54; Robinson, *Southern California's First Railroad*, 29–31.

18   *Los Angeles News*, 17 December 1867, 21, 25 February, 19, 27 March 1868; *Los Angeles Republican*, 15 February 1868; Franklin Hoyt, "The Los Angeles & San Pedro: First Railroad South of the Tehachapis," *California Historical Society Quarterly* 32 (December 1953): 327–28; Remi Nadeau, *City-Makers: The Men Who Transformed Los Angeles from Village to Metropolis during the First Great Boom, 1868–1876* (Garden City, N.Y.: Doubleday, 1948), quote on 26–27.

19   Hoyt, "The Los Angeles & San Pedro," 329; Lionel A. Sheldon, "Biographical Sketch of Phineas Banning," 1888, 9–10, MSS C-D 771, BANC; Banning & Company ledgers, vols. 110 and 111, Banning Company Collection, HEH; Matthew Keller to J. Lancaster Brent, 6 August 1868, document BT142, Joseph Lancaster Brent Papers, HEH; June Margaret Crampton, "A History of the Los Angeles and San Pedro Railroad" (master's thesis, University of Southern California, 1929), 17, 20; *Alta California* (San Francisco), 27 June 1867. On Tichenor, see Alonzo Phelps, *Contemporary Biography of California's Representative Men* (San Francisco: A. L. Bancroft, 1881), 400–403; Lyman L. Palmer, *History of Mendocino County, California* (San Francisco: Alley, Bowen, 1880), 419–21, 432. On Banning's mining interests and those companies, see *Los Angeles Star*, 12 August 1863; *Syracuse Herald*, 14 March 1934; entries for La Abundancia Mining Company, January and June 1870, vol. 107, and the Eureka Mining Company, 24 May 1870, vol. 106, Banning Company Collection, HEH; Arthur B. Perkins, "Mining Camps of the Soledad," part 1, *Historical Society of Southern California Quarterly* 40 (June 1958): 167.

20   *Alta California* (San Francisco), 23 July 1868; *Los Angeles Star*, 3 July 1869; Hoyt, "The Los Angeles & San Pedro," 329–33; Robinson, *Southern California's First Railroad*, 35–52; Holly Charmain Kane, "Arriving in Los Angeles: Railroad Depots as Gateways to the California Dream" (master's thesis, University of Southern California, 2007), 8–12.

21   *Los Angeles News*, 28 May, 11 June, 10, 24, September 1870, 9 September,
     25 November 1871; *San Luis Obispo Tribune*, 11 June 1870; Hoyt, "The
     Los Angeles & San Pedro," 329–42; Robinson, *Southern California's First
     Railroad*, 58–77.

22   *Weekly Arizona Miner*, 3 December 1870; *Los Angeles News*, 3 December 1870;
     Nadeau, *City-Makers*, 89–91; John R. Signor, *Beaumont Hill: Southern Pacific's
     Southern California Gateway* (San Marino, Calif.: Golden West Books, 1990),
     8–9.

23   Sheldon, "Biographical Sketch of Phineas Banning," 10; William Hyde to
     H. D. Bacon, 29 November, 2, 3, 4 December 1869, Hyde to John M. Fry,
     11 December 1869, box 1, William B. Hyde Papers, SU; Larry Mullaly and
     Bruce Petty, *The Southern Pacific in Los Angeles, 1873–1996* (San Marino,
     Calif.: Golden West Books and the Los Angeles Railroad Heritage Founda-
     tion, 2002), 11.

24   *Los Angeles News*, 5, 12 February 1870; Robinson, *Southern California's First
     Railroad*, 79–81; Nadeau, *City-Makers*, 71–74.

25   *Los Angeles News*, 13, 27 July 1872; Phineas Banning to Wilson, 21 December
     1871, and L. J. Rose to Wilson, 26 December 1871, box 15, Benjamin D. Wilson
     Papers, HEH; copy of Thomas D. Mott and Benjamin D. Wilson to Leland
     Stanford, 5 May 1872, box 1, Sepulveda/Mott Collection, SCWHR; Robinson,
     Southern California's First Railroad, 81–84.

26   Robinson, *Southern California's First Railroad*, 84–85; Robert M. Fogelson,
     The Fragmented Metropolis: Los Angeles, 1850–1930 (Cambridge, Mass.:
     Harvard University Press, 1967), 52–54.

27   L. J. Rose to Wilson, 24 July 1872 (quote), box 16, Benjamin D. Wilson Papers,
     HEH; Los Angeles County Board of Supervisors, Minutes of Meetings, 5: 5,
     6 August, 7 September 1872, Los Angeles County Board of Supervisors
     Office, Los Angeles, Calif.; *Los Angeles News*, 10 August, 14, 21 September
     1872; Frank B. Putnam, "Serape to Levi … Southern Pacific," *Historical Society
     of Southern California Quarterly* 38 (September 1956): 213–14.

28   Hyde to Los Angeles County Board of Supervisors, 14 September 1872, Hyde
     to George E. Gray, 1 October 1872, Hyde to Leland Stanford, 10 October 1872
     (quote), Hyde to Collis P. Huntington, 10 October (quote), 7 December
     (quote), 8 December (quote) 1872, box 1, William B. Hyde Papers, SU.

29   Phineas Banning to Wilson, 26 October 1872, box 16, Benjamin D. Wilson
     Papers, HEH; *Los Angeles Star*, 23 October 1872; *Los Angeles News*,
     19, 26 October 1872; Hyde to Huntington, 8 December 1872, box 1, William B.
     Hyde Papers, SU; R. M. Widney, "Which Subsidy Shall I Vote For, or Should
     I Vote for Both?" (1872 pamphlet), reprinted in *Historical Society of Southern
     California Quarterly* 38 (December 1956): 347–62; Robinson, *Southern Cali-
     fornia's First Railroad*, 86–89; Putnam, "Serape to Levi," 216.

30   Nadeau, *City-Makers*, 232. On the Southern Pacific's tax assessment, see
     Los Angeles County Board of Supervisors, Minutes of Meetings, 7: 9 March,
     23 July 1881, 8: 10 May, 6 November 1883, Los Angeles County Board of
     Supervisors Office, Los Angeles, Calif.; *Los Angeles Herald*, 23 July 1881;
     Los Angeles Times, 21 September 1882, 19 April, 5 June, 7 November 1883.

31   *Los Angeles Herald*, 20 November 1873, 17 October 1874; Phineas Banning
to Benjamin D. Wilson, November 28, 1874, David D. Colton to Wilson,
4 December 1874, box 17, Benjamin D. Wilson Papers, HEH. On the transfer
of the LA&SP to the Southern Pacific, see Robinson, *Southern California's
First Railroad*, 90.

32   *Los Angeles Herald*, 8 May 1874, 12, 20 January, 6 March, 25 June 1875,
22 January 1876; Collis P. Huntington, *Letters from Collis P. Huntington to
Mark Hopkins, Leland Stanford, Charles Crocker, E. B. Crocker, Charles F.
Crocker, and D. D. Cotton* [*sic*], *from August 20, 1867, to* [*March 31, 1876*],
3 vols. (New York: n.p., 1892–94), various letters regarding Sen. John P. Jones
dated 1875 in vol. 3; Paul Spitzerri, "The Road to Independence: The Los
Angeles and Independence Railroad and the Conception of a City," *Southern
California Quarterly* 83 (Spring 2001): 23–58.

33   Agreement between Phineas Banning and Common Council of Yuma Village,
14 April 1877, box 18b, Banning Company Collection, HEH; Collis P. Huntington to David D. Colton, 25 December 1876, box 9, Henry E. Huntington Collection, HEH; David F. Myrick, *Railroads of Arizona*, 3 vols. (Berkeley, Calif.:
Howell-North Books, 1975–84), 1:14–19, quote on 16.

34   Phineas Banning to Lucy Banning, 6 January 1877, box 6, 1985 Addendum,
Banning Company Collection, HEH; Myrick, *Railroads of Arizona*, 1:17;
James H. McClintock, *Arizona*, 3 vols. (Chicago: S. J. Clarke, 1916), quote
on 1:290. The *San Francisco Chronicle*, 22 November 1883, printed details
of Banning's payments from the Southern Pacific based on David Colton's
correspondence with the Big Four.

35   Huntington to David D. Colton, 27 September 1875 (quote), in Salvador
Ramirez, *The Octopus Speaks: The Colton Letters* (Carlsbad, Calif.: Tentacled
Press, 1982), 197; Thomas Sheridan, *Arizona: A History* (Tucson: University
of Arizona Press, 1995), quote on 116; Jay J. Wagoner, *Arizona Territory 1863–
1912: A Political History* (Tucson: University of Arizona Press, 1970), 256–57.

36   Phineas Banning to Mary Hollister Banning, 15 August 1877, box 6, 1985 Addendum, Banning Company Collection, HEH; Myrick, *Railroads of Arizona*,
1:18–19; Sheridan, *Arizona*, 116–17; McClintock, *Arizona*, 1:290–93; David
Lavender, *The Great Persuader* (Garden City, N.Y.: Doubleday, 1970), 318–27.

37   Phineas Banning to Matthew Keller, 2 August 1878, box 5, 1985 Addendum,
Banning Company Collection, HEH; Mark Hopkins, *Letters from Mark Hop-
kins, Leland Stanford, Charles F. Crocker, and David D. Colton, to Collis P.
Huntington, from August 27th, 1869, to December 30th, 1879* (New York:
J. C. Rankin, 1891), 208–9; Benjamin C. Truman to Joseph Brent Banning,
6 February 1905 (quote), box 18b, Banning Company Collection, HEH.

38   Charles Crocker to Collis P. Huntington, 6 October 1882 (quote), box 2,
Charles Crocker Correspondence, HEH.

39   On the Southern Pacific Railroad's economic and political practices, see,
among many others, George Mowry, *The California Progressives* (Berkeley:
University of California Press, 1951), esp. 1–22; William Deverell, *Railroad
Crossing: Californians and the Railroad, 1850–1910* (Berkeley: University of
California Press, 1994); and chapter 8, below.

CHAPTER SEVEN

1   *Los Angeles News*, 16 January 1867; *Wilmington Journal*, 6 April, 25 May 1867.

2   Charles S. Lovell to Col. R. M. Scott, 6 September 1866, box 1273, Quartermaster Consolidated Correspondence File, RG 92-225, USNAW; H. B. Wharfield, *Fort Yuma on the Colorado River* (El Cajon, Calif.: for the author, 1968), 156; Erna Risch, *Quartermaster Support of the Army: A History of the Corps, 1775–1939* (Washington, D.C.: Office of the Quartermaster General, 1962), 473; Frank Rolfe, "Early Day Los Angeles: A Great Wagon Train Center," *Historical Society of Southern California Quarterly* 35 (December 1953): 309–10, 316–37; James F. Rusling, *Across America: or, The Great West and the Pacific Coast* (New York: Sheldon, 1874), 330; Remi Nadeau, *City-Makers: The Men Who Transformed Los Angeles from Village to Metropolis during the First Great Boom, 1868–1876* (Garden City, N.Y.: Doubleday, 1948), 39–40.

3   *Wilmington Journal*, 18 June, 27 September 1866; John W. Robinson, *Gateways to Southern California: Indian Footpaths, Horse Trails, Wagon Roads, Railroads and Highways* (Arcadia, Calif.: Big Santa Anita Historical Society, 2005), 123–24; John Albert Wilson, *History of Los Angeles County, California* (Oakland, Calif.: Thompson and West, 1880), 74–75; J. J. Warner, Benjamin Hayes, and J. P. Widney, *An Historical Sketch of Los Angeles County, California* (Los Angeles: Louis Lewin, 1876), 124.

4   L. J. Rose Jr., *L. J. Rose of Sunnyslope, 1827–1899: California Pioneer, Fruit Grower, Wine Maker, Horse Breeder* (San Marino, Calif.: Huntington Library, 1959), 93; Felix Riesenberg Jr., *The Golden Road: The Story of California's Spanish Mission Trail* (New York: McGraw-Hill, 1962), quotes on 166; Captain William Banning and George Hugh Banning, *Six Horses* (New York: Century, 1930), 365–69; *The First Los Angeles City and County Directory, 1872*, reprint ed. (Los Angeles: Ward Ritchie, 1963), n.p.

5   Banning & Company business records, 1864–67, vols. 90–102, Banning Company Collection, HEH; research files on Wyatt Earp, box 16, Stuart N. Lake Papers, HEH; Donald Chaput, *Virgil Earp, Western Peace Officer* (Encampment, Wyo.: Affiliated Writers of America, 1994), 13. The Earp story is mentioned in Stuart N. Lake, *Wyatt Earp: Frontier Marshal* (Boston: Houghton Mifflin, 1931), 21–22; Oliver Vickery, *Harbor Heritage: Tales of the Harbor Area of Los Angeles, California* (Mountain View, Calif.: Morgan, 1979), 47–50; Lee A. Silva, *Wyatt Earp: A Biography of the Legend; Vol. 1, The Cowtown Years* (Santa Ana, Calif.: Graphic, 2002), 46–50.

6   Phineas Banning to Benjamin D. Wilson, 2 March 1872, box 16, David D. Colton to Wilson, 4 December 1874, box 18, Benjamin D. Wilson Papers, HEH; J. M. Guinn, "Los Angeles in the Later Sixties and Early Seventies," *Annual Publications of the Historical Society of Southern California* 3 (1893), 63–68, quote on 67; *Los Angeles Daily Herald*, 20 November 1873, 7 January, 18 July, 17 October 1874; Blanche Christie, "Phineas Banning with Special Reference to the Development of Transportation in Southern California" (master's thesis, University of Southern California, 1933), 109–13.

7   Aliso Tract Map, January 1869, Map Collection, SCWHR (my thanks to
Betty Uyeda for bringing this map to my attention); Articles of Incorporation, Aliso Homestead Association, 1869, box 2, Los Angeles County Incorporation Records, SCWHR; Minutes of the Los Angeles Common Council,
3 June 1875, 9:368, and Banning Street file, box C-2533, LACRC. By the 1890s,
the area surrounding Banning Street had become a rough part of town, and
reports of crime and violence associated with residents of Banning Street
were common in city newspapers. In 1924 it was part of a barrio district
quarantined because of an outbreak of pneumonic plague. Banning Street
still exists, although it has been shortened over the years to accommodate
industrial plants. On the 1924 plague epidemic, see William Deverell, *Whitewashed Adobe: The Rise of Los Angeles and the Remaking of Its Mexican Past*
(Berkeley: University of California Press, 2004), 172–206.

8   Patent application 175,266 (1875) on the United States Patent and Trademark
Office website, http://patimg2.uspto.gov/.piw?Docid=00175266&idkey=
NONE (accessed 27 January 2010). Also on the Google Patents website at
http://www.google.com/patents?id=HNVSAAAAEBAJ&dq=175266
(accessed 27 January 2010); entry in ledger, 1869–70, vol. 109, Banning Company Collection, HEH; *Los Angeles Daily Herald*, 2, 18 February 1876.

9   Index to Deeds (1865–85), Los Angeles County Recorder's Office, Norwalk,
Calif.; John S. Griffin to Benjamin D. Wilson, 22 November 1873, Wilson to
Griffin, 24 November 1873, box 17, Benjamin D. Wilson Papers, HEH; Hiram
A. Reid, *History of Pasadena* (Pasadena: Pasadena History Company, 1895),
77–78; Harold David Carew, *History of Pasadena and the San Gabriel Valley*,
3 vols. (Chicago: S. J. Clarke, 1930), 1:276–78.

10   Phineas Banning to General R. O. Taylor, 20 November 1867, copy of Nathan
Porter to General E. O. C. Ord, 16 June 1869, Bvt. Brig. Gen. James F. Rusling,
"Report of Inspection of the Depot and Post at Drum Barracks, Wilmington,
Cal.," February 1867, and other material in box 527, Quartermaster Consoli-
dated Correspondence File, RG 92-225, USNAW; Asst. Adj. Gen. J. C. Kelton,
Special Orders No. 186, 11 November 1871, extract from Quartermaster
General M. C. Meigs to Gen. Robert Allen, 29 January 1872, and extract of
report in Adjutant General's Office in Washington, D.C., 4 March 1872,
box 14, Benjamin D. Wilson Papers, HEH.

11   Phineas Banning to David Alexander, 15 January 1873, Richard C. McCormick
to Banning, 29 March 1873, Phineas Banning to Wilson, 3 August 1873,
box 17, Benjamin D. Wilson Papers, HEH; Aurora Hunt, *The Army of the
Pacific: Its Operations in California, Texas, Arizona, New Mexico, Utah,
Nevada, Oregon, Washington, Plains Region, Mexico, etc., 1860–1866* (Glendale, Calif.: Arthur Clark, 1951), 47–48.

12   *Los Angeles Daily Herald*, 20 August 1878; Hunt, *Army of the Pacific*, 48.

13   Land grant agreement, 2 January 1875, box 18, Addendum II, Benjamin D.
Wilson Papers, HEH; *Los Angeles Daily Herald*, 14 May 1874; Wilson, *History
of Los Angeles County*, quote on 145; Muriel Aloha Tracy, "The Life of
Benjamin D. Wilson" (master's thesis, University of Southern California,
1934), 86–92.

14   Phineas Banning to Benjamin D. Wilson, 22 January 1866, box 11, Benjamin D. Wilson Papers, HEH; photocopy of Benjamin C. Truman to Joseph Brent Banning, 6 February 1905, box 18b, Banning Company Collection, HEH; Sarah Bixby-Smith, *Adobe Days* (1925; repr., Lincoln: University of Nebraska Press, 1987), 119–20.

15   Benjamin D. Wilson to Phineas Banning, 16 December 1870, box 14, John S. Griffin to Wilson, 12 January 1872, J. P. Widney to Wilson, 12 January 1872, box 15, Benjamin D. Wilson Papers, HEH; Banning to Senator Cornelius C. Cole, 12 October 1871, box 3, Cole Family Papers, UCLA.

16   *Los Angeles Star*, 26 August 1871, 27 February 1872; *Los Angeles News*, 27 April, 16 November 1872; *Los Angeles Daily Herald*, 4 October 1873; Phineas Banning to Benjamin D. Wilson, 4 January 1873, Phineas Banning to David Alexander, 15 January 1873, box 17, Wilson to several California congressmen, 1876, box 19, Benjamin D. Wilson Papers, HEH; Wilson, *History of Los Angeles County*, 142–43.

17   *Los Angeles Daily Herald*, 21, 23, 25 January, 12 February 1881; Memorials to Congress, 1877, 1881, Joseph P. Widney Scrapbooks, SCWHR; John H. Krenkel, "Development of the Port of Los Angeles," *American Neptune* 25 (October 1965): 263. Always the entrepreneur, Banning saw another potential government contract in providing rocks for the breakwater in 1883: "There's millions in it," he wrote to a potential business partner, although neither lived long enough to take advantage of the opportunity. Phineas Banning to James de Barth Shorb, 26 July 1883 (quote), box 8, James de Barth Shorb Papers, HEH.

18   Articles of Incorporation, Wilmington Canal and Reservoir Company, 1872, box 66, Los Angeles County Incorporation Records, SCWHR; Phineas Banning to Benjamin D. Wilson, 12 April 1870, box 14, 11 February, 19 April 1872, box 16, Benjamin D. Wilson Papers, HEH; Robert Cameron Gillingham, *The Rancho San Pedro: The Story of a Famous Rancho in Los Angeles County and Its Owners, The Dominguez Family* (Los Angeles: Cole-Holmquist, 1961), 254–55; *Los Angeles Daily Herald*, 19 August 1881; *Los Angeles Times*, 8 November 1883. As noted later in this chapter, Phineas's nephew William L. Banning was the son of John A. Banning Jr.

19   *Los Angeles Daily Herald*, 20 February 1878; copy of act to incorporate Wilmington, 20 February 1872, box 16, Benjamin D. Wilson Papers, HEH; Benjamin C. Truman to Joseph Brent Banning, 6 February 1905, box 18b, Banning Company Collection, HEH; J. Ross Browne, *A Tour Through Arizona, 1864; Or, Adventures in the Apache Country* (repr., Tucson: Arizona Silhouettes, 1951), 34; Wilson, *History of Los Angeles County*, 143. A. A. Polhamus recalled that Banning was the major force behind the Wilmington incorporation; A. A. Polhamus to Charles Healey, 24 March 1902, box 2, Banning Company Collection, HEH.

20   Survey, deeds, agreements and other material regarding tidelands in box 2, Banning Company Collection, HEH; copy of act authorizing Phineas Banning to purchase certain tidelands in Los Angeles County, 1872, box 17, James de Barth Shorb to Benjamin D. Wilson, 8, 23, 25, 28 February 1878, George H. Smith to Wilson, 4 March 1878, box 21, Benjamin D. Wilson Papers, HEH; *Los Angeles Daily Herald*, 21 January 1880 (quote).

21   *Los Angeles Daily Herald*, 10 April 1874 (quote), 1 January 1875.

22   *Los Angeles News*, 14 August 1868; *Los Angeles Daily Herald*, 20 December 1873, 21 January 1874; *Los Angeles Star*, 4 February 1879; *San Pedro Shipping Gazette*, 6 October 1883; Richard Webster Barsness, "The Maritime Development of San Pedro Bay, California, 1821–1921" (PhD diss., University of Minnesota, 1963), 248–49; William Andrew Spalding, *William Andrew Spalding, Los Angeles Newspaperman: An Autobiography Account* (San Marino, Calif.: Huntington Library, 1961), 51–53, quote on 52.

23   Balfour, Guthrie and Company to Phineas Banning, 21 January 1880, letterbook 5, Goodall, Perkins & Company to Phineas Banning, 12 October 1881, box 18a, 28 February 1880, letterbook 5, J. C. Stubbs to Phineas Banning, 9 April 1881, S. Gage to Phineas Banning, 23 August 1881, box 18a, A. N. Towne to Phineas Banning, 16 December 1878, 20 January 1879, letterbook 4, 12 February 1880, letterbook 5, 19 July 1880, letterbook 6, H. B. McClellan to Phineas Banning, 14 August 1880, letterbook 6, 13, 23 December 1880, box 18b, Banning Company Collection, HEH. There are many other such letters in the collection. Some of Phineas Banning's replies can be found in box 1, 1985 Addendum, Banning Company Collection, HEH.

24   *Los Angeles Express*, 23 April 1880; *Los Angeles Daily Herald*, 11 January 1881; *Los Angeles Times*, 7 May 1882; Larry Mullaly and Bruce Petty, *The Southern Pacific in Los Angeles, 1873–1996* (San Marino, Calif.: Golden West Books and the Los Angeles Railroad Heritage Foundation, 2002), 24–27; John W. Robinson, *Southern California's First Railroad: The Los Angeles and San Pedro Railroad, 1869–1873* (Los Angeles: Dawson's Book Shop, 1978), 97.

25   *Los Angeles Daily Herald*, 9, 10, 11 November 1881; *Los Angeles Times*, 11 February, 6 March 1885; Walter D. Stephenson to Phineas Banning, 10 November 1881, box 18b, Banning Company Collection, HEH. On previous negotiations between Phineas Banning and the initial applicants of the 1881 franchise, see J. H. McKune to W. H. Perry, 17 December 1881, Phineas Banning to Wallace Woodworth, 31 December 1881, unknown to Woodworth, 18 April 1882, box 10, Wallace Woodworth Collection, SCWHR.

26   *Los Angeles News*, 8 August 1865; *Los Angeles Daily Herald*, 14 June, 7 July 1881; *Los Angeles Times*, 5, 13, 26 (quote) June, 20 July, 8 August 1883.

27   Articles of Incorporation, Wilmington Transportation Company, 1884, box 9, Wilmington Development Company, 1884, box 10, Los Angeles County Incorporation Records, SCWHR.

28   Copy of James Menzies to Mr. Wilson, 4 October 1883 (original in files of British Consul of Los Angeles), box 8, 1985 Addendum, Banning Company Collection, HEH.

29   *Los Angeles Times*, 29 February, 20, 21 March 2008; Rusling, *Across America*, 332–34, quote on 333; James J. Yoch, *Visionary on the Golden Shore: Phineas Banning in Southern California, 1851–1885* (Wilmington, Calif.: Banning Residence Museum, 2002), 41–42.

30   A. A. Polhamus to Joseph Brent Banning, 4 April 1905 (quote), box 18b, Banning Company Collection, HEH; Los Angeles County Assessor Records, 1867, SCWHR.

31   Joyce Freeman Loranger, "Phineas Banning: The Stories vs. the Record,"
      Shoreline 27 (August 1999): 16. Maymie Krythe mentions the trip at this time,
      but, as Loranger has deduced, has the wrong date for Bessie's birth and death
      based on an incorrect gravestone. See *Port Admiral: Phineas Banning, 1830–
      1885* (San Francisco: California Historical Society, 1957), 163. Bessie's remains
      were later moved to Wilmington Cemetery.

32   *Alta California* (San Francisco), 13 January 1868; *Los Angeles Star*, 20 June
      1868; Joyce Loranger, "Women of This House—Who Were They?" (lecture for
      Banning Museum Residence volunteers, 2007), copy in possession of author.

33   Lucy H. Tichenor to Margaret Wilson, 28 January 1868, box 12, Benjamin D.
      Wilson Papers, HEH; *Los Angeles News*, 12 February 1868. The wording of
      Tichenor's letter suggests that there might have been other Miss Mariannas
      (possibly before Rebecca died), but the author has not found any evidence of
      them. Phineas Banning must have been very frustrated with his situation, and
      soon after his return to Wilmington in February he was charged and convicted
      of assault and battery on an unnamed victim. The offense could not have been
      that serious, however, as he was only fined $5. Minutes of Justice of the Peace
      Proceedings, 1863–68, 527, Los Angeles Area Court Records, HEH.

34   Joyce Freeman Loranger, research notes on Mary Elizabeth Hollister, 1994, in
      possession of the author; J. M. Guinn, *History of the State of California and
      Biographical Record of Santa Cruz, San Benito, Monterey and San Luis
      Obispo Counties* (Chicago: Chapman, 1903), 311–12; Yda Addis Storke,
      *A Memorial and Biographical History of the Counties of Santa Barbara,
      San Luis Obispo and Ventura, California* (Chicago: Lewis, 1891), 326.

35   Arthur M. Ellis, comp., *Historical Review, Seventy-fifth Anniversary, May 5,
      1929, Los Angeles Lodge, no. 42, F. & A. M.* (Los Angeles: Los Angeles Lodge
      42, 1929), 31–32, 103; Loranger, research notes on Mary Elizabeth Hollister.

36   Harris Newmark, *Sixty Years in Southern California, 1853–1913* (New York:
      Knickerbocker, 1916), 368; Phineas Banning to Mary E. Hollister, 5, 22 Au-
      gust, 11 November, 31 December 1869, and undated, box 6, 1985 Addendum,
      Banning Company Collection, HEH; Margaret Wilson to Benjamin D. Wil-
      son, 1 November 1869 (quote), box 13, Benjamin D. Wilson Papers, HEH.
      The wedding is noted in the *Los Angeles Star*, 26 February 1870 and *San Luis
      Obispo Tribune Weekly*, 26 February 1870. The site of the nuptials, now called
      the Stowe House, is frequently used for weddings.

37   Joyce Loranger, research notes on Sanford Family, BRM; Joyce Loranger
      (former BRM research specialist), interview by the author, 14 November
      2007; J. M. Guinn, *A History of California and an Extended History of Its
      Southern Coast Counties*, 2 vols. (Los Angeles, Calif.: Historic Record Com-
      pany, 1907), 2:1840–41; *Illustrated History of San Joaquin County, California*
      (Chicago: Lewis, 1890), 252.

38   Loranger, "Women of This House—Who Were They?"; *Los Angeles Daily
      Herald*, 31 July 1874, 28 March 1875, 18 February 1876; Kilbee Brittain, *The
      General Phineas Banning Residence Museum*, rev. ed. (Wilmington, Calif.:
      Friends of Banning Park, 2008), 35. Harriet might have eventually moved
      back to her home state of Missouri by 1870. Ellen's remains were later moved
      to Rosedale Cemetery in Los Angeles.

39   *Los Angeles Daily Herald*, 24 October 1880, 3 May, 24 July 1881.

40   Newmark, *Sixty Years in Southern California*, 356; *Los Angeles Daily Herald*, 24 July 1881; *Los Angeles Times*, 15 September, 3 October 1883; "Roll of Certified Attorneys," 1850–1922, 5 vols., RG–Supreme Court of California, CSA. Joseph acted as a lawyer at least once for his company in the 1890s, but certification as a lawyer for that situation would not have been required.

41   Phineas Banning to Hancock Banning, 21 June 1884, box 12, Banning Company Collection, HEH.

42   *Los Angeles Daily Herald*, 20 August 1880 (quote); *Los Angeles Times*, 12 February 1911; research files, BRM; Mesick Cohn Waite Architects, "Historic Structure Report: General Phineas Banning Residence, Wilmington, California," 1992, 27–30, BRM; U.S. Census Office, 9th and 10th Census, (1870 and 1880), Wilmington Township, Calif., as scanned by Ancestry.com, http://www.ancestry.com; Wilson, *History of Los Angeles County*, 98.

43   Phineas Banning to Mary E. H. Banning, 26 January 1873, and others, box 6, 1985 Addendum, Banning Company Collection, HEH; Mary E. H. Banning to Margaret Wilson, 8 October 1874, box 18, Benjamin D. Wilson Papers, HEH.

44   Joyce Loranger, research notes, BRM; Lionel A. Sheldon, "Biographical Sketch of Phineas Banning," 1888, MSS C-D 771, 11, BANC; Phineas Banning to Hancock Banning, 27 May 1884, box 12, Banning Company Collection, HEH; *Los Angeles Times*, 31 July 1883.

45   U.S. Census Office, 9th Census (1870), Wilmington Township, Calif.; *Los Angeles Daily Herald*, 19 July 1879; Warner, Hayes, and Widney, *An Historical Sketch of Los Angeles County*, 67.

46   *St. Paul Pioneer Press*, 9 November 1877; Arthur Naftalin, "The Tradition of Protest and the Roots of the Farmer-Labor Party," *Minnesota History* 35 (June 1956): 58; Martin Ridge, *Ignatius Donnelly: The Portrait of a Politician* (Chicago: University of Chicago Press, 1962), 176–77; Joseph A. Burnquist, ed., *Minnesota and Its People*, 3 vols. (Chicago: S. J. Clarke, 1924), 1:301.

47   *St. Paul City Directory* (St. Paul, Minn.: R. L. Polk and A. L. Dancer, 1884); T. M. Newsom, *Pen Pictures of St. Paul, Minnesota* (St. Paul, Minn.: for the author, 1886), 505.

48   Phineas Banning to William Lowber Banning, 17 April 1871, box 2, 1996 Addendum, Banning Company Collection, HEH; *Los Angeles Times*, 19 January 1882.

49   Phineas Banning to Mary E. H. Banning, 26 January 1873, box 6, 1985 Addendum, George Robert to Mary E. H. Banning, 2 September 1880, box 18b, R. Pollard to Phineas Banning, 15 January 1879, letterbook 4, Banning Company Collection, HEH; Phineas Banning to Benjamin D. Wilson, 8 May 1873, box 17, Benjamin D. Wilson Papers, HEH; Phineas Banning to John D. Bicknell, 27 September 1880, and others, box 4, John D. Bicknell Collection, HEH; Phineas Banning to Robert Edgar Jack, 16 July 1874, box 3, Jack Family Papers, CPSU. A large file of material related to the estate of Joseph Hubbard Hollister, including correspondence with the Bannings, can be found in boxes 2, 3, 4, and 5 of the latter collection.

50   Mary E. H. Banning to Robert Edgar Jack, 21 July 1874, box 3, Jack Family Papers, CPSU. The sheep industry in Southern California is described in Robert G. Cleland, *The Irvine Ranch of Orange County, 1810–1950* (San Marino, Calif.: Huntington Library, 1952) 65–66, 69; Ben C. Truman, *Semi-Tropical California: Its Climate, Healthfulness, Productiveness, and Scenery* (San Francisco: A. L. Bancroft, 1874), 71–72.

51   Deed, Andrew Glassell to Mary E. H. Banning, 24 October 1874, vol. 3, Index of Deeds, Los Angeles County Recorder's Office, Norwalk, Calif.; Rancho Santiago de Santa Ana map and other material, box 25, Solano-Reeve Papers, HEH; Virginia Carpenter, *Ranchos of Orange County: Chronologies of Early California* (Orange, Calif.: Paragon Agency, 2003), 51–57.

52   *Phineas Banning v. H. N. Alexander et al.*, case 1082, 1864, box 32, Los Angeles Area Court Records, HEH; Phineas Banning to Robert Edgar Jack, 15 January, 29 March, 9 April 1875, box 3, Jack Family Papers, CPSU; *Los Angeles Daily Herald*, 10 September, 5 December 1875.

53   Cleland, *Irvine Ranch*, 78; Phineas Banning to Robert Edgar Jack, 12 March 1876, box 3, Jack Family Papers, CPSU; Bert Haskett, "History of the Sheep Industry in Arizona," *Arizona Historical Review* 7 (July 1936): 20–21; Edward Norris Wentworth, *America's Sheep Trails: History, Personalities* (Ames: Iowa State College Press, 1948), 250; Tom Hughes, *History of Banning and San Gorgonio Pass* (Banning: Banning Record, 1938), 13, 21.

54   Ransom B. Moore biography file, CSL; Robinson, *Gateways to Southern California*, 136. On one of the early and important settlers in the Banning area, see John R. Brumgardt, "Pioneer by Circumstance: James Marshall Gilman and the Beginnings of Banning," *Southern California Quarterly* 62 (Summer 1980): 143–59.

55   Hughes, *History of Banning and San Gorgonio Pass*, 20–21, quote on 21; Robinson, *Gateways to Southern California*, 137; Jane Davies Gunther, *Riverside County, California, Place Names: Their Origins and Their Stories* (Riverside, Calif.: J. D. Gunther, 1984), 40–41.

56   Correspondence between John D. Bicknell and Winfield Scott Hancock, January 1877, box 3, John D. Bicknell Papers, HEH; Robinson, *Gateways to Southern California*, quote on 137; James T. Brown, *Harvest of the Sun: An Illustrated History of Riverside County* (Northridge, Calif.: Windsor, 1985), quote on 72; *Los Angeles Times*, 4 January 1885; Hughes, *History of Banning and San Gorgonio Pass*, 22; Gunther, *Riverside County, California, Place Names*, 41–43; Kenneth M. Holtzclaw, *Banning* (Charleston, S.C.: Arcadia, 2005), 7.

57   Jay J. Wagoner, "Overstocking of the Ranges in Southern Arizona during the 1870s and 1880s," *Arizoniana* 2 (Spring 1961): 23–27; Wentworth, *America's Sheep Trails*, 249–50; Thomas Sheridan, *Arizona: A History* (Tucson: University of Arizona Press, 1995), 131–34.

58   Charles R. Johnson to Cave J. Couts, 21 March 1867, document CT1289, 22 August 1869, document CT1348, Cave J. Couts Papers, HEH; Phineas Banning to J. Lancaster Brent, 3 August 1865, document BT10, Matthew

Keller to Brent, 17 August 1865, document BT140, Joseph Lancaster Brent Papers, HEH; Judson A. Grenier with Robert C. Gillingham, *California Legacy: The James Alexander Watson–María Dolores Domínguez de Watson Family, 1820–1980* (Los Angeles: Watson Land Company, 1987), 207–8; *Los Angeles News*, 18 July, 2 September 1865, 12 July, 10 December 1867, 23 October 1869, 25 November 1871, and many others; *Los Angeles Times*, 14 October 1923 (King obituary).

59 *Alta California* (San Francisco), 20 December 1867.

60 Deverell, *Whitewashed Adobe*, 11–48; Leonard Pitt, *The Decline of the Californios: A Social History of the Spanish-Speaking Californians, 1846–1890* (Berkeley: University of California Press, 1971), esp. 229–96; William David Estrada, *The Los Angeles Plaza: Sacred and Contested Space* (Austin: University of Texas Press, 2008), 85–98.

61 Wilson to Banning, 16 December 1870, box 14, Banning notes on George J. Clarke to Wilson, 24 January 1871, box 15, Banning to Wilson, 15 February 1872, box 16, Benjamin D. Wilson Papers, HEH.

62 Phineas Banning to Wilson, 17 December 1865, box 11, Benjamin D. Wilson Papers, HEH; Frederic Cople Jaher, *The Urban Establishment: Upper Strata in Boston, New York, Charleston, Chicago and Los Angeles* (Urbana: University of Illinois Press, 1982), 604; Phineas Banning to Senator Cornelius C. Cole, 12 October, 1, 2 November 1871, box 3, Cole Family Papers, UCLA.

63 Phineas Banning to J. C. Stubbs, 25 March 1880, Phineas Banning to Romualdo Pacheco, 17 March, 8 April 1880, box 1, 1985 Addendum, George C. Perkins to Phineas Banning, 3 June 1879, 13 January 1880, letterbook 5, Romualdo Pacheco to Phineas Banning, 3 January, 23 February 1880, letterbook 5, Banning Company Collection, HEH; *Los Angeles Daily Herald*, 6 April 1878.

64 P. Davis to Phineas Banning, 7 January 1872, box 11, William M. Gwin to Benjamin D. Wilson, 6 March 1874, box 18, Benjamin D. Wilson Papers, HEH.

65 *Los Angeles Republican*, 21 March 1868; *Los Angeles Times*, 20 August, 26 September 1882; Harvey White Magee, *The Story of My Life* (Albany, N.Y.: Boyd, 1926), 96.

66 Winfield Scott Hancock to Phineas Banning, 8 December 1874, box 2, Antonio F. Coronel Collection, SCWHR; Hancock to Matthew Keller, 1 January 1876, box 1, Matthew Keller Papers, HEH; *Los Angeles Daily Herald*, 22 September 1880.

67 W. S. Montgomery to Phineas Banning, 29 July 1880, letterbook 6, Banning Company Collection, HEH; *San Pedro News Pilot*, 23 November 1911.

68 Newmark, *Sixty Years in Southern California*, 501–2; *Alta California* (San Francisco), 13 May 1876; *Los Angeles Daily Herald*, 17 November 1880 (quote); *Los Angeles Times*, 10 June 1882; Glassell & Smith to Phineas Banning, 2 September 1881, box 18a, Banning Company Collection, HEH; Phineas Banning to Benjamin D. Wilson, 12 August 1863, box 9, Benjamin D. Wilson Papers, HEH; Christie, "Phineas Banning with Special Reference to the Development of Transportation in Southern California," 117–20; Nadeau,

City-Makers, 25–26. On Banning's military appointments, see *Los Angeles Star*, 19 December 1857, 11 June 1859; "California Militia Staff Brigadier General, 1861–1866," 15:5, 124, and "Register of Commissions," 17:5, 18:26, California Adjutant General Office, California Military Records in the State Archives, 1858–1923 (on microfilm at the Los Angeles County Library, Rosemead, Calif.).

69   Col. James J. Ayers, *Gold and Sunshine: Reminiscences of Early California* (Boston: Gorham, 1922), quote on 300; A. A. Polhamus to Joseph Brent Banning, 4 April 1905 (quote), box 18b, Banning Company Collection, HEH; *Los Angeles Daily Herald*, 20 August 1880 (quote), 21 August 1881 (quote).

70   *Alta California* (San Francisco), 31 August 1873 (quotes). The "twelve hundred oysters" was obviously an exaggeration, although the number was probably quite high.

71   Grenier, *California Legacy*, quotes on 208; John Shore to J. Lancaster Brent, 11 July 1865, box 2, Joseph Lancaster Brent Papers, HEH.

72   Ayers, *Gold and Sunshine*, quote on 300; Winfield Scott Hancock to Matthew Keller, 1 January 1876, box 1, Matthew Keller Collection, HEH; George Hugh Banning, interview by Joyce Loranger, n.d., copy of notes in possession of the author; Hancock Banning Jr., notes of his reminiscences, 1978, BRM. An inventory of some of the liquor in the Banning residence in 1880 is described in Yoch, *Visionary on the Golden Shore*, 45.

73   Edward L. Watkins to J. Lancaster Brent, 28 August 1875, document BT327, Joseph Lancaster Brent Papers, HEH; Watkins to Phineas Banning, 27 March 1876, box 19, Watkins to Benjamin D. Wilson, 8 (quote), 13, 25 (quote) May, 5 June (quote) 1876, box 20, Benjamin D. Wilson Papers, HEH.

74   *Los Angeles Daily Herald*, 14 March 1878; Benjamin D. Wilson correspondence with Phineas Banning in boxes 3–20, Benjamin D. Wilson Papers, HEH; Muriel Aloha Tracy, "The Life of Benjamin D. Wilson" (master's thesis, University of Southern California, 1934).

75   *Los Angeles Daily Herald*, 12 April 1881; correspondence and diaries in boxes 1 and 4, Matthew Keller Collection, HEH; Jane Apostol, "Don Mateo Keller: His Vines and His Wines," *Southern California Quarterly* 84 (Summer 2002): 93–114.

76   *Los Angeles Times*, 10 June 1882.

77   *Los Angeles Times*, 8, 21 August 1883, 10 March 1885 (quote); Phineas Banning to James de Barth Shorb, 2 (quote), 6, 11, 26, 30 (quote) July 1883, box 8, James de Barth Shorb Papers, HEH; Sheldon, "Biographical Sketch of Phineas Banning," 13; Newmark, *Sixty Years in Southern California*, 548.

78   Banning Power of Attorney, 19 May 1884, box 18a, Phineas Banning to Hancock Banning, 7 April, 27 May, 16, 18, 21 (quote) June 1884, box 12, Banning Company Collection, HEH; Phineas Banning to James de Barth Shorb, 19 August 1884, box 8, James de Barth Shorb Papers, HEH. On the curative effect of these hot springs and associated vacation amenities, see William Alexander MacCorkle, *The White Sulphur Springs* (New York: Neale, 1916).

79   Transcript of Joseph Brent Banning to William Lowber Banning, 27 March
      1885, BRM; *Los Angeles Times*, 4 January, 10 March 1885; *San Francisco
      Examiner*, 9 March 1885.

80   Sheldon, "Biographical Sketch of Phineas Banning," 17; *Los Angeles Times*,
      13 March 1885 (quote); Krythe, *Port Admiral*, 230–31, although much of this
      description of the funeral is conjecture. Banning's body was later moved to
      Rosedale Cemetery in Los Angeles.

81   Rusling, *Across America*, quote on 331; *Los Angeles Daily Herald*, 19 August
      1879 (quote), 19 March 1885 (quote).

82   Browne, *A Tour Through Arizona*, quote on 34; Steven P. Erie, "How the
      Urban West Was Won: The Local State and Economic Growth of Los
      Angeles, 1880–1932," *Urban Affairs Quarterly* 27 (June 1992): 519–54.

Chapter Eight

1   *Los Angeles Times*, 14 April 1885; Hancock Banning Jr., "The Banning Family
     in Southern California," interview by Dellene M. Tweedale, 1971, transcript,
     Center for Oral History Research, UCLA, quotes on 168.

2   *Los Angeles Times*, 13 October 1885; Joseph Brent Banning to William Lowber
     Banning, 8 March 1886, Nancy Morse Banning Call Collection; John D.
     Bicknell to William and Joseph Brent Banning, 18 February, 23 October,
     3 November 1886, letterbook 2, John D. Bicknell Papers, HEH.

3   *Los Angeles Times*, 4 April 1885, 31 July 1887, 16 June 1888; *Banning v.
     Banning*, 80 Cal. 271 (1889); Hancock Banning, "The Banning Family in
     Southern California," quote on 170; William Banning to Smith, Winder &
     Smith, 11 April 1890, letterbook 20, and copy of Phineas Banning probate
     case 3902 and *Banning v. Banning* material, box 2, Mary E. H. Banning to
     Col. S. O. Houghton, 7 February 1888 (quote), letterbook 3, 1985 Addendum,
     Banning Company Collection, HEH; Mary E. H. Banning to John D. Bicknell,
     21 July 1887, box 7, John D. Bicknell Papers, HEH. The Bicknell Papers
     contain many letters regarding specifics of Banning property management
     during the probate period.

4   William S. Banning to William Lowber Banning, 20 June 1887, box 2, 1996
     Addendum, Banning Company Collection, HEH. On Frederick Ayer,
     see Edwin P. Conklin, *Middlesex County and Its People: A History*, 5 vols.
     (New York: Lewis, 1927) 3:85–86; Frederick Ayer, *Reminiscences of Frederick
     Ayer* (Boston: Merrymount, 1923); Scott C. Steward, *The Sarsaparilla Kings*
     (Cambridge, Mass.: for the author, 1993).

5   *St. Paul Pioneer Press*, 27 November 1893; *Los Angeles Times*, 18 December
     1893.

6   Banning State Park brochure, BRM; Elizabeth van Schaick-Banning,
     The Book of Banning (Westminster, Md.: Willow Bend Books, 2005), 347;
     June Drenning Holmquist, "Strands in the Web of History," *Minnesota
     Volunteer* 35 (May–June 1972): 15–20.

7   Bicknell to William Lowber Banning, 2 July 1888, box 7, John D. Bicknell
     Papers, HEH.

8   William Lowber Banning to Bicknell, 26 July 1888, box 7, John D. Bicknell
     Papers, HEH.

9   *Los Angeles City and County Directory, 1886–87* (Los Angeles: various pub-
     lishers, 1886), 196; *Who's Who in the Pacific Southwest,* 25; Banning Family
     Collection of Photographs, Parts I and II, CL180 and CL451, HEH; Joseph
     Brent Banning to Fred E. Hotchkiss, 28 March 1894, letterbook 31, Banning
     Company Collection, HEH.

10   *Los Angeles Tribune,* 13 March 1887; research files, BRM; Joseph Brent Ban-
     ning to Katharine S. Banning, 17 October 1894, deed to Lot 2, Block A, Bonnie
     Brae Tract, and family notes in box 2, and notes in scrapbook 10 and scrap-
     book 30, 1996 Addendum, Banning Company Collection, HEH; *Receipts from
     Katharine's Kitchen: Personal Recipes of Katharine Stewart Banning* (Wilm-
     ington, Calif.: General Phineas Banning Residence Museum, 1978), 17.

11   *Los Angeles Times,* 19 March, 25 November, 3 December 1901, 2 January 1902,
     23 August 1905, 5 February 1910; clippings in scrapbook 29, 1996 Addendum,
     Banning Company Collection, HEH; Margaret Leslie Davis, *Childrens
     Hospital and the Leaders of Los Angeles: The First 100 Years* (Los Angeles:
     Childrens Hospital Los Angeles, 2002), 25, 31–32, 123, 228, 231, quote on 32.

12   Carol G. Wilson, *California Yankee: William R. Staats—Business Pioneer*
     (Claremont, Calif.: Saunders, 1946), 21–23; Hancock Banning to Anne
     Banning, 2 May 1895, and newspaper clippings, EBA; *Los Angeles Times,*
     14 April 1885, 13, 17 September 13, 17, 1904.

13   Megs Meriwether to Robert J. Banning, 7 June 1978, box 7, 1985 Addendum,
     Banning Company Collection, HEH; Henry Markham Page, *Pasadena: Its
     Early Years* (Los Angeles: privately printed by L. L. Morrison, 1964), 96, 102
     (quote), 123.

14   William A. Spalding, *History and Reminiscences, Los Angeles City and
     County, California,* 3 vols. (Los Angeles: J. R. Finnell & Sons, 1931), 3:203–4;
     Stanley P. Hirshson, *General Patton: A Soldier's Life* (New York: Harper
     Collins, 2002), 6–30; Robert H. Patton, *The Pattons: A Personal History
     of an American Family* (New York: Crown, 1994), 22–83.

15   *Los Angeles Times,* 16 November 1890; George S. Patton correspondence,
     1866–79, box 25, Addendum II, Benjamin D. Wilson Papers, HEH; Patton,
     The Pattons, 62–78. Correspondence between some of the members of
     Susan Glassell Patton's family from the 1820s to the 1860s can be found in
     boxes 9 and 10, 1985 Addendum, Banning Company Collection, HEH.

16   William Thornton Glassell, *W. T. Glassell and the Little Torpedo Boat
     "David"* (Los Angeles: privately printed, 1937); J. Thomas Scharf, *History of
     the Confederate States Navy from Its Organization to the Surrender of Its Last
     Vessel* (New York: Rogers & Sherwood, 1887), 750–68; William H. Roberts,
     USS New Ironsides in the Civil War (Annapolis, Md.: Naval Institute Press,
     1999), 80–82.

17   *Los Angeles Times,* 23 January 1938.

18   Joyce Loranger, research notes, BRM; Herbert C. Andrews, comp., "Record of Ancestry of Mr. and Mrs. Hancock Banning," typescript, 1904, compiled for Mrs. Hancock Banning and the Colonial Dames, box 13, Banning Company Collection, HEH.

19   Hancock Banning to Anne Banning, 14, 30 August 1895, 8 December 1896, 28 December 1897, Hancock Banning to Hancock Banning Jr., 10 November 1896, EBA; Selena Ingram, diary entry for 5 May 1911, box 2, Selena Gray Galt Ingram Papers, HEH. Some of Anne's health problems might have been associated with postpartum depression, but the timing of her sanitarium stays did not always correlate with the births of her children.

20   Franklin Harper, ed., *Who's Who on the Pacific Coast* (Los Angeles: Harper, 1913), 524; W. W. Robinson, *Lawyers of Los Angeles* (Los Angeles: Los Angeles Bar Association, 1959), 82–84, 162, 317, 332; Martin Blumenson, *The Patton Papers*, 2 vols. (Boston: Houghton Mifflin, 1972), quote on 1:25; Hancock Banning to Anne Banning, 3, 14 November 1893, 2 August 1895, EBA.

21   U.S. Census Office, Population Schedules, 12th Census (1900), City of Los Angeles, as scanned on Ancestry.com, http://www.ancestry.com; *Los Angeles Times*, 4 December 1933.

22   *Los Angeles Times*, 22 April 1894, 1 July, 13 September, 13 October 1901, 28 December 1902, 17 February, 21 March 1904; *La Paloma* material in box 5, 1985 Addendum, and photograph of *La Paloma* and label, box 19, Banning Family Collection of Photographs, Part II, CL451, HEH.

23   *Los Angeles Times*, 22 August 1889; files on land purchases by the Banning brothers in boxes 1, 4, and 6, Banning Company Collection, HEH.

24   William S. Banning to William Lowber Banning, 28 May 1890, letterbook 20, William S. Banning to Lawrence Fogel, 17 February 1892, letterbook 21, William S. Banning to William Staats, 8 May 1896, letterbook 24, "Banning Rancho Log Book," scrapbook 41, 1996 Addendum, Banning Company Collection, HEH; Conejo Ranch photographs in boxes 4, 5, and 20, Banning Family Collection of Photographs, Part II, CL451, HEH; William Lowber Banning Jr., *A Two Weeks Coaching Party in Southern California in April 1889* (St. Paul, Minn.: for the author, 1889), and *A Coaching Party to Southern California* (St. Paul, Minn.: for the author, 1889).

25   Title Insurance Company property description of Banning brothers, 7 November 1894, and copy of indenture of Banning brothers to Banning Company, 31 October 1894, box 1, Banning Brothers Statement of Assets and Liabilities, 18 December 1893, letterbook 22, William S. Banning to Henry T. Gage, 27 November 1894, letterbook 24, Banning Company Collection, HEH; Hancock Banning to Anne Banning, 14 August 1895, EBA. On the Santa Catalina Island purchase, see the next chapter.

26   *Dominguez de Guyer v. Banning*, 167 U.S. 723 (1897); William S. Banning to Byxbee & Clark, 14 September 1894, letterbook 23, William S. Banning to F. K. Rule, 5 July 1897, letterbook 25, Banning Company Collection, HEH; J. L. Willcutt to John D. Bicknell, 5 August 1889, box 8, Stephen M. White to John D. Bicknell, 5 December 1895, 24 March 1896, box 14, John D. Bicknell Papers, HEH; William S. Banning to Stephen M. White, 4 June 1897 (quote),

box 17, Stephen M. White Papers, SU. The Los Angeles Terminal Railway acquired land on nearby Rattlesnake Island to make into its entrance to the harbor.

27   William S. and Hancock Banning to Joseph Banning, 12 February 1892, letterbook 21, Banning Company Collection, HEH; Hancock Banning to Anne Banning, 3, 4 November 1893, EBA; *Los Angeles Times*, 26 April 1900.

28   *Los Angeles Times*, 19 November 1897, 21 February 1929, 4 January 1956; Marshall Stimson, *Fun, Fights, and Fiestas in Old Los Angeles: An Autobiography* (Los Angeles: privately printed, 1966), 43 (on the rivalry between Mary's suitors); correspondence between Mary H. B. Norris and Hancock Banning, box 12, William S. Banning to John Rosenfeld's Sons, 21 February 1900, letterbook 26, Banning Company Collection, HEH.

29   Katharine S. Banning, notes on Lucy Banning, n.d., "Phineas Banning" file, box 4, 1996 Addendum, Banning Company Collection, HEH.

30   William S. Banning to Mary E. H. Banning, 24 July 1889, box 2, 1996 Addendum, William S. Banning to John Bradbury, 24 October 1894, letterbook 23, Banning Company Collection, HEH; *Los Angeles Times*, 5, 8, December 1893; Hancock Banning to Anne Banning, 18 November, 5 December (quote) 1893, EBA.

31   *Los Angeles Evening Herald and Express*, 14 May 1938, 6 December 1954; "Beautiful Women and Healthy Children," *Capital*, 28 December 1895, 23; William Pugsley, *Bunker Hill: Last of the Lofty Mansions* (Corona del Mar, Calif.: Trans-Anglo Books, 1977), 12; W. W. Robinson, *Los Angeles from the Days of the Pueblo* (San Francisco: California Historical Society, 1959), 68.

32   *San Francisco Chronicle*, 3 (quote), 4 (quote), 5 July 1897; *San Francisco Call*, 11, 13 (quote) July 1897.

33   *Los Angeles Times*, 18 (quote), 19 July 1897, 7 December 1901; *San Francisco Call*, 18 July 1897; *New York Times*, 20 July 1897, 18 November 1911.

34   Copies of Lucy Banning Bradbury to her brothers, 5 July 1987, and Hancock Banning to Major William B. Hooper (lessee of Occidental Hotel, San Francisco), 10 July 1897, RJB.

35   *Los Angeles Times*, 7 December 1901, 19 November 1902 (quotes).

36   *Los Angeles Times*, 14 February, 26 September 1903, 20 January 1905, 1 July 1907; *San Francisco Call*, 21 September 1906; *Los Angeles Examiner*, 7 April 1928.

37   Mary E. H. Banning to John D. Bicknell, 27 September, 22 November 1886, box 6, 21 July 1887, box 7, Bicknell to Mary E. H. Banning, 30 September 1886, letterbook 2, John D. Bicknell Collection, HEH; Marco R. Newmark "Phineas Banning, Intrepid Pioneer," *Southern California Quarterly* 35 (September 1953): 274.

38   *Los Angeles Times*, 2 September 1895, 26 January, 22 March 1896, 29 October 1898, 31 March, 6, 13 April 1899, 1 June, 3 August 1901, 17 April, 28 July 1904, 8 January 1905, 1 April 1934; Anna E. Satterlee, "The N.S.D.A.R.," *Out West Magazine* 43 (February 1916): 65–66; 1893 ship passenger list, box 6, 1985 Addendum, Banning Company Collection, HEH.

39   Robert M. Fogelson, *The Fragmented Metropolis: Los Angeles, 1850–1930*
      Cambridge, Mass.: Harvard University Press, 1967), 109, 119, 121–22.

40   *Los Angeles City and County Directory, 1886–1887*, 196; Hancock Banning to
      Clark Brothers, 7 January 1889, Hancock Banning to W. C. Halstead, 25 May
      1889, and other correspondence in letterbook 7, William S. Banning to
      J. F. Bakewell & Company, 27 April 1892, letterbook 21, wharf franchises in
      box 2, Banning Company Collection, HEH.

41   *Los Angeles Times*, 9 March 1890; U.S. Census, Population Schedules,
      9th Census (1870), Wilmington Township, 15, as scanned on Ancestry.com,
      http://www.ancestry.com.

42   Deeds and other material regarding Adelaida M. Banning in box 12, Joseph
      Brent Banning to Adelaida M. Banning, 16 April 1894, letterbook 31, William S.
      Banning to Frank Cox, 30 December 1907, William S. Banning to Frank H.
      Lowe, 25 January 1909, letterbook 29; Banning Company Collection, HEH.

43   J. M. Guinn, *A History of California and an Extended History of Los Angeles
      and Environs*, 3 vols. (Los Angeles: Historic Record Company, 1915), 2:81–82;
      William S. Banning to Frank Mellus, 29 April 1892, letterbook 21, William S.
      Banning to Mellus, 8 August, 4 September 1895, letterbook 23, William S.
      Banning to Mellus, 25 April 1898, letterbook 25, Banning Company Collec-
      tion, HEH; Mellus to Banning Company, 16 April 1898, box 2, James J. Mellus
      Collection, SCWHR.

44   List of officers in 1893, letterbook 23, William L. Banning to William G. Hal-
      stead, 13 March 1883, box 2, 1996 Addendum, Banning Company Collection,
      HEH; *Los Angeles Times*, 18 August 1910, 11 May 1934.

45   Grace Heilman Stimson, *Rise of the Labor Movement in Los Angeles* (Berkeley:
      University of California Press, 1955), 81–87, 256–69, 289–318; William S. Ban-
      ning to Mary Hollister Banning, 6 October 1886 (quote), box 12, William S.
      Banning to J. A. Muir, letterbook 23, Banning Company Collection, HEH.

46   On the Bannings' perceptions of this partnership, see Joseph Brent Ban-
      ning to William L. Banning, 2 April (quote), 2 February (quote) 1893, letter-
      book 31, William S. Banning to William L. Banning, 23 January 1893 (quote),
      letterbook 21, William S. Banning to John Rosenfeld's Sons, 10 December 1897
      (quote), letterbook 25, Banning Company Collection, HEH. For examples of
      the working partnership, see William S. Banning to Louis Lissak, 20 May
      1890, letterbook 20, William S. Banning to Frederick Banning, 11 March 1893,
      William S. Banning to William Lowber Banning, 20 April 1893, letterbook 22,
      copy of J. A. Muir to William S. Banning, 19 May 1894, letterbook 23, Ban-
      ning Company Collection, HEH; *Los Angeles Times*, 19 April, 8 August 1899.

47   William S. Banning to T. P. Burnett, 25 February 1892, letterbook 21, William S.
      Banning to John Rosenfeld's Sons, 15 July 1896, letterbook 24, William S. Ban-
      ning to James B. Fraley, 4 February 1898, letterbook 25, William S. Banning to
      William G. Halstead, 22 March 1899, letterbook 26, Hancock Banning Jr.,
      label on photograph 342, box 3, Banning Family Collection of Photographs,
      Part I, CL180, HEH.

48   William S. Banning to Thomas Shaw, 6 April 1894, William S. Banning to Henry T. Gage, 27 November 1894, William S. Banning to Andrew Young, 2 August 1895, letterbook 23, William S. Banning to Edward Mahar, 16 November 1895, letterbook 24, Banning Company Collection, HEH; Banning Company (1894) file, box 47, Los Angeles County Incorporation Records, SCWHR.

49   *Los Angeles Times*, 8 August 1899, 15 May, 24 August 1901; William S. Banning to J. M. Hanford, 19 July 1895, letterbook 23, agreements to drill for oil and run oil rigs, box 19, Statements of Assets and Liabilities, Banning Brothers, 18 December 1893, letterbook 22, Banning Company Collection, HEH; Hancock Banning to Anne Banning, 25 July 1895, EBA; San Pedro and Wilmington Water Company (1900), file 3104, box 78, Los Angeles County Incorporation Records, SCWHR; John M. Houston, *San Pedro City Dream: An Account, by Its Own Records, of an Attempt to Be an Independent City; Part I (1888–1896) and More Stories of Old San Pedro* (San Pedro, Calif.: San Pedro Historical Publications, 1980), quote on 62.

50   Vanderbilt file, box 5, S. T. Gage to Phineas Banning, 23 August 1881, box 18a, newspaper clipping, ca. 1889, box 5, 1985 Addendum, Banning Company Collection, HEH; "The 'Vanderbilt' Arrives . . . ," *Los Angeles County Museum Quarterly* 18 (Winter 1961): 16–17.

51   *California Blue Book and State Register* (Sacramento: California State Printer, 1889–1911), 1895: 157; correspondence in boxes 1 and 2, John Tracy Gaffey Papers, BANC.

52   *Los Angeles Times*, 21 September 1898; *Los Angeles Herald*, 16 October 1898; Royce Delmatier et al., *The Rumble of California Politics, 1848–1970* (New York: John Wiley & Sons, 1970), 99–124; Tom Sitton, *John Randolph Haynes: California Progressive* (Stanford, Calif.: Stanford University Press, 1992), 24–26.

53   Los Angeles County Board of Supervisors Minutes, 12: 11 March 1889, 13, 22 November 1890, 20 January 1891, 17: 21 November 1893, 18: 16 July 1894, Los Angeles County Board of Supervisors Office, Los Angeles, Calif.; *Los Angeles Times*, 13 August 1888, 13 March 1889, 22 May 1892, 15 March 1893. For a recent interpretation of the Southern Pacific as much less politically powerful in California than has been traditionally believed, and as much more of a positive force in protecting the state's environment, see Richard Orsi, *Sunset Limited: The Southern Pacific Railroad and the Development of the American West, 1850–1930* (Berkeley: University of California Press, 2005).

54   Charles Crocker to Collis P. Huntington, 25 October 1883, box 2, Charles Crocker Correspondence, HEH.

55   *Los Angeles Times*, 6 September 1892; Charles Crocker to Henry Z. Osbourne, 18 November 1888, box 1, Henry Z. Osbourne Papers, HEH; Richard Webster Barsness, "The Maritime Development of San Pedro Bay, California, 1821–1921" (PhD diss., University of Minnesota, 1963), 384–90; William Deverell, *Railroad Crossing: Californians and the Railroad, 1850–1910* (Berkeley: University of California Press, 1994), 93–100.

56   *Los Angeles Times*, 18 December 1895; Stephen M. White to John Gaffey, 14 January 1895, box 92, Abel Stearns Papers, HEH; clippings and copies of telegrams in Stephen M. White scrapbooks, SCWHR.

57   Joseph Brent Banning to William L. Banning, 2 February, 20 April (quote) 1893, letterbook 31, William S. Banning to William Lowber Banning, 23 January 1893, letterbook 21, William S. Banning to Joseph Brent Banning, 11 March 1893, letterbook 22, Banning Company Collection, HEH. William also noted the partnership with the railroad, reminding a Southern Pacific official that "We took a very active part in favor of Santa Monica." William S. Banning to J. A. Muir, 25 January 1893 (quote), Banning Company Collection, HEH.

58   *Los Angeles Times*, 3 March 1897, 28 April 1899 (quote); Charles Dwight Willard, *The Free Harbor Contest at Los Angeles* (Los Angeles: Kingsley-Barnes and Neuner, 1899), 208–11; Deverell, *Railroad Crossing*, 100–120.

59   William S. Banning to Senator Leland Stanford, 18 December 1890, box 5, William S. Banning to Edwin Stanton, 28 October 1892, William S. Banning to George Hinds, 7 November 1892, letterbook 21, William S. Banning to Thomas H. Williams, 21 January 1899, William Banning to Gov. Henry T. Gage, 3 July 1899, William S. Banning to J. A. Muir, 16 March 1900, letterbook 26, William S. Banning to George Hatton, 25 November 1902, letterbook 27, Banning Company Collection, HEH; William H. Mills to Henry Z. Osbourne, 11 January 1896, box 4, Henry Z. Osbourne Papers, HEH.

60   William S. Banning to William Lowber Banning Jr., 26 April 1897, letterbook 22, William S. Banning to William A. Morgan, 29 August 1894, letterbook 23, William S. Banning to John Cline, 25 August 1896, William S. Banning to Joseph Brent Banning, 4 September 1896, William S. Banning to A. Chesebrough, 3 December 1896, William S. Banning to Joseph Brent Banning, 5 January 1897, letterbook 24, William S. Banning to John D. Bicknell, 4 June 1897, letterbook 25, William S. Banning to Joseph Brent Banning, 24 April 1900, letterbook 26, William S. Banning to State Senator Charles Belshaw, 9 February 1903, letterbook 27, Joseph Brent Banning to Myron Herrick, 6 November 1896, letterbook 24, Joseph Brent Banning to Gov. Henry Markham, 29 October 1892, letterbook 31, Banning Company Collection, HEH; William S. Banning to James de Barth Shorb, 19 October 1892, Hancock Banning to Shorb, 30 October 1892, box 8, James de Barth Shorb Papers, HEH.

61   Stephen M. White to John D. Bicknell, 14, 16 February 1887, box 2, John D. Bicknell Papers, HEH; Hancock Banning to Senator Stephen M. White, 7, 29 June 1898, box 17, Stephen M. White Papers, SU; William S. Banning to Senator Stephen M. White, 26 March 1898, letterbook 25, Banning Company Collection, HEH.

62   Assemblyman Brewster C. Kenyon to Henry Z. Osbourne, 5 March 1897, box 6, Henry Z. Osbourne Papers, HEH.

Chapter Nine

1   For important scholarly treatments of tourism in America in this period, see, among others, John F. Sears, *Sacred Places: American Tourist Attractions in the Nineteenth Century* (New York: Oxford University Press, 1989); John Jakle, *The Tourist: Travel in Twentieth-Century North America* (Lincoln: University of Nebraska Press, 1985); Jon Sterngass, *First Resorts: Pursuing Pleasure at Saratoga Springs, Newport, & Coney Island* (Baltimore: Johns Hopkins University Press, 2001), esp. 112–45; Theodore Corbett, *The Making of American Resorts: Saratoga Springs, Ballston Spa, Lake George* (New Brunswick, N.J.: Rutgers University Press, 2001); and Marguerite S. Shaffer, *See America First: Tourism and National Identity, 1880–1940* (Washington, D.C.: Smithsonian Institution, 2001). On Western tourism, see, among others, Earl S. Pomeroy, *In Search of the Golden West: The Tourist in Western America* (New York: Knopf, 1957); Hal K. Rothman, *Devil's Bargains: Tourism in the Twentieth-Century American West* (Lawrence: University Press of Kansas, 1998); David M. Wrobel and Patrick T. Long, eds., *Seeing and Being Seen: Tourism in the American West* (Lawrence: University Press of Kansas, 2001); Hal K. Rothman, ed., *The Culture of Tourism, the Tourism of Culture: Selling the Past to the Present in the American Southwest* (Albuquerque: University of New Mexico Press, 2003).

2   On California, see Jakle, *The Tourist*, 239–41, quote on 239; Pomeroy, *In Search of the Golden West*, 16–30, 112–25, 145–47; and Phoebe S. Kropp, *California Vieja: Culture and Memory in a Modern American Place* (Berkeley: University of California Press, 2006), 47–102. On Southern California, see Paul F. Allen, "Tourists in Southern California, 1875–1903" (master's thesis, Claremont Colleges, 1940); Melinda Elizabeth Kashuba, "Tourist Landscapes of Los Angeles County, California" (PhD diss., University of Southern California, 1986); Dydia DeLyser, *Ramona Memories: Tourism and the Shaping of Southern California* (Minneapolis: University of Minnesota Press, 2005); Milton Lawrence Culver, "The Island, the Oasis, and the City: Santa Catalina, Palm Springs, Los Angeles, and Southern California's Shaping of American Life and Leisure" (PhD diss., University of California, Los Angeles, 2004). Among the numerous tourist guidebooks from the turn of the century extolling the Southern California setting are *Newman's Information Guide, A Condensed and Accurate Guide to Los Angeles* (Los Angeles: T. Newman, 1906); and *Handy Guide and Reference Book to Los Angeles and Vicinity* (Los Angeles: Commercial Printing House, 1897).

3   Mrs. M. Burton Williamson, "History of Santa Catalina Island," *Annual Publications of the Historical Society of Southern California* 6 (1903): 14–31, quote on 14; Adelaide LeMert Doran, *The Ranch That Was Robbins': Santa Catalina Island, California: A Source Book* (Los Angeles: for the author, 1963), 9–13. "26 Miles Across the Sea," of course, is the first line of "26 Miles (Santa Catalina)," written by Bruce Belland and Glen Larson and recorded by the Four Preps in 1957. It has become a theme song for the island.

4   Harry Kelsey, *Juan Rodríguez Cabrillo* (San Marino, Calif.: Huntington Library, 1986), 157–59; Richard Buffum and Marjorie Buffum, *Catalina Saga:*

An Historical Cruise around Santa Catalina Island (Balboa Island, Calif.:
Abracadabra, 2003), 14–25.

5   Williamson, "History of Santa Catalina Island," 14–26; *Los Angeles Star*,
6 August 1853, 6 October 1855; *Los Angeles News*, 2 November 1866; Doran,
The Ranch That Was Robbins', 48–71.

6   Williamson, "History of Santa Catalina Island," 26–29; J. Duncan Gleason,
Islands of California: Their History, Romance, and Physical Characteristics
(Los Angeles: Sea Publications, 1951), 20; *Los Angeles Express*, 2 September
1880; Frank Lecouvreur, *From East Prussia to the Golden Gate* (New York:
Angelina Book Concern, 1906), quote on 309; Harris Newmark, *Sixty Years
in Southern California, 1853–1913* (New York: Knickerbocker, 1916), 250. See
also chapters 5 and 7 above.

7   Phineas Banning to James de Barth Shorb, 23, 27 May, 1 June (quote),
2, 11, 26 July 1883, box 8, James de Barth Shorb Papers, HEH.

8   *Los Angeles Star*, 30 May 1868, 5 August 1877; *Los Angeles News*, 13 June 1865,
6 July 1872; *Los Angeles Herald*, 23 December 1874; *Wilmington Enterprise*,
25 June, 20 August 1874; Rosemary Lick, *The Generous Miser: The Story of
James Lick of California* (Los Angeles: Ward Ritchie, 1967), 59–60; Ernest
Windle, *Windle's History of Santa Catalina Island*, 2nd ed. (Avalon, Calif.:
Catalina Islander, 1940), 17.

9   Henry T. Finck, "Santa Catalina Island," *Nation* 49 (17 October 1889): 307–9,
and (24 October 1889): 327–29; *Los Angeles Tribune*, 3 May 1889; *Los Angeles
Express*, 27 February 1891.

10   Hancock Banning to William G. Halstead, 25 May 1889, letterbook 7, Wil-
liam S. Banning to Col. Charles F. Smith, 21 December 1889, letterbook 8,
William S. Banning to George Shatto, 1 March 1889, letterbook 7, 28 August
1890, letterbook 20, *Catalina Jewfish*, 3 August 1889, in scrapbook 23, 1996
Addendum, Banning Company Collection, HEH; copy of George Shatto to
James Lick Trust, 1 September 1890, box 9, John D. Bicknell Papers, HEH;
Los Angeles Express, 20 July 1889.

11   William S. Banning to H. E. Mathews, 3 September 1890, William S. Banning
to W. W. Stow, 4, 9 December 1890, 9 January 1891, William S. Banning to
Mathews, 5 March 1891, letterbook 20, Banning Company Collection, HEH;
William S. Banning to James de Barth Shorb, 5 May 1890, box 8, James
de Barth Shorb Collection, HEH; H. E. Mathews to John D. Bicknell,
5 February, 27 March 1891, and many others, box 10, Bicknell to Mathews,
4 February, 31 March, 7 July 1891, and many others, letterbook 7, 25 August
1891, letterbook 8, John D. Bicknell Papers, HEH.

12   *Los Angeles Express*, 19 January 1892; copy of agreement between Joseph
Brent Banning and George Shatto for the purchase of Santa Catalina Island,
31 December 1891, William S. Banning to Walter Vail, 1 January 1892, William S. Banning to J. M. Elliott, 28 June 1892, William S. Banning note,
7 November 1892, letterbook 21, Banning Company Collection, HEH. Shatto
would die less than a year after the sale in a Los Angeles railway accident.
See *Los Angeles Express*, 17 June 1893.

13   *Los Angeles Times*, 16 March, 16 April 1892; William S. Banning to W. A. Morgan, 14 March 1892, letterbook 21, copy of petition supporting a Banning wharf, 27 February 1892, Banning Company Collection, HEH.

14   William S. Banning to T. B. Burnett, 27 January 1893, letterbook 22, Banning Company Collection, HEH; *Los Angeles Times*, 8 April 1893.

15   Santa Catalina Island advertisement (1896), box 5, Banning Company Collection, HEH; *Pasadena Star*, 1 June 1895; *Los Angeles Express*, 20 July 1894, 10 January 1899; *Los Angeles Times*, 4 August 1897, 6 August 1972; *Los Angeles Herald*, 17 July 1894, 1 June 1897; *Capital* (Los Angeles), 20 July 1895, 5; *Red Bluff Times*, 3 December 1930; Doran, *The Ranch That Was Robbins'*, 122–31. Jeannine L. Pedersen, *Catalina Island* (Charleston, S.C.: Arcadia, 2004), 49–53, contains many historic photographs of these amenities and locations.

16   *Los Angeles Times*, 15 June 1896; Pedersen, *Catalina Island*, 19–39, 47; Doran, *The Ranch That Was Robbins'*, 117–18, 126.

17   *Los Angeles Express*, 26 January 1894; *Los Angeles Times*, 11 February 1894; *San Francisco Examiner*, 17 February 1894; Joseph Brent Banning to Frederick E. Banning, 31 January 1894 (quote), letterbook 31, Banning Company Collection, HEH.

18   *Los Angeles Times*, 2 June 1895; Marshall Stimson, *Fun, Fights, and Fiestas in Old Los Angeles: An Autobiography* (Los Angeles: privately printed, 1966), 46–47, quote on 47; Pedersen, *Catalina Island*, 26–29; Culver, "The Island, the Oasis, and the City," 113–14.

19   *Los Angeles Times*, 7 June, 22 July 1894; *Pasadena Star*, 8 January 1894; Doran, *The Ranch That Was Robbins'*, 118.

20   Los Angeles County Board of Supervisors, Minutes of Meetings, 15: 29 August 1892, 31: 18 March 1902, 50: 11 May 1914, 56: 16 February 1916, Los Angeles County Board of Supervisors Office, Los Angeles, Calif.; A. W. Potts to Joseph Brent Banning, 19 July 1892, box 11, William S. Banning to Joseph Brent Banning, 5 January 1897, letterbook 24, Charles F. Holder to Joseph Brent Banning, 21 October 1902, scrapbook 38, 1996 Addendum, Banning Company Collection, HEH; Frank V. Rider to Henry Z. Osbourne, 14 November 1898, box 7, Henry Z. Osbourne Papers, HEH; *Los Angeles Times*, 1 January 1901. On the problem of overfishing, see D. C. Beaman, "Sport at Catalina—Can Its Waters Be Fished Out?" *Outdoor Life* 9 (February 1902): n.p.; Culver, "The Island, the Oasis, and the City," 119–20.

21   *Pasadena Star*, 24 July 1893; *Los Angeles Times*, 14 May 1901, 21 March 1905; William S. Banning to George S. Patton, letterbook 28, Banning Company Collection, HEH; Buffum and Buffum, *Catalina Saga*, 54–56.

22   William S. Banning to Edwin Stanton, 13 February 1893, William S. Banning to H. E. Mathews, 30 September 1893, letterbook 22, newspaper clipping, April 1894 (quote), scrapbook 23, 1996 Addendum, Banning Company Collection, HEH; Buffum and Buffum, *Catalina Saga*, 117–20; Pedersen, *Catalina Island*, 42–43.

23   William S. Banning to William L. Banning, 13 July 1892, letterbook 21, William S. Banning to Banning Advertising Co., 27 December 1898,

letterbook 26, Banning Company Collection, HEH. Examples of California newspaper stories include *Los Angeles Herald*, 15 April 1894; *Pasadena Star*, 17 February 1894; and *San Francisco Examiner*, 31 July 1893. Eastern newspaper stories of the 1890s include *Atlanta Constitution*, 30 June 1895 (quote) and *New York Tribune*, 19 November 1894.

24   William S. Banning to James Horsburgh Jr., 11 October 1892, letterbook 21, William S. Banning to Charles F. Holder, 7, 29 December 1894, letterbook 23, Joseph Brent Banning to Holder, 11 December 1894, letterbook 31, William S. Banning to Holder, 29 February 1904, letterbook 28, William S. Banning to Joseph Brent Banning, 22 May 1913, box 5, Holder to Joseph Brent Banning, 6, 26 December 1907, scrapbook 38, 1996 Addendum, Banning Company Collection, HEH. On Southern California tourism at the time, see, among many others, Culver, "The Island, the Oasis, and the City," esp. 127–28.

25   Santa Catalina Island Company, file 1826, box 47, October 1894, Los Angeles County Incorporation Records, SCWHR.

26   *Los Angeles Times*, 14 December 1893; Hancock Banning to Anne Banning, 29 August 1895, EBA; James Zordich, "Phineas Banning and the W. T. Co.," *Water Lines* 4 (1st Quarter 1989): 7.

27   Joseph Brent Banning to William L. Banning, 2 February 1893, letterbook 31, William S. Banning to John H. Dialogue & Sons, 2 October 1897, William S. Banning to James B. Fraley, 4 February 1898, letterbook 25, William S. Banning to William G. Halstead, 22 March 1899, letterbook 26, Banning Company Collection, HEH; label on photograph 345 (quote), box 3, Banning Family Collection of Photographs, Part I, CL180, HEH; James Zordich, "Santa Catalina Island Company: The First Quarter Century," *Water Lines* 9 (1st Quarter 1994): 6.

28   *Los Angeles Times*, 4 December 1893, 29 January 1899, 7 February 1901; Hancock Banning to Anne Banning, 28 December 1897, EBA; Joseph Brent Banning to William L. Banning, 25 April 1893, letterbook 31, Hancock Banning to Smith and Young, 17 July 1893, letterbook 22, William S. Banning to Frank Carey, 11 August 1908, letterbook 29, Hancock Banning to George H. Smith, 18 August 1911, letterbook 3 (in box 2 of the 1985 Addendum), Banning Company Collection, HEH; Buffum and Buffum, *Catalina Saga*, 49–51. Hancock Banning reported to one respondent that architect George Wyman was going to order Catalina soapstone for the Bradbury Building, but evidence of the sale or use of this material on the structure has not come to light. See the highly detailed description of the design, construction features, and trimmings of this edifice, and its contractors and suppliers, in the *Los Angeles Herald*, 1 January 1894.

29   William S. Banning to Walter Vail, 30 March 1892, and Vail to William S. Banning, 4 April 1892, box 5, William S. Banning to C. W. Gates, 16 April 1894, William S. Banning to Vail and Gates, 19 April 1894, letterbook 23, Banning Company Collection, HEH.

30   William S. Banning to H. E. Mathews, 26 April 1894, letterbook 23, Banning Company Collection, HEH; *Los Angeles Times*, 3 December 1906, 27 January 1908.

31   Banning Wool Company, file 2547 (1898), box 64, Los Angeles County Incorporation Records, SCWHR; *Los Angeles Times*, 2 August 1901, 29 January 1902, 11 February 1903; Frank H. Lowe to William S. Banning, 24 February 1908, letterbook 80, Hancock Banning to Joseph Banning, 15 May 1911, box 3, 1985 Addendum, Hancock Banning to George S. Patton, 28 May 1904, box 12, 1985 Addendum, Banning Wool Company Minutes, 1898–1907, ledger 197, Banning Company Collection, HEH; Edward Norris Wentworth, *America's Sheep Trails: History, Personalities* (Ames: Iowa State College Press, 1948), 203; Buffum and Buffum, *Catalina Saga*, 31–32.

32   William S. Banning to Edwin Stanton, 2 March 1897, letterbook 24, William S. Banning to Hancock Banning, 17 January 1897, box 3, 1985 Addendum, Banning Company Collection, HEH; Joseph Brent Banning's cottage, photograph 94, box 2, Banning Family Collection of Photographs, Part II, CL451, HEH; *Los Angeles Times*, 16 August 1898, 28 June 1902; Joseph Brent Banning home at Descanso photographs 2005-0275 and 1983-0036, CSL.

33   *Los Angeles Times*, 29 June 1902, 26 June, 14 August 1903, 21 March 1904, 8 August 1905.

34   Selena Ingram, diary entries, 1903–11, boxes 1 and 2, Selena Gray Galt Ingram Papers, HEH; *Los Angeles Times*, 4 September 1901.

35   Minutes of Meetings, Los Angeles County Board of Supervisors, 22: 15 June 1996, Los Angeles County Board of Supervisors Office, Los Angeles, Calif.; *Los Angeles Herald*, 21 March 1895, 6 June 1897; Windle, *History of Santa Catalina Island*, 71, 152.

36   *Los Angeles Herald*, 15 August 1897; hotel liquor license to Banning Bros. at Avalon, July–September 1893, box 6, William S. Banning to Joseph Brent Banning, 5 January 1897 (quote), letterbook 24, 20 August 1902, letterbook 27, William S. Banning to Edward Mahar, 10 April 1900, letterbook 26, Banning Company Collection, HEH.

37   William S. Banning to Joseph Brent Banning, 1 July 1896 (quote), letterbook 24, 28 August 1900, letterbook 26, William S. Banning to Hancock Banning, 8 May 1905, letterbook 28, Banning Company Collection, HEH; Hancock Banning Jr., "The Banning Family in Southern California," interview by Dellene M. Tweedale, 1971, transcript, Center for Oral History Research, UCLA, 93.

38   William S. Banning to Hancock Banning, 17 September 1906, letterbook 28, Banning Company Collection, HEH; Minutes of Meetings, Los Angeles County Board of Supervisors, 56: 13 March 1916, Los Angeles County Board of Supervisors Office, Los Angeles, Calif.; Windle, *History of Santa Catalina Island*, quote on 96.

39   Sterngass, *First Resorts*, 105–7, 271–72; Corbett, *The Making of American Resorts*, 144–55; Culver, "The Island, the Oasis, and the City," 105–8.

40   William S. Banning to H. E. Fletcher, 21 May 1904, letterbook 28, Banning Company Collection, HEH; *Los Angeles Times*, 22 August 1905 (quotes); *Los Angeles Express*, 21 August 1905.

41   William S. Banning to O. O. Orr, 5 May 1900, letterbook 26, Banning Company Collection, HEH; Orvar Löfgren, *On Holiday: A History of Vacationing* (Berkeley: University of California Press, 1999), 5, 105–6.

42   William S. Banning to Hancock Banning, 25 July 1892 (quote), William S.
      Banning to Edwin Stanton, 27 March 1893, letterbook 21, William S. Banning
      to Bicknell & Trask, 12 May 1893, William S. Banning to Edwin Stanton,
      27 July 1893, letterbook 22, newspaper clipping, ca. May 1895, scrapbook 23,
      1996 Addendum, Banning Company Collection, HEH.

43   William S. Banning to Joseph Brent Banning, 5 June 1896, William S. Banning
      to A. A. Bynon, 2 July 1896, letterbook 24, Joseph Brent Banning statement,
      n.d., Frank H. Lowe statement, 24 June 1896, box 5, Banning Company Col-
      lection, HEH; *Los Angeles Times*, 8, 17 July 1896.

44   William S. Banning to George H. Smith, ? April 1897, letterbook 24, William S.
      Banning to Joseph Brent Banning, 17 May 1899 (quote), 10, 22 August 1889,
      letterbook 26, Banning Company Collection, HEH; *Los Angeles Times*, 18 Au-
      gust 1897, 24 October 1898, 25 July, 15, 17, 23 August 1899, 24, 31 January 1900.

45   *Los Angeles Times*, 27 September, 4 October 1899, 15, 24 January 1900, 7 May
      1901.

46   William S. Banning to Joseph Brent Banning, 7, 9 (quote) July 1896, letter-
      book 24, 31 August 1900, letterbook 26, William S. Banning to George E.
      Weaver, 26 January 1900, letterbook 26, William S. Banning to Edwin Stan-
      ton, 22 October 1901, letterbook 27, Banning Company Collection, HEH.

47   *Los Angeles Times*, 2 February 1903; William S. Banning to W. H. Kelso,
      2 February 1903, to C. M. Belshaw, 9 February 1903, and to John H. Nelson,
      6 March 1903, letterbook 27, Banning Company Collection, HEH.

48   *Los Angeles Times*, 23 June, 19, 22, 23 September 1906; *San Francisco Chroni-
      cle*, 23 September 1906 (quotes).

49   *Los Angeles Times*, 3 (quote), 6, 10, 28 October 1906, 16, 31 July, 1 August 1907;
      Hancock Banning to Harry Chandler, 2 August 1907, letterbook 79, Banning
      Company Collection, HEH.

50   *Los Angeles Times*, 11 August 1901, 22 March, 12 April, 15 August 1903;
      William S. Banning to William L. Banning, 26 October 1899, and William S.
      Banning to William Staats, 13 March 1900, letterbook 26, William S. Banning
      to William Mulholland, 23 March 1903, letterbook 27, Joseph Brent Banning
      to Edwin Stanton, 7 April 1903, letterbook 32, Joseph Brent Banning to
      Theodore Lukens, 19 November 1900, letterbook 55, Banning Company
      Collection, HEH.

51   George S. Patton to Frederick Law Olmsted [Sr.], 18 February 1903 (quote),
      notes of John C. Olmsted and Mr. Jones at Santa Catalina Island, 3–6 April
      1903, Joseph Brent Banning to Olmsted Brothers, 15 April 1903, file 2394,
      microfilm reel 91, box B123, Records of the Olmsted Associates, LCW; copy
      of Olmsted Brothers to Santa Catalina Island Company, 25 February 1903,
      box 5, 1985 Addendum, William S. Banning to Olmsted Brothers, 19 March
      1903, letterbook 27, Banning Company Collection, HEH.

52   John C. Olmsted report to Banning Brothers, 1 June 1903, file 2394, microfilm
      reel 91, box B123, Records of the Olmsted Associates, LCW.

53   Charles T. Healey to John C. Olmsted, 30 November 1903, Olmsted to
      Healey, 8 December 1903, Frederick L. Olmsted Jr., memorandum to

partners, 4 March 1919, J. B. Lippincott to Frederick L. Olmsted Jr., 8 March, 21 April 1919, file 2394, microfilm reel 91, box B123, Records of the Olmsted Associates LCW; Edwin Stanton to William S. Banning, 20 March 1905, box 5, 1985 Addendum, Banning Company Collection, HEH.

54   William S. Banning to Edwin Stanton, 13 February 1905, letterbook 28, Banning Company Collection, HEH; Windle, *History of Santa Catalina Island*, 68; Pedersen, *Catalina Island*, 36–37, 46.

55   *Los Angeles Times*, 15 May 1903, 16 February, 3 July 1904; *Los Angeles Herald*, 16 February 1904; William S. Banning to Robert Ingram, 14 September 1903, letterbook 27, Banning Company Collection, HEH; Buffum and Buffum, *Catalina Saga*, 154–59, 165–69.

56   William S. Banning to H. E. Mathews, 8 September 1893, letterbook 22, 5 December 1894, letterbook 23, William S. Banning to Charles F. Ayer, 31 December 1895 (quote), William S. Banning to Charles Crocker, 5 October 1896, William S. Banning to J. A. Muir, 10 October 1896, letterbook 24, Banning Company Collection, HEH; *New York Times*, 23 June 1895.

57   *Los Angeles Times*, 2 July 1901; indenture, 21 January 1905 (agreed as of 31 May 1901), box 5, Banning Brothers to George S. Patton, 9 February 1901, box 6, Banning Company Collection, HEH.

58   *Los Angeles Times*, 6 September 1901; William S. Banning to Charles M. Clinton, 30 December 1901, 11 March 1902, letterbook 27, Banning Company Collection, HEH.

Chapter Ten

1   Hancock Banning III, interview by the author, 4 April 2007; Robert J. Banning, interview by the author, 7 October 2007; Robert H. Patton, *The Pattons: A Personal History of an American Family* (New York: Crown, 1994), 106, 206.

2   William S. Banning to Hancock Banning, 12 October 1903 (with notes added), 11, 14 June 1905, copy of Hancock Banning to William S. Banning, 9 February 1903, Joseph Brent Banning to George S. Patton Sr., 14 July 1905, Patton to Henry E. Huntington, 15 July 1905, box 3, 1985 Addendum, Banning Company Collection, HEH; Santa Catalina Island Company board of directors meeting minutes, 28 September 1903, SCICA.

3   Katharine S. Banning to Hancock Banning, 20 October 1905, copy of Hancock Banning to Katharine S. Banning, undated [October 1905], box 3, 1985 Addendum, Banning Company Collection, HEH.

4   Joseph Brent Banning letters, 1907, letterbook 32, Frank H. Lowe to George W. Shaw, 3 May 1907, letterbook 78, William S. Banning to George S. Patton Sr., 7 October 1908 (quote), letterbook 29, William S. Banning to Joseph Brent Banning, 4 March 1909, letterbook 30, Joseph Brent Banning to Hancock Banning, 24 August 1908, William S. Banning to Hancock Banning, 25 August 1908, 18 January 1909 (quote), box 3, 1985 Addendum, Banning Company Collection, HEH; Santa Catalina Island Company board of directors meeting minutes, 3 May 1904–16 January 1907, SCICA; Selena Ingram,

diary entries for 15 October 1908, box 1, 10 August 1909, box 2, Selena Gray
Galt Ingram Papers, HEH; William Alexander MacCorkle, *The White Sulphur Springs* (New York: Neale, 1916), 74–87.

5   Copy of William S. Banning to Katharine S. Banning, telegram, 29 June 1909,
letterbook 30, and 2 July 1909, box 12, William S. Banning to Hancock Banning, 7 July 1909 (quote), box 3, 1985 Addendum, Hancock Banning to Hancock Banning Jr., 7 October 1909, letterbook 1, box 2, 1985 Addendum,
Banning Company Collection, HEH; Katharine S. Banning, notes on photograph in scrapbook 6, box 18, Banning Family Collection of Photographs,
Part II, CL451, HEH; Selena Ingram, diary entry, 10 August 1909 (quote),
box 2, Selena Gray Galt Ingram Papers, HEH.

6   Hancock Banning to Santa Catalina Island Company Board of Directors,
13, 14 November 1907, and "Report #2," box 3, 1985 Addendum, copy of
Hancock Banning, "Prefix to Memorandum 'A,'" 1917, box 5, Banning Company Collection, HEH.

7   Agreement between the Banning Brothers, 15 November 1907, box 1,
Hancock Banning to Banning Company, 14 November 1907, box 2, William
Dunn to George H. Smith, 26 March 1909, box 3, William S. Banning to
Joseph Brent Banning, 23 January 1909, William S. Banning to Hancock Ban-
ning, 24 February 1908, letterbook 29, Joseph Brent Banning to Hancock
Banning, 27 December 1907, letterbook 33, Banning Company Collection,
HEH; Hancock Banning to Hancock Banning Jr., 3 February 1908, Hancock
Banning to William S. Banning, 23 February 1908, letterbook 6, box 1, Joseph
Brent Banning to Hancock Banning, 28 February 1908, William S. Banning to
Hancock Banning, 7, 21 February, 2 April (quote), 16 June 1908, box 3, 1985
Addendum, Banning Company Collection, HEH.

8   Hancock Banning to James A. Gibson, 19 January 1911, copies of Hancock
Banning to William S. Banning, 19 January, 5 December 1911, William S. Banning to Hancock Banning, 7 June, 29 November 1911, Hancock Banning to
George H. Smith, 26 June 1911, Hancock Banning to Joseph Brent Banning,
8 April 1912, box 3, copy of Hancock Banning to A. M. Shields, 25 July 1912,
letterbook 4, box 2, 1985 Addendum, Banning Company Collection, HEH;
Santa Catalina Island Company board of directors meeting minutes,
12, 14 December 1911, SCICA.

9   Copy of Hancock Banning to William S. Banning and Joseph Brent Banning,
8 June 1909, Katharine S. Banning to Hancock Banning, 20 October 1905,
box 3, 1985 Addendum, Banning Company Collection, HEH; Selena Ingram,
diary entries, 23 November 1903 (quote), box 1, 10 September 1909 (quote),
box 2, Selena Gray Galt Ingram Papers, HEH.

10   *Los Angeles Times*, 12 February 1911 (quotes); Joyce Loranger, research notes,
in possession of author; Hancock Banning to Katharine Banning, 26 December 1917, box 5, Banning Company Collection, HEH.

11   Santa Catalina Island Company, File 1826, box 47, Los Angeles County Incorporation Records, SCWHR; *Los Angeles Times*, 29 June 1905; Adelaide
LeMert Doran, *The Ranch That Was Robbins': Santa Catalina Island, California: A Source Book* (Los Angeles: for the author, 1963), 75; James Zordich,

"Santa Catalina Island Company: The First Quarter Century," *Water Lines* 9 (1st Quarter 1994): 7.

12   *Los Angeles Times*, 30 August 1904, 25 July 1905; Selena Ingram, diary entries, 16, 19, 20 November 1906, box 1, Selena Gray Galt Ingram Papers, HEH; William S. Banning to Hancock Banning, 24 March 1908, letterbook 29, William S. Banning to Otto M. Kahn, 4 November 1910, box 3, 1986 Addendum, Banning Company Collection, HEH.

13   Copy of Hancock Banning to William E. Dunn, 2 December 1910, box 3, 1985 Addendum, copies of Hancock Banning to Katharine S. Banning, 26 December 1917, and Hancock Banning, "Management," memorandum, 12 August 1918, box 5, Banning Company Collection, HEH.

14   William S. Banning to Frank H. Lowe, 29 October 1908, letterbook 29, William S. Banning to George S. Patton Sr., 7 October 1908, letterbook 30, William S. Banning to Hancock Banning, 24 May 1910, box 3, 1985 Addendum, Joseph Brent Banning, "Memorandum of Policy," 16 January 1911, box 5, Banning Company Collection, HEH; *Los Angeles Times*, 15 July 1910; Joseph Brent Banning, note on photograph 1155, box 14, photographs and notes in scrapbook 6, box 18, Banning Family Collection of Photographs, Part II, CL451, HEH.

15   *Los Angeles Times*, 19 May, 13 June 1913; Doran, *The Ranch That Was Robbins'*, 196–207.

16   *Los Angeles Times*, 8 November 1908; William S. Banning to Joseph Brent Banning et al., 2 November 1908, William S. Banning to Al Carraher, 10 November 1908, letterbook 29, William S. Banning to Hancock Banning, 13 November 1908, William S. Banning to Santa Catalina Island Company Board of Directors, 17 November 1908, box 3, 1985 Addendum, Banning Company Collection, HEH; William S. Banning to Al Carraher et al., 25 November 1908, 1, 29 December 1908, copy of Committee to William S. Banning, 27 November 1908, General Files, CIM.

17   Freeholders Improvement Association of Avalon, file 10153, box 260, Los Angeles County Incorporation Records, SCWHR; list of members, Freeholders Improvement Association of Avalon, n.d., Vaughan Ormsby to William Hunt, 16 December 1909, General Files, CIM; Zordich, "Santa Catalina Island Company," 17.

18   William S. Banning to Edwin Stanton, 1 December 1908, letterbook 29, Hancock Banning to A. M. Jamison, 7 June 1912, letterbook 4, box 2, 1985 Addendum, Banning Collection, HEH; *Los Angeles Times*, 19 November 1911.

19   *J. H. Miller and E. Donaldson v. Wilmington Transportation Company* briefs and decisions, 1913–15, and *Wilmington Transportation Company v. California Railroad Commission*, 1913, box 5, Banning Company Collection, HEH; Railroad Commission of the State of California, *Decisions of the Railroad Commission of the State of California* 3 (1 July 1912–31 December 1913): 43–61, 125; Railroad Commission of the State of California, *Report*, 1 July 1914–30 June 1915, 9, 13, 323; *Los Angeles Times*, 20 December 1914, 1 December 1915.

20   Copy of petition to Los Angeles County Board of Supervisors, 30 April 1895, box 5, Banning Company Collection, HEH; *Los Angeles Times*, 19 May 1913 (quote). With its new powers, the Board of Supervisors passed an ordinance banning the delivery of liquor in some precincts within unincorporated areas of the county in October 1913.

21   *Los Angeles Times*, 19 May 1913 (quote); William S. Banning to Gibson, Trask, Dunn & Crutcher, 3 March 1908, letterbook 29, Banning Company Collection, HEH; Doran, *The Ranch That Was Robbins'*, 106–9.

22   *Los Angeles Times*, 17, 18, 19 July, 26 August 1913; Zordich, "Santa Catalina Island Company," 8.

23   *Los Angeles Times*, 18 July, 11 August 1913; Joseph Brent Banning to David P. Fleming, 15 August 1913, box 5, Banning Company Collection, HEH.

24   *Los Angeles Times*, 13 January, 22, 24 March, 14 June 1914. By the end of March 1914, the Avalon city treasury contained $1,404.71, with over $1,067 in unpaid bills and a new list of expenses to pay. See copy of Avalon City Council meeting minutes, 10 April 1914, box 1, Frederick Baker Collection of Avalon City Council Minutes, UCLA.

25   *Los Angeles Times*, 1 January, 14 June (quote) 1915; Amended Articles of Incorporation, Freeholders Association of Avalon (1915), file 10153, box 260, Los Angeles County Incorporation Records, SCWHR.

26   *Los Angeles Times*, 30 November, 1 December 1915; Ernest Windle, *Windle's History of Santa Catalina Island*, 2nd ed. (Avalon: Catalina Islander, 1940), 93; Richard Buffum and Marjorie Buffum, *Catalina Saga: An Historical Cruise around Santa Catalina Island* (Balboa Island, Calif.: Abracadabra, 2003), 182–83; Jeannine L. Pedersen, *Catalina Island* (Charleston, S.C.: Arcadia, 2004), 58–60. The secondary sources differ on the number of hotels destroyed.

27   William P. Banning Jr. to Hancock Banning Jr., 27 Ma 1971, box 4, 1985 Addendum, *Islander* (Avalon, Calif.), 7 December 1915, clipping in scrapbook 23, 1996 Addendum, Banning Company Collection, HEH; Hancock Banning Jr., label on photograph 533, 1917, box 5, Banning Family Collection of Photographs, Part I, CL180, HEH; *Los Angeles Times*, 6 December 1915; Hancock Banning Jr., "The Banning Family in Southern California," interview by Dellene M. Tweedale, 1971, transcript, Center for Oral History Research, UCLA.

28   *Los Angeles Times*, 1 December 1915; undated *San Pedro News-Pilot* clipping (December 1915), scrapbook 23, 1996 Addendum, copy of Hancock Banning to William S. Banning, 20 December 1915, 2 January 1916, box 3, 1985 Addendum, option to George S. Patton Sr., 31 December 1915, box 4, 1985 Addendum, Hancock Banning to William S. Banning, memo, 3 January 1916, and Hancock Banning to E. Cole, 3 January 1916, box 5, Banning Company Collection, HEH.

29   *Los Angeles Times*, 6 January 1916 (second quote); Gibson, Dunn & Crutcher, "Brief of Defendant," Wilmington Transportation Company, case 381, Railroad Commission of the State of California, December 1915 (first quote on p. 5), box 5, Hancock Banning to Hancock Banning Jr., 11 May 1916, box 12, William S. Banning to Hancock Banning, memorandum, 15 February 1916, William S. Banning to Hancock Banning, 25 March 1916, box 3, 1985 Addendum, Banning Company Collection, HEH.

30   *Los Angeles Times*, 13 October 1916; Santa Catalina Island brochure (1916), scrapbook 23, 1996 Addendum, Banning Company Collection, HEH. The Bannings also claimed that their profits were down that year because the LaFollette Act, which went into effect in November 1915, restricted the total number of passengers allowed on its two steamers to just more than half of previous number and thus required them to make more trips. See Gibson, Dunn & Crutcher, "Brief of Defendant," 30–32, box 5, Banning Company Collection, HEH.

31   Copies of Hancock Banning to William E. Dunn, 20 December 1916, box 5, and 19 December 1916, copy of Hancock Banning to William S. Banning, 12 January 1917 (quotes), box 3, 1985 Addendum, copy of Hancock Banning, "Prefix to Memorandum 'A,'" 1917, box 5, Banning Company Collection, HEH.

32   *Los Angeles Times*, 30 April, 14 December 1917, 28 April 1918; Banning Company, "Statement of Earnings and Expenses, December 31, 1917," box 1, Banning Company Collection, HEH; *Islander* (Avalon, Calif.), 2 July 1918; Zordich, "Santa Catalina Island Company," 9; Buffum and Buffum, *Catalina Saga*, 176–78.

33   John A. Jakle, *The Tourist: Travel in Twentieth-Century North America* (Lincoln: University of Nebraska Press, 1985), 101–45; Hal Rothman, *Devil's Bargains: Tourism in the Twentieth-Century American West* (Lawrence: University Press of Kansas, 1998), 143–67; Earl S. Pomeroy, *In Search of the Golden West: The Tourist in Western America* (New York: Knopf, 1957), 125–31, 145–47; Jane Wilson, *Gibson, Dunn & Crutcher, Lawyers: An Early History* (Los Angeles: Gibson, Dunn & Crutcher, 1990), quote on 343; Melinda Elizabeth Kashuba, "Tourist Landscapes of Los Angeles County, California" (PhD diss., University of Southern California, 1986), 82–85.

34   Hancock Banning, "Management," memorandum, 12 August 1918, box 5, copy of Hancock Banning to David P. Fleming et al., 22 December 1918, box 3, 1985 Addendum, Banning Company Collection, HEH.

35   Hancock Banning Jr., "The Banning Family in Southern California," interview by Dellene M. Tweedale, 1971, transcript, Center for Oral History Research, UCLA, quote on 136; *Los Angeles Times*, 5 November 1914, 13, 19 February 1919; agreement between William S. Banning and Blankenhorn-Hunter Co., 17 February 1919, box 1, copies of minutes of special meetings of the Banning Company and the Santa Catalina Island Company, 17 February 1919, box 11, Banning Company Collection, HEH; Wilson, *Gibson, Dunn & Crutcher*, 345.

36   Hancock Banning Jr., notes on envelope of William P. Banning Jr. to Hancock Banning Jr., 27 May 1971, box 4, 1985 Addendum, Banning Company Collection, HEH; Santa Catalina Island Company board of directors meeting minutes, 17, 18 February 1919, SCICA; Zordich, "Santa Catalina Island Company," 10.

37   Copy of Hancock Banning to William S. Banning, memorandum, 4 February 1919 (quote), copy of Hancock Banning to Senator Rosenberry, 3 February 1919, Hancock Banning, draft statement to *Los Angeles Herald*, 15 February 1919, box 3, 1985 Addendum, agreements on sale of Banning

Company, February 1919, James A. Gibson to William S. Banning, 15 March 1919, box 1, William S. Banning to Commissioner of the Internal Revenue Service, 30 June 1921, box 11, Banning Company Collection, HEH.

38   Wilmington Transportation Company, board of directors meeting minutes, 18 February 1919, SCICA; William E. Dunn to William S. Banning, telegram, 8 January 1920, James A. Gibson to David P. Fleming, 12 June 1920, box 1, William S. Banning to Commissioner of the Internal Revenue Service, 13 May 1921, box 11, Banning Company Collection, HEH; *Los Angeles Times*, 19 March 1919, 27 May 1920; William Sanford White and Steven Kern Tice, *Santa Catalina Island: Its Magic, People and History* (Glendora, Calif.: White Limited Editions, 1997), quote on 34.

39   Catalina Island Conservancy website, http://www.catalinaconservancy.org (accessed 7 March 2008); Buffum and Buffum, *Catalina Saga*, 188–90; Milton Lawrence Culver, "The Island, the Oasis, and the City: Santa Catalina, Palm Springs, Los Angeles, and Southern California's Shaping of American Life and Leisure" (PhD diss., University of California, Los Angeles, 2004), 140–93.

Chapter Eleven

1   John Whiteclay Chambers III, *The Tyranny of Change: America in the Progressive Era, 1900–1917* (New York: St. Martin's, 1980), esp. 105–14; Richard L. McCormick, "The Discovery that Business Corrupts Politics: A Reappraisal of the Origins of Progressivism," *American Historical Review* 86 (April 1981): 247–74. Among a wealth of other major sources on U.S. Progressivism are John D. Buenker, John C. Burnham, and Robert M. Crunden, *Progressivism* (Cambridge, Mass.: Schenkman, 1977); and Sidney M. Milkis and Jerome E. Mileur, eds., *Progressivism and the New Democracy* (Amherst: University of Massachusetts Press, 1999).

2   Steven P. Erie, "How the Urban West Was Won: The Local State and Economic Growth in Los Angeles, 1880–1932," *Urban Affairs Quarterly* 27 (June 1992): 519–54; Daniel Jon Johnson, "A Serpent in the Garden: Institutions, Ideology, and Class in Los Angeles Politics, 1901–1911" (PhD diss., University of California, Los Angeles, 1996), 77–425. The power of the elite is described in often-exaggerated terms in Frederic Cople Jaher, *The Urban Establishment: Upper Strata in Boston, New York, Charleston, Chicago and Los Angeles* (Urbana: University of Illinois Press, 1982), 654–85; Robert Gottlieb and Irene Wolt, *Thinking Big: The Story of the Los Angeles Times, Its Publishers and Their Influence on Southern California* (New York: G. P. Putnam's Sons, 1977), esp. 189–201; and Mike Davis, *City of Quartz: Excavating the Future in Los Angeles* (New York: Verso, 1990), 101–21.

3   Robert Fogelson, *The Fragmented Metropolis: Los Angeles, 1850–1930* (Cambridge, Mass.: Harvard University Press, 1967), 108–34, 205–13, 229–36; Martin J. Schiesl, "Progressive Reform in Los Angeles under Mayor Alexander, 1909–1913," *California Historical Quarterly* 54 (Spring 1975): 42–49; Martin J. Schiesl, "Politicians in Disguise: The Changing Role of Public Administrators in Los Angeles, 1900–1920," in Michael H. Ebner and Eugene M. Tobin, eds., *The Age of Urban Reform: New Perspectives on the Progressive Era*

(Port Washington, N.Y.: Kennikat, 1977), 102–16; Albert Howard Clodius, "The Quest for Good Government in Los Angeles, 1890–1910" (PhD diss., Claremont Graduate School, 1953), 19–30, 128–539; John Allswang, "The Origins of Direct Democracy in Los Angeles and California: The Development of an Issue and Its Relationship to Progressivism," *Southern California Quarterly* 78 (Summer 1996): 175–98; Thomas J. Sitton, "Walter F. X. Parker and Machine Politics in Los Angeles, 1903–1910" (master's thesis, California State University, Fullerton, 1973); George Mowry, *The California Progressives* (Berkeley: University of California Press, 1951), 1–85, 105–273.

4   Joseph Brent Banning to Banning Company, 30 March 1909, box 12, William S. Banning to Walter F. X. Parker, 25 February 1908, letterbook 29, Hancock Banning to Cornelius Pendleton, 20 January 1909, letterbook 1 in box 2, 1985 Addendum, Banning Company Collection, HEH; *Los Angeles Times*, 10 October 1906.

5   Copy of Hancock Banning to William S. Banning, 21 November 1911, box 3, 1985 Addendum, Banning Company Collection, HEH; Selena Ingram, diary entry, 5 December 1911, box 2, Selena Gray Galt Ingram Papers, HEH; Tom Sitton, *John Randolph Haynes: California Progressive* (Stanford, Calif.: Stanford University Press, 1992), 109–12.

6   *Los Angeles Times*, 21 March 1911.

7   Copy of Hancock Banning to Anne Banning, 8 December 1896, EBA; *Los Angeles Times*, 28 June 1912.

8   Democratic Party material in box 22, Addendum II, Benjamin D. Wilson Papers, HEH; George S. Patton Sr. file, box 2, John Tracy Gaffey Papers, BANC; copy of John R. Haynes to John F. Neylan, 11 October 1916, box 17, Meyer Lissner Papers, SU; "Character Sketches—George S. Patton," *Graphic* 21 (27 August 1904): 2–3; *Los Angeles Express*, 27 November 1897; Robert H. Patton, *The Pattons: A Personal History of an American Family* (New York: Crown, 1994), quote on 159.

9   J. J. Pettigrew to Treasurer, Friday Morning Club, 14 March 1912, letterbook 4 in box 2, 1985 Addendum, Banning Company Collection, HEH; Clark Davis, "An Era and a Generation of Civic Engagement: The Friday Morning Club in Los Angeles, 1891–1931," *Southern California Quarterly* 84 (Summer 2002): 138–56.

10   *Los Angeles Times*, 21, 24 May 1913, 7, 17 August 1914. On the 1913 city election, see Sitton, *John Randolph Haynes*, 117–19.

11   Sitton, *John Randolph Haynes*, 93–94.

12   *Los Angeles Times*, 21 March 1911; *Los Angeles Tribune*, 11 September 1911; *Los Angeles Herald*, 11 October 1911; Jane Apostol, "Why Women Should Not Have the Vote: Anti-Suffrage Views in the Southland in 1911," *Southern California Quarterly* 70 (Spring 1988): 35; George S. Patton Sr. speeches, box 28, Addendum II, Benjamin D. Wilson Papers, HEH.

13   *Los Angeles Times*, 17 August 1914; Selena Ingram, diary entry, 13 August 1911, box 2, Selena Gray Galt Ingram Papers, HEH; copy of Hancock Banning to William S. Banning, 24 October 1911, box 3, 1985 Addendum, Banning Company Collection, HEH.

14   On municipal ownership in Los Angeles in these years, see Fogelson, *Fragmented Metropolis*, 229–46; Sitton, *John Randolph Haynes*, 51–61.

15   Richard Bigger and James D. Kitchen, *How the Cities Grew*, vol. 2 of *Metropolitan Los Angeles: A Study in Integration*, ed. Edwin A. Cottrell, 16 vols. (Los Angeles: Haynes Foundation, 1952), 122, 158–64; Richard W. Barsness, "The Maritime Development of San Pedro Bay, California, 1821–1921" (PhD diss., University of Minnesota, 1963), 403–5.

16   Bigger and Kitchen, *How the Cities Grew*, 158–64; Don A. Shotliff, "San Pedro Harbor, or Los Angeles Harbor? Senator W. H. Savage and the Home Rule Advocates Fail to Stem the Tide of Consolidationism, 1906–1909," *Southern California Quarterly* 54 (Summer 1972): 127–54.

17   *Los Angeles Times*, 20, 25 March, 16 April 1906; William S. Banning to J. M. Elliott, 16 November 1908, letterbook 29, Banning Company Collection, HEH.

18   *Los Angeles Times*, 4 August 1909; Shotliff, "San Pedro Harbor, or Los Angeles Harbor?" 136–52; Steven P. Erie, *Globalizing L.A.: Trade, Infrastructure, and Regional Development* (Stanford, Calif.: Stanford University Press, 2004), 55.

19   *The Statutes of California and Amendments to the Codes* (Sacramento, Calif.: State Office), 1862: 197–99, 1871–72: 108–16, 446–48; Clinton Gurnee to Phineas Banning, 23 March 1880, letterbook 5, William S. Banning to William Kerchoff, 31 May 1894, letterbook 23, deeds and surveys of tidelands property, box 2, Banning Company Collection, HEH; *Los Angeles Herald*, 20 February 1879; Barsness, "The Maritime Development of San Pedro Bay," 474–75; John H. Krenkel, "The Port of Los Angeles as a Municipal Enterprise," *Pacific Historical Review* 16 (August 1947): 285–97.

20   Copies of William S. Banning to Brig. Gen. A. McKenzie and E. E. Calvin to Brig. Gen. A. McKenzie, n.d. [ca. 18 August 1905], D. E. Hughes to Capt. Amos A. Fries, 1 September 1908, box 107, RG77, Records of the Office of the Chief of Engineers, U.S. Army Corps of Engineers, 1896–1943, USNALN; *Los Angeles Times*, 23 February 1906.

21   Thomas E. Gibbon to Banning Company et al., 27 March 1907, Banning Company to Secretary of War William H. Taft, 9 December 1907, William S. Banning to Joseph Brent Banning and Hancock Banning, 17 February 1908, Hancock Banning to Banning Company, 14 November 1907, box 2, Hancock Banning to George H. Smith, 12 May 1909, box 3, Banning Company Collection, HEH; *Los Angeles Times*, 11, 21 November 1908; Capt. Amos A. Fries to Thomas E. Gibbon, 30 June 1908, box 36, Bergman Collection (Thomas E. Gibbon Papers), HEH.

22   William S. Banning to George S. Patton Sr., 23 June 1908, letterbook 29, Hancock Banning to Banning Company, 13 May 1908, agreement between Banning Company and Southern Pacific Railroad Company, 16 June 1908, minutes of special meeting of Banning Company authorizing the sale of tidelands, 16 June 1908, box 2, Hancock Banning to William S. Banning, 15 May 1908, letterbook 6, box 1, William S. Banning to Hancock Banning, 25 August 1908, box 3, 1985 Addendum, Banning Company Collection, HEH.

23   William S. Banning to Robert Ingram, 3 June 1908, copy of Los Angeles Chamber of Commerce Harbor Committee to Capt. Amos A. Fries,

23 January 1907 (quote), box 2, Banning Company Collection, HEH; "Proceeding of Public Hearing of San Pedro Harbor Line Board, June 18, 1908," box 107, RG77, Records of the Office of the Chief of Engineers, U.S. Army Corps of Engineers, 1896–1943, USNALN.

24   *Los Angeles Times*, 8 October 1909, 5 January 1911; "Opinion of the Court, *California v. Southern Pacific Railroad et al.*," Superior Court case 64535, 3 January 1911, box 17, Bergman Collection (Thomas E. Gibbon Papers), HEH; copy of George H. Smith to James A. Gibson, 23 August 1909, box 3, Banning Company Collection, HEH; Barsness, "The Maritime Development of San Pedro Bay," 479.

25   Franklin Hichborn, *Story of the Session of the California Legislature of 1911* (San Francisco: James H. Barry, 1911), 297–314; Marshall Stimson, *Fun, Fights, and Fiestas in Old Los Angeles: An Autobiography* (Los Angeles: privately printed, 1966), 258–59.

26   *Los Angeles Times*, 10 July 1911, 9 March, 18 April 1912, 16 April, 21 December 1913, 14, 20 January 1914, 22 February 1916; *Banning Co. v. California*, 240 U.S. 142 (1916); *Catalina Islander*, 12 August 1925; Barsness, "The Maritime Development of San Pedro Bay," 480–82.

27   *Los Angeles Times*, 17 December 1913, 12 August, 3 November 1916, 4 July 1917; *Los Angeles Daily Journal*, 8 January 1914; copy of Smith, Miller and Phelps to Leslie Hewitt, 20 September 1911, K. A. Miller to Hancock Banning, 9 July 1915, copy of K. A. Miller to William S. Banning, 16 December 1915, box 3, copy of K. A. Miller to F. T. Woodman and Board of Harbor Commissioners, 3 July 1916, box 4, Banning Company Collection, HEH.

28   On the petroleum issue, see Ernest R. Bartley, *The Tidelands Oil Controversy: A Legal and Historical Analysis* (Austin: University of Texas Press, 1953), esp. 59–78.

29   William S. Banning to Edward Mahar, 5 October 1909, box 5, Banning Company Collection, HEH.

30   Fogelson, *Fragmented Metropolis*, 117–19; Los Angeles Board of Harbor Commissioners, *The Port of Los Angeles* (Los Angeles: Board of Harbor Commissioners, 1913), 45–51, 109–14; Capt. Amos A. Fries, "San Pedro Harbor," *Out West* 27 (October 1907); 301–31; Merry L. Thompson, *The Miracle of a Muddy Tideflat* (Wilmington, Calif.: General Phineas Banning Residence Museum, 1980), 23–24.

31   *Los Angeles Times*, 12 December 1906, 1 January, 27 May 1909; William S. Banning to E. E. Calvin, 2 October 1908, letterbook 29, William S. Banning to H. V. Platt, 7 April 1909, letterbook 30, dredging agreement between Marshall Harris and the Banning Company, 16 October 1908, box 2, William S. Banning to North America Dredging Co., 29 March 1909, box 4, 1996 Addendum, Banning Company Collection, HEH.

32   William S. Banning to Hancock Banning, 16 January 1913 (quote), box 12, Banning Company Collection, HEH; *Los Angeles Times*, 20 October 1908, 18 June 1909; Larry Mullaly and Bruce Petty, *The Southern Pacific in Los Angeles, 1873–1996* (San Marino, Calif.: Golden West Books and the Los Angeles Railroad Heritage Foundation, 2002), 33–38.

33   Selena Ingram, diary entries 1903–8, box 1, Selena Gray Galt Ingram Papers, HEH; copy of Robert Ingram to William Hood, 7 March 1905, box 5, Banning Company Collection, HEH.

34   William S. Banning to Howard Huntington, 13 May 1904, letterbook 28, Banning Company Collection, HEH; Grace Heilman Stimson, *Rise of the Labor Movement in Los Angeles* (Berkeley: University of California Press, 1955), 257–59.

35   *Los Angeles Times*, 24 August 1906; Stimson, *Rise of the Labor Movement*, 302–3.

36   William S. Banning to H. V. Platt, 25 January 1907, William S. Banning to John D. Bicknell et al., 25 November 1908, letterbook 29, Banning Company Collection, HEH; *Los Angeles Times*, 25 July 1912, 28 March 1919; Louis B. Perry and Richard S. Perry, *A History of the Los Angeles Labor Movement, 1911–1941* (Berkeley: University of California Press, 1963), 165–81. On the boarding house proposal: the railroad decided to raze the building instead.

37   *Los Angeles Times*, 27 May 1920; Banning Company, file 1825 (1894), box 47, Los Angeles County Incorporation Records, SCWHR.

38   Townsend Land Company, file 9772 (1908), box 250, Los Angeles County Incorporation Records, SCWHR; William S. Banning to Hancock Banning, 8 October 1908, letterbook 29, George Smart to Stephen Townsend, 31 July 1908, letterbook 80, Banning Company Collection, HEH; *Los Angeles Times*, 11 May 1909. The timing of the creation of this company coincided with Hancock's desire to divide all of the Banning property among the three brothers, and he did bring up the possibility of dividing the Newport Ranch holdings but did not pursue it. See Hancock Banning to William S. Banning, 13 April 1908, letterbook 6 in box 1, 1985 Addendum, Banning Company Collection, HEH.

39   Joseph Brent Banning to Hancock Banning, 28 February 1908, 7 November 1908, William S. Banning to Hancock Banning, 7 February 1908, box 3, 1985 Addendum, William S. Banning to Joseph Brent Banning, 17 February 1908, letterbook 29, Banning Company Collection, HEH.

40   *St. Paul Dispatch*, 5 February 1910; *Los Angeles Times*, 29 June 1906, 9 July 1907, 5 February 1910; Santa Catalina Island Company, board of directors meeting minutes, esp. 14 February 1916–23 January 1917, SCICA.

41   *Los Angeles Times*, 12 December 1914; *Los Angeles Examiner*, 13 December 1914; clippings and letters in scrapbooks 29 and 33, 1996 Addendum, Banning Company Collection, HEH.

42   Photograph 93.1, box 2, Banning Family Collection of Photographs, Part II, CL451, HEH; Katharine S. Banning, notes in scrapbook 2, 1996 Addendum, Banning Company Collection, HEH; Scott C. Steward, *The Sarsaparilla Kings* (Cambridge, Mass.: for the author, 1993), 38, 84.

43   Hancock Banning to George S. Patton Sr., 22 February 1908, Hancock Banning to William Staats, 13 March 1908, letterbook 6 in box 1, 1985 Addendum, Banning Company Collection, HEH.

44   *Los Angeles Times*, 16 April 1897, 22 September 1907; *Los Angeles Herald*, 27 January 1907; C. M. Davis and T. Newman, comps., *Los Angeles, California Illustrated* (Los Angeles: Chamber of Commerce, 1899), n.p.; George Hugh Banning, "As I Remember Wilmington," memorandum (quote), copy in Joyce Loranger research files, in possession of author; John S. McGroarty, *Los Angeles, From the Mountains to the Sea*, 3 vols. (Chicago: American Historical Society, 1921), 3:776.

45   George Hugh Banning, "As I Remember Wilmington" (quote); George H. Smith to Albert Crutcher, 6 April 1911, box 6, Hancock Banning to William S. Banning, 20 February 1908, letterbook 6 in box 1, 1985 Addendum, Banning Company Collection, HEH; *Los Angeles Times*, 31 October 1909; Selena Ingram, diary entries for 13 June, 23 September 1907, box 1, Selena Gray Galt Ingram Papers, HEH; James J. Yoch, *Visionary on the Golden Shore: Phineas Banning in Southern California, 1851–1885* (Wilmington, Calif.: Banning Residence Museum, 2002), 102–6.

46   Copy of E. W. Nichols to Hancock Banning, 21 February 1911, box 12, Hancock Banning to Rev. R. B. Gooden, 15 August 1912, letterbook 4 in box 2, 1985 Addendum, Banning Company Collection, HEH.

47   *Los Angeles Times*, 8 May 1906, 19 April 1907, 30 June 1917 (quote); *Los Angeles Times* clippings, 1894–99, in "Early Assistance League of Southern California" file, ALSCA; Gloria Ricci Lothrop, "Strength Made Stronger: The Role of Women in Southern California Philanthropy," *Southern California Quarterly* 71 (Summer/Fall 1989): 165–66.

48   *Los Angeles Times*, 27 October 1912, 18 October 1913, 17 January 1914; Selena Ingram, diary entries, 1903–8, box 1, Selena Gray Galt Ingram Papers, HEH.

49   George Hugh Banning, "As I Remember Wilmington"; copy of Hancock Banning to Baron Alfred de Ropp, 19 March 1919, box 14, copy of Hancock Banning to William S. Banning, 30 September 1909, box 3, 1985 Addendum, Hancock Banning to George H. Smith, 19 April 1912, letterbook 4 in box 2, J. J. Pettigrew to Anne Banning, 4 July 1911, letterbook 3 in box 1, Hancock Banning to Rev. S. J. McPherson, 9 September 1913, and Hancock Banning to Miss C. H. Baker, 15 August 1913, letterbook 5 in box 2, 1985 Addendum, Banning Company Collection, HEH.

50   Hancock Banning to Hancock Banning Jr., 18 January 1915, box 12, Banning Company Collection, HEH; *Los Angeles Times*, 16 February 1915; Harper Franklin, ed., *Who's Who on the Pacific Coast* (Los Angeles: Harper, 1913), 524.

51   U.S. Bureau of the Census, Population Schedules, 13th Census (1910), listings for Los Angeles City, as scanned on Ancestry.com, http://www.ancestry.com; McGroarty, *Los Angeles, From the Mountains to the Sea*, 3:555–56; *Southwest Blue Book* (Los Angeles: Lenora King Berry, 1918), 34. One of the Browns' cousins, Russell Errol Train, was appointed head of the Environmental Protection Agency during the Nixon Administration, and has continued his activism as a nationally prominent environmentalist in the twenty-first century. See J. Brooks Flippen, *Conservative Conservationist: Russell E. Train*

and the Emergence of American Environmentalism (Baton Rouge: Louisiana State University Press, 2006).

52   Selena Ingram, diary entries, 1902–8, box 1, Selena Gray Galt Ingram Papers, HEH; Patton, *The Pattons*, 87–284.

53   Los Angeles County Board of Supervisors, Minutes of Meetings, 40: 24 June, 8 July 1908, Los Angeles County Board of Supervisors Office, Los Angeles, Calif.; William S. Banning to Charles F. Lummis, 14 April 1905, William S. Banning to L. W. Blinn, 19 September 1905, letterbook 28, William S. Banning to E. E. Calvin, 11 April 1910, box 5, Banning Company Collection, HEH.

54   Building permit (1912), Building Records Section, Los Angeles City Department of Building and Safety Metro Office, Los Angeles, Calif.; notes on letterhead of William S. Banning, 7 June 1938, scrapbook 10, 1996 Addendum, Banning Company Collection, HEH; newspaper clipping (*Los Angeles Examiner?*), December 1912, RJB; Yoch, *Visionary on the Golden Shore*, 131. On Carroll H. Brown, see *Los Angeles Times*, 20 October 1885, 1 January 1896, 1 January 1897; Henry F. Withey, *Biographical Dictionary of American Architects (Deceased)* (Los Angeles: Hennessey & Ingalls, 1956), 80.

55   Map of William S. Banning property in Compton, box 13, 1985 Addendum, Banning Company Collection, HEH; notes on photograph 411 (quote), box 4, Banning Family Collection of Photographs, Part I, CL180, HEH.

56   Selena Ingram, diary entries for 2, 3 August 1913 (quotes), box 2, Selena Gray Galt Ingram Papers, HEH.

57   Selena Ingram, diary entries, 1903–8, box 1, 1909–15, box 2, Selena Gray Galt Ingram Papers, HEH; Katharine S. Banning, labels on photographs in box 4, Banning Family Collection of Photographs, Part II, CL451, HEH.

58   *Los Angeles Times*, 2 February 1903, 21 October 1910; Mary E. H. Banning, account book, 1906–11, Rare Book Collection, BRM.

59   *Los Angeles Times*, 23 February 1913, 1 November 1914 (quote); Bertha H. Smith, "California's First Cubist House," *Sunset* 35 (August 1915): 368–76; Thomas S. Hines, *Irving Gill and the Architecture of Reform: A Study in Modernist Architectural Culture* (New York: Monacelli, 2000), 71, 123–26.

60   *Los Angeles Times*, 14 September 1918, 23, 24 August 1919.

61   William S. Banning to F. W. Thompson, 26 April 1907 (quote), letterbook 29, Banning Company Collection, HEH; *Los Angeles Times*, 10 February 1920; *Southwest Blue Book* (1918), 23.

62   *Los Angeles Times*, 13 February, 2, 4, 8 May 1918; Mary H. Banning Norris probate file P373115 (1956), Los Angeles County Archives, Los Angeles County Recorder's Office, Norwalk, Calif.

63   *Los Angeles Times*, 21 September 1906 (quote), 1 July 1907, 17 November 1911. The newspaper reports on Lucy's assertion that Mace mistreated her are mentioned in Selena Ingram, diary entries for 4, 5 November 1910, box 2, Selena Gray Galt Ingram Papers, HEH. Lucy's first husband, John Bradbury, died in 1913 after a three-year illness (*Los Angeles Times*, 21 August 1913).

64 *New York Times*, 18 November 1911; *San Francisco Examiner*, 2 April 1912 (quote); *Los Angeles Times*, 28 August 1919.

65 Clippings and ephemera, scrapbook 32, 1996 Addendum, Banning Company Collection, HEH. On the sinking of the *Lusitania*, see Thomas A. Bailey and Paul B. Ryan, *The Lusitania Disaster: An Episode in Modern Warfare and Diplomacy* (New York: Free Press, 1975).

66 Hancock Banning Jr., notes on photograph 380 (quote), box 4, Banning Family Collection of Photographs, Part I, CL180, HEH. Banning identified Demmler as the German consul, but the city directories merely list him as a general agent for a fertilizer company.

67 William A. Spalding, *History and Reminiscences, Los Angeles City and County, California*, 3 vols. (Los Angeles: J. R. Finnell & Sons, 1931), 2:123. Joseph Brent Banning's youngest son, William Phineas, was a teenager when the war broke out and spent the war in college.

68 Ibid., 3:419; Hancock Banning to Hancock Banning Jr., 12 January 1917, box 12, Banning Company Collection, HEH; *Who's Who in the New Deal: Southern California Edition* (Los Angeles: New Deal Historical Society, 1938), 281.

69 Spalding, *History and Reminiscences*, 3:419; Manuel Pineda and E. Caswell Perry, *Pasadena Area History* (Pasadena, Calif.: J. W. Anderson, 1972), 165.

70 Hancock Banning Jr. to Helen Miller, 7 December 1918 (quote), transcribed and edited by Robert J. Banning, RJB; *Los Angeles Herald*, 14 January 1919.

71 Patton, *The Pattons*, 143–58, 166–84; Stanley P. Hirshson, *General Patton: A Soldier's Life* (New York: Harper Collins, 2002), 65–131; Martin Blumenson, *The Patton Papers*, 2 vols. (Boston: Houghton Mifflin, 1972), 1:293–680.

72 *Los Angeles Times*, 7 April 1917. On the home front in America during the war, see David M. Kennedy, *Over Here: The First World War and American Society* (New York: Oxford University Press, 1980).

73 *Los Angeles Times*, 7 August 1918; *Los Angeles Times* newspaper clippings, 1917–19, in "Red Cross" scrapbook, ALSCA; Ruth Burke Stephens, "An Observer in a Red Cross Shop," *Graphic* 52 (10 July 1918): 10–11; McGroarty, *Los Angeles, From the Mountains to the Sea*, 2:15–18. On Anne's production of *Patience*, see Selena Ingram, diary entries for 6, 26 September, 20 October 1914, box 2, Selena Gray Galt Ingram Papers, HEH.

74 *Los Angeles Times*, 18 January, 2 October 1918.

75 *Los Angeles Times*, 7 April, 10 May 1917; *Los Angeles Examiner*, 4 November 1917; John J. Byrne to Katharine S. Banning, 3 May 1917, Katharine S. Banning to Mrs. Robert Wood, 23 May 1917, scrapbook 13, newspaper clipping (*Los Angeles Herald?*), 27 July 1917, scrapbook 2, 1996 Addendum, Banning Company Collection, HEH.

76 *Los Angeles Times*, 27 November 1917; *Los Angeles Examiner*, 6 December 1917; papers regarding the "Bill's Comfort Bags" business in scrapbooks 14 and 18, 1996 Addendum, Banning Company Collection, HEH.

Chapter Twelve

1   On the United States in the 1920s, see, among others, Ellis W. Hawley,
     The Great War and the Search for a Modern Order: A History of the Ameri-
     can People and Their Institutions, 1917–1933 (New York: St. Martin's, 1979);
     David Joseph Goldberg, *Discontented America: The United States in the*
     1920s (Baltimore: Johns Hopkins University Press, 1999); and Niall A. Palmer,
     The Twenties in America: Politics and History (Edinburgh, U.K.: Edinburgh
     University Press, 2006).

2   See, among many others, Kevin Starr, *Material Dreams: Southern California*
     through the 1920s (New York: Oxford University Press, 1990); and Tom Sitton
     and William Deverell, eds., *Metropolis in the Making: Los Angeles in the 1920s*
     (Berkeley: University of California Press, 2001).

3   *Los Angeles Times*, 1, 4, 5, 6, 7, 22 November 1920.

4   *Los Angeles Times*, 11 November 1920, 16 March 1921.

5   *Los Angeles Times*, 13 July 1977; copy of Hancock Banning to James A. Gib-
     son Jr., 6 May 1919, copy of Hancock Banning to David P. Fleming, 3 July 1919,
     Hancock Banning to Anne Banning, 20 August 1923, and other material in
     box 14, Banning Company Collection, HEH, Selena Ingram, diary entry,
     14 January 1919, box 3, Selena Gray Galt Ingram Papers, HEH; Los Angeles
     Board of Harbor Commissioners, *Annual Report* (Los Angeles: Board of
     Harbor Commissioners, 1923–24).

6   *Los Angeles Times*, 6, 8, 10, 11, 13 August (quotes) 1925; *Catalina Islander*,
     12 August 1925; copy of Hancock Banning to Jackson A. Graves, 23 August
     1922, Hancock Banning Jr. to Dr. Wernigk, 7 August 1925, box 7, 1985 Adden-
     dum, Banning Company Collection, HEH.

7   *Los Angeles Examiner*, 13 August 1925.

8   *Los Angeles Times*, 24 July 1926, 3 June 1927; *San Francisco Chronicle*,
     12 January, 1 June (quote) 1927.

9   Kazumasa Yoshida, *Maboroshi no Isan (Elusion of Inheritance)* (Tokyo:
     Sanichi Shobo, 1996), n.p. in translation, BRM; *Los Angeles Times*,
     26 October 1926, 23 January 1928; *Los Angeles Examiner*, 21 February 1929.

10   *Los Angeles Times*, 21 January, 4 May 1928; *San Francisco Examiner*,
     4 May 1928 (quote); *Los Angeles Examiner*, 7 April 1928 (quote).

11   *Los Angeles Times*, 17, 19, 21 February, 19 March, 4 May 1929; Rebecca Lee
     Dorsey, unpublished memoir, 283, copy at BRM; Eugene Francis, "Lucy
     Banning's Primrose Path," *American Weekly*, 20 March 1949, 24–25; Cecelia
     Rasmussen, "'Man Crazy' Lucy Banning Was Rich and Free-Spirited,"
     Los Angeles Times, 5 September 2004, B-3.

12   *Los Angeles Times*, 11 November 1930, 5 January 1931, 30 September 1933,
     23 April 1940, 11 February 1942, 1 August 1947; *Los Angeles Examiner*,
     15 September 1933, 10 October 1946, 17 December 1946; Yoshida, *Maboroshi*
     no Isan, n.p.

13   *Los Angeles Times*, 24 December 1924.

14   *Los Angeles Times*, 11 June 1927, 8 October 1928; Robert H. Patton, *The
Pattons: A Personal History of an American Family* (New York: Crown, 1994),
206–11. A Los Angeles–area Banning far removed from the Phineas line, but
possibly connected to his descendants, also died in this decade. Pierson
Worrall Banning was born in Chicago and came to Los Angeles in 1910 as a
researcher and writer. In 1908, he had compiled and written a history of the
Banning family, aided by the Southern California members of the clan. The
book was never published, but fifteen typescript copies were distributed to
major libraries throughout the United States. A superpatriot who investigated alleged German espionage in Los Angeles County during World War I
and later led a movement to ban books in California that did not teach history "from the American standpoint," he became better known for inventing
an award for a book he published in 1924 that was attacked by the American
Medical Association. *Los Angeles Times*, 16 November 1920, 12 May,
23 August 1923, 30 March, 3, 4, 6, 13 April 1924, 8 July 1927; *Who Was Who
in America, 1897–1942* (Chicago: Marquis's Who's Who, 1966), 54.

15   Mary H. Banning Norris to Hancock Banning, 28 June 1923, box 3, 1985
Addendum, Banning Company Collection, HEH; Elizabeth Banning
Ames, interview by the author, 14 January 2006; Marianne Alyce Banning
Adey, interview by the author, 10 January 2006; *Los Angeles Times*, 2 May
1938, 4 January 1956.

16   Copy of William S. Banning to Robert B. Armstrong, 19 February 1920,
to Harry Chandler, 19, 24, 26 February 1920, and to William Wrigley Jr.,
8 March 1920, William S. Banning letterbook, box 5, 1985 Addendum,
Banning Company Collection, HEH.

17   Copy of James A. Gibson to Henry Keller, 2 April 1920, box 20, William S.
Banning to Henry Keller, 4 October 1921, Keller to William S. Banning,
28 December 1944, letterheads of Francis P. Graves & Company and Graves,
Banning & Company, 1927–28, and other material in box 21, Banning Company Collection, HEH.

18   *Los Angeles Times*, 16 December 1920, 18 October 1925, 3 January 1926,
28 August 1927, 31 March 1929; *Catalina Islander*, 26 October 1927;
George C. Wheeler to William S. Banning, 17 June 1930, box 20, John C.
Macfarland to Hancock Banning Jr., 7 July 1931, box 21, Banning Company
Collection, HEH; photographs 395, 397, and others, box 4, Banning Family
Collection of Photographs, Part I, CL180, HEH.

19   *Los Angeles Times*, 4 April 1926.

20   "Bill's Comfort Bag for Men in the Service—Its History," *Islander* (Avalon,
Calif.), 23 July 1918; Katharine S. Banning, "Bill's Comfort Bags," U.S. patent
130828, 1 July 1919, and "Comfort Bags of Katharine S. Banning," Dominion
of Canada patent serial number 195959, 13 January 1920, Robert P. Crane
to Katharine S. Banning, 21 January 1919, R. A. Applegate to Katharine S.
Banning, 13 September 1927, scrapbook 22, Mrs. Joseph B. Banning business
records, 1918–23, scrapbook 27, 1996 Addendum, Banning Company Collection, HEH.

21   James Taylor Dunn, "St. Paul's Schubert Club: Musical Mentor of the
      Northwest," *Minnesota History* 39 (Summer 1964): 52; advertisement in the
      Minnesota Guardsman 1 (August 1893): 17; Nancy Morse Banning Call, inter-
      view by the author, 25 June 2007; William F. Banning, telephone interview by
      the author, 2 October 2007.

22   William F. Banning, telephone interview by the author, 2 October 2007;
      National Cyclopaedia of American Biography, 63 vols. (New York: James T.
      White, 1898–1984), 38:472; *Los Angeles Times*, 8 June 1937; *Los Angeles Exam-
      iner*, 3, 8 June 1937; unidentified clipping in box 8, 1985 Addendum, Banning
      Company Collection, HEH.

23   *Los Angeles Times*, 28 October, 18 November 1921, 1 February 1924, 28 Au-
      gust 1927, 26 January 1928; "Anne Ophelia Smith Banning" research file,
      Tea Room Guest Books, and Location Bureau books, ALSCA; receipt
      for use of "Banning Place" by Goldwyn Pictures Corporation, 5 September
      1920, box 15, Banning Company Collection, HEH.

24   *Los Angeles Times*, 15 December 1920, 15 January, 11 June 1922, 10 November
      1923; Selena Ingram, diary entry, 17 January 1920, box 3, Selena Gray Galt
      Ingram Papers, HEH.

25   *San Francisco Chronicle*, 28 June–5 July 1920; *Los Angeles Times*, 5 April 1925.
      On Parrot and Cryer and the 1925 election, see Tom Sitton, "The 'Boss'
      Without a Machine: Kent Kane Parrot and Los Angeles Politics in the 1920s,"
      Southern California Quarterly 67 (Winter 1985): 367–87.

26   *Los Angeles Times*, 4 December 1921, 21 June 1925 (quote), 5 December 1926.

27   *Los Angeles Times*, 6 March, 2 August 1921; Hancock Banning to Mrs. Wil-
      liam Le Moyne Wills, 1 October 1923 (quote), box 7, 1985 Addendum, Ban-
      ning Company Collection, HEH.

28   *Los Angeles Times*, 4, 31 March, 7, 10 April, 2, 4 May 1926.

29   *Los Angeles Times*, 29 October 1926, 27 June 1927.

30   Hancock Banning to Mr. Thatcher, 20 February, 26 October 1908, letterbook
      6 in 1985 Addendum, copy of E. W. Nichols, superintendent of Virginia Mili-
      tary Institute, statement, 21 February 1911, Hancock Banning to Hancock
      Banning Jr., 27 February 1911 (quote), Hancock Banning to George H. Smith, 8
      March 1911, box 12, Banning Company Collection, HEH.

31   Manuel Pineda and E. Caswell Perry, *Pasadena Area History* (Pasadena,
      Calif.: J. W. Anderson, 1972), 165.

32   Ibid.; *Los Angeles Times*, 22 April, 19 October 1919, 2 January 1927; Hancock
      Banning Jr. to Hancock Banning, 16 November 1920, box 12, Banning Com-
      pany Collection, HEH; Elizabeth Banning Ames, interview by the author,
      14 January 2006.

33   *Los Angeles Times*, 7 June 1917, 24 September 1933; Selena Ingram, diary
      entries for 6 June 1933, 8 June, 19 August 1926, box 3, Selena Gray Galt In-
      gram Papers, HEH; Russell Holmes Fletcher, ed., *Who's Who in California,
      1942–1943* (Los Angeles: Who's Who, 1941), 570–71. Eleanor was a very close
      friend of Selena Pope Ingram, and their very frequent activities together are
      mentioned in the diaries of Selena's mother, cited in this endnote.

34   E. W. Taylor Jr., *Bench and Bar of California, 1937–1938* (Chicago: E. W. Taylor Jr., 1937), 225–26; *Who's Who on the Pacific Coast* (New York: A. N. Marquis, 1949), 584; Jane Wilson, *Gibson, Dunn & Crutcher, Lawyers: An Early History* (Los Angeles: Gibson, Dunn & Crutcher, 1990), 439–42.

35   *Los Angeles Times*, 27 May 1916, 1 June 1919, 28 April 1920.

36   *Los Angeles Times*, 28 April, 1, 2, May 1920.

37   *Los Angeles Times*, 27 April, 25 May 1919, 27 October 1925; George Atcheson Jr. and George Hugh Banning, *Adonis Falls* [play program] (Berkeley: University of California Class of 1919, 1919), RB 274321, HEH; George Hugh Banning, *Found in a Derelict: "Queen of the Night" and Other Poems* (Los Angeles: Murrell, 1919), quote on 1, RB 83882, HEH; George Hugh Banning, *Spun Yarn* (London: Methuen, 1923).

38   *Los Angeles Times*, 8 January 1923; *London Times Literary Supplement*, 9 April 1925, 248; George Hugh Banning, *In Mexican Waters* (London: Martin Hopkinson, 1925).

39   Captain William Banning and George Hugh Banning, *Six Horses* (New York: Century, 1930); research notes and images in all boxes of the George Hugh Banning Collection, BRM. Reviews of the book include: Henry Steele Commager, *Books*, 11 May 1930, 4; Milo M. Quaife, *Yale Review* 20 (Winter 1931): 399; and K. Frank Dobie, *Nation*, 13 August 1930, 182–83.

40   Additional publications based on *Six Horses* include Captain William Banning and George Hugh Banning, "Some Aspects of Staging in the Golden State before the Coming of the Overland Mail," *Touring Topics* 21 (July 1929): 26–31; and "Wheel Tracks of the 'Jackass Mail': A Chronicle of the Perils and Problems of the First Transcontinental Stage Line," *Touring Topics* 21 (November 1929): 21–25, 54; and George Hugh Banning, "Stage Wheels Over the Padres's Trail," *Westways* 26 (July 1934): 16–17, 33–34. As noted above, George wrote the essays attributed to both him and William.

41   Hancock Banning to Hancock Banning Jr., 27 February 1911, box 12, family photographs, notes, program of performance, ca. 1905, and other material in scrapbook 1, 1996 Addendum, Banning Company Collection, HEH.

42   *San Francisco Shipping Register*, 21 March 1925, clipping in scrapbook 83, Morse Family Scrapbooks, HEH; William A. Spalding, *History and Reminiscences, Los Angeles City and County, California*, 3 vols. (Los Angeles: J. R. Finnell & Sons, 1931), 2:123.

43   *Los Angeles Times*, 12 October, 10 December 1922; *San Francisco Examiner*, 22, 28 August 1898, clippings in scrapbook 83, and other material in earlier volumes, Morse Family Scrapbooks, HEH; John Frederick Morse, M.D., *The First History of Sacramento City* (1853; repr., Sacramento, Calif.: Sacramento Book Collectors Club, 1945).

44   Nancy Morse Banning Call, interview by the author, 25 June 2007; Marian Lowry Banning, interview by the author, 3 December 2005.

45   *Los Angeles Times*, 24 May 1921, 14 November 1929, 15 March, 30 September, 30, 31 December 1930; U.S. Department of Commerce, license of Master of Steam Vessels, 29 September 1926, file L-684, R. J. Chandler, memorandum

to "All Concerned" at Los Angeles Steamship Company, 17 January 1931, box 3, 1996 Addendum, Banning Company Collection, HEH; Matson Navigation Company, news release (announcing Joseph Brent Banning Jr. retirement), 12 April 1954 (quote), Banning file, *Los Angeles Examiner* Collection, Department of Special Collections, University of Southern California Library. Los Angeles, Calif.

46   Selena Ingram, diary entries for 4 February 1914, 24 September 1917, box 2, Selena Gray Galt Ingram Papers, HEH; *Los Angeles Times*, 2 December 1927; Justice B. Detwiler, ed., *Who's Who in California, 1928–1929* (San Francisco: Who's Who, 1928), 109.

47   *Los Angeles Times*, 20 July 1922.

48   Fred M. Keller to William Phineas Banning, 13 January 1928, box 83, Henry Workman Keller Papers, UCLA; Spalding, *History and Reminiscences*, 2:123. According to his spouse, William Phineas Banning also played some role in the purchase of the seat on the New York Stock Exchange for his brother-in-law and partner, Francis Graves. Evangeline Grier Banning, diary entry, 27 November 1927, Evangeline Grier Banning Diary, 1924–28, MLB.

49   *Los Angeles Times*, 11 November 1920; William M. Grier Jr., *The Griers: Pioneers in America and Canada, 1816–1991* (Denver: Grier, 1991), 105–6; Doane Robinson, *History of South Dakota, Together with Personal Mention of Citizens of South Dakota*, 2 vols. (Logansport, Ind.: B. F. Bowen, 1904), 2:1248–49.

50   *Los Angeles Times*, 8 December 1921; Marian Lowry Banning, interview by the author, 3 December 2005.

51   Starr, *Material Dreams*; Sitton and Deverell, *Metropolis in the Making*.

52   Nancy Morse Banning Call, interview by the author, 25 June 2007; Mary Jane Grier, diary entry, 18 June 1931, Mary Jane Grier Diary, and Evangeline Grier Banning, diary entry, 1 February 1927, Evangeline Grier Banning Diary, 1924–28, MLB.

53   John C. Macfarland to J. Stuart Neary, 8 October 1928, Neary to Macfarland, 4 December 1928, box 21, G. O. Gartz to William S. Banning, 8 April 1936, box 20, Banning Company Collection, HEH. There is also speculation that William might have ordered the move from the Barn because the surrounding neighborhood was changing or because new city zoning laws would soon outlaw keeping horses there. See James J. Yoch, *Visionary on the Golden Shore: Phineas Banning in Southern California, 1851–1885* (Wilmington, Calif.: Banning Residence Museum, 2002), 131.

54   Nancy Morse Banning Call, interview by the author, 25 June 2007; Karen E. Hudson, *Paul R. Williams, Architect: A Legacy of Style* (New York: Rizzoli, 1993), 45, 230; David Gebhard and Robert Winter, *An Architectural Guidebook to Los Angeles*, 5th ed. (Salt Lake City, Utah: Gibbs Smith, 2003), 162.

CHAPTER THIRTEEN

1   Arthur M. Schlesinger Jr., *The Age of Roosevelt* series, 3 vols., including *The Crisis of the Old Order, 1919–1933*, *The Coming of the New Deal*, and *The Politics of Upheaval* (Boston: Houghton Mifflin, 1957, 1959, 1960); T. H. Watkins, *The Great Depression: America in the 1930s* (Boston: Little, Brown, 1993); David Kennedy, *Freedom from Fear: The American People in Depression and War, 1929–1945* (New York: Oxford University Press, 1999).

2   On the New Deal, see the works cited in n. 1, and the following, among many others: Allan M. Winkler, *Franklin D. Roosevelt and the Making of Modern America* (New York: Pearson/ Longman, 2006); Ronald Edsforth, *The New Deal: America's Response to the Great Depression* (Malden, Mass.: Blackwell, 2000); Elliott A. Rosen, *Roosevelt, the Great Depression and the Economics of Recovery* (Charlottesville: University of Virginia Press, 2005).

3   Leonard Leader, *Los Angeles and the Great Depression* (New York: Garland, 1991), esp. 1–18; William H. Mullins, *The Depression and the Urban West Coast, 1929–1933: Los Angeles, San Francisco, Seattle and Portland* (Bloomington: University of Indiana Press, 1991); Kevin Starr, *Endangered Dreams: The Great Depression in California* (New York: Oxford University Press, 1995); Thomas Joseph Sitton, "Urban Politics and Reform in New Deal Los Angeles: The Recall of Mayor Frank L. Shaw" (PhD diss., University of California, Riverside, 1983), 32–150.

4   *Los Angeles Times*, 6 October, 10 (quote), 17 November 1929, 10 February, 20 March, 25 April, 9 October 1932, 1, 16 March, 2 October 1933, 17 November 1935 (quote), 19 February 1936.

5   *Los Angeles Times*, 26 January, 7 February, 10 March, 21 July 1933. On California in the 1930s, see Royce D. Delmatier et al., *The Rumble of California Politics, 1848–1970* (New York: John Wiley & Sons, 1970), 230–99; Starr, *Endangered Dreams*.

6   *Los Angeles Times*, 6 April 1921, 29 October 1929, 22 September 1931, 12 March, 25 June, 16 September 1932; Harry Chandler to Anne Banning, 24 October 1934, MABA.

7   *Los Angeles Times*, 20 November 1932, 18 September 1936, 10 May 1937 (quote). On the 1937 Los Angeles election, see Sitton, "Urban Politics and Reform in New Deal Los Angeles," 151–64.

8   *Los Angeles Times*, 5 December 1931, 23, 25 September, 20, 22 October 1940; *Los Angeles Examiner*, 23 September 1940; Elizabeth Banning Ames, interview by the author, 14 January 2006.

9   *Los Angeles Times*, 6 October 1929, 18 May, 25 July, 24 September 1933.

10   *Los Angeles Times*, 26 March 1936, 17 March, 4 November 1938; Robert J. Banning, interview by the author, 7 October 2007.

11   *Los Angeles Times*, 27 September, 9 October 1934, 7 March 1936.

12   *Los Angeles Times*, 23 December 1937, 10 January, 25 March, 5 April, 14, 20, 21, 31 (quote) October 1938; Starr, *Endangered Dreams*, 121–55.

13   Eleanor Banning Macfarland to Senator William Gibbs McAdoo, 31 August 1938 (quote), box 9, William Gibbs McAdoo Papers, HEH.

14   *Los Angeles Times*, 19 February, 21 October 1936, 23 January 1938, 20, 29 January, 9, 15 March 1939; Oliver Vickery, *Harbor Heritage: Tales of the Harbor Area of Los Angeles, California* (Mountain View, Calif.: Morgan, 1979), 12–14, quote on 14; Joyce Loranger, research notes (quote), BRM; *Who's Who in the New Deal: Southern California Edition* (Los Angeles: New Deal Historical Society, 1938), 240; Gloria Ricci Lothrop, "Strength Made Stronger: The Role of Women in Southern California Philanthropy," *Southern California Quarterly* 71 (Summer/Fall 1989): 143–94.

15   *Los Angeles Times*, 29 June 1932, 11 April 1937, 22 March 1939.

16   *Los Angeles Times*, 5 February, 13 August (quote) 1933, 23 April 1935.

17   *Los Angeles Times*, 22 November 1934, 12 January 1936; *Southwest Blue Book* (Los Angeles: Lenora King Berry, 1924–42); Hancock Banning III, telephone interview by the author, 10 May 2008.

18   *Los Angeles Times*, 27, 30 November, 4 December 1932; F. W. Thom to Anne Banning, 7 July 1932, Paul Curtis to Anne Banning, 25 November 1932, and other correspondence and inventories in box 13, Banning Company Collection, HEH; Hancock Banning Jr., "The Banning Family in Southern California," interview by Dellene M. Tweedale, 1971, transcript, Center for Oral History Research, UCLA, 129–30.

19   Townsend Land Company statements and correspondence, 1931, box 3, 1996 Addendum, and clipping, *Swett and Crawford Review*, February 1935, p. 4, box 13, 1985 Addendum, Banning Company Collection, HEH; Hancock Banning Jr., "The Banning Family in Southern California," 140–47; Manuel Pineda and E. Caswell Perry, *Pasadena Area History* (Pasadena, Calif.: J. W. Anderson, 1972), 165.

20   "Places and Personalities," *California Arts and Architecture* 45 (February 1934): 26; Russell Holmes Fletcher, ed., *Who's Who in California, 1942–1943* (Los Angeles: Who's Who, 1941), 570–71.

21   *Los Angeles Times*, 29 May, 12 June, 28, 30 (quote) July 1940; *New York Times*, 28 July 1940; Elizabeth Banning Ames, interview by the author, 14 January 2006.

22   *Los Angeles Times*, 23 November 1934; *Los Angeles Examiner*, 24 November 1934, 10, 12 March 1936; Senator William Gibbs McAdoo to George Hugh Banning, 27 March 1937, 4 April 1938, George Hugh Banning to Jerry Voorhis, 29 March 1946, George Hugh Banning to Senator Sheridan Downey, 9 December 1946, MABA; *Who's Who in the New Deal*, 281; Jane Apostol, *South Pasadena: A Centennial History* (South Pasadena, Calif.: South Pasadena Public Library, 1987), 107. George Hugh Banning's writings in the 1930s include *Sailor Ways* (New York: Thomas Nelson & Son, 1932) and "Stage Wheels Over the Padres's Trail," *Westways* 26 (July 1934): 16–17, 33–34.

23   Marianne Alyce Banning Adey and Douglas Banning, interviews by the author, 10 January 2006.

24 Ibid.; interviews by the author with Robert J. Banning, 7 October 2007, and Hancock Banning III, 4 April 2007; George Hugh Banning to Richard Dinkelspeil, 12 January 1949, box 2, Gelett Burgess Correspondence, BANC; Hancock Banning Jr., label on photograph 350 (quote), box 4, Banning Family Collection of Photographs, Part I, CL180, HEH; Hancock Banning Jr. to John C. Macfarland, 30 July 1942 (quote), RJB; Marianne Alyce Banning Adey, interview by the author, 10 January 2006; George Hugh Banning to William S. Banning, 22 October 1943, box 4, 1996 Addendum, Banning Company Collection, HEH.

25 *Los Angeles Times*, 11 December 1938; clippings and notes in scrapbooks 3 and 7, box 1, 1996 Addendum, Banning Company Collection, HEH.

26 *Los Angeles Times*, 2 January 1930, 26, 27 July, 1 September 1932; R. J. Chandler memorandum to "All Concerned" at Los Angeles Steamship Company, 17 January 1931, box 3, 1996 Addendum, Banning Company Collection, HEH.

27 Louis B. Perry and Richard S. Perry, *A History of the Los Angeles Labor Movement, 1911–1941* (Berkeley: University of California Press, 1963), 362–65. On the history of the 1934 strike in California, see also Mike Quin, *The Big Strike* (Olema, Calif.: Olema, 1949); Starr, *Endangered Dreams*, 84–120.

28 Ibid.; Joseph Brent Banning Jr. to Vice President and General Manager, Merchant's and Manufacturers' Association, 30 March 1934, in Senate Committee on Education and Labor, *Documents Relating to Intelligence Bureau or Red Squad of Los Angeles Police Department* [1940] (New York: Arno, 1971), 23548–49.

29 Perry and Perry, *A History of the Los Angeles Labor Movement*, 365–67; Charles Queenan, *The Port of Los Angeles: From Wilderness to World Port* (Los Angeles: Harbor Department, 1983), 79.

30 *Los Angeles Times*, 9, 12, 13, 14, 16, 27 May 1934; Perry and Perry, *A History of the Los Angeles Labor Movement*, 367–71.

31 *Los Angeles Times*, 14 November 1934, 31 January 1937, 14, 24 March 1938; *San Pedro News-Pilot*, 28 March 1938; Perry and Perry, *A History of the Los Angeles Labor Movement*, 391–94.

32 *Los Angeles Herald-Express*, 12 February 1933; *Los Angeles Times*, 2 February 1941; *Southwest Blue Book*, 1932–42; Francis P. Graves Jr., telephone interview by the author, 20 May 2008.

33 *Los Angeles Times*, 4 February 1934 (quote); *Los Angeles Examiner*, 17 February 1934; Katharine S. Banning, notes in scrapbook 24, 1996 Addendum, Banning Company Collection, HEH; Mary Jane Grier, diary entries for 9–31 December 1933, Mary Jane Grier Diary, MLB; William M. Grier Jr., *The Griers: Pioneers in America and Canada, 1816–1991* (Denver: Grier, 1991), 105–6.

34 *Los Angeles Examiner*, 27 July 1939; *Los Angeles Times*, 2 January 1948; Marian Lowry Banning, interview by author, 3 December 2005.

35 *Los Angeles Examiner*, 13 March 1930, 30 October 1938; *Los Angeles Times*, 20 December 1931, 17 May 1932, 7 August 1933, 28 January, 6, 24 June 1934;

Carroll O'Meara, "Captain Wm. Banning and the Art of Stage Coaching," *Out West Magazine* 91 (December 1933): 167–68, 171; Robert O. Foote, "Overland Stage Coach Club," *The Horse*, July–August 1941, 23–25.

36   *Los Angeles Times*, 2 December 1931; Elizabeth Banning Ames, interview by the author, 14 January 2006.

37   William P. Banning Jr., "Uncle's" (typescript, October 1983), quote on [ii], photocopy at BRM; interviews by the author with Douglas Banning, 10 January 2006, Elizabeth Banning Ames, 14 January 2006, Hancock Banning III, 4 April 2007, Nancy Morse Banning Call, 25 June 2007, and Robert J. Banning, 7 October 2007.

38   *Los Angeles Times*, 22 May 1938; Robert J. Banning, interview by the author, 7 October 2007.

39   *Los Angeles Times*, 13 October 1975; William P. Banning Jr., "Uncle's," 26, 45.

40   John C. Macfarland to Anne Banning, 28 January 1929, with statements of accounts of Hancock Banning heirs, 1929–43, and reports on oil royalties to 1947, box 17, Banning Company Collection, HEH; Hancock Banning III, telephone interview by the author, 10 May 2008.

41   Copy of D. M. Anderson to Hancock Banning Jr., 12 July 1938, statements of accounts of Hancock Banning heirs, 1929–43, and reports on oil royalties to 1947, box 17, Banning Company Collection, HEH.

42   *Los Angeles Times*, 16 December 1922, 13, 15 May, 10 June 1926. For another case involving the Bannings and the tidelands issue at this time, see *Los Angeles Times*, 24 June 1924. The harbor commission also pushed for a law to tax the Mormon Island property, which Hancock Banning claimed was not part of the 1917 lease agreement. See Hancock Banning Jr., "The Banning Family in Southern California," 140–44; *Los Angeles Times*, 21 July 1926.

43   *Los Angeles Times*, 29 June 1929, 5, 6 March, 3 September 1930, 7 June, 6 July, 2, 3 November 1933; *Los Angeles Examiner*, 3 March 1930. On Macfarland's work on the tidelands issue, see Jane Wilson, *Gibson, Dunn & Crutcher, Lawyers: An Early History* (Los Angeles: Gibson, Dunn & Crutcher, 1990), 440–41.

44   *Los Angeles Times*, 15 January, 25 April, 7 October 1935, 6 January 1938, 15 February 1939; *Borax Consolidated, Ltd. et al. v. City of Los Angeles*, 296 U.S. 10 (1935).

45   James J. Rawls and Walton Bean, *California: An Interpretive History*, 5th ed. (New York: McGraw-Hill, 1988), 289–93; E. J. Amar, "What Oil Did for the Harbor," *Southern California Business* 14 (November 1935): 14–15.

46   Correspondence between Mary E. H. Banning and Mary H. Banning Norris, 1909, box 12, Mary H. Banning Norris to Hancock Banning, 26 June 1923, box 3 of 1985 Addendum, Banning Company Collection, HEH; *Los Angeles Times*, 6 March, 28 August 1934; Kenny A. Franks and Paul F. Lambert, *Early California Oil: A Photographic History, 1865–1940* (College Station: Texas A&M Press, 1985), 101–2.

47   Lease agreement between Ventura Refining Company and William S. Banning, 17 April 1916, box 19, Banning Company Collection, HEH; *Los Angeles*

Times, 16 May 1935, 19 May 1936; Jack Courtney, "Cristóbal Was No Treasure Hunter," *Westways* 28 (April 1936): 22–23.

48   Walter J. Crown, "Wilmington Oil Field," *Summary of Oil Operations— California Oil Fields; Annual Report of the State Oil and Gas Supervisor* 26 (July 1940–June 1941): 5–6; Franks and Lambert, *Early California Oil*, 110–11. On the subsidence issue, see "California Depression," *Scientific American* 182 (January 1950): 30; Hancock Banning Jr., label on photograph in box 4, Banning Family Collection of Photographs, Part I, CL180, HEH; Xenophon Constantine Colazas, "Subsidence, Compaction of Sediments and Effects of Water Injection, Wilmington and Long Beach Oil Fields, Los Angeles County, California" (master's thesis, University of Southern California, 1971), 1–4; Hancock Banning III, telephone interview by the author, 10 May 2008; *Los Angeles Times*, 9 September 2008.

49   Copy of William S. Banning, petition to Board of Harbor Commissioners, 7 March 1939, John Hurndall to William S. Banning, 15 December 1939, William S. Banning to Gremac Oil Company, 7 May 1940, John C. Macfarland to Hancock Banning Jr., 21, 23 February 1945, and lease agreements with several oil companies, 1936–45, box 19, Banning Company Collection, HEH; *Los Angeles Times*, 30 March 1939, 11 February 1940; *Los Angeles Daily Journal*, 3 January 1945. On the oil tidelands issue, see Ernest R. Bartley, *The Tidelands Oil Controversy: A Legal and Historical Analysis* (Austin: University of Texas Press, 1953); Paul Sabin, *Crude Politics: The California Oil Market, 1900–1940* (Berkeley: University of California Press, 2005), 54, 58–61. Coincidentally, in 1947 the U.S. Supreme Court decided a case on the ownership of California tidelands and oil drilling that addressed some of the same issues that arose in the Banning cases some thirty years earlier. On the Banning Ranch property, see Hancock Banning III, interview by the author, 4 April 2007; Townsend Land Company, file 9772, box 250, Los Angeles County Incorporation Records, SCWHR.

50   William L. O'Neill, *A Democracy at War: America's Fight at Home and Abroad in World War II* (New York: Free Press, 1993); Michael C. C. Adams, *The Best War Ever: America and World War II* (Baltimore: Johns Hopkins University Press, 1994); Kennedy, *Freedom from Fear*, 381–858.

51   Kevin Starr, *Embattled Dreams: California in War and Peace, 1940–1950* (New York: Oxford University Press, 2002); Arthur C. Verge, *Paradise Transformed: Los Angeles during the Second World War* (Dubuque, Iowa: Kendall/Hunt, 1993); Tom Sitton, *Los Angeles Transformed: Fletcher Bowron's Urban Reform Revival, 1938–1953* (Albuquerque: University of New Mexico Press, 2005), 51–80.

52   Hancock Banning Jr. to William S. Banning, 22 December 1943, box 4, 1996 Addendum, Banning Company Collection, HEH.

53   Notes by Katharine S. Banning in scrapbook 13, 1996 Addendum, Banning Company Collection, HEH; *Pasadena Star-News*, 20 October 1941.

54   Interviews by the author with Marianne Alyce Banning Adey and Douglas Banning, 10 January 2006, Francis P. Graves Jr., 20 May 2008 (telephone), Robert J. Banning, 7 October 2007.

55   Robert H. Patton, *The Pattons: A Personal History of an American Family* (New York: Crown, 1994), 246–48, 262, 269–70; *Los Angeles Times*, 20 March, 12 June 1940; wedding invitation for Beatrice Ayer and Lt. John K. Waters, 1934, box 3, 1996 Addendum, Banning Company Collection, HEH; James L. Mooney, ed., *Dictionary of American Naval Fighting Ships*, 8 vols. (Washington, D.C.: Navy Dept., Office of the Chief of Naval Operations, Naval History Division, 1959–81), 5 (1970): 66–68.

56   Matt C. Bischoff, *The Desert Training Center/California–Arizona Maneuver Area, 1942–1944: Historical and Archaeological Contexts* (Tucson, Ariz.: Statistical Research, Inc., 2000), 9–50. Among many, many secondary sources on Patton and World War II, see Patton, *The Pattons*, 249–87; Martin Blumenson, *The Patton Papers*, 2 vols. (Boston: Houghton Mifflin, 1972), vol. 2; Stanley P. Hirshson, *General Patton: A Soldier's Life* (New York: Harper Collins, 2002), esp. 240–680.

57   Ibid; *Los Angeles Times*, 4 April 2006.

58   *Time* magazines in box 2, Call-Sisk Collection, SCWHR; Nancy Morse Banning Call, interview by the author, 25 June 2007; Marion Fitzhugh Macfarland Worthington statement, ca. 2007 (quotes), RJB.

59   *Wilmington (Del.) Journal*, 25 February 1943 (quote); *Long Beach Press-Telegram*, 10 February 1943. The SS *Phineas Banning* was eventually scrapped in 1967.

Chapter Fourteen

1   On postwar America, see, among many others, James T. Patterson, *Grand Expectations: The United States, 1945–1974* (New York: Oxford University Press, 1996); William Henry Chafe, *The Unfinished Journey: America Since World War II* (New York: Oxford University Press, 1991); Glen Jeansonne, *A Time of Paradox: America from the Cold War to the Third Millennium, 1945–Present* (Lanham, Md.: Rowman & Littlefield, 2007); Richard M. Abrams, *America Transformed: Sixty Years of Revolutionary Change* (Cambridge: Cambridge University Press, 2006).

2   *Los Angeles Times*, 13 March 1944; William P. Banning Jr., "Uncle's" (typescript, October 1983), 29, photocopy at BRM; Nancy Morse Banning Call, interview by the author, June 25, 2007.

3   *Los Angeles Times*, 28, 29 January 1946; Joseph Brent Banning Jr. to Robert Burnham, 30 May 1944, box 4, 1996 Addendum, Banning Company Collection, HEH; George Hugh Banning to Joseph Henry Jackson, 5 May 1944 (quote), box 1, Joseph Henry Jackson Papers, BANC; "Famed Stagecoach Driver Dies," *Desert Magazine* 9 (April 1946): 35.

4   William P. Banning Jr., "Uncle's," quote on 45; William Banning, 1946 federal income tax return, box 20, and will, box 29, Banning Company Collection, HEH.

5   *Los Angeles Examiner*, 24 March 1944; *Los Angeles Times*, 24 March 1944. In 1928 Adelaida's nephew, the son of Banning family friend James Mellus, had

made headlines when he discovered the body of his wife murdered by her paramour. The story had been a scandal, particularly in the affluent Hancock Park neighborhood where the Melluses then lived (and where many Bannings would soon live), and became one of many sensational homicides associated with Los Angeles in the public mind. *Los Angeles Times*, 30 April 2006.

6   *Los Angeles Times*, 29 October 1950, 20 December 1951; Marianne Alyce Banning Adey, interview by the author, 10 January 2006; copy of death certificate for Anne Banning, research files of Joyce Loranger, copy in possession of author.

7   *Los Angeles Times*, 12 November 1954.

8   *Los Angeles Times*, 4, 6 January 1956.

9   *Los Angeles Times*, 25 January 1956, 7 March 1969, 8 April 1970; *Sacramento Bee*, 8 April 1970.

10   *Los Angeles Times*, 6 November 1963, 15 November 1965.

11   Banning family genealogy notes, RJB.

12   Ibid.; *Los Angeles Times*, 4 December 1982.

13   *Los Angeles Times*, 28 July 1966; *Who's Who on the Pacific Coast* (New York: A. N. Marquis, 1949), 584.

14   *Los Angeles Times*, 18 October 1989; Marianne Alyce Banning Adey, interview by the author, 10 January 2006; Ruth Lockett to John Anson Ford, 30 September 1935, box 33, John Anson Ford Papers, HEH.

15   *Los Angeles Examiner*, 16 July 1949; Hancock Banning III, interview by the author, 2 June 2005, 4 April 2007; James P. Felton, ed., *Newport Beach 75, 1906–1981: A Diamond Jubilee History* (Fullerton, Calif.: Sultana, 1981), 9, 167.

16   *Los Angeles Examiner*, 11 January 1954; *California Historical Society Notes* 29 (November 1972): 3.

17   Elizabeth Banning Ames, interview by the author, 14 January 2006.

18   *Los Angeles Times*, 16 April 1956; Marion Fitzhugh Banning Mack, interview by the author, 31 May 2008; Elizabeth Banning Ames, interview by the author, 14 January 2006.

19   Douglas Banning, interview by the author, 10 January 2006.

20   Biographical data on Richard Call and Nancy Morse Banning Call can be found in *Marquis Who's Who* 2007, available at the Biography Resource Center website, http://galenet.galegroup.com/servlet/BioRC (accessed 21 May 2008). See also Margaret Leslie Davis, *Childrens Hospital and the Leaders of Los Angeles: The First 100 Years* (Los Angeles: Childrens Hospital of Los Angeles, 2002), 123, 183.

21   *Los Angeles Times*, 3 December 1972, 19 June 1978, 21 August 1988; Asa V. Call, "Notes With Asa Call," interview by Amelia Fry, 1975, transcript, Regional Oral History Office, BANC; Bob Gottlieb, "Memories of Asa Call, L.A.'s Back-Room Mr. Big," *Los Angeles*, August 1978, 100–103; Alice Catt Armstrong, *Who's Who Executives in California* (Los Angeles: Who's Who Historical Society, 1963), 8; William S. Banning to Robert Ingram, 3 June 1908, box 2, Banning Company Collection, HEH.

22   Francis P. Graves Jr., telephone interview by the author, 20 May 2008.

23   *Los Angeles Examiner*, 28 August 1949, 30 August, 15 September 1950; *Los Angeles Times*, 20 June 1954, 16 September 1994; Marian Lowry Banning, interview by the author, 3 December 2005.

24   *Los Angeles Examiner*, 24 March 1947, 25 September 1950, 16 August 1951; William F. Banning, telephone interview by the author, 2 October 2007; *Southwest Blue Book* (Los Angeles: Lenora King Berry, 1961–85).

25   On the original purchase by Mary E. H. Banning, see chapter 7 above.

26   California Secretary of State website, Business Search, s.v. "Beeco," in Business Entities section under Business Programs menu, http://kepler.sos.ca.gov (accessed 4 June 2008); *Los Angeles Times*, 1 August 1952; copy of Beeco, Ltd. Articles of Incorporation (1958), MLB; interviews by the author with Hancock Banning III, 4 April 2007, and John Haskell, 30 April 2007.

27   Ibid.; *Los Angeles Times*, 26 September 1963, 2 August 1964, 15 June 1969, 11 June 1972, 13 September 1973, 6, 25 April 1974, 14 February, 27 December 1975, 23 May 1976; John Haskell, memorandum to Mary Banning Norris heirs, 25 April 1978, box 8, Banning Family Collection of Photographs, Part I, CL180, HEH.

28   *Los Angeles Times*, 14, 25 February 1981.

29   *Los Angeles Times*, 9 August, 28 September 1981, 25, 27 January 1982. Former Beeco official John Haskell believes the residents protesting the Beeco project were more concerned with losing their view of the ocean than with additional traffic; John Haskell, interview by the author, 30 April 2007.

30   *Los Angeles Times*, 10 February, 13, 16, 28 March, 4, 13 April, 4, 26 September, 27 October, 4 November 1982; John Haskell, interview by the author, 30 April 2007.

31   *Los Angeles Times*, 18 March 2008; John Haskell, interview by the author, 30 April 2007.

32   *Orange County Register*, 3 August 2008.

33   Joseph Brent Banning to Hancock Banning, 6 June 1907, letterbook 32, Herbert C. Andrews, comp., "Record of Ancestry of Mr. and Mrs. Hancock Banning," typescript, 1904, box 13, and letters of A. A. Polhamus, Herman Hellman, and Ben C. Truman to Joseph B. Banning, 1905, box 1 of 1996 Addendum, Banning Company Collection, HEH; Pierson Worrall Banning, "The First Banning Genealogy" (typescript, Chicago, 1908), copy at LAPL.

34   *Los Angeles Times*, 29 November 1931; El Molino Viejo file, box 14, 1985 Addendum, Banning Company Collection, HEH; Hancock Banning Jr., "The Banning Family in Southern California," interview by Dellene M. Tweedale, 1971, transcript, Center for Oral History Research, UCLA.

35   Nadine Ishitani Hata, *The Historic Preservation Movement in California, 1940–1976* (Sacramento, Calif.: California Department of Parks and Recreation, Office of Historic Preservation, 1992).

36   Mesick Cohn Waite Architects, "Historic Structure Report: General Phineas Banning Residence, Wilmington, California" (1992), 14–146, BRM; Simie Seaman et al., *Wilmington* (Charleston, S.C.: Arcadia, 2008), 24–25; Kilbee

Brittain, *The General Phineas Banning Residence Museum*, rev. ed. (Wilmington, Calif.: Friends of Banning Park, 2008). On the architectural style and its historical context, see James J. Yoch, *Visionary on the Golden Shore: Phineas Banning in Southern California, 1851–1885* (Wilmington, Calif.: Banning Residence Museum, 2002), 74–125.

37 *Los Angeles Times*, 21 July, 23 November 1930, 28 January 1934; correspondence, June–December 1927, Banning Park file, box C-743, LACRC.

38 *Los Angeles Times*, 26 January, 7, 24, 31 May, 6 June 1936; *Los Angeles Examiner*, 12, 15 March 1936.

39 Seaman et al., *Wilmington*, 115; annual reports of the Los Angeles Recreation and Parks Department, 1945–70, box C-2019, LACRC; *Grizzly Bear*, January 1940, 15; Oscar Lewis, *Here Lived the Californians* (New York: Rinehart, 1957), quote on 185; *Los Angeles Times*, 21 October 1963.

40 Nancy Morse Banning Call, interview by the author, 25 June 2007; *Los Angeles Times*, 31 March 1952, 29 January 1976.

41 *Los Angeles Herald-Examiner*, 18 April 1977; *Los Angeles Times*, 8 April 1984; Marian Winter, "Phineas Banning's Dream House," *Shoreline* 9 (April 1982): 5–8; annual reports of the Los Angeles Recreation and Parks Department, 1977–92, box C-2019, LACRC; Christine V. F. Shirley, "Banning Residence Museum," *Terra* 18 (Summer 1979): 3–11. The study of the history of the house and its condition in 1992 is contained in Mesick Cohn Waite Architects, "Historic Structure Report: General Phineas Banning Residence" (1992), BRM.

Conclusion

1 "About the Port: Facts and Figures," Port of Los Angeles website, http://www.portoflosangeles.org (accessed 2 June 2008 and 26 April 2010).

Appendix A

1 Zella Armstrong, comp., *Notable Southern Families*, 6 vols. (Baltimore: Genealogical Publishing, 1974), 1:25; Leroy B. Banning, *Banning Branches* (Bowie, Md.: Heritage Books, 1994), 4–5; Elizabeth van Schaick-Banning, *The Book of Banning* (Westminster, Md.: Willow Bend Books, 2005), 301–2, 310, 314. Much of this information initially came from Pierson Worrall Banning, "The First Banning Genealogy" (typescript, Chicago, 1908, copy at LAPL), and has not been completely verified.

2 R. R. Palmer, *A History of the Modern World* (New York: Knopf, 1965), 142–54; D. A. Crowley, ed., *History of Wiltshire*, 17 vols. (London: Institute of Historical Research, 1999), 16:81. Most of the Banning genealogists believe Edward was born about 1620 and came to America by 1650. However, his own father was probably born about 1620, and since Edward fathered a child in 1700, it is more likely that he was born in at least the 1640s or later and arrived in Maryland between 1660 and 1675.

3   Leslie Keddie and Neil Keddie, abstractors, *Land Office Rent Rolls, Talbot County, 1666–1680* (Salisbury, Md.: Family Tree Bookshop, 2001), 65; deed, Robert Smith to Edward H. Banning, 20 October 1691, vol. 5, p. 338, General Land Index, 1662–1799, Clerk of the Circuit Court, Talbot County Courthouse, Easton, Md.; *Archives of Maryland*, 72 vols. (Baltimore: Maryland Historical Society, 1883–1972), 7:92; Henry C. Peden Jr., *Colonial Maryland Soldiers and Sailors, 1634–1734* (Westminster, Md.: Willow Bend Books, 2001), 15; Henry C. Peden Jr. and F. Edward Wright, *Colonial Families of the Eastern Shore of Maryland* (Westminster, Md.: Willow Bend Books, 2000), 5–7.

4   Edward Banning probate file, vol. 1, folio 263, Register of Wills, Talbot County Courthouse, Easton, Md.; Banning, *Banning Branches*, 5. A number of other Bannings living in the British colonies in the late 1600s through the 1700s can be found in published census and vital statistics sources in the Maryland Room of the Talbot County Free Library, Easton, Md., DHS, DPA, and HEH.

5   Peden and Wright, *Colonial Families of the Eastern Shore of Maryland*, 5–6.

6   Robert W. Barnes, comp., *Maryland Marriages, 1634–1777* (Baltimore: Genealogical Publishing, 1976), 8; Peter Wilson Coldham, *Settlers of Maryland, 1679–1783* (Baltimore: Genealogical Publishing, 2002), 8; Banning, *Banning Branches*, 97.

Appendix B

1   *Los Angeles Times*, 12 June 1940; *New York Times*, 10 April 1946; Elizabeth Macfarland Brown Nordlinger, telephone interview by the author, 8 June 2008.

2   Marion Fitzhugh Banning Mack, telephone interview by the author, 31 May 2008; genealogy notes, RJB.

3   Marianne Alyce Banning Adey, interview by the author, 10 January 2006.

4   *Los Angeles Examiner*, 20 July, 29 November 1954; Katharine Alice Banning Sisk, telephone interview by the author, 13 May 2008. Biographical data on Daniel Arthur Sisk can be found in the *Marquis Who's Who* 2007, available online at the Biography Resource Center, http://galenet.galegroup.com/servlet/BioRC (accessed 21 May 2008).

5   Francis P. Graves Jr., telephone interview by the author, 20 May 2008.

6   Ibid.; genealogical notes, RJB.

7   *Los Angeles Examiner*, 12 September 1948; William M. Grier Jr., *The Griers: Pioneers in America and Canada, 1816–1991* (Denver: Grier, 1991), 106–7; Marian Lowry Banning, interview by the author, 2 May 2008.

8   *Boston Globe*, 30 June 2008; *Who's Who in America, 1999* (New Providence, N.J.: Marquis Who's Who, 1998), 4011–12.

SELECTED BIBLIOGRAPHY

Manuscript and Reference Collections
Archives and Special Collections Department, Los Angeles Harbor College. Wilmington, Calif.
    Los Angeles Harbor Area Collection

Assistance League of Southern California Archives. Los Angeles, Calif.
    Assistance League of Southern California Records
    Anne Ophelia Smith Banning Research File
    Bannings and Other Families File

Bancroft Library, University of California. Berkeley, Calif.
    Gelett Burgess Correspondence
    John Tracy Gaffey Papers
    Benjamin Hayes Papers
    Joseph Henry Jackson Papers
    Miscellaneous California Dictations
    Edward Otho Cresap Ord Papers

Banning Residence Museum Library. Wilmington, Calif.
    Banning Family Papers
    George Hugh Banning Collection
    Banning Residence Museum Staff and Volunteer Research Files
    Christine Shirley Collection

California State Library. Sacramento, Calif.
    California Biography Files
    Ephraim W. Morse Papers

Catalina Island Museum. Avalon, Calif.
    Freeholders Improvement Association of Avalon File
    Local History Collections
    Personalities Files

Delaware Historical Society. Wilmington, Del.
    Biography Indexes and Files
    Rumsey Family Collection

Delaware Public Archives. Dover, Del.
    Delaware Family Files
    Ridgely Family Collection
    Joseph Brown Turner Collection

Free Library of Philadelphia. Philadelphia, Pa.
    Philadelphia newspapers, rare books, directories, and maps

Henry E. Huntington Library. San Marino, Calif.
    Banning Company Collection and Addenda
    Banning Family Collection of Photographs, Parts I and II
    John D. Bicknell Papers
    Joseph Lancaster Brent Papers
    Cave J. Couts Papers
    Charles Crocker Correspondence
    Thomas E. Gibbon Papers (Bergman Collection)
    Jackson A. Graves Papers
    Henry E. Huntington Collection
    Selena Gray Galt Ingram Papers
    Henry Keller Papers
    Matthew Keller Papers
    Kerchoff-Cuzner Mill and Lumber Company Records
    Stuart N. Lake Papers
    Los Angeles Pioneer Oil Company Documents
    Theodore P. Lukens Papers
    William Gibbs McAdoo Papers
    Morse Family Scrapbooks (California scrapbook 83)
    Henry William O'Melveny Papers
    Henry Z. Osborne Papers
    George S. Patton Papers
    James de Barth Shorb Papers
    Solano-Reeve Papers
    William A. Spalding Papers
    Abel Stearns Papers
    Benjamin D. Wilson Papers

Library of Congress. Washington, D.C.
    Records of the Olmsted Associates

Los Angeles Public Library and Municipal Reference Library. Los Angeles, Calif.
    California Biography File
    Luther Ingersoll Historical Collection

Maryland Room, Talbot County Free Library. Easton, Md.
    Local History and Genealogy Special Collections

Minnesota History Center. St. Paul, Minn.
    Alexander Ramsey Papers
    Jay Cooke Papers (transcriptions from the Pennsylvania Historical Society)
    Ignatius Donnelly Papers
    William Branch and Company Records

San Diego Historical Society Archives. San Diego, Calif.
    Biography Files—Judge Benjamin Hayes

Santa Catalina Island Company Archives. Avalon, Calif.
    Santa Catalina Island Company Records
    Wilmington Transportation Company Records

Seaver Center for Western History Research, Natural History Museum of
    Los Angeles County. Los Angeles, Calif.
    Call-Sisk Collection
    Antonio F. Coronel Collection
    James J. Mellus Collection
    Sepulveda/Mott Collection
    Stephen M. White Scrapbooks
    Joseph P. Widney Scrapbooks
    Wallace Woodworth Collection

Special Collections, California Polytechnic State University. San Luis Obispo, Calif.
    Jack Family Papers

Special Collections, Stanford University Library. Stanford, Calif.
    William B. Hyde Papers
    David Jacks Papers
    Meyer Lissner Papers
    Stephen M. White Papers

Special Collections, University of California. Los Angeles, Calif.
    Frederick Baker Collection of Avalon City Council Minutes
    California Ephemera Collection
    Cole Family Papers
    Joseph Mesmer Papers
    W. W. Robinson Papers
    Henry Workman Keller Papers

Special Collections, University of Southern California. Los Angeles, Calif.
    Los Angeles Chamber of Commerce Collection
    Los Angeles Examiner Collection

Wilmington Branch, Los Angeles Public Library. Wilmington, Calif.
    Local History Collection

Wilmington Public Library. Wilmington, Del.
    Local History Collection

Privately Held Banning Family Papers
    Marianne Alyce Banning Adey
    Elizabeth Banning Ames
    Marian Lowry Banning
    Robert J. Banning
    Nancy Morse Banning Call

Interviews by the Author
    Robert J. Banning: 26 June 2004, 2 April 2005, 7 October 2007
    Nancy Morse Banning Call: 18 May 2005, 25 June 2007
    Hancock Banning III: 2 June 2005, 4 April 2007, 10 May 2008 (telephone)
    Marian Lowry Banning: 3 December 2005, 2 May 2008
    Marianne Alyce Banning Adey: 10 January 2006
    Douglas Banning: 10 January 2006
    Elizabeth Banning Ames: 14 January 2006
    John Haskell: 30 April 2007
    William F. Banning (telephone): 2 October 2007
    Joyce Loranger: 14 November 2007
    Eleanor Henry (telephone): 16 December 2007
    Katharine Alice Banning Sisk (telephone): 13 May 2008
    Francis P. Graves Jr. (telephone): 20 May 2008
    Marion Fitzhugh Banning Mack (telephone): 31 May 2008
    Elizabeth Macfarland Brown Nordlinger (telephone): 8 June 2008
    Patricia Moore (telephone): 10 September 2008

Oral History Transcripts
Banning, Hancock, Jr. "The Banning Family in Southern California." Interview by
    Dellene M. Tweedale, 1971. Unpublished oral history transcript, Center for
    Oral History Research, UCLA.

Government Documents
California. Adjutant General. *Report of the Adjutant General of the State of Califor-
    nia, 1864–1865.* Sacramento: State Printer, 1865.

———. Adjutant General. *Report of the Adjutant General of the State of Califor-
    nia, 1865–1867.* Sacramento: State Printer, 1867.

———. Adjutant General. California Military Records in the State Archives,
    1858–1923. Microfilm, 35 reels, copy at Los Angeles County Library, Rose-
    mead, Calif.

———. California Census of 1852. Typescript transcript of original at CSA, Genealogical Records Committee, Daughters of the American Revolution of California, 1934–35. Microfilm at HEH.

———. Governor. *Governor's Message; and Report of the Secretary of State on the Census of 1852, of the State of California.* San Francisco: State Printer, 1853.

———. Military Department. Indian War Records. CSA.

———. Military Department. Civil War Volunteers Records. CSA.

———. Railroad Commission. *Decisions of the Railroad Commission of the State of California* [journal].

———. Senate. *Journal of the Senate during the Sixteenth Session of the Legislature of the State of California, 1865–1866.* Sacramento: State Printer, 1866.

———. Senate. *Journal of the Senate during the Seventeenth Session of the Legislature of the State of California, 1867–1868.* Sacramento: State Printer, 1868.

———. State Agricultural Society. *Transactions of the California State Agricultural Society during the year 1874.* Sacramento: State Printer, 1875.

———. *The Statutes of California and Amendments to the Codes* (Sacramento, Calif.: State Office, 1860–72).

Delaware. Delaware Land Records Index. DPA

Los Angeles, City of. Board of Harbor Commissioners. *The Port of Los Angeles.* Los Angeles: Board of Harbor Commissioners. 1913.

———. Board of Harbor Commissioners. Annual Reports, 1924/25–1930. LACRC.

———. City Council. Files, 1940–79. LACRC.

———. Common Council. Minutes, 1858–59. LACRC.

———. Common Council. Files, 1857–75. LACRC.

———. Recreation and Parks Department. Annual Reports, 1945–92. LACRC.

———. *Los Angeles City Charter* [revised to 1873 and 1878]. LACRC.

Los Angeles County. Assessor Records, 1864–75. SCWHR.

———. Board of Supervisors. Minutes of Meetings. Los Angeles County Board of Supervisors Office, Los Angeles, Calif.

———. Deeds. Los Angeles County Recorder's Office, Norwalk, Calif.

———. "Great Register of Los Angeles County," 1867–1908. SCWHR.

———. Court Records, 1850s–ca. 1880s. HEH.

———. Court Records, 1850s–ca. 1900. SCWHR.

———. Incorporation Records. SCWHR.

New Castle County, Del. Index to Deeds. New Castle County Recorder of Deeds Office, Wilmington, Del.

Talbot County, Md. General Land Index, 1662–1799. Clerk of the Circuit Court, Talbot County Courthouse, Easton, Md.

———. Register of Wills. Talbot County Courthouse, Easton, Md.

United States. Army. Office of the Inspector General. Records. Record Group 159. USNAW.

———. Army. U.S. Quartermaster General. Records. Record Group 92. USNAW.

———. Army. Corps of Engineers. Records of the Office of the Chief Engineer, U.S. Army Corps of Engineers. Project Administration Records, 1896–1947. Record Group 77. USNALN.

———. Census Office. Population Schedules. 5th Census. 1830. New Castle County, Del., microfilm roll 12, LAPL.

———. Census Office. Population Schedules. 6th Census. 1840. New Castle County, Del., microfilm roll 33, LAPL.

———. Census Office. Population Schedules. 7th Census. 1850. New Castle County, Del., microfilm roll 1. LAPL.

———. Census Office. 7th Census, 1850. *Statistical View of the United States.* Washington, D.C.: A. O. P. Nicholson, 1854.

———. Congress. House. 35th Cong., 1st sess., 1857–58, series 951, H. Doc. 96, XI:458. Copy at HEH.

———. Congress. Senate. *Reports of Explorations and Surveys to Ascertain the Most Practicable and Economical Route for a Railroad from the Mississippi River to the Pacific Ocean, 1853–4.* 33rd Cong., 2nd sess., 1856, Ex. Doc. no. 78. 12 vols. Washington, D.C., Government Printing Office, 1855–61.

———. Department of Commerce. Bureau of the Census. *Historical Statistics of the United States, Colonial Times to 1957.* Washington, D.C.: Bureau of the Census, 1960.

———. Department of the Interior. Census Office. *Eighth Census.* Washington, D.C.: Government Printing Office, 1864.

———. Department of the Interior. Census Office. Population Schedules, 8th Census, 1860, San Pedro Township, 480. Microfilm at LAPL.

———. Department of the Interior. Census Office. *The State of the Population of the United States . . . Ninth Census (June 1, 1870).* 3 vols. Washington, D.C.: Government Printing Office, 1872.

———. Department of the Interior. Census Office. *Statistics of the Population of the United States at the Tenth Census (June 1, 1880).* Washington, D.C.: Government Printing Office, 1883.

———. War Department. *The War of the Rebellion: A Compilation of the Official Records of the Union and Confederate Armies.* 70 vols. Washington, D.C.: Government Printing Office, 1880–1901.

Newspapers

Los Angeles Examiner	*Los Angeles Express*	*Los Angeles Herald*
Los Angeles News	*Los Angeles Star*	*Los Angeles Times*

Court Cases

Banning v. Banning, 80 Cal. Rep. 271 (1889)
Banning Co. v. California, 240 U.S. 142 (1916)
Dominguez de Guyer v. Banning, 167 U.S. Rep. 723 (1897)

Reference and Unpublished Sources

Archives of Maryland. 72 vols. Baltimore: Maryland Historical Society, 1883–1972.

Atcheson, George, Jr. and George Hugh Banning, *Adonis Falls* [play program]. Berkeley: University of California Class of 1919, 1919. RB 274321, HEH.

Banning, Phineas. "Settlement of Wilmington." San Francisco, 1883. Transcribed and edited by Edward P. Newkirk. MSS C-E 139, BANC.

Banning, Pierson Worrall. "The First Banning Genealogy." Typescript, Chicago, 1908. LAPL.

———. "My Ancestors to the Missing Link." Typescript, 1910. LAPL.

Banning, William P., Jr. "Uncle's." Typescript, October 1983. Photocopy at BRM.

Barnes, Robert W., comp. *Maryland Marriages, 1634–1777.* Baltimore: Genealogical Publishing, 1976.

Beers, D. G. *Atlas of the State of Delaware.* Philadelphia: Pomeroy & Beers, 1868.

Blumenson, Martin. *The Patton Papers.* 2 vols. Boston: Houghton Mifflin, 1972.

Bushman, Claudia L., Harold B. Hancock, and Elizabeth Moyne Homsey, eds. *Proceedings of the Assembly of the Lower Counties on Delaware, 1770–1776, of the Constitutional Convention of 1776, and of the House of Assembly of the Delaware State, 1776–1781.* Newark: University of Delaware Press, 1986.

Coldham, Peter Wilson. *Settlers of Maryland, 1679–1783.* Baltimore: Genealogical Publishing, 2002.

Dakin Map Company. "Los Angeles, California." 1883 and 1889. SCWHR.

Delaware Public Archives Commission. *Delaware Archives.* 5 vols. Wilmington, Del.: various publishers, 1911–19.

Detwiler, Justice B., ed. *Who's Who in California, 1928–1929.* San Francisco: Who's Who, 1928.

The First Los Angeles City and County Directory, 1872. Facsimile. Los Angeles: Ward Ritchie, 1963.

Fletcher, Russell Holmes, ed. *Who's Who in California, 1942–1943.* Los Angeles: Who's Who, 1941.

Governor's Register, State of Delaware. Wilmington, Del.: Public Archives Commission of Delaware, 1926–.

Harper, Franklin, ed. *Who's Who on the Pacific Coast.* Los Angeles: Harper, 1913.

Hexamer, Ernest and William Locher. *Maps of the City of Philadelphia.* Philadelphia, Pa.: E. Hexamer & W. Locher, 1858–60. Available on the Greater Philadelphia GeoHistory Network website, at http://philageohistory.org/rdic-images/.

Hopkins, Mark. *Letters from Mark Hopkins, Leland Stanford, Charles F. Crocker and David D. Colton, to Collis P. Huntington, from August 27th, 1869, to December 30th, 1879.* New York: J. C. Rankin, 1891.

Huntington, Collis Potter. *Letters from Collis P. Huntington to Mark Hopkins, Leland Stanford, Charles Crocker, E. B. Crocker, Charles F. Crocker, and D. D. Cotton [sic], from August 20, 1867, to [March 31, 1876].* 3 vols. New York: n.p., 1892–94.

Keddie, Leslie and Neil Keddie, abstractors. *Land Office Rent Rolls, Talbot County, 1666–1680.* Salisbury, Md.: Family Tree Bookshop, 2001.

Los Angeles City Directory. Los Angeles, Calif.: various publishers, 1872–1942.

McElroy's Philadelphia City Directory. Philadelphia: A. McElroy, 1837, 1844, 1851, 1854, 1867.

Mesick Cohn Waite Architects. "Historic Structure Report: General Phineas Banning Residence, Wilmington, California." Typescript, 1992. BRM.

Mooney, James L., ed. *Dictionary of American Naval Fighting Ships.* 8 vols. Washington, D.C.: Navy Dept., Office of the Chief of Naval Operations, Naval History Division, 1959–81.

National Cyclopaedia of American Biography. 63 vols. New York: James T. White, 1898–1984.

Newmark, Maurice H., and Marco R. Newmark. *Census for the City and County of Los Angeles for the Year 1850.* Los Angeles: Times-Mirror, 1929.

Peden, Henry C., Jr. *Colonial Maryland Soldiers and Sailors, 1634–1734.* Westminster, Md.: Willow Bend Books, 2001.

———. *The Delaware Militia in the War of 1812.* Lewes, Del.: Colonial Roots, 2003.

———. *Revolutionary Patriots of Delaware, 1775–1783.* Westminster, Md.: Family Line, 1996.

Peden, Henry C., Jr. and F. Edward Wright. *Colonial Families of the Eastern Shore of Maryland.* Westminster, Md.: Willow Bend Books, 2000.

Rasmussen, Louis J. *San Francisco Ship Passenger Lists.* 4 vols. Colma, Calif.: San Francisco Historic Records, 1967.

Robinson, W. W. *Maps of Los Angeles: From Ord's Survey of 1849 to the End of the Boom of the Eighties.* Los Angeles: Dawson's Bookshop, 1966.

Saint Paul City Directory. St. Paul, Minn.: various publishers, 1856, 1875, 1890.

Sanborn Map Company. "St. Paul, Minnesota." 1885, corrected to 1890. MHC.

Sheldon, Lionel A. "Biographical Sketch of Phineas Banning." 1888. MSS C-D 771, BANC.

Taylor, E. W., Jr. *Bench and Bar of California, 1937–1938.* Chicago: E. W. Taylor Jr., 1937.

Virdin, Donald Odell. *Some Pioneer Delaware Families.* Arlington, Va: Virdin, 1977.

Valinger, Leon, Jr., comp. *Calendar of Kent County, Delaware, Probate Records, 1680–1800.* Dover, Del.: Public Archives Commission, State of Delaware, 1944.

Valinger, Leon, Jr., and Virginia E. Shaw, comps. *A Calendar of Ridgely Family Letters, 1742–1899, in the Delaware State Archives.* 3 vols. Dover, Del.: Public Archives Commission, 1948–61.

Who's Who in the New Deal: Southern California Edition. Los Angeles: New Deal Historical Society, 1938.

Who's Who in the Pacific Southwest. Los Angeles: Times-Mirror, 1913.

Who's Who on the Pacific Coast. New York: A. N. Marquis, 1949.

Wilmington Directory for the Year 1845. Wilmington, Del.: Lewis Wilson, 1845.

Wilmington Directory for the Year 1853. Wilmington, Del.: Joshua T. Heald, 1853.

Wright, F. Edward. *Colonial Families of Delaware*. Vol. 1. Westminster, Md.: Willow Bend Books, 1999.

———. *Maryland Eastern Shore Vital Records, 1648–1725*. Silver Springs, Md.: Family Line, 1982.

Dissertations and Theses

Allen, Paul F. "Tourists in Southern California, 1875–1903." Master's thesis, Claremont Colleges, 1940.

Barsness, Richard Webster. "The Maritime Development of San Pedro Bay, California, 1821–1921." PhD diss., University of Minnesota, 1963.

Christie, Blanche. "Phineas Banning with Special Reference to the Development of Transportation in Southern California." Master's thesis, University of Southern California, 1933.

Colazas, Xenophon Constantine. "Subsidence, Compaction of Sediments and Effects of Water Injection, Wilmington and Long Beach Oil Fields, Los Angeles County, California." Master's thesis, University of Southern California, 1971.

Crampton, June Margaret. "A History of the Los Angeles and San Pedro Railroad." Master's thesis, University of Southern California, 1929.

Culver, Milton Lawrence. "The Island, the Oasis, and the City: Santa Catalina, Palm Springs, Los Angeles, and Southern California's Shaping of American Life and Leisure." PhD diss., University of California, Los Angeles, 2004.

Holstein, Walter E. "A History of Wilmington from the Spanish Period to 1931." Master's thesis, University of Southern California, 1931.

Kane, Holly Charmain. "Arriving in Los Angeles: Railroad Depots as Gateways to the California Dream." Master's thesis, University of Southern California, 2007.

Kashuba, Melinda Elizabeth. "Tourist Landscapes of Los Angeles County, California." PhD diss., University of Southern California, 1986.

Kurutz, Gary F. "Don Benito Wilson: A Pioneer in Transitional Southern California, 1841–1854." Master's thesis, University of San Diego, 1972.

Pugh, Byron Grant. "History of Utah–California Wagon Freighting." Master's thesis, University of California, Berkeley, 1949.

Sitton, Thomas Joseph. "Urban Politics and Reform in New Deal Los Angeles: The Recall of Mayor Frank L. Shaw." PhD diss., University of California, Riverside, 1983.

———. "Walter F. X. Parker and Machine Politics in Los Angeles, 1903–1910." Master's thesis, California State University, Fullerton, 1973.

Tracy, Muriel Aloha. "The Life of Benjamin D. Wilson." Master's thesis, University of Southern California, 1934.

Westbrook, Charles Ruggles. "The Securing of a Transcontinental Railroad Tie for Los Angeles and the Development of the Adjoining Port Facilities, from the Founding of San Pedro to 1881." Master's thesis, University of Southern California, 1966.

Books and Articles

An Illustrated History of Los Angeles County, California. Chicago: Lewis, 1889.

Andrews, C. C. *History of St. Paul, Minnesota.* Syracuse, N.Y.: D. Mason, 1890.

Apostol, Jane. "An Army Bride Goes West." *Southern California Quarterly* 72 (Winter 1990): 303–20.

———. "Don Mateo Keller: His Vines and His Wines." *Southern California Quarterly* 84 (Summer 2002): 93–114.

———. *South Pasadena: A Centennial History.* South Pasadena, Calif.: South Pasadena Public Library, 1987.

———. "Why Women Should Not Have the Vote: Anti-Suffrage Views in the Southland in 1911." *Southern California Quarterly* 70 (Spring 1988): 29–42.

Ayer, Frederick. *Reminiscences of Frederick Ayer.* Boston: Merrymount, 1923.

Ayers, Col. James J. *Gold and Sunshine: Reminiscences of Early California.* Boston: Gorham, 1922.

Bancroft, Hubert Howe. *History of California.* 7 vols. San Francisco: History Company, 1884–90.

Banning, George Hugh. *Found in a Derelict: "Queen of the Night" and Other Poems.* Los Angeles: Murrell, 1919.

———. *In Mexican Waters.* London: Martin Hopkinson, 1925.

———. *Sailor Ways.* New York: Thomas Nelson & Son, 1932.

———. *Spun Yarn.* London: Methuen, 1923.

———. "Stage Wheels Over the Padres's Trail." *Westways* 26 (July 1934): 16–17, 33–34.

Banning, Leroy B. *Banning Branches.* Bowie, Md.: Heritage Books, 1994.

Banning, William, Captain, and George Hugh Banning. *Six Horses.* New York: Century, 1930.

———. "Some Aspects of Staging in the Golden State before the Coming of the Overland Mail." *Touring Topics* 21 (July 1929): 26–31.

———. "Wheel Tracks of the 'Jackass Mail': A Chronicle of the Perils and Problems of the First Transcontinental Stage Line." *Touring Topics* 21 (November 1929): 21–25, 54.

Banning, William Lowber, Jr. *A Coaching Party to Southern California.* St. Paul, Minn.: the author, 1889.

———. *A Two Weeks Coaching Party in Southern California in April 1889.* St. Paul, Minn.: the author, 1889.

Banning-Bradley and Allied Families. Hartford, Conn.: States Historical Society, 1930.

Barrows, H. D. "Don David W. Alexander." *Annual Publications of the Historical Society of Southern California* 3 (1897): 43–45.

———. "Los Angeles Fifty Years Ago." *Annual Publications of the Historical Society of Southern California* 6 (1905): 203–7.

Barsness, Richard W. "Los Angeles' Quest for Improved Transportation, 1846–1861." *California Historical Society Quarterly* 46 (December 1967): 291–306.

———. "Railroads and Los Angeles: The Quest for a Deep-Water Port." *Southern California Quarterly* 47 (December 1967): 379–94.

Bates, J. C., ed. *History of the Bench and Bar of California.* San Francisco: Bench & Bar, 1912.

Baur, John. "John Goller: Pioneer Angeleno Manufacturer." *Quarterly Publications of the Historical Society of Southern California* 36 (March 1954): 14–27.

Beaman, D. C. "Sport at Catalina—Can Its Waters Be Fished Out?" *Outdoor Life* 9 (February 1902): n.p.

Beattie, George William, and Helen Pruitt Beattie. *Heritage of the Valley: San Bernardino's First Century.* Pasadena, Calif.: San Pasqual, 1939.

Bell, Horace. *On the Old West Coast: Being Further Reminiscences of a Ranger.* Ed. Lanier Bartlett. New York; Grossett & Dunlap, 1930.

———. *Reminiscences of a Ranger: or Early Times in Southern California.* Santa Barbara: Wallace Hebberd, 1927.

Bigger, Richard, and James D. Kitchen. *How the Cities Grew.* Vol. 2 of *Metropolitan Los Angeles: A Study in Integration,* ed. Edwin A. Cottrell. 16 vols. Los Angeles: Haynes Foundation, 1952.

Bischoff, Matt C. *The Desert Training Center/California–Arizona Maneuver Area, 1942–1944: Historical and Archaeological Contexts.* Tucson, Ariz.: Statistical Research, Inc., 2000.

Blegen, Theodore C. *Minnesota: A History of the State.* Rev. ed. Minneapolis: University of Minnesota Press, 1975.

Blew, Robert W. "Vigilantism in Los Angeles, 1835–1874." *Southern California Quarterly* 54 (Spring 1972): 11–30.

Brewer, William H. *Up and Down California in 1960–1864.* Rev. ed. Berkeley: University of California Press, 1974.

Brittain, Kilbee. *The General Phineas Banning Residence Museum.* Rev. ed. Wilmington, Calif.: Friends of Banning Park, 2008.

Browne, J. Ross. *A Tour Through Arizona, 1864; Or, Adventures in the Apache Country.* Repr., Tucson, Ariz.: Arizona Silhouettes, 1951.

Buffum, Richard and Marjorie Buffum. *Catalina Saga: An Historical Cruise around Santa Catalina Island.* Balboa Island, Calif.: Abracadabra, 2003.

Burdette, Robert J., ed. *Greater Los Angeles and Southern California: Their Portraits and the Chronological Records of Their Careers.* Chicago: Lewis, 1906.

Burnquist, Joseph A. A., ed. *Minnesota and Its People.* 3 vols. Chicago: S. J. Clarke, 1924.

Burris, Evadene A. "Building the Frontier Home." *Minnesota History* 15 (March 1934): 43–55.

"California Depression." *Scientific American* 182 (January 1950): 30.

Carew, Harold David. *History of Pasadena and the San Gabriel Valley.* 3 vols. Chicago: S. J. Clarke, 1930.

Carpenter, Virginia. *Ranchos of Orange County: Chronologies of Early California.* Orange, Calif.: Paragon Agency, 2003.

Carr, William H. A. *The du Ponts of Delaware.* New York: Dodd, Mead, 1964.

Case, Walter H. *History of Long Beach.* Long Beach, Calif.: Press-Telegram, 1935.

Casebier, Dennis G. *The Mojave Road.* Norco, Calif.: Tales of the Mojave Road, 1975.

Castle, Henry A. *Minnesota: Its Story and Biography.* 3 vols. Chicago: Lewis, 1915.

Chaput, Donald. "The Civil War Military Post on Catalina Island." *Southern California Quarterly* 75 (Spring 1993): 37–50.

———. *Virgil Earp, Western Peace Officer.* Encampment, Wyo.: Affiliated Writers of America, 1994.

Clary, William W. *History of the Law Firm of O'Melveny & Myers, 1885–1965.* 2 vols. Los Angeles: privately printed, 1966.

Cleland, Robert G. *California in Our Time, 1900–1940.* New York: Alfred A. Knopf, 1947.

———. *The Cattle on a Thousand Hills: Southern California, 1850–1870.* San Marino, Calif.: Huntington Library, 1941.

———. *The Irvine Ranch of Orange County, 1810–1950.* San Marino, Calif.: Huntington Library, 1952.

Cleland, Robert G., and Frank B. Putnam. *Isaias W. Hellman and the Farmers and Merchants Bank.* 2nd printing. San Marino, Calif.: Huntington Library, 1980.

Clements, E. D. "Banning and Allied Families." *Americana Illustrated* 26, no. 4 (1932): 516–81.

Cole, Cornelius. *Memoirs of Cornelius Cole.* New York: McLoughlin Bros., 1908.

Colonial Families of the United States of America. 7 vols. Baltimore: Seaforth, 1912.

Conkling, Roscoe P. The *Butterfield Overland Mail, 1857–1869: Its Organization and Operation over the Southern Route to 1861; Subsequently over the Central Route to 1866; and under Wells, Fargo and Company in 1869.* 3 vols. Glendale, Calif.: A. H. Clark, 1947.

Conrad, Henry C. *History of the State of Delaware.* 3 vols. Wilmington, Del.: the author, 1908.

Courtney, Jack. "Cristóbal Was No Treasure Hunter." *Westways* 28 (April 1936): 22–23.

Coy, Owen C. *California County Boundaries: A Study of the Division of the State into Counties and the Subsequent Changes in Their Boundaries.* Berkeley: California Historical Survey Commission, 1923.

Crowe, Earle. *Men of El Tejon: Empire in the Tehachapis*. Los Angeles: Ward Ritchie, 1957.

Crown, Walter J. "Wilmington Oil Field, *Summary of Oil Operations—California Oil Fields; Annual Report of the State Oil and Gas Supervisor* 26 (July 1940– June 1941): 5–11.

Daggett, Stuart. *Chapters on the History of the Southern Pacific*. 2nd ed. New York: Augustus M. Kelley, 1966.

Davis, Margaret Leslie. *Childrens Hospital and the Leaders of Los Angeles: The First 100 Years*. Los Angeles: Childrens Hospital of Los Angeles, 2002.

Davis, Mike. *City of Quartz: Excavating the Future in Los Angeles*. London: Verso, 1990.

Davis, William Heath. *Seventy-five Years in California*. San Francisco: John Howell, 1929.

Delgado, James P. *To California by Sea: A Maritime History of the California Gold Rush*. Columbia: University of South Carolina Press, 1990.

Delmatier, Royce D., et al. *The Rumble of California Politics, 1848–1970*. New York: John Wiley & Sons, 1970.

Deverell, William. *Railroad Crossing: Californians and the Railroad, 1850–1910*. Berkeley: University of California Press, 1994.

———. *Whitewashed Adobe: The Rise of Los Angeles and the Remaking of its Mexican Past*. Berkeley: University of California Press, 2004.

Deverell, William, and Tom Sitton, eds. *California Progressivism Revisited*. Berkeley: University of California Press, 1994.

Dixon, Elizabeth I., ed. "Early San Fernando: Memoirs of Mrs. Catherine Dace." *Southern California Quarterly* 44 (September 1962): 219–66.

Doran, Adelaide LeMert. *The Ranch That Was Robbins': Santa Catalina Island, California: A Source Book*. Los Angeles: the author, 1963.

Duke, Marc. *The du Ponts: Portrait of a Dynasty*. New York: Saturday Review, 1976.

Dumke, Glenn S. *The Boom of the Eighties in Southern California*. San Marino, Calif.: Huntington Library, 1944.

Dunn, Alice Monfort. "People and Places on Old St. Paul." *Minnesota History* 33 (Spring 1952): 1–6.

Eberlein, Harold Donaldson, and Cortlandt V. D. Hubbard. *Historic Houses and Buildings of Delaware*. Dover, Del.: Public Archives Commission, 1962.

Ellis, Arthur M., comp. *Historical Review, Seventy-fifth Anniversary, May 5, 1929, Los Angeles Lodge, no. 42, F. & A. M*. Los Angeles: Los Angeles Lodge 42, 1929.

Erie, Steven P. "How the Urban West Was Won: The Local State and Economic Growth of Los Angeles, 1880–1932." *Urban Affairs Quarterly* 27 (June 1992): 519–54.

Essah, Patience. *A House Divided: Slavery and Emancipation in Delaware, 1638– 1865*. Charlottesville: University Press of Virginia, 1996.

Estrada, William David. *The Los Angeles Plaza: Sacred and Contested Space.* Austin: University of Texas Press, 2008.

Federal Writers' Project, Works Progress Administration, comp. *Delaware: A Guide to the First State.* New York: Viking, 1938.

———. *Philadelphia: A Guide to the Nation's Birthplace.* Philadelphia: William Penn Association of Philadelphia, 1937.

Feldberg, Michael. *The Philadelphia Riots of 1844: A Study of Ethnic Conflict.* Westport, Conn.: Greenwood, 1975.

Finck, Henry T. "Santa Catalina Island." *Nation* 49 (17 October 1889): 307–9, and (24 October 1889): 327–29.

Fogelson, Robert M. *The Fragmented Metropolis: Los Angeles, 1850–1930.* Cambridge, Mass.: Harvard University Press, 1967.

Foote, Robert O. "Overland Stage Coach Club." *The Horse,* July–August 1941, 23–25.

Forbes, Alexander. *California: A History of Upper and Lower California from Their First Discovery to the Present Time.* Repr., New York: Arno, 1973.

Francis, Eugene. "Lucy Banning's Primrose Path." *American Weekly,* 20 March 1949, 24–25.

Frank, Herman W. *Scrapbook of a Western Pioneer.* Los Angeles: Times-Mirror, 1934.

Franks, Kenny A., and Paul F. Lambert. *Early California Oil: A Photographic History, 1865–1940.* College Station: Texas A&M Press, 1985.

Frey, Robert L., ed. *Railroads in the Nineteenth Century.* New York: Facts on File, 1988.

Fries, Amos A., Capt. "San Pedro Harbor." *Out West* 27 (October 1907): 301–31.

Furness, Marion Ramsey. "Childhood Recollections of Old St. Paul." *Minnesota History* 29 (June 1948): 114–29.

Gates, John D. *The du Pont Family.* Garden City, N.Y.: Doubleday, 1979.

Genealogical and Biographical Records of the Banning and Allied Families, Prepared for Miss Kate Banning. New York: American Historical Society, Inc., 1924.

Giffin, Helen S., and Arthur Woodward. *The Story of El Tejon.* Los Angeles: Dawson's Bookshop, 1942.

Gillingham, Robert Cameron. *The Rancho San Pedro: The Story of a Famous Rancho in Los Angeles County and its Owners, The Dominguez Family.* Los Angeles: Cole-Holmquist, 1961.

Glassell, William Thornton. *W. T. Glassell and the Little Torpedo Boat "David."* Los Angeles: privately printed, 1937.

Gleason, J. Duncan. *Islands of California: Their History, Romance, and Physical Characteristics.* Los Angeles: Sea Publications, 1951.

Gottlieb, Robert, and Irene Wolt. *Thinking Big: The Story of the Los Angeles Times, Its Publishers, and Their Influence on Southern California.* New York: G. P. Putnam's Sons, 1977.

Grassman, Curtis. "The Los Angeles Free Harbor Controversy and the Creation of a Progressive Coalition." *Southern California Quarterly* 55 (Winter 1973): 445–68.

Graves, Jackson A. *My Seventy Years in Southern California, 1857–1927.* Los Angeles: Times-Mirror, 1929.

Gray, Paul Bryan. *Forster vs. Pico: The Struggle for the Rancho Santa Margarita.* Spokane, Wash.: Arthur Clark, 1998.

———. "Francisco P. Ramirez: A Short Biography." *California History* 84 (Winter 2006–7): 20–39.

Grenier, Judson A., with Robert C. Gillingham. *California Legacy: The James Alexander Watson–María Dolores Domínguez de Watson Family, 1820–1980.* Los Angeles: Watson Land Company, 1987.

Grenoble, Penelope. "Banning Museum—Where History Lives." *Westways* 77 (May 1985): 29–31, 73.

Grier, William M., Jr. *The Griers: Pioneers in America and Canada, 1816–1991.* Denver: Grier, 1991.

Guinn, J. M. *Historical and Biographical Record of Los Angeles.* Chicago: Chapman, 1901.

———. *A History of California and An Extended History of Los Angeles and Environs.* 3 vols. Los Angeles: Historic Record Company, 1915.

———. *A History of California and an Extended History of its Southern Coast Counties.* 2 vols. Los Angeles, Calif.: Historic Record Company, 1907.

———. *History of the State of California and Biographical Record of Santa Cruz, San Benito, Monterey and San Luis Obispo Counties.* Chicago: Chapman, 1903.

———. "Los Angeles in the Adobe Age." *Annual Publications of the Historical Society of Southern California* 4 (1897): 49–55.

———. "Los Angeles in the Later Sixties and Early Seventies." *Annual Publications of the Historical Society of Southern California* 3 (1893): 63–68.

Gumprecht, Blake. *The Los Angeles River: Its Life, Death, and Possible Rebirth.* Baltimore: Johns Hopkins University Press, 1999.

Gunther, Jane Davies. *Riverside County, California, Place Names: Their Origins and Their Stories.* Riverside, Calif.: J. D. Gunther, 1984.

Hancock, Harold B., ed. "The Kent County Loyalists." *Delaware History* 6 (September 1954): 92–139.

Harnsberger, John L. "Land, Lobbies, Railroads and the Origins of Duluth." *Minnesota History* 37 (September 1960): 89–100.

Haskett, Bert. "History of the Sheep Industry in Arizona." *Arizona Historical Review* 7 (July 1936): 3–50.

Hata, Nadine Ishitani. *The Historic Preservation Movement in California, 1940–1976.* Sacramento, Calif.: California Department of Parks and Recreation, Office of Historic Preservation, 1992.

Hichborn, Franklin. *Story of the Session of the California Legislature of 1911*. San Francisco: James H. Barry, 1911.

Hindes, Ruthanna. "Delaware Silversmiths, 1728–1830: New Discoveries." *Delaware History* 19 (Spring–Summer 1981): 127–55.

Hines, Thomas S. *Irving Gill and the Architecture of Reform: A Study in Modernist Architectural Culture*. New York: Monacelli, 2000.

Hirshson, Stanley P. *General Patton: A Soldier's Life*. New York: Harper Collins, 2002.

Hoffecker, Carol E. *Delaware: A Bicentennial History*. New York: W. W. Norton, 1977.

———. "Nineteenth Century Wilmington: Satellite or Independent City?" *Delaware History* 15 (April 1972): 1–18.

Hofsommer, Don L. *Minneapolis and the Age of Railways*. Minneapolis: University of Minnesota Press, 2005.

———. *The Southern Pacific, 1901–1985*. College Station: Texas A&M University Press, 1986.

Holder, Charles Frederick. *An Isle of Summer: Santa Catalina, Its History, Climate, Sports and Antiquities*. Los Angeles: R. Y. McBride, 1901.

———. *The Channel Islands of California: A Book for the Angler, Sportsman, and Tourist*. London: Hodder, 1910.

Houston, John M. *San Pedro City Dream: An Account, by Its Own Records, of an Attempt to Be an Independent City; Part I (1888–1896) and More Stories of Old San Pedro*. San Pedro, Calif.: San Pedro Historical Publications, 1980.

Hoyt, Franklin. "The Los Angeles & San Pedro: First Railroad South of the Tehachapis." *California Historical Society Quarterly* 32 (December 1953): 327–48.

Hubbard, Lucius F., et al., eds. *Minnesota in Three Centuries*. 4 vols. New York: Publishing Society of Minnesota, 1908.

Hudson, Karen E. *Paul R. Williams, Architect: A Legacy of Style*. New York: Rizzoli, 1993.

Hughes, Tom. *History of Banning and San Gorgonio Pass*. Banning, Calif.: Banning Record, 1938.

Hunt, Aurora. *The Army of the Pacific: Its Operations in California, Texas, Arizona, New Mexico, Utah, Nevada, Oregon, Washington, Plains Region, Mexico, etc., 1860–1866*. Glendale, Calif.: Arthur Clark, 1951.

Hutchinson, W. H. *Oil, Land, and Politics: The California Career of Thomas Robert Bard*. 2 vols. Norman: University of Oklahoma Press, 1965.

Illustrated History of San Joaquin County, California. Chicago: Lewis, 1890.

Jaher, Frederic Cople. *The Urban Establishment: Upper Strata in Boston, New York, Charleston, Chicago and Los Angeles*. Urbana: University of Illinois Press, 1982.

Jordan, David M. *Winfield Scott Hancock: A Soldier's Life*. Bloomington: Indiana University Press, 1988.

Kelsey, Harry. *Juan Rodríquez Cabrillo*. San Marino, Calif.: Huntington Library, 1986.

Kemble, John Haskell. *The Panama Route, 1848–1869*. Berkeley: University of California Press, 1943.

Kirker, Harold. *California's Architectural Frontier: Style and Tradition in the Nineteenth Century*. San Marino, Calif.: Huntington Library, 1960.

Kneiss, Gilbert H. "Phineas Banning and the Los Angeles and San Pedro Railroad." *Railway and Locomotive Historical Society Bulletin* 97 (October 1957): 27–54.

Kornweibel, Theodore, Jr. "The Occupation of Santa Catalina Island during the Civil War." *California Historical Society Quarterly* 46 (December 1967): 345–57.

Krenkel, John H. "Development of the Port of Los Angeles." *American Neptune* 25 (October 1965): 262–73.

———. "The Port of Los Angeles as a Municipal Enterprise." *Pacific Historical Review* 16 (August 1947): 285–97.

Krythe, Maymie. *Port Admiral: Phineas Banning, 1830–1885*. San Francisco: California Historical Society, 1957.

Lake, Stuart N. *Wyatt Earp: Frontier Marshal*. Boston: Houghton Mifflin, 1931.

Lavender, David. *The Great Persuader*. Garden City, N.Y.: Doubleday, 1970.

Layne, J. Gregg. *Annals of Los Angeles: From the Arrival of the First White Men to the Civil War, 1769–1861*. San Francisco: California Historical Society, 1935.

Leader, Leonard. *Los Angeles and the Great Depression*. New York: Garland, 1991.

Lecouvreur, Frank. *From East Prussia to the Golden Gate*. New York: Angelina Book Concern, 1906.

Lee, Ellen K. *Newport Bay: A Pioneer History*. Fullerton, Calif.: Sultana, 1973.

Lick, Rosemary. *The Generous Miser: The Story of James Lick of California*. Los Angeles: Ward Ritchie, 1967.

Lillard, Richard G. *Eden in Jeopardy: Man's Prodigal Meddling with His Environment, The Southern California Experience*. New York: Alfred A. Knopf, 1966.

Lincoln, Anna T. *Wilmington, Delaware: Three Centuries under Four Flags, 1609–1937*. Rutland, Vt.: Tuttle, 1937.

Loranger, Joyce Freeman. "Phineas Banning: The Stories vs. the Records." *Shoreline* 27 (August 1999): 3–30.

Lothrop, Gloria Ricci. "Strength Made Stronger: The Role of Women in Southern California Philanthropy." *Southern California Quarterly* 71 (Summer/Fall 1989): 143–94.

Lucid, Robert F., ed. *The Journal of Richard Henry Dana, Jr.* 3 vols. Cambridge, Mass.: Harvard University Press, 1968.

Ludwig, Ella A. *History of the Harbor District of Los Angeles*. Los Angeles: Historic Record Company, 1926.

Lyman, Edward Leo. *The Overland Journey from Utah to California: Wagon Travel from the City of Saints to the City of Angels*. Reno: University of Nevada Press, 2004.

Magee, Harvey White. *The Story of My Life*. Albany, N.Y.: Boyd, 1926.

Mansfield, John. "Recollections of Los Angeles—1875 to 1885." *Annual Publications of the Historical Society of Southern California* 3 (1893): 69–73.

MacCorkle, William Alexander. *The White Sulphur Springs*. New York: Neale, 1916.

Matson, Clarence H. *Building a World Gateway: The Story of Los Angeles Harbor*. Los Angeles: Pacific Era, 1945.

Mayo, Morrow. *Los Angeles*. New York: Alfred A. Knopf, 1933.

McClintock, James H. *Arizona*. 3 vols. Chicago: S. J. Clarke, 1916.

McDowell, Don. *The Beat of the Drum: The History, Events and People of Drum Barracks, Wilmington, California*. Santa Ana, Calif.: Graphics, 1993.

McGroarty, John S. *California of the South: A History*. 5 vols. Chicago: S. J. Clarke, 1933–35.

———. *Los Angeles, From the Mountains to the Sea*. 3 vols. Chicago: American Historical Society, 1921.

McWilliams, Carey. *Southern California Country: An Island on the Land*. New York: Duell, Sloan, and Pearce, 1946.

Melendy, H. Brett, and Benjamin F. Gilbert. *The Governors of California: Peter H. Burnett to Edmund G. Brown*. Georgetown, Calif.: Talisman, 1965.

Metzler, Evelyn Jackson Tubbs. "The Lowbers of Kent County, Delaware: Moving South from New Amsterdam (New York) to Kent-On-Delaware." *Maryland and Delaware Genealogist* 19, no. 3 (July 1978): 80–81.

Morrison, Annie L., and John H. Haydon. *History of San Luis Obispo County and Environs*. Los Angeles: Historic Record Company, 1917.

Mowry, George. *The California Progressives*. Berkeley: University of California Press, 1951.

Mullaly, Larry, and Bruce Petty. *The Southern Pacific in Los Angeles, 1873–1996*. San Marino, Calif.: Golden West Books and the Los Angeles Railroad Heritage Foundation, 2002.

Munroe, John. *History of Delaware*. 5th ed. Newark, N.J.: University of Delaware Press, 2006.

Myrick, David F. *Railroads of Arizona*. 3 vols. Berkeley, Calif.: Howell-North Books, 1975–84.

Nadeau, Remi. *City-Makers: The Men Who Transformed Los Angeles from Village to Metropolis during the First Great Boom, 1868–1876*. Garden City, N.Y.: Doubleday, 1948.

———. *Los Angeles: From Mission to Modern City*. New York: Longmans, Green, 1960.

Nagle, Mary Dunning. "A Sweeny Sampler." *Minnesota History* 41 (Spring 1868): 29–33.

Naftalin, Arthur. "The Tradition of Protest and the Roots of the Farmer-Labor Party." *Minnesota History* 35 (June 1956): 53–63.

Nelson, Howard J. *The Los Angeles Metropolis.* Dubuque, Iowa: Kendall-Hunt, 1983.

Newmark, Harris. *Sixty Years in Southern California, 1853–1913.* New York: Knickerbocker, 1916.

Newmark, Marco R. "Early California Resorts." *Historical Society of Southern California Quarterly* 35 (June 1958): 129–52.

———. "The Life of Jonathan (John) Temple." *Historical Society of Southern California Quarterly* 36 (March 1954): 46–49.

———. "Phineas Banning, Intrepid Pioneer." *Southern California Quarterly* 35 (September 1953): 265–74.

Newsom, T. M. *Pen Pictures of St. Paul, Minnesota.* St. Paul, Minn.: the author, 1886.

Olesen, William L. "The Birth and Growth of Shipbuilding in the San Pedro Bay Area." *Shoreline* 13 (April 1986): 9–13.

O'Meara, Carroll. "Captain Wm. Banning and the Art of Stage Coaching." *Out West Magazine* 91 (December 1933): 167–68, 171.

Orsi, Jared. *Hazardous Metropolis: Flooding and Urban Ecology in Los Angeles.* Berkeley: University of California Press, 2004.

Outland, Charles F. *Stagecoaching on El Camino Real: Los Angeles to San Francisco, 1861–1901.* Glendale, Calif.: Arthur Clark, 1973.

Overholt, Alma. *The Catalina Story.* Avalon, Calif.: Catalina Island Museum, 1962.

Packman, Anna Begue de. "Landmarks and Pioneers of Los Angeles in 1853." *Quarterly Publications of the Historical Society of Southern California* 26 (March 1944): 57–95.

Page, Henry Markham. *Pasadena: Its Early Years.* Los Angeles: privately printed by L. L. Morrison, 1964.

Palmer, Edwin O. *History of Hollywood.* Hollywood, Calif.: A. H. Cawston, 1937.

Patton, Robert H. *The Pattons: A Personal History of an American Family.* New York: Crown Publishers, 1994.

Pedersen, Jeannine L. *Catalina Island.* Charleston, S.C.: Arcadia, 2004.

Perry, Louis B., and Richard S. Perry. *A History of the Los Angeles Labor Movement, 1911–1941.* Berkeley: University of California Press, 1963.

Peterson, Harold F. "Early Minnesota Railroads and the Quest for Settlers." *Minnesota History* 13 (March 1932): 25–44.

Phillips, Catherine Coffin. *Cornelius Cole: California Pioneer and United States Senator.* San Francisco: John Henry Nash, 1929.

Pineda, Manuel, and E. Caswell Perry. *Pasadena Area History.* Pasadena, Calif.: J. W. Anderson, 1972.

Pitt, Leonard. *The Decline of the Californios: A Social History of the Spanish-Speaking Californians, 1846–1890.* Berkeley: University of California Press, 1971.

Pitt, Leonard and Dale Pitt. *Los Angeles A to Z: An Encyclopedia of the City and County*. Berkeley: University of California Press, 1997.

Prudhomme, Charles J., and Thomas F. Keaveny. "Early Days in Los Angeles County II.—Phineas Banning and Historic Wilmington." *Grizzly Bear* 20 (March 1917): 6–7.

Putnam, Frank B. "Serape to Levi . . . Southern Pacific." *Historical Society of Southern California Quarterly* 38 (September 1956): 211–25.

Queenan, Charles. *Long Beach and Los Angeles: A Tale of Two Ports*. Los Angeles: Harbor Department, 1983.

———. *The Port of Los Angeles: From Wilderness to World Port*. Los Angeles: Harbor Department, 1983.

Ramirez, Salvador. *The Octopus Speaks: The Colton Letters*. Carlsbad, Calif.: Tentacled Press, 1982.

Raup, Hallock F. "Rancho Los Palos Verdes." *Quarterly Publications of the Historical Society of Southern California* 19 (March 1937): 7–21.

Read, Isaac. "The Chagres River Route to California in 1851." *California Historical Quarterly* 8 (March 1929): 3–16.

Receipts from Katharine's Kitchen: Personal Recipes of Katharine Stewart Banning. Wilmington, Calif.: General Phineas Banning Residence Museum, 1978.

Records of the Court of New Castle of Delaware. 2 vols. Lancaster, Pa.: Wickersham, 1904–35.

Reed, H. Clay, ed. *Delaware: A History of the First State*. 2 vols. New York: Lewis Historical Publishing, 1947.

Reid, Hiram A. *History of Pasadena*. Pasadena, Calif.: Pasadena History, 1895.

Rice, Lee M., and Glenn R. Vernam. *They Saddled the West*. Cambridge, Md.: Cornell Maritime, 1975.

Rice, William B. *The Los Angeles Star, 1851–1864: The Beginnings of Journalism in Southern California*. Berkeley: University of California Press, 1947.

Ridge, Martin. *Ignatius Donnelly: The Portrait of a Politician*. Chicago: University of Chicago Press, 1962.

Ridgely, Mabel Lloyd, ed. *What Them Befell: The Ridgelys of Delaware and Their Circle in Colonial and Federal Times; Letters 1751–1890*. Portland, Maine: Anthoensen, 1949.

Ripley, Vernetta. "The San Fernando Pass and the Pioneer Traffic that Went Over It." *Quarterly Publications of the Historical Society of Southern California* 29 (March 1947): 34–48.

———. "The San Fernando Pass and the Pioneer Traffic that Went over It." *Historical Society of Southern California Quarterly* 30 (June 1948): 111–22.

Risch, Erna. *Quartermaster Support of the Army: A History of the Corps, 1775–1939*. Washington, D.C.: Office of the Quartermaster General, 1962.

Roberts, William H. *USS New Ironsides in the Civil War*. Annapolis, Md.: Naval Institute Press, 1999.

Robinson, John W. *Gateways to Southern California: Indian Footpaths, Horse Trails, Wagon Roads, Railroads and Highways*. Arcadia, Calif.: Big Santa Anita Historical Society, 2005.

———. *Los Angeles in Civil War Days*. Los Angeles: Dawson's Book Shop, 1977.

———. *Southern California's First Railroad: The Los Angeles and San Pedro Railroad, 1869–1873*. Los Angeles: Dawson's Book Shop, 1978.

Robinson, W. W. *Los Angeles from the Days of the Pueblo*. San Francisco: California Historical Society, 1959.

———. *Lawyers of Los Angeles*. Los Angeles: Los Angeles Bar Association, 1959.

Rose, L. J., Jr. *L. J. Rose of Sunnyslope, 1827–1899: California Pioneer, Fruit Grower, Wine Maker, Horse Breeder*. 1959. Repr., San Marino, Calif.: Huntington Library, 2003.

Ryden, George H., ed. *Letters to and from Caesar Rodney, 1756–1784*. Philadelphia: University of Pennsylvania Press, 1933.

Rusling, James Fowler. *Across America: or, The Great West and the Pacific Coast*. New York: Sheldon, 1874.

Sabin, Paul. *Crude Politics: The California Oil Market, 1900–1940*. Berkeley: University of California Press, 2005.

Salvator, Ludwig Louis. *Los Angeles in the Sunny Seventies: A Flower From the Golden Land*. Los Angeles: J. Zeitlin, 1929.

Sammack, Emil G., and Don O. Winslow, eds. *Dover: The First Two Hundred and Fifty Years, 1717–1967*. Dover, Del.: City of Dover, 1967.

Scammell, J. M. "Military Units in Southern California, 1853–1862." *California Historical Society Quarterly* 29 (September 1950): 229–49.

Scharf, J. Thomas. *History of the Confederate States Navy From its Organization to the Surrender of its Last Vessel*. New York: Rogers & Sherwood, 1887.

———. *History of Delaware, 1609–1888*. 2 vols. Philadelphia: L. J. Richards, 1888.

Scott, Allen J., and Edward W. Soja, eds. *The City: Los Angeles and Urban Theory at the End of the Twentieth Century*. Berkeley: University of California Press, 1996.

Scott, Jane Harrington. *A Gentleman as Well as a Whig: Caesar Rodney and the American Revolution*. Newark, Del.: University of Delaware Press and Cranbury, N.J.: Associated University Presses, 2000.

Seely, Bruce E. "Wilmington and Its Railroads: A Lasting Connection." *Delaware History* 19 (September 1980): 1–9.

Sheridan, Thomas. *Arizona: A History*. Tucson: University of Arizona Press, 1995.

Sherwood, Midge. *Days of Vintage, Years of Vision*. San Marino, Calif.: Orizaba, 1982.

Shirley, Christine V. F. "Banning Residence Museum." *Terra* 18 (Summer 1979): 3–11.

Shotliff, Don A. "San Pedro Harbor, or Los Angeles Harbor? Senator W. H. Savage and the Home Rule Advocates Fail to Stem the Tide of Consolidationism, 1906–1909." *Southern California Quarterly* 54 (Summer 1972): 127–54.

Signor, John R. *Beaumont Hill: Southern Pacific's Southern California Gateway.* San Marino, Calif.: Golden West Books, 1990.

Silka, Henry P. *San Pedro: A Pictorial History.* San Pedro, Calif.: San Pedro Bay Historical Society, 1984.

Sitton, Tom. "The Bannings on the Magic Isle: Santa Catalina Island, 1892–1919." *California History* 87, no. 1 (2009): 6–23.

———. "The 'Boss' Without a Machine: Kent Kane Parrot and Los Angeles Politics in the 1920s." *Southern California Quarterly* 67 (Winter 1985): 367–87.

———. *John Randolph Haynes: California Progressive.* Stanford, Calif.: Stanford University Press, 1992.

Sitton, Tom, and William Deverell, eds. *Metropolis in the Making: Los Angeles in the 1920s.* Berkeley: University of California Press, 2001.

Smalley, Eugene. *History of the Northern Pacific Railroad.* New York: Putnam, 1883.

Smith, Bertha H. "California's First Cubist House." *Sunset* 35 (August 1915): 368–76.

Spalding, William A. *History and Reminiscences, Los Angeles City and County, California.* 3 vols. Los Angeles: J. R. Finnell & Sons, 1931.

———. *William Andrew Spalding, Los Angeles Newspaperman: An Autobiography Account.* San Marino, Calif.: Huntington Library, 1961.

Spitzzeri, Paul R. "Judge Lynch in Session: Popular Justice in Los Angeles, 1850–1875." *Southern California Quarterly* 87 (Summer 2005): 83–122.

———. "The Road to Independence: The Los Angeles and Independence Railroad and the Conception of a City." *Southern California Quarterly* 83 (Spring 2001): 23–58.

Splitter, Henry Winfred. "Los Angeles in the 1850s as Told by Early Newspapers." *Quarterly Publications of the Historical Society of Southern California* 31 (March/June 1949): 114–18.

Stanley, Gerald. "Civil War Politics in California." *Southern California Quarterly* 64 (Summer 1982): 115–32.

Starr, Kevin. *Americans and the California Dream, 1850–1915.* New York: Oxford University Press, 1973.

———. *The Dream Endures: California Enters the 1940s.* New York: Oxford University Press, 1997.

———. *Embattled Dreams: California in War and Peace, 1940–1950.* New York: Oxford University Press, 2002.

———. *Endangered Dreams: The Great Depression in California.* New York: Oxford University Press, 1995.

———. *Inventing the Dream: California Through the Progressive Era.* New York: Oxford University Press, 1985.

———. *Material Dreams: Southern California Through the 1920s.* New York: Oxford University Press, 1990.

Stenzel, Franz. *James Madison Alden: Yankee Artist of the Pacific Coast, 1854–1860.* Fort Worth, Tex.: Amon Carter Museum, 1975.

Stephens, Jess E. "San Pedro Harbor: A California Commercial Wonder and What the Experts Say about It." *Out West* 4 (July 1912): 27–31.

Stephens, Ruth Burke. "An Observer in a Red Cross Shop." *Graphic*, 10 July 1918, 10–11.

Stimson, Grace Heilman. *Rise of the Labor Movement in Los Angeles.* Berkeley: University of California Press, 1955.

Stimson, Marshall. *Fun, Fights, and Fiestas in Old Los Angeles: An Autobiography.* Los Angeles: privately printed, 1966.

Storke, Yda Addis. *A Memorial and Biographical History of the Counties of Santa Barbara, San Luis Obispo and Ventura, California.* Chicago: Lewis, 1891.

Sumner, Ann. "Pioneer Families of Los Angeles: The Banning Clan." *Los Angeles Historical Review*, October 1929, 5, 16.

Thompson, Gerald. *Edward F. Beale and the American West.* Albuquerque: University of New Mexico Press, 1983.

Thompson, Merry L. *The Miracle of a Muddy Tideflat.* Wilmington, Calif.: General Phineas Banning Residence Museum, 1980.

Tomlinson, John G. "Intellectual Adventures: A Century of Faculty Thought and a Law School Permanent in Nature." *USC Law*, Spring 2000, 4–13.

Totten, Ruth Ellen Patton. *The Button Box: A Daughter's Loving Memoir of Mrs. George S. Patton.* Columbia and London: University of Missouri Press, 2005.

Townsend, E. D. *The California Diary of General E. D. Townsend.* Ed. Malcolm Edwards. Los Angeles: Ward Ritchie, 1970.

Trask, Blanche. "The Heart of Santa Catalina." *Land of Sunshine* 4 (September 1897): 153–59.

Truman, Ben C. *Semi-Tropical California: Its Climate, Healthfulness, Productiveness, and Scenery.* San Francisco: A. L. Bancroft, 1874.

Tullidge, Edward W. *History of Salt Lake City and its Founders.* Salt Lake City, Utah: E. W. Tullidge, 1886.

Turhollow, Anthony F. *A History of the Los Angeles District, U.S. Army Corps of Engineers, 1898–1965.* Los Angeles: U.S. Army Engineer District, 1975.

Tyler, Mary Marjorie. "Banning and Aliied [*sic*] Families." *Americana* 22 (January–December 1928): 88–118.

Van Schaick-Banning, Elisabeth. *The Book of Banning.* Westminster, Md.: Willow Bend Books, 2005.

Upham, Warren, and Mrs. Rose Barteau Dunlap. *Minnesota Biographies, 1655–1912.* St. Paul, Minn.: Minnesota Historical Society, 1912.

Verge, Arthur C. *Paradise Transformed: Los Angeles during the Second World War.* Dubuque, Iowa: Kendall/Hunt, 1993.

Vickery, Oliver. *Harbor Heritage: Tales of the Harbor Area of Los Angeles, California*. Mountain View, Calif.: Morgan, 1979.

Wagoner, Jay J. *Arizona Territory 1863–1912: A Political History*. Tucson: University of Arizona Press, 1970.

———. "Overstocking of the Ranges in Southern Arizona during the 1870s and 1880s." *Arizoniana* 2 (Spring 1961): 23–27.

Warner, Col. J. J., Benjamin Hayes, and J. P. Widney. *An Historical Sketch of Los Angeles County, California*. Los Angeles: Louis Lewin, 1876.

Weigley, Russell F., ed. *Philadelphia: A 300 Year History*. New York: W. W. Norton, 1982.

Welsh, Peter C. "Merchants, Millers and Ocean Ships: The Components of an Early American Industrial Town." *Delaware History* 7 (September 1957): 319–36.

Wentworth, Edward Norris. *America's Sheep Trails: History, Personalities*. Ames: Iowa State College Press, 1948.

Wharfield, H. B. *Fort Yuma on the Colorado River*. El Cajon, Calif.: the author, 1968.

White, William Sanford, and Steven Kern Tice. *Santa Catalina Island: Its Magic, People and History*. Glendora, Calif.: White Limited Editions, 1997.

Widney, R. M. "Which Subsidy Shall I Vote For, or Shall I Vote Against Both!" *Historical Society of Southern California Quarterly* 38 (December 1956): 347–62.

Willard, Charles Dwight. *The Free Harbor Contest at Los Angeles*. Los Angeles: Kingsley-Barnes and Neuner, 1899.

Williams, J. Fletcher. *A History of the City of St. Paul and of the County of Ramsey, Minnesota*. St. Paul, Minn.: Minnesota Historical Society, 1876.

Williams, William H. *Slavery and Freedom in Delaware, 1639–1865*. Wilmington, Del.: Scholarly Resources, 1996.

Williamson, Mrs. M. Burton. "History of Santa Catalina Island." *Annual Publications of the Historical Society of Southern California* 6 (1903): 14–31.

Wills, Jocelyn. *Boosters, Hustlers and Speculators: Entrepreneurial Culture and the Rise of Minneapolis and St. Paul, 1849–1883*. St. Paul. Minn.: Minnesota Historical Society Press, 2005.

Wilson, Carol G. *California Yankee: William R. Staats—Business Pioneer*. Claremont, Calif.: Saunders, 1946.

Wilson, Harry. *Wilson's Guide to Avalon the Beautiful and the Island of Santa Catalina*. Avalon, Calif.: the author, 1913.

Wilson, Jane. *Gibson, Dunn & Crutcher, Lawyers: An Early History*. Los Angeles: Gibson, Dunn & Crutcher, 1990.

Wilson, John Albert. *History of Los Angeles County, California*. Oakland, Calif.: Thompson and West, 1880.

Wilson, Neill C., and Frank J. Taylor. *Southern Pacific: The Roaring Story of a Fighting Railroad*. New York: McGraw-Hill, 1952.

Windle, Ernest. *Windle's History of Santa Catalina Island*. 2nd ed. Avalon, Calif.: Catalina Islander, 1940.

Winter, Marian. "Phineas Banning's Dream House." *Shoreline* 9 (April 1982): 5–8.

Winthur, Oscar Osborn. *Express and Stagecoach Days in California.* Stanford, Calif.: Stanford University Press, 1936.

Wolcott, Marjorie T., ed. *Pioneer Notes from the Diaries of Judge Benjamin Hayes, 1849–1875.* Los Angeles: McBride, 1929.

Woolsey, Ronald C. "Crime and Punishment: Los Angeles County, 1850–1856." *Southern California Quarterly* 61 (Spring 1979): 79–98.

———. "Disunion or Dissent? A New Look at an Old Problem in Southern California Attitudes toward the Civil War." *Southern California Quarterly* 66 (Fall 1984): 185–205.

———. *Migrants West: Toward the Southern California Frontier.* Sebastopol, Calif.: Grizzly Bear, 1996.

Workman, Boyle. *The City That Grew.* Los Angeles: Southland, 1935.

Yale, Charles G. *Pacific Coast Harbors: A Description of the Harbors, Landings, Roadsteads and Chutes on the Coast Line of California, Oregon and Washington.* San Francisco: n.p., 1879.

Yoch, James J. *Visionary on the Golden Shore: Phineas Banning in Southern California, 1851–1885.* Wilmington, Calif.: Banning Residence Museum, 2002.

Yoshida, Kazumasa. *Maboroshi no Isan (Elusion of Inheritance).* Tokyo: Sanichi Shobo, 1996.

Zordich, James. "Phineas Banning and the W. T. Co." *Water Lines* 4 (1st Quarter 1989): 1–3, 7, 12.

———. "Santa Catalina Island Company: The First Quarter Century." *Water Lines* 9 (1st Quarter 1994): 1–11.

Zwinger, Ann. *John Xántus: The Fort Tejon Letters, 1857–1859.* Tucson: University of Arizona Press, 1986.

List of Illustrations

INDEX

Illustrations are indicated in bold-face type. References to Phineas Banning are abbreviated as "PB."